Elysium Britannicum, or The Royal Gardens

PENN STUDIES IN LANDSCAPE ARCHITECTURE

John Dixon Hunt, Series Editor

This series is dedicated to the study and promotion of a wide variety of approaches to landscape architecture, with emphasis on connections between theory and practice. It includes monographs on key topics in history and theory, descriptions of projects by both established and rising designers, translations of major foreign-language texts, anthologies of theoretical and historical writings on classic issues, and critical writing by members of the profession of landscape architecture.

Elysium Britannicum, or The Royal Gardens

JOHN EVELYN

Edited by John E. Ingram

University of Pennsylvania Press

Philadelphia

*Publication of this volume was assisted by grants from the
Getty Grant Program and the Graham Foundation for Advanced Studies in the Fine Arts.*

10   9   8   7   6   5   4   3   2   1

Published by
University of Pennsylvania Press
Philadelphia, Pennsylvania 19104-4011

Library of Congress Cataloging-in-Publication Data
Evelyn, John, 1620–1706.
Elysium Britannicum, or The Royal gardens in three books / John Evelyn ; edited by
John E. Ingram.
     p.   cm. — (Penn studies in landscape architecture)
Includes bibliographical references (p.).
ISBN 0-8122-3536-3 (alk. paper)
1. Evelyn, John, 1620–1706. Elysium Britannicum.   2. Gardens—England—Design—
History—17th century.   3. Gardens—Europe—Design—History—17th century.
4. Landscape architecture—England—History—17th century.   5. Landscape
architecture—Europe—History—17th century.   I. Title: Royal gardens in three
books.   II. Ingram, John E.   III. Evelyn, John, 1620–1706. Elysium Britannicum.
IV. Title.   V. Series.
SB470.E9 E93   2000
712.6'0942'09032—dc21
                                                                99-054571

Title page illustration: Portrait of John Evelyn, from *Sylva*, 1664, frontispiece.

Contents

Summary of Editorial Conventions Used in the Transcription

~~text lined through~~	Text lined through by Evelyn
{text in wavy brackets}	Interlineations by Evelyn
[text in square brackets]	Editorial comments, notes, or clarifications by editor
[text in boldface]	Used to indicate page numbers of the original manuscript, and to alert the reader in the footnotes whether material is marginalia, or inserted on separate pieces of paper, or combinations of both
(text in parentheses)	Evelyn's use of parentheses
text in italics	Text underlined by Evelyn
footnotes (Arabic numerals)	Evelyn's marginalia and text additions on separate pieces of paper
endnotes (Roman numerals)	Editor's annotations for identification or clarification

Evelyn's more common spelling conventions are used interchangeably: then/than; se/see; of/off; on/one; gard[i]ner; ii/ij.

Evelyn used both "&c" and "etc"; this has been regularized to "etc" throughout the text.

John Evelyn and
His "Elysium Britannicum"

JOHN E. INGRAM

the Noblenesse & State of the piece . . . has putt an edge and Keenenesse on our appetites to see the whole made publique.

John Evelyn was, according to the *Dictionary of National Biography*, perhaps the seventeenth-century's quintessential virtuoso. The definitions of a "virtuoso" and the scientific culture of the time have changed considerably in the century since that entry was written; but Evelyn remains an object of fascination and study, recognized as one of the key personalities of a crucial transitional period in the evolution of the modern intellectual world. He was a founding member of the Royal Society in 1660 and a leading participant in its debates for several decades, author of more than thirty major publications, welcomed at the English court at home and in exile and received by foreign royalty and aristocracy, correspondent of scientists and clerics, friend of Samuel Pepys and Sir Christopher Wren, and staunch defender of the Anglican Church against its enemies during the Interregnum. Evelyn was uneasy about his status and achievements, famously suggesting "coxcomb" as a scornful alternative to "virtuoso," and that uncertainty may well be important to the history of the manuscript presented here.[1]

Evelyn was born at Wotton in Surrey in 1620 and died there in 1706, having inherited the family's estates from his elder brother in 1699. The middle son of Richard and Eleanor Evelyn, John was born into a comfortable life, the result of a family fortune built initially on the introduction into England of the manufacture of gunpowder by his grandfather George, and then maintained and expanded through timely and astute investments in land. Although John Evelyn never became especially wealthy, he was with few exceptions always in at least comfortable circumstances, as a consequence of which he had the leisure to pursue a wide range of interests.

When Evelyn was four years old, his father, fearing the plague, sent the boy from Wotton to live with his maternal Stansfield grandparents at their estates in Lewes, Sussex, near the sea. Evelyn returned to Wotton as a sixteen-year-old prior to going up to Balliol College, Oxford, where he was enrolled as a Fellow Commoner. At Oxford from 1637 to 1640 he did well in the classics and in the godly and Protestant study of religion, a combination characteristic of the age and of profound importance to the formation of his thought. Throughout the rest of his life Evelyn continued to adhere to this combination as the foundation of learning, even as he welcomed the Baconian agenda of new learning and the new sciences.[2] His surviving commonplace books reveal little about his nonacademic life at Oxford, Evelyn having neatly and extremely effectively blotted out those entries in his accounts of his younger days.

The same caution appears in the work for which he is most famous, his *Diary*, which was regularized in the 1680s. He appears always to have had a wary eye to posterity's reading of his life and career, removing the inconvenient and rewriting the record where he judged it necessary.

With his older brother George, Evelyn settled in lodgings at London's Middle Temple in 1640, but despite his father's wishes, the law was not to be his field of study. As the second son of a wealthy landowner, Evelyn received a considerable allowance, which he used in the early 1640s to travel initially to Holland and France. During this time, the conflict between king and Parliament had turned to civil war, and Evelyn found himself emerging into independence just as his chosen party was on the point of utter defeat. It might be thought that, like Marvell's "forward youth," Evelyn would forsake study for the battlefield (and he appears to have joined the king's forces briefly); but he may have been among the considerable number of those who found their repugnance for internecine strife stronger than their partisan allegiance. Evelyn elected to resume his tour of Europe, obtained permission to travel abroad, and returned to the continent in 1644 to extend his travel through Holland to the Spanish Netherlands, various Italian states such as Venice, Switzerland, and then a return to France. In the course of these travels he met Thomas Howard, Earl of Arundel, perhaps the epitome of the English collector, who provided the younger man with a set of notes on "what curiosities I should enquire after in my Journey."[3]

Evelyn had avoided combat by his absence from England, but he was clearly committed to the Stuart cause and his choice necessarily had consequences: an adherent of the monarchy in a country controlled by the king's opponents, Evelyn was frustrated in his desire for a career in public service. Initially he found employment upon his return to England (1647 to 1649) monitoring the interests of the exiled Sir Richard Browne, Charles I's "Resident" in France, but the execution of the king in January 1649 may well have forced him to abandon his country and join other royalists abroad.

The English court in exile welcomed him, as did many of the royal and noble families in the countries he visited. His travels and residence in France had acquainted him with European centers of learning for both the arts and sciences, resulting in an expanded and appreciative *Weltanschauung* that influenced his subsequent study and writing. Evelyn acquired certificates of matriculation at Padua and Leiden universities, but refused the office of syndic at Padua because (characteristically) it was chargeable and interfered with his travel plans. At the same time he bought curiosities and cabinets in which to store them. Even more significant for the composition of the "Elysium Britannicum" was Evelyn's systematic book collecting and his adoption of a mode of manuscript note-taking and digesting. He became acquainted with leading figures in intellectual, cultural, and scientific circles, and was drawn into relationships designed to facilitate the exchange of ideas and information. Once more one sees the connection with the "Elysium Britannicum," which in some respects is more of a collaborative compendium of knowledge than the work of an individual.[4]

Even at this early stage of his life, Evelyn's interest in gardens and landscape design is noteworthy, as he remarked on the positive and negative features of the great gardens of Europe, jotting his observations, rather greatly embellished after the fact, in his personal "kalendarium" or diary. He had, according to the *Dictionary of National Biography*, earlier made "various improvements in the gardens" at Wotton in 1642–1643 as he avoided the notice of the parliamentary authorities in London. In 1647

Evelyn married Mary Browne, Sir Richard Browne's thirteen-year-old daughter. John and Mary Evelyn had eight children, of whom four died in childhood, sad passings that Evelyn recorded in his diary with more emotion than is usual for this objective chronicler of events.

The execution of the king and the failure of the 1650 rising by his son, later Charles II, appeared to put an end to royalist hopes, and many of the exiles (Thomas Hobbes, for instance, as well as Evelyn) looked for ways to return to England, making terms with if not accommodating themselves to the republican regime led by Oliver Cromwell. Evelyn returned to England permanently in 1652, having conveyed his decision to do so late in the previous year in a letter to William Prettyman, his wife's uncle. Characteristically, despair at the frustration of his ambitions and the yearning for a space in which to turn away from uncongenial reality are expressed in relation to a garden: "I shall therefore bring over with me no ambitions at all to be a statesman, or meddle with the unlucky Interests of Kingdoms, but shall contentedly submit to the losse of my education, by which I might have one day hoped to have bin considerable in my Country. A Friend, a Booke, and a Garden shall for the future, perfectly circumscribe my utmost designes."[5] In this mood of quiet gloom he settled his family at Sayes Court, an estate that came to Mary and John from Sir Richard.[6] Here he again contrived to absent himself and his family from the notice of the Interregnum authorities and devoted his attention and energy to establishing some of the most renowned, cosmopolitan, and "modern" garden landscapes in seventeenth-century England, creating in effect a laboratory for landscape design and plant cultivation.

Evelyn was not a hermit, however (though in 1659 he did propose a hortulan monastic establishment where he and a select group would "desire nothing more than to give a good example, preserve science, & cultivate themselves").[7] He came to the notice of intellectual communities in London and Oxford that flourished throughout the Interregnum and from which the founding membership of the Royal Society would be drawn. He met and corresponded with Robert Boyle, with the intelligencer Samuel Hartlib, and with Dr. John Wilkins of Wadham College, all of whom had central roles in the fostering of scientific collaboration and the dissemination of knowledge for the betterment of humankind.[8] Evelyn did not fully commit himself to any of these groups; in all likelihood, he found himself unable to participate in their more radical political stances. However, he had access to their networks through which he met others with similar interests, and these groups provided him with stimulus and encouragement (as well as some skeptical criticism) as he embarked on the extraordinary project that was to become the "Elysium Britannicum."

After the Restoration in 1660, Evelyn's circle of acquaintances included many levels of society, from English royalty to the celebrated woodcarver he championed, Grinling Gibbons. He knew and worked for the English monarchy until his death, serving Charles II, James II, William and Mary, and Anne. His greatest royal intimate was Charles II, however, under whom he served as commissioner for those wounded in the Dutch War of 1665–1667. He was also appointed a commissioner of the Privy Seal and became a member of the Council for Trade and Plantations through which service he met William Blathwayt, who was Secretary to the Lords, chief bureaucrat for the new English colonies in North America, another "curious" collector of plants and specimens, and creator of renowned gardens at Dyrham Park. Through Blathwayt and Evelyn's cousin, Daniel Parke, Evelyn corresponded with John Walker, a major supplier of Virginia's flora and fauna to English natural history enthusiasts, who looked after the gardens at the College of William and Mary in Virginia. There are many references to "Verginian" plants in the "Elysium Britannicum," information about which Walker may have transmitted to Evelyn.

Among Evelyn's closest friends was Samuel Pepys, the more popular diarist of the seventeenth century and architect of the English navy, who, according to the Evelyn scholar Geoffrey Keynes, considered Evelyn "a man so much above others."[9] He met and worked with Christopher Wren as early as the 1660s, when the Sheldonian Theatre was being constructed at Oxford, but more closely and for a protracted period of time during the rebuilding of St. Paul's Cathedral and most of London following the devastating fire of 1666. Charles II commended Evelyn for not abandoning his duties during the smallpox plague of 1666, when at its height the epidemic was taking upward of seven thousand lives a week, or during the conflagration and its aftermath. Evelyn, inspecting the damage, noted in his diary that his hair was singed and his feet pained by the heat of the cobblestones, from a fire so intense that the lead on the roofs ran into the street, heating the stones to red.[10]

During his eighty-five years, Evelyn met and corresponded with scientists, literary figures, and religious authors. Pepys and Wren have been mentioned, but notable also were Samuel Hartlib, Robert Boyle, William Oughtread, John Ray, Abraham Cowley, John Beale, John Wilkins, Richard Bentley, and other members of the Royal Society. Many of his correspondents appear in his marginal annotations to the "Elysium," as he continually attempted to update and augment his information through cullings from new publications, personal correspondence, and experiments he witnessed at the Society and elsewhere. Evelyn was a founding member of the Royal Society and served on its committees for many years, but true to a sometimes reticent nature or an astute political and economic sensibility, he refused to take on the position of president. He had earlier also graciously avoided similar appointments offered by the king and members of his government, appointments that would have been full of duties but devoid of remuneration.

With his permanent return to England in 1652, Evelyn devoted time to the study of architecture and mezzotinting, to theological inquiry and political pamphleteering, to building his library collection and cabinet of curiosities, and to other topics of learning and scientific inquiry. His major area of interest, however, and the subject that called to him for at least the last fifty years of his life, was gardening in all of its many facets. These included not only the creation of "Princely gardens," but also such advanced schemes as plantings that would improve the quality of the air around London, encouragements to seize the benefits of eating more green vegetables, and the proposals that argued the advisability (indeed, necessity) of practicing forest conservation through reforestation, in the wake of the use of vast quantities of wood for military purposes by the republican regime of the Interregnum, to the dismay of many landowners.[11] Each of these topics resulted in a major publication: *Fumifugium: or the Inconveniencie of the Aer and Smoak of London dissipated, together with some Remedies* . . . (1661), *Acetaria: A Discourse of Sallets* (1699), and *Sylva; or A Discourse of Forest-Trees, and the Propagation of Timber in his Majesties Dominions* (1664).

In his bibliographical study of Evelyn, Geoffrey Keynes lists ten major publications relating to gardening and horticulture published during Evelyn's lifetime. Of these, at least three, *Sylva*, *Kalendarium Hortense* (1664), and *Acetaria*, were originally, in whole or in part, sections of his projected monumental study of gardening, "Elysium Britannicum, or The Royal Gardens in Three Books," but these three works were issued separately, because Evelyn never succeeded in bringing the opus as a whole to a publishable state. The Royal Society had ordered Evelyn to prepare *Sylva* for publication, and it was the Society's first. *Sylva* was the means by which Evelyn's fame as the supreme man of gardens (and, more important perhaps for the present "green" generation, one of the principal progenitors of the conservation movement) remained secure through at least the early nineteenth century.

* * *

The current edited transcription of the "Elysium Britannicum, or The Royal Gardens in Three Books" is based on a single bound volume (Evelyn MS 45). The main text appears to be a fair copy of the work, that is, a text that is correct and essentially finished for publication. It is in Evelyn's hand. However, the author subsequently altered even this fair copy over more than a forty-year period as he introduced thousands of changes and additions. Evelyn enlarged this portion of the work by at least one-third through the additions he made on separate slips and sheets of paper, annotating each such addition carefully with the page number of the fair copy text and a matching symbol to note the exact place in the text for the inserted text. The volume also contains manuscript material in other hands that Evelyn likely intended to include in some manner in the final version of the work: for example, a two-page set of instructions "to govern bees" (see Appendix 4), extracts from Pierre Morin's catalog of anemones and other flowering "curious" plants[12] (see Appendix 8), and Sir Thomas Hanmer's comments on the cultivation of tulips, very probably in Hanmer's own hand (see Appendix 7).[13]

The fair copy portion of the manuscript was likely completed in several stages beginning in the 1650s and continuing through the early or mid-1660s, although it would remain ultimately unfinished, or at least, unedited. Graham Parry has suggested that it was begun around 1657.[14] Such a time frame is supported by comments in one of Evelyn's letters to Sir Thomas Browne, dated 28 January 1660: "And now to shew you how farr I am advanced in my worke, though I have drawne it in loose sheetes, almost every chapter rudely, yet I cannot say to have finished any thing tollerably, farther than chapter XI. lib. 2, and those which are so compleated are yet so written that I can at pleasure inserte whatsoever shall come to hand to obelize, correct, improve, and adorne it."[15] This would bring the manuscript to at least page 167 of the extant text. Again, some twenty years later, in an 11 July 1679 letter to John Beale, Evelyn, in my opinion, is referring to the "Elysium Britannicum":

When againe I consider into what an ocean I am plung'd, how much I have written and collected for above these 20 yeares upon this fruitfull and inexhaustible subject (I mean Horticulture) not yet fully digested to my mind, and what insuperable paines it will require to insert the (dayly increasing) particulars into what I have already in some measure prepared, and which must of necessitie be don by my owne hand, I am almost out of hope that I shall ever have strength and leasure to bring it [i.e., the "Elysium Britannicum"] to maturity.[16]

I suggest that the fair copy text of the "Elysium Britannicum" may have been produced in several stages: there are noticeably different inks used throughout separate sections of the manuscript, some lighter brown, some very dark brown turning to black; and the character of the handwriting changes within the fair copy text, especially evident between the earlier chapters of Book I, and the chapters on garden layout and decoration in Book II. Conversely, the number of changes Evelyn made in the first and last quarters of the fair copy text indicate that the fair copy text as it survives reflects a fairly concentrated period of writing. It is precisely in the areas of experiment, discovery, and philosophical inquiry into nature that Evelyn introduced the vast majority of his changes and additions. It cannot be coincidence that the first and last quarters of the surviving manuscript account for approximately two-thirds of the marginalia and insertions, with the remaining text having only a third of such changes. Thus, the chapters on celestial influences, the seasons, and the natures of soil, as well as medicinal plants, decorative flowers, and nonnative plants, have many more changes and added material than chapters devoted to the subjects of landscape design and garden ornament.

Moreover, in keeping with Evelyn's stated intention to "obelize, correct, improve, and adorn" the "Elysium," he crossed out entire pages of the fair copy text as new information came to hand, and indeed noted at the beginning of Chapter 3 of Book I: "My purpose was quite to alter the philosophical part of this first booke" (ms. p. 6). Again, Evelyn often reminded himself in a marginal note that for additional improvements to a specific chapter's subject matter he should consult his contemporaries, such as Marcelo Malpighi, Robert Boyle, or Nehemiah Grew to update his discussion of the elements (6), Rusden and Martin Lister for bees and insects (200), and Hanmer and Pierre Morin for information on flower propagation and cultivation (Book II, Chapter 16).

Evelyn continued his "dense overwriting" of the manuscript until close to his death at the age of eighty-five.[17] The latest dated annotation in the text is for 1702, on page 161: "Here consult Bernard Lamy Translated into English, printed 1702: you have in your library at Wotton, Pag 122, 123" (see Fig. 27).[18]

After his death in 1706, Evelyn's library and papers, including the "Elysium Britannicum," remained more or less in the Evelyn family despite the "assistance" of individuals such as William Upcott and some of Evelyn's own descendants. Upcott (1779–1845), sometime sub-librarian at the London Institution, was also a book collector and scholar who with William Bray (1736–1832), a noted antiquarian, edited and published Evelyn's diary in 1818. In 1814 Upcott received from Evelyn's great-great-granddaughter by marriage, Lady Mary Evelyn, an essential "free hand" to investigate the Evelyn family papers. The papers and books of "Sylva" Evelyn, as he was known,[19] were apparently of special interest to Upcott, for when his own library was auctioned in 1846, many of Evelyn's manuscripts and books were found in the collection, leading to Upcott's Janus-like reputation as both malefactor and benefactor of the Evelyn collection. However, as Geoffrey Keynes noted in his bibliographical study of Evelyn, it could be claimed that Upcott was indeed a real benefactor for the Evelyn collection, because the family, at least by the early nineteenth century, was perhaps somewhat "unmindful" and carefree about the importance of John Evelyn's bibliographical and manuscript legacy.[20] Whether the manuscript of the "Elysium Britannicum" was numbered among the Evelyn papers and books that were part of the Upcott auction remains unknown at the present time.

In due course, following the ravages of auctions and editors, as well as family complacency through two centuries, the entire collection of books and papers was placed on deposit at Christ Church, Oxford, in 1951 by a collateral descendant, appropriately named John Evelyn. The Christ Church Library continued to house the

Evelyn collection of papers until 1995, when the British Library purchased the entire collection. The books had earlier been sold at auction in 1967, with the British Library acquiring many volumes that contained Evelyn's annotations or important association value.

The extant remnant (MS 45) of the manuscript of the "Elysium Britannicum" contains 342 consecutively numbered pages, with one major lacuna comprising pages 25 through 36, and some misnumbered additional pages inserted toward the end of the volume. Written principally in English, the text has numerous quotations in Latin and Greek, ranging from the classics on gardening, such as Virgil's *Georgics*, to contemporaneous authors, such as Abraham Cowley; there are also a few glosses written in imperfect Hebrew. The manuscript is bound in a single small folio volume approximately thirty-one centimeters high by twenty centimeters wide. The codex's binding is likely of mid-nineteenth-century fabrication; it is half-bound black morocco with paper-covered boards. The volume as a whole shows rather repeated handling.[21]

In addition to the fair copy text of 342 pages, there are numerous inserted sections of textual material, ranging in length from several lines of text on a "sliver" of paper to thirteen folio-sized pages of text and illustration. The total amount of additional text resulting from separate insertions, marginalia, and interlineations would amount to more than one hundred pages of fair copy text, not including the more than one thousand single word changes Evelyn incorporated throughout the fair copy. It is understandable why Evelyn failed to have the entire text made ready for publication during his lifetime, even with the support and interest of his colleagues at the Royal Society and Oxford, although parts of the work were published separately.[22]

Evelyn included more than eighty illustrations for the work, some requiring entire pages, such as the two-page collection of garden tools (see Figs. 8 and 9). Other drawings occupy large portions of folio pages, such as the phonotactic cylinder and the music to be played on it (see Figs. 35, 36, and 37). More frequently, however, Evelyn drew rather more modest illustrations, scaled down to fit into the margin of the main text, or even the margin of an insertion (see Figs. 2 and 3). His illustrations are almost all done in ink, except two in faint pencil on the subject of echo chambers (see Figs. 31 and 32).

The majority of the text block remains secure, although several gatherings at the beginning of the volume have come free of their sewn binding; in addition, several pages, including the printed prospectus that serves as the volume's table of contents, have begun to lose text through constant folding and unfolding as well as the general handling that the pages have received over the course of more than three centuries.

The table of contents is of bibliographic interest in its own right because it began its life as a broadside announcing Evelyn's grand design of the "Elysium Britannicum" and exists in several versions. The copy in the "Elysium" codex[23] has had page numbers added to the various chapters that may indicate that the original manuscript of the "Elysium" had included at least five hundred additional pages. Indeed, Evelyn noted in his preface to *Acetaria*, in an oblique reference to himself, that the manuscript had grown "to so enormous an Heap, as to fill some Thousand Pages."[24] Although the manuscript numbers added to the printed table of contents page correspond exactly to those in the existing text, there is some doubt in this editor's mind that Evelyn completed a fair copy text for all the books and chapters listed in the contents. Because of information given below and in Frances Harris's essay, one might conjecture that the remaining page numbers, for which the text is not extant, may be only estimates for the conjectured lengths of the chapters, and therefore Evelyn may never have actually finished a fair copy of the entire text because of his desire to bring to completion the most up-to-date statement of the gardener's art and science.[25]

A preliminary review of three boxes of Evelyn's miscellaneous papers in 1992 at Christ Church revealed no immediately identifiable additions to the current text, except for two small pieces of paper that evidently became separated from similar pieces of paper that had been previously tipped into the codex. With the permission of Christ Church Library, the two pieces were transferred to their respective locations in the codex and are included in the transcription. Portions of the remaining fifteen boxes of miscellaneous papers then in the Evelyn archive at Christ Church, which Michael Hunter had earlier examined with some success for potential additions to the main manuscript of the "Elysium" (MS 45), were subsequently consulted by this editor after they were purchased by the British Library.[26] (See below and Frances Harris's essay for the role of these and other materials in the creation of the "Elysium Britannicum".) Since Upcott removed at least one section of the "Elysium," other sections may also exist, but have not yet been identified as belonging to the original manuscript.[27] Indeed, in a separate set of pages attached immediately after the contents page, Evelyn has set down "A Table leading to the notes in the loose Sheetes to be inserted into the Elysium Britannicum" (see Appendix 1). The table lists references to 220 pages of notes to be distributed throughout the entire original text of more than 867 pages indicated in the table of contents; this reference is to MS 38, for which see Frances Harris's essay.

Because of the occasionally negative but generally well-intentioned treatment that the manuscript received at the hands of members of the Evelyn family, Upcott, Bray, and several auctions, and mindful of the arguments that Harris makes in this volume, I question whether Evelyn had completed an entire fair copy version of the text that was as far along in editorial revision as the surviving portion, MS 45. In addition, because up to the present time no single piece of the manuscript has been located that would link itself to the missing text via page number or placement symbol, it is not likely that there are any missing pages to be identified beyond what has been fairly conclusively determined by Harris and others to be significant parts of the raw documentation that Evelyn would have used for the text.

At Frances Harris's suggestion, three manuscript items were examined in February 1998 to ascertain whether they might be, or should be, made an integral part of this edited transcription: Evelyn MS 38, Evelyn Papers Miscellaneous Manuscripts XI (a group of unnumbered loose papers), and British Library Additional Manuscript 15950. Although a few additional portions of the text were identified (via page number and matching location symbol) for this edition of the "Elysium Britannicum," the remainder of the material does not appear to fall into the same category of "intentional" or "publication-ready" text as is contained within MS 45. Rather, these materials could be viewed as the raw data (or as Evelyn marked them on MS 38: "Rude Collections to be Inserted into the Elysium Britannicum") from which Evelyn would have developed text in a similar state of completeness as MS 45. As noted above (and very clearly described by Harris in this volume) nowhere in any of these papers do page numbers or location symbols appear, devices that Evelyn consistently used to attach his numerous insertions to the correct place in the text. Whereas MS 38 contains book and chapter references that link the subject matter to the respective chapters that are missing but noted on the prospectus page or table of contents, it was impossible to link definitively those items that were identified by book and chapter to the respective extant text. Although the other two manuscripts contain one or two instances where there is a page number with a location symbol, the matching symbol does not appear on the corresponding page of MS 45. There is therefore little doubt that these three sources contain valuable information to indicate the intellectual content and directions that Evelyn had intended for the missing portions of the "Elysium Britannicum," but they should only be viewed as potential sources for Evelyn to have synthesized into a finished text and should not be considered integral parts of MS 45, which arguably reflects a finished text awaiting an experienced editor.[28]

The appendices to this volume contain inserted material that is quite extensive in length, selected based on my sense that Evelyn had simply inserted the material at a logical point in his text with the aim of future editing for inclusion in the text proper or for placement in the appendices of the "Elysium." At some future point, in a differently edited text of the work another editor will exercise her or his best judgment on how Evelyn would have brought the text to an acceptable state for publication.

In her introduction to John Evelyn and his "Elysium Britannicum" at the 1993 Dumbarton Oaks colloquium, Therese O'Malley quoted Stephen Switzer, one of the eighteenth century's greatest gardeners, on Evelyn's place in garden history: "As [Evelyn] began, so he continued till his death, a great lover and observer of gard'ning. . . . In short, if he was not the greatest Master in Practice, 'tis to him is due the theoretical part of Gard'ning. . . . His own Works, which are publick, are a clearer Demonstration of the Greatness of his Genius, than any Monument I can raise to his Memory."[29] After more than three hundred years, Evelyn's most important unpublished manuscript is now available to readers, researchers, garden historians, and anyone who delights in the hortulan arts.

Notes on the Transcription of the Manuscript of "Elysium Britannicum"

The present editor's original transcription of the "Elysium" was a line-by-line literal transcription, with no wrapping of text, that is, each transcribed line ended where the manuscript line ended. Exceptions to this rule were all interlineations, marginalia, and inserted text. This system reflected the practice of Evelyn, who made no attempt beyond the fair copy text to set left and right margins. Catchwords, that is, a word or words, printed at the foot of a page to direct the bookbinder to the first word of the following page, were also retained as in the original. The current version of the transcription has wrapped the text with a view to making the main text more readable, and eliminated catchwords except where the catchword differed from the word actually used. Evelyn also used catchwords to lead into inserted text; these words are retained.

Suggestions from an initial selection of scholars interested in the "Elysium" at a Dumbarton Oaks Round Table in March 1991 led to a revision of the text that follows generally accepted standards for transcription of similarly dated manuscripts.[30] As a consequence, I silently expanded abbreviations for words such as *with*, *which*, *the*, *that*, *them*, even the word *colour* in one of the inserted texts, and so on, and reduced all superscripts to standard text. Text that Evelyn underlined has been italicized for better readability.[31]

Evelyn changed his mind about phrasing and spelling in words, phrases, and sentences, and there are inconsistencies throughout the text, beginning with the title page and running through the last page. Evelyn's spelling has been retained without standardizing variants, although, in the interest of clarity, interpolations have been used: [*sic*] or modern spellings in square brackets [ ]. I attempted faithfully to recapture Evelyn's lined-through text (several thousand instances) and noted Evelyn's own additions and substitutions by means of wavy brackets { }. My own interpolations into the text are within square brackets [ ]. Parentheses ( ) reflect Evelyn's own use.

A peculiarity of Evelyn's updating of his text was his penchant for adding more text in the margin or on an inserted piece of paper than the available space could handle. Again, his seemingly interminable, almost obsessively compulsive additions to certain areas of the text, most notably in the section describing the plants in the coronary garden, proved very challenging; on some days only one or two pages of text could be transcribed. Equally trying were Evelyn's marginal notes, sometimes in the faintest of pencil, especially his annotations citing sources of additional reading. He also did not restrict his marginalia to the fair copy text, but managed to add marginal notes even to his insertions, in effect, glossing the glosses.

For all marginalia and text additions made on separate free or tipped in pieces of paper, I have noted the mode of addition and the location in the text at which the addition was made. In all, Evelyn made more than 750 marginal notes and insertions, ranging from simple citations of a classical author and/or work, such as Virgil and his *Georgics* and Lucretius's *De rerum natura*, to modern authors such as Francis Bacon and Abraham Cowley. There are also multipage additions, such as Evelyn's four-page design of a "physical garden" inserted at page 329 (see Appendix 10), and his dozen or so pages on hydraulics and other waterworks (see Appendices 2 and 3), and a number of multipage insertions in other hands (see Appendices 4 and 6). In some ways, Evelyn's marginalia, inserenda, and addenda are the most interesting parts of the work, for in many instances their contents represent the products of the best and the brightest of authors on these subjects for almost half a century.

For the Latin and Greek excerpts, complete author and title citations, including chapter and line numbers, are supplied where they could be identified, so that readers may consult the original texts. The Hebrew alphabet, astrological signs that Evelyn used to indicate the months for various planting activities, and other symbols are also reproduced in the published text.

Evelyn's idiosyncratic spelling in general, and in particular his creative genius for using several versions of proper names for people, places, and plants (many of which were obscure or arcane), provided innumerable opportunities to use the reference resources at Christ Church Library with great success. However, several words and phrases remain to be clarified in the future, and are marked as [indecipherable] in this volume. Text that had been lined or circled through, or for which the ink or pencil has blurred, presented a particular challenge, for such words, although originally clear, were more difficult to read than Evelyn's own scrawl in his marginalia and insertions. Single question marks alert the reader to the lack of absolute certainty in the transcription of individual words. Because Evelyn also used question marks in his text, in all cases where there could be a misinterpretation, additional notes have been given in the published text.

The Manuscripts of the "Elysium Britannicum"

FRANCES HARRIS
British Library, Department of Manuscripts

While this first published edition of the main manuscript of the "Elysium Britannicum" has been in progress, John Evelyn's archive, of which it is a part, has been acquired by the British Library and is for the first time being systematically arranged and cataloged.[1] In the course of this work, it has become clear that rather more survives of the "Elysium Britannicum" than the main text here published. The manuscripts relating to it, in fact, fall into four distinct groups. As an addition to the main text, transcribed here by John E. Ingram, and pending a full catalog of the whole Evelyn archive, it may be useful to have an interim description of all of these manuscripts, how they relate to each other, what they reveal of the successive stages of the work, and what additions they provide to the main text.

The first mention of the "Elysium Britannicum" by Evelyn comes in the dedicatory epistle to his translation of Nicolas de Bonnefons's *Le jardinier francois*, published in December 1658, although he states there that the design had been conceived "long since,"[2] perhaps when he first began to lay out his gardens at Sayes Court in 1652. In 1659 he circulated the first version of a synopsis or prospectus of the work among Samuel Hartlib's circle. Various responses were received, the most significant being from Henry Oldenburg,[3] the future secretary to the Royal Society, and John Beale, the West Country clergyman, and writer on husbandry, who was to become Evelyn's most prolific correspondent. The latter, in a long and important letter, suggested the addition of six or seven additional chapters, including one on "the riches, beauty, wonders, plenty, & delight of a Garden festivall," another on the "transmutation of flowers," and another on "Mounts, Prospects Precipices and Caves."[4] No copy of Evelyn's first synopsis appears to survive, but "to avoyde the infinite copying of some of my curious friends,"[5] he had another printed, this time with Beale's suggested additions incorporated, some of them almost verbatim. There is a copy of this second version, once part of the Evelyn archive, in Additional Manuscript 15950, f. 143. From this source it was published in successive nineteenth-century editions of Evelyn's diary and correspondence,[6] and so has until now been the most accessible and familiar version. The group of manuscripts of which it forms a part is further discussed below.

Early in 1660 Evelyn circulated this synopsis more widely, to a group of Oxford experts[7] and to Sir Thomas Browne, among others. The composition of the work itself appears to have been considerably advanced at this stage, but it had not reached the form in which it now survives. In his long covering letter to Browne, which has become the best known description of the project, Evelyn explained that, "Though I have drawne it in rude sheetes, almost every chapter rudely, yet I cannot say to have finished any thing tollerably, farther than chapter XI. lib. 2, and those which are so compleated are yet so written that I can at pleasure inserte whatsoever shall come to hand to obelize, correct, improve, and adorne it."[8]

Immediately after this Evelyn printed yet another version of the synopsis, this time inserting (as Book II, Chapter 18) a new section on "stupendious and wonderful plants" that he had first mentioned in his letter to Browne. It is this version of the synopsis, now printed as part of John Ingram's transcription, that Evelyn used as the table of contents to the main text of the "Elysium Britannicum" (see Appendix 1). It contains various manuscript additions in Evelyn's hand, including page numbers for the beginning of each chapter and a continuous sequence of Roman chapter numbers (I–XLVII), in addition to the three Arabic sequences for each of the three "books" of the work. He has added the note that these Roman numerals cross-refer to the chapter numbers added to his commonplace notes for the "Elysium," in bundles marked with the symbols of a pentacle in a circle, two triangles, and a double circle intersected with a line. Some of this commonplace material survives and is described below.

Evelyn continued to work on the "Elysium Britannicum" intensively for several more years, though much interrupted by Royal Society work and other commissions.[9] In fact he extracted the whole of the "Kalendarium Hortense," the last chapter of Book II, for inclusion in his treatise on forestry, *Sylva*, the first publication officially sponsored by the Royal Society. *Sylva* was a compilation not dissimilar to the "Elysium Britannicum," and its popularity and influence must have encouraged him. Yet by 1668 he was admitting privately that it might be beyond his resources to treat the subject of horticulture so comprehensively, though he felt that he was "engag'd too far to retreate with honour."[10] In fact the project was now so widely known that its imminent publication was referred to in the *Philosophical Transactions of the Royal Society*.[11]

In 1670 work again came to a standstill when Charles II commissioned Evelyn to write the official history of the Dutch war. After this uncongenial task had been officially discontinued in 1674 Evelyn returned to the "Elysium," collecting and collating fresh material and occasionally quarrying it for short publications. But with his advancing years the sheer quantity of matter he had amassed became increasingly daunting to him. To John Beale he admitted in 1679:

When again I consider into what an ocean I am plunged, how much I have written and collected for above these twenty years upon this fruitful and inexhaustible subject . . . not yet fully digested to my mind, and what insuperable pains it will require to insert the (daily increasing) particulars into what I have already in some measure prepared, and which must of necessity be done by my own hand, I am almost out of hope, that I shall ever have strength and leisure to bring it to maturity.[12]

Despite further prompting from the Royal Society in 1684 to finish his great work, "a book very much desired,"[13] the last of Evelyn's publications derived from the "Elysium" was to be *Acetaria: A Discourse of Sallets*, published in 1699 when he was almost eighty.[14] It was prefaced by one final version of the synopsis, now headed "The Plan of a Royal Garden: Describing, and Shewing the Amplitude, and Extent of that part of Georgicks, which belongs to Horticulture," and including a new chapter in the third book on "garden burial." Evelyn then went on to explain why he never had been and now never would be able to bring the project to completion:

> this is that which abortives the perfection of the most glorious and useful undertakings; the unsatiable coveting to exhaust all that should or can be said upon every head. . . . There ought to be as many hands, and subsidiaries to such a design (and those masters too) as there are distinct parts of the whole . . . that those who have the means and courage, may (tho' they do not undertake the whole) finish a part at least, and in time unite their labours into one intire, compleat, and consummate work indeed.

Descriptions of the four groups of surviving manuscripts of the work follow. One, originally part of the Evelyn archive, has been in the British Library's collections for many years; the others all remained in the archive at Christ Church, Oxford, until its acquisition by the Library in 1995 and will be assigned British Library Additional Manuscript numbers when cataloging is complete. But for the present purpose I have used the numbers assigned during the period of their deposit at Christ Church.

Evelyn MS 45

Evelyn MS 45 is the principal manuscript of the "Elysium Britannicum," originally composed in three "books," of which the present volume provides a complete transcript of all that survives. It clearly began as the autograph fair copy which Evelyn intended, in the optimistic early years of the project, to send to the press; it even includes a double-page opening of beautifully drawn garden implements from which the engraver was to work. The text as it now survives must have originated in the early 1660s, since it represents a stage further than that described to Sir Thomas Browne in January 1660 and predates the extraction of the "Kalendarium Hortense" in 1663 (published in 1664), the page number for which is given in the table of contents. However, many later insertions have been added, both as interlineations and marginal notes and on separate slips; these are discussed further below.

But the crucial point to note is that less than half of this manuscript as it originally existed now survives. We know from the pagination added by Evelyn to the table of contents that it originally ran to more than eight hundred pages, possibly more than one thousand. But of these, pages 25–36 of Book I, on soil and compost, and everything after page 342—that is, from Book II, Chapter 18, "Of Wonderfull and Stupendious Plants"—are missing. This includes all of Book III.

The losses from Books I and II are probably to be accounted for by their removal for piecemeal publication; as a rule the manuscripts that Evelyn actually sent to press are not preserved in his archive. To this extent their contents are not really lost. The missing pages of Book I formed the basis of his *Philosophical Discourse of Earth*, delivered to the Royal Society in 1675 and published the following year.[15] Part of Book II, Chapter 19, on "Olitory and Esculent Plants" and "Sallets," was published in *Acetaria*. The section of Chapter 20 on winemaking is probably to be identified with the "Directions concerning Making and Ordering of Wines," which Evelyn added to *The*

English Vineyard Vindicated, published on behalf of John Rose in 1666.[16] As we have seen, the "Kalendarium Hortense," which formed the last chapter of Book II, was first published in 1664 as an appendix to *Sylva*, and in many editions thereafter.

The reasons for the total loss of Book III can only be conjectured, since no part of it is known to have been published and it has not been found among the material removed from the archive by the nineteenth-century collector William Upcott. On the evidence of the successive versions of the synopsis, Book III appears to have undergone the most changes, the order of the chapters being altered and new ones added. It must therefore have become much more disordered than the rest, and perhaps also, like several of the supplementary manuscripts described below, became badly damaged by damp, so that it did not seem worth preserving. But we will never know for certain.

It is likely, however, that much of the content of one of the longest chapters of Book III, that on "the Gardiners Elaboratory, and of distilling, and extracting of Waters, Spirits, Essences, Salts, Resuscitation of Plants, with other rare Experiments, and an account of their Vertues," was derived from another of Evelyn's projects of the early 1660s. In Paris in 1651 he had attended the chemistry lectures of Nicolas Le Fèvre, and when these were published in 1660, he undertook a translation of them, the first portion of which survives in his archive as MS 61. Le Fèvre's work as published included detailed instructions for carrying out particular processes, many of them involving plants. It is at this point that the manuscript of Evelyn's translation becomes fragmentary. As he was also working intensively on the "Elysium" at the time, it seems likely that he decided to incorporate the translated material into it, and although it is now lost we can infer at least some of the content from Le Fèvre's published work. It is suggestive that the few pages of experiments on vegetable matter which do survive in MS 61 include a sketch plan and elevation of a garden laboratory and its equipment which very probably represents that in Evelyn's garden at Sayes Court.[17]

MS 38

This volume consists of Evelyn's collection (originally 221 pages, now 155 folios) of additional, mostly autograph, material to be incorporated into the "Elysium Britannicum." It bears his annotation, "Rude Collections to be Inserted into Elysium Britannicum, Referring to the several Chapters of what is beg[un]" (f. 150v). This material is particularly worth attending to because it includes many insertions intended for Book III, of which the main text is now missing.

In his reading and correspondence from the 1660s until the end of his life, Evelyn was constantly discovering more items of information to add to his great work. Some he inserted into the manuscript itself as marginalia or on separate slips, connected with the main text by a variety of symbols, of which the simplest was an asterisk. Others he noted down in the order he found or read them, using a collection of miscellaneous scrap paper, in some cases the blank portions of address leaves of letters to himself and his father-in-law. Since there were too many of these notes to be incorporated as slips into the manuscript, he preserved the leaves uncut, annotating each entry with its correct location. Some of these annotations take the form of abbreviated subject and chapter headings, but most are book and chapter references in Arabic numerals, separated by a hyphen; as Evelyn notes at the beginning of MS 45: "Note that in the loose papers . . . the first stands for the book, the second for the Chapter: as 2–8 in the margent: that is the second book; chap 8. viz Transplants, & so of the rest." He then paginated the entire collection of loose leaves in his own hand, 1–221, and used these page numbers to compile a corresponding key in chapter order which he inserted at the beginning of the main manuscript, immediately following the table of contents, thus bringing together all the material for insertion into each chapter. The key is headed, "A Table leading to the notes in the loose Sheetes to be inserted into the Elysium Britannicum" (see Appendix 1).

The material in MS 38 comes from a variety of sources, including published works, private communications, and his own commonplace books (e.g., f. 6, "See for an Engine or water-worke, my Booke of Receipts Mechanical: paragraph 68").[18] Many of the notes are only a few lines in length; some run to a paragraph or more. As is clear from the key just mentioned, they include additional material for every chapter in the main manuscript, ranging from a new draft page for the introductory chapter (f. 136v), to passages on subjects as diverse as compost, water, grafting, transmutation, greenhouses, grottos, statuary, and artificial echoes, and many notes on actual gardens, ancient and modern. Also included are some original letters and lists of plants sent to Evelyn by friends and associates; these are listed below. When acquired by the British Library the whole collection, which then had a disintegrating binding of a much later date, had suffered badly from damp and was extremely fragile. The paper has now undergone extensive conservation, but some fading and discoloration remain, and parts of the text require patience to decipher.

An itemized summary of contents is as follows:

ff. 1–10, 14–16v, 19–24v. Notes for incorporation into all three books of the "Elysium Britannicum," with abbreviated subject and chapter headings added in the margin for each item, referring to those in the table of contents in MS 45, f. 1. Includes (f. 22) a page of notes headed "Villa."

ff. 11–13v, 17, 25–57, 59–65, 76–78, 81–98, 115–125, 127–132, 136–149v. Notes for incorporation into all three books of the "Elysium Britannicum," with book and chapter numbers in Arabic numerals added in the margins for each item (e.g., "2-1" for Book II, Chapter 1). Includes several lists of plants (ff. 93, 95, 147–149v) not in Evelyn's hand.

ff. 18, 153–155. Notes with Roman chapter numbers in the margins, referring to the continuous sequence (I–XLVII) added by Evelyn in manuscript to the table of contents in MS 45.

f. 58. Letter from Cuthbert Horsley to "Madame" [Lady Tuke?], 20 April 1670, with a passage marked by Evelyn for insertion in Book II, Chapter 19.

ff. 66–74v, 79, 126, 133–135. Letters from John Beale to Evelyn, 19, 22, 29 October 1670; 11 December 1668; n.d.; 9, 12 November 1662, discussing the "Elysium Britannicum" or matters relevant to it, some passages marked by Evelyn with the book and chapter numbers (these supplement the long sequence of the Beale-Evelyn correspondence elsewhere in the archive which contains further references to the "Elysium Britannicum").

f. 75. "An Extract of Mr [Henry] Oldenburg Letters Paris" [1660s?], containing a message for Evelyn concerning a French work giving advice about the situation of a garden.

ff. 99–114. Letter headed "Madrid 12 June 1668," much faded but describing the gardens of Spain, in the hand of Edward Montagu, First Earl of Sandwich, at that time ambassador in Spain, with passages marked by Evelyn for insertion chiefly in Book III, Chapter 9.[19]

f. 150v. An original wrapper for this bundle of notes, marked with a flower symbol.

ff. 151–152. List of books and authors consulted in the compilation of "Elysium Britannicum."

Of the 221 pages numbered by Evelyn in MS 38, the following pages are missing: 62, 72, 74, 77–78, 81, 100, 103(?), 111, 124, 127, 143, 183, 192–195, 198–201, 218. Of these, pages 72, 77, 81, 111, 124, 143, 193, and 218 are now among the third group of notes relating to the "Elysium Britannicum," described in the following section.

British Library Add. MS 15950, ff. 142–174

This group of thirty odd leaves was among the large collection of manuscripts removed from the Evelyn archive in the early nineteenth century by the collector William Upcott, who claimed to have had permission from its owner, Lady Evelyn, to do so. When Upcott's manuscripts were sold at auction in 1846, several items were bought back by the Evelyn family and several others acquired for the (then) British Museum, Department of Manuscripts. The latter are now numbered Add. MSS 15889 and 15948–15951.[20]

An itemized list of the "Elysium" items in Add. MS 15950 is as follows:

f. 142. Part of a wrapper with the note in Evelyn's hand, "Belonging to Elysium Britannicum/Materia substrata for Hortus & Elys/not yet inserted," with further note "This large Bundle Containes the severall Parcels and Bundles marked ✪ ⊖⊖ ❀."

f. 143. The second version of the printed synopsis or prospectus for "Elysium Britannicum," described above.

ff. 144–145. A bifolium, originally MS 38, page 143, with a variety of notes, chiefly for insertion into Book III.

f. 146. Description and measurement of pall-malls in Paris in the hand of Evelyn's father-in-law, Sir Richard Browne, 1660, marked for insertion into Chapter XVIII (Book II, Chapter 6, on walks, terraces, etc.).

f. 147. Originally MS 38, page 218: a series of notes, chiefly for insertion to Book II, Chapter 19, concerning groves, labyrinths, etc.

f. 148. A receipt, not in Evelyn's hand, headed "To make the perfect oyl called Balsamina," and marked for insertion into Chapter XXXVII (Book III, Chapter 2, concerning the gardener's laboratory).

ff. 149–156, 164–172. A variety of short notes marked with the symbol of the circled pentacle, for insertion into several Roman chapter numbers.

f. 158. "A Note of Garden-Tooles," 18 November 1670, marked for insertion into Chapter XIII (Book II, Chapter 1, "Of the Instruments belonging to a Gardiner").

f. 159. List of plant names with references to Robert Sharrock.

f. 160. Originally MS 38, page 124: a sequence of notes, several marked for insertion into Book II, Chapter 13, concerning insects.

f. 162. Originally MS 38, page 111: a list, headed "Bibliotheca," of books concerning plants and gardens.

f. 169c. Originally MS 38, page 72: for insertion into Book I, Chapter 2, concerning a gardener's qualities.

f. 169d. Originally MS 38, page 81: for insertion into Book II, Chapter 19, concerning fruit trees.

f. 170c. Originally MS 38, page 77: passages for insertion into several chapters of Books II and III.

ff. 173–174. Two garden designs, marked with the circled pentacle, for insertion into Chapter XVII (Book II, Chapter 5, concerning knots, parterres, etc.); the first, originally MS 38, page 193; the second, annotated by Evelyn: "see in your notes of Husbandry for the true draught of the Garden at Says Court before the bowling ground was made."

Unnumbered Loose Papers

In addition to the above collections, the archive contains a further group of unnumbered loose insertions for the "Elysium Britannicum," probably of a later date than most of MS 38 and left unpaginated. They are on sheets of different types, some of pocketbook size, and each is annotated with the chapter number in Roman numerals to which it relates, and with the commonplace bundle symbol of interlocking circles. Some sheets are also headed "Hortus," "HE," or "S." Evelyn's key to these abbreviations, now in Add. MS 15950, f. 80, shows that "S" indicates that the notes were for inclusion in the next edition of *Sylva*, and "HE" that they were "to be inserted in what I begun and intended about Gardning & Horticulture, under the Title of Elysium or Paradise." The collection comprises insertions for many chapters, but the most significant relate to Book I, Chapter 10, concerning earth; Book II, Chapters 15 and 16, concerning conservatories and flower gardens; and Book III, Chapters 6, 7, and 8, on "Hortulan Laws," "Hortulan Study," and "Hortulan Entertainments."

ELYSIUM BRITANNICUM[i]
OR THE
ROYAL GARDENS
IN
THREE BOOKS

Præmissis præmittendis, etc.
BOOK I.

---

1. **[Margin note]** part of this is printed. *Syl*[va]

BOOK III.

---

2. **[Margin note, printed]** This is already publish'd, being but a Chapter of
this work.

FINIS

J EVELYN

Elysium Britannicum.

The First Booke.

A Garden {derived and} defined, with its distinctions & sortes.

When ~~the~~ Almighty {God} had exiled our Fore–fathers out of Paradise, the memorie of that delicious place was not yet so far obliterated, but that their early atempts sufficiently discover'd how unhapp~~y~~{ily} they were to live without a Garden: And though the rest of the World were to them but a Wildernesse,[1] Adam instructed his Posteritie how to handle the Spade so dextrously, that in processe of tyme, men began, with the indulgence of heaven, to recover that by Arte and Industrie, which was before produced to them Spontaneously; and to improve the Fruites of the Earth, to gratifie as well their Pleasures and contemplations, as their necessities and daily foode.[2] True it is, that it was somewhat long before they had arrived to any considerable perfection in this Arte {the first and noblest part of Agriculture}; Since, we learne out of *Festus*, that in Citie or Country, a Garden was at first taken but for a poore and simple *Villa*[3] and deriv'd its reputation from the expeditious groth of the Plantation; *Hortus, quasi ortus, quod semper ibi aliquid oriatur.*[4] For, whereas other fields yielded their returnes but once in the yeare, this was *numquam sine fructu.* Some will have it of ὀρθος, and the arte *Orthographia*; because all things are to be planted in even lines; it may passe for a conceite of the *Etymologist*;[5] ~~whilst~~ others {againe} of the Gr: χορτος grasse and hearbs,

---

1. **[Insertion on facing page]** and that God had destin'd them this employment for a sweete & most agreable purition of their Sinns

2. **[Insertion on facing page]** for ~~even~~ {doubtlesse} even in the most innocent state, ~~thing~~ though ther was no individual {in itselfe} imperfect, yet {~~even~~} these perfections were to be discovered by Industry, & perhaps were not actualy existent & exerting their natures, & productions, ~~when~~ {till} by {his ingenuity} ~~culture~~ they should afterwards be cultivated by such ~~combinations &~~ applications, {marriages} ~~&~~ combinations & experiments as his {deepe} knowledge in nature ~~sho~~ should prompt him to

3. **[Insertion on facing page]** Pro quovis prædio suburbana; or rather as Plin: L: 19. c. 4: In ~~tam~~ XII Tabb legum nostrarum (says he) nusquam nominant Villam semper in significatione Ea Hortus: ~~in hor~~ & then, in Horti vero hæredium, quam rem comitata est Religio quadum; Hortusque et fores tantum contra invidentium facinationes dicare videmus. But Horti instructi were compleate Plantations to which nothing was wanting house or furniture, ~~as we~~ & thus purposely an heritage as we may learn out of Cicero: Offic: ~~de horti~~ speaking of those which Pythius bought

4. **[Margin note]** Isador: Gloss: l: 17. c. 10.

5. **[Insertion, crossed through, on facing page]** rather as *Festus* quod ibidem

locus ad plantas alendas et custodiendas;[6] or of ἑρχτος *Scaliger* ὁρχος, *Horctus,* and by *Euphonia,* Hortus. *Hesychius* ὁρχος κηπος και φυτων σιχος, deriving it ἀπο της ὁρχησεως:[7] But *Valla* more *Grammatically,* Hortus in the Singular [8] and Plu: for a *Kitchin-Garden:* Horti in the Plurall onely. For a Gardens of Pleasure, *Voluptatis, amœnitatisque gratia parati:* being what we in *English* name a Garden κατ' ἐξοχτω:, and without adjuncts, and the Sound, by some, conceived to be the offspring of the Heb: גן ghan; others of ἀρδειν, often irrigated: but We, rather from the *Picard* French (who much excell in this profession) *Giardin;* or {if not more} probably the **[page 2]** [9] *Saxon* Garte whenc the Moderne Languages, Giardino, Jardine. as from the former, *Huerto, Orto,* etc.[10] But, leaving these nicities to the industrious *Roote-diggers* from whenc soever the Name might spring, amongst the antient and honester *Romanes;* it signified no more then a place guarded, and fenced to sow Herbes in, as that which afforded them {alterum macellum, as *Pliny,* or successionem necessarium as Plin: Nonius Agricolæ succidiam alteram[ii] as Horac, or what he calls} what *Horace* calles

[iii]*Sine arte Mensam.* a Sallet, and to Bed, *Expedita res et parata semper.* So frugally did our Fore-fathers live,[11] till the *Horti Urbani* instituted by *Epicurus,* {that {same}

---

viri ad bella apti quique arma capere possunt orirentur: but this in a more ample sense; in the more stricte any cultivated place destind to the culture of plants: {but} Hor then Hortus in the singular was for the Olera & Sative furniture, Horti in the plu: for the our flouer Garden, as now disposd into walkes, planted with trees for shade & pleasure: Then againe

6. **[Margin note]** whenc sometymes Virens Agellus etc

7. **[Insertion on facing page]** Ὀρχατω pomarium: an Orchard, Habuimus in Camdenianus. Sunt sane ὄρχω et ὄρχατω Homeriem verba, unde tanto probabilius ad Anglos transitus. Dubito tamen an illa vera origo. Dubitandi caussa, quod Belgæ OEKTGAERD & OOKTGAERD; ut U et BOOMGAERD: et Germani BAUM GART: OBS GART: (LUST GARTE: Paradisus:) dicunt. Unde proverbiale est, etiam Anglie est verbum compositum: OR-CHARD, vel ORCH-YARD: (ut VINE-YARD, et MIN-YARD) ut τὰ OOKT, et EK sint ejusdem, ex Græca ὀπώρα originis: cuius τὸ to apud Belgæ, in f. mollitum remanseris; τὸ p. apud Anglos, q.d. ὀπωροφυλάκιον vel ὀπωράριον. Vide Mer: Caus Causabon Le quat: ling: Comment p: 314. [Meric Casaubon, 1599–1671, *De quatuor linguis commentationis pars prior quœ, de lingua Hebraica, et de lingua Saxonica,* London, 1650.]

8. **[Margin note]** LL. 3. 9.

9. **[Margin note]** Se the Saxon characters

10. **[Margin note]** & by translation & Metaph it signifies bene custodita virginitas & so the Jewes use the word: as well as poets. Se Diog: in *Stilpone* et in lampsaceno Carmine: et Hortulus apud Apuleum & the poets in a naturall sense as may be gathered from that of Plautus **[continuation indicated but not present]** Horti maxime placebant quia non egerunt igni parcentque ligno Ex horto Plebi macellum quanto innocentiore victu! Plin [19.19] κῆπος is properly a garden of pleasure which *Epicurus* first transferred out of the country into the Citty of *Athenes.* Therefore Pliny calls him Hortorum Magister. where Horti by all antiquity from holy ground

11. **[Margin note]** & therefore Pliny [19.19]: ne quam esse in domo matrem familias

Hortorum Magister as Pliny styled him} were by Contemplative men, and *Philoso-phers* refined to their successive improvement, and present magnificency. So that to define a Garden now, is to pronounce it *Inter Solatia humana purissimum.* A place of all terrestriall enjoyments the most resembling *Heaven*, and the best representation of our lost felicitie. It is the common Terme and the pit from whenc we were dug; We all came out of this parsly bed. At least ~~so~~ {according to} the creed of the Poet. For

> Hinc ubi quæque loci regio opportuna dabatur
> Crescebant uteri terram radicibus apti
> Quos ubi tempore maturo patefecerat ætas
> [12]Infantum.
> Twas hence, as every place was qualified
> The Wombes of Earth were full of rootes, which when
> Her Reckning was out, she op'ned then
> And tender Babes produc'd:

[13]*Olerum more,* as *Censorinus*; or if *Anaximander* were the first that invented the *Genesis* of the fermented Earth, it was not without companie, and a prospect of our origi-nall, analogical to our pedigree out of holy writ. *Nam omnis*[14] *caro est ut gramen, et omnis gloria hominis, ut flos graminis* etc. {to say nothing of the originall of our common mother, {growing} as a plant ~~growing~~ out of {the side of} Adam

[15]{For} ~~And~~ It was then indeede that the *Protoplast* only remained happy, whilst he continued in this *Paradise* of God;[16] and, truely, as no man can be very miserable that is master of a Garden here; So {will} no man {be} ~~will~~ ever be ~~be~~ happy, who is not sure of a Garden hereafter. From thence we came, and thither we tend; where the first Adam fell, the Second arose. Thus in the mysterious Sense {Horti by all Antiquity for Holy Ground} Παραδεισος Pomarium, The Church Catholic on Earth: *Voluptas sacra, Cœlum, locus beatorum,* the [17]Triumphant in Heaven. ~~For~~[iv] {And} what shall we add more? They were planted by the hands of God, honourd with the presence of our Saviour, and the greatest miracle of our Religion: Kings, and Philosophers, and Wisemen spent their choycest houres in them; and when they would frame a Type of Heaven, because there is nothing in Nature more worthy and illustrious they describe

---

(for this care also the women
were wont to look after) ubi indiligens esset hortus.
(not thriving without it)
though some ~~turne~~ {construe} it to a worse sense.

12. **[Margin note]** Lucret: L: 5 [807–810]
13. **[Margin note]** de die natali: c. 3. Camerarius Med: hist: Tom. 1. L. 4. c. 13. Diodor[us]: Sic[ulus]: L. 1.
14. **[Margin note]** 1: Pet. 1. 24
15. **[Margin note]** Here introduce A: Cowleys verse: 2d stanza to you: When God did man to his own likeness make etc.
16. **[Margin note]** in the whole Earth God found not any place more happy then a Garden
17. **[Margin note]** 22 Luc: 43 2. Apoc 2. 7 Aug: Eusebius Fr: Jun.

a Garden, and call it ELYSIUM; Instances sufficient to verifie our *Definition* with all its *Epithetes*, and *Encomiums*. But since a Garden is now a name of a large significa-tion; it will become the *Œconomie* of our present designe, to distinguish them by their several kinds; and thereby ~~to~~ shew you, what we intend to pursue in the following discourse.

Those who are most pleased with distinctions have constituted fowre, or five sortes of Gardens. As the *Parterre* **[page 3]** [18] *knot* and *Trayle-worke* for one: The *Coronarie* or Flower-Garden for a second: The *Medicinal*, or Garden of Simples for a Third: The Ortchard, {Olitory} and Garden of {Fruite &} *Esculent* plants for a Fowerth and Fift.[19] And these destinctions were hapily convenient enough for those that wholy attend upon either; as the *Ortchard* for the Fruiterer; the *Olitorie* for the *Cooke*; ~~and the third~~ for the *Botanist* the third, and the other for the *Florists*, such as make profession of selling and making gaine by their beauties, as some that we have knowne, who have sold their curiosities of this nature at such prodigious and excessive rates, that it has bin thought expedient by the state ~~itself~~ {of Holland} that no man should give above a thousand *guilders* for a *Tulip*, and modifie that ἀνθομανια; for to that intemperance and raritie were men arrived even in this innocent diversion.

And {now} though we hold that *Hortus instructus* an accomplished Garden, should consist of a mixture of all the~~se sortes~~ {particulars} which we have enumerated {and to show orchards, groves, Hills, Arbors, Walkes etc. ~~and even natural Temples~~}; there being nothing more agreable than varietie, well, and judiciously dispos'd: yet we shall in this designe treat ~~onely~~ {principaly} of the three first {with their severall Appendices & Ornaments} as having already published an account of the other in a [20] worke aparte;[v] and, for that we intend this Booke chiefly for the divertissement of Princes, noble-men and greate persons, who have the best opportunities and effects to make Gardens of Pleasure, though the *Particulars* therein described, may (we hope) be of exceeding use also, and emolument for persons of all Conditions whatsoever, who are either Masters of, or delight in Gardens.

---

18. **[Insertion on separate piece of paper marked for, but not attached at, page 3]** Even in hedging & Ditching, men of improv'd sense & forecast, that com-prehend lines & numbers, & seasons will be master workmen among other labour-ers; Wase [Christopher, 1625?–1690]: Considerat: concerning Free-Schools [Oxford, 1678]; etc. p: 49 speaking of the advantages of learning to all sorts of Mechanics etc: for Elys: p: 3. he should above all be a good Geometritian; & skilld in Surveying

19. **[Margin note]** Here something may be said of *Pomœrium* which dos by no means signite *pomarium*, but was a certaine space of ground reserv'd without a citty wales, as we learn out of Livy: Henc Festus quasi promurum.

20. **[Margin note]** French Gardener 1659.

CHAP. II

{For this Cap. consult Mo[nsieu]r de la Quinteni}[vi]

Of a Gardiner, and how he is to be qualified.

{God Almighty was the first Gardiner we have Scripture said: *Ornaverat autem plantis Jehova Deus Hortum* etc. Gen. 2.8 Ab *horto* fit Hortunus says Plin: L: 25. c. 2}

There are so many Accomplishments requisite to the perfection of an excellent Gardiner, that I know not whither[1] the {Orator in Cicero or} very Architect of *Vitruvius* ought to be more universal: For, as *Philo* the *Athenian* Builder, was not more admired[2] for his Worke then for his abilitie to discourse of it; So neither dare we esteeme him an accomplished Gardiner, who is not capable to render an account of his skill, beyond the ordinary Talent of men, who assume and take upon them that glorious name and Profession. In effect, we finde, that without Gardens, Buildings and Palaces *manus tantum sunt opera, nec sapiunt naturam*; and 'tis well ~~observed~~ {pursu'd} by my Ld: Bacon that men were at the height of[3] Building, before they were ~~exact~~ {tollerable} in Gardining. *quasi elegantia illa Hortorum esset res perfectior* {as if Gardining were the more excellent ~~& superior~~ {& accomplisht}}. And now though to arrive at this, we do not oblige our Gardiner to make his Circle through those *Duodecem necessaria* with that exactnesse which this *Dictator* requires in his Architect, *ut haberet pro laboribus Authoritatem*:[4] yet some of them may at no hand be omitted; namely, That He be of an ingenious a{n}d docile spirit, diligent and patient; That he be skillfull in Drawing and **[page 4]** Designing; in *Geometrie*, the *Opticks*, *Astrologie*, and *Medicine*; and if not in all these accurate, at least should he be *leviter imbutus*; especialy, in the facultie of Drawing, that he may be capable to invente, and imitate *Compartiments, Trayle-workes, Moresqu's, Foliage* etc. for the furniture and ornament of plots, and the severall ordinances of his Parterrs; and therefore to *Ebbozzar*, and dextrously {to} worke off from Smale into Greate, according to the *Type* and *Ichnography* of the designe. Truely, this of Drawing and the rest, are of so high importance, that what *Plato* caused to be inscribed upon the *Architrave* of his Schoole dore, would be set with as much reason over that of our Garden, Ἀγεωμέτρητος *nemo*; especialy, so far as concernes the modell, proportion and Discipline of those many singularities which enter into this {incomparable} Arte. The *Optic* is an assiduous attendant upon the Former, and instructs our Gardiner in *Perspective*, of extraordinary use for the ~~proportions~~ Symmetrie, breadth, and altitude of Wales, Palisades, Walkes, and innumerable other pleasant and noble diversions.

---

1. **[Margin note]** Vitr: L. 1. c. 1

2. **[Margin note]** Cic: 1. de Orat

3. **[Margin note]** – Serm: Fidel: [*Fr. Baconi de Verulamio Sermones fideles, ethici, politici, œconomici, sive, Interiora rerum accedit faber fortunæ &c.*, edition unidentified.]

4. **[Margin note]** Vitr: L. 1. c. 1.

By *Astrologie*, we learne the celestiall Influences, the nature of the Winds, Weather, æquinoxes, etc. Without some tincture in Medicine, Gardening is a voluptuous and empty Speculation: But by a competent knowledg therein, a Gardiner becomes one of the most usefull members of Humane Societie.

Chiron, and *Æscylapius* and *Apollo* himselfe {have} were esteem'd as Gods among men, and have bin chiefly celebrated for their Skill in Plants, there being so many incomparable {admirable & sovraigne} Remedies to be deriv'd out of the *Vegetable Family*, over which our Gardiner præside{'}s, not as a Beast to looke and feede on them onely; but to contemplate and to applie them in all their usefull varieties: To comprehend the nature of the *Earth*, and her productions: To be able to discourse of the *Elements* and to penetrate into the nature energie and reason of things with judgment and assurance. In a word, What is our Gardiner to be, but an absolute Philosopher! [5]It is therefore an egregious errour, says the[6] noble Verulam, that Princes and greate–men committ themselves to the advice of ignorant Gardiners, who manage things indeede with excessive cost, but litle judgment, and {and} so as not at all conducing to the amœnitie of the place. And therefore {upon this} the wise *Cato* was wont to say, *male agitur cum Domino, quem Villicus docet*, that the Gentleman was but in a sorry condition, who was always taught by his Servant, which applicable to the present instance, caused *Ischomac{h}us* to tell *Socrates*, discoursing one day upon this Argument, that it was easier to make, then to find a good Gardiner;

{To shew} Since what our former Author has concluded of *Architecture*, we may {as} justly pronounce of the Arte of Gardining, That, it is, *Scientia pluribus disciplinis, et* **[page 5]** *variis eruditionibus ornata* etc. An Arte which hath many Artes, and Sciences, attending upon her. For And on this account *Marcus Varro* calls it a Science; *nam, illud procul a vero est, quod plerique crediderunt, facillimam esse nec ullius acuminis Rusticationem.* Reckning them extreamely mistaken, who conceiv'd this Arte an easy and dull {insipid} study. It was their simple culture onely, with so much difficulty retrived from the {late} confusions of a bloody intestine warr, & put in reputation, which made the Poet say

> *verbis ea vincere magnum*
> *quam sit, et angustis hunc addere rebus honorem.*[7]
> whilst we affirme, rather a paine 'twill be
> To find out words suiting the dignitie
> of this our subject.

For, *nihil homine libero dignius*, says Cicero, *nihil tam*[8] [9]*Regale*: But having already dispatch'd this in the præface We now define our *Phyturgus* or Gardiner, To be a *Per-*

---

5. **[Margin note]** & the Mystery about which he is examined
6. **[Margin note]** Serm. Fidel
7. **[Margin note]** Geor: 3. [289–290]
8. **[Margin note]** pro Milone
9. **[Margin note]** or as elsewhere he speakes of the Law of Nature, so may we of this Mystery, Non Scripta, sed natattus & little after to which I may add with him; ad quam non docti sed facti; non institutione sed imbuti sumus & here **[continued**

son skillfull in the Arte of Gardning: The knowledg whereof consisting in the former *Præcognita's* hath for its End Utilitie, Delight, and Beauty.

Now, to improve a thing to this transcendency, Three principles are requisite: First, a good purse; Secondly, a judicious Eye; and thirdly, a skillfull hand. The first we will name *Hortulanus Sum{p}tuarius*, understanding [10] the person at whose charge and for whose ~~use~~ {divertissement} the Garden is made. The Second, *Hortulanus Ingeniarius*; who, though he may be fitly styled the *Surveyer* (as from whose dictates and directions the Garden is contrived) yet is he in truth, properly, The Gardiner, by way of excellency, as in whome all the fore mentioned accomplishments concurr and center. The third and last, is, *Hortulanus Manuarius*, a compellation more suitable to the immediate Labourers, though applicable also, to Masons, Statuaries, Plumbers, etc, and as many subsidiaries as are any way ~~appli~~ employable ~~to~~ {in} {~~the~~} conduct{ing} of the worke for its final perfection. So that still, we see, *instruunt facilius, quam inveniunt Artificem*; {& that} Such a Workeman is not easie to light upon. ~~But~~ {And therefore} we have {here} endeavor'd to shew you, how he should be qualified ~~and~~ {and} which we have the rather illustrated with all his Accomplishments; That the *Gentlemen* of our Nation (for whose sakes we have diverted other studies with this Worke) may not thinke it any dimunition to the rest of their Education, if to be dignified with the Title of a *Good–Gardiner*, be esteemed none of the least of their *Encomiums*.[11]

[Page 6 crossed out to end of page]

Figure 1. Illustration on a piece of paper inserted at page 5 of how the gardener of the grand seignior "rides through the streetes of Constantinople."

on separate piece of paper] And here Theocritus as one observes calls our Gardner ἐμειβετο Διός, Διᾶς ἀγρώτης by a divine Epithetum, there were Civil Greekes, & who understood the dignity of our function Says Cowley; ~~& it may be~~ but these were the days when Empps & Kings ~~used the spade~~ {were gardners} ~~sometimes~~, & ~~as one says~~ cultivated the Earth laureate vomere, et triumphali aratore

10. **[Margin note]** Hortulanus, qui horti curam habet. κηπευτής or κηπωρός, Hortilio, Horti custos, & cultur virentis agelli etc: Olitor for the Kitch Gardner. Viritarij for the Gardner of pleasure & Topiarij that governd the Contrspalie & hedges: deinde Ulptans de fundo instructo

11. **[Separate piece of paper]** I will now shew you how the Grand Segr: Gardner rides through the streetes of Constantinople in State **[illustration, see Fig. 1]**

~~One~~ {Two} Servants hold his stirrups, the other leads his horse

The Bostange – Bashaw or principle Gardner of the Grand Sigs Seralio: Se: [Sir Paul] Rycaut p: 40. [*The History of the Turkish Empire from the Year 1623 to the year 1677 Containing the Reigns of the Three Last Emperours, viz., Sultan Morat or Amurat IV, Sultan Ibrahim, and Sultan Mahomet IV, His Son, the XIII Emperour Now Reigning*, edition unidentified.]

{For these chapp. consult Malphigii[vii] & Dr. Grew,[viii] with Mr Boyles Origin of Forms[ix] etc. Dr Cudworth[x] etc}

Of the Principles and Elements in generall.

{according to the Spagyrist & Corpuscular Account.[2]}

[3]To the Culture of a Garden, the Knowledg of the Nature of the *Elements* is of absolute necessitie, and especially of the Earth, which being of all the rest the most *heterogeneous* (considered in the bulke it ~~now~~ appeares to us),[4] is the most difficult to

---

1. **[Margin note]** My purpose was quite to alter the philosophical part of this first booke.

2. **[The following material is designated for page 6, but Evelyn did not indicate where in the text it should be placed.]** Ad: p: 6 of the Principles & Elements in generall: c: 3.

{Since the virtues of plants are chiefly to be knowne by the elementary qualities & that properly speaking these Elements are the life & Spirits in which the astral or invisible*} To assigne which are the certaine Principles & true Causes of Things in order {call them Principio with the Chymists, or Principiata with the {early} Philos:} to the following subject, especially as they concern the order of Generation & Vegetation & government of Plants may be rather laudably attempted than positively concluded, so various is Argument & so different the Hypotheses of Philosophers: But since in these abstruse disquisitions, we may safely aquiesce in what so ever dos most rationaly solve the Phœnomenon, we shall rather choose to present you with what the more modern Enquirers have furnished us upon this Argument, & which seemes to be so probably established, than to engage in disputes which were endlesse, & which would swell this chapter {alone} to a just Treatise. We shall therefore say [some word?] of the common and vulgarly received Principles of the Peripatetes, some thing of the Cartesian **[continued on verso]** The Cartesians ~~compose~~ {produce} all things of Body, figure & motion **[end insertion]**, but more largely of the Spargyricall & Corpuscularie, altogether warning[?] ma[g]netical & Astrological Suppositions, & consider them as Analytically & yet as briefly as we are able. Parmenedes & some other made but one Principle, and divers learned men even of later **[insertion indicated but not present]** The Peripatetics have long enogh taught us that all things are composed of *invisible virtue of things & ~~sep~~ spermatical enemys dos lurke[?], producing everything according to the Sperme, the invisible lobules & offspring of the vegetable nature is nothing but the invisible fruite of the ~~Eart~~ Elements & astrall virtue, the products of the invisible Vertues conceald under sensible bodys, as the human soule in our bodys; Thus has every sorte of fruite their sensible astras or seedes from where they spring. But to assigne

3. **[Margin note]** Aristotle first

comprehend: Also the variety of *Climates*; the degrees of Heate and Cold; the qualities of the Aire, and of the Water; all which exceedingly cooperate and ~~agree~~ {signifie} to th' accomplishment of our designe; seing the causes of all Generation, germination and commencement of things so ~~much~~ {universally} result from their mixture and temperaments; as, on the contrary, their *d*i{*γ*}*scrasis* and exorbitancy, is the occasion of their ruine and dissolution. Our intente is not here to discourse, but very briefly, of the subtile nature of *Principles*, such as *Philosophers* describe them to be before they compose the Mixts; that is, by reducing them to those πρῶτα σώματα Atomes; but as they are vulgarly sti{y}led, and most sensibly knowne by the name of *Elements* (though upon strict intuition they prove but mixts) *viz*, Fire, Aire, Earth and Water; where-off the two last compose that goodly Globe upon which we intend our plantation, which the Aire and the Fire or *Æther* with the glorious influences of the celestial constellations inviron.

Now the Principle of all these Principles is nothing less then Nature herselfe. The Roote, Sp~~awne~~{erme}, *Entelechia* and Soule of all things, and the first li{n}ke to the ~~divine~~ {sublimest} Throne; seing the energie of matter is not that which in the body physical we find everyday ~~such~~ obnoxious to corruption; but ~~is~~ {is} that invisible Seede or Sp~~erme~~{awne} covered under that ~~case~~ {integument} or ~~shell~~ {skin} of the body, the offspring of a more sublime original by which it becomes {permanent &} immortal; so that even the very destruction and death of this external *phœnomenon* which imprisons this virtue, always produces some other ~~thing~~ individuall, and is never at repose 'til it againe revert to its sourse and original; as is evident in the {seeming} perishing of seedes and rootes if they specifie not according to our expectation, or ~~before~~ {do any ways prevent} their spring and resurrection, ~~according~~ {suitable} to that of St Paule, *quod tu seris, non viviscit* [5]*nisi mortuum fuerit.*

Now this spiritual substance (for as we sayd, there is a substance besides corporeal matter, which is the Soule, seminal forme and *Archeus*) ~~with~~ {produces} three distinct substances, or rather denominations (and therefore some do call them *second matters*) {distinct onely we say} for indeede, they are not essentialy different *inter se*; since that would subject them to manifold inconveniencies, hindring both the generation and augmentation of compounds & the variety resulting from mixts: They are therefore unical in *Essence* **[page 7, crossed out to *]** though differing in Name according to the varietie of qualities and effects. As when from its natural Fire, 'tis called *Sulphure*; from its Humidity and alimentation *Mercurie*; from its radical Siccity, by which it cements and constipates things, *Salt*[.] In a word, it is that *Universal Spirit of the World*, so much talked of, but little understood, by such as from the canting ignorance, or envie of some writers, have taken it for a *Chymical Chimæra*

vox, et præterea nihil.

not considering even as to our subject in hand, that Paradise being planted the third

---

4. **[Margin note]** for we speak not here of the Elements as altogether simple, which {to us} are ~~purely~~ {rather} intellectually conceived, then well express'd
5. **[Margin note]** 1. Cor: 15. 36.

day of the Creation,[6] the maturitie and perfection of the Earthly productions were
before the Sunn and influences of the heavenly bodies, which though they governe
in their annual courses by removing all impediments, and inciting this Seminall and
plastic virtue; yet doe they little or nothing in their primerous specification; which,
after the Almighty *Fiat* is ~~doubtlesse~~ {rather} the worke of this universall cause, determin'd by certaine parts of the Earth, indowed with severall qualities, which acting
together ~~cau make~~ {cause} each individual to emerge. We know that *Fernelius* ascribes
the original of all Formes to the heavens, others to the Aire, {& Water} and some to
the universal agent onely, determining both the Specificall & generical virtue thereto;
but we ~~have, and~~ shall hereafter examine them more punctualy, being satisfied for the
present that what we affirme is no such imaginarie notion, but ~~next under~~ a powerfull emanation from the ~~first~~ {primarie} Cause, seene by few, but felt by every body,
and flowing throgh all the workes of the creation, according to that of the poet

> Spiritus intus agit, totamque infusa per orbem
> Mens agitat molem.
>   Virg. [*Aen.* 6.726][xi]

For no sooner is a thing deprived of this Principle, Seminal and plastic virtue ~~(for that
it is that which we intend by the universal Spirit)~~ but forthwith it expires, becomes
uselesse and good for nothing; as is to be seene in Vitriol despoiled of its Salt and
expos'd againe sub dio for reanimation; {& even the very mould of our Gardins becomes altogether sterill & emaciat by being perpetually worked and exhausted til it
revive & receive new forces from this rich and benign heate} for this principle specified into any matter, can never revert to its first universalitie, without ~~it first~~ deserting
that *Idea*, which the body had communicated to it; and therefore, Vitriol is no more
vitriol, nor a Plant or Flower, Plant, or Flower, when it is once dissposs{ess'd} of this
Soule.[7] *

Now the manner of this Spirits operation by meanes of the three ~~primarie~~ {pri-
marie} Substances, with which it composes all ~~other Individuals~~ {the vulgar Ele-
ments}, though of extraordinary difficulty to investigate, consists in its specifing or

---

6. **[Margin note]** 1. Gen: 1: 12. 13. Ambr: Hexam: L. 3.

7. **[Insertion, lined through, on separate piece of paper, seemingly a re-
working of the paragraph in the fair copy text.]** exanimated & disposse'd of this
Soule. Now the manner of this Spirits operation by meanes of the three primary Substances with which it composes the vulgar Elements, though of extreame difficulty
to investigate, consists in its specifing or modifing the parts of {the grosser} Matter
by particular and seacret textures, evolutions dilations and mixtures; and (as the *Spagyrist* adds) c~~onformance~~{rresponds} to that *Idea* which it takes of the severall *Matrices*
which receive it determining them to the severall formes in which they appeare to us;
which *Idea* once assumed, 'tis deduc't into various particulars, so as each thing has its
particular spirit by which every species formes {to} itselfe a constant body, conformable to its owne nature, unlesse some accidental impediment {powerfully} intervine.
During the composition of these mixts, this universal principle retaines the nature of
that which invests it according.

modifing the particles of Matter, conformable to that Idea which it ~~receives~~ {takes} of the severall Matrixes, which chance to receive it, together with ~~the~~ particular and seacret textures evolutions {dilations} & mixtures, ~~with an infinite series of accidental causes, which assigned by God doe waite upon every thing~~, determining them to the Severall formes in which they appeare to us; as anon we shall more fully describe.

Hence, during the composition of *Mixts*, this *principle* retaines the nature of that which invests it, **[page 8, crossed out to end of page]** according to the Idea acquired, and communicates the virtue and qualities thereoff to the things which result from the composition; soone discovering by the activity puritie, solidity, volatilitie {thereof}, etc to what familie they belong; especialy, if by the most effectual instruments of separation (which, what it is, *Chymists* do best understand,) their courser garments, or fetters rather, be{ing} taken off, they approach neerer to their ~~libertie~~ {Emancipation} and reunion; as it is manifestly discovered, by one drop of any *Essence*; take that of the *Rose* or *Violet*, which [8] will impart a ~~greater~~ {freer}, and more delicious Sent, more refresh the heart and spirits {to which it now claimes a neerer affinity}, then whole bushels of Roses or Violets plucked from the bush or plant.

Such as are exercised in these kind of Speculations neede not be ~~told~~ warned that by *Salt, Sulphur* and *Mercurie* we do not meane those {concrete juices and} grosse substances commonly knowne by those names; and sold in the Shops, which are indeede but the results of grosser principles, proceeding from Masses of Atomes, coalescing in a certaine order, and position, which presents them to the Sensories under those names and externals; but as considered apart, and ~~wholy~~ {more} separated from the mixts by which our *Mercurie* opens the most obstinate and compacted bodies by its insinuating ~~figure~~ virtue, exciting the heate to fermentation, and devouring the salt, to which yet it is united. It is hot, and it is cold; ~~for it acts~~ {yet} not {as acting} by Elementarie qualities, but by a proper specific, as the Sunn softens, humectates, and hardens according to the composure of its object: for so {likewise} our ☿ [Mercury] preserves the water and other things from corruption, gives it activity; finaly, being duely mix't, and not constrained to exceede by any Agent extraordinary (for then he plaies the *Devill* and becomes a principle of destruction) gives groth, multiplies, and corroborats the faculties of all compounded bodies whatsoever.

{Farther} ~~Now~~ {to} the grosser Elements {compounded of and} investing these principles, the ☿ [symbol for Mercury] contributes, besides his liquor, which is a subtile and acide Spirit, the Colour to things, as plants and Floures, which is variegated according to the union and disposition of their rougher particles; and the modification of the light {up}on their Superficies. Our Sulphur is an oylie, natural, and vital fire, and therefore, whilst it remaines pure and *ætherial*, it floates upon the Phlegme and the spirits or ☿ [Mercury]. It is the matter of fiery *Meteors* above, and *Corruscations* beneath; it resists cold and never congeales; 'tis incorruptible, dulcifies the acrimony of Salts, vanquishes the acidity of the ☿ [Mercury], and in the Contexture of mixts, helpes to bind the Earth, which would else be nothing but dust and ashes. For it atempers the Siccitie of the Salt, and the fluidnesse of the ☿ [Mercury] by its sweete and balsamic substance, imparting that *genial* Warmth ~~which assembles and coagulates things together and~~ {and} from {which} hence proceedes those odoriferous

---

8. **[Margin note]** deliver'd from those grosser parts which depress

undulations of {the} Sents ~~from~~ {of} Flowers and other bodies, pleasant or offensive according as this is gradualy mixed with its companions: For odor is onely **[page 9, crossed out to end of page]** the diffusion of this Essentiall *halitus* wafted through the {thinner} medium to the mammillarie processes.

But these Substances, being extreamely volatile, are fixed by our Salt, and hindered from their naturall levitie Sublimation; and therefore it is allwayes the very last thing which we find in the resolution of all compound~~ed~~ bodies;[9] in which we discover two substances, the one, in forme of Simple *Earth*, devoyd of all qualities but weight and siccitie: the other, of an incombustible Salt, relenting onely in ~~fire~~ water. It is a body immutable and transcending in virtue, which it exercises according to the substance ~~which~~ it encounters; for the more *terrestrial* is fix't, the more *airie* volatile; the most *waterie* participat's of both: and all this we detect in the *common Salt* which we use, *Sal Ammoniac* and *Niter*. And it was very requisite to Speculate into these particulars after this Sort, as previous to these operations which are in due place to succeede, for from here it is[10] that the savors and tasts of things result, which like the former, varie, remitt, and intende proportionably as ~~it is~~ {they} {are} blended with the two former substances; allways understanding a subingression of the grosser particles into the various and spongy contexture of the Tongue in these effects:

For so we desire to reconcile whatsoever we may have spoken to the well restored doctrine of *Epicurus*; from which however, the notions seeme {~~somewhat distinct &~~} Hermeticall and to interferre upon a superficial view, we neither do, nor intend to receede. But to proceede; The Simple is purely *Salt*; that which is mixt with *Sulphur* is sweete; with *Mercurie* Egre; and compounded with them all, bitter, asper, sower etc. these substances being no where incountred solitarie, as truely inseparable: For, though (as we sayd) the ☿ [Mercury] disolves the ☿ [Mercury] yet this *Sulphure* coagulates the *Mercurie*, whilst our acrimonious and penetrating Salt associates and marries them together. In Summ, Salt is that which fertilises the Earth {is the most manifest in all our artificial composts} becomming with the *Sulphure* a vital *Balme* for the *Vegetables*; hence the Earth too much humectated with immoderate raines, {remitts &} looses its fecundity: It generates *Animals*, and hardens *Minerals* if not mixed with excesse; for then it corrodes and destroys as fast: Finally, it is, accurately inquir'd into the very center base & Sperme of all productions. Now as touching that more corporeall matter which the vulgar understand by the name of the *Elements*, as they be all of them parts of the whole, they are likewise connaturall, though distinguish't to us under the name of principles, appearing as so many severall differences of rare and dense quantities, which blending one with another by their mutual activitie, produce the *physical* mixt bodys and grosser compounds, more or lesse sincere **[page 10]** as the particles are united. And thus we come to have so many Severall Sorts of Earth, moulds, reines, Waters etc, as we find in turning up {the gleabe} and examining the ~~gleabe~~ Soyle for our Gardens: But it is the subingression of the parts of something else, which endowes any of these with the {substantial} qualities which we ascribe to them: Seing, as we sayd, there is amongst all these *Principles*, {but} one, which is

---

9. **[Margin note]** & ~~yet the most manifest in~~
10. **[Margin note]** Lib: 3. cap: 3

the most divine and active, yea so transcendently subtile as hardly to be discerned of corporeall existence, which is it, that by these powerfull effects produces ~~out of the former *mixts*~~ those *second-matters* whereoff we have at large discoursed, and, which as the forme, spirit and Soule of nature, gives {all} ~~every~~ thing{s} {their due} *fermentation*, that is, *Motion* and emissions whereby they act one upon another {& have life} according as they are more or lesse quickned by and susciptible of it. And this is that which the *Chymists* would signifie by *Ideifing* an *Universall Principle*. ~~By~~ {through} the mediation of particular receptacles, and the *Characters* engraven on them; by which they produce us those varieties, ~~which~~ {that}, not only our Gardens do shew us; but, which all the world presents us with.[11] {But} ~~The processe whereoff if we have endeavoured to explaine in Severall manners, and more sensibly, it will somewhat commute for the prolixitie of this Chapter.~~

---

11. **[Margin note]** for as Varro truely affirmes; the Principles of Gardning are the principles of all Nature, all the Elements, & contains in it more real Philosophy than any Art, Science, or Profession whatsoever & as Cic.: acknowledges dos proxime accedere; and it

CHAP. IV

Of the Fire

It may appear strange to some, and besides our Institution, that we should wander into these discourses, after our promise of brevitie: but since we pretend not here to write to *Cabbage-planters*; but to the best refined of our Nation who delight in Gardens, and aspire to the perfections of the Arte {& for Institution}, we thinke our selves obliged to assert the necessitie, which we have not made without just reason, of our Gardiners more then ordinary qualifications: For truely, did we not already believe him to be a person somewhat acquainted ~~in~~ {with} these Speculations the Subjects are so copious and withall so usefull that we should be constrained to extend our discourses to much longer periods. In briefe therefore, since all things verge to their natural center, 'tis manifest they are transported by a natural virtue concealed in their owne entraills, which can be no other then that magnetisme which every Element hath in it selfe, exercising their polar energies (as we may say) both in attracting what is amicable and correspondent to them, and repu{e}ls{l}ing the contraries. **[Page 11 crossed out to end of page]**

We attribute ascent to fire when being disengaged from other mixts and resigning to the more ponderous it mounts up~~wards~~ {towards} its owne *Spheare*, which like the rest of the Elements flourishes with its particular substances and fruits, whence some affirme, that these celestiall Constellations, whose numbers and lusture we so much admire {& contemplate} are no other then so many various receptacles in which the universall Soule as an *homogeneous* Substance, assumes a most perfect *Idea* before it descends to be corporified in the particular *matrices* of the inferiour Elements, from whence we come to comprehende that abstruse *Maxime* of the *Smaragdine* Table: *Nihil est ~~Sup~~{inf}erius, quod non fit superius*, and *è contra*, that every thing hath its star and *Signature*, which being knowingly applied ~~reflect~~ {produce} wonders as the learned Gaffarel[xii] {& others} has{ve} shewed in stupendious instances,[1] and effects so considerable, that did men, and especially, Gardiners well examine they would emerge the most accomplished *physitians* in the World. It is by the ascent of this fire {volatile, liquid & hott} that the clouds are sustain'd in the Second Region, 'til it having passed through that vapour {it} descend~~s~~ in showers as being deprived of its support.

This Fire, or Spirituall *Sulphur* being darted by the uncessant influences of the starrs, as the proper vehicle of the *universall Spirit*, insinuating it selfe through all the parts of matter {actu[ates?] &} produces every creature & by introducing into each individual its owne forme {(}to the reception whereof the matter is prepared,{)} assumes ~~to it selfe~~ the bodyes which we behold in so many varieties. ~~There be some~~

---

1. **[Margin note]** curiositez inouyos: c. 5. Theophrast phytogr. L: 1. c. 8.

who conceive {Or let us rather suppose} that it {this Spirit} begins to corporifie it selfe first in the aire in forme of dew etc, and by this meanes precipitating into the water, or earth, by the efficacious Character of some particular receptacle, and the formative {plastic} power {which ever contain [?] it} takes to it selfe a Minerall, Animal or Vegetable body; which {(}happning to dissolve by virtue of some powerfull Agent{)}, refines its *Sulphure* in such sort, that the *æther*, which is nothing else but a most pure and active *Sulphure*, attracts it againe; which being reinfluenced by those celestial bodies, is sent downe againe to recorporifie as before, and fertilise the Earth, and the Seminal masses {& dispositions} contain'd in it; which without this assiduous rotation would eternaly stand in neede of new miracles as perpetually exhausted: And this is that which not onely communicates that primary activity, fresh and succedaneus vigour to Seeds, plants and flowers; but affords also towards the never ceasing supplies to of the flames of *Ætna, Vesuvius,* the *Stromboli* and other *Vulcano's*; the virtues of hot and acid fountaines and inexhaustible *Bathes,* which have burnt and boyl'd so many ages, and are likely to continue so 'til the universal ecpyresis & conflagration of the world; {But besides these sublime fires, there are the more inferiour also, which as much contribute to that prodigious fertility of some places; according as it is more or lesse intense & copious: for if (as Arist[ot]l holds,[)] that neither the raines nor the rootes of trees exceede one another in depth (which we seldom find to be above 10 foote, whatever some report of the Cædars of Libanon), much is certainely to be attributed to {the} these subterranean fires, which as another kind of ἀντηλιον diffusing its head every way; & there can be no other so good reason about it, {aledgd} for the continuall fertillity of all the Apulean & Calabrian Campannian Italy {&} Sicily etc: than to this, for it is not the[i]r Vicin[i]ty to the Sun etc: so we also find it in divers parts of Somersetshire & above the Balt, & {about} the Acola[?] in Greenland, & upon the ises[?] at some warme **[continued in margin]** {warm} fountaines on the summit of high hilles, where the vapur is condenst in its passage:
[Page 12, crossed out to end of page]

CHAP. V.

Of the Aire and Winds.

The Second face of the Matter of this Universe reduced to forme is *Aire*, which, though a pure substance in respect of the other two Elements is yet of different constitutions, especially towards the Earth, where, as fitter for respiration {& nutriment}, it is {becomes} more thick, yet so as extreamely capable of extension and compression, and therefore replete {if not} with interspersed and disseminated vacuities {or at least with spirituall substances} as all other bodys are: And though it be comparatively light; yet it is ponderous of its owne nature and descends towards the earth from where {there} it is evaporated, extending and delating it selfe to the very *æther* itselfe & concurring to the worke of the Universall Spirit.[1] It serves for the respira-

---

1. **[Insertion on separate piece of paper]** Some opine {and that truely} that plants receive more nutrition from the Aire & water than from the Earth itselfe.* I have seene vines & other considerable plants set far into dry Earth, their rootes coverd with great buildings & walles, nay under the pavement of Kitchins & other warm places whose branches being spread abroad on the out wales have wonderfully flurished, as if it onely needed ayre & water to the armes: & certainly it is that nitrous defect in ayre which chiefly contributes to the vegetation; for Earth calcined till that Spirit be mortified produces nothing till new exposure to the ayre which infallibly impregnats it; & some Trees have ben knowne to grow & thrive which have ben planted upon flat & impenetrable stones & hard rock, without any earth, like the ~~Barbed &~~ Canary Vine, & we see how the Sedums & house leekes thrive upon the very sides of houses. So it receives the iradiations of the heavens, but most conspicuous in the Aloes, which being dry even to a manifest shrinking & even parching manifestly recover its Vigour, virve & fattnesse expos'd to the air onely, whereas ~~If~~ one spunefull of water would infallibly rot it, & this is no small Arcanum. For nothing would grow not only in our Gardens **[continued on separate piece of paper]** Nothing would grow not onely in our Gardens, but in the world, were there not a power in the Aire, penetrating & altering, bringing with it Selfe a nutriment which multiplies, & in it is a wonderfull Sperme, & Seede {as it were} congealed & constringed, & it, like a vegetable Magnes attracts to itselfe the nourishment of the Water, which affords a radiall moisture to all Seedes, which they hold to be a virtue of the 280th part in all Seedes, & therefore advise that in planting Trees, Gardners should ever turne the attractive poynt ~~of Tr~~ Northward: which attractive poynt they discern by putting a ~~piece~~ boule of wood into a vessell of water for that part will still be upmost. verte
* **[On separate piece of paper]** it selfe. ⧸A It has ben ~~held~~ {indeed esteemed} to have partly an Active, partly a passive power, in reference to which 'twas cald Jupiter, to that sd Juno: of which Seneca has something L: 3. qu[estionum]: nat[uralium]: c. 14.

tion of Animals and for the refocillation and refreshment {if not most to the very generation as it is so easily convertible into water of which hereafter} even of plants.

Here we observe, that *Gilly-flowers* and many ~~others~~ flourish best in open and free Aires, as being most impregnat with an *Idea* altogether celestiall and spirituall, which revives and cherishes them. For albeit plants are not ~~endow'd~~ endow'd with functions altogether so sensible as the vital and animal as having neither *lungs nor {animal} organs* of respiration {for they will spring awhile even sealed up in Glasse} yet possesse they something *analogicall* and very conformable to them [2](as we shall shew hereafter), ~~though but obscurely~~, by which they attract this spirit and ~~the~~ {its} *vehicle* so benigne to them: The contrary whereoff we perceive ~~when they are~~ {being} too severely imprisond, or covered with earth, or dung; when they tarnish, blanch, {are} suffocated and finaly corrupt {here insert Dr Sharrock p: 84:}[3]

To us that are conversant on Earth, the Aire is hot and moyst though what we respire be fresh & coole by the mixture, dilation and compression of it; the superiour parts are likewise very hott, as approaching the *æther*; but the centrall & intermediall ~~parts of it very cold~~ by consequence very cold. The Wind is onely an agitation of the particles of Aire, or rather a flux thereof, caused by the plenty of exhalations, attributed to the external and internal operations of heate upon the *terraqueus* Globe; and imbu'd with the qualities of the vapours through which ~~they~~ {it} passes; so as the same winds are ~~sane~~ {wholesome} and insalubrous according to {the variety of} accidents; sometymes wafting cold and nitrous *atomes*, blasts, and medews producing wormes, killing, & nipping, {~~burning~~} scorching, ~~and~~ {and} retarding the [4] beauty and

---

~~& that we put wind & ayr~~ We usually mingle them but he distinguishes Aera marem indicant, quia ventos &, or rather with Ennius in Varro. 4: de L[ingua] L[atina: book 5, paragraph 65]: Ista est is Jupiter quem dico, quem Græci vocant Aerem, qui Ventus est, et nubes inber postea, Atque ex inbere frigus, Ventus post fit, aer denuo. Anaximenes thought it a God. So Tulij de Nat[ura]: deor[um]: by reason of its boundlesse activity, & St Aug. de Civ[itate]: dei: c. 11. says that Diogenes, one of Anaxemens's scholars, acknowledgd air to be the material that all other things derived ther beings from, & that ~~from~~ {for} this 'twas Compos divinæ rationis: Anaxagoras sayd that Seedes were in the Ayre ~~as Theophrastus~~ I have Seene

   2. **[Margin note]** cap: 12.

   3. **[Insertion on separate piece of paper]** [Robert Sharrock, 1630–1684] Ad. p. 12. *Aire*

Such effect has the aire on Colours, that {even in things artificial} some {~~This~~ mixtures & application} ~~of~~ will not take effect but in particularly disposed places, such (for example) as the ~~bleues~~ Persian blues {& damasks & frabicks} at Florence, which (though the ayre be there so pure) will be woven but in ~~one~~ certaine loomes, though other places of the same towne have ben tryed with all due circumstance as far as art could devise; & then even in that very place & roome where it ~~is so~~ succeeds so well, the shifting of the wind alters it, & they immediately shutt up the windows when it blows & give over the worke: This I instance ~~to show~~ not onely to show off what import choyce of ayre is, but to lead the curious to farther experiments: & to ~~establish some~~ cultivate {the} philosophy of it.

   4. **[Margin note]** penetrabile frigus aderit.

maturitie of our flowers and fruite when they seeme to flatter us with the fairest expectations: Especially the ~~Eta~~ *Etesian* and anniversary winds spiring from the {North &} *North East*[5] for at the least fourty days about March, ~~comming~~ {proceeding} from the *Russian* tracts, where the snows and the yce are not yet dissolv'd: {A}and the {furious} *prodromi* about *Midsomer* the concussions whereoff leave their markes all the yeare after. And though it be certaine that by agitating the grosser aire, they preserve it from putrifaction; yet are they extreamely pernicious to our Gardens.[6] The South wind is hot and moist, Sulphury, furious and too opening; yet convenient for {drying & preparing the ground} the advancement of vegetable groths; as the foremention'd (when not over intense) retards the præmature arival of the Spring, 'till the Sunn be advanced to a posture capable to preserve what is tempted forth, & by ~~the~~ {its} periodique revolution, exposed to the aire. {This Wind is excellent for the stirring and di} **[Page 13, crossed out to end of page]**

The *East Wind* is indeede esteem'd of temperate qualitie upon many parts of the *Continent* which have large tracts of *Terra-ferma*; and therefore to be considered with caution, when we will deduce to practise the writings and directions of *Exotick* Authors upon our Subject; but we find to our sad experience, that in *England*, it is one of the most noxious winds to our Gardens (whatever *Virgils* counsell be concerning the site of Vineyards) as frequently blowing so long at the *Spring* that it nipps and dries the flowers and blossums of our choycest fruits. ~~and~~ hindering ~~the~~ {that gentle} aspiration {it destroys Graffs & is no season for that worke when it **[continued in margin]** blows ingenders wormes in timber they cutt & in pulse then sown} when the West and genial *Zephyre*, the[7] most benigne and temperate of all the {rest} ~~other~~, were most{re} to be desired, as the most ~~fa~~ kind and favoarable to productions.[8] All these with their *collaterall* should then be dilligently observed by our Gardiner, and may be prevented, improv'd, and modified with his care, and according to the situation and accidents of the place; for waters, mountaines, plaines, woods, minerals, citties,[9] etc. ~~We affirme againe, that the knowledge thereof is so considerable, as by~~

---

5. **[Margin note]** There the name Ester with us says learned men

6. **[Margin note]** whence the poet councells ~~never to stirr our ground Borea~~ tellurem Borea rigidam Spirante Geor [2.316] never to stirr the Earth whilst the North blow.

7. **[Margin note]** The Charriot of Odors & ravishing delights of Gardens

8. **[Margin note]** This wind also blowing in decrease of ☾ is excellent to lay compost or gravel in, as making it more thirsty & open: Se L: Bacon req: 668

9. **[Insertion on separate piece of paper]** Citties etc: Since as we noted, Winds spiring from palustrall and unhealthy places bear along with them those fumous & pulverulent adherences which proceede from a certain humid & tenacious matter which poyson & discolor our Plants especialy {when} the South Winds blow ~~it has ben~~ which also produce noxious Insects {& by calling forth moisture too fast {&} in blossoming times dos other harme: Se Browne exp: 562} It has ben observed by some expert Vespillions that where men that dye of the pestilence were buried, that the plants growing about the place, grew rusty & full of insects; thought to proceede from the halituous fumes of the venomous Carcusses penetrating the pores of the Earth & invading the rootes & infesting the ayre: For the ayre agitated by the wind

~~frequent experience~~ we find, that plants are much more obnoxious to winds, then to the very hardest and severest frosts, and shall better ~~insure~~ {support it} to be transplanted during the one then the other, not to mention those *Arsenical* and Scorching ~~blasts~~ {Sypherations} which sometymes infect, consume, and dry them more up in the space of few minutes, then had they bin a moneth plucked up by the rootes, or exposed to the {eye of the} Sun:[10] We therefore no farther pursue the necesity of these precepts, but recommend {you to} the advice of the Poet   Geor: 1 [51–53]

> Ventos et varium cœli prædiscere morem
> Cura sit, ac patrios cultusq; habitusq; ~~recuset~~ {locorum}
> Et quid quæq; ferat regio, et quid quæque recuset
> > > To know
> All Winds and Seasons, let it be our care
> What every region can, or cannot beare.

I conclude this Chapter with this facile prognosticator to detect the degrees of wett & dry, or any change of Weather: Take the Stipulo[11]

---

can carry things a wonderfull distance, to say nothing of the Athenian plague brought ~~there~~ out of Æthiopia into Egypt & then into Greece: Or to come to more benigne instances, those who who [sic] write of the Malucco plants report that the Scent of the Cloves & Cinnamon have been smelt 200 miles distant.*

   From these & other ~~instances~~ {examples} we ~~affirme~~ learne how much it concerns our Gardner to comprehend the philosoph of the ayre & Winds; & we find by wofull experience that plants are much more obnoxious[.] Hence he is to learne how to govern his situation, & to plant early blossoming fruite in the least exposd places[.]

* **[Insertion on same piece of paper]** And by the same meanes as we have shewed in raising artificiall deawes L: 2: c: 21 & the drawing of moisture from neighbour places, & by superfusions of cheape Aromatic Aires may be altered & prove of use to powerfull Influences both upon our Gardens, & the Spirits of our Gardners themselves.

   10. **[Margin note]** As in the *Azores* when the wind fretts the very yron, & the tiles of houses to pouder: as *Varenius* reports: so penetrating are the Salts they convey.

   11. **[Margin note indecipherable. Insertion of seemingly identical content on separate piece of paper:]** Take the stipula or spirall beard of the wild Oak {vine}, or rather ~~of~~ the cod of a wild Vetch, place it on a style, as in the fig: A.B. So as one extreame may be fix't on a piece of a stick or the like; then put on the other point of it: viz. B. a small ~~pi~~ slip of paper form'd like a magnetic index viz, B.C. placd horizontaly on A. Touch this Oak beard or Vetch with the least ~~wet~~ moisture & 'twill untwist itselfe so as to move the Needle; which when dry will revert the contrary way again: The reason is plaine from the dilatation causd by the moisture, & the natural distortion of the style which shrinks againe as the moisture is extracted new so insensibly **[illustration, see Fig. 2]**

But this ~~experi~~ Instrument is improved by concealing the style in a convenient box {pierct to intro[duce?] ayre}. The poynt {& Indix} of it only opening upon the ~~litt~~ lid or Cover with a Circle divided about it:

Figures 2 (above), 3 (below). Illustrations of "hygroscopes" "to detect the degrees of wett & dry, or any change of Weather" in the margin of an insert at page 13.

And thus has our Gardner a perpetual notic of all aerial vicicitudes, whether causd by the cold, heate, wettnesse or drynesse, wind or the like: or as it is yet farther advanc'd by what Mr: Hooke [Robert Hooke, 1635–1703] has brought into the report of the R[oyal]: Society after the way describd by Emanuel Magnan, to which may be added the Hygroscope for {inventd by the R: S:} to find out its pressure; both accurately describd in the History of the R.S. part: 2. p: 173. But this property have also all those plants & herbes which grow in wreathes, such as all the Convolunts, Brionies, Lupits, Lupines etc. And they are worthy our Gardner observations, & may serve to arme him against many accidents of the weather as it intends or remits, denotes the quality of the ambient aire & even different quality of the wind, The Rhomb if you place it to the Rhomb: so as to be highly usefull for planting, Sowing, Galling, & for to good purpose of direction in the governing your tender plants & rare plants especially such as you keepe house in the Winter Conservatory, of which se L: 2. c. 15. **[illustration, see Fig. 3]**

CHAP. VI

Of the Water

Those who have thought *Water* to be the first {material cause} and chiefest Principle of all natural things as the wise Milesian and others did {& particularly Theophrastus} have had many partisans {as to this of the Seedes of Plants} who in our apprehension had greate reason on their side; especialy, when we do steadily consider how many things are produc't from the condensation ~~of vapours and~~ coagulations {and motion} of vapours, & how susciptible they are of {all the} qualities. How wonderfully will a plant grow, put forth and flourish in water alone! The mature productions, that are to be raised by the severall temperaments of it, and ~~innumer~~ {the swarmes} ~~able~~ {of living} Creatures which {proceed from} reside and live in it, give sufficient countenance to their opinion, {& presumption} as containing in it selfe (for we now discourse of the vulgar{ly cald} Elements), innumerable receptacles, producing ~~those~~ those vast diversities of fruits, Animals, Insects, Vegetables, most of all perspicuous in the *Sea Lentill*, whose roote ~~grows in~~ {extends even to} the boosome of Neptune himselfe {besides} Corulls, mineralls, pearles, Sponges shells, ~~and~~ Salts {& things innumerable} in abundance: so that Sea or marinated water overflowing the Earth, when ~~drye~~ {once her bosome become dry againe}, exceedingly fertilises ~~it~~: {& improves her.} ~~And~~ **[page 14, crossed out to end of page]**

For, though at present it seeme to kill whatsoever growes upon it; yet being once well dreind and evaporated, {it} becomes of all dressings the most incomparable, {naturall} as is sufficiently apparant in our Marshes, nitrous imbibitions, and composts of which there is much to be ~~affirmed~~ {lirnt} from daily experience.[1]

~~Now~~ *Water*, strictly speaking, is coagulated *Aire*, moyst and fluid, but unequally, as 'tis more or lesse rarified. It is {esteemd} an insipid Liquor, devoyed of other com-

---

1. **[Insertion on separate piece of paper]** *Ad: p: 14 Water*
Upon this consideration, & the evident activity of Salts, I cannot ~~reject~~ but take notice of ~~the opinion~~ {those} who affirme the Sea to be as the heart of the ~~World~~ sublunary World, whence the Waters passe by seacret wayes into the Earth as by arteries, ~~carring ou~~ carrying the vitality of its salts into its body, from whence it returnes insipid by the rivers & greater channells to recruite at that inexhaustible fountaine, & by the way serving to allay the indispositions of ~~Animals~~ other Creatures who drinke of it ~~to aba~~ who find themselves heated by the over activity of Salt; & this we call quenching of thirst. And this motion of the water has something analogical to it of the blood in animals ebbing & perpetually flowing by a circular motion by which it takes as it were a new substance {& Spirit} passes the heart, & then revisites the body, by all these seacret {& aparent} deferends of Arteries & vaines till it want a new supply at the same fountaine. But to come to the vulgar definition, Water strictly speaking

pounds, but indifferent to the qualities; the first Substance produced by the activity of the Fire, and precipitating in deaw after reasonable condensation; the matter of clouds, raines, and fountaines; {and sometymes the dispersor of the seminall masses {themselves whether} drawne up with the vapour, & againe descending with it or as a coadjutor to the worke of the universall Spirit}; and so necessary to {in} this œconomie of nature that it is the very bridle and moderator of the *Spirits*, abating their *acidity*, and the fiercenesse of the *Salt*; it hinders the inflammation of the *Sulphure*; and imparts that usefull mixture {& ligature} to the *Earth* from them both; and therefore a principal ingredient of use and benefit to our *Gardiner*, as discovering thereby the qualities which it encounters through all its *percolations*. It furnishes that liquifaction and humidity necessary to generations becoming the *vehiculum* of that aliment, which is ~~sucked~~ {derived} ~~by~~ {to} the rootes, and distributed into the branches so that

²   sine certis imbribus anni

Lætificos nequeat fetus summittere tellus etc

     Unlesse some Annual showers ~~descend~~ {it lend}

The Earth her welcome of Springs cannot send.

And therefore of exceeding consequence it is that the waters which we use in our *Gardens*, be good, seing as they may be over cold, lapidescent, hungrie, sulphurous, Vitriolic, {vitrous} aluminous corrupt etc. so they will affect our plants; hinder, or accelerate their productions, as they are well or ill ~~qualified~~ concocted and qualified[.] ³

---

2. **[Margin note]** Lucret: 1.1. [192–193]

3. **[Insertion on separate piece of paper]** Ad: P: (14) Water.
~~But~~ How much farther ~~Water~~ this principle may concerne even the generation of plants, let {our} ~~Philosopher~~ Gardner philosophize: To us it seemes most stupendious that some trees which grow in the most arid & barren places, as well as ~~moist~~ uliginous & moist (for example the Birch) ~~should~~ & I am told both Oake & Ash etc:) should in one day yield 8 or 10 pound of liquor from one branc onely, nay in 14 or 14 days so much clear liquor ~~observating~~ which an observatant of the tree, ~~som~~ as to preponderat the whole bulke of an huge growne tree, stem, branches, roots & all; where some would affirm that Trees (& why not all other {hortulan} productions) *ex sola aqua fieri*, which water they suck from the ~~Earth~~ nitrous earth which bears them; & urge it farther for that it is evident nothing of the earth impairs or is ~~consum'd~~ insum'd

[Insertion continued on a separate piece of paper] ~~But~~ How much farther ~~Water~~ this principle may Theophrastus speakes of the {sudden sprouting} of trees that grew after the inundation of the Abderension bankes as if the water onely bred them:

It was from the fecundity of water that the Ægyptians adore their hydriam or ~~water~~ pitcher. Certainly the enquiry upon the whole subiect of Germination, & which principles are its true Causes is exceeding difficult, were that once don, the altering of species or Formes would not be hard; however in our opinion water seemes the most probable cause.

Here my Ld: Bacon urges by frequent instances that for nourishment water is

Now as the purest *aire*, so the best *Water* is that which is lightest, of good savor, and smell; fresh, humid, firme, limpid, trickling in smallest dropps; not slimy, not easily altering the colour of the recipient; soone evaporated; voyde of sediment, staine or clouds; if it cleanse perfectly well, be easily tinged; if it ingender no moss or flakes, and such as usually runs *South* and *East*, exposd to the aire and Sunn. In fine, the best experiment we know of examining all this, is, by præcipitating a few dropps of the oyle of *Tartar per diliquiuum*, into it, and filtrating it; if it be {im}pure and ~~excellent~~ {vitrous} you shall find it in the paper, and by the coagulation & resideue of the water; if good and excellent, by neither. To conclude, it is commonly an indication of good mould, where the water is good. But of all other, proper for the *Gardiners* use, that of *Raine* is the best; ~~es~~ and especially that which hath bin reserved at the *æquinoxes* {Air which is a seminall viscosity above all to be esteemd & indeed the proper aliment of Vegetables} as being most of all impregnat with the *universall Spirit*.

[4]{The following is an extract of Dr Sharroks Experiment of the successe of plants set in Water:}

[Page 15, crossed out to end of page]

---

almost all in all, & that the Earth serves onely to keepe things upright, & save it from over heate & cold: Thus Lu: Nat: Hist: Exp: 411. And againe he maintains exp: 647: that the Earth is not necessary to the first sprouting of plants, & affirmes that they will come faster on the water than the Earth, which though judiciously ~~taught~~ suggested is not to be over streigned to the neglect of Soyle etc:

[Insertion continued on yet a third separate piece of paper] Drie Earth in an Oven so as not the least moysture remain, weigh it accurately: set gourds in it, water them with fountaine water a little warm'd, or raine water better, which also weigh; when the Gourd is ripe, drie the Earth as at first, weigh it againe, & youl not find above 3 [an ounce] wanting, thou[g]h the gourd weigh many pounds: & what addition of substance there is probably made, not onely by the swelling of malted barley but the dust; & by its sprouting, in which solely water is made use of, every one sees, which dos in some sort confirm that opinion that the Earth is not {the prime} necessary, to the sprouting of plants what ever it may be to the progresse.

4. **[Margin note]** Sharrac p: 53 . 54 ad p. 56:

CHAP. VII.

Of the Earth.

We are now at last come to set foote on the Ground, and are landed on the *Gardiners Element* indeede. Where the *Earth* is situate, {or how it moves} as to the *Hypothesis's* which have exercis'd the contemplations of the profound *Astronomers*, we will not here much concerne our selves; provided that it be gratefull, and that we have enough of it; since the enjoyment and benefits which our Gardiner receives from it, gives him sufficient reason to favour their opinion, who have thought, that all the other Elements were created {for this} alone seing, whatever they possesse, seemes onely to reguard her Service: For hither descend the Influences of the heavens, penetrating the greatest of her Abysses and profundities: The Fire, and the water never repose within her Cavernes and channels, all of them conspiring to furnish her with supplies, concoct, ferment, impregne and make her a fruitefull Mother. The *Universall Spirit* ~~him~~ itselfe seeming to court the *Earth* more then all the rest of his Mistrisses, as most delighting in her embraces, {whither by} specifing in those Severall mixts, {~~whither~~} by virtue of those particular characters contain'd in the receptacles of her body, by which ~~irradiating~~ {encountring} a mundified, well prepard and qualified womb, it becomes a *Metall, Animal,* or *Vegetable* more or lesse perfect, different, Sweete, & Specious; or any other processe of modifing the parts of matter, by which the passive and active virtues of their parents produce them, appeare, and endow them with natures more or lesse durable, whereby they arive to their destin'd perfection, or immature and untimely Catastrophes.

In briefe, the Earth, though first in our designe, is last of all the Elements as well volatile as fixt; being, to discourse as a Philosopher, {a kind of mix in of certaine imperfect bodys} denude of all {manifest} qualities, siccity and adstriction onely excepted, and therefore sterill and improlifique {of itselfe};[1] It is sayd to be a thickn'd

---

1. **[Margin note]** That is till by help of the 3 principles & celestiall Spirit, that which is disposd growe perfect seede:

[Continued on separate piece of paper] Upon they {Spagyrists} affirme that Nature disposing {of} all principles (as a Monarch) causes them to act on each other, as the Fire on the Aire producing Sulphur; Aire on ~~fire~~ Water bringing forth Mercury, The Water on the Earth producing Salt, but the Earth having nothing to act on produces nothing of her self, but is contented to remain the receptacle, or at best but the nurse to bring up what she beares without any active & materiall contribution. Hence she is sayd to be a thickened & hardned Water but there be who affirme her to be nothing else but Niter*, ~~in whose bowells are many~~ {& if so then certainely she may} contribute something more of her owne to the production of plants than they imagine:

and hardend Water, as it holds gradation with the rest of the Elements, dry, cold, and sluggish 'till stirrd up and ~~fermented~~ {irradiated} by that Superiour agent, it be rendred apt to ingender all the other qualities ascribable to it, and so becomes ponderous, & salt, rocky, unctuous, contiguous, fat ~~and~~ firtile and usefull for all productions. But taken in the common notion {of unintelligible qualities which we onely mention}, and as it beares proportion with the rest it is cold and drye; the *Water*, cold and humid; the *Fire* hot and dry; the *Aire* hot and moyst: so that two of them though ever *Antagonists*, ~~yet~~ doe {yet} ~~they~~ so mutualy *Symbolise* as that the Water with the Earth in coldnesse; the Earth with Aire in siccitie; each *Element* participating with two, they become at length inseparable, and thereby avoyd that deffect or superfluity which would else result from an universall hostilitie.

Now that this generous Spirit hath its operation in the Earth, let our Gardiner take out of the profoundest of her Entraills what quantities he pleases, Sift and Searce It the most exquisitely, and expose it once to the embraces of this powerfull *Agent*, and he shall soone perceive the effects **[page 16 crossed out to end of page]** by a Seasonable production without any matter or seminal masses to worke upon, cast into it by hand {~~though yet we do not affirme but that it engage be a maine composition of a multitude of formes & substances~~} and that not onely in one, but innumerable species, according to the *Climate*, and other accidents, which qualifie it for such varieties; {~~At least~~} So the {greate} ~~virtue there is~~[2] hidden in the vegetant Salt contributing with the other principles to its genetive faculty invincible, and not to be destroyed, however treated; but that even in the very cinders ~~of it~~ Phœnix like, it reinvigorates, give we it but tyme, and rest, and that it be not deprived of the celestiall embraces. ~~or hindred by the sloth and inducing of~~ {which either finds the matter in her pregnant} womb, which he irradiats & quickens or else injects it by some hidden & seacret conveyance; near is the heate & spirit in the center of the Earth a Small cause of her various impregnations etc:[3]

---

* which the raines ~~dissolving~~ comming on dissolves the {particular} seedes in her womb whose attractive fire or Spirit rather feedes on the ~~milky &~~ oyly part of the moisture or astrall balsam, & radical humidity as some {mysticaly} tearne it.

2. **[First insertion indicated, but not present. Second insertion on separate piece of paper]** should conceive {even} without Seede (& for ough[t] we know Animals too) ~~De~~ A Friend of mine made {this} experiment He ~~cut~~ {cutt} a banke & drew off the spring in a small chanell out of a large pond For it is not improbable that this firtil womb & very ranke soyle, the ranke Soyle produc'd for many yeares quite differing kinds of plants; & not one plant of the first yeares production to be 2d [? paper edge torn] in the 3d: the like we ~~find~~ {observe} in all arable land ~~turnd~~ {converted} to pasture: by ~~which~~ [? edge torn] & what it might do in other species, which a recent soyle may {possibly} bring for[th] [edge torn] after the ~~first~~ first separation, as where greate inundations of Seas [&] [edge torn] rivers ~~breake out~~ {inundate}, we determine not: We know what is sayd of the sli[me?] [edge torn] of Egypt & some parts of Africa {what some ~~grave~~ {both historians & poets} thither have conceived even of man's original:} & how little credit it now gaines. But this we incline to believe, that there is at least so powerfull a Virtue hidden in the Vegetant Salt.

3. **[Insertion on separate sheet of paper]** And what more pregnant argument

can now be assigned for the assertion of the power & providence of God, against the half Atheists of our age, who with the poet

Jam adeo fract' est ætus effœtatque tellus Luct: 1 cf [2.1150]

pretend a decay {for such} in Nature: The Earth is still the same prolefique Mother, & the Heavens ~~& the Elements~~, the same Indulgent father: Boccart [Samuel Bochart, *Geographia Sacra*, Frankfurt, 1674] assures us from oculer experience & good testimony, that even to this day in the holy Land, the vines and other Trees, bear as fair fruits as ever; & what the Indies produce of stupendious in those kinds we have everyday brought us, besides what we reade in Authors of undou[bted] verity; So true is that of Pontanus (de rebus cœlestibus) that what seemes to impair in our plans, is recompensed in another would be in all {to [ideal proportion?] of nature} were due culture & Industry applied: To this Columella assents [? edge torn] L: 1. c. 1. where he styles the Earth diurnam et eternam fruenta & Pliny L: 28. c. 3. For as Grotius learnedly & piously if once singular things ~~pr~~ be deprived of Gods providence, the generall & universal will certainly come to ruine & destruction. But we give instances of the Earthly Vigour in more particle & connections in the 18 Chap: of our 2d booke where we treat expressly of the stupendious & wonderfull plants. We shall onely add that the Heathen admiring the Effects of Nature in this Rural Deity, not knowing how to give {a} name sufficiently comprehensive cald it *Pan* & The Earth is that true Pandora of the Poets pressing out her near dryed breasts in milions of streames, to feede & repair her {numerous} Offspring: & well was the word γαια or γη of the verb γαιω to excell & {be glorious} ~~(& perhaps then our *gay*)~~ upon the ~~florid~~ mount of her ~~daily~~ {daily} florid {gay} & beautifull productions.

Of the Celestiall influences, particularly, the Sun, and Moon; and of the Climates.

{It has not ben improperly affirmed, but the very rootes of Trees grow in Heaven, though planted on Earth, whither considered in relation to their nourishment, received from the Celestial *Influences*, or their Almighty Creators benediction. Hence Plato}[1]

Touching the Influences of the *Celestiall bodys*. They are certainely of grand importance, as to their effects and energies upon the Labours of our industrious *Gardiner*: For, as from them proceedes those healthfull and benigne *Aspects*, whilst they reguard us in pure and amicable irradiations; So likewise their destructive and maligne ~~Syderations~~ {in} *blasts, mell deaws, corruscations*, and other insalubrous *Syderations*; ~~and~~ {for} the Meteors themselves which contribute to all this are no other then the maladies and indisposures of the *Macrocosme*, as well as of the lesser World; so that a *Pyromantic* who could attaine to a certaine cognisance of the *Principles* before ~~spoken of~~ {describ'd}, and of the nature of the *Celestiall Influences*; to know of what *Sulphure* the *Lightnings*; and other *meteors* are compos'd; of what *Salt* the *Thunderbolt*; of what *Mercury* the *Raines*, might also be able to divine and augure concerning their prodigious Effects and greately prevent the mischiefe which they produce; and therefore, a Mysterie not to be slightly passed over by our studious *Gardiner*. We have already shewed how there is an invisible fire which is the Soule of the Universe. But there is also {a} visible ~~fire~~ which we may call the Soule of our Gardens, of all the Celestial inhabitants the most vigorous and active instrument; It {is} the ~~life of the World &~~ the Eye of the World, ~~and~~ the gemme of heaven, {&} the measure of Tyme, ~~and the Life~~ & the very life of nature herselfe; for it ~~nourishes~~ renews, nurses, augments, changes, fecundates, & vivifies the Seedes and the plants; the virtue of its beames transpierces the Earth, comforts her womb {and taking off all extraneous moysture} & sets the parts in motion. {& perfects concoctions} and he that effects all this is that benigne, masculine, diurnal, warme & splendid starr of starrs: where he touches not, nothing matures ~~so that were it art~~ {nothing arrives to perfection but not for} him, not onely our *Gardins*, but ~~man~~ {even our *Gardner*} himselfe would cease & come to nothing; So

---

1. **[Insertion on separate piece of paper]**

~~A Gardiner ought to understand the declination rising & setting of the Starrs.~~

Plato placd Astronomy the 3d amongst the Arts {because the knowledg of} opportunities & Seasons were so requisite in all our actions: I am sure in none more then in Gardning: The moone as being most neere to Earth has greate operation on Vegetables: ~~Then by Athenians calld Phyllida~~[?] [page torn]

truely is that affirm'd, *Sol et Homo generant hominem*. For as the *Sun* approaches, we behold the Earth, (hastning as it were, to the ~~to the~~ long'd for embraces of her welcome **[page 17, crossed out to end of page]** husband) to ferment, swell and every day grow biger, 'til being no longer able to containe the fruit of her teeming womb, she breakes forth into her thousand productions; peopling the fields, the woods, and the mountaines with those varieties of flowers, plants & trees; besides what she spawnes in innumerable other births, culminating with their celestial *Genitor* to their ~~elated~~ {admired} lust're and {elated} perfection; 'till satiated with her embraces and now retrograding at ~~the~~ {his} *Tropick*, The Mother which bare and nursed them, languishing at the departure of her beloved, withdraws that nourishment which before she aforded them; as being now no more able to support the charge of so numerous an ~~offspring~~ {Family}, 'till he revisite her againe at the next revolution of the Yeare.

Next to the *Sun*, hath the *Moone* wonderfull Effects upon inferiour bodys, influencing them with a power and virtue to attract nourishment, according as she is pleas'd to communicate her selfe; movving, and by her moyst imbibitions resolving those *Salts* before mention'd, which may be some cause of the brackishnesse and plenitude of Waters, more or lesse, as she maskes or discloses her pale countenance, where ~~in~~ like {wise} ~~manner~~ some {have} affirm'd that the Seas receive {even all of} their enigmaticall reciprocation, ~~which~~ {because they} hapen to augment and deminish as they participate of her light and influence and even in the *Æquinoxes*, and most temperate Seasons when this productive Salts act with so much vigour in trees, plants and all the vegetable Familie, most eminent in Spring and Autumne, when this Principle is more fluid, then when it is imprison'd and condensed by the excesse either of heate or cold.[2]

These two conspicuous *Luminaries*, created by the Almighty *Architect* for Signes and Seasons, there is no man may pretend to the perfection of an excellent *Gardiner*, which is ignorant of the annuall, periodicall, menstrual and diurnal Course and motions of them; so far at least, as to observe their different illuminations, aspects and mutual configurations; the strength and virtue whereoff intend, and remitt, according as they are respectively posited: And that the *Moone* and ~~Pla~~ the rest of the Planets

---

2. **[Insertion on separate piece of paper]** Ad: p: 17 moone:
{It is observed indeede that there is more aboundance of deaw in the full moone then at other tymes; & therefore Alemon (in Plat: Sympos: L: 3. gath: ult makes δρόσοω ἄερος θυγατέρα καὶ Σελήνης that deaw was the daughter of the Moone & the Ayre.} Some aspects of the Moone & Planets by their drawing forth their Heate & moysture, induce putrefaction, & something contribute to the ~~increas~~ birth & increase of hurtfull insects; & some againe excite the Spirits of Seedes & plants to put forth, & these in such Consignations it is proper to sow in ♉ [Taurus] for instance, ♑ [Capricorn] by a △ [trine] or ✶ [sextile] in the signes ♋ [Cancer], & so in ♎ [Libra] & ♑ [Capricorn], & to plant trees in ♒ [Aquarius] of which I dare give our Gardner but a hint because I am no friend to Astrological nicities in these matters: & that generally warme & moist weather is {certainly} the best for all these ~~master~~ operations what ever the Aspect or the Signe be; although I cannot here but take notice of the renownd effect of Pæonie rootes in Epilepticall fitts, being gatherd when the Moone passes under *Aries*.

are sometymes neere, sometymes at more distance from us in rerelation to *Excentricitys* and *Epicycles* in their ☌ [conjunction] and ☍ [opposition]; and as indeede we more sensibly discover by the greater effects. Now as there is betweene the *Sun* and the primary *Planets* a wonderfull cognation; so is there likewise betweene these two greater Lights and the *Earth*; manifesting it selfe by a kind of *magnetisme*, if at least the *Earth* (as some affirme) containe certaine fibers, which do diametrically, and perpetually attend and respect this usefull Planet. {But to passe this} B̶u̶t̶ as the *Moone* is of all the rest neerest to the *Earth*; so hath she a very greate influence upon the Labours and endeavors of our *Gardiner*, during the intire course of her periodic moneth:[3] We t̶h̶e̶r̶e̶f̶o̶r̶e̶ {usually} call her *New*, when she first apeares, augmenting to the seaventh day, and then we name it the *First quarter*; as many after, arriving to her perfection, she presents {us} with a *full* countenance; thence, as she decaies in beauty, and growes lesse, in 7 daies, she is in the *last quarter*, and in Seaven more, quite antiquated: all which is d̶o̶n̶ {perform'd} in the **[page 18 crossed out to end of page]** revolution of 27 dayes and about 8 howers.[4] And these are observations so requisite, that our *Gardiner* shall soone d̶e̶t̶e̶c̶t̶ {discover} it by the Effects, when he is to take up, cutt, Graffe, Transplant or Sow; for Seedes committed to the Earth at the end or beginning of the *Moone*, produce lusty and goodly plants, those in the full Low & Shrubby. **[Six lines of text heavily circled over and indecipherable]**
For it is an antient observation & we shall find it material

Ipsa dies alios alio dedit ordine Luna
Felices operum.
      [Virgil *Georgics* 1.276]
The Moone did not all Daies alike daine
Successfull for each worke.[5]

As to the {force of} *Eclipses* and their so much cry'd up effects upon inferiour bodys, we acknowledg to p̶u̶t̶ {place} no great stresse in them: For every night is a longer

---

3. **[Insertion on separate piece of paper]** γίνεται καί δε ὅσπερ ἄλλος ἥλιος ἐλάττων she is (as Aristotle some where says) a kind of diminitive Sun:
The illumination of the Moone begens from its first apparition, but the measure of it is uncertaine, because sometimes she appeares from the 4th day after c̶a̶p̶t̶u̶r̶e̶ coition; sometimes from the 3d, yea & sometimes from the very first, so as she is then sayd to be ἕνη καὶ νέα, vetus et nova; but these being for Lyncean eyes
4. **[Insertion on separate piece of paper]** So as the lunary yeare consists of 12 Synodical Moneths or 354 days, some odd hours & Scruples, eleven dayes lesse than the Solar; & is not rectified till the cycle of 19 yeares is Effluxed.
5. **[Insertion on separate sheet of paper]** Therefore these observations are given
1. Humidis locis interlunio serito, et circa interlunium quætriduo, Plin: L: 18. c. 22. [75]
2. Arborum radices plenam lunam aperito: idem:
3. Omnia quæ caduntur, carpuntur, tonduntur, innocentius decrescente Luna, quam crescente, fiunt: id: etc. verte

{and black} Eclipse; our houses, the trees, and the clouds do the same without observation or consequence: nor much more in the influences of particular *Starrs*, as they are fansi'd to governe, particular *plants*, but in the greater *Constellations*, they serve, for tymes, inspire a various forme into the Creaturs, (operating by various Effluxes both on the Earth & each other} they warme the Earth, and midwive ~~the~~ her productions; being with the rest of the *Planets* (the Suns *Coadjutor*), ~~and~~ deferents of the universall Soule; and thus the rising and setting of the *Fixed-Starrs* are cause of greate alterations.[6] ~~and~~ {for} it was altogether ridiculous to denie that the *Hyades* and *Pliades* were not rainy and nebulous {or at least forerunners of such seasons}: Leo and the Canicular fore {runners of} heate and drouth; *Orion* tempestious and humid, {the rising Goate obnoxious to winds and},[7] and so of the rest; ~~not to speake here of their operations on~~ the{ir} motion and explications of flowers, according as they heate, coole and moysten; it is wonderfull in plants, but it is {even} stupendious in stones, as the miraculous *Phases* of the *Selenites* and some [8]other demonstrate; ~~But~~ of which more in due place. {In the mean time to comprehend}[9]

This *Theorie*, then is so necessarie for our *Gardiner* that without some knowledge in it, he shall be exceedingly to seeke, when he would either cultivate the Earth, improve, or gather the fruits of it; And therefore in our rainy and unseasonable Cli-

---

6. **[Insertion on separate sheet of paper]** alterations; nor is it by their light onely, but other specifing qualitys transfered by that vehicle, which becomes more or lesse benigne as they are associated; for so Saturn & Mars neere to Jupiter, Venus, or Sol are kindred of the Malevalence, & therefore not without admirable providence has God placed that glorious Planet twixt Mars & Saturne, Sol twixt Mercury & Mars, 'twixt Luna & Mercury Venus ~~as~~ Mediatrix as it were; nor visite they all the parts of the Globe alike, but turning on their proper center, obvert different parts to the Earth, & being also excentrical are now neerer, now more remote, ~~so as~~ according as the divine Decorum has admirably ordered. And though we built not fundamentally on these observations of the planetary effects, yet to thinke that the celestiall bodys (which are doubtlesse complexed of elemental principles as other bodys are) do not operate on these inferiour things were madnesse, & it were altogether ridiculous to deny that the Hyades

7. **[Insertion on separate sheet of paper]** and in Pausanias {in Corinthians} you ~~have~~ read how greate the force of the Erratic when in conjunction, as joyned with either Sol or Luna; as Sol with Saturn cloudy & turbid aire Jupiter & ☿ [Mercury] temperate, Venus & mars showres, sometimes lightning {Mars & Saturn pestilential & exitial} etc. especially if the Moone be in conjunction; nor are the least & most imperceptible of the fixed without marvelous effects if coupled with the Planets: for the Fixed starrs like Women are sterill & barren of themselves, till impregnated by some {of the} planets: And here we might treate of their motions.

8. **[Margin note]** Se: Lib: 3. c. 1.

9. **[Insertion on separate sheet of paper]** to comprehend the perfect motions & operations ~~to~~ were a difficult taske whatever some pretend; for if we do not fully know the effects & nature even of our very plants which we daily handle & cultivate, & which are the subject of our Gardners studys, how shall we ever hope to detect any {thing} certaine of the the flowers of Heaven, the starrs so far out of our reach; & therefore we only touch their more eminent ~~effe~~ qualities & effects.

mates, {happy} inventions may be found out to prevent inconveniences, ~~to~~ redubble the vigour of the Sun, and protract the *Autumne*; to præocupate the *Spring* and moderate the *Winter*, and ~~Mr Beale has~~ xiii {it will be} shew'd ~~us~~ how to make such choyce {even} of *Plants* as may warme the ayre for others, more tender & lesse hardy. {& how to plant to the best advantage}[10]

Touching the *Climates* (which *Geographers* define to be certaine spaces of Earth, according to the increment of *Solstitiall* Days, distinguish'd 'twixt North and South, or that tract of land comprehended betweene the two Circles *Parallel* to the *Æquatuor*, (whereof the *Antients* made Seaven the *Neotericks* 24, and as many *Anti-Climats*, so as in all they are rekoned 48) We in short ascribe them to this inequality of the *Celestiall Influences*, and especialy of the *Suns* elevation, which creates these differences ~~whence~~ {as render} the Southern tracts ~~are~~ most obliged to him where his beames ~~being~~ **[page 19 crossed out to end of page]** darting with lesse obliquitie, maintaine perpetuall Spring, whereby, as a Situation approaches the warmer *Climates*, they excell one another in the grandure, goodnesse, and variety of fruite; the Sun attracting, dring, depuring and concocting the Spirits, which with us are over much sobbed and diluted with superfluous crudities, unless art and very greate industry interpose, as in our elevation of *Melons*, *Amaranths* and other curiosities; the *Climat* alone in Spaine ripning the *Oranges*, when there is scarse a leafe upon the tree in *Swethen*; And yet we do not affirme (with Virgil) that all plants do require distinct climats, or attribute the Effects and productions of Severall places to them, or the mere activity of the *Constellations*; but as we have already evinced, to the qualities of their *Receptacles* and Seminaries, when, as the most learned Browne xiv rightly[11] observes they best maintaine the intention of their *Species* and where, if they meete not a Concurrence, and be not lodged in a convenient *Matrix*, they are not excited by the efficacie of the Sun, or benignity of the *Climates*: for although supreame powers cooperate with inferiour activities, and may contribute to the plastic ~~con~~figurations of things; yet are they determin'd by particular agents, and defined from their proper Principles; so as what is a *stone* in one place, may be a *plant* or *animal* in another, according as the matter and the Mould are prædispos'd.

---

10. **[Insertion on separate sheet of paper]** for example that those fruites which have the sun rising on them till 3 houres after noone are best for the more delicate fruits, & such as you would have early; for the Sun begining to rise on them concocts by degrees {& insenses} & heates & scorches not at once as others do which dart more immediately: besides such as have not the early Sunn, are too ~~much &~~ long settled in the deaw of the night: Those which are more robust may endure the western aspect; & all watry fruites as Rose Chiles, Bergremotts, can indure from morning to evening sonn. other pares content themselves with the afternoone Sunn; & Abricotts will do well enough, yet the East is better, provided you secure the blossoms by curtaines if the winds blow, it freezes, or is too ~~ho~~ scorching, all which is obnoxious to: But in very scorching weather, even neere ripening time, tis counselable to sett skreenes before them from 10 a clock till 3. of Matts or boughes, 2 yards distant that the ayre may fan, & the Sun not scorch them. & for the same reason refresh the rootes with mungy stuff, which for beauty sake you may strewe over with mould: or moist mosses.

11. **[Margin note]** Pseudodox Epid: L: 6. c. 7.

CHAP. IX.

Of the fower Seasons

{It was truely sayd ~~of our~~ Annus fructificat, non tellus; the Earth & Soyle dos much, but the Seasons do more, it will therefore be of high importance that our Gardner both observe & prepare for them because the {due} knowledge of them will instruct him how {he is} to entertaine them when they happen to be either propitious or a sense, let him therefore understand briefly & plainly that the Solary etc}

The *Solary* Yeare we account to be that intervall of Tyme in which the Sun doth with its *Seeming* proper motion pervade the 12 Signes of the *Zodiaque*; by which he imparts those various temperaments to the Earth, according ~~to~~ {as} he approaches {to} or departs from our severall *hemispheares* and *horizons* which we distinguish into fower equal parts, or Seasons of the Yeare, giving to each of them three Moneths, whereoff six to the particular intemperatures and inconstances of hot and cold, defficient, or excessive, and the other six, to a greater and more agreable mediocrity and ~~thus~~ in this equipage

> ~~in se sua per vestigia volvitur annus~~
> ~~His owne steps back, the circling Yeare doth tread.~~

~~We commence with the Spring, as in which many *Divines* (though all accord not) have supposed the first Garden was planted by *God* himselfe. It beginns from the Hiemna Æquinox to the Summer Solstice at which tyme the Sun ascends through~~ ♈ ♉ ♊ [Aries, Taurus, Gemini] ~~the Vernal Signes: It is of qualitie hot and humid, but unequally; because the warmth sweetly increases.~~

> It Ver, et Venus, et Veneris prænuntius ante
> Pennatus graditur Zephyrus vestigia propter:
> Flora quibus mater præspargens ante viai
> Cuncta coloribus egregijs, et odoribus opplet.

[Page 20 crossed out to end of page]

> Inde loci sequitur Calor aridus, et comes una
> Puluerulenta Ceres, et Etesia flabra Aquilonum:
> Inde Autumnus adit; graditur simul Euius Euan:
> Inde aliæ tempestates, ventique sequuntur.
> Altitonans Volturnus, et Auster fulmine pollens
> Tandem Bruma nives adfert, pigrumque rigorem
> Reddit: Hiems sequitur, crepitans ac dentibus alger.
> [1]The Spring goes forth, and Venus walking by

---

1. **[Margin note]** Lucret: L: 5. [737–747]

Wing'd Zephyre, Venus prodromus doth flie
Before, and Mother Flora strews the way
With exquisite perfumes, and colours gay:
Next Drouth Succeedes, and him accompanies
The dusty Ceres, and th' Elesian breeze
O'th' North. Then Autumne comes, by whom dos tread,
The joviall Bacchus, who is followed
By other Seasons: Then the Winds do hast,
The roaring Nor–west, thundring South, and last
Winter with chattering teeth in order goes
Rigid with cold, and clad with brumal Snows.

^{xv}And in this order we commence with the *Spring* as in which sundry *divines* (though all accord not) have suppos'd that the first *Garden* was planted by *God* him-selfe. We reckon it from the Winter *Æquinox* to the Summer *Solstice*, at which season the Sun ascends through ♈ [Aries] ♉ [Taurus] and ♊ [Gemini] the *Vernal* Signes. {& that all the astrations are in efficacy} It is regularly, of qualitie hot and humid, ~~because~~ which causes it to impart a gentle & gradual warmth, convenient for the opening of the pores of the Earth, & her productions, which the Severity of the winter had im-prisond and locked up;² and if in this proceedure ~~of the Spring~~ any thing impeach the nature of the Season, as that in stead of the pregnant, benigne & supple showers, there ~~comes downe~~ {descend} haile, frosts, ~~and~~ impetuous and piercing Winds, which checque and retarde this delicious and promising Season, we are to receive it as a chastisement from *God*, as a bridle to our intemperance, and may better prevent it by prayers, then precepts.

But otherwise the Sun *culminating* over our *Horizon*, daily heates the Earth more and more, inciting and renewing her vegetative faculty, which accompanied with other virtuous and attractive *Constellations*, ~~exhales~~ {causes her to exhale forth} the cold & superfluous moysture, which had layn in her bosome during ~~the~~ {his} absence ~~of the Sun~~ concocting and converting it into showers, and a dew impregnated with the *Universal Spirit*, which descending in gentle irrigations upon her, becomes that powerfull Agent, the father {& life} of all productions: So that when ever we find a *Spring* to be calme, warme and moyst, we soone behold the effects of it to present us with the most glorious enamell, wherewith *Nature* is used to diaper **[page 21, crossed out to end of page]** and embroider our Gardens with flowers and fruits in the greatest variety and perfection: Thus with the poet

Ver adeo frondi nemorum, ver utile Sylvis,
Vere tument terræ, et genitalia semina poscunt.
                              Virg: [*Georgics* 2.323–324]
The Springs the tyme that cloaths the woods with leaves
That Swells the Earth, ~~and~~ {which} genial Seede receives:

---

2. **[Margin note]** & now the sperme of Autumne ascends ~~into~~ {to nourish} the Vegetable Kingdom.

{tis then} and the propitious *Zephyre* attempering the fervour of the Amorous Planet, courting the Blossums & flowers, kisses them open, expands their beautys & perfumes the aire with their delicious and ravishing effluxes.³ It is now then that our Industrious *Gardiner* should bestirr himselfe in {stirring up the Earth which was in Autumn dug & extirpating weede there left &} sowing and planting or else thinke no more of it till three moneths after for when once the Sap creepes up by the barke of the trees, and that the bud begines th' annunciation of leaves and blossomes, it will be too late to betake him selfe {with successe} to this employment. Now is the Season of *Graffing*, now likewise to *prune & cutt, disbranch, plash, bynd*, and not whilst the rigorous frosts may indanger the destruction of our labours when the ignorant expose the wounds of their amputations to their tyranie; now may our Gardiner begin to open his tender plants and shew them the ayre by degrees; but not expose them till the Season be well advanced: In Summ

> Vere novo gelidis canis cum montibus humor
> Liquitur, et Zephyro putris se gleba resolvit
> Geor: [1.43–44]
> When first the Spring dissolves the mountaine snow
> And Earth grows soft againe, when West Winds blow.

Our Gardiner is to lay aside all buisinesses and avocations whatsoever, to cultivate his ground, and pursue his employments. & the Summer is the Second period of the yeare, beginning from the *æstive Solstice* to the *Autumnal Æquinox*, in which the Sun passes the three Summer Signes ♋ ♌ ♍ [Cancer, Leo, Virgo]. This Season is hot and dry, and therefore the most proper for the concocting and ripening of the fruits, and gratifiing{es} the industrie of our laborious *Gardiner* with the expectations of a bountifull & luxurious Autumne. Now is the tyme of discreetly watering & refreshing his thirsty plants, to *Inoculate* the more curious, especially in the Morning and Evening, unlesse some extraordinary showers humectating the Earth, ferment, and produce a Second Spring, as it sometymes happens, irrigating the languishing plants & flowers, which now begin to put forth a fresh, in signe {toaken} of joy and gratitude. From this *Æquinox* to the *winter Solstice* we calculate the *Autumne* or third parte of the yeare, in which the Sun accomplishes the signes of ♎ ♏ ♐ [Libra, Scorpio, Sagittarius]. A Season cold and moyst, yet temperate, and agreable, 'till towards its expiration, that the Earth sensible of the unkind departure of **[page 22, crossed out to end of page]** her Beloved begins to lay aside her festivall robes & glorious mantling; in sign testimony whereof, the Trees and the plants forsake their verdure and shead their ornaments. The continuall sighing of the Earth sending up her exhalations, they descend againe in teares, which being (as at the Spring) qualified by the *Sun*, and other *constellations*, his companions, exceedingly refresh and abate those excessive heates which his conversation had raised excited in her during the Summer ardour embracements & more neere embraces, which the Earth receiving kindly from

---

3. **[Margin note]**
O ver! o pulchræ ductor pulcherrime gentis
O Florum Zerxes innumerabilium! Cowley

him, would, if the now approaching *Winter* did not too much envye her fecundity, reccompense in new productions both of flowers and fruits, as in some more propitious Countrys she dos; however, she failes not bringing to maturity her present charge, perfecting both the fruits and the seedes {in} the Vineyards, the Ortchards and the Gardens; in fine where ever she has not bin prevented by the unkindnesse {of the Season}, or the ignorance of our Gardiner. And therefore from the very first approach of this ~~gratefull~~ Season, having gratefully received the effects of her bounty and his owne Industry, let our vigilant *Gardiner* begin to take up and prepare his *Nurseries* for⁴ *Transplantation*; especially, after a soaking raine, that they may yet roote, and take hold of the ground before the frosts surprise him, for {now} after a while Geor: [2.317]

> Rura gelu tum claudit hyems
>> Winter locks up the ground with frost

So as the rootes cannot spread, put forth, nor extend them selves. We say, as soone as ever the leafe begins to wax yellow and tarnish; and not to expect till the *perrucks* of the Trees are fallen of, as many, for want of experience doe: And if they be perennial-greenes let him begin this worke the earlier, unlesse (as the mould may be) he reserve them for the Spring, to which, if the Season prove very moyst our ~~experience~~ frequent trialls {rather} inclyne us. Now all is a Season for the commiting divers *Seedes* to the Earth, to lay, and plunge such branches as you desire to propagate and encrease, *Myrtils, Lawrells, Arbutus, Jessamines*, etc: Now to begin the preparing of *Composts*, {of stirring & digging the Earth & opening her bottome, take out weeds, leaves, etc} that the Spiritous and *nitrous* Raines of this Season; the frosts and the Snows of the Winter, and the rich influences of the heavens may ~~qua~~ mature & qualifie it for future employments.⁵ In Briefe, now is the tyme to accomplish whatsoever the severitie and unkindnesse of the Winter may frustrate; which beginning from the *brumall Solstice* and reaching to the *vernal æquinox*, is caus'd by the Suns ascention through the cold Signes of ♑ ♒ ♓ [Capricorn, Aquarius, Pisces], ~~cold~~ {frigid}, drie, and improper for Generation: For the Sun reguarding the Earth at such a distance, leaves as it were all things ~~in a profound~~ Sleeping in their *Causes*, without motion & manifest activity; however Nature be still awake nothing is able to charme her restlesse Spirite; for even **[page 23]** those very icy chaines that bind the Earth and pane the waters, rob her of her ornaments & (for the tyme) expose her to contempt,⁶ contribut to her reinforcement when once she comes to be stirred up, and emancipated of her fetters {& hermetique seale} in which she has rather taken her rest, then sleepe, & being restor'd to liberty proceeds with greater vigour {for now the spermatic humidity {impreg-

---

4. **[Margin note]** query some afirme ise & snos[?] better

5. **[Margin note]** & by internaling warmth both cherishes & reinvigorates the roote being in the bowels of their mother; from here Hip[pocrates]: ventres hyme [hieme] callidiores & we find caves to be there the best & most naturall of stoves etc. [Seemingly, a rephrasing of words from Hippocrates's *De aere aquis locis*.]

6. **[Margin note]** provided they come early, gradualy & seasonably (for late winters do all the mischiefe)

nated in Autumn} dos as it were circulate}. In the meane tyme, the sharpnesse of the Frosts, and Severitie of the Season, has destroy'd many of her Enemies, Weeds and noxious insects: The Snows are as a bed of downe to her in the extremity of the Cold, and conserves those Seedes which it threatens to destroy, securing them from the devouerers both ~~without~~ {domestick} and ~~within~~ {forraine}. {Illa seges demum votis respondet avari agricolæ, quæ bis Solem, bis frigora sensit. Georg: 1 [47–48]}

And now as compassionating the toyles of our assiduous *Gardiner*, this Season affords him some repose; at least, an opportunity to prepare for the following Spring. But he must not forget to cary in early and carefully all his tender plants, and such as being fixed in *Cases*, *Pots*, etc. belong to the *Conservatory*, and require Covert; especialy in our Climat, till the kindnesse of the returning *Spring* invite them forth {againe}

> Atque in se sua per vestigia voluitur Annus
> Virg: [*Georgics* 2.402]
> And his steps back, the Circling Yeare doth treade.

CAHAP. X. [*sic*]

Of the Mould and Soile of a Garden.

What Herodotus

The Earth dos generaly lye in beds, or couches *stratum super stratum*, in divers thicknesses; but for the most part, next to the surface, it is at least a foote thick, in some places deeper, more or lesse, which is ever the mould the most prolific, and naturaly endow'd for production of *Plants*, as having bin temper'd and prepar'd by the activity, qualities, and operations of all those *principles* which we have before discoursed of; and so, from one degree to another, all the rest of the successive and subjacent beds. {The usual sorts of mould are the pulla, alba, Topacea, rubrica, columbina, rufa of all which the pulla is the lightest & best for flowers, as most resembling rotten wood or willow earth, but of all these}

The excellent Earth or mould is blackish, fat, porous, light, ~~yet~~, holding firmely together, and in grosser clodds, yet easily separable: Of this sort there are three which[1] differ in foundation; the one, which is the next ~~best~~ mingled with a sprinkling of stones, hard, and brittle is the best: For such a Mould as being loose, ~~and~~ admitts the refreshment of the raine, is very proper for Trees and Plants which require greate nourishment, and store of moysture. Declining in perfection from this, there is Earth of a darkish grey colour, somewhat tawny; and thence from bad to worse, it holds of a yellow red, growing pale, proportionably, as you mine it deeper, where it abounds with stones, 'till it in fine, arives to the hard, and impenetrable Rock.

[Page 24] Another Sort is also obscure, and approaches next in goodnesse to the first; more easie for culture, as consisting of a more delicate graine, voide of stones; It has such a mixture of loame and sand, as renders it both light and moyst; of all other, the most excellent for *Flowers*, and commodious for *Gardens* of Pleasure.

There is another inclining to both the former, which is fat, something gravelly, intersparsed with Flints; better for the foundation of a house then for our purpose.

A fourth Sort is altogether sandy, having a bottome of clay, which easily admitting the heate of the Sun, and the water of immoderate raines, parches and chills, interchangeably, producing mosse exceedingly, and {is} very corrupt. The most pernicious mould of all the former. There is a kind of devouring clay which is so hungry, as it preys upon every thing that touches it, and is applyd to reforme it converting it into its owne nature in a very short space.

The grosser sandy mould, of a more darke hue, and ressembling the mould which the moles and Ants have turnd up, having no ligature, ~~and~~ is rejectable upon the former ~~reasons~~ account.

There is also an unctuous and more slippery clayie surface, which hath a *basis* of

---

1. **[Margin note]** promptum est oculis perdicere [prædiscere] Georg: 2 [255]

chalke; but it is good for little, as totaly insiped; for that the body of it, being too compact, admitts not of the heavenly Influences; so that the fower last, are to be esteemed the very {basest} {worst} of moulds. {But let us heare my Ld: Bacon Exp: 665. Cent. 7² ˣᵛⁱ

However, there are expedients to reforme even the worst {basest & worst} of these; and it is in the power of an experienced Gardiner: If he give them a profound trenching, heaping up the mould in *Pyramids*, and mounts, and exposing them to the aire, water, frosts, Snow and *Celestiall influences*: And therefore, this should be begun in a dry Season; be it cold or hott; especially, {at} the commencement of *Autumne*, and reiterated before the Earth become too ponderous and slugish: And in this processe he must mingle it with store of litter, fearne, leaves, halfe consum'd, and the like; for that will heate and accellerat concoction. If the Earth be sandy, fatten and embody it with Cow dung made very fine, & well evaporated; working it in wett, and humid Seasons and leting it soake aboundantly; then leave it coverd with this compost before the raines descend in too greate excesse, least it {which may} dissolve the Salts, and virtue of the manure into it; and therefore chalke, and marle are excellent to dresse such ground withall calcinations of turfe, stones, and ashes {especially of Sea weede} if such materials be at hand:ˣᵛⁱⁱ And after this sort {processe} may all sorts of imperfect moulds be treated. In Summ, If it be too hard, molifie it; if too loose to give it ballast, body and ligature; if to me{a}gre, to impinguat and fatten it; if too rich and luxurious, to emaciate and bring it downe; if over moyst, to dry; if over wett & raw, to draine and concoct it; if excessive

---

2. **[Insertion on separate piece of paper]** Ad p. 24. Cent. 7 The differences of Earth (says he) & the [edge of paper torn] of them are mostly to be diligently inquired: that which shew us doe eas[ily?] is commanded & yet some of that kind of herb will be very dry & hard before the sh[owers?.] The earth that casts up from the plough a greate clod is not so good as at breaks rises in smalle: Mouldy & mushy Earth is not good; that which smells well over Digging & ploughing is a mudd approvd, as containing the juice of vegetables almost ready prepard. **[Insertion on same piece of paper]** To which we add that old one of if the excavated earth more or lesse fill the pitt out of which tis dugg, upon which Lauremburg affirmes is observd at Witeberg in Ger: where it {the mould} lye so close as not to fill the hole, the Corne that is sowne dos de soone degenerate into Rye: & that Rye sowd in Thuringia, {(}where the earth is of a swelly & more spongy nature) it comes in 3 yeares to be corne {wh[e]ate} **[end insertion]** It is thought by some {tis Plinys 1: c: 5} that the ends of raine bowes fall more upon one kind of earth than another; as it may well be: for that that earth is most viscide, & therefore a hopefull signe the boornesse of the herb shews the poornesse of the soile, especially if more darke of colour: But if they shew withered or blasted at top, it denotes the Earth to be cold, & so dos mossinesse of trees, etc: that whereoff the grasse is soone parched with the Sun, is commonly forc'd Earth, & barren in its owne nature: The tender & chessome & mellow Earth is best: being meere mould 'twixt the extreames of clay & sand, especially if not loamy & binding. The Earth that after raine will scarce be ploughd is commonly fruiteful, for 'tis cleaving & juicy: etc. so farr he says: & so far of the sorts: we will now shew what expedients there may be to reforme where the oake thrives naturaly the Earth & soile excellent; by these & other natural Augures, the Soile may be knowne:

[Pages 25 through 36 are missing, but there are miscellaneous text insertions on pieces of paper evidently meant for insertion into the missing text as follows]

[Page 25 insertion] And as Earth dos dispose to plants: so dos the emission of some plants disclose ~~ther~~ {of what} nature ~~of~~ the soile is: thus[?] we find in the thistle, ever a sign of fertil grasses. {& where the Oake thrives of itselfe} thyme of good pasture, strawberys & betony dispose to Wood, camomile that is mellow & fit for Corne; Mustard sede that it is strong & apt for wheate, Burnet for meadow; Malows for rootes etc:
[Insertion to page 25 insertion] In short fatt earth for the culinary herbs, Macram {& the light} for plants, & trees, & the naturall or middle sort of Earth for flowers:
[end to insertion to page 25 insertion] These natural Auguries are therefore to be carefully observed.[xviii]

Ad p: 25: Soile

But to this the best expedient were to trye our Grounds (some time before we bestow over much cost on them) where they spontaneously or rather over officiously produce: For some you shall find are addicted to one thing, some to another. Some produce Broome, Gorst, Juniper, Ivy, Holly & Yew ~~& other~~[.] 'Tis probable these may more easily entertaine the Seedes of Pine, Firrs, Cedars, Spanish broome, etc: as we find in Devonshire that the grounds which beare but their shrubby ~~Fuzzes~~ {Gorst} repayes them with a very large Fuzz of speedier groth, & such as they use not onely for a substantial field, but even for joysts & partitions to their humble houses. So as we see much may be expected from this kindnesse of the soile:

It is certain says my Ld: Bacon that Earth take[n] out of foundations [paper torn] wells, etc: & exposd, will put forth sundry herbs; but it will require [paper torn] as if a fathom deepe the first year, if deeper much, one or two [foote more? paper torn] The nature of plants so taken up, follows the nature of [paper torn] fine {it produces}. Soft herbs; as grasse, plantains, etc: if coarser & hard[ier?] [paper torn] thistle etc: If the Earth be taken out of shady & watry [paper torn] herbs of fatt & juicy substances, as pennyweed, houseleeke [paper torn]

[Paragraph crossed out] Some plants have againe a part of ther nature ~~from the~~ if not from the earth simply, yet from the peculiar streames, which arise from subterranean parts, & which may be ~~in that place~~ confined to that place & no where else to be found with all the concomitant circumstances: some from peculiar deawes from the surface, as well vegetables as other: Some from the heate & digestiion of birds & foule which passing through the stomac of the ostrich (as the Chymists phrase it) may be inflamed into a more

In proposals therefore of transplanting spices & exotic Vegetables etc from either of the Indies, it were to be wished that as much of the very Earth where they grew might be transported in balast with them, not onely for Essayes, but to ~~ente~~ discover to us the nature of the Soile, & to assist us in imitating it; but for the entertaining of what we sow & plant in it, which may probably nourish it, till the rootes have taken some hold, & begin to be acquainted with the Earth, & aire of our Country:

By that inimitable description of Vergils, old happy & industrious Gardner Georg: 4:

~~Namq sib~~   cui pauca relicti
jugera etc

Gardners are of all others encourag'd to practise upon light hollow lands, abandond by the Husbandman for its too præcipitous ferment, & though it beare nothing of itselfe worldly the tillage, because with a little helpe of compost it may be converted into the most beautifull & most profitable of Gardens: especialy the odoriferous furniture. ~~and~~ for ~~speedy~~ {vigorous} groth, & delicious fruite; though happly neither so large or lasting as in stronger lands: The Compost proper for this is sheeps dung; for ~~though~~ some Earthes appeare to be totaly barren, ~~yet it~~ {& other, though not altogether so unfruiteful yet} wants ~~vigor~~ {salacity} to conceive {& vigor} [to] produce anything to the purpose; ~~for whatever earth~~

You shall easily discover whither your Soile be of itselfe prolifique, if you find it perpetualy conceiving & bringing forth some particular plants or other: I say ~~not~~ ~~g~~ particular, for tho the Earth never so sanguine & vigorous, yet it brings not for all manner of plants indefinitely, but such onely as most inclin'd to above others.

And now having dispatcht what we thought fit to præmise of the Principles, Influences, Seasons, etc: let our Gardner have a tast of what the Antients Philosophiz'd in their Mysterious doctrine: Palladius L: 1 says **[continued on separate piece of paper]** ad paper to pag: 25 Soile

~~Jupiter signifies the Seminal power~~

Palladius: L: 1. says that bene colendi value consists in {aer} water, ~~a~~ earth & Industry, that is Pluto, Proserpine, Jupiter, & Hercules, because of his labour, which a hieroglyphic of the Rape of Proserpine dos rarly present ~~by~~ which we may judge of the wisdom of the antient fictions; the Hierog: we have out of Heliac tables ~~of~~ Hieronym: Alexandri: where ~~the~~ Ceres is the magna frugum mater or the Ceres:[?] The lamp she holds, vis Solis, which ~~matrum~~{es} all productions. The dragons or serpents drawing her chariot. Soleus agronum or the insita vis terræ producing fruite:

The Nymphs Minerva, the Lunary effects: Dian the humid ~~fe~~ power of the moone, & Proserpina the Fruites, herbs & plant: Pluto signifies Sol inferus, ~~or the~~ ~~hybernal heate~~ seu hybernus: The 4 horses drawing his chariot the 4 Seasons over which he presides: Hercules the industry & labour belongs to the field, or as some tyme it selfe: Jupiter the seminal power, proceeding from heaven, the bushel of flower etc flung downe & desposd the Winter, when flours perish: The chariott & wheeles the celestiall motions, necessary to agriculture much more we could add, together with the ~~Sch~~ Emblems or Schematisme but we [?] the reader, ~~& much more of this~~ ~~kind could we add of the learned significations of these Insects the vilest Scarabe~~ ~~especialy, see the Hieroglypiall interpreters especialy Riverius~~ [xix]

(1) Ad P: 25: Composts

To confide in dung onely I have been taught is a greate error & it [is?][page torn] evident that in old tyme, & Hesiods dayes They seemed to have little or no use at all of stercoration which though some attribute to the natural fertility of his Country & that dung is not to be had in all places, nor for all uses of cult[ure?] being the buisynesse of vermine, yet there was more than one reason for it, there being as we have formerly shewed many other expedients to dresse & ~~prepare~~ {impregnate} our Ground, more effectuall, naturall, & vigorous then the best dung, & that by mechanical ayds, as by contusion galling verifing, exposures to frosts, aire, & influences,[xx] some by coverture & drynesse, some by intermixture of liquors, some by repos~~ing~~ & ~~the~~ ~~for bea~~ forbearance of lust & impregnation for a season as we see in our worn–out exhausted & clay fields {which enjoy the Sabbaths.} And ~~we~~ as for our Gardens of pleasure (which is the maine subject of this Worke) the fairest beauties of that pasture

rather require a fine quick friable & well wrought field then a ground rankly dunged.
To the first proposition therefore take of the most barren greety Earth you can find,
whither ~~taken~~ dug out of a very deepe & barren pit, or having also drayned out all
the nitrous ~~&~~ Saline & masculine parts of it, pulverize the greety parts (which may be
dispatched by a rude Engine, which letts fall a kind of hammer or flinty beetle at the
motion of a wheele) let this earth thus ~~pul~~ reduc'd to pure dust, & frequently churnd
be expos'd for one Summer & a Winter to the influences) by this labour & rest from
vegetation, we shall find that it will in one yeare gather a prompt purging:[xxi]

And by this toyle may ground be altered from its former nature (yea though ~~a~~
{the} toughest binding {& most unkind} clay) to be made [to] beare carrotts, Tur-
nepes, & the largest sort of rootes, which ~~delight~~ {require} a light hollow & loose
ground: Other Soiles are fertilized from centrall agitations & heate which exceedingly
alter & impregnate grounds; which if too hott may be allayed with a feminine mixture, for oftentimes hott & over spiritual composts do much poysen hott & cholery
grounds {as we shall shew} & that quantity of Salt which makes a cold & moist ground
~~preg~~ fruitfull will destroy the contrary as Dr: {Gabriel} Plott[xxii] shewes us, & therefore it require good heede to direct where lime, where Salt, Ashes, Sand ~~&~~ Clay &
Marle [are?] [edge torn] fittly applicable & for what speciall uses: For it is the same in
{these} ~~Grounds as in Animals~~ vegetable productions, as in the Animals, where com-
plexions must be suited, & the ~~not observance~~ {neglect} of this through avarice of
greate portions & other sordid circumstances make many a family childlesse: It has
ben ~~And~~ {sayd} that a thin sifting of ashes has enriched all the high pasture, but when
it was strewed too thick it became totaly barren: & sometimes againe the want of
depth, falt of mixture too dry, too close, moyst or cold is the cause of ~~dwarfynesse &~~
sterility i[f not?] [edge torn] dwarflynesse at least: But as to external indications from
the comm[on] [edge torn] opinion, {as} that hot & choleric ground is red or browne,
cold & dry blackish cold & moist whitish, hott & moist ruddy, not only the ~~Antient~~
late [torn] Antients have ben greatly mistaken, & Columella[xxiii] dos smartly re[proch?]
[torn] his forefathers for it: satis admirari non possum (says he) cum [torn] [alios tum
etiam] Cornelium Celsum etc. Nam ut fortissimæ pecudis diver[sos et pæne] [torn]
innumerabilis, sic etiam robustissimæ terræ plurimes [torn] [et varios] calores sortitæ
sunt. And this we find true by experience [The?] [torn] learned Laurenburg: Hortic:
L: 1. c. 4[xxiv] ~~divested~~ di[vested?] [torn] **[continued on verso]** [soil]e (by varying the
depth of digging at 3 severall depths the 1, 2d & 3d [yea]re) to perpetuate the Vigor
in the soile of sufficient depth: & so it [f]requently falls out that the proper remedy
of a barren, shallow, or hungry surface, will be found by them that make constant
tryall of some degree [of] depth in the same soyle, but a single tryall of any one kind
of lay or ~~over~~ hasty tryall before the Winter frosts or Summer Sun, or due Season
(according to L: Bacon Exp) hath prepared the Soile, may be insufficient:

But that we may ~~happen to~~ {finish} the more antient account of Soyles, we referr
~~you~~ our Gardner to Varro L: 1: c. 9: Columella L: 2: c. & C; 10: & Lib: 3: c. 1 etc: To
Palladius L:1: Tit: 5. 7: To Theophrastus L: 2. To Pliny: L: 10: c. 2: & L: 16: c. 44: & the
most accomplished of all the best of Gardners & Poets Vergil: Geor: L: 2: [177–178]

Nunc locus arvorum ingenijs quæ robora cuiq
Quis color, et quæ sit rebus natura ferendis etc

Especially from ver: 226:

Nunc quo quamque modo possis cognoscere dicam etc

which it behoov ~~to~~ us ~~to~~ {so as to} reade & consider at leasure: ~~We come therefore at last to speake of the Qualities And now having dispatched what we have thought fitt to peruse of the Elements, the Influences & Seasons, let us heare how the Antients philosophized upon them But of this Mysterious doctrine Palladius says~~

We come therefore at last to speake of their Qualities. **[separate insertion follows on same piece of paper]** when we mentiond Swine Dung, ~~'twas~~ {'tis to be noted that} of old 'twas it were esteemd greately for a special property of dedcorating fruite attributed as my Ld: Bacon thinks to the moisture & little acrimony: {but} this with a mixture of bran or chaff, layd up for some moneths to rott, is a greate nourisher & comforter to fruite trees: **[separate insertion follows on same piece of paper]** The stalkes & leaves of lupines, especially layd about [torn] or to dig them into the ground; especially for corne; so the [torn] of Vines each on land.

[Page 26 insertion] Ad: p: 26: Comp.

But besides these Composts my Ld: Bacon (whose ayds we professe to look in as often as they occurr throughout this treatise) reckons up a second, even to a sixt kind, as the spreading of sundry kinds of Earths, as marle chalke Seasand, Earth upon Earth, pond–earth & the mixture of them: of these marle is thought best as fattest & lesse {over} heating. Sand next, as salter, & Salt is held the first rudiment of life: Chalke (as heating) best on clay & ~~on~~ cold {& moist} grounds & then let it lye sometime before you turne it in. {to grow friable & ~~mellow~~ mealt}: Earth on Earth, it being surface unexhausted earth, tis compost of itself, ~~&~~ as being nitrous naturaly; fatt pond earth with a mixture of chalke is also excellent: Thus briefly: A 3d sort is by other substances that are not meere earth, as Ashes; Soote (not cynders, for that is too dry & effete): also Salt discreetely sowne etc: The 4th is suffering Vegetables to ~~dry~~ dye into the ground, as they use in stubble & peases haume {braken} etc: cast on the ground at beginning of Winter; so leaves of Trees mixt with chalke & dung to hearten them, & keepe them from sowring the ground to which they are prone: The 5t is heate & warmth, as by dashing[?] & burning of living heath sedge etc: hence walls & enclosures, & exposure to the South, and coverings of pastures with bushes or the like mends grounds; & my Ld: says the very warmth of sheep as well as their compost: & therefore some blame even the clearing such grounds from stones:

The last is irrigation, both by letting in & shutting out waters {at pleasure}, & certainely, this has since my Ld: Bacons tyme, ben found to be one of the greatest improvements, that ever was tryd, especially when the water is fatt & not gritty, {over} cold or harsh, & that it ~~des~~ straine {or desend} from hanging rich ground, & hence it is that valies are universaly more luxurius than either hills or high grounds: {note that some are for tempering lime with blood; [3]as admirable for vines but let it be what Sr: H: Plats [xxv] cautions that he suffer the first accidental heate to passe over, least it indanger the total burning}* But these are visible helpes, we come next to {the} more refined with those who undertake to marshall the vigour of Composts [xxvi] * A Composition of Lime with light sand dos excellently, and changes even the very Nature of soiles.

---

3. **[Margin note]** Gab. Platt tresr.

[Page 27 insertion]

Ad: p: 27 Composts:

For {(as one observes)} though we find that all the materials enumerated to cause it, (with many others which might be produc'd) yet we are to seeke of any certainty what is indeed the prime {&} virtual cause, as what it is of the vulgar Elements {or of the Spagyrists Principles} be it Dung, Ashes, Marles, lime; while something Accidental, or Essential, Material, or immaterial, {Visi} ~~corpo pri~~ corporeal, or Spiritual {Visible or invisible} principal or Organical; ~~visible whether any of the Spagyrist principles~~ whither by Vapors Effluvias or Atomes, Salts, Urine, Embrionate or non specifical, or by ferments, Acidities, or indigested & unspecificated masses, from Spermatic vapours ascending from the center, or Influences celestial, or from water onely impregnated & fermented; or finaly from the divine benediction alone.

[4]Here {then} comes in an examination of Salts by tribes. 1 Nitrous 2 Vinnous, in which are included 3 all dungs, Hornes, shreads, etc: 4 Common Salt & Sea–Sands 5 Kaly Salt, ether, Kelps, Mineral Salts, as of stones, lime, Marle Chalk, ~~Vitriol~~ Fuller earth, Vitriol etc: And since some of these are deleterious, as the last mentiond if they super abound, it is questionable (says one) whither any Salt dos universaly nourish all plants, or whether some best agree with one, others with another & upon the cleare determination of this dos the grand arcanum of imbibitions depend:

But here two difficultys appeare, first since it can produce no vegetables in Salt alone without Water to dissolve it, that the Seede or plant may feede on it, & 2 Earth to embrace as in a womb & keepe it steady: the question will be what earth abstract-edly is, since it appeares by its viscosity, that it is not sand (as some would have it) then if it be salt, how may it be separated from it: If Water, how comes it to be un-able to nourish without fresh additions: If Earth ~~be~~ disclaime all these, what is it, & its energy to this effect: This says ~~my~~ {an} Author is of maine consequence, since these imbibitions signifie yet nothing, if ~~th my~~ {our} Earth be before impregnated with another Salt different from what the plant imbibed dos require. It is likewise to be considered that ~~raine~~ Water, especially raine water, hath a Salt ~~in it~~ or life in it-selfe without any artificial additions before what neede is there of them which seeme so much lesse actually vital[.] Then againe as there is no nourishment or approach to vegetation without Moysture, so can there be no life without motion & actual warmth. This is common as well in ~~vegetable~~ animals as Vegetables; for let the be neare so much & good earth, Salt, & Water, if the Season be cold & inactive, there is no vegetation: On the other side the soyle must be prepared[.] And the most severe & sharp cold & in which nothing germinates, yet nourish many plants, as we see in Cypresse, bays & other perennial greenes: Therefore what is ~~princi~~ {more} or lesse principal in this abstruse worke, & what part to attribute to each must be considered & deeply weighed before we can come scientifically to know what it is promotes vegetation: & 2ndly we must seriously ~~consider~~ propond whither the subject of Fer-mentation & things that serve to {excite &} entertaine & treate be not of one kind

---

4. **[Margin note]** Se: Mr: Hartlibs legacy p. 47. [Samuel Hartlib, *Samuel Hartlib His Legacie, or An Enlargement of the Discourse of Husbandry Used in Brabant and Flaunders Wherein Are Bequeathed to the Common-wealth of England More Outlandish and Domestick Experiments and Secrets in Reference to Universall Husbandry*, London, 1651.]

the Subject of nutrition or another to avoyd the confusion: 3dly ~~wh~~ how various the sorts of this notion is ~~emiting~~ resulting happly from the diversity of the Salts or other Subjects which cause it, & what the effects {& consequences} of these motions may be as to the variety of figure upon the subject of nutrition. Finaly he must {study &} looke into the cause of the frequent ~~& apparent~~ to appearance accidents of Vegetation as why some plants seeme spontaneous to the place, others not, why some thrive not but in ~~company~~ consort with others, as with Corne, others of the mud of cast, & **[continued in margin]** others in the water onely: why some againe defray {as it were} & abolish the Vegetative Virtues & where they have ben sown as Hempe Oats etc: These intracts are ~~the~~ difficultys worthy Philosopher heads & hands, whilst we usualy content our selves to know in Generall.

[Page 28 insertion]

Ad: p: 28: Composts

The burning to ashes of the ground & all that grows on it be it turfe, stubble, halme, fearne, weedes, sedge, rootes, fare [=fair] wood, is admirable; & the mixture of this with even a barren clay makes it almost resemble the richest ~~mate~~ Marle {Se Virgil 1 Geor [84]}

Sæpe etiam steriles ~~visam~~ incendere profuit agros, etc. shews you all the excellent reasons for it

lastly

To this we add the pasturing {& feeding} of Ground where fruite grows, as a natural manure; ~~but we will~~ where greate & large plantations are arid to the uttmost groth; but the cutting & mowing of these grounds is altogether exhausting & prejudicial:

[Page 29 insertion, incorrectly inserted between pages 56 and 57]

I will now conclude with some cautions for the adjusting ~~the Composts~~ & application of Composts, for even in this, as in prescribing of the best nourishment or medicine, errors may be committed: Where therefore the Earth is obnoxious to heate & its effects, which is to chap much, especially when the mou[l]d is clay, or if it burne much, as when tis sandy. Then lime, salt, Ashes, pidgeons & other hott dung, exhalt its feavor, & make it more hott: Where none of these Symptums appeare, but contrary, then these are the proper remedys & improvements, & therefore let our industrious Gardner ever examine the quality prædominant, & then endeavor to abate it: a little observation of this would quickly make better Gardners & better husbandmen then we find, who throw on any thing that is cald dung without judgement or description, not considering that the grounds are as nice as their owne bodys, & subject to ~~the~~ many of the same infirmitys. Note therefore that cow dung is fattest & best for leane earth & dry, usd before winter: Sheepes is also very fatt, but hotter, & is best for cold soiles, use it in November: Horse is not so fatt, but very hott, & therefore best for plants not trees, & in moist places: use it in Octob: else it induce burning: Swine dung is the coldest of all, & best for burning ground; use it later near the spring: Pigeons must be let coole; spread before you use it, therefore not good freshly made use it early at beginning of winter & use it in Spring unlesse to comfort old rootes, lay it earlier.

[Continued on verso]

but to apply them to the severall purposes of plants as well as places (which generally if cold would [be] spiritd with horse dung pigeons & poultry, if hott, with cow dung limed) Fruite trees do well in {well consumed} composts of Swine dung: but {all Trees universally well with cow–dung} Flo: with that of Cow dung & Sheepes, ~~for~~ the first for Auricula especially mingled with willow or ~~weed earth burned~~ {weede} Earth such as ~~lies~~ has long layn under heapes of bovines; the 2d for Gillyflo: Tulips & other bulbs would not have much of these helpers, but that of naturall earth taken from under foder'd pasture & if too rich, qualified with Sand:

In ablaqueation uncover within an inch of the rootes, then a layer of good Neates dung. do this in September: & so by degrees ~~moneth~~ moneth after moneth till approach of Spring: be still covering all with the Earth againe upon it: be sure your dung touches nothing of the naked Tree or rootes immediately: this infinitely recovers & recreates Fruite Trees.

[Page 37]

[Of the Generation of Plants.] ^{xxvii}

In the meane while {mere terrestrial {& crasse} part which compose} the Rootes are inclind, and contorted in search of {the} aliment to maintaine what they support; in which action yet, we find them to affect the superficial ~~partes~~ rather then penetrate {the} lower & more frigid parts of the earth. ~~By~~ {And from} these flexures as there happen to be more knotts & ventricles whither naturally or by ~~accident~~ Art, the more succkers and offsets ~~spring~~ {burst} out: And as this flame & Spirit is more copious ascending through the hide ~~fo~~ of the now formed trunk {&} boughs, it carries up the aliment with it, which breakes out at {throu} their severall pores & overtures ~~of the~~ which are more or lesse frequent, as the body is more or lesse rare, whither ~~by~~ {from} the nature of the tree, or its treatement of the Gardner. ~~for~~ {in} pruning, cutting and topping, which are the greater openings makes them spread wonderfully, and come very thick:

Here ~~Gassendus dos~~ ^{xxviii} {'tis} well observe that Fir–trees, Pines etc whose parts are closed with a resinous substance, and the passage and texture of their bodys perpendicular and not so oblique, as the Oakes, and other crosse–grain'd woods, amplifie {& spread} onely at the top, whilst their gemms or buds break out from the very interiour substance of the lignous part of the tree, perforating the rind or integument, and a little diverting the course of the juice which it spends in the leafe.[1] And ~~that~~ {as} some leaves are of ~~more~~ {nerer} affinity with the more solid and internall parts of the barke,[2] the longer & the more perenniall is their verdure; The rest, obnoxious to the penetration of frosts & invasion of the weather become more fraile and deciduous, unkindly forsaking the branches at Autumne, which bore them all the Summer whilst the rest, preserve their beauty, 'till the stalke & foote of the bud growing too big, displaces and thrusts them off, and 'till the ~~faileur~~ {supplie} of that nourishment, ~~which~~ failes, which made them flourish; not so much by any descency of the Sap, ([3]as the mistake certainely is), as through its slow ascent for want of sufficient heate to ~~draw up~~ *meteorise*, and exhalt it; although we firmly believe that a

---

1. **[Margin note]** which are larger or narrower, few or many as the sap issues slower or in more aboundance.

2. **[Margin note]** more compact & close in their pedicles, & the more tough & viscous the juice. The longer greene they containe as we se in the holy [holly] Firrs, juniper

3. **[Margin note]** much lesse the extinction of its vertue, which is rather sopite & inactive, than any ways destroyed or imagine its motion, like that of a sealed Weather glasse so as it dos not descend out of the Tree but compared to air running more, sometimes lesse: etc.

considerable part of the juice of Vegetables, descends from the heavenly influences
into all the prominent and remoter parts, and dos not onely proceede from the rootes,
and this conjecture is well fortified by the plentifull and most efficacious distillation
of the *Birch* and other trees more from the branches, then any other part, as neerer to
its celestiall originall: Nor dos the *Sap* passe onely by the pith (another {epidemicall}
errour); but by the barke, and all other channells, {thereby} contributing a mutual
{& universall} *transudation* ~~through~~ {through the tree} ~~all~~; nor yet againe by the barke
alone; as is perspicuous in the Corke tree & some others, ~~after~~ which grow {& thrive}
after excortication, though more in deede, ~~by~~ {through} that, then any other passage,
because of its laxity; and the very radication of a bud in the wood; as is noted in Implastration & inoculating trees, sufficiently evinces its through fare {even} ~~through~~ {a
traverse} the most firme & solidest parts of it.[4,5]

The Branch, leafe and other members of a plant, are by an accurate anatomisa-
tion, discerned to be envelop't **[page 38]** And curiously ~~rolled~~ {swadled} up together,
compleately formed, and wanting onely tyme, & heate to explaine & mature them; &
when the branches are a little more adult, the rudiments {& evidence} both of flower
and fruite; The like is to be detected in bulbous and greater rootes, especially what
tyme they begin to germinate & put forth. Now the Flower {which is the *gaudium*

---

4. **[Insertion on separate sheet of paper]** Here we may note that Theophrastus attributes 3 peculiar juices or aliments to the compleating of the vegetable period:
~~one sorte~~ of which one kind maintains the germination, the 2d is destin'd to the
Seedes, the 3d to the pulp or edible part & fruit; & ~~if~~ hence tis deduced that where
the most nourishment goes there the ~~augmentation~~ augmentation follows, as if into
the woody part, the branches spared & the fruite is the lesse, if into the pulp, the
Seede the lesse, if to the Seedes, the pulp is lesse: for the reason too the softer & laxid
trees bere more constantly plentifully, then the harder & superanuatd

5. **[Insertion on separate sheet of paper]** ad p:37: Generation of Plants
In this processe {both} the branches of trees ~~have~~ & their stemms I conceive to have
a double motion, the one out right & formed as it were[,] the other circling, which
gives an annual superinduction of barke in a spirall manner **[illustration of spiral]**,
by which meanes what was the last yeares, comming now to be under the cuticle of
this yeare grows into more hard & solid wood, ~~& this dos~~ This ~~appeared by a~~ might
be evinced to much probability by what was shewed King Charles the 1 at Oxon:
in a piece of a Tree which being settled before his Mats [Majesty] had names graven
upon ~~a piece of barke~~ the very timber where squared, a good depth into the heart of
it beneath the barke: ~~But to preceeds the Branch etc:~~
And here we may a little consider those *Instantiæ conformes* (as my L: Bacon happily
calls them) of the Vegitable intumesceral & {circumferential} extrusion of its parts
as well above, as beneath, as appeare in the very little, & but as it were, accidental
diffrence of Branches from the roots; seing a branch invested with Earth becomes a
roote, & {vice versa} ~~a roote in the ayre would become a branch as his Ldship teaches~~
so as a roote is but a branch in the Earth, & a branch a roote in the ayre: & Pliny
speakes of a moly roote 30 foote long growing downe & yet cropt off, for they could
not attain its bottome: L: 25: c. 4.
But to proceede The Branch, leafe & other members

plantæ & for runner of pregnancy} grows upon the tender ~~fruite~~ (& almost) indiscernable fruite, as on the top of a button, from the exuberances of whose spirituall substance (for it is exceedingly *halituous* & volatile) it emerges; 'till at last the Fruite increasing, pushes it off; or ~~some~~ {oft}tymes (immaturely) some immoderate cold or heate: For now the Fruite receives the nourishment of the whole tree to it selfe in a manner[6] the purer portion whereoff being exquisitely elaborated becomes the seede ~~&~~ {defended by the περικαρπιον & pellicula &} concentring in the middle as the result & utmost effort of all the particles, ~~which~~ after this compleate circle is finished; for whilst the plant was growing, nourishing, and taking roote, there was other employment & diversions; ~~for~~ so that its virtues could not {thus} unite; ~~in this manner~~ and in these receptacles are the atomes so ~~place~~ marshall'd, as that every, the least parti{cle} of the plant is existent, though in an extraordinary presse, close & admirable ~~manner~~ method (as before we have discoursed) 'till the heate, and the moysture causes them to swell & amplifie themselves, running through the former processe; ~~as~~ {the} nourishment making the new parte to adjoyne, & in time, to perfect its shape & forme, though at first appearing, but with a little spire & a payre of leaves. {which being but the Secondines as it were of the Seede perish & give way to other: as is evident in the Seede of the Ash & greate kernels to a well arm'd Eye which may detect}[7]

---

6. **[Insertion on separate sheet of paper]** & the Spirits calld forth to the outward parts & equaly spread, the grosser part digested by these Spirits, by a scarce perceptible inception of putrefaction, as my Ld: Bacon hints, or rather the next disposition to it, arives to its perfect, & consummate maturity.

7. **[Insertion on separate piece of paper]** detect the {almost atomical} Secondismes as they ~~live~~ lye {in some more extended, in others} curiously enveloped like the fœtus in the mothers womb, fed & nourished with a ~~stalke~~ slender ~~staff or~~ threid or navil string ~~reaching~~ {reaching} to the stalke {though through the hardest stones & nutts} & these made turgid with the ~~moisture~~ adventitious moisture break out & deliver themselves & erect themselves sometimes carrying their secondines ~~on their heads~~ & even their very shells & stones upon their heads **[illustration, see Fig. 4]** Cf the Ash & maple by a microscope & these being {so} come up as we shewed, as their stock of new moisture thrust them forth put out leaves & parts of different forms from the first which till then were folded up in real, though almost undiscernable points.

[Insertion continued on another piece of paper] Now {in} plants we may observe sundry peculiarities in which they differ from one another as that the olive hath its oyly part in the out side only; whereas other fruite have it in their fruit or kirnell: The Firr has it both in the Kirnell & body: though my Ld Bacon allow it to have no kernell, which is a mistake: The Pomegrand & pine reserve the grains & ~~nut~~ kirnell

Figure 4. Illustration of seeds and their enveloping "skins" in an insertion at page 38.

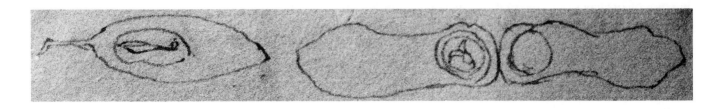

And {thus} here[8] is the ultimate designe of Nature, and the decree of heaven in these admirable and stupendious productions; for when the stemm begins to wither, the fruite is at its consistence, though it {grow} something more in maturity; 'till, in conclusion (if not tymely gathered) it falls off, and sows it selfe, ~~and~~ passing the former processe againe by a perpetuall rotation.

> [9]*Nam* Specimen sationis, et insitionis origo
> Ipsa fuit rerum primum natura Creatrix
> Arboribus quoniam baccæ, glandesque caducæ
> Tempestiva dabant pullorum exanima subter. etc:
> For the invention of sowing, and
> Of Planting, Nature first, herselfe (who all
> Created) taught; For from the trees did fall
> Berries, and Acorns, whence in Season did
> A numerous offspring, underneath succeede.

And thus, what we have spoaken of Trees and plants, we are also to understand of Flowers, which, according to their caducity, perish and fade away; the ligature & foote, & appendices ~~being~~ {by} which the ~~flower~~ {pretty} cup **[page 39]** of the flower, is sustaind & nourished, being dryed, or the huske gaping when it is not more able to containe the ~~bignesse~~ {dimensions} of its ~~Seedes~~ {numerous} progenie.

Lastly, as ~~in~~ all {other} sublunary things; so ~~in~~ {have} plants also there ~~is the~~ Increment, status, ~~and~~ decrement or decay: To the first of these Periods, they proceede with more or lesse ~~haste speede~~ {velocity} {haste}, as they are of more strict & denser parts, ~~of~~ or of slighter contexture; and so receive a speedier or slower diflusion [sic] of aliment. This is apparant in Box, and Willow, the {one of} a harder, & the {other of} a ~~softer substance~~ {more tender Substance}: But as they spring, so they continue **[line illegible due to striking through]** ~~according to the old~~ {Verifing that ~~knowne~~} {well knowne} saying *Soone ripe, Soone rotten*, & which holds as well in Men as in plants: {And here to add something of their age}[xxix] ~~But of this, as of their numericall progression, and declension, we conceive it not our part at present~~

---

in distinct & admirable receptacles; some have curld leaves as Cabbage Endive lettuce etc: Some have leaves investing the Stalke as well as fruite, as one sort of palme, & the Artichock, none such a spread as the Woodbines etc: which says my Lord B: may be an ample field for Contemplation, shewing that in the frame of Nature ther is in the production of some species a composition of matter which may be diversified in some, & add mills of little variety in others, & these may be good hints to experiment as one thing is found to have affinity with others. We might proceed to the observation of rootes, which love to penetrate as the Oake, of Trees the Ferne & Sorrell of plants, which affect shallow ground as the Ash, Birch & most graminous plants but this shall suffice: For here is the ultimate designe etc

8. **[Margin note]** By Tertull[ian]: Eligantly de Anima [19.3] they et frutices inoculantur, et folia formantur, et germina ~~formantur~~ inflantur, et flosculi inornantur, et suci condiuntur, etc

9. **[Margin note]** Lucret: L: 5. [1361–1364]

concern'd to enlarge on. By the *state* of plants, we meane {would signifie} their utmost effort, groth and maturity, which are all of them severall as to tyme; yet not meaning by this any period or instant in which they do not either improve or decay; seing, as in all other things, the ende of one is the beginning of the other; but farther then which, they do not extend, but, immediatly, though insensibly, dwindle & grow impaire, either through age, defect of sufficient nourishment & want of heate sufficient for its bulke {& quality}; by sicknesse, and decay of principle parts: But, especially, if violently invaded, with mortall & incurable infirmities, *Sphacelisms, Carbunculations, exustion* of budds, and other extinctions of the native heate which makes all motions {whatsoever} to cease de cease and determine.¹⁰

And thus we may {might} conclude the Generation of Plants, from the most naturall, rationall & comprehensive *Hypothesis* of the most learned, which we have {studiously} examined could we without injustice to some others, whose fames {names} are glorious in the world trumpet of *Fame*, passe also what they have also erected upon some of one {the} former *Principles*. That these Seminall and apt masses, convening under the Earth, in proper, but variously dispos'd and characteris'd recipients; being (as we affirm'd) actuated and fermented by the universal Spirit (which imparts to them both heate and moysture) they come to put forth themselves in a circular motion, piercing the womb of their teeming mother in a perpendicular progresse towards the Surface, because there the pressure is loose, and lesse impenetrable towards that part {side} of the particles of matter: seing, else the operation would be everywhere equall & sphericall unlesse impeded by the obvention of some harder substance **[page 40]** rock or stone, which may hinder, or cause it to search for the fresh aire by some indirect & oblique course. This, say they, being actuated and digested by that innate Soule, inclos'd and supplied with fitting moisture, is that which imparts motion and increment to plants, and to all other productions, as specifie into such differences and configurations, correspondent to the various Characters of their terrestriall receptacles, accompanied with the multifarious causes before explain which gives {renders} them their determinat formes. This, if it happen to be a plant, the aire

---

10. **[Insertion on separate sheet of paper]** We spake at the beginning of how plants were propaga But not onely (as we sayd) are plants propagated by Seedes, but some by by Succkers, & some by {other} violent Sep Separations & this is effected by the remanent virtue {confusedly yet} still remanent in the Separated part, which usualy going to formerly destin'd to the rootes, searching & recurring towards the lower parts {some of which} & finding it wanting roote is as it were expected {but found wanting} thrust footh [forth] themselves into the earth & so produce new rootes & so th fasten & may & perfect what was defective by which it comes to be a plant of the same kind where it was taken: Those which propagate Thus are layers, cuttings, & even graffs themselves in {after} a sort propagatd*: But succkers have already some part of the mother rootes adhering to them & are more easily elevated because these seminal or rather radical atoms are readdyly placed {& attending} to put forth & take hold of the earth & draw fit nourishment for the maintenance of its kind stock *(when some affirme that rootes are not efficient cause of the life of a plant, which se learnedly disputed by Laurenburg: L: 1. c: 9:) [Peter Lauremberg, *A Petri Laurembergii . . . Apparatus plantarius primus tributus duos libros* (Frankfurt am Main, 1632), edition unidentified.]

& Sun, ~~beating on~~ {invading} its externall parts, superinduces *that* which on the surface invests it, and we name the *rind* or *barke*. The rest of the parts abiding in the Earth, being likewise somewhat agitated, spread forth those feete which we call the *Roote*; & by which it fixes and maintaines its vigour, feeding upon the same influences, which at first produced it; and having obtain'd this liberty from the *cell* which restraind it, the inward and circular activity begins also to manifest it selfe, by breaking forth into branches & armes, which as so many raies dart from the centerall beame, producing leaves which ~~as~~ {like} so much Gumm–worke are formed of that glutinous and tenacious humor, {that} which ~~sluses~~ diffuses it selfe over all those interstices, woven in that curious and subtil networke, which, as so many veines convey both the matter and nourishment: But the most exquisitely elaborated juice, advances into buds, blossomes and flowers, whose bottomes the fruites do knitt, and in their centers lye carefully guarded & wraped up, those Seedes and Causes, which the God of Nature has bountifully ordaind to propagate its Species, & is the ultimate designe. Now a plant arived to this perfection, and the Seede againe commited to the Earth in a proper Season, Nature in like manner nurses & educates it, 'till conducted through the same Course, it attaine the desired maturity, as before: And albeit some Plants are not thus propagated by Seedes; but by Rootes and Setts. {as well} Yet are they but very few; and their roote is to them in lieu of Seede; since it derives its first originall from the Elements, & this Principle of the Universe inducd with those impregnating virtues: For, after the same Sort, Animals are bred, some by appropriate Sperme others, without it, & by ~~the~~ {the} putrifaction, mutuall action & passion of the Elements, ~~And~~ 'till in fine, ariving to their præfixed period, dissolv'd, they returne againe to their respective Principles, leaving their Bodys to the Earth, and their Spirits to the Astrall originall from whenc they came; Mans onely excepted, which proceeding immediately from God, returnes againe to him that made it.[11,12] ~~And now utrum horum manis accipe:~~ ~~{Choose whichever of these you think best}~~ By this tyme we suppose our Gardiner

---

11. **[Margin note]** Here insert Dr Sharrocks p. 35 & 56 add 60; 74 & 77. [Robert Sharrock, *The History of the Propagation & Improvement of Vegetables by the Concurrence of Arts and Nature Written According to Observations Made from Experience and Practice*, 2d ed., Oxford, 1672.]

12. **[Insertion on separate sheet of paper]** So far then we have proceeded to examine the Hypotheses of these Philosophers of the prime motions & conceptions of Vegitation to its ultimate maturity & perfections **[insertion continued on a separate piece of paper]** to which we might add ~~aboundance~~ {a number} of subtil ~~arguments~~ {discourse} ~~to prove~~ {concerning} the {essential &} specifique differences {forme & perspective} of plants as to their vegitable life & nature & vertues; & whither ~~they~~ {these} proceed rather from their matter than their formes; whither it is by vertue of their specifique soule that Plants seeme so much to differ in colour taste smell etc: passes through all the effects of the vegitable life: & ~~whith~~ what ~~share~~ the {subordinat} forma corporietatis (as they call it) signifies {to this difference by which plants are sayd to exist ~~when yet deprived of their vegitable life~~ may & ~~to act~~ sensibly to act upon occasion (as we see in the heate of {dry} [grasse?], the purgative quality of rhubarb so long gatherd) when yet they ~~are~~ are all deprived of their vegitable life. & what might farther be said of all the other functions of the vegetable soule as to its nutrition & increase & recreation, all which we sense to be don by the {same} act of

[page 41] may have received some beame of Light, usefull to a farther intuition into the Mysteries of Nature, as she is the subject of his daily contemplation; and beginns withall, to be sensible that if we have appeared somewhat Scrupulous of admitting him, without due reguard to his accomplishments, premis'd in the Second Chapter of this instant Worke, it has not bin for want of just consideration to the merites of the subject. So that now receiving him as qualified to proceede with sufficient intelligence of that which is to follow, and to derive those ~~those~~ advantages from this discourse, which it shall faithfully, and candidly present him withall: We in the next, advance to the more Artificiall part of his profession, as it relates to practice, in pursuance of our Designe, and to justifie the Title. {I conclude this chap: & booke with the learned Dr: Merrett Anatomy of the dissimilar parts of plants as I find them in his Pinax: P. 156}ˣˣˣ

The End of the First Booke.

---

the Vegetable Life: ~~How~~ which the heate by which plants are thus believed to act be elementary, be rather more celestial & spiritual. In what peculiar seate or parte of our plants their soule is seated or rather universally disposed which the like curious disquisition of {say not one which but volumes of disputes might be congested} manner of disputing might be considered: But we shall passe over these fruiteless trifles to the more speculative and [satisfie?] ourselves with the mention of them onely. **[End insertion]**

{In the mean time} Those who would delight **[insertion indicated but not present]** Concerning æquivocal generation of plants without Seedes {of which we touched in the entrance of this Chapter} I shall not enter into that discourse here, (being not well satisfied as to any of these extraordinary productions) though we reade of divers plants which have sprung up in places, where never were any before, as Jo: a Costa tells us in his description of Peru & Nova Hispania L: 4: [José de Acosta, *The Natural and Moral Historie of the Est and West Indies*, London, 1604.] Nor shall we dogmatise whither the Earth have actual or potential Seede in her which then appeare upon the domineering of certain constellations, or some other universal cause which come to be determin'd to such & such Individuals from the Indoles and nature of the Soyle ~~which man~~ according as tis variously disposd & qualified as the yeare & Season may fall out for drouth, moisture, heavens influences etc. but certaine it is there ~~may~~ {dos} lye very much hid to us, & we {daily} see strange ~~things~~ accidents of this nature, & especially as the Earth may be treated & fecundated ~~as we shall shew in this treatise~~ which ~~is~~ {was} never idle since the Almighty benediction ~~of which St Ambrose~~* quam vehemens vox! germinet terra ex sese ~~seemes to inferr~~ which St Ambrose seemes to inferr a kind of spontaneity. But as we sayd ~~these are~~ to unfold these particulars & detect them in the Causes *Invida præclusit Speciem Natura videndi* {Lucretius: L: 1 [321]} Nature is very nice in discovering to us, as indeede having nothing which she conceals from men with more reservation, yet not out of the poets envy, but to excite our {modest &} enquirys & increase our admiration of the workes of God: it shall {therefore} have sufficed us to have solv'd the phœnomenon as we have ben able & by this tyme our Gardner etc: **[Margin note]* Hexam: L: 4

[Margin note] Se D: Morison plant that grew after Lond: conflagration

The Second Booke.

Of the Instruments belonging to a Gardiner, and their various uses.

Since *Gardining* is one of the noblest and most refined parts of *Agriculture*, and hath, as all other *Arts* and Professions certaine Instruments and tooles properly belonging to it, and without which we can hope for little Successe in our Labours

> Dicendum est quæ sint duris agrestibus arma
> 1. Geor. [160]
> We now produce the hardy Gardners Tooles.

And truely, we are not asham'd to bring them forth, since besides the honour they have derived from antiquitie we reade that princes have borne them in the royall standard as Orosius[1] reports it of the Indian Kings of *Benomotapa* who[1] had for their Imperiall Ensigne a *Spade* above two *darts*, to signifie not onely their preferrence of peace before warr, but their affection to an Art so useful and divertissant[2] Hesiod and Homer have celebrated them for the same reasons:

And when {C. Fugius Cresinus} that ~~In~~ industrious Romane had produc't before the *Senate* his spades and his Mattocks, his ploughs and other Instruments so strongly and exquisitely made, rarely fitted & well contrived; being accused for Sorcery, because he had[3] a better crop then his envious Neighbour, they acquitted the Defendant with disgrace to this Adversary. We will now therefore begin to speake of the Supellex hortulana and to enumerate and describe such *Utensils* **[page 42]** as appertaine to the Gardiners profession, and their Severall employments. ~~And first~~[4]

---

1. **[Margin note]** Lib: 1: de Re: Indicæ.
2. **[Insertion on separate sheet of paper]** I had rather have says the noble Cowley: two spades Saltier in a field proper, than all the Lions & the Eagles of Princes, & the plough is of more dignity then the Scepter: **[Margin note]** in his desc: of Agriculture[.] [Cf. Abraham Cowley, Essays, 4, in The *Workes of Abraham Cowley* (London, 1678): "But if Heraldry were guided by Reason, a Plough in a Field Arable, would be the most Noble and Antient Armes."]
3. **[Margin note]** Plin: L: 18. c. 6
4. **[Insertion on separate piece of paper]** & possibly this may seeme a low & ignoble Subject, yet he that should undertake to expand the old instruments of this Art, or make addition by some new Invention (as in ~~one~~ {not a few} we have here attemptd) & esspecialy afford some hints & Mathematical touches from the Mechanicall powers of their figures & contrivance {~~which for be which for beauty would not prætermit~~} would not only do a gratefull worke to Gardners; but meet ends

1 Amongst all the Instruments belonging to our Artist, the *Spade* is the principall: The *bit* thereoff should be w[r]ought of excellent steele, not brittle, of a competent, not over large Size and concavity: the graft (as of all other tooles) of Ash, well and lightly wrought: of a fittinge poise: for these are particulars of maine concernement both as to handinesse and expedition: But we referr it to your election and experience. Also Shovells etc: to dig, trench, open, pare and cast out the mould as occasion requires.

2 The Rake is the next, of use for levelling breaking the clodds and refining the ground: Of these therefore there should be severall Sizes: Some whereof ~~the~~ with teeth very close sett, some at greater distance; some flatter, others rounder, longer. shorter, both in head, teeth, and handle; as for the Service of narrower paths and passages betweene the beds and divers other employments.

3 There is another Sort of Ra{c}kle which is found of Singular expedition for the suddaine extirpation of weedes in pathes and Alles, where the accurate handy weeding is not so necessary; as under close–walkes, in Groves & places lesse obvious. It may be form'd of the blade of a broaken *Syth* a foote in length, thick upon the back, and sharp on the edge, towards which let it be somewhat curved: This Instrument fitted with its handle like a Rake being drawne backwards, dos at once so clense the ground of Weedes by cuting them off, and explaining the rugged inequalities of the Earth, as far exceeds our usuall *Haues* which with the violence of the stroake, renders the ground full of holes & extreamely mangles it.

4 Though there are also *Haues* to be provided of all sizes especially the least, not above 2 or 3 Inches broad, very commodious in thinning, cleansing and earthing many sorts of plants, and for sundry other purposes.

5 A Forke or *Trident* of Yron for the loosening and extirpation of Dog–grasse, bird–weede, Arcangel, and other obstinate and noxious Weedes.

6 A Mattock and Pick–axe to breake up the gravell, grub the rootes of trees and open hard and rocky grounds.

7 A Crow of Yron with a spoone to make and clense holes for the setting in and fixing of poles, posts, stakes and Palisades.

8 Sieves of wire of severall finenesses, for the Seifting of mould upon Seedes and for the cleansing of them, {& also to sift & clense seedes themselves.}

9 A wire Hurdle to cast ~~and~~ trye and refine coarse earth, & to sorte and prepare the gravell for Bedds & Walkes.

10 A water Levell, or some other with the *Dioptra* for levelling the *Area* of any Ground; or to be planted on a **[page 43]** *Tipas* as the plaine Table is usd to be & so deepe that [5]

---

of our Criticks & Politer Scholars; But this we being obliged to pretermitt as not altogether belonging to our Institution, ~~I~~ & to avoide prolixity, ~~I beginn with due speede~~ I proceede to the enumeration of what is necessary, And first

5. **[Margin note]** This W: levell neede be about 5 foote long bord quite thick & stopt with an immovable stopple at one extre[me], the other with a caske to put the water in; & with two smale pin holes at the surface ends so if setting it till the water plays at both these holes it will be levell & will need no diaptera thus **[illustration, see Fig. 5]** or fill it with a tunnell at one of the smale holes: the holes about as big as goose quill. (a) (b) are the holes:

Figure 5. Illustration of a water level in a margin note at page 43.

the wind disorder not the Water: The like also may be performed with the Semicircle etc: described by *Mr: Blith*.[ii]

11 Also another Levell of 6 foote long, made of drie and firme wood, with its plumett etc:

12 A Rule of 12 foote 6 inches, to place the stakes or pinns, and to applye the levells upon, if occasion require, in laying of walkes, and ~~upon~~ {for} other uses.

13 A scale or halfe perch divided into 8 foote 1/4 both to measure withall, and for the making and drawing of short lines in Traile–worke and parterrs.

14 Parallels to work off from patterns.

15 A Circumferenter or Plaine table, with its chaine etc. for the plotting and setting out of greater plantations etc:

16 A Reele of wood or yron furnished with a line of ~~smale~~ {midling} {whip} Cord {of the best water–wought hemp} well waxed to preserve it from shrinking and to containe in length 50 fathomes.

17 A Drawing–poynt to trace and designe withall, being a round staff of 6 foote long, steeled at the top with a poynt, light and fit to worke withall.

18 Compasses of Wood, the Shankes 3 foote in length, shod with yron poynts, to divide, draw circles, parterrworke, and for other uses; and therefore described to open from Inches to feete, with a skrue to fix them.

19 A Pin or peg of some hard wood, halfe a foote in length, ~~shod~~ poynted, to set in the Earth: This pin must be headed with a flatt top of 3 inches square upon which to fix the immoveable foote of the Compasses, that it sinke not in working upon the ground.

20 Planting sticks and Dibbers of wood and Yron, some poynted, others indented, others plaine and flatt, with markes and divisions on them, and holes at each marke, to fix a pegg fitted to severall depths.

21 A Taravelle, which is an Instrument made of Yron 3 foote in length, fashion'd like a Crow, but somewhat broader, having an handle of wood, and in the yron part, holes made at severall distances for pinns of yron or wood as in the dibbers above described; onely they must be stronger and longer, that the Instrument may be pressed into the ground with the foote if neede require for the Planting of Vines, {and other} shrubbs. etc.

22 A Set of Planting teeth which is an Instrument made like the head of a Rake, but with the teeth somewhat bigger, and not so poynted, in length 4 Inches; distant 5, the head 4 foote long, and fitted with an handle both to ~~thr~~ presse the teeth into the Earth & take them out; exceedingly usefull for dispatch. {especially for beanes, pease, or tender rootes: for which you may have the teeth of severall bignesses:}

23 A Planting Lattice which is a frame made of fir {or oake} like the wood of an Harrow, of 6 foote in length, 3 in breadth, each square at competent distance for *bulbous rootes*; One side of this frame to be made with ~~a~~ sharpe ridges **[page 44]** that being applied to the bed, it may leave an impression, being somewhat pressed downe. An Instrument of great dispatch for the regular planting and setting of rootes & flowers, for which the French make use of it, and to avoide the frequent removing of the line. etc.

24 The Gouge, made of a strong curved yron–plate, one foote in length, and open about 4 Inches, the edges on both sides acute, and at the poynt very sharpe: This must be fitted to an handle of wood, a little bending for the more easie extraction of Rootes and plants, together with the mould: which is don by thrusting it downe on

both sides of the plate, and turning it, till the clod be sufficiently loosned: much to be preferred before the flatt gouge.

25 The *Extractory Imtrex* or *Italian* ~~tube~~ *Gouge*, which is form'd also of a reasonable thin yron plate {or laton:} yet somewhat stiff: the diameter of 6 Inches, in length 10, fitted with 3 or 4 loopes or hasps, which, when the tube is pressed with the hand, may so adjust that it may be closed and fastned with a pin or *stile* of yron. It must likewise have two handles fixed to the upermost margent: the neither part of this Instrument must be sharp, with an edg to cutt and enter the earth when pressed and forced above. It is of admirable effect and exceedingly commodious for the taking out and transplanting of rootes when they are in flower without the least disordering them. Thus, First gather up the Leaves and stalkes, so as they may best be comprehended within the hollow of the Tube, then presse it downe ~~easi~~ equally on all parts to a requisite depth, and so draw forth the Roote with mould and all, and transpose it into the place which you have before prepared ready to receive it, opening the plate by drawing forth the pin or wyre which closed the loopes, that it may gently slide out, without the least violence or concussion, and then closing it with mould to the rest of the bed, give it a little water.

26 A Trowell after the Masons shape, others narrower, more poynted & all different sharpnesses, to plant, take up and cutt the fibers of rootes withall.

[6] 27 A Turfing spade, of steele and well edg'd, made somewhat broader & flatter then an ordinary spade, thinner and with a curved neck fitted into a wooden handle. {Also another not above half so big & broad, made hollow, quite sharp, onely the edge, & sides to strengthen it of ~~yron~~ steele; this of excellent **[continued in margin]** use to pare weedes in waterables etc: the opening or vacuum being made that the weedes & earth may better fall through.}

28 The Edging Plough, the Coulter to be fixed onto an yron jacket, yet so as to move it to what depth you please, not exceeding 3 Inches: And this Sockett to be fastned to a handle of willow 5 foote long, a little bending, **[page 45]** Lastly, there must be a wheele of brasse of fowre Inches high, to run at the end of the Sockett upon a pin or *axis* of yron. Or else, an Edging knife may be made with the Poynt of a sithe, fastned obliquely into a wodden grasp.

---

6. **[Insertion on separate piece of paper]** At num (27) Turning–Spade:
To which may be added Mr: Blithes, with a bit looking up as much more as our ordinary spades do, with a curious thin shoo ~~between~~ bow'd up also, the bitt exceeding well steeld & broader at the point or neather end of the bit, then at the over end by 1/2 an Inch, which will take up turfe ~~in~~ all of a thicknesse: & for other uses. **[illustration, see Fig. 6]**

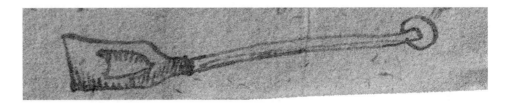

Figure 6. Illustration of a turning spade in an insertion at page 44.

29 Siths of several Sizes, some not so falcated & crooked, some narrower and thinner for fine carpet.

30 Others almost straite, and fitted with even handles for tall palisade hedges; and workes out of reach.

31 Rollers, for Gravell Walkes, the best are made of the hardest Marble, and such as are procured from the ruines of many places in *Smyrna* when old *Columns* of demolish't *Antiquities* being sawd off, towards the *vine* of the *Pedistall* and at the part or *Modell* where the shaft deminishes, makes excellent Rollers: Our English Portland or kentish stones are too soft, and weare flatt in a very short tyme if the gravell be anything sharpe, and unlesse you preserve the stone very drie, being apt to imbibe the wett and grow tender. The fore described Rollers may be procur'd by the friendship of some Merchand trading into the Levant. But the very best of all are to be bought in Holland made of cast yron, or from our Furnaces, where gunns are cast: from one to two foote diameter, 2 . 3 . or 4 foote in length, for severall walkes; If of stone: of Yron a foote 16 or 18 inches is sufficient; if deeper they may be cast hollow: These are forever.

32 We have seene Rollers contriv'd into a moveable Engine, which ran on wheels, the Rollar to be lifted up and downe by a pully and a Winche for the rolling of Bankes of Turfe and the Sides of Tarraces which could not commodiously be beaten. Rollers of Wood for Carpet walkes, Alles etc: of heart Elme, two foote diameter, if lesse, covered with sheete lead: and to prevent cracking boared through with a hole of 2 Inches diameter. The handles of yron.[7]

33 Rammers and Beaters of Elme, for the levelling of knobbs & inequalities at the commissures of the Tarre, when newly layd, or swelling: and for the fixing of stakes, Palisads etc:

34 Sheares, made of excellent Steele, close rivetted, light, & well handled: Of these there should be two sorts, one a lesser paire, and for the clipping ~~the~~ more tender worke.

35 A paire of Reachers {Sunt enim rebus novis, nova ponenda nomina: Cic: L: de N: deo.} which are sheares fixed upon a staff of ~~five~~ {10, 15, or 20} foote long, both the handles of **[page 46]** the Sheares being yron, and one halfe a foote exceeding the other is to be made fast on the head of the staff, about the middle of that handle let there be fitted a ~~bra~~ {brasse} pulley, with a tongue or Spring bearing moderately against the shorter handle, from the extreamity whereoff there must passe a line over the pully, ~~and~~ {which} hanging downe all the length of the staff, being pulld, doth cause the sheares to close, cutt and open, at what height you please, according to the length of the staff: and wonderfully usefull for the clipping of hedges, Arbours, trees, and tall palisads, without the trouble of a ladder, and to cutt of the tops of inaccessible twiggs on which the Caterpillars do fasten their webbs. {also to reach a tall ~~fruite~~ flo: or bunch of grapes or other fruite a bushel contrived to hand so neere as it may fall into it without bruising.}

36 A Hand bill, Hookes, large knife, Pruning knives straite and crooked. {one whereof

---

7. **[Margin note] [illustration, see Fig. 7]** Shover to breake worme cods dry on Carpet:

Figure 7. Illustration of a "Shover to breake worme cods dry on Carpet" in margin of page 45.

with the use & parts you have at large described by Columella L:4 c: 25. & meant by
~~Vergil: 2: Georg~~ the Poets}⁸

37 The pruning Pincers, which are a large paire of Pincers, the edges 3 inches, made
very sharp and of excellent steele, the handles 10 inches long; of greate use to prune
& cutt of such branches as grow in ~~places~~ {those parts} of wall fruite–trees, & palisad
hedges, where you cannot come to strike or force.

38 A pruning hooke {set on a handle 4 foote in length} made somewhat like a Battell–
Axe with edges to cutt both wayes, upwards thrusting, and downeward pulling, especially such branches as grow from the stem, and that without the use of the Ladder
which many tymes prejudices the boughs.

39 An Hatchett, Greate and Smale hand Saw, Chizells, to cutt off a branch close to
the stock: shaving knives, Augers, Plyers, Mallet, Beedle, Wedges, etc: to Cutt, shave,
boare, pull out, twist, drive, cleave & for innumerable other uses both in making and
repairing of Instruments, and other affaires about the Garden.

40 Graffing and Inoculating Instruments.

41 Ladders of severall sizes for length and strength One made with a stage to plash,
bind, and doe high–worke upon, also to serve for the gathering of fruite. {These are
~~by~~ Vitruvius's *Scalæ erismate fultæ* and appropriated to this worke & to the pruning of
the taller trees as *Junius* applys it.}

42 Watering Potts of severall capacities, some portatile, others more fixt: One of
Copper with a dubble neck, the Cullenders of exceeding smale boare for the better
dispersing the water without violating the plant or ~~holle~~ washing the dirt into hollownesses. {& such as with a small orifice as they may graduate the impetuosity **[con-
tinued in margin]** of the water so as it fall as gently as a mist on tender seedlings by
pressing your thum harder or gentler upon it.}

43 The Foixt ⁱⁱⁱ [watering truck] is to be made of a Barill of what capacity⁹ you thinke
fit, so as it may be either transported by wheeles, or otherwise borne: let this vessel
be lined with sheete lead exquisitely sothered, well and strongly hooped with 4 yron
circles; to this let there be contrived **[page 47]** one pipe of leade or brasse of halfe
inch diameter, reaching from the head of the vessel to within a quarter of an inch
of the bottome, ~~let~~ & the upper part of this pipe rise halfe a foote above the head,
to which it is fixed, & crosse the top of the pipe place to plyable spoutes which may
move upon a skrue, having ~~also~~ a stop-cock underneath; these spouts perforate to the
boare of a gooses quill. Moreover, at convenient distance let there be fixed a dubble
pumpe with their suckers, and handles of brasse and yron, these must be contrived
within the body of the Vessell, and made to worke at the same tyme, the one drawing
in water through a neck or pipe of coach leather skrued ~~into~~ with a soccket to the
bottome edge of the Barill, & extending to the fountaine or well, the other drawing

---

8. **[Margin note]** Falce data Frondator erat, vitisque putator: Ovid: Met: 14
[649]

Rusticus et curvo Saturni dente relictam persequitur Vitem attondens, frugit que
putando: Vir: Geo: 2. [406–407]

9. **[Margin note]** reforme this by Dr: Wilkins: [John Wilkins, perhaps his
Mathematical Magick or The Wonders That May Be Performed by Mechanical Geometry (London, 1680).]

in the Aire and compressing the Water, till being no longer moveable ~~the stop–cock be immediately shutt which~~ another stop–cock passing through the lower sockett afore sayd be immediately shutt: Then opening that which is ~~place~~ intercepts the neck of the upper pipe, Let the Gardiner direct the Spoute to the height, or place requisite. It is hardly imaginable, how effectuall, easie, expeditious and naturall this watering, resembling Raine, is, for being directed at the farther part of a Bed or Garden and the Spout fixed to a poynt, it will (without any farther attendance) according as the aire dilates, refresh and water the whole bed regularly, and with greate delight to the beholder. Besides this, it will also reach the topps of the highest trees, destroy Caterpillars, and other noxious Insects: In summ, of all the Gardiners Instruments, this ~~most~~ is the most elegant, usefull, and Philosophicall.

44 There are other Cyringes, to be used in buccketts for the refreshing of ~~the lower~~ Dwarfes and lower trees, & to clense them from the dust & the Insects.

45 Cisterns of lead, or Wood for Infusions, imbibitions, ~~and~~ reserves of Water and Insolation.

46 Cases of Wood, Oake well pitched within, and painted without, of severall capacities, for such Trees, and plants as are yearely to be carried into the Conservatory & store; Let them be made broader at the bottom then at top, with yron loopes fitted for barrs to remove them, or handles, according to their weight and bignesse.

47 Cases to Sow choyce Seedes in, to preserve them from the Worme: Some upon wheeles to alter the aspects, and change places: Also with covers like the round lid of a trunke, and with holes for passage of the Aire. etc.

48 Flower potts, Layer potts, Earthern cisternes to set flower potts in, Earthern Tubes for the transferring of plants, etc.

[page 48] 49 Capps of Earth, and of straw, to cover tender plants and flowers, which you either cannot or neede not remove.

50 A Frame of Wood of the Widenesse of a Flower–bed, the height one foote, with sticks fastned ~~a twhart~~ a thwart the upper brim; to beare ~~up~~ a Cover of reedes or matresse, fitted, bound and adjusted: This is of greate use for the covering and preservation of choice Seedes, newly sprouted, and to secure them from the frosts of Spring and Autumne. {& the intense parching of the Summer.}

51 Bells of Glasse, some Close, others with a tunnell for the admission of aire; Bells and Tubes of Earth Straw etc to shade plants, preserve them from haile etc:

52 *Chasses* or frames Glasse to preserve flo: & Plants from the cold winds, yet expose their beauties, especially *Tulips* etc: {& some of these with small casements to intremist & exclude ayre like chymicall registers:}

53 A Bed–Stead furnished with a tester and Curtaines of Greene, or some other colourd Taffata to draw over and preserve the choycest flowers, being in their beauty, from the parching beames of the Sunn: The frame of six foote ~~le~~ in length, 4 in breadth.

54 Canopies of Glasse, made of Glaziers worke, and put into a frame, capable to cover a *Hott–bed*, {at 1 foote height} and one of the sides made to open and shut with Casements; for the attempering of the aire ~~and~~ government & elevation of choice Seedes: {But those are best which are shapd like a clearks deske, the deepest side (to be placed North) clossd with a board:}

55 Frames to lay Matrasses, Panells of Reede, or straw upon, if the cold {or heate} be very intense and neede so require.

Figure 8 (overleaf). Illustrations of garden tools and implements on page 50.

Figure 9 (overleaf). Additional tools and implements illustrated on page 51.

Elysium Britannicum.

The Instruments presented to the Eye by the Sculptor, and referring to the numbers as they are described.

56 A good Grind stone, Whetstones, Rubbing stones Files to grind, sharpen, & set the edges of your Instruments withall.

57 Wheele–barrows of Severall capacities, some close, some open before, for the carring of Turfe. ~~Earth~~ mould, gravell and other materialls.

58 An Hand–barrow to transport and cary withall, without leaving the Impression of the Wheele.

59 A Cart to carry greater quantities of Earth, Compost and other materialls etc.

60 Baskets of all Sizes, some lined with leather to carry dust & preserve the allys from fowling, Weeding basketts etc:

61 Vintage Baskets, made flat at one side, to weare with harnesse at the back, very convenient for divers purposes; especially the carring of dung and earth to the bedds etc:

[page 49] 62 Scarr–Crows and *Terriculamenta* t'affright the birds, made ~~of~~ {with} horse bells, hanging upon a string which having feathers fastned crosseways 'twixt every bell, sett them a ringing and trembling being plaied upon by the least breath of aire or wind; the line extended betweene two stakes.

63 Also hand and wind clappers of wood for the same purpose.

64 A Case of drawers {of Satin} divided into neasts, and inscribed, for seedes and rootes etc. {with a lidd.}

65 A box of Lamells, or Tallies, which are pieces of lead or narrow plates of 5 Inches long, figured with numbers, to prick in next the stalke of the choycest flowers & plants, and referring to the Register.

66 A Register or booke wherein are the names of all the flowers and plants in the Garden.

67 Mole–Graines, Tubes {Trap Cages}, Field–trappes, {especially those made with holes in the block & the wrire springs fastned with threid boiled in oate meale:} Samsons Posts Netts etc for the destruction of Birds & Vermine.

68 Mattrasses, Reedes, Poles, Oziers, Brasse and Yron Wyre Broomes, etc to Cover, make Palisad worke, bind, sweepe etc: Lastly,

{69 The Rill plough for Kitchin garden Seedes to be order'd at what distance you please:

70 Infusing Vessells for dungs as sheepes dung etc to be steepd in Water:}

A House fitted to place, and preserve all these Instruments in, safly, and without Confusion, with a Chamber and Lodging for the Gardiner. In briefe

> Omnia quæ multo ante memor provisa repones
> Si te digna manet divini gloria Ruris.
> > 1. Geor: [167–168]
> All these before ~~hand~~ must be procur'd by thee
> If fame thou seeke by noble Gardnerie.

[pages 50–51] The Instruments Presented to the Eye by the Sculptor, and referring to the numbers as they are described. **[illustrations, see Figs. 8 and 9]**
[page 52]

Of the Situation of a Garden, with its extente.

{Wisely did our Master Varro call ~~the fir~~ Situation the first part of Agriculture; but it is}

 It is hardly to be expected that all lovers of Gardens, whose Habitations are already fixed, should be provided of such Situations as were in every particular perfect, and accommodated to all the ~~all~~ opportunities of Pleasure and ornament to be desired, *adeo nihil est ab omni parte beatum.* And therefore, though this Chapter be destin'd for the direction of such as are yet to choose, but are {otherwise} provided of all requisite abilities to make their election (as for the most part Princes and greate Persons are), yet may it indifferently Serve to shew, how he which dos not enjoy all those conveniences, of place, or fortune, may by the mediation of Art, supplie in greate measure, what nature, or his lesse propitious fate, has denied him. A Place whose gentle declivitie {Sub radice montis (says ~~Varro~~ {Cato}) & leviter inclinata planities says Palladius}[1] were insensibly towards the South, so as the Sun might visite it, at three of the Cardinal poynts, and by this meanes project his raies more perpendicular (which is the temper we are industriously to court in this our northern Climate), were a situation to be chosen before all others; because this descente will be a considerable shelter from the Septentrionall Winds so prejudiciall to Gardens, especially if the Dwelling–House and Mansion be built on that side, which should command the prospect regularly: And if by this meanes or the nature of the Soyle; it should be suspected too much obnoxious to the eye of the Sun, (a most pardonable accident in ~~this~~ our country) the Waters, and the Glades (which are at no hand to be dispensed withall upon this occasion) will soone be brought to qualifie and attemper it; together with the groves and enclosures: For having wood and Water at command, there is nothing to be despair'd of, which can fall into {our} designe. But though for the rarer plants and trees the South have the præheminency, it is yet acknowledged that the East and West are both tollerable enough for fruite; the west side having an Eastern aspect discovers by the verdure of the trees, and politenesse of the stemm, how gratefull and benigne the rising sun is to it:

And the East Wales which respect the west produce also goodly fruite: But it is to be understood of such Situations as have the Eastern Winds accidentally broaken and mittigated by some rising ground behind it: for if the Sun at his first ascent, passe, and refract through the exhalation of Marshes, or stagnated waters, or that they lye north of the Garden **[page 53]** you will soone find the inconvenience of it, both in the aire, and in your Flowers; whereas if they be South or west, it is nothing so considerable; because those vapours following the course of the Sun are drawne away from your

---

 1. **[Margin note]** but to the height of elegiac and judgement the younger Pliny in the description of his sweete Thuscia: Ep: L: 5 [6] Apollinaro ~~ab~~ Villa in Colle imo sita prospecit quasi ex summo ita leniter et sensim clivo fallente, consurgit, ut cum ascendere te non putes, sentias ascendisse for the rest to its ~~aspect etc.~~ defence from the winds & aspects to the sun etc. Se the intir discussion of it in our 3: book cap: 9.

Garden and quickly dissipated. But, besides this, is the Situation of a Garden very considerable in respect of the Climate; of which we have already amply discoursed; ~~likewise~~ and it wil be our Gardiners greate[2] advantage, and no little marke of his perfection; so to order his ground, and the accidents about it, that assisting Nature with the addition of Arte, he bring it to such a temper as may best qualifie it for universall productions; by which industry, almost all the inconveniencys of our Climate may be rectified, & places brought to a very kind, and hospitable disposition. Of grand importance to this is the fertility and nature of the Earth, which in the next place should be accurately examin'd; That the mould be good, according to the severall indications præscribd in the 10th chap: Lib:1:

Nor should we be satisfied with superficialls, but see that the second and third beds be proportionable to the rest, abating for the severall depths: For though Flowers, and some other Plants, wil prosper and do well enough in shallow mould; yet trees, and the greater shrubbs require more profunditie, that the rootes may be well fed, expatiate and fortifie themselves.

Above all let our Gardiner be curious that the water be excellent, in plenty, and at command; and therefore, we thirst after a Sourse that may breake forth of some chalky eminence, or serpenting in a channell of amber colourd and smoth pibbles, it irrigate the subjacent ground rather in a swift then slower progresse: Wee say in aboundance to furnish the many uses both {of} necessity and ornament; and from a spring sufficiently elevated, for the ease both of the purse, and the body: For there may be occasions and tymes, when it would be requisite to inundate even some considerable part of the Garden; and where such collines {crowne &} environ a place, so as not to interrupt the Prospect, but at agreable distances; There it is that we expect those temperat & salubrous breezes, which so gently refresh both our Gardens & our ~~bodys~~ {Spirits}; whereas, if the hills be mountainus, and the vallys profound, the repercussion & reverberation of the Sun chases the exhalations, renders it sulphury, pestilentiall and impetuous.

Situations are likewise reformed, by melioration of the Earth, by artificiall reflections, plantation of trees, erecting of Shelters, disposing of the Levell, ~~and~~ preparation of the mould, & by severall other artifices. Lastly, touching the Extent and circuit of the Ground, it is also to be modified {as able} to the designe of the person and the Gardiners projection; for if the intent be onely to make a parterr, compartiment, or Coronary Garden, and his ~~intention~~ {fancy} be {narrow &} particular, a lesser {& more regular} compasse will **[page 54]** suffice;[3] But for a Royall & universall Plantation, & to make an *Elysium* indeede, neither one forme, or Situation of Ground will accommodate {the proposition} nor a smaller [4]proportion, then a thousand Geometricall paces in [5]circumference; {The D: of Orleans's in Luxembourg is 70 akers ~~though~~ in ~~area it~~ itselfe} Though some thing very princely, may be contrived in thirty akers; allways supposing it be exquisitely kept: For not onely dos that hold in profit but in the pleasure and delight allso of Gardens *Melior est culta exiguitas, quam magnitudo neglecta.*

---

2. **[Margin note]** cap: 8: Lib: 1.

3. **[Margin note]** a tollerable ground cannot be lesse then 500 foote square for Ortchard & Flo: of which 100 to the flo: Garden:

4. **[Margin note]** c: 3: et:

5. **[Margin note]** Se: L: 3: c: 9. ~~ult~~ See ult.

CHAP. III

Of Fencing, Enclosing, plotting and disposing the ground.

[1]The Ground, Situation and Extent determin'd, the next to be considered is the {Munition} Securing and fencing of our Garden;[2] for which {And yet} we {shall} neither consult *Columella* or *Palladius* or others of the Antients, whose hedges {or Wind walls} though never so artificially {erected} disposed & planted can be no sufficient guard for our Out–Workes, but a good, strong and substantiall Wall of two foote in thicknesse, and thirteene foote in height, either of brick, stone or such materialls as may neither decay, nor leave any uneven & rugged surfaces, receptacles for Snailes, and other noxious Insects. To this purpose let the foundation be well layed {examined} and the mortar excellently prepared.[3] The coping without and erect within; But it shall not be necessary to insert it with hookes, or blocks of wood for the support of Palisads, & cancelled quarters, unlesse it be in that part onely which shall be destin'd for fruit, in which the direction set downe in the *French Gardiner* may be of use; because we suppose it but a portion of our Villa {*Elysium*} (whereoff we do not treat in this place expressely) and would husband our Expenses: But in separating particular plotts, for particular Gardens within the grand Zeraglio or Enclosure, we do by no meanes, approve of Walling, {if walls, parapetts and pedistalls} not onely to avoyd the charge; but for that it greately detracts from the grace and beauty of the *whole*, and will make them appeare but like so many courts or pounds unlesse it be for the private flower Gardens, & of choyce plants, such as are contiguous to the flankes of the Mansion house, which indeede should be contrived to all the advantages of Retirements, & freed from all other intercourses.

Rather therefore, let such partitions be made of Contr' Espaliers[4] and palisads hedges of Alaternus, Holly, {paliuras} pyrocanta, Lawrells {cypresse, juniper}, Hornebeame, Elme, the Garden purple–flour'd Willow, the peach–blosomed thorne, {white thorne, Berberies} some hedges of fruites, or the like, which will in convenient tyme {will} fortifie and become a sufficient Fence, & {gracefull} partition; especially, where there is nothing to violate the Inclosures **[page 55]** but reasonable creatures. {Also a mixt hedge may be made of quinces, apples, cherys, Filberts, Cornelias, peach etc.

---

1. **[Margin note]** mend palisads by Contrespaliers Poole [pole?] hedges

2. **[Margin note]** Talis humus, vel parietibus, vel sepibus hirtis claudatur, neu sit picori, neu pervia furi Col: L: 10 [27–28]

3. **[Margin note]** the lime made of flint (if to be had) & so beaten as not to be seene in the mortar: the joynts close layd, & with little mortar:

4. **[Margin note]** the antients calld them pergulæ rectæ to distinguish them from the Murales or wall Cattices for fruite so much in use in France

all interwoven one in another & bearing fruits: & if you let some of them rise in standards as the chery, cornelia etc: it will neede no stakes but become it & may be there}

Now because stakes and palisads are in divers places chargeable, and the frequent repairing of them dos {many tymes} dissorder the plants; it were good {so} to prepare them before hand, that ~~so~~ they might last, 'till the hedg or enclosure{s} be arived to some fitting stature, and consistency, capable to support themselves without them, by that tyme they come to decay. And to effect this, you shall scorch & rost the poles in a piercing flame, continually turning them round, 'till they have contracted a hard and coaly crust upon them {superficies} ~~{as at *Venice* they {now} harden their piles upon which they superstruct their palaces}~~ For since all putrifaction beginns *ab humido*, it must needes be a most excellent meanes to preserve them; and it would be tried, if for this purpose, it were not better to smother the poles (first cutt out in stakes, sharpned & proportiond as you would have them) under the Earth as for Charr{k}ing of Coale; by which the acid Spirit, ~~coming~~ issuing forth with the vapour, might revert into them (as Glauber somewhere notes) which must needes be an excellent preparation to make them resist putrifaction, & the asaults of ~~the~~ {time &} weather.[iv]

Palisads may be likewise made of the white Mulbery, and other fruits without poles; if being planted {so} as to crosse in forme of Rhombs & Lozenges of about a foote wide. The barke be incised with a little of the wood where the decussations are, and {then} tyed together at the Season, by which they will, in a short tyme, incorporate and become a lively pa~~lisade~~{rtition}, or growing pale, and of greate beauty, being carefully kept pruned betweene the Vacuities: but of these hereafter. {Lastly, for the more ample & natural enclosures, occasion may prompt, & necessity enforce to protect **[continued in margin]** some places with mounds & bankes of Earth & some would be chosen for Ornament; these I would have invested with Ivy by sowing the berrys at the foote in rills & kept weedd till it had quite covered the Earth which I would keepe clip'd in good order & so shall you have a beauty which the poet saw when he sang Hedera formosior alba.}

We come then now to the Plotting and disposing of the Ground; in which we shall not pretend to ~~prescribe~~ {introduce} all that may enter into it under the notion of Ornament; because that were infinite, and will be the greate designe of this whole discourse: What {is} in generall ~~is~~ to be sayd, is, that it would be so contrived and set out, as that Art, though it contend with Nature; yet might ~~it~~ by no meanes justle it out: There being nothing lesse taking, then an affected uniformity in greate & noble Gardens, where Variety were chiefly to be courted; and which Sr: H: Wotton[v] has well observed: For seing Nature dos in the universall œconomy of things præceede Arte, and that Art is onely Natures ape, and dos nothing but by the power thereoff, as having first received all ~~her~~ {its} principles from her Schoole (for thus the Physicks are ever before the Mathematicks) what can be more just and regular, then that she should also præside in the world about which our Gardiner (so much obliged to her) is {perpetually} conversant? **[page 56]** At no hand there{fore} let our ~~Gardiner~~ {Workman} enforce his plot to any particular Phantsy, but, contrive rather how to apply to it the best shape that will agree with the nature of the Place; and studdy how even the most imperfect figure, may, by the Mysteries of Arte and fantsy, receive the most gracefull ornaments, and fittest for a Garden; yet {in this} proceed~~ing~~{ure}, as not to inflame unnecessary expences {so}, nor to Spoile {it} with another extreame, by a wastfull frugalitie: But when Nature will be more proper; then to {take} leave {of}

Art, & save {the} charges. To comprehend all which the better, we will here endeavor to ~~shew ye~~ leade you {up} to such a Prospect of a plot of Ground (no phantasticall *Utopia*, but a reall place) ~~&~~ {as} then which, nothing were almost farther to be desired, ~~as~~ to what Nature can contribute, and as it requires little of Art to render it the most ~~accomplished~~ {illustrious}, & proper for a most ~~illustrious~~ {accomplished} Elysium: Nor will we travaile abroad for this {fine} sight; The Instance shall be out of our owne Country, {&} as I received the description from a Worthy Person.[vi]

There is amongst the severall eminences upon which The Antient *Britanns*, the *Silures*, or at least the *Romans* did extreamely affect to plant themselves {~~either~~} for safty & delight a place {~~now~~} ~~called~~ {~~by the name of~~} ~~Backbury, belonging to the Prices in the~~ {belonging to a worthy person consisting of a Mount & other Greek} This mount is of a vast and prodigious height; the ascent is by severall wayes; some more oblique, some by more gentle degrees, windings and meanders (not unresembling that renowned pensil Garden of *Semiramis* neare *Chaona* in *Media* described in Chap: 7: lib: 3 of our Elysium) and there are likewise frequent rests, or if one desire it, ascents more direct; or one may take a gentle round, or walke up the hill by plaine and smooth passages without bush, thickett, or any obstacle, or by more then semi-circling {& anfractuous} Trenches which are yet perfectly drie and ~~of coverd~~ carpeted with so short a mossy grasse, as cannot bedeaw the feete in any tyme of winter; ~~and ye~~ not withstanding which, these avenues are so deepe, and the extreames so fenced; that our friend has there followed his studies most part of the Winter, sheltred and protected from all winds, & importunity of weather:

For the brimms of these trenches are all along skreened with goodly oakes, forming a naturall close walke or Gallery: upon the Summite of this Hill (the aire seeming allways serene and pleasant) is an ample greene plaine of a Square figure, and every way crowned with thicketts of Oakes, the bordures whereoff are ~~every way~~ all the winter long decked with a frienge of primeroses. violets, **[page 57]** and some other lively {& redolant} plants: At a furlong distance from this sweete and naturall Garden, ~~is~~ {breakes} a most horrid and deepe precipice, fitted for Solitary Grotts and Caverns, and upon the top of this is a prospect over a most desolate Country, called the Vale of Misery, full of poore & ~~wretched~~ {wild} Cottages {seated} ~~up~~on many lesser hills, nemorous and perruked with woods, and other vast objects of rocks, caves, mountaines, and stupendious Solitudes fitting to dispose the behoulder to pious Ecstacies, silent &[5] profound contemplation. Whilst all the other views from the Garden are of quite different prospects from this and indeede from each other, as into most rich vales & other {ravishing} varieties. Now this square hath already the perfect resemblance of an antient Flower–Garden, and to reinforce the pleasure of it, there is another hill of almost equall height emulating *Horeb*, *M: Sinai*, or if you will, *Parnasus* (Such as in Scripture would be called the Mountaines of God, *propter excellentiam*) from the poynt whereoff, one may with a cleare lowde voyce hold conferrence with another, though disjoyn'd by a very deepe & profound bottome passing betweene them. At the foote of this Hill stands the Mansion, and from the side of it gushes forth a rich and pure Fountaine of excellent Water, which (being apt to be improved to all the advantages

---

5. **[Margin note]** Se. Dr: Casaub: Enthus: c. 2 . 3. [Meric Casaubon, *A Treatise Concerning Enthusiasme, as It Is an Effect of Nature . . .* , London, 1655]

of Pleasure for the Gardens), conveys it selfe through the house in a naturall streame, passing to the Garden and fields & making no more stay then is required. The dwelling is situated in the midway to a rich pasture by a most pleasant rivers side, where are the *Viridaria* provided. The *Arable* and *Ortchards* after choyce of wayes leading downe to the River side whither, upon a greene and under shade, or *sub dio* and in the open aire. The *Garden plot*, though thus situate upon a Rock, is yet apt to be perpetually verdant, and may be amplified to what extent the Owner pleases; & the hill seems naturally firtile, & extreamely commode for Medicinal Simples, Vineyards etc winding about a Vale in the middle, proper for the shelter of ~~Laurells~~, {Daphnones} *Cypresseta, Myrteta,* ~~Vepreta~~ and other thicketts & *vepreta* of perenniall greenes; {fit onely for the Muses & the Graces} In Summ, a Place so blessed by Naturall Situation, & varieties that with a competent spot of ground lying contiguous to it; it were capable of being made one of the most august and magnificent Gardens in the World, as far exceeding those of Italy & France, so prodigall of Arte and full of Ornament as they surpasse our best in England by superlative degrees; especially, when to render **[page 58]** it the uttmost accomplishments, it {might} have likewise the addition of Walls, Archtitecture, Particos, {Terraces}, Statues, obelisks, Potts, Cascades, Fountaines, Basons, Pavilions, Aviaries, Coronary Gardens, Vineyards, Walkes, and other Artificiall Decorations, in their true & ~~proper~~ {genuine} places {all which may be introduced} without excesse of charge; because Nature has already bin (as we may {truly} say,) so Artificiall; & as the noble *Spencer* in a better straine, has seemed to describe his Templing Bower of Blisse, as if he had assumed his *Idea* from [6]this very place: For

> There the most dainty Paradise on ground
> It selfe dos offer to his sober eyes
> In which all pleasures plentiously abound
> And none dos others happinesse envie;
> The Painted Flowers, the Trees upshooting lye,
> The Dales for shade; the Hills for breathing space.
> The trembling Groves, the Christall running by,
> And that which all faire workes doth most aggrace
> The Art, which all that wrought, appeared in no place.

> One would have thought (so cunningly the rude,
> And scorned ~~ground~~ {parts} were mingled with the fine,
> That Nature had for wantonesse ensude
> Art, and that Art at Nature did repine,
> So striving each the other to undermine
> Each did the others worke more beautifie;
> So diff'ring both in Wiles, agreed in fine:
> So all agreed through sweete diversitie.
> This Garden to adorne with all varietie.

~~{as the most elegant Propertius has phansy'd his Mistris; & a rare Idea for our Gardiner to follow {or focus} in the universal dispose}~~

---

6. **[Margin note]** L. 2. Canto: 12.

Or if you will have it in poeticall prose, such a plot as the most accomplished *Sidny* makes Kalander to[7] entertaine the Prince Palladius. It was (saith he) neither field, nor Garden, nor Ortchard, or rather it was both field, Garden, and Ortchard: For as soone as the descending of the staires had deliverd them downe, they came into a place cunningly set with trees of the most {tast} pleasing fruites; but scarcely they had taken that into consideration, but that they were suddainely stept into a delicat greene, at each side of the Greene a thicket, and behind the thickett againe new beds of Flowers, which being under the Trees, the Trees were to them a Pavillion, and they to the trees a Mosaicall Floore; so that it seemed that Art therein would needes be delightfull by counterfeiting her enemie Errour, and making order in confusion etc.

Many such like descriptions we might {here} add; but **[page 59]** these shall suffice {us} not onely to shew how well these brave genious's understood it, but, wherein dos in truth consist the excellency of all Hortulane perfection. And all this we do propose as Instances by which {our Gardener may} comprehend what it is we would signifie by an irregular plot, fit to be made a noble, princely and universall Garden & Elysium indeede; {as more at large in the last chap: of the 3d booke: c: 9th} Likewise to shew how much Situations contribute, & how little some narrow hearted people understand their owne felicity; whilst many are in the very way to the most excellent pleasures of this kind, if ~~our of~~ {by} an affected and stiff uniformity they did not spoile their Gardens, undoing themselves with filling up hollows, plaining of precipices, and raising mole–hills in comparison; & then againe levelling other places, whose excellency was as they found it to their hand; and where the Artist should be vigilant to apply all that may contribute to those agreable mixtures we have before described; disposing and placing the parterrs, Relievos, Walls, ~~Pa~~Eminencys, Waters, yea even the very Trees, Plants, Flowers and Severall *Areas* to their best advantage; that so the shades and the lights may fall and diversifie in sweete and gracious varieties; & which may be effected with a greate deale more facillity, where the site is uneven by Nature, or easily so made by Art; then by those starch't and affected designes which we behold in many of our Cockney Plantations, ~~which~~ that looke like Gardens of Pastboard & March–pane & which smell more of Paint then of flowers & {natural} verdure: {Aspice quos summittit humus formosa colores, et veniant ederæ sponte suæ melius: Surgat et in solis formosius, arbutus antris, **[continued in margin]** et sciat in dociles currere lympha vias: litora nativis persudent picta lapillis, et volueres nulla dulcius arte canant. Propert: L: Eleg: 2. a most admirable *Idea* for our Gardiner to consider.}

Howbeit there ought to be very greate reguard had of the Symmetrie and intermixture of these Varieties; least in stead of a Garden we make a Wildernesse onely {&} that it be contrived so as a prospect being had of the *whole* from the first stage of the Mansion. There may result a sweete & agreable correspondency in the parts, though considered by themselves, they ~~are~~ {seeme} altogether irregular & heterogene: Such a plot has a perfect resemblance of the Universe it selfe, of which contemplative men & such as best skill how to enjoy the virtuous delights of Gardens are never sated ~~withall~~, but find always something of new and extraordinary to entertaine their thoughts withall. And now, though of all the formes of Gardens, we find the Square

---

7. **[Margin note]** Arcad: L: 1.

~~& parallelogram~~ to be most usuall; yet the oblong {& parallelogram} which is one of its species, is doubtlesse more convenient as to the circuit of the out Wales; because of protracting the Walkes, Allys, and prospects: But we do by no meanes oblige our Workeman to either: For if, even *that* be irregular as for the taking in of some naturall Rock, hill, Fountaine, or other convenience, it may sometymes happen to his greatest advantage; In the meane tymes **[page 60]** that such portions of the *whole* as are to be employ'd for the Severall Members, be cast into almost all the Species of Squares, circles, crooked & oblique lines; yet so as they do at no hand intercept the principall walkes and Allys; which besides that they are to have universall communication, do with their length alone aford a pleasant and most gracious perspective, whilst they serve to decline and concurr in a poynt, especially ~~inf~~ planted with {tall} trees, then which nothing can be more ravishing and agreable.

For such figures, ~~are~~ as be formed of straite lines onely {they} are extreamely vulgar, and can afford us none of those varieties, which we have so much celebrated & reccommended; not withstanding an ingenious Gardiner may be able to find some beauty and grace in any forme, by appling his invention and judgment to it, whither square, oblong, round, Elliptic, polygone, or anyway rectangular, or irregular; as we shall touch upon severall occasions. Onely we do for the present put in this caution, that in case you affect the quadrangular, you give it (if possible) some what more of longitude then latitude; because an effect of naturall perspective will else too much contract and foreshorten it at the front, & from ~~any~~ {all the} more superiour views & avenues, which ~~it~~ {would be} a very greate errour in a Garden of Pleasure. {If in the inclosure you wall in Theaters or Neeches let them be noble & ample of at least 160 foote wide & 90 .f. diametr & the **[continued in margin]** gates or issues (if proper as to lead you out into some large & long walke or field) should be 6 foote at least, & best of yron open to see your ranges of Trees & prospect: etc}

In the meane tyme to facilitate this necessary disposure of the *whole* to all the advantages enumerated: let our Gardiner in the very first place plot it out exactly by an Instrument; and that not ~~onely~~ with the plaine table onely; ~~but reduce~~ {as they} usually surveigh; but reduce it into geometricall feete accurately, together with all its naturall varieties; that so ~~by the~~ he may designe, and contrive all the severall members to their best advantage, without that confusion, which, if he presume to worke upon the place immediately, without the *Carte*, he shall never effect, but with ~~egregious~~ {extreame} Errours & extraordinary Expences. Now, though, for the accomplishing of what hath bin sayd, the filling up vacuities, raising of bankes disposing of materialls & the like, it were much to be wished that our Gardiner had more then a Superficiall Skill in the Mathematicks: Yet, will it be tollerable, that he be not altogether ignorant how to calculate the most ordinary dimensions & operations which concerne the Superficies onely. As that if his Figure be *oblongue* or *Square*, one side being multiplied by the others, it produces the content. **[page 61]** If *Triangular*, the *Base* multiplied by the breadth, the moitie of the product be ~~the content~~ {what he searches}: That every *Rectilineary Regular* or *Equiangular Scheme* as the *Pentagon, Hexagone* etc be as easily measured by taking the whole *circle* for the *Base*, and the line beneath the center at one of the sides, for the height: and lastly, if the Figure be Irregular, yet *Rectilineary*, or of more then fower sides, it be measured by reducing it into *Triangles*, and then ~~measuring~~ {calculating} them a parte, the *Contents* united: Every {of} which operations may with perfect exactnesse & facilitie be performed, as our Learned *Oughtred* has demonstrated in ~~cap: 6~~ his Circles of proportion Chap: 6, treating of Duplicated

& Triplicated proportion; or by the two Rules for Calculation; yea, even with the plaine measure alone, as it is reformed by him in Cap: 8, to which I referr, our industrious Worke man.[vii] {For the rest, the Ordinary Squale, a {Water} levell & a line will ~~for this~~ furnish to the plotting of ~~squares~~ common figures, observing your sides & diagonals for the **[continued in margin]** head, center & angles at which the Gardner is to fix straite & lasting stakes to be his guide til the worke be finished:}

These things præmised; concerning the disposall of the ~~Soyle~~ {Ground}, we have but a word to add; having already in the chapp. of Soile and stercoration instructed ~~how those~~ our Gardiner, how those parts which he designes for new plantations, are to be husbanded, and as ~~you are~~ {he is} taught to bring it into ease by the frequent stirring and turning up the gleabe, which will infinitely contribute to a speedy fertilitie, by exposing and freeing the prolificall Salts from its restie ligature & alloy which hinder the earth from ventilating and receiving those blessed and impregnating influences, which purifies and renders it luxurious: Breake then such places up, and manure them early in *Autumne*, and againe, about January, turne the ground three or fower tymes {more} clensing & exactly purging it of all noxious weedes, rubbish and impediments whatsoever.[8] But we referr you ~~rather~~ to what {hath bin} sayd already *Ne actum agamus.* and {so} conclude this Chapter.[9]

---

8. **[Margin note]** but if you keepe it thus stirring in midsomer also it will by September following be so mellow & tractable, as nothing can be more desired and in that worke at first opening the ground go shallowest at first, suppose for the 1 yeare neere 2 foote trench: 3 for the 2d yeare, or deeper the third (unlesse the mould be gravelly clay or sand) still casting what you last dug & come from the deepest part upon one side of your trench to cover the next with, by this method your mould will in tyme be restored at a greate depth exposd thus to the Influences by turnes which will impregnate it: I have ben told they have a plow in Holland dos this at once turning in the old & more worn–out Earth, & suppling it with the fresh thus mellowing & improving the ground by stirring it, & very little use of composts.

9. **[Margin note]** Consider if it were not better to make a chap. for propagating Ever greens & other rare greens.

CHAP. IV.

Of a Seminary, and of propagating of Trees Plants, and Flowers.

It may be thought an immethodicall transposition, that we {should} begin our Planta-tion, before we have made our Way to it, and that we did not first designe our Walkes and Alles, before we proceede any farther. And truely we have already suppos'd that the Gardiner has **[page 62]** no sooner ~~set out his ground~~ finished his draught, and observed our late directions, but that in the next place he proceedes to plot it out upon the ground & *area* itselfe by the helpe of Instruments, lines, stakes, trenches and other markes, in order to the employing of Labourers and masons about levelling, raising, walling, delving and other workes, subservient to the greate designe: But for that these ~~are~~ cannot be finished without time and much labour; that there will be employment for Carts, Sledges, barrows, horses and a continuall concourse, which would potch, and extreamely deface the ground, we thinke it sufficient in the first place to delineate and lay out ~~the~~ our Walkes, Allies, Parterrs, and the rest of the sev-erall members of the Garden in grosse; and for a while to respite their finishing, in the interim that we industriously provide Materials for the Plantations, that so there being no time lost, there be a sufficient & speedy furniture of Trees, shrubbs, Plants & Flowers of convenient and different groths, fitting for their severall designations; since we do not pretend; nor will it be seasonable to plant all at once, though the Plotts were already fitted & prepared for it.

So soone therefore as the Wall is erected, if not before, (for *ædificare diu cogitare oportet, conserere cogitare non oportet sed facere*, says *Cato*)[viii] let our Gardiner make choice of a convenient part of the Ground, well secured from the meridian Sun; yet so, as to be somewhat visited by the Easterne rayes, & hardly one poynt upon the North; for, though these are quarters, which, according [1]to our former cautions, we have reason to suspect, for their rigour and unkindnesse to fruite: yet, we hold, that it is better to place a seminarie in such an aspect as may produce hardy plants; that so, when they shall come to be removed into their severall stations in the Garden, they may not onely be prepared for all weathers and expositions, but thrive much the better, when they shall come to dwell in a more propitious aire, and participate of a gentler edu-cation. {for} We can upon experience affirme, that by this hardy elevation of Plants, Myrtill, Orange trees etc. some very tender & choice shrubbs, have bin made to in-dure such severities of the Weather, as would immediately have ~~killed~~ {sterred} those, of the same kind, which had not bin accostomed to it.

And, for this reason, neither should the soile it selfe of the Nurserie be made

---

1. **[Margin note]** C. 5: Lib: 1.

altogether so rich and luxurious, as where we doe intend to transplant; at least that it by no meanes exceed it. ~~It is Virgils advice so~~ {Let us heare the poet.}
[page 63]

> At si quos haud ulla viros vigilantia fugit
> Ante locum Similem exquirunt, ubi prima paretur
> Arboribus seges.
> Geor: 2. [265–267]
> He then who would a vigilant Gardiner be,
> Must find a place out for a Nurserie
> Resembling that he plants in.

But we give no farther[ix] directions here concerning the dressing of the Seminary, then, that it being considered, how ~~smale and~~ close the rootes of the Seedes will ~~stand~~ {crowde} before removall, the mould be made somewhat richer; seing they cannot but stand in neede of more nourishment and care, then trees or plants whose rootes have roome to spread at greater distances in search of it.[x]

Now because there may be some just objections against this situation, and that divers Seedes and rootes require lesse shade and more heate; it will also be necessary to make another seminary in some warmer part of the Garden for this purpose, and in a more free and open aire: Likewise, for the preparing of hot beds and artificiall accelerations, which cannot be too much exposed to the eye of the Sun. All these being well inclosed, should at the beginning of Winter be trenched, and exquisitely clensed, that the earth, which has layne so long restie, may, being now sufficiently loosned, incited, and fittly cultivated take pleasure in entertaining the Seedes which shall be throwne into it: But let the severall plots be cast into beds so proportion'd before the Sowing that they may commodiously be weeded {or rather turn'd up with the spade} as oft as neede requires; which will be very frequent; since there is nothing more pernicious to young plants, then the neglect of purging them.[xi] The beds thus prepared.[xii] cast in your Seedes and set your kernells, thinner or closer as the ~~nature~~ {stature} and bulke of their kinds require. {in the light ground pressing the surface a little with your Spade:} The generall Season of this worke is the beginning of the Spring, that saying of *Plinie* being very considerable: *Sementem festinatum sæpe, Serotinam semper decipere.*[xiii] Hasty Sowing dos de[c]eive our Gardiner sometimes, the late dos deceive him always.[xiv] Secondly that the Moone be either old, or very young; to which the *Count Brembati* adds a[2] caution, not to committ Seedes to the ground {for} eight daies either before or after Eclipses, affirming that it greately deminishes the rootes of bulbous plants: Lastly, that the Earth be moyst, the weather ~~be~~ serene & open.

But though we {generally} give the preheminence to the Spring, especialy for the more ~~proper~~ tender and delicate plants; yet is the Autumne a more proper Season **[page 64]** for many hard and compacted Seedes, which will strike and take good roote within the Earth, while the coldnesse & asperitie of the Winter suffers them not to sproute above it: But then there must {be} very greate care ~~be~~ to preserve them from the mice and other vermine, which are prodigious devouerers of all Autumnal

---

2. **[Margin note]** Proteo Legato c. 3: Lib: 3.

Seminations. Some there are who have sowne their Seedes in the middest of winter; but very improsperously; though the stove has bin applied, and tempered with exceeding care & industrie. But in all Seasons a due preparation of the Seedes and kernells will exceedingly advance their groth; and of these preparations there is great varietie, according to the Nature of the Seede, and the severall imbibitions. {& though I am very little for them, as never having seene such effects as they take up} {Yet} ~~For~~ some are macerated in water alone; some with mixtures of hony, dung, {soote} salt, milke, {blood}, Spirits, {juice of sedum boyld} etc. {but here consult L: Bacon: nat hist: cent: r: exp: 402 etc. & ~~liber~~ c 1: of our third book in this treatise:}

The hardier Seedes in water and unslaked lime, filtrated, adding a very smale portion of *aquæ vitæ*: in which they may ~~remaine~~ {be soaked} 3 or 4 ~~daies~~ {times}. ~~every~~ Being carefully dried with a cloath at every infusion. If the Seedes be very drie, and old, macerate them in water, fermented with a little yest & clarified through a filter. {or in lime water} The more tender may be cast into ~~warme~~ {new} milke ~~new~~ {warme} from the Cow, or in milk and water, so as it be daily changed.

Some have reccommended mans blood, frequently renewed for the maceration of the Seedes of flowers to cause them produce miraculous effects; but it is altogether imposture. Glutinous Seedes, such as yuf [yew] etc should be washed, {& clensd of the mucilege} and rubbed with a drie cloath to prevent mouldinesse. *Pine Aples* & nutts {such as holy berys, yew, Alaternus, etc:} may be steeped two or three daies in water alone. {But this rule is worth all, let the drye seedes & kernells be kept moyst, the moyst dry, the mucilegious washed & dryed **[continued in margin]** keepe the dry Seede in Earthen Vessells, the moyst in sweete Gourds & all them in a box of Laton from the Mouse & Vermine: such a box divided in nests, wrapping the seedes in paper etc:} *Democritus* affirmes that we should breake the berries of *myrtils* to give the Seedes liberty, but with care that they suffer no contusion: the same may happily be don to the yef, pines, Almond, Date, and other hard seedes; but ~~to~~ {in} our experience with little advance or safty. {Some reccommend lifting with a knife a little} *Wallnutts, Chestnutts, Acorns* etc may be barrelld or potted {or kept in a smale cellar in barills} up {during the whole winter} with husks and all in earth, or sand; having bin first steeped in cows milke warme, 24 howres; ~~Curi~~ Some macerate their *Chestnutts* a whole moneth in water: others lay them in beds of Earth, Sand, Sawdust, moyst dung etc:

It is evident that Seedes, or berries, being kept in heapes, after due imbibitions 'till they begin to ~~swell and~~ **[page 65]** ferment and swell a little, will suddainely spire, and (being sowne) peepe up in a very short tyme, greately preventing such as are but crudely injected.[3]

---

3. **[Insertion on separate piece of paper]** For the ~~tyme~~ {Season} of Semination generally the Spring Ver tument terræ et genitalia semina poscunt Virg: 2: Geor [324]

In the Summer very few things: Autume many ~~especially Seeds such~~ especially such as those are apt to sow themselves: In winter few or none {especially ~~after~~ before Christmas:} of all which particulars se our Calendar Cap: 23. of this booke to forbear repetition:

As to Lunations the common rules are, what you would have grow tall & big,

But before Semination it will be requisite that the ground receive a second dressing, that it be refin'd, and hurdled if neede be; and then the beds & quarters trodden out, your Seedes may be sowne in lines, if it be of the greater sort; if very smale, more at randome, and scattering; because it is so difficult to cast it into the rill thin enough: And when the plants apeare about an inch above ground, you may then safely drawe and prick them into lines and ranges at pleasure, for the more commodious clensing them from weedes, allowing them distance {of} hand breath or more according to their qualities and future stature. {Fruit kernels for such at 1 foote distance **[continued in margin]** a foote from each other: but every 3d ranke 1 foote 1/2 . the better to come to graffing & clensing, let them stand N: & south & make trenches not holes⁴} This don in a fit, that is, moyst {& warme} Season will cause them to

———————————————————

take the full moone. & decrease: such as most trees; such whose flowers you only desire, New moone & increase: The reverse of which rules produce contrary effects:

For the Manner Pliny teaches us to set out our right hand & foote together in scattering the Seede more equally:

Some Seede you must sow thick, as Scurvy grasse, chusewell[?], Nasturtiums, cardus benedict[us], marjoram etc: cabbage, ~~aniseed~~ endive, hyssop, etc: & such as may be drawne & transplanted: & such as are very minute with sand or Hilles for better dispersing on dryd Earth which is as good: But pease, reddish, scorzenera, Onions, the thinner the better.

[Continued on verso] Some plants thrive best being sowed amongst others, as parsneps, onions, Petroselinums, etc: which mature one after another & do no injury to each other. When Seeds are sown, the next care is to preserve them from cold, ~~ver~~ birds, vermine, for which looke c: 27.

4. **[Insertion on separate piece of paper]** ad p: 65 Fruite Trees Nursery & in dry places begin the worke at Autume, & in moyste after Xmas:

For stocks for Dwarfes & Walles fruite {peare, peach, plums, etc} set your stockes 2 foote asunder & cutt them 3 inches from the Earth to make them spread fresh to graff on: But the pared of[f] stock {cut} a foote & halfe high, for you must graff in the old wood which is longer a growing alike to neere a great, for {to} inoculate in the stock is not proper: In May nip of the budds, & let but one bourgeon remaine on each twig for one shoote onely, & chop the ground a little once in June (9)[?] an half digging, then cover it with ferne, yet so as not to choke the small ~~stocks~~ seedlings, in October take off the Ferne or rake it in ranges, & a little rigole between which the seedlings grow that the raine may soake them better, & the Earth you take out for the rill cast on your ferne, but be carefull not quite to uncover the rootes of your seedlings: March following cover & rake all even ferne & Earth cutt & mingled: they will make their rootes exceedingly, use this course 2 yeares after they have ben graffed: if they thrive not with the dung then the 3d yeare in November, (i) cast it mixed with earth about the whole Nursery. When your stockes begin to be big enough clense them of the branches 6 or 8 inch high, & then meddle no more with them: Plums, cherys, quince eplucke not till March the 2d yeare, & then leave them not above one or 2 branches to each foote then cutt them 8 inch high, ready to graffe

[continued on verso] by that tyme the wound is healed: so also save that pard of [pared off] stock: Quince & plum may be graffed in 2 yeares, the rest in 3 or 4 yeares:

Figure 10. Planting instructions for gourd-like seeds, illustrated on page 65.

take immediate hold [5]on the ground and soone prepare them for transplantation as their severall groaths require, there being now space enough to take them up {earth & all} without violating their rootes which is (in some plants especially) of exceeding consequence. {But being of any reasonable groth before you thus thin them, cutt the downe right roote pretty close, & it will cause it to spread, **[continued in margin]** & if it be a Fruite tree extreamely facilitate its ultimate Transplantation. Some kinds excepted.}

Stones and kernells would be set towards the ende of Feb: two inches deepe at 4 inches asunder, in even lines, & every species a parte: But in burying these & all other Gourd like Seedes, you shall not plant the sharp poynt upright; but rather couch them *ad latus* sidelong. The reason whereof the following figures doth better discourse, then any other description, to demonstrate how præpostrous the common errour is {by making the rootes & stemm to fetch a compasse about the seed etc:}[6]

[illustration, see Fig. 10]

Kirnells may be set in Octob: Novemb: stones in Feb: March. {But best immediately after they fall off their fences[.]) If the kirnells, berry or Seede be of any choice or rare kind, sow, set, and burie them in potts of earth to preserve them from vermine, and to this effect, it were not amisse that all the edges of the Seminarie beds were enclosed with flat stones, broad, & close tyles.

The appling of boards and weights together with some tongue upon the stones {& weights} themselves, ranged only upon the surface of the bed, is reccommended in our *French Gardiner* with good successe, for this opened at the Spring will doubt-lesse discover a greate magazine of sprouted & forward plants, to be redressed and fixed in the Earth at spring at that Season, {provided the ground be not very ver-minous}[.] **[page 66]** Wallnutts and Almonds should be set, where they are to abide forever; because upon the least motion in transplanting they are exceedingly endan-gered, and much retarded of their groth. Whither the *Sumera*, or Seedes of Elme will produce Plants, we know has bin pretended by some: but essaied without success: Such as have a desire to make farther experiment, should gather it, says *Curtius*, about the Kal: of March, before the leafe comes, & when it begins to looke of a redish-yellow hue, and then drie it two days in the shade. {Sow it on moyst ground, in Scotland I am assured it growes successfully, but however the chipps of Elme cutt of from a branche **[continued in margin]** with some of the barke & placed or secured

---

5. **[Margin note]** crabfish:
6. **[Margin note]** Se Malpuigius[.] Se Lauremb: L: 1 c. 17: p: 100

in moyst furrowes or rills an inch deepe{ly} will furnish a plentifull nursery: do this latter end of September[7] if at least it be not a mistake printed in our Sylva from Dr: Sharroks suggestion:} *Chessnutts, Haizells, Acorns, Mast, Ashen-Maple, Sycomore,* hegs, etc are produced being set, or sowne in furrowes of a hand breadth deepe; & the line two foote distant, that they may be howed, weeded, drawne, and transplanted. {Note that the best Season for sowing as to the temper of the mould is 2 or 3 days after a raine: with this Canon: that in dry places you sow early, in moyst later}

When these severall plants are risen to a competent height, it will be requisite to establish, to comfort, & refresh them with a little fine seifted mould, dispersed amongst them: for now will the roots be subject to loosening; being elevated either by ~~the~~ frosts, or the ordinary swelling of the Earth after thawes, & at other tymes; also to keepe them from spending too much in branches: for which cause, some buds at the sides, may be rubbed off. Thus let them stand till about *June,* at which tyme you shall bestow a half digging or stirring ~~upo~~ on your Seminarie, betweene the lines and alleys, Spreading {as before} some mungie stuff, halfe rotten ferne or the like over the beds, to refresh & moysten the rootes during the excessive heates, which will greately advance them: And in March following, you may mingle this compost (which will by that tyme become sweete, short & well consum'd) with the loose Earth, chopping it in and raking it over. {but use not much dung till the 3d yeare, for reasons we alledge:} But for as much as we pretend not in this designe to treate {altogether} of Ortcharde fruite, but of such trees ~~onely~~ {chiefely}, as are proper for the decoration of a Garden of Pleasure, for avenues, Walkes, Groves, thicketts and other embellishments; we rather referr to those who have expressly written of them & to our often mentioned *French Gardiner.* ~~and pursue this Chapter Therefore~~

There shall one part of the Seminary be destin'd for the elevation of tall trees & such as are most proper for shade, Groves, Woods, Walkes, etc: You have bin already instructed how their severall Seedes, Acorns & kirnells are to be ~~disposed~~ prepared & set: Being then sprung up, you shall now and then cherish them with a slight dressing, but without pruneing for the first **[page 67]** three yeares, and then, about mid-october or sooner, plant them forth, cutting them within an inch of the ground where they are to continue. The Second yeare in March you shall prune and cutt {them} againe halfe a foote from the Earth, leaving them but one shoote: & thus let them stand for good and all.

White thorne & such shrubbs {proper} for *Vepreta* are to be intermixed with the tall trees to invite the Birds, and should be prepard as you are taught, the whole winter before, though they also come well enough of Setts;[8] but of these sorts of Thorne, there is one which beares a blossome like a peach tree, which is exceeding beautifull, and to be preferred before all the rest. And thus we have done with such trees and plants as spring of Seedes, and which *Servius* calls *Plantarias.*

We come next *ad plantas* ~~which &~~ such as are produced of trees themselves. *Elmes, Poplars* etc wil be ~~well~~ best produc't of Suckers or roots; and so with the ~~Lime &~~ *Abiel* trees, {& Lime[9]} of all other the most beautifull and fit for walkes and approaches,

---

7. **[Insertion on separate piece of paper]** but in Frame it comes without difficulty, & may be removed in 3 yeares.
8. **[Margin note]** of large setts & single rowes
9. **[Margin note]** ~~by cutting a gorge in it & covering it with earth~~

which are in aboundance to be procured out of *Holland*, where they are sold at reasonable rates, barrelld up and transplan{or}ted: {Or you may raise innumerable by cutting a roote close to the ground & covering the top with earth.} The *Witch–Haisell, Birch, Horne–beame* etc may be taken out of the woods in young rooted plants, set in rows at eighteene inches a sunder, all these may be cutt {within a foote} when you transplant them; The *Aspen* {& Birch} only excepted which will not {so well} endure it: *Oakes & Beech* may be likewise drawne out of the woods and {immediately} planted either in Nursery; or rather in the places where you will have them continue.[10,11]

There are besides these drie trees, beds to be prepared for Ever–greenes; which, though they may for the most part of them be sowne, like hawes; yet we have ever found, that one indifferent case produce more in a smale compasse, then many pounds cast the {an} ordinary bed of larger extent, abandon'd to the worme, and other accidents. And therefore, as well for these, as for the raising of Flowers, we advise our Gardiner to provide himselfe with store of cases, boxes of wood, large panns, jarrs, and earthern pots etc filled with good mould, and such as is mingled with the rotten stuff to be found in hollow willow trees, sifted from the dry unconsumed sticks, and embodied with a lomy moyst and feeding mould; or such as is mingled with the rotten is mingled with the you are shewed how to prepare and sever for those curious uses in our Chap: of Composts and stercoration.[12] The proper Season for committing these seedes to the Earth is in the new Moone of March and Aprill.

Now these Cases and Vessels must be placed in the shade having handles by which to transport them if the weather be so hard prove too hard, cold, or washing; and that the mosse meanaces to invade them.

[Page 68] Having all things thus provided: you may in Beds or Cases at the Spring sow. *Alaternus, Anagallis, Arbutus, Bays, Barba Jovis, Belvederes, Cedar, Chondrille incarnat: Chrysanthemum, Valentinum Clusij, Cistus* (or upon the hot–bed for more surety), *Carobes, Cyanus* of all colours to have flo: in Summer, *Cypresse*; especially the Male, *Cytisus Maranthus, Fir, Genista, Gilly–flo:* of all sorts; *Juniper,* the *Rose–Lawrell Laurustinus; Common Lawrell, Lentiscus, Lilac, Limons, Muscipula,* for Summer and Autumne flo: *Nasturtium Indicum,* (or the hotbed), *Nigella of Damascus,* and other sorts for the flo: *Oranges, Pinkes, Phyleria, Scabious* for flo: in Summer & Autumne, *Senna, Sesamoides coronopus, Seseli Æthiop: Thlaspis Cand:* for flo: in Summer & Autumne, *Violets, Yufs,* and many others.

[13]For Seedes which are exotick, and the most tender sort Let our Gardiner prepare an *Annuall Hott–bed,* erected in the hottest part of the Seminary; And this bed we would have dubble wattled, or matted about, rather then paled [14]wisped, or otherwise inclosed, as we have seene some {many}; not onely to preserve the straw and

---

10. **[Insertion on separate sheet of paper]** The best season of planting them are early in Autume & especially your quick–setts, & set in {all} planted as shallow as may consist with their standing

11. **[Margin note]** here add {visite Sylva} the discourse you gave into the Society for the Commissioners Octob: 1662

12. **[Margin note]** cap: 11: lib: 1.

13. **[Margin note]** se how made in Cap: 9: Se also L: 3. c. 1

14. **[Margin note]** describe it before

the litter from scattering; but ~~for~~ [15]to cast in, and apply fresh dung for the exciting of the spent or languishing heate, as occasion requires, without any dissorder to the Bed, over which we rather approve of a curved Frame of wood glazed of convenient distance for reflection and with casements to open {& shut upon occasion} then the perpetuall use of Bells or glasses, unlesse it be for such plants as require the utmost degree of this artificiall heate to raise and entertaine them. This frame may be covered with matts, and ~~fitted with~~ straw as neede requires: A description of these frames you have in Cap 1 num: 54. 55. The Bells of Glasse would be made with a tunnell to let the aire in at Top, as in num 51. least the heate of the Bed tarnish and suffocate the plant, as our Melon–planters do well observe; and to avoyde the tilting up of the bells, which frequently disorders the bed, and is a very unconstant remedy.[16]

Upon the hot–Bed in Spring, these Seedes are proper to be Sowne. *Africanus flos, Amaranthus* of all sorts, *Amomum Plinij, Balsalmum masc: Canna Indica, Cistus* (or in potts), *Dactyles, Geranium triste, Hedisarum Clipeatum, Heliotrope,* (or in the plaine bed), the Humb[l]e *plant, Lentiscus, Marjoram Sweete,* to have it early; *Miserian, Myrtiles, Nasturtium Indicum,* or in potts; *Ilex, Olive, Piper Ind: Pomum Aureum, Pomum Æthiopicum, Pomum Spinosum, Pistachiam* nutts; The *Sensitive plant* and such like:[17] But for more security ~~and for~~ prevention of the worme, and all other accidents, our advice is that you sowe those which are the most rare of these sorts in potts by themselves, **[page**

---

15. **[Margin note]** Se also how made {better} Sharrok p. 10

16. **[Insertion on separate piece of paper]** But there is another bed to be made chiefly for flowers & annuals which require ~~neither so hasty raising~~ a more natural & lesse hasty ~~raising~~ germination, and that is what I shall cover in this booke calld by the name of Second hot bed, or straw–bed because the ingredients are onely straw & {good} mould, to which if you mingle some bran it will be much the better: Make it thus, in some warme corner of your Garden, take a quantity of barly straw, lay it in a trench hollowd as for a melon ridge, upon this a layer of dry bran, some mingle it: seift on this ~~two~~ 3 inches of fine mould, & it is made: over this fit a wicker frame to support the matts at night & you have a bed both for divers domestique & exotique seedes & plants far superior to ~~the fo~~ that which is ~~made~~ {form'd} of horse dung which precipitates some things, especialy flower seedes too ~~soone~~ hasty; it being of a middle temper, between the first hot bed, & the natural earth, in this therefore you may sow ~~Seedes~~ divers of your lesse ~~tender~~ delicate plants, as Nasturtium Indicum, palme Christi, Flos Africanum & divers of those hereafter mentioned, yea Orange, lemmon, Cedum etc & generaly most exotic flower Seedes

[Continued on verso] But for such plants as require a wonderfull intense heate, as some raritys do; ~~which is the 3d~~ Rx: fresh horse dung, one foote thick, on that a stratum of barly straw, & Bran, half foote: then 2 inches pigeon dung, on that your sifted mould 2 inches more: Hoope it over, & cover it all over with lith ~~24 hours~~ {a day} & night, & when of fit temper sow in or prick in your Seedes.

Note that in all H: bedds, a stake ~~fix~~ thrust down to the bottom so as to be moved & taken out upon occasion, serves to bring up the warme vapor under your glasse to the greate comfort of the plant if it require it: To temper your bed, make an hole, or holes at the sides to exhaust the vapour.

17. **[Margin note]** finaly even all Salads that you would have come very early.

69] plunging them to the brimms in the hot–bed, the Seedes having bin duely macerated in warme milke or some other menstrue, as before you are instructed.[18]

The following Seedes may be sowne in Spring or Autumne, either in the open
beds, or cases. *Alaternus, Anemonies*, also during Summer itselfe, *Antirrhiron, Auriculus,
Bay–bery, Chame–Iris, Crowne Imperiall, Cyanus*, of all sorts, *Cyclamen, Digitale, Eringium
planum, Fraxinella, Heliborus albus, Hepatica*, Larks–heele, Laurellberry, (preserv'd from
cold), *Muscipula, Nigella of Damascus*, & other; *Pyracanth*, Poppys, *Pulsatella, Scabious
Montan: Thlaspi Cand., Tulips*, and divers others, for which we referr you to Cap:
16: 21.[19]

There are other Seasons in which some do adventure to Sow; but we have mention'd the cheife and the safest; especially for those seedes which we know; As for
those which we know not, such as are many tymes sent us from ~~th~~ beyond the Seas,
and forraine Countries; it will be best to divide them into three equall portions, and
to sow one part in Autumne in the plaine Earth, ~~or in~~ {or in} potts, and ~~hot–Bed~~ the
two other ~~sow~~ in the Spring in plaine Earth, potts and hot–bed, by which meanes 'tis
likely that some of them will rise in one of the Seasons. Moreover, if they be annuall
plants, which are apt to suffer of frosts, they must of necessity be sowne in the Spring:
If more hardy, in the Autumne. If they be Seedes of perenniall plants sow them before
their mother plants shote, whither they be obnoxious to frosts, or not; But we referr
you to the Chapters before mention'd. {& to the directions in our Calendar c: 23}
The most part of the Seedes above specified, Spring up some later then others, with
their huskes {or Shells} upon their heads; and therefore, though you see them not ~~rise~~
{appeare} so suddainely as others, & as you expected; yet you are not to despond of
their resurrection: For some, which are inclosed with a harder coate, & integument,
will remaine long under ground before they peepe. (Thus we have sometymes expected the *Juniper, Cedar, Service, Ife* etc almost two yeares, and yet they come up at
last:) Some rise within a moneth; as the *Cypresse, Alaternus*, {some sorts of} *Phyleria*
etc, some which find smaler resistance in their receptacles, rise in {a} few dayes; And
therefore, our advice is, that such Seedes as are invested with hard and empty integu-
ments be well macerated, or sowne in the hot bed, as we have already showne, to

---

18. **[Insertion on separate sheet of paper]** Amongst the more strange things,
the propagation of the Yucca is yet a seacret since it is neither multiplied by cutting, grafting, or layering, but by breaking off (not cutting) the eyes or duggs which
swell out of the sides of an old roote not much unlike to Irish potatos but somewhat
sharppe snouted & having fleshy strings to them; let these be set in a pott of good
earth at spring, almost quite covered with mould, all but the very upmost ~~greene~~
greene spire & plunge the pot into the hott bed to the bud rises in the spring: Here
consult L: 2: c: 16: concerning the Japonius lilly, Tuberose & other rare plants which
belong to these directions:

19. **[Insertion on separate sheet of paper]** Some plants will not come up in
the spring & therefore are onely to be sow'd in Autume; of which kind are chervill,
Angelica, Rubarb, etc. Note that Bay berrys are sowd of ~~Seede~~ berrys in Aprill, &
2 years after transplant it: & is also propagated by slips in September taking of such
as sprind out from the bole of the Tree, & laing them as you do laurells in a shady
moist place in a year they will have strooke roote:

facilitate their production; But it oftentymes happens, that Seedes are totally lost, or come up very unseasonably; and this fortunes for the most part, when they are too deepely interred, which is a fault with many; especially, if the Seede be smale and soft, as *Cypresse*, the Seedes of {many} flowers etc:

Now to prevent this, it will be expedient to set up two or three smale pins of wood to such a height as you thinke fit; and then to seift the mould upon the Seedes, 'till it lye levell with the markes: But if, as your plants begin to **[page 70]** peepe, you perceive by their instabillitys, that they were not sowne deepe enough; you may re-peate this Seifting 'till it be sufficient, pressing it downe a little about them, to fix and erect them the better. In Winter, and during the colde Northerne Winds, it will be requisite to cover such as you do not cary into the Conserve or store, with ~~th~~ Matts, and the instruments described in Cap:1: num. 47.50.55. And, if the Snow have pre-vented you, to strike it off carefully, least a rude hand do breake any of your plants, which are then extreamely brittle. In the parching and intollerable heate of Summer, you may cover them with wett–matts, {or canvas tents} or set them (if moveable) in the shade; for some howers at least.

We should have told you that if the Season prove drie, as it {dos} many tymes is in Spring, it will be necesary to irrigate and water your Seminary; For the Earth must be kept moyst 'till the Seedes are sprowted. It is evident that Cypresse Seedes should be watered every third day at last, 'till they peepe; and we cannot but wonder why *Pliny* should affirme, that they prosper not, if on the same day they be sowne, the raine falls on them: it is doubtlesse either a mistake, or some superstitious observation. {but being of competent height, they love not much water, This tree ~~loves~~ abhors dung, but affects a light mould; nor should the mould be often stirred **[continued in margin]** pines on the contrary love the Earth to be loosend.}

There are divers Trees, but especially of the Ever–greenes which are propagated also by Laying and Submersion as *Alaternus, Bays*, {the leaves strip off & set in Spring) *Laurells, Myrtil, Oleander, Jessamines, Pomegranades, Woodbynd* and many others; Sloaping the branch, or laying the very cuttings in some moyst and shady place of your Nurs-erie {with the shinning leafe upmost}; But then you shall do well to couch them at some joynt ~~cutti~~ slitting them a little upwards, bruising or pricking it at least where the incurvation is, and with a hook fastning it to the ground, as we shall shew at large: But if they be cuttings onely, it shall be sufficient to strip off the leafe so far as you in-tend to immerge them, and to expose the shining and polished part of what remaines, ~~out~~ upmost; laying them somewhat sloping, and at least three parts in the earth:

About the latter end of August is a proper Season for this worke; especially for the more hardy plants, *Carnations*, & some other flowers: But *Myrtills, Jessamine*, and the more delicate, must be layd about mid–July; being carefully defended from the North {&} East Winds, scorching heates, and greate drouths; for which reason they should be perpetualy irrigated, and kept moyst. {Se Sharrok p. 50. 55. 57:}[xv] {Savine}[20]

---

20. **[Insertion on separate piece of paper, incorrectly noted to be inserted at page 71]** Savine planted of the slip in a rich shaded mould, in {Spring or} October ~~or later~~ & requires never to be removed out of its place: it being difficult to take: let the slip have some roote if you can:

[21]It is further to be noted: that as any of your Beds, Potts or Cases rise too thick of plants, so as to cumber one another by their having bin ill sowne, they may be ~~when drawne~~ drawne out (whilst very young) and thinned; being againe immediately pricked either into ~~beds~~ the same, or some new Bed, prepared for them;

[Page 71] And then it will be convenient to range them in lines, at fitting distances for the better weeding them; and that they may abide without other trouble, till they are capable of being transplanted, which this separation will extreamely facilitate; especially in such plants as much suffer upon removall, unlesse the earth and all can be transferred with them: Such as are the *Cedar, Pines*, etc with divers other, which seldome thrive after a naked irradiation, though planted with all the care {& circumspection} that is possible. {Here insert Mr: Sharroks catalogue p: 4: & compare it with Lawrenbergs which he calls perennial because they sow themselves: Se: Launb: L: i. c: 17: p: 103}

And here we should speake something concerning the various sorts of ~~planting~~ graffing; but because it is so amplie layd downe and conspicuous in our *Fr: Gardiner*, a very briefe repetition shall suffice. {Consult Sharrok: c: 5. p 61 etc. ad 72 etc. & first of the sorts of graffing}[22] Your stocks being now become of a competent groth

---

21. **[Margin note]** Periwinkle grows of slips & is excellent to keepe up bankes & mounds, it killing weeds & furthering the mould.

22. **[Insertion on separate piece of paper]** {cf where some of this may not be better placed}

1 ἐγκεντρισμὸς the proper Insition or ordinary graffing in cleft, properest for those trees whose pores are recti, & that draw up the nutriment through their fibers in a cylindrical tenor: as pears & Apples, Cherys etc, {Feb &} new moone of March. **[Insertion on a separate piece of paper]** There is also another sort of insition which is graffing by two sorts of graffing at once viz, in the cleft in the one side & Whip-stock {or pact-graffing} on the other: in this the Graffe is to be neere as big as the stock: this, though a little more difficult **[illustration, see Fig. 11]** yet soone covers the ~~stock~~ head & is stronger.

It is reported one may propagate graffs from almost any decayed tree, especially such as are apt to ~~shoote~~ {take} rootes from their bur knotts, which may be graffed in every branch of the thicknesse of one arme, & these graffs when growne out 2 or 3 yeares may be sawne off, & set in the Earth at the burr, & out grow ordinary stocks & graffs, & if the arme be long enough when you cutt of the first stock & graff: you may graff againe, as long as the branch affords knots & competent length, as a foote or so for the stock tree: **[illustration, see Fig. 12]** when the graff is taken & the head well covered separat the stock att a, leaving a little of the wood below which you may peele almost to the burr or prick to make it roote the better, & so you may bill the burr: Such an arme you see will afford 3, or 4 stocks to graff on: **[end insertion of insertion to the insertion]**

2 ἐφυλισμὸς or infoliation when you graff twixt the stocke & rind proper for large & antiquad trees, whose stemms, or other parts you would preserve:

3 ἐνοφθαλμισμὸς which is implastration of the bud, proper for the tendrest & delicate fruites: & there Plin: calls it omnium insitionum fertilissima: {there is also another kind of inoculation which Stephens calls ~~Fistulation~~ infistulation* Moreover

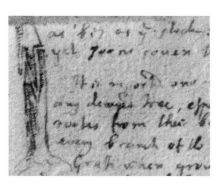

Figure 11. Illustration of "graffing in cleft" inserted at page 71.

as of three or fowre years standing; {or able to put forth a shoote of a yard long in one yeare}²³ you may graff in the cleft upon them, either for Tall or Dwarf Trees: Instruments for this Worke are the Saw, Knife & Wedg and the plaster. {here insert the

---

those who observe φυτο magnetisme advise (nor is it to be rejected) that you place the austral fibers of your Cyon to the same point of the stocke, & so of the rest of the fibers: [Perhaps Phillip Stephens, ca. 1620–1679, *Catalogus horti botanici oxoniensis alphabetice digestus, duas*, Oxford, 1658.]

That you joyne those of natural similitude; since tis observed that ~~few~~ no tree will ~~unite with the~~ contract with the Taxus, but the fig & mulbery & platanus; The Mulbery with the Chessnut & the Beech; Apple with wild pear, pear with quince, Medlar with crab, Elme with the white poplar, {Peech} pear with the Almond etc: The Ever–green Oak with the ordinary Oak: The Azerole on the white thorne.

* infistulation which is by ~~leav~~ taking off the barke & leaving the bud, & clapping the barke of another tree upon it, ~~for as the 2d bud stick upon the~~ with the bud on, so as this new bud invest the other or stic upon it:

[Insertion continued on separate piece of paper] Some for the more certaine & suddaine taking of the bud, prescribe ligatures beneath it, yet so as by soft bolsters to favour that part of the stock your budds are on: that so the Sap, both ascending & descending (as they call it) may chiefly furnish by that more easy intercourse & current: others speake of barking the stock above the bud for the same effect: other Rules concerning inoculating

A stocke inoculated {12 or} 14 days (Season good) before Midsomer if the head be then immediately cutt off will shoote a faire shoote that yeare: though the common practise leave it till the following Springs: but I suppose a topping and disbranching of the head, leaving sufficient to lead up the sap better than total decapitation till your bud be lusty & safe.

23. **[Insertion on separate sheet of paper]** Some plant every stock with one leading branch to draw up the sap, & after a years groth, then graff on it, leaving one or two leaders, but none so high as to over top your Cions, & cutt not the leaders away till your Cions be well taken.

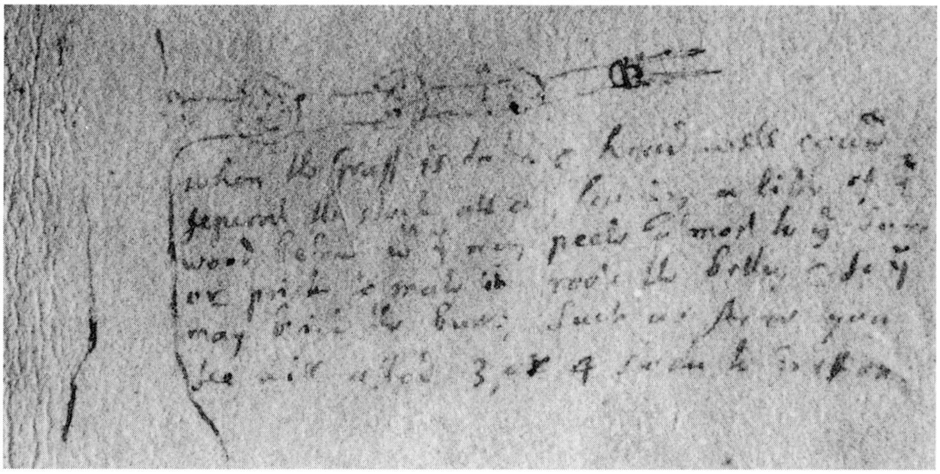

Figure 12. Grafting in a decayed tree, illustrated in an insertion at page 71.

severall ways in your MSS.} {For dwarfs} Cutt your stocke something approaching the earth that the Graff may, as it were, even roote itselfe with it: {& yet it would be considered whither **[continued in margin]** this be in all cases advisable for the improvement of the fruit the sap having lesse way to percolat through the stock: But for Dwarfs it is very expedient: And there is also a graffing in the very roote itselfe. for graffing too high}[24]

Elect your Graffs {or Cions} from those top branches, which grow on the East side of a bearing and generous tree, cutting them in the waine of the Moone, and a serene aire.[25] The Season for this worke begins about the end of January, 'till the expiration of February; {& even in March} ~~This manner of Graffing~~ 'tis a manner more ~~expedient~~ {appropriate} for standard Fruite Trees. ~~for~~ the furniture of an Ortchard, ~~and dos therefore little concerne our present worke.~~ {of which see: c: 19: L: 2:[26]} Inoculation is a more refined way of Graffing, and 'tis effected by dextrously taking off, and inserting the bud of one Tree, betweene the wood and the barke of another, ~~placed at one~~ collaterally placed on the stocke; of all other the most expedient for *Espaliers*

---

24. **[Insertion on separate piece of paper]** For graffing too high robs the tree of much nutriment which is wasted on the stock; therefore dwarfs are commended, especialy where no under crop is expected, & where the exposure is in the weather; besides the frosts have not the same power over low graffings.

Graffing on too old ~~tree~~ & large stocke indanger the heart for tainting, before the barke can sufficiently close the wound.

25. **[Insertion on separate sheet of paper]** 3 or 4 good budds next the foote {or knob} of your Cions is enough, & so you may make divers of one twig if you be not stored

26. **[Insertion on separate piece of paper]** If you graff old trees, cutt not the head too close, 'twill be difficult to cleave, but in france they take out a whole piece & fit the Graffe to it, & so they cleave little of it: 'tis advised you head it not too neere the stemm, because so difficult to cover, & indanger ruine: but leave in some parts {small} branches on the top of the tree to draw up the sap, but when your graffs be taken & have made a good shoote, in march {after} cutt the branches you spared off close to the trunk: but 'tis yet better in old trees to cutt the heads a little high, & let them put out new branches, on which graff the 2d yeare; & such high graffs you must defend from winds & birds which will violate them: There is also graffing twix the barke for such old trees:

For the Soile, pears would have a deepe rich mould; for they grow tarnished & hard & swell within they come to gravell & they penetrate: Apples contrary are content with shallow mould: Quince in sweete fresh {strewn} earth, & moist; but in dryer earth the fruit is better, though smaller: Plums love drye ground stony, so dos the Almond: cherys in sandy & sweete for they go not deepe: in short, ~~moyst~~ to render fruite delicate, the moist {as plumms peaches} would be planted in dry, the harsher & dryer in moyster as peares Apples etc. of these there are yet farther divisions for even these also differ in these qualities & are to be buried accordingly: & hence proceeds the reason **[continued on verso]** that there is {frequently} such differences in fruite of the same kind, & even in one & the same Garden as is easily seene in the Burgamott. B:

and Wall–fruite; and of greate importance for the propagation of *Oranges, Lemmons, Roses* and other curiosities. Take therefore the Bud (with[27] leafe and all to hold it by), from a full and lusty shoote of the same yeare; but gather it neare to the Syen of the præcedent yeare. Then your stock stripped of all its smale twigs, the height of halfe a foote, {on the young wood} about the Season that they use to cutt trees, choose the fairest part of the barke,[28] fashion & cutt the *Escutchion* ~~of~~ about an Inch long ~~like~~ a quarter broade;[29] And see that in taking it off the Sproute of the bud hold intire within. {that it look purplish not white or woadly[30][.] Then incise the stock like a ~~Roman~~ Capital T, the length of your Shield and gently loosen the backe with the poynted handle of your knife {which let be of bone or box for Yron taints the sap} without Scraping the wood or Sappy filme remaining;[31] then place your Escutchion, thrusting it downe 'till the head of the shield joyne with the incision & ~~be~~ lie even and flat upon the wood.[32] This perform'd, bynd it athwart with raw hemp {or bast} above and below the bud, leaving the Eye a decent compasse about it free, and unconstrained: ~~the~~ & within in a moneth after {bind some leafe over it to keep it from scorching} you may loosen the binding, by cutting the ligature {behind} and letting it fall of itselfe.(2)[33] When the bud has a little shot, you may prune it at the top, to make it branch, and then you may also cutt the wood of the stock remaining about the shield, covering the wound **[page 72]** [34]with a plaister or else attend 'till almost

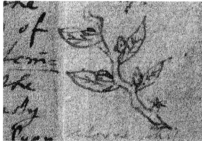

Figure 13. Margin illustration of example of inoculation, inserting the end of one tree between the wood and bark of another, on page 71.

---

27. **[Margin note] [illustration, see Fig. 13]**

28. **[Margin note]** some fix the new bud in the place of ~~the old~~ an old bud, but tis not good for it hinders closure:

29. **[Insertion on separate piece of paper]** for which a paire of compasses flat & sharp at ends with an edge: ~~take the just bredth of~~ cut away the barke at just bredth & compasse, with the same also take off the bud exactly fitt for the place in your stock etc:

30. **[Insertion on separate piece of paper]** if you see a hole through, tis good for nothing:

31. **[Insertion on separate piece of paper]** Some make this overthwart beneth, ~~& the b~~ or invert the [inverted T] as better inclosing the bud

32. **[Margin note]** Note some clip the edges of the barke on which the bud grows with a pair of sizars into a square forme or oblong; & tis better than with a knife because in laying it downe to cut it you loose the belly of the inside & then twill never take.

33. **[Insertion on separate piece of paper, originally bound upside down into the volume]** Lauremberger describes an instrument which dos at once & in a trice dispatch this curious worke & that is of steele made with 4 edges very sharp in forme of a Rhomb or thus **[illustration, see Fig. 14]** or somewhat biger than the diamond spot in a card (or of any other figure) presse this upon a budd branch, then {cleave} cutt out the bud, then presse your Instrument on your stock, & take of the barke, then apply your budd in its ~~barke~~ {rhomboid barke} & all & twill so exactly fitt, that being tyed with raw hemp {& plaster it} etc: it {will} speedily take:

34. **[Margin note]** if you put on two budds, let them be at each side, not one over another; it will deforme the tree: & if both take, preserve but one: be sure to inoculate always in dry weather, else you endanger all.

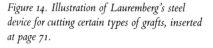

Figure 14. Illustration of Lauremberg's steel device for cutting certain types of grafts, inserted at page 71.

the expiration of winter, when the approaching sap will of it selfe cure it, without more trouble or danger.

The proper Season for this worke of Implastration is so soone as upon incision & triall you find the barke dos easily quitt the wood, an indication that 'tis prowde and full of juice as it frequently happens about {July or} the beginning of August.[35]

---

35. **[Insertion on separate piece of paper]** To these we may add these rules: {1 that the wind be not {North or} easterly for the East wind will cause the contrary side to peele} 2 that such sorts as soonest budd be soonest graffed, as cherrys, plums: about Jan:. 3 Let neither your graffs be bisulic forked, nor too proud & turgid: 3 [*sic*] choose such as are fairest & fullest of budds {4 or 6} of the last yeares shoote, {(it too is off not good)} not too long cutting of the top at the bud. 4 Graff no stock till it have ben removed, that the rootes spread the better. 5 Graff kind on kind {ὁμόιων [*sic*] ἐις ὁμόια} as Apples on Crabe, peare & the wild peare (i) such as are raised of kirnells: cherrys on black cherry stock, Plums {& Abricots & Peach} on the white peare plaistered[:] The red Roman Nectar on an Abricot that has formerly ben inoculated on the plumm: The Almond stock is subject to gumm, & dos not take well replaced: For Dwarfs se: c: 19: L: 2 {but it produces faire fruite, but not so durable: 'tis best to set the Almond when you will inoculate.}

6 Choose Cyons for Graffs from the ~~best~~ most {lustily} bearing sunny branches & full of budds, & of trees that have born fruite. {Let the foote be of old wood, if to graff on a very hard & old stock}

7 Apply budds quickly for 'tis dangerous to let them take ayre.

8 Graff straight cions deeper into the stock; but if either stock or cions be crooked shallower: & so if you graffe too early; because deeper graffing maintaines moysture ~~till~~ in your cions till the sap rise briskly: {let part to part answer, as wood to wood, & rind to rind:}

9 Stocks may be cutt early fitt to graffe, & then when the sharpe Weather is past graffed so you leave one branch neere the head to bring up the sap, but some wax it over, & a moneth after cutt it againe an inch lower.

10 Cions cutt of early as in Novr: or Decr: being layd in earth may be graffed with successe till even Aprill, have formed so even {or leavd or budded} the stock be; for being dry they appetite the sap the more greedily: {never graff the same day you cutt your scion:}

11 Cutt your stock sloping {to the North that it dry not too soone & to resist the wind better} like a deer foote, to awaite the raine, & to cover better:

12 For Seasons at beginning of the yeare in the wood of the shoote, when the sap is up, graff twixt barke & wood; when tis proud, inoculate.

[Continued on verso] And here I may satisfie some of the use of Dwarfes, grafted first on the Quince & brought into reputation ~~for the~~ for the many perfections of security from blasts, Winds, Maturity etc: by the Curat of Henonuille: who for {these &} Espale stocks commends for Apples the parelese stocks, which spend little in wood, & is very apt to make fruitfull trees; & they are raised as we saye of ~~cuttings~~ layers & cuttings like the codling.

[Insertion on another piece of paper] Graffs may be graffed on stocks ~~in~~ {brought out of ground into} a warme roome, & then the stocks set & have pros-

{This is the noblest & most princely way for propagation, & fitt for kingly hands: of them Virgil: 2: Geor: [73–82] **[continued in margin]** Nam qua se medio trudunt de cortice gemmæ 4 verses & then nec longum tempus etc. verses et non sua poma.} Propagation is made also by Approch[36] and it is indeede of admirable ~~use~~ {expedition} in our Garden of Pleasure, ~~the~~ and for ~~the~~ increasing of the more delicate and choice plants; especially the various sorts of {Ever–}greenes & Shrubbs:[37] To effect this, place your stock neere to a Tree that's already well growne, and Sawing off the head of your stock at a competent height & cleansing it a little neere the middle bend either a branch or the intire head of the shrub into it somewhat slope–wise, paring the branch or wood neere the pith underneath, where it is most contiguous to the stock, and so adjust them that the wood and the rinds may mutually encounter. Thus fitted, bind them together with Bast or raw hemp; and with a plaster or hood of loame secure the wounds for a moneth ~~or~~ two {or three}, 'till perceiving it begin to swell, it give you notice that 'tis tyme to cutt {off} the tree or branch a little below the graffing place, covering the wound as ~~bef~~ before, either with loame mixed {well} with horse, ~~&~~ {hogg or} cow dung, or a Plaster ~~of~~ compos'd of Wax and Turpentine {& a little butter} incorporated together. {Upon which (when you have headed your Graffs) strew some Earth dryed **[continued in margin]** Some also bind the stocks with bast before the head: & cutt it about August: but this is needlesse.}

The best Season for this worke is about the beginning of September, and to free them, the end of October: {Some continue them a full yeare} nor is there a more ~~excellent~~ {profitable} expedient for the sudaine propagation of more fruits, Oranges, Lemons, Jessamines, Myrtils etc whose intire heads one would sometimes preserve, as in this figure it appeares

[illustration, see Fig. 15] [38]

[39]The last manner of Propagation, usefull ~~for~~ {in} our Nursery, is by submer-

---

pered: Cyons too tender & soft are squeezed in the stock, therefore ~~cutt your Cyon~~ fitt your Cyons wedg out of the old wood or below the gnob: In a tender or over young stock graff lower them in a lustier:

You may upon occasion Graff in Aprill & May, ~~by delibra~~ twixt barke & wood in an old tree Cutt the trees head off, ~~upon the~~ separate the barke by a wedg, set in your graff: but cutt it back with but one shoulder, halfway almost the pith, & but just raze or guide ~~the barke side~~ {the barke off} to opposite side: then set wood to wood, & barke to barke: tie your stock with a band to fix the cyon the better, & then use your plaster to keepe out weather: your Cyons for this reason must be gathered a moneth or 2 before & layd in Earth till you need them: This worke is calld *delibrationer*.

36. **[Margin note]** or *Ablactation*

37. **[Margin note]** as also the graffing of any sort of tree upon which stock you please, presented by Columella, but never perfected in his booke:

38. **[Note for illustration]** This Square Case should be bored at Topp, not bottom

39. **[Insertion on separate piece of paper]**

For the Government of your Graffs what you graff in cleft for standards, ~~take~~ cleene it of buds, all but one as soone as they sproute, that but one then remaine, but after let them alone ~~because it will spread the sap too fast~~ till the 3d yeare after, &

Figure 15. Instructions for grafting rare fruit trees, illustrated on page 72.

sion or Layers.[40] The parents of an incredible increase both in Plants and Flowers, especially the perenniall greenes & Carnations which much abound in moysture. It is another kind of Ablactation, effected by the binding of a branch or slip to the ground, and either a little Slitting, or incising {it} under a Joynt, {upwards} fasten it to the earth, {or trench} with a hoocke, and **[page 73]** cover it with {rank} mould, after this, being often refreshed, it will in a short tyme strike faire rootes, and then you may sever it from the Mother & immediately transplant it.[41]

But in case the Branch be too high for this humble flexure, it may be passed thrugh a Basket or Smale Barell, or traverse an earthern Vessel made of that shape, and about the bignesse of a Carnation–pot; but before it be set in the kilne to be baked, let a hole of a reasonable size be made at the side thereoff, and then cutt the

---

then stay till Aprill, & then 3 or 4 inch from the stem 3 or 4 foote high give them onely a {bruse or} wind to stop the sap & divert it to the stem, & the next year in the same month, cutt them close, & so do from yeare to yeare take away all irefull branches, till the head be formed at what height you please, viz 6 foote is enough; & this may be don in March: Some stocks do more in 2 yeares than others in 4.

For such as be troubled, prune not the {wild} stock till after winter, when the Escutchion is ready to sprout, & meddle not with the shoote unlesse it produce no branches: then stop it at 1/2 a foote by pinching it {often} ~~with your nailes~~ oft & to make it furnish a foote:

Replant not dwarf pears till the {3 or} 4 yeare when well cured; but peaches after one yeare.

40. **[Margin note]** of which thus Vergil: Geo. 2. [26–27] Sylvarumque alte pressos propaginis arcus exspectant et viva sua plantaria terra. (Arcus then is before & from it pasture in the Earth)

41. **[Margin note]** if it be a lusty branch, slit it the farther up {halfe through} & pierce the barke above it with a bodkin: shootes of the same yeare take soonest, slit it at a knot or joynt if possible: if the plant be not ever greene abate the top: Some commend a very straite ligature of waxed paste thrid or wyre a little above the slitt to stop the sap & make it strike roote the sooner

Figure 16. Method for grafting fruit trees, illustrated on page 73.

the [*sic*] whole vessell in two parts; these you will find extreamely commode for the comprehending of such branches as grow out of ordinary reach, the twig passing this overture, and the segments fastned firmly together by some hoopes or Wyres, & the vessel in the meane time supported, or hanging at a competent height, for which it should be contrived with eares, or Socketts, or both as the figure {here} describes it

[42][illustration, see Fig. 16] [43]

You must suppose that first there be some part of the barke of the branch stripped off, an inch or two in breadth, according to the groth of the wood, or it may be

---

42. **[Margin note]** Circumpositions are for upper branches which cannot be layred: Thus, early in Spring ere budds come out bind good Earth in a linnen about a bough: or make a wooden box bored with holes & with a notch for the branch or a small bushell so as the earth hold about the branch: pricking & gauling that part which is invested, let this so abide till the next spring & then cast it off; it will have rooted; & may be transplanted with case or bushell & all, & so you may have fruite the same year:

[continued on separate piece of paper] 'tis as old as Pliny, a prompt who calls it *audax ingenium*, & is an excellent & prompt expedient, which I admire is no more made use of

43. **[Margin note]** For ever–greenes take the shootes of the past Spring & not the old wood; & though few take roote well till next Spring, yet this season prepares & soakes it, as especialy the Arbutus, phillipella augustofol: yellow Jasmin etc: & some againe will never make roote thus as the Zizypha Candida or beade tree Cytisus lunatus, paliurus Azedracti, but are raised from seedes. The Cytisus of slips in June, taking shoote of the Spring add handfull dung, in moyst & shady places, Lay all layers in rich moist shady earth, as in mould well dunged that has bin rotting 3 or 4 yeares: & is exceeding fine. When you remove & cutt off your layers set them at first in {some} shady place a while more rather kept moyst not over wett for feare of rotting the tender fibers, then after 15 days as long in the open air, & last of all in the Sunn but mid Aug for things to be planted in Spring (as green etc) is best. Se: Cap: 16:

~~rung~~ galled of with a wyre which is a very neate way of excortication in this worke, or you may prick it full of holes the tree being tender; and passe it at some joynt if possible, last of all fill the vessell with good moyst earth, securing ~~the vessell~~ {it} as you are taught, that the wind disturbe it not, till having struck sufficient rootes it be taken downe, and when severed from the Mother ~~be~~ transplanted with mould and all, by drawing of the hoopes & gently separating the segments of the vessell. The proper season for this worke is from May till the commencement of August, and at the entring of November you may saw it from the Mother: Or there may {be made} with as good Successe, ~~be~~ very large Layer–pots ~~made~~, such as they use for Carnations, ~~with~~ fitted with an yron plate indented to run within a sockett thus

[illustration, see Fig. 17]

[Page 74]

[44]In this sort are Gilly–flowers propagated in aboundance being layed in potts of a lesser size and so Pomegranads Jessamines, Myrtills, & divers other choyce shrubs may be presently increased. {Propagation is also made by viuiradices Stolons or Suckers: of which the poet: 2: Geo: [17] pullulat ab radice aliis densissima Sylva}[45] ~~Finaly~~, many plants are augmented by slips onely, with a little part of the old wood, as the Box, Baie, Rosemarie, Lavender, Thime,and other tender plants, giving the poynt or joynt of the slip a little twist to make it sensible of the earth, ~~for~~ & for which a moyst and warme Spring is the onely sure season. {here insert Mr: Sharroks p: 50. here insert Mr: Sharrocks {Appendices & Asetts etc: from pag: 43 ad p: 49. Slips 51. 52. Sharrok} Also by cuttings alone,[46] thus Baies, Laurells, yea Myrtills & some other plants, placed in the moyst and shady earth, as we have before described it in particular treating of perenniall–greenes. {~~here insert Mr: Sharrocks p. 51 ad p. 55~~ cutt at first rise of sap; cutt at a joynt deepe layd & sloping & often refreshed][47]

Finally, the Truncheons of some Trees, such as Alder, Withy, Mulbery, {Olives, Quince}[48] etc, being plunged {into the ground} and interred {a foote deepe upright},

Figure 17. Method for propagating plants using pots filled with earth, illustrated on page 73.

---

44. **[Margin note]** Do all in Spring:

45. **[Insertion on separate piece of paper]** & he mentions the Cherrys, Elmes, Laurells, etc: & these may be puld from their mother {with a peduncle or small part of roote adhering} in if not Spring {or} Autume, full moone, & immediately planted; the way to multiply these we shall speake of ~~in divers~~ on divers occasions: & give the catalogue:

46. **[Margin note]** Hic plantas tenero abscindens de corpore matrum deposuit sulcis – L: 2: Geor: [23–24]

47. **[Insertion on separate piece of paper]**
Some to make cuttings, take the seon bruise the ~~end~~ greate end with a wodden mallet upon a block: some prescribe a plaster for the cut part to hinder the sap from wandering: Rx: Ceræ 3 [ounce] terebines: 2 3 [ounces]: Refine comm: fiat Emplat but it is more the raines: at the expiration of winter cut of the {small} topps of your layer

[insertion on separate piece of paper] I have bin a assured that a{n} ~~Mulbery~~ {Abricot} will grow of cutting, if set about Feb: let it be tryd of others.

48. **[Insertion on separate piece of paper]**
Another & never failing way to be furnished with Q: stocks is to cutt downe some old Tree {of the particular kind} in March within 2 fingers of the ground, &

a little onely of the poynt or end appearing {a span} above {ground}, will increase & put forth Suckers {if watered} to admiration. {well refreshed with rich water, {& weeded}} {Bast Mulberys may also be raised by budding or graffing: & even the succkers would be chosen from bearing trees [49]

And thus have we in briefe described most of the usuall, and usefull wayes, of Propagating Trees, Plants & Flowers, for the peopling of our Seminary; and the furniture of our Elysium, in their severall ~~expediences~~ {Instances}: by which meanes Trees

---

there will rise an aboundance of suckers which when a foote or 2 high cover them 6 or 8 inches up with earth & moisten it frequently & they will roote plentifully & be soone fitt for your ~~nurs~~ Nursery & in 2 years more fitt to graff on: They are to be preserved for peares for all the perfections of that fruite

49. **[Margin note]** Let the branch of a mulbery be as big as one arme a yard long: in two years it will yield you setts fit to transplant letting the stump remaine to produce more:

[Continued on separate piece of paper] There growes a kind of burr–knot at the foote of every branch of a Mulbery tree, where it grows out of the tree: cutt this close off with the knot, set it in March or very beginning of Apr: twill grow: It is reported Mulbery stocke receive any Graffs: quince **[end insertion of insertion]**

Medlars are to be produced from suckers, or may be grafted on the thorne, or budded for large fruite. Here set Mr: Sharroks universal figure p: 70 with the explanation:

[Continued on separate piece of paper] Lastly there is {yet} another way {of propagating} per terebrationem, though rarely practised, & that is by boring holes with an auger in a good big trunction of Willow whilst green & sappy, bore them at a foote distance, in these holes, sett fast in twigs or branches of Apple trees, peares, etc: a little of the barke peeld at the end: then bury the trunchion in the ground, & at Spring take it out, & saw off the trunk twixt any branch, without hurting the twiggs, & then bury every twig with its part of the trunction againe, & you will have fruite the next yeare: By the way of terebation you may perserve [preserve] pretty things as you will see in L: 3: c. I.

[illustration, see Fig. 18] The picture shews where they are to be cutt off, or you may do it at first, but then your trunction will not keepe its moysture so intyre:

Figure 18. Method of propagating fruit trees by terebration, illustrated on a piece of paper inserted at page 74.

~~are~~ & Flowers are not onely wonderfully increased, but meliorated, and extreamely refined. For Graffing dos open the pores of the wild & sative stock, passing the Sap & juice through finer percolations, & rendering it very delicate & more fruitefull: In summ, it is that to Trees and Plants, which a noble and generous Education is to men themselves. {An Emphyteutic plaster to head graffs in the cleft, which to preserve them from injury Rx: common rosin: 1 ℥ [ounce], wax 2 ℥ [ounces]: Birdlime 2 ℥ [drams] Butter 5 ℥ [ounces] ad form Emplat: Or take a sufficient quantity of Bees wax, with a little pitch & oyle, mealt & cast them into cold water, & temper them witth your hands:}

CHAP. V.

Of knotts, {Fretts} Parterrs, Compartiments, Bordures, and Embossements.

Our Seminary is now furnished, it thrives {apace} & there is store of Materiall,

ergo age nunc cultus   Lets fall to th' worke.

The flattest Embelishments of Gardens are *knotts* {Fretts} and *Parterrs*, but they ~~may~~ {should} at no hand be disposd, save where they may be view'd from the noblest roomes ~~at~~ {of} Entertainement, {Galleries} & lodgings of the Mansion; because they require to be seene horizontally, & where, if the worke be rich and well ~~ordered~~ {understood}, it will appeare like a glorious embrodery; especially, if to the excellency of the invention, there be industry and skill in the clipping and entertaining.

~~Therefore~~ Let therefore the file never exceede two inches **[page 75]** in diameter, cutting it curved above & ~~not~~ {by no meanes} flatt, as much as possibly resembling the embrodery of twist, shaping it broder & narrower as the foliage, stature flower & moresco requires. It has bin a greate dispute amongst Gardiners what were the best materiall to be employd in this worke. Mr. Parkinson[xvi] has enumerated many, & ~~resolves~~ {pitched} at last upon Box: And truely, since in our Climate, the smale leavd Myrtill (which in Italy and the hott Countrys they use in this worke with admirable Successe) will not endure the cold and exposure, he has certainely resolved upon the very best: There is a low, narrow leavd fine Sort, calld *Dutch-Box*, which is beautifull, hardy & slow of groth; and the objection (which indeede is in a Garden very considerable) of the ill sent which now & then it casts i{s}f very much corrected, if not wholy taken away, ~~if~~ {by} the Parterrs, {being} ~~are~~ kept according to the directions above, and not sufferd to grow ranke, as we can testifie upon experience. But it is the subjection of this curious maintaining it, & assiduity, which has almost banished it ~~with~~ out of our Gardens {in England} as an ornament altogether out of fashion, because indeede so ill understood as {being} commonly ~~let~~ {suffered to} grow into course & rude hedges of a foot square, & that in stiff and meane workes, to the great prejudice of one of the most glorious embelishments of our Elysium: For what can be more ravishing then to behold a goodly *area* richly adornd with this Phrygian ~~ornament~~ {worke} continually growing, & eternally greene, naturall & artificiall, & which may be either wrought together, or gracefully intermixed, with beds & quarters of flowers, *vireta, shrubs,* ~~& other~~ *relievos* & other ornaments, according to the fantsy, & judgment of the ~~Gardiner~~ Artist! For there is no worke about the Garden, which requires a more exquisite hand, both in the Planter Inventer & Governer then this; and therefore it greately ~~behoves~~ {concernes} our *Phyturgus* to be skillfull & dextrous in drawing & designing, especially, of *Grotesco, Foliage* and *Compartiments* whereoff it chiefly consists, & by which, he may be able to compose *Impresses, Mottos, Dialls, Escutchions, Cyphers* and innumerable other devices with wonderfull felicity & effect. {in Square, round or mixt workes:}

But first the worke is to be design'd upon paper, and pasted on a thin board, cancelled with lines and figured ~~especially~~ {perfectly} correspondent to the {scale of the} *area*. Let the plot then be exactly well dug, levell'd, and carefully trodden, ~~and lastly~~ refined with a Rake, that ~~there be~~ no impressions appeare, so as the workeman may go ~~litely~~ lightly upon it without indenting the ground: This prepar'd, cast the Area by the helpe of your *paralells* into as many squares as your designe containes, which being figured, you may with your drawing poynt, line & compasses trace out upon the plott: This don, about March, you may fall to planting, be it with box, or {any} other verdure **[page 76]** But our Workeman would be adv{vert}ised, that he make not the devise too busie; for that dos frequently shew very ~~well~~ beautifully upon the *paper*, which will make no {such} effect on the *Parterre*. And therefore we esteeme those the best for this purpose which can be so contrived, that *parts & foliages*, ~~may be~~ or *Grotesques* may be added on, detracted as best agrees with ~~your~~ fantsy, without defacing {of} the whole. The same would be observed in *Trayle-worke*, which is another kind of intermixture cutt out upon the Turfe or Carpet & by some much approv'd of. In planting the box, there are, who strip away the leaves, & do not wind the roote or slip; but, in our judgement some would be spared, ~~and which there~~ There is yet one exception {more} against *box*, that the rootes, when they come to spread, suck away from the flowers, and emaciate the ground: But Mr. *Parkinsson* has instructed us how to prevent this, by cutting them with a certain sharpe spade without dissordering the earth[1] at all; We have seene the ordinary *Frith*, and *dubble Daisie* do exceedingly well in this kind of ornament. When your parterr is thus planted, and the heads of the box clipped into exact ~~shape~~ {forme}, if the *Interstices* or *terrace* be layed over with some ~~gloriously~~ {splendidly} colourd Sand, it will make {a} very glorious {effect}: Or there may some of these spaces be a little embossed with mould, planted with low growing Flowers of various Colours which will resemble a rich & ~~well~~ noble Tapistry.

The *Area* destin'd for the *Parterr* should ever extend to the whole front of the Palace or mansion respecting the Gardens, of what figure or demension soever it be. *Compartiments* are {narrow &} thinner *knotts* running along the sides of Allies, in which *flowers, Cypresse, shrubbs*, etc may be planted at pleasure. *Bordures* are the most simple of ornaments, & are commonly for edges, and under the outmost wales. These we name *Embossements*, which like to *Bordures*, are made with a gracefull swelling and *Relievo*; either by themselves, or, as we sayd, intermixed in the *Parterrs* in which they succeede perfectly well: But they should by no meanes be layed too high, halfe a foote is sufficient in the very ridge, unlesse the *Bordure*, or Circle be for Cammomile, or Carpets of turfe; but for Flowers a lesser declivity, or the Smalest Section of an *Arch*, seing the designe is onely to bring such flowers in sight at once, as in *plano*, could not appeare to one that were walking at any reasonable distance.

These *Embossements, Bordures*, and *Beds* may either be framed about with Oaken-{zinct} planke, indented, or plaine, the part above painted[2] & {the inside &} that be-

---

1. **[Margin note]** veronica:
2. **[Margin note]** in oyle ~~with~~ in stone Colour viz white lead in linseed oyle in but first primd with red lead & vernich
[Insertion on separate piece of paper] every 6 or 8 foote should have a stump of 2 foote long 4 inch square well pitch'd these droen into the ground; the rails to reach to them should be at least 5 inches broad: & so raised to these stumps or the posts as

neath pitched: But this is to be understoode of the principall *Flower-Garden*, in which it were much more usefull, then {in} the *Parterre*, because it would dissagree with the rest; and if the worke be of curved lines (as it is impossible it should be otherwise to be {sweete &} naturall) the materialls will not {easily} comply {with the figures;} but with extreame cost, & continuall dissorder: Therefore, let such **[page 77]** *Embossements* as enter into the *Parterr* be bordurd with the same verdure of the knotts. {And} Here we cannot but commend for this worke, the *Partrig-Ey'd* or *Spanish Pinke*, because it is ~~exceedingly beautifull~~ hardy, and being close clipped & well refreshed,[3] during the excessive heate, supplies the want of Box, and may possibly be preferred before it; especially, for *Bordures* and to keepe up the Beds in the Coronary Garden, where being permitted to grow at somewhat more liberty, when it comes to blow the wonderfull beauty of the flower will infinitely exceede all other frenges, & be more Symbolicall to the rest of the flo{ury} ornaments. {also lavender cotton dos well & {Thym, Hyssop} any plant which growes thick & is patient of clipping but of Beds for ~~the Olitory plants se~~ Flo: & Olitory plants Se Capp: 16: 19:}

Under this title might be also properly introduced sundry other ornaments of Gardens, especially such as have any Rising, and it would be enquired into, what approch of Trees may be allowed for the ornament of these workes, for it is our opinion that *Viridaria*, *Vireta*, ~~*Vipreta*~~ *Walkes, Mounts, Groves, Fountaines* etc be the more principall, & all *Parterrs* and *Flowry Areas* but the trimmings and accessories of a noble Garden: The same ~~is to~~ {may} be concluded of *Pyramids, Cabinetts, Pavillions, Skreenes, Freezes, Niches, Pillars,* {*Pedistalls*}, *Corniches* and other parts and compositions of *Architecture*, chargeable and difficult to maintaine but by such as are skillfull in tha{e} Arte, ~~thr~~ Fabricques of the Carpenter, {Sculptors &} Mason: {& of the industrius Gardner of poole worke the uprights **[continued in margin]** & collateralls, of Ash or Chessnut poles bound with wyre; & the more flexible ribbs to expresse beasts, birds etc in Topiary worke of Haizell peeld & smokd in the Winter, & then invested with what plants you think fit, especially Ever-greenes, Juniper, Alaternus, box etc: or of the other[?] privet, white thorne etc: Se cap: 7:} Of this sort are likewise *Statues, Repositories,* ~~*Precipices*~~, *Balustrades, Pergolas, Palisade-worke,* and a greate number of other ornaments, which we have assigned to particular Chapters, of wonderfull grace and mag[n]ificency for the retaining, diverting, and taking of the eye of the Spectator, which should not be glutted at once with the same object, but pleasingly confounded, and entertained with the most gracefull varieties both naturall and artificiall. Place here the ~~fig~~ {draughts} of the Parterrs.

---

to be an inch above them, & set by a levell: But if you can procure these with the posts to be made of {heart} yew sawd to a thicknesse & plan'd nothing were more lasting: let the ~~railes~~ {posts} be well ramm'd in; & the boards appear 4 inches above the Walkes, & one Inch higher than the inmost bordure if for Flo:

Some have don thus with free stone to immense cost, but both the tyle & brick breake with the frost: & also accident; but Klinker or flush brick (well burnt) layd in tarris is above all stone work in the world for this Worke

3. **[Margin note]** we do not approve of bone {goose or sheep} pibbles etc: the frosts break them & weeds will disperse them. Tyles brittle brick (if klinker & layd in Tarras) best of all, better than even marble

CHAP. VI.

Of Walkes, {~~Palisads~~} Terraces, Carpets, and Allees, Bowling greenes, ~~B~~eares, Maills, Their materialls and proportions.

{And elatienes Walkes in Gardens we find as antient use: Cicero speakes of them in {1} Oratore & so dos the younger Pliny ~~& that they usd them as we to meditat & study Tum Scavolans~~[?]}

The necessitie and use of Walkes and Allies are parts so essentiall in all Gardens that there will be no neede of shewing you in how many respects they are requisite: Since it is by them alone that the severall Parts and distinctions of a Garden are as well formed as by hedges, Wales, Palisads and other enclosures whatsoever: ~~And~~ not to mention the most agreable use they afford us for health, exercise, pleasure {&} buisinesse & conversation: And therefore we esteeme one of the principall mysteries of our Gardiner to be able to make and proportion them skillfully; that their length and breadth ~~are~~ hold an agreable correspondency; so as **[page 78]** they neither seeme too narrow, broad, flat, ~~or~~ round or uneven, which are all of them vices {sedulously} to be prevented by the Artist.

And in the first place most agreable and magnificent ~~will it be that there bee~~ {are those walkes which are} made ~~a the most spacious and noble Walke~~ {exactly} fronting with the middle poynt or projecture of the Palace, where the doore ~~leading~~ {opening} into the ~~Garden pergola~~ {Portico} stands levell with the area of the Parterre, and the walke stretch it selfe {*a perte di vieue*} quite through the whole enclosure; The want of such a Walke in front is a very considerable defect in the Garden of the *Palace of Orleans* at *Paris*, caused through the interception of the wall of the *Carthusian* Convent. The pleasure of this greate Prince {herein} religiously submitting to his pietie & devotion, whilst the imperfection might easily be supplied by errecting some magnificent ~~portico~~ Pergola of good Architecture, or a piece of excellent Perspective, after the example of that at Ruell wherof we shall speake hereafter.

There ought likewise to be made an {ample} Walke leading quite about the whole Imparkement, or out Wales, besides those which are to be set out, passing to the particular *Enclosures*, *Labyrinths*, *Groves*, *Mounts* etc every of which, even to the smalest *Alle* & *bed Path* should have a universall intercommunication, there being nothing more odious & prepostrous then to necessitate a returning by the same steppes, which many tymes compells the ~~Companie~~ encountring of some Companies and Persons that would {otherwise} avoyde it, & be private.

And as there is to be a correspondency 'twixt the breath and length of Walkes, so should the height of their collaterall hedges, Palisad's and Trees observe a just and proportionate Symmetrie, whither they be open or close. For Cover'd Walkes do make the Allee seeme broader to the Eye than the open and free; and therefore should they be design'd narrower in proportion to the length, which, likewise will much facilitate the Arch–ment above.

[1]On the Contrary, if the Palisads {& Contr'Espaliers} of open and airy Walkes be very high, which is exceeding gracious, & ~~may be~~ best made of *Alaternus, Holly,* ~~and~~ *Lawrell,* & other winter–greenes (as in tyme we shall shew), the area would be much ~~broader~~ {more spacious}, the ~~height~~ altitude of the Palisade or pole hedges containing two thirds of the breadth of the Allees. {u[n]lesse ~~that is of such as you will have~~} If the Walke be of a very greate length, it is better to exceed in widenesse, then to offend in the contrary defect: Thus, the middle Walke of the Thuilleries **[page 79]** which is planted with stately Elmes is 30 foote {in} breadth and of far more beauty than the two collaterall of Platanus, which is onely 20. though {it be} 600 foote long. To give then a genenerall & positive Rule in this case, Let the proportions of {long} Walkes be so ordered, ~~as~~ that what in *Perspective* we name the *poynt principall,* may, as one walkes continue without straitning the area; for there is nothing more August then to behold a Walke so contracted after one is a little engaged {& that hides the gaping} ~~then to see it gape~~ at both the extreames;

But this is infinitely improv'd if the {side} plantations be of tall & goodly Trees, such as *Elmes,* {Platan, Horsechessnut:} *Limes, Pines* etc which not onely seeme to meete, but do effectually embrace one another {& canopie} at their {spreading} tops {*Umbram hospitalem consociare amantes* as Hor:} as we find in that stately middle Walke of the *Thuilleries,* The *Maille* at *Tours,* and upon the goodly *Ramperts* of *A[n]twerp, Lucca,* {Barn elmes by Lond:} & divers other places then which nothing dos render a Walke more venerable & magnificent: Though for the middle Allee of our Garden, perpendicular to the Front, as we described it, a more open & free aire may for the benefit of the prospect be {happly} more agreable.

If the Walkes ~~be made~~ {extend themselves} (as more frequently through spacious Parkes and Fields then in our ordinary Gardens) to the length of 2000 or 2500 foote, it will become them to have 44 and 50 foote in breadth: The Trees planted at the Sides with dubble ranges ~~of trees~~ at 12. 16. & 18 foote distance {or more}, according to their severall kinds: for if they be *Wallnutts, Chessenutts* or *Oakes,* they will beare 25 and 30, 40 and 50 foote asunder;[2] and {the like} in single ranges, unlesse you will dubble the files with some lesse spreading trees for the foote walkes, which the middle ranges be set out for the principall Avenues and stately ascents to palaces and country houses: {Elmes & lime trees do well much neerer, **[continued in margin]** nay I have known goodly of such at 12 & 15 foote asunder: pines at 24 foote:}

But to returne to our Garden Walkes, ~~I~~ {We} ~~suppose~~ {may allow} the largest ~~will not to exceede~~ {to be of} 30 or 35 foote ~~I~~ in breadth, if they {much} exceed not 1200 foote in length; if 900 24[,] for those of 600 22 or 22½ of 300 20. of 180 18 *et sic deinceps,* which ~~are~~ {though} somewhat larger proportions then ~~I~~ {we} find generally given {yet} you {will be {more} pleased with the effects, For thus} the Palisads Alles of Hornebeame in Luxembourg at Paris being about 680 Ordinary ~~pa~~ walking paces

---

1. **[Margin note]** by Palisads we meane that which covers the Walle {or serves in stead} Contrespale & Espaler, ~~that which~~ a pole–hedg standing by itselfe & opposite to the other though sometimes as promiscuously, but the sense is plain:

2. **[Margin note]** ~~though chestnutt will do well much nearer~~

(i) 1360 foote allowing two foote for each pace is ~~but~~ {over} 30 foote broade; and that next the Charthusians Wall 2080 but 22, which ~~is~~ {were} truely some what of the narrowest, were it not destind for an out walke, & for competent shade, according to the præcept we have already set downe: But such Walkes as approach the Center of the Garden as about the Parterr etc ought to deminish of the breadth in proportion as they **[page 80]** contract themselves 9 foote to 50 etc unlesse ~~the~~ {some} *Fountaine, Theater,* or other *Relievo* cause you with discretion to amplifie it for the convenience of the Spectators & ~~grace of~~ {for accession to} the ornament³

Walkes which are exceeding spacious and long, being terminated with *Palisads,* or Trees, have regularly their *Servile Walkes* or Alles to attend them on both sides, containing halfe the breadth of the principles; But if bordures of Flowers be superadded (which we would reccommend to perfume the aire, & {be} fitted for the severall Seasons) in this case let them not exceede one quarter, or somewhat lesse: {But} In this manner, flowry bordures accompanie the narrower Allees and walkes which divide and traverse the severall members of the Garden with lesse disproportion, then, when out of the larger we fall into them. To conclude, in the proportion of Walkes, the greatest reguard is to be had to the breadth, ~~near~~ in which it is lesse criminall to excede, then to contract & pinch ~~the walkes~~ {them} as many do; for as much as the Gardens, *Palisads, Hedges, Carpets, Watertables* & *Enclosures* will in tyme incroch insensibly upon them.

But now since the Materialls, mixture ~~and~~ making & {foundation} of our Walks, especially, those of *Gravell* (wherein our Country dos certainely exceede all that we have seene in Europe or heard of) ~~is what~~ {are particulars} we have obliged our selves to describe; though we do not take upon ~~ourselves~~ {us} to produce infallible Rules; because the severall Materialls {of places} abound with as various natures which may greately facillitate the worke, or render it difficult & ineffectuall: We will yet to the best of our Tallent set dow[n] the most ~~infallible~~ {expedient} directions, & such as will {certainely} prove infallible if the Stuff be not very deffective.

The Walkes and Alles set out & proportioned as you are instructed, let the Labourers dig, clense ~~and~~ accurately pick & make ~~even~~ levell the ground, empting ~~the~~, carring away the mould a convenient depth; {⁴} upon the{se} Trenches {so likewise

---

3. **[Insertion on separate piece of paper]** But why should I not record his Mats: Walkes ~~at~~ in St James's & Greenwich which may for their Statelinesse & comly dimension compare with any of them we have celebrated: In St: James's Parke the Walke or strade next the Maill being about 8 score rodd in length, is 44 f broad & the trees at 24 foote: The broadest Walke next Westminster on the other side of the Canall is 60 ft: ~~ex~~ trees at 24 f: The Walke longer than the other, & the Strades at each head of the same length, & next the Canall: 44 wide & trees 22. distant:

4. **[Insertion on separate piece of paper]** In the ~~middle line~~ {verges or margent} of this you shall sinke ~~another~~ {two other} trenches of two foote ~~deepe~~ {square (or proportionable to the Walke)} ~~& as broad sinking~~ making them upon a pent ~~hardly perceptible, though the~~ as much as the ground will suffer, & at every 100 paces sinke a pitt of 4 foote if the water hinder you not, in these trenches & likewise in these pitts lay in flints, pibbles, brik–batts, and other the larger sort of stones, as hollow yet as firmly as you can, not minding any accurate order, & these if the Gardens be in-

upon all the rest which you design for the water} you shall spread a bed of lime, ~~or~~ chalke, [rubbish], old bricks, pottshards, flints, rough gravell, {broken glasse} or whatsoever hard, & impenetrable rubbish you can procure, {layd especially thick at the edges where the moisture breeds most weedes} which will be of greate effect to resist the weede and abate the Worme; ~~let this~~ being well beaten & rammed {downe}[5] then if the Gravell, must first be cast, or **[page 81]** skreen'd (which is the most preferrable) lay a bed of the coarsest first, & upon that the finer, provided[6] it be such as is binding of it selfe:[7] for being naturally ~~blended~~ intermixed with a competent proportion of Loame, it will not onely be superiour to all other compositions; but save much expence, whereas, if it want sufficient ligature, it will be the best way to make severall essays with different & various quantities of the brightest Loame,[8] till you have ~~detected~~ {found out} the true proportion, which you will {soone} detect by the hardnesse and binding, ~~of it~~ after it has bin a while watered and rolled; For this admitts of no infallible rule: Thus, suppose one loade of loame be blended with two or three of Gravell; & as we shall proceede ~~anon~~ anon. But first must the loame be {beaten &} reduced to powder, soone after it is dug; for else it will with lying grow exceedingly hard, ~~&~~ churlish and untractable; & if it be too soft and clammy it is as bad: There may also be occasion to mingle it with sand, whereoff that which is to be procured from the Sea were best, as most binding; but not {so fitt} for colour.[9]

Well, the Ground thus prepar'd, & your mixture right, spread of the coarsest halfe a foote thick, which may be wheeled or carted in: One lusty Labourer is able to spread as much as fower can {well} supplie: when this bed is layd & coursely raked, let it be very well trodden; which done, lay as much of the ~~finest~~ {most} refined (for we suppose the ground to be {already} abated according to the depth and quantity of the stuff which you will employ: sixteene inches is a competent ~~thicke~~ depth) and whilst the workmen are spreading and raking it, let them be well followed with

---

fected with springs or too much water will be a meanes to cure it: And as upon these Trenches

5. **[Margin note]** Some commend Oake saw dust or saw dust of Firr a Coate of it one inch thicke to be layd between the 2 Coates, which by a sowernesse proceeding from it from report kills wormes:

6. **[Margin note]** Insert: we are told that it has bin tried to mix Gravell with dust of Free stones & that it resists weedes & is very beautifull also with glasse dust to be had at the glasse houses & sow salt under: & Soape ashes:

7. **[Insertion on separate piece of paper]** Such as that which is calld the Cattbraine as some call it or the amber loam'd which is a sort of yellow ~~bright~~ transparant & bright gravell, small & {naturaly} mixed with {such a} such a proportion of loame & sand as binds of it self like a pavement exceedingly beautifull to look & walke on.

8. **[Margin note]** where there is not loame clay beaten to powder may supply, the colour onely will likely be darker:

9. **[Insertion on separate piece of paper]** Shell walkes[:] First lay 2 Inches thick of loame finely raked & even, then halfe an inch of beaten shells grossly; & raked; then roule & fine it & fix it: It has a property to cutt the wormes; & is to be found in the Ille of Thanett & other places by the Sea shore; but nothing like good Gravell.

watering potts powring {plentifully} upon what they have finished. But there is {in this} great Arte required, ~~an even~~ {steady} hand, and exact eye to give the Walke its ~~due~~ {decent} Swelling, & in which truely our Gardiners in England are very defective, making them so round & ridgid; that they are not onely too uneasie to walke upon; but unsightly to look on. Therefore, having first determin'd the poynts of the middle and sides, by stakes erected at severall distances, extend three lines from one extreame to the other, so as they may passe the head, of the stakes: If the designe be without declivity long ways, the lines must be examin'd with a Levell; if with ascent, by the proportion of that ascent which you will give it: In either case, if the line be six inches from the first course of Gravell (which I suppose to be halfe a foot deepe) the rubbish 4. ten in all, the Collaterall Lines shall not exceede three: & {from} this you will find **[page 82]** a very gracefull swelling to result in a Walke of 21 foote broade, which we do ~~make~~ {constitute for} our Instance. ~~For th~~ {Nor} indeede it cannot be to insensible provided it carry off the raine & water which falls from heaven:

{But} This, as too ~~smale~~ {humble} and low an Arch may some happly condemne; ~~bu~~{Ye}t let ~~such~~ {them} not {hastily} determine till they have experimented the grace and effects of it, as we have don in the best, and most magnificent Walkes of Europe, where they are not made of so drye and binding materialls as ours, ~~are~~ {and} which in most places they ridge rather ~~th~~ like plow'd Lands, then Walkes and decent Allees. ~~And after this proportion~~

After this {Calculation} of a Walke of 21 foote over, will take up two good loads of Gravell (reckning 20 Barrow to a loade) every 5 foote in length: A Walke of 14 foote, one. To a Walke of 7 foote, a loade every twenty foote, 9 inches being depth sufficient for Alles of that demension. And after these proportions ought our Gardiner to proceede in Walkes and Allees of lesser or greater breadth and extent.

If {in} the first Rollings one follow, and plentifully wash the Roller, it will exceedingly harden the Walke; and if, when all this is don, it prove not yet firme enough, a slighte coate of ~~slight~~ {fine} gravell well refined, mingled with a little sand may be cast upon it & rolled in: for all the art consists in binding it fast, so as it neither indente with the feete, or rise with the trailing of the Ladys gownes; & if it have any other perfection, it is that the colour be agreable; for there is some gravell shiny & transparent like amber: but if that cannot be obtained, the Seifting of coloured & bright sands upon it, will some what supplie that deffect, though with nothing that beauty and permanency.

There is likewise exceeding {greate} care to be taken, that in the first rolling of Walkes, the stone be continually kept ~~going~~ {moving}; that so it may be settled without impression; that the cillinder be exact & heavy enough; for which it will require a diameter of 28 inches, and a length of 4 foote. Also that the person who rolles, rolle it now & then crosse wayes, to do which well, there is a dextrous slight, so as the turning raise not up the Gravell, or leave any baulkes. This will wonderfully settle them, being {well &} skillfully handled.

Lastly that no poynted or highheeld shoes presume to march upon it (and I would they were banished ~~all~~ out of {our} Gardens forever) 'till it be thoroughly hardned. In *France* the Walkes are for most part made like our ordinary Barne–floors, mixed with plaster & loame; **[page 83]** {But} The Gravell which they use is sharp, & nothing worth; though it is probable they might find better; And, as we are informed, the late *Mons: Belieure* (who had bin formerly *Embassador* here in ~~England~~ {our Country}) has layd some Walkes with Gravell, emulating {even} our best in England.[xvii]

But, in Italy, they breake chalke and loame together, which they moisten with the fresh lees or mare of the oyle–presse, tempering them together, & then ramming it exceedingly, they last of all sprinkle it with the same liquor againe, & thus let it drie in, by which meanes it neither chaps in the heate, nor thaws with cold, neither is it obnoxious to weedes, or vermine. And yet with all this charge, do they nothing approch our Walkes in England, which might yet be infinitely improved, if, instead of Gravell, they were made of the smallest *Sparr* found in our *Lead–mines*, which, where it may be procured, is such a materiall, as exceedes {all} comparison, both for use, richnesse, & of lustre, and all other perfections imaginable. It is a kind of *Talke*, the *Matrix of the Leadoare* to which it frequently adheares: Such as are very curious might obtaine it by shipping, & it would be good Ballast, nor, could the charge be excessive.

Concerning Walkes of Sand, brick dust etc: we shall not say much, because they lye loase, are obnoxious to the winds & waters; if there be the least descent; yet in case of necessitie, they are made, & are usefull, and gracefull enough in narrow Allees, where it may be often coated and refreshed without trouble, and so as the *area* lie levell, as in *Galleries, coole, & close Walkes*,[10] where superinduced with a fine & beautiful mosse, which is very soft and agreable. These may likewise be made of various colours, but such as for black and blew, with the dust of slatts, Coale, {sope ashes} etc: And the barke of the Tanpitt{ners}, after they have don with it, may be of use for {some} Allees, for it lookes of a pretty colour, preserves the ground from cleaving, kills weedes, and in three yeares {tyme} proves good compost, & may then be taken off, employ'd else where, and be {againe} renewed. There are also severall sorts of coloured pibbles, which may be paved like mosaique floores, & fixed into the ground prepared with some loame or other fitting ligature: But all the fore mentioned loose walkes should be so contrived, that neither the Sun, nor the winds may easily discompose them.

And here for as an necessary advertisement we give this caution. that the (as before we touched) the Walke contiguous to the dore, which enters from the house opens into the Garden, be layd even even & levell with the *area* of the Mansion, and by no meanes rising or declining, however practised to the contrary in many places of England, who preferr an {Elevated} Tarrace before **[page 84]** the grace of the *Fountaines*, naturall & artificiall *Perspectives* of the Gardens: And therefore, though the rest of the enclosure lye with an agreable declivitie towards the South, as we have desire it should, yet let the area of the Walke in Front lye parallel with the *Parterr*; so far, at least, as the knott extends, and then it may insensibly decline; The *Tarraces*, flanking upon Collaterally with the *parterr*, as we have describe it in the plott of our *Villa*: L:3. c. 8. For though a Tarrac {or portico} with an ascent, be proper at the Front towards the Court, at no hand is it so, on the front of the Garden, where the prospect below should be free to the *Fountaines*, and the view universall from the *Galleries* and roomes of Entertainement; otherwise, the Garden seemes like a pit, the *Cascade* of the *Tarrac* and descent of stepps, drowning both the fabrick and the *Parterr*. Nor will what may be objected from {the} forraigne examples of *St Germains en Lage*, incomparable *Maisons* etc in *France Tivoli*, & some other places in *Italy* be of any validity here: Since it is

---

10. **[Margin note]** insert: Brick allyes are best made of brickbatts ram'd in in good big morsells[.] pe[a]t Coale makes best Allys: etc:

the Situation alone, which has constrained them to ~~it~~ {that Subjection} especially that of *St Germains*, which is rather a *Series of Cascads* then to be at all esteem'd a Garden; ~~for indeede~~ And the steps at *Frascati* descend not to any Garden; for there is indeed none considerable about that admirable place; but to the *Grottos*, *Theater*, *Hill*, and *Wood* ~~and~~ immediately ascending, & {wholy} interrupting the contrivance of any straite walke, which *in plano* {had} could not have bin omitted, and is where it happens the formall reason of our assertion; seing 'tis to be supposed, that the rising of the *Avenue* and front of the House, wearing the *Ascendent* he ~~be~~ {ought to be} reccompens~~ing~~{ed} {him} with an even Walke and an agreable prospect, though the Gates and severall overtures of the Courts and Palace, and not immediately to descend againe which is both painefull, and renders the passage like the bottome of a Well through which nothing appeares but the Skie {& the water}. And thus[11] much shall suffice to have bin spoaken {of} ~~concerning~~ *Gravell-walkes* ~~and~~ *Allees & Avenues* as they concern the Argument in hand:

Those we call ~~Walkes~~ Carpets, Walkes which are invested and covered with Gravell or Turfe; and the difference betweene these and the other of Gravell, is, that they are never layd round or Swelling; but flatt & very levell. Those Walkes which you designe for a Carpet, should be first ~~coursely~~ dugg, clensed & {course raked}, trodden, {&} then fine raked and made very even: And upon this is the Turfe to be applied which, being cutt into just and tractable quarters, ~~must~~ {may} be accurately joynted {by laing} earth to earth, so as the slop of the edges mutually correspond, **[page 85]** and the commissures be with a hand bettle beaten very close till it come perfectly to the levell, which you are {diligently} to examine with a line strained from one extreame to the other, and now and then with the Triangle, or some such like instrument. When it is thus all layed, sprinkle it well with the water-pott and {beate with a flatt beater} rolle it aboundantly, continuing this ~~worke~~ labour 'till the edges are grow united together, ~~and~~ when the Sith must {often} goe it over & have ~~low~~ it as low as may be.

But before this worke be ~~begun~~ {undertaken}, care is to be had[12] in the ~~choice~~ {election} of {fitting} Turfe: choose therefore that which produces the finest and best collour'd Grasse, which matts, & grows thick, is free from weedes, daisies, wild Time, mosse etc such a swar~~d~~{th} as is usually found upon the barren Heaths & Downes, whose foundation is chalke or sand, and where the perpetuall feeding of sheepe keepe it low and very delicate. In such a place cutt your Quarters with the Paring knife or Plough describ'd in cap: 1. num: 28. running by an even line {& then crossing the

---

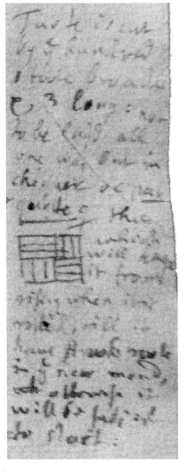

Figure 19. Instructions for setting turf in a "chequer or parquette" pattern in a margin note at page 85.

11. **[Margin note]** Taraces of Masonry should be made with frequent nices & pillasters, which if of free-stone interrupt it, brick give a good plane. Steps to such ascents should be 15 inch brod & 5 1/2 high: of Free-stone or Clinker and this is that which my Ld: Verulam calls obletamentum ex Gramineto, which he commends for their dubble pleasure, the Eyes ~~than which nothing~~ being frequently moved & well kept then which nothing is more delightfull, & through such a greene plott he should have the entry into the Garden Graminetum in Introitu:

12. **[Margin note]** Turfe is cut by the hundred foote broade & 3 long: not to be layd all one way but in chequer or parquette **[illustration, see Fig. 19]** & thus which will keepe it from rising when it is rolled, till it have struck roote in the new mould, ~~which~~ otherwise it will be subject to start:

lines} yet holding the Instrument {somewhat} sloping (for in the same posture must you joyne them) and then with a Turfing Spade loosen & take them up from the ~~Earth~~ ground ~~being~~ allowing them about an inch and halfe thicknesse, ~~and~~ one foote in breadth; & three for the length, carefully rolled up, and gently ~~carried~~ conveied.[13] It is in the very rolling up that you shall perfectly discerne the qualities of it; for there is a sort which is very stringy, the mould friable & brittle, which will not endure the making up: But let these cautions suffice. Some to prevent the exuberance of its groth, & the greate inconveniency of Worme casts if it be to lye upon a rich soyle, do by sand, and other meanes, {Salt, cole dust, soape ashe or a layer of lime an inch thick} moderate, and sterilize the Earth, and ~~it~~ {the invention} is not to be dissaprov'd.

There is another way of producing carpet upon walkes and Greenes, without Turfing; and that is by sowing the place (so prepared as above) ~~above~~ with hay–seede onely: let it be sowne upon the treading, & then fine raked {over}; {& if the} and this often tymes succeedes so well as hardly to be discerned from {the layed} Turfe; especially provided it be of the finest Seede: To procurre which, goe not to the common hay lofts; but let Boys be employd, about the tyme that the Grasse is ripe, to gather & strip off ~~what they find~~ the finest of that which they find growing upon the higher pastures, not that which grows in the Meadows: for without this Industry & care, your Grasse will come full of weedes, {insert} & be little better then what is usually scraped together from the Sweepings of spent *Mews*, & from the Inns & Stables; which is of all other the most infectious. It is incredible what halfe a score Boys will gather & strip in a few dayes:

But to prepare the ground exactly for it, being first well dug, ~~&~~ clensed, & ~~le~~ made levell, give it a slight raking, then ~~sow it~~ tread it, rake & sow it; tread {it} a second tyme & lastly finely rake it. Thus, when the spires are well come up, ramm downe all the knobbs & risings, and **[page 86]** roll it sufficiently, ~~and last of all~~ {to conclude} mowe it about the spring very frequently, {keeping it} continually beate~~ing~~ and rolling it 'till it produce a fine Carpet emulating even the best {of} Turfe.

Walkes are likewise made of Cammomile, which must be planted with rootes within two inches one of another, & that in lines; then cutt the extravagant heads, & roll, ~~&~~ beate, {& weede} it often.

Lastly there are Walkes of Mosse which if it be of the bright & shining sort, & ~~not as~~ very shallow, makes an excellent carpet. It is to be produced by {the} strewing of brick dust, or sand upon Loame, & keeping it very moyst & shadie; & therefore, easily {to be} ~~wh~~ procured under close walkes, Galleries etc where the Sun dos not penetrate: They neede nor {wetting nor} cutting but are sometymes to be rolled; & ~~seldome~~ were it not for the dampnesse of their nature, & earthinesse of the smell, they might be of more esteeme, however in Summer they are very tollerable & agreable. There are Walkes {also} of Marble & other stone, of the diamond & Square cutt, of one of more Colours, forme & shape, which may properly be ~~employed~~ layd on the Walke which extends itselfe {by} the whole side of the Front, & is immediately contiguous to the area of the Edifice, either in ~~the~~ *Tarras* or *sub dio*:[14] They are of incomparable

---

13. **[Margin note]** & but so many at a tyme as you can well lay in a day or two; because of one drying:

14. **[Margin note]** These are the Hypætræ of Vitruvius: L: 5. & by Plin: 1. 36 cald subdialia pavimenta

use, ~~are~~ fit at all Seasons, preserve the Garden from potching in wett weather & sort well with our designe: but for that the paving {& particular laing} of them belongs {properly} to the Masson. ~~I~~ {We} referr them to the {skillfull} workemen.

And here {we conceive} it will not be impertinent to speake something concerning *Bowling-Greenes*, ~~that~~ {since the} incomparable divertissement which they afford us, is singular to the *English* Nation above all others in the World.[15] The making of these requires no other præcepts then what we have {already} layd downe in our description of Carpet walkes: {Onely} the demensions are to be regulated conformably to the companies which frequent them; Such as are made for private use may very well be contrived within the Enclosure of our *Elysium* & neede not be altogether so large as those which are prostituted to publique {the} Gamsters: However to give ~~you~~ universall satisfaction herein, we have calculated the demensions of some of the most famous about ~~London~~ our *Metropolis*. {Lo: Barclays: at Dundans in {Surry} 50 yards one way, 60 the other: a good Patterne:} **[Page 87]** This onely is to be added {as} wherein ~~they~~ {*Bowling greens*} differ from our method in *Carpet Walkes*; that for the diversitie of *Casts* rather then to gratifie the Eye.

Those Greenes are {held} most in ~~esteeme~~ {reputation}, which are either so artificially, or accidentally layed, as to afford the ~~most~~ {greatest} variety: ~~of casts~~ {and this is}, caused by frequent but almost imperceptible ~~risings & fallings~~ elevations & depressions, at competent distances; we say imperceptible, because it is most notorious, they are not onely {lesse} ungracefull, but likewise require ~~lesse~~ {more} skill in the Gamster then when he can evidently discerne the deception; therefore you shall many tymes see your cunning *Rookes* run out in a sweeping shower of Raine to find out the declivities & risings, by the naturall ~~course~~ {current} of the Water in those Greenes, where the irregularities are {otherwise} indiscernable to the eye.

We advise that the precincts & enclosures of Bowling Greenes be made with a banke of Turfe of 4 foote high, bevell, and indented with a seate theatricall, of competent measure; These {do} best deaden a hard throwne Bowle: Upon this banke, let there be a palisade of some ever Greene, kept parapett hight; that the Spectators, which walke without it & are not engaged in the *Partie*, may behold the Sport, & how the Game goes, without {at all} interrupting them:

There are of greate use in Citties certaine Square plotts destind for this recreation, which are naked & without Grasse, & have thence their name of *Bares*: And truely they are beautifull, & supplie the defect of the others during the Winter halfe yeare from *Octob: to Aprill* & since they may likewise be introduc't into our *Elysium* where we would have nothing difficient that contributes {either} to health & ornament, we will heare describe {unto you} the making of them. First, if the Ground be not of it selfe sufficiently levell (for ~~then~~ you neede {else} only take off the sward), give it a course digging, picking it extreamely cleane; then rake and levell it; yet so, as it have a competent ~~rising~~ {swelling} in the middle from which center the whole ground must be abated for the equall & speedy carring of the raine: Then {doe} treade it well; after that {over} lay it with a coate of mould exquisitely sifted, ~~all over~~ {in

---

15. **[Margin note]** ~~May~~ But yet we read that the Romans (who had all sorts of pleasures in their Gardens, thatt could ~~ref~~ any way refresh & contribute to health besides Hypocaustra, Vivaries, etc: their Sphænstheria also.

which mix some quantity of Soape ashes} about three fingers thick, rake & treade it; then rake it ~~finely~~ {againe} universally with a very fine ~~rake~~ {toothe}; last of all, strew it over thinly with Sand, and rolle it aboundantly with a good & a weighty roller: It is usuall also in these *Bares* to make some variety of casts by raising some smale eminences neare each corner of the Square, **[page 88]** and to banke and plant it about, as we have shewed in that of the Bowling Greenes. As concerning coverd Allees, to be found in Citties, Prisons & ~~drye Countrys~~ {obscure places}, because they commonly end in drink~~ing associations~~ & idle associations, we disdaine to doe the honour of a description.

But there is another healthfull and ~~noble~~ {princly} recreation more frequented in forraine Countries, then our owne, which for that ~~they are~~ {it is} made by {the} conversion of Walkes into ~~them~~ {it}, and sometimes found in noble Gardens, & very practicab~~le~~{ll}, ~~in our~~ we thinke it not amisse to speake something of, before we conclude this chapter. *Paille mailles* are certaine Allees exceedingly protracted, and edged at the side with boards: & with arches of yron at each end through which to strike the Balles. But, we shall more perfectly describe them by these {ensuing} particulars.

Let a place be made choyce of, which may extend a walke upon an exactly levell floore 500 geometricall paces[,] 2500 foote in length, or longer, if conveniently may be; (for that is indefinite.) Make this Allee 24 foote in breadth; Then edge it round [16]about with 3 Inch ~~& halfe~~ Oaken planke; to be fastned to {certaine} stumps of ~~cer~~ timber {fixed} in the Earth: {as you doe the bordures of ~~bedd~~ **[continued in margin]** flowre beds 2 foote high above ground, the ends 4 foote, the plankes are to be spiked into the puntions {of oake} & joynd with pinns at edges: The ~~posts~~ stakes or puntions 4 or 5 foote distant; & to be 4 inch square timber pitched where they are driven into the Earth: **[end margin insertion]**} ~~At e~~ At each end erect an Arch of Yron {moveable} of ~~4~~ {2} foote & halfe high, & ~~one foote~~ {9 inches} wide, {set into a piece of timber lind with yron} within 14 foote of the extreamities; Then {when you take down the Arch, stop the holes with peggs to keepe out water & Earth:} at the same distance ~~to the~~ {towards} the opposite face of the Arch, insert two square smale stones even with the floore, & 8 foote from the plankes; And last of all, another stone 50 foote from these placed just in the middle of the floore.[17] The balls, {of french box 3 inch in diameter french box is tougher} and head of the Mailles, are made of ~~box~~, {oake verruld with yron} and the {also a spoone **[continued in margin]** of different lengthes to fitt the Gamester, the handle of Ash small neere the head or hammer by degrees that the flexablenesse may fit it for the greate swingh the head of tough oake 5 Inch long, 2 diameter feruld at end half inch broad, the very handles of the Malls are to be wreathed about with as rich leather as Raccketts are.[18] The spoone is made

---

16. **[Margin note]** the side planke marked at every 100 paces with figures as tenis courts are cf

17. **[Margin note]** the 2 first are called the striking of stones the farthest the passing stone

18. **[Insertion on separate piece of paper]** These differ from the Goffe [golf] Malls (which are to use in ~~allys~~ large & wide Walkes of Grasse well cutt, or sometymes in wide fields & on downes) by the turning up of its head like a does foote, the better to hitt the ball in the grasse

of box fit for the ball, & with a long handle: this to passe the post with. **[end margin insertion]**} Rules of Play best knowne to the Gamster; nor concernes it our farther inquirie: This onely wee add, that the floores {may be} ~~are~~ made after the same manner as we have set downe in *Bares*;[19] & must be dilligently swept & kept rolld upon all occasions, ~~yet~~ with this caution {also} that there be some overture {in} at {the} {~~side middle or as you think fitt, made by a narrow slitt in the middle of a stone over a draine; the drain of brick the stones halfe a foote admitt an yron grate of halfe a foote square or rather a plate with small holes in it:~~} competent distances for the draining away of the raines which fall, & may by their stagnating very much incommode the floore.[20] But though we describe our *Paill Maille* to extend it selfe to such a length {in perpendicular;} yet in a case of necessitie, it is not forbidden to make {sometimes} a flexure. That of the citty of *Tours* in *France*, which is certainely the goodliest in the world, take it for the ~~length~~ {extent} & incomparable plantation of the lofty Elmes, which **[page 89]** cover it like a gallery for neere an *English* mile in length, Those of *Bloys* ~~that~~ and in *St Germains Parke* are without any bending {at all}: & so were ours at *St James's*, New–hall in Essex & divers other places: But that in the Gardens of the *Thuilleries* in Paris hath a flexure of 160 ordinary paces; and that in the *Palais Royall Gardin*, two bendings of 180 and 370 paces, resembling this figure,

[illustration, see Fig. 20][21]

That likewise at the *Arsenall*, has a turning up not so oblique of 160 paces: It is in the whole length 736 paces ~~wide~~ & about 20 foote {or 9 paces} broade: in this forme

[illustration, see Fig. 21]

And so is that in *Marse* field at *Geneva.* and divers other places: By all which we see that they are {many times} contrived to accommodate with the places, where there is not length enough to extende them in perpendicular, as at Tours {there is,} which ~~was th~~ is {doubtlesse} the most perfect figure, & ~~the~~ most desirable: {But amongst

---

19. **[Insertion on separate piece of paper]** Or with sand & loame beaten till well confirmed, this don frequently, but then you must not walk on it till dry.

20. **[Insertion on separate piece of paper]** To order this right the floore of the Malle must be made most imperceptibly hollow (otherwise its perfection were to be as even {& levell} as calm water) & under that at the first making, must be ~~a~~ {a gutter or} chanells of brick a foote under ground {8 inch wide }*

[continued in margin] & at competent distance: {to each of these, viz, every 10 paces a collaterall gutter of the same dimensions} a square draine of 4 foote diameter steand also with bricks which is to be at the side of the mall without the ~~brick~~ planke {six foote deepe} to which the water is carried the channells {made} at reasonable distances, should have a grate or rather plate of yron full of small holes: this not above a foote square & to lye as even as the area that it may not impede the fling of the balls. {but what we have prescribed for the cure of over moisture even in ordinary Gravell allys etc may also be as expedient here and lesse costly:}

* covered with brick without mortar that the Wett may sink in, but the bottome & sides with mortar

21. **[Margin note]** Note that the {stones (for so those parts must be, for feare of deading the Play[?])} planted at the flexures must be a full yard in height for the mounting of the ball when it comes to turne:

Figures 20, 21 (facing page). Illustrations of the pall-malls at the Palais Royal Garden (above) and the Arsenall and Tuileries (below) on page 89.

89

couer it like a gallery for neere an English
mile in length; those of Bloys, and
St Germains Parke are without any bending:
& so were ours at St Iames's, New hall &
&c & diuers other places: But that in the Gar
dens of the Thuilleries in Paris hath a flexure
of 160 ordinary paces; and that in the Palais
Royall Garden two bendings of 180. and 370
paces, resembling this figure,

noting the plantings be so
at the flexures must
be a full yard in
height, for the mounty
of the ball when it
comes to heare.

that likewise at the Arsenall has a turning off
not so oblique of 160 paces: It is in the whole
length 736 paces about 20 foote broade.
In this forme

And so is it in Marse field at Genova
and diuers other places; By all which we see that
they are many times contriued to accomodate with the places, where there is not length enough to extend them in
perpendicular, as at Tours, which is the
most perfect figure & most desirable. But it will
It would be needlesse to add, that plantations
& somtymes double & treble ranges of the most copy
& shady trees, are alwayes attendants to these Paille Mailles, for the grace & magnificence of the walker
and to refresh our Gamsters.

CHAP. VII.

Of Groves, Labyrinths, Dædales, Cabinets,
Cradles, Pavilions, Galleries, Close-walkes
and other Relieve's.

It may be objected to our want of aduertancy, that hauing
so lately deferred to speake of walkes, we should finish them
in the preceeding Chapter. To this we reply, that the parterrs
Knotts, Bordures & compartiments which lye contiguous to
the Mansion, and afford the most imediate & agreable prospect

them all}²² It ~~will~~ would be needelesse to add, that plantations & sometymes dubble & trebble ranges of the most lofty & shady trees, are allways attendants ~~to~~ {on} the *Paille Mailles*, for the grace & magnificence of the Walkes, and to refresh ~~the~~ {our active} Gamster.

---

22. **[Insertion on separate piece of paper]** But amongst them all I know none that exceedes, hardly approches that which his Ma[jes]ty: has made at St: James park which containes in length 160 rodd & is 26 f: broad: The floore is made with ~~loame, sand: & then strewd over which See~~ {loame, & then beaten cockle–shells strewd} halfe inch thick & beaten & rolled in, which renders it a floore beyond all that I have seene;

{but as a flo: as you make a barne flo: of good sifted mould lime, loame, & sea coale proportionally mixed {& tempered} with water layd in a competent thicknesse, then beaten with a beate square with a long sloping handle, & drawne to & when wett then rolld long & crosse:}

Had this Mall about 30 {or 40} yards more in length as it might have for the space & reach, it were without reproch & would containe 3 good streetes:

To this is a walke of Elmes 44 f: brod on one side, & another on the other of limes at 24 foote asunder:

Of Groves, Labyrinths, Dædales, Cabinets, Cradles, Pavilions, Galleries, Close–Walkes and other Relievo's.

It may be objected to our want of advertancy, that having so lately deferred to speake of walkes, we should finish them in the preceeding Chapter. To this we reply, that the Parterrs, Knotts, Bordures & Compartiments which lye contiguous to the Mansion, and afford the most immediate & agreable prospect **[page 90]** to the roomes of Entertainement, it was requisite, that the Walkes, Alles and Terraces leading to and about them should follow in the next place; and especially to give some diversion to the Ladys, and encouragement to the Owner, whilst the rest, which is yet imperfect to make our *Elysium* compleate, remaines unfinished, and will take up a longer tyme: Add to this, that the materialls to be used in order thereunto may well be brought in, mould and rubbish carried forth by other wayes, and gates left for this purpose in the first construction of the Walle, without the least interruption of what we have {already} brought to perfection.

We have hitherto discoursed of some ornaments and accessories to Gardens, especially in the two or three last chapters; we come now to the more principall parts, for such we esteeme the naturall ~~ornaments~~ {decorations} of [1]Groves, Labyrinths, thicketts & what *Pliny* calls *horridior Naturæ facies*, which after a wonderfull diversitie from the compt, polite and uniforme partes of the *Walkes* and *Parterrs*, is of all other the most noble, sollumne and divertissant of Garden ornaments. To speake then of Groves, Wildernesses, Summer houses, Closewalkes, etc as most gracefully succeeding the Knotts and Compartiments (whereoff we have already treated) if in the originall disposure of the plott, we find them not already planted by Nature, (preferrable to all artificiall additions {whatsoever}) the fittest place to raise & make them in will be on the flankes of the ~~Terraces~~ {Parterrs}, somewhat in Front, collaterall to the through and longest walke, which we designed in the former Chapter opposite to the Gate of the Mansion; but at some distance {for, *Premum in exitu* as **[continued in margin]** My Ld: Bacon would have groves & wildernesses at the farther part of the Garden} and if possible on some eminence of ground, interserting Fields, Crofts, Theaters, & frequent openings & smaler inclosures, whose bordures and bankes would be filled with ordinary flo: especially such as are apt to perfume {& improve} the ayre, as pinkes, primroses, violets, Cowslips, {lillys} Narcissus, etc: The hedg-rowes set with fragrant, fruite–bearing beautifull or very profitable Trees, in which case we do admitt the Ortchard furniture into our Gardens of Pleasure, provided that the Trees be

---

1. **[Margin note]** Plin: 24. c 1.

straite, and very well chosen: And by these will divide our severall larger partitions, pastures and plotts for beanes, pease, & such blossome–bearing graine yea for hopps & Sallys if neede bee; some of these subdivided againe by plantations of fragrant **[page 91]** shrubbs of all kinds, whole Palisads of Gessamine² Rosemarie, {Sweete bryer}, Woodbynd, {Vines}, within which, there may be Squares & beds of the more ~~beautifull~~ {redolent} flowers, especially the Clove Gilly–flo: {bankes of Cammomille & large fields of tyme³} by this meanes the ayre and wind being perpetually fannd from so many encircling & encompassing hedges {blossomes & fragrant Trees} should never approach the region, which is properly designed to be flowery, without greate varietie of perfumes; nor those who walke in our Garden without variety of objects, ~~suitable to the~~ affecting and delighting the ~~chiefest~~ senses: ~~of descriptions~~ For thus the {naturall} Groves, parterrs, Viridaria, ~~Fountaines~~ {hills}, {statues}, Mounts, {~~Grotts~~}, fields, {Walkes} [&] statues, Grotts, Fountaines, streames {large} & frequent enclosures would reppresent the beholder {with} a prospect of a noble & masculine majestie far surpassing those trifling bankes and busy knotts of our ordinary Gardens consisting ~~of~~ of stiff and meane designes; the worke for their uniformity, and excessive charge[.]

To returne then to our {former} Argument, since amongst all the ornaments of our Elysium there ~~is~~ {are} none more magnificent & gracefull then what trees afford

Sicelides Musæ, paulo majora canamus
Non omnes Arbusta juvant humilesque Myricæ
Si canimus Sylvas, Sylvæ sunt Consule dignæ.⁴
[*Eclog.* 4.1–3]

~~Having therefore mu~~ If therefore Nature have not bin so propitious as to furnish the place you would assigne for ~~a~~ Groves etc; They may be elevated in these three manners. First by plowing and enclosing it, and so permitting it to rest as they do Copples, this is the Vulgar and Naturall way. The second is by sowing with Acorns, nutts, keys, mast, hawes and berries, after the ground has bin well broken up & cultivated {the yeare} before ~~hand~~, so as you would prepare it for wheate; baulking & abating with the plough, for such Walkes and Alles ~~which~~ {as} you will reserve: But, if the Plott be not extraordinary large, rather by treating it with the spade, by which meanes it will be the easier clensed of whatsoever may obstruct the groth of the intended wood. Thus prepared ~~and sowen~~ with the materialls above mentioned, either immediately after their gathering, or reserved till spring, as you are taught in Cap: 4: Set or sow

---

2. **[Margin note]** Se: {L: 3} cap. 9:

3. **[Margin note]** violets the white especialy, which are in flo: twice a yeare Apr: & Aug: Musc rose, fragrariæ whose leaves emitt a Cardiac halitus. Rubus odoratus parietaria lutea. Flores Tibæ Lavender also Walles of Cammomilles, mint, pimpinnell & Serpillum which being walked upon break forth their ~~perfumes~~ {odors}, & in summ whatever perfumes & tinges the aire: for the breath of flo: is sweeter in the aire then in the hand.

4. **[Margin note]** vide Virg: [In his quotation from the *Eclogues* Evelyn has changed "sint" to "sunt".] Erithræ voc Sylva etc. [Nicolaus Erythreus] & Pet[ronius]: crinitus de Honest. discip. 4: c 5.

the ground in Rills or trenches drawne halfe a foote deepe with the howe in even lines, covering them with the rake, as they doe for beanes and pease in the field:

Some thinke it best to sow the seedes on the banke in rowes, and to set on the top as well as on both the sides, For all these cases, you must have a speciall care to clense them at their first rising, & preserve them **[page 92]** from Weedes; & thus in a short tyme you will have a plentifull crop of trees, which comming up too thick you may thin and transplant at pleasure into other places about your grounds; letting the rest stand till the third year, when the little Oakes {& Ashes} may be cutt within an Inch of the ~~ground~~ Earth with a very sharp bill for feare of shaking & abusing the tender roote: This ~~being~~ don in the old moone & when the weather is faire, will make the shoote of the next spring to come very beautifull & straite.

Lastly, by planting of young plants in Autumne, or Spring, the more dry and such as loose their leafe, as soone as it falles from the mother tree; the more moyst in the latter season, as the Ever–greenes etc. Take therefore such plants out of the Nurserys, coppses and young woods as have faire stocks & good rootes & transplant them in your ground prepared as before in competent fosses at three foote distance, cutting them within halfe a foote of Ground {(birches excepted which cutt not)} & carefully weeding & dressing them the three or fower first yeares, untill the shade of these young impes suffocate and vanquish the weedes & trash which deprives them of their nourishment. The first yeare will require but little labour besides weeding, but in the following they must be supplied with plentifull refreshments in the hot seasons, softning & stirring the mould about the rootes & applying of rotten ferne to keep them moyst, especially, if the Spring & Autumne prove very drie, and binding but after this they will be able to shift for themselves;

Plants for the more sound mould are Oake, Elme, Ash, Sycamor, Maple, Beech, Crab, Thorne: For the moyster or boggy, {Birch} Poplar, Willow, Sallow, Osier, etc, most of which will grow by Trunchions, & then plant them by raising fosses: Some also spring of cuttings and Layers as the Willow, Sallow, Horse–Chessnutts, Withy, Woodbynd, etc: *Blith* would have trees set in dubble Ditches like Quicksetts: But of this for more full directions consult our fourth chapter.

And now, though we have shewed in what order & method Groves & thicketts may be most ~~expeditiously~~ {compendiously} raised; yet we ~~thinke~~ reccomme[n]d the confused & irregular planting of them far before the ranging of them in lines; because the~~y~~ Eye is not in this worke pleased with continuall order, which is too naked & subject to leave many eye–sores when any of them chance to dye, whereas by the other way the sight is bounded or lost in pleasing obscurities, hollownesses & umbrages naturall & sollomne. {~~so as the~~ {elegant} ~~Propertius fansys his Mistris & may be good to imitate in all our Garden workes.~~}

And to shew what is possible to be don in this kind as to the groth and stature of some trees: *Count Maurice* the late Governour of *Brasile* planted a Grove in his Garden of Friburge, **[page 93]** containing 600 Coc{c}as trees of 80 yeares groth and 50 foote high to any bough, which he brought upon[5] Floates & engines 4 miles, planting them so prosperously; that they bare aboundantly the very first yeare as *Gaspar Barlæus* has related in his description of that *Princes* expedition:[xviii] But this is a par-

---

5. **[Margin note]** Mons de Fiat Marishall France did the like etc.

ticular & extraordinary example, neither so practicalle nor usefull, we proceede then next to *Labyrinth* and *Dædales* which in English we meane by *Mazes*. They are made either by cutting them out of larger thicketts, or else are sowne & planted in formes and plotts contrived with the greatest intricacy, windings & meanders leading to a certaine Center in imitation of that famous Labyrinth of Creete so much celebrated by the Poets: One Aker of ground set out for this worke is capable of continuing a walke of a mile in circute provided the palisads or hedges be not over thick: But first they must be exactly plotted upon the Area, and then poled, or else sowne in trenches onely, the hedges frequently interserted with standard trees:

Let such a trench be a yard wide, & neere two foote deepe, casting the good mould (which is ever the first) upon one side, and the next on the opposite, two or three monethes before you plant for reasons already given: & when you plant remember to fling in the first earth next upon the rootes, & cover & fill up the trench with the rest of the mould, leaving the stemm of your plants, but a little out the earth; & yet ~~not~~ burring [burying] the roote as shallow as possibly you can, without exposing it too much, & which you shall the lesse feare, if you keepe them covered with some moyst stuffe, fearn or the like to secure them from the invasion of the Sunn, as you are already taught: & thus they may stand till they grow up, and are fit to forme into hedges, or be applied to the Palisads & *contr' Espalieres* as {we shall} hereafter ~~we shall~~ shew. For the Allees betweene the broadest neede not exceede 18 foote, and those of 12 are tollerable, but 9 is the leaste proportion: Be carefull not to suffer that they over hastily aspire & shoote up 'till the sides and the bottomes be well furnished: understanding this of hedges which are two or three foote in thicknesse; so as the grosse stemm of the plant be sufficiently hidden, easily effected by frequent cutting, pruning & clipping till they have attained 6. or 7 foote in height: In the meane time the standards of taller wood may be placed at 9. or 12. foote distance.

By *Cabinetts* we signifie Arbours & Summer houses {~~wheroff some are open &~~ ~~subdiales~~} if they be covered, *Pavillions* from their structure & use; *Cradles* are the shorter close walkes or higher **[page 94]** *Relievo's* {Domes} & Cupoles in the {Corridore} *Galleries* {Ambulationes of old} & longer close Walkes concamerated with foliage *sub Fornice viridi* for {shade &} inumbration; {these are properly *Pergolæ* which were either erect or camerated} And such they had of old, *Theocritus* [6] calls the worke τήν φυλλάδα; and in *Plinys* tyme some were covered, or rather lined beneath with the specularie stone, which we take to be a kind of *Talke*, & of this Specularia integumenta, Juvenal

> Quæ vehitur clauso latis specularibus antro.
>   Sat: 4. [21] cf

There were some of infinite cost, and no lesse ~~pleasure~~ {delight} to walke under & enjoy the verdure, though the weather were never so wett {& unpleasant} abroad.[7]

---

6. **[Margin note]** L: 17 36

7. **[Margin note]** under these they had of old Hamads or beds ment haply by the poet: 11: querno Instructosque thores obtentu frondis inumbrant. & here were the stibadia & herby benches {& beds stuffed} to eate upon in hott weather. [*Aen.* 10.66; text should read "extructosque toros"]

{My Ld: Bacon would have close walkes so placed & contrivd that blows the wind how it will, one may be in the lee of it.} They are all of them made after the same manner, either fram'd of quarters, or poles as you make Palisade hedges cancell'd at a foote square, and bound with wyre of what height the *Architect* will designe them: For *Close-walkes* 12 foote is a gracefull proportion for height, and *Cupolas* of the third poynt are very noble.

If you frame the worke of quarters, let the timber be of Oake, ~~sawed or~~ cleft of 6 inch Square which is best for lasting. This for the punchions: Fower Inches broad & 2 inch thick for the thwart pieces; spiked or pinn'd together & let in at such distances as may render it most firme & durable: But, as these are exceeding chargeable if the length & capacity of the worke be much; so are they nothing in our conceite so naturall and agreable as the former which do ~~do~~ not obscure so much of the foliage & verdure, and though they last not so long, yet they are easily repaired, & {do} many tymes before they decay support the plants so long, as being well governd, prun'd & plashed they are able to maintaine themselves, without impeaching their shape, & to stand with lesse frequent supporters.

For this worke poles of ground Ash & Chessnutt are the best: The stakes would be 5. or 6. inches about the collaterall 3. the breadth & height of the walkes to be proportiond as we formerly noted, ~~&~~ having reguard to the nature & groth of the plant which is to circumvest them.

Cabinetts, *Summer houses*, and *Pavillions* may be made of what dimensions you thinke fitt taking in the usuall cautions, & ~~in them there may be Niches~~ {may be contrived into squares}, Angles, Circles, or any other forme, adorn'd with *Niches*, in the verdure it selfe, for statues, Seates, Fountaines, Tables of Marble, chaires of the Antique fashion the feete resembling {the leggs of} Lyons, Goates etc[.] These **[page 95]** Cabinets may be also Cupola'd above, open or close in the center to let in a gloomy light, or they may be canopied with Ivy at excessive heights, as we remember to have seene it at *Verona*; also with *Fenestrages*, Windows, one or more porches: {I have seene them coverd by one tree, as Elme, Lime, etc: by half cutting the branch & bending them down in forme of an umbrilla, & so stayd at fitting distance by straite quarters thus **[continued in margin] [illustration, see Fig. 22]** so as tis placed in the middle of a circle has been the cover & the seats made about the stem; & a single Hornebeame which covers a seate in the Garden of H–Court perplex'd as it is the very imitable}

We have already spoaken in Chap: 6 concerning the hedging & palisading of those ~~Ambulationes~~ subdiale Ambulatories & open Walkes, calld by *Vitruvius Hypæthras*, & whose sides are the *Camerary pergulas* whither covered or erect; ~~And per~~ though pergolas are also such Bowers, as are covered with Vines, frequent in every Garden; therefore we passe them over here briefly and for their furniture reccommend our Gardiner to what we have sayd about planting of hedges for Labyrinths etc with this repetition onely, that Galleries and all covered Walkes must be made much narrower then the open, and the trench made neere a foote from the *Palisades* which should be droven into the firme ground, the poynts prepard & hardned {in fire} and pitched so farr as they are to penetrate the earth. {But these hedges are to be reduced into 3 sorts 1 so high as to termin at the sight a second sort parapet high so as to leane over, a 3d very low & dwarfish **[continued in margin]** so as onely to divide the quarters not hinder sight freely:

And though (as has bin shewed) any of these Relievos may be planted & covered

Figure 22. A plane tree at Hampton Court Palace, illustrated in margin at page 95.

with such shrubbs & plants as grow frequently in the woods, & loose their leaves in winter, such as *Birch, Elme, Hornebeame, Maple* etc yet are none of these comparable to those which are perpetually greene: Yet the Granade, white Jessamine, dubble white rose, Lilacs {Woodbynd} and some {few} other ~~annually greene~~ shrubbs may be admitted for variety, & sweetenesse: The same we hold also of Labyrinth, and for the under {under} woods, ~~and~~ thicketts & *Vepreta* of Groves consisting of Tall trees, such as Oake, Elme, Beech, Chessnutt, Service etc, the ground whereoff we would have {in some places} planted with all sorts of greene and pleasant shrubbs, Simples, Flowers, such as will thrive in the shade, as Cowslips, Prim–roses, Violets, Strawberries, Hurtles, Pinkes, Wood Sorrell, also with Rosemary, bays, knee holly & *Agrifolia*, white thorne & hawes to invite the birds, and for Covert, not forgetting frequent Woodbynd & Sweetebrier: For thus have we sometymes beheld a very tall wood of ~~dry~~ {goodly} Trees {whose leaves had forsaken them} having in the middest of winter an under wood or Coppse of perenniall Greenes, no lesse divertissant to the eye in that cold {& naked} season then coole fresh & usefull in the heate of Summer.

But it dos wonderfull add to the sollomne venerablenesse of Taller Groves if in some place neere the Center, the Trees be planted, or abated ~~in a large~~ so as to reppresent a large and goodly *Circus* ressembling some *Amphitheatre*;[8] as in other parts of the wood lesser naturall Arbours such as the *poet* describes ~~when~~ **[page 96]** in his tempting Bower of blisse.

> Where in the thickest covert of that shade
> There was a pleasant Arbour, not by art,
> But of the trees owne inclination made,
> Which knitting their ranke branches part to part,
> With wanton Ivy twine tangled a thwart
> And Eglantine, & Caprifole emony
> Fashion'd above within the inmost part
> That neither Phoebus beames could through them throng
> Nor Æolus sharp blast could worke them any wrong
> > Spenc Lib: 2. Cant: 12.

The proper ornaments of these are the statues of Eremites, Narides, {Orpheus} Pans, Satyres; the resemblances of Lyons, Beares, {Wolves} Foxes, {Goates, Boares etc} cutt out artificially in stone and painted (for in no other case admitt we of painted statues a barbarity unpardonable in the Arte) to be placed amongst the thicketts, & at the mouth of Caves, naturall or artificiall Grotts, over growne with mosse & Ivy; ~~naturall~~ Insitions upon the barke of the smother trees, inscrib~~ing~~{ed} with names, sentences, verses,[9] etc, {tease the fantsy} do much contribut to the sweete & melancholy delight of Groves; & which is greately reinforced by some fountaines comming

---

8. **[Margin note]** & in some the Romans had Hippodromi or Menagers planted about with trees, as may be learned out of Pliny, & in his description of his Thusia cf. M. [indecipherable]

9. **[Margin note]** as that of Virgil out of Theocritus – tenerisque meos incidere amores arboribus: [*Eclog.* 3.103] crescent illæ crescentis amores [*Eclog.* 10.54]

out of the naturall rock, or precipitating from some roaring Cascade, with mossie
bankes, glades, and Valles (for it is better if such tall woods grow upon variety of uneven grounds) bare {of bushes} at bottome for a good distance, and giving now and
then a through passage to your Eye into the subjacent {sceanes of} meadows, lakes,
ponds, & collines; not to say much at present of Sepulchers, Oratories, & whatsoever
~~may~~ {dos} render it sacred & sollomne, & such as may best compose the mind for
devotion and ~~serious~~ profoundest contemplation.

And amongst the former Relievos of *Statues* for this and other furniture both of
woods & ~~Gardens the other~~ severall parts of Gardens, ~~is to be reckoned up~~ {we are not
to omitt} [10]the *Topiary* art {Topium} or Tunsa Viridaria as {Vitruvius &} Pliny calls
them, invented first by that greate favourite of *Augustus Cn: Matius a Roman knight*:
& celebrated by the Antients Topiarium laudavi, ita omnia convestiuit hedera. says
Cic: ad Quintum Fr: For ~~of~~ {in} this worke we find they were wont to reppresent their
Deorum Simulacra, the *Trojan Warrs & Adventures of Ulysses*: And in our {latter} Ages
it has bin much used, both abroad & in England, wittnesse his *Majesties* Gardens at
Hampton Court **[page 97]** the quicksetts whereoff were cutt in the shapes of severall
Animals, the Kings Armes etc: & so {it} was in the Gardens of severall noble persons;
but none of these comparable to those of *Monsr: Chandelar* neere *Chartres* in *France*
where the Hedges & frames of Box and other greenes ~~hedges~~ were shorn into the
shapes of the 7 *Wisemen*, *Hercules* Labours, the 3 *Graces*, *Convivia Deorum*, *Accubitus
Romanorum*, *Busts*, Statues, ~~&~~ heads, {Castles, Battlements} & *Pyramids* innumerable:
So as in some places his Garden reppresented an Army etc. {which **[continued in
margin]** calls to my mind the Gyants plac'd before the Physical Garden at Oxford ~~as~~
{because} celebrated by that witty poem (whoever was Author) which begins *Although
no brandish'td Cherubins are here / Yet sons of Adam venture not too neere etc*:} Although to
speake our thoughts, we do least of all esteeme this kind of ornament, as being both
chargeable & tedious to maintaine, & for the most part, through neglect or art in the
Gardiner lamely & wretchedly reppresented, and therefore, but sparingly to be introduced, and never to be formed of any materiall which cannot supporte themselves
without sticks & frames which are continually starting and at fault. If any {Myrtle}
Juniper, yuf, {pyracanth, privet} & Box are the best of the greenes, & of the drye
shrubbs the ~~Privet~~ white–thorne. {of which may be made knobbs, & piramids at the
corner of bedds, which also my Ld: Bacon approves:}

Lastly, to Topiarium belongs also Cabinets, ~~and~~ Closewalkes, and the open,
whose hedges are kept {& formed} by the shearer {heretofore} a peculiar {Gardners}
trade ~~called eith~~ {&} amongst the Romans called *Topiarij*[11] so difficult & singular it
was then esteemed; and thus we have beheld Men, Horses, {divers beasts &} foule,
& ill made & deforming ~~a~~ good Gardns though we do not alltogether decrie the
moderat use of this worke, especially in Pyramids, Globes, Embossements, Battlements, Nieches, Skreenes & Triumphall Arches, magnificent & very noble ornaments

---

10. **[Margin note]** Vitr: L: 1: c. 5. Nat: Hist: L: 6. c.16. Plin. Jun ~~Epist~~ in severall
Epistles

11. **[Margin note]** of which Vitruvius L: 1. c: 5. speaks of reppresentations of
the Trojan Warr the story of Ulysses etc: all much in that worke so antient it seemes
it was

skillfully ~~and~~ erected & govern'd with care; that the Columns, Architraves, Freezes, & Corniches etc; be first framed, of polles, or quarters {with exact Symmetrie according to Arte, the more delicat flexed parts for ribbs of beasts {skelettons for} men etc: of Haizell ~~pee~~ peel'd & smoked in Winter, & all bound with wyre etc:}, & then planted with ever greenes, as we once saw a very noble skreene of this worke at the entry of a Garden at *Caen* in *Normandy*, and indeede their propper places are at the *Vestibuls*, & entries into particular Gardens & Enclosures that the eye may not on the suddaine be let into the view of the whole.

Lastly, there ~~*Pinacothecas*~~ {Peristyles} and Relievos of stone for {pinacothecas of} statues, Vasas, Columns & repositories of rarities, in which there is many tymes employed aboundance of Art & Measure, ~~whether errected~~ built & carved of stone, & with ranges of Pillars & pillasters, arched towards the parterrs, & to be ascended by some few stepps, paved with Marble & pietra comessas {& emblematic worke} below, & painted ~~afres~~ a fresca on the vault: Flat & balustraded above all {with the podial & merione} from {which} Aerie one may take a view of the whole Garden. In these stand the most precious marbles & statues partly on pedestalls twix the Intercollumniation, & partly in {Thecas or} Niches in the **[page 98]** dead wall opposite to them with frequent cases of Orange Trees & other delicious Ever greenes interposed, then which nothing can be more delicious & magnificent for Sommer refreshment: And some of these are but the Porticos to Greater Repositories, ~~bui~~ which are built of two or 3 storys high serving for {Musick roomes} *Liberaries, & Chimelias* of rare Pictures & naturall Curiosities, dispos'd in Galleries, ~~&~~ chambers & clossetts, all of them disjoynd from the Palace or Mansion of the Owner, & sometymes built in the middle or some remoter part of the Garden, encompassed with groves etc, & serving for a most sweete Retirement at the pleasure of the Master. Examples of all which we have very frequently in the Italian Gardens, and especially the noble Villas of Aldobrandinos, Mont'altos, Ludovisios etc. The orthography whereoff we give in the ensuing figures, with some other inventions for Terraces, Peristyles & Repositories of this nature, leaving the particular members to the skillfull Architect, upon whose province we thinke not fit to usurpe on this occasion, & {for that} there are other Relievos of which we shall speake in the following chapters, whilst we conclude the ~~Catalogue~~ present, with this Catalogue, and some necessary directions concerning Trees and shrubbs for the planting of Groves, Cabinetts, Closewalkes, & other Relievos of this nature, ~~& of~~ which we have ~~spoaken at~~ bin the Subject of this discourse.

Abeal or white Poplar, {Acatia} Ash, Asp, Alder, Beech, Birch, Barbery, Sweete Brier, Chesse–nutt, Chery–black, {bird cherry} Elme, Filbert, [~~indecipherable~~]. Haisell, Witch Haisell, {or Quic–beam} Haw, Hornebeame, {Horse Chessnutt} Jassmine, Lime, Maple, Mulbery, Oake, Platanus, Poplar, Pomegrand, ~~Quick–beame~~, Service, Sloe, Sicomor, [blank space] Wall–nutt, Willow, Wood–bynd, Vines. {Of these proper for Walks are the Oake, Elme, lime, Chessnutt & Alaternus, above all which though hardly raised of seedes with us, comes very well of layers, & the horse–chessnutt is next: Of these, the Ash, Mulbery and Wall–nutt may be forborne in Groves, because {the two first} ~~they~~ are late ere they put forth their leaves and shead them early; & for the most part the Wallnut is an extravagant tree, & suffers nothing to thrive under its shade, which by some is also esteemed unwholesome {but falsley}; yet being planted at greate distances if they be choice & straite trees, they become the approches & avenues of places ~~very~~ {admirably} well, are profitable and of stately as-

pect: The Shade of the Ash is also held **[page 99]** unpropitious, ~~whatever~~ {however}
the poet has celebrated it

> Fraxinus in Syluis, pulcherrima Pinus in hortis
> Virg: [*Eclog.* 7.65–68]

The Sycomore leafe falls early, and being very broad & spongy extreamely foules the
walkes, though otherwise not to be despised. The Willow and Alder are fitter for
Boggs & marshy places: but preferrable to all the forementiond for Groves are the
Oake, Lime, Elme, Chessnutt, Beech, Service, etc. Trees proper for Walkes, Cabinetts
& Palisads, are the Hornebeame, which furnishes with leaves to the foote, and may
be kept shorne; straite plants being set at ~~a yard~~ {one foote} distance, they last very
long, & do not grow extravagant being thus governd[.]

That goodly Espallier Walke in Luxembourg at Paris is made of this Tree. Maple
likewise and Elme are fitt for this worke, we have seene very tall trees of Elme plashed
and thicknd like a hedge of 40 foote high, by which has bin made an extraordinary
fence against the wind & weather, far exceeding any Walke whatsoever.[12] {They also
set Cypresse at every 10 foote distance amongst the palisads of Hornebeame **[con-
tinued in margin]** which being suffered to grow round or square, seem like so many
peers or pilasters, though I do not in other cases allow the mixture of falling & perenial
leaves but in hedges of ever greens all such relievos, especially if of ~~another~~ {different}
colour do very well. These Palisads they also clip taper which furnishes & fortifies
the mould but so makes perpendicular ~~here insert the discourse of Trees given by
you to the Society for the Commissioners of the Navy. 1662 October.~~ Examine these
by the Herbal} The rest, especially the Birch, Asp, Quickbeame {Haisell} etc may be
intermingled in groves for thickett & variety, with frequent Woodbynd & Thorne
for Vepreta etc. If the Grove consist of one sort alone (which we do not condemne)
Oake or Beech are most pleasant; Chess–nutt and Birch for a neede; To the former
more plyable uses may be added Jessamine, Filbert, Senna, Tamaris, Pome–granade,
Syrinx or pipetree of both colours. The Guelder & all sorts of other Roses.

Ever–greenes[xix]
Arbores semper Virentes

Accommodable for Groves *Cypresseta, Myrteta, Daphnenes* etc: which ought to be
plantations apart from the taller Woods of Dry trees, and neerer ~~to the~~ in prospect to
the Mansion not farr from the Parterre are the severall kinds of *Abies* or *Firr, Alaternus,
Arbutus, Arbor vitæ, sive Thuyæ, Agrifolium,* Holly, *Buxus, Cupressus, Carube sive siliqua
dulcis, Cedrus, Conifera Libani, Ilex glandifera, Ilex coccigera sive Kermes, Juniper,* {maj: &

---

12. **[Insertion on separate piece of paper]**

In palisads {or hedges} of Evergreenes the Cypresse especialy: let the Gardner
be curious ~~about~~ to plant onely the femals which do not agree in this worke, by reason of the different tenore of their branches; the males growing {more} ~~up ward~~ out
ward & collaterall, the female erect, ~~&~~ they may be distinguished by the leafe {ever}
where & have it some what resembling lig: vitæ:

minor} *Laurus dommestica,* or common bays, *Cæcarea, Indica, Pinus,* wild Bay, *Rosea, Nerium* or *Oleander, Laura, Cerusus* or *Cherry bay, Lentiscus,* The *Orange, Limon, Citron, Myrtills* of severall sorts, *Olea, Phillyrea, Picea, Pinus, Pinaster* or *Pseudopinus, Pyracantha, Sabina* or *Cedrus Baccata, Suber* The Corke, *Taxus,* ~~Tamari~~ *Terebinthus,* and sundry others as more amply in Cap: 15{4} {where we have countd them alphabetically & with the varieties.}

Fructices & shrubs *Semper virentes*

Chamærrhudendros Alpigena Dwarfe Rose Bay of the Alps **[page 100]** *Celastrus, Cistus,* Holly, Rose, *Cneorum Mathioli* white rockrose: *Dorycinium Monspeliensium, Erica,* Heath *omnis generis, Genista,* Hispan: Hedera *Jasminum, Oxycedrus Phœnicea,* crimson prickly cedar *Rosmarinus, Ruscus, sive Bruscus* knee holme, *Sabina Scorpius sive genista Spinosa,* Fuzzes, *Seseli Æthiopicum frutex. Clematis* Daphnoeides perevincia, Smilax aspera. And many others {Se cap: 14:} To be planted & set amongst those, and to cover the ground under both the taller trees & shrubbs, in Groves & thickets of Perenniall greenes, take these following.

Frutices et Herbæ Semper virentes

Aloe folio mucroniato, prickly sea house leeke, *Alipum montis Ceti* herb terrible, *Barba Jovis,* silver bush. *Chamælea tricoccos, sive oleago vel oleustellus,* Widow wail, [13]*Chamælea Germanica, sive mezereon, Chamærriphus,* little wild date tree. *Cepea Paucij, Cytisus semper virens,* evergreene shrub trefoile, *Cytisus Maranthæ sive cornutus, Halymus,* sea purslan, *Ladon, Ladanum, Laurus, Alexandrina sive hyppoglossum,* hors tongue, *Laureola, Opuntia, sive ficus Indica, Sedum arborescens, semper vivum majus stachia Monspeliensium, Tarton raire, Thymelea, Tragacantha,* goats thorn, *Viscum,* Miseltoe. [14]*Yucca.* etc: See C: 14

Herbæ Semper virentes *Abrotonum femina,* {*Absynthium*} *Anonis sive Resta Bovis, Amaracus, Borago Semper virens, Capillus veneris, Caryophullus, Caryophyllus marinus, Cepæa Paucij, Chamædrus sive Teucrium, Chamemelum, Chelidonium majus, Cneorum albus olea folio, Coclearia, Crithmum marinum* Sampier, *Jacobea marina, Hissopus, Lavandula, sive stoechas, Leucoium, Malva arborescens, Majoram rotundo folio, Nasturtium, Pimpinella, Psyllium, Pulegium, Ruta, Salvia, Satyreja sempiterna radice, Sedum diversi generis, Sterpillum, Viola Lutea,* and many others. {Of all which See C: 14:} For with divers of these may the whole ground be covered, and if the various coloured *Larkes–heeles* be sowne amongst them here and there, it will raise (together with *Primroses, Cowslips, Violets, Pansys,* {*Strawberries*} *dubble Daisies* etc) such an embroderie as will extreamely affect and delight the beholder; and besides they do at first serve to suppresse the {subnascent} weedes and grasse.

[Page 101] Such of these Greenes as grow shrubbie, and are portable in cases, may be set in the conservatory in such order as (according to the capacity of the place) to make Walkes and Allees betweene their ranges: As the *Oranges, Citrons, Limons, Arbutus, Myrtills, Granads, Cedars, Ilex, Oleander, Pinaster* with those other lower shrubbs, which will not endure the cold and exposure; to be set in potts and vasas amongst them by a uniforme order. We remember to have once seene a very large Grove of Orange trees, which, with infinite paines, were thus ranged in a vast Conservatory, and in the Sommer set abroad in such order as they took up some Ackers

---

13. **[Margin note]** Buxus arbor auratus apicibus auratus Chamæ–buxus
14. **[Margin note]** Vermicularis frutex.

of ground, all of them in cases: we have already spoken of Myrtle, which is a very old tree, that has never bin housed for above 20 yeares, to encourage the hardy education of ~~some~~ plants for some generations: {but they thrive best neere the Sea, it is venus tree, & venus orta mar} The *Fir, Pine, Cedar, Arbutus, Laurell, Bay, Cypresse, Yuf, Box, Juniper, Phylerea, Alaternus, Spanish broome,* ~~Balsame~~ {*Savine*}, *Privet* resist all weathers: For *Palisade–hedges,* and *Contr'Espaliers Cabinets, Closewalkes, Mazes* etc there is none to be compared to the *Alaternus's* of severall sorts which we first brough[t] into use and reputation for these workes in England: The *Agrifolium* exceedes all ~~the Ever~~ {the perenniall} greenes whatsoever for hedges of Service. They are to be raised of seede like hawes, and are entertaind at what height one pleases without frames or Palisads to support them; in summe they exceede all walls or fences whatsoever, eternally verdant, and decor'd with a naturall Corralle, ~~the~~ berrys which make both a glorious shew, and invite the birds: A Grove of *Lawrell* alone will become of wonderfull stature if suffered to grow in standards, and Bays will aspire to a prodigious stature if dilligently cultivated: Groves of *Cypresse* do rarely well, and may be governd without poles {or binding} by frequent topping the master & middlemost stemm, & clipping the ~~leaves~~ branches. Thus for the *Cypresseta.* But for Palisads they must be planted within a foote & halfe of each other and shorne flatt by line; & than this there is nothing more beautifull for hedges and walkes. The *Pyracanth,* is a stout fence, but its leafe is of an unpleasant greene, and too extravagant; *Juniper* may be governd in all respect like *Cypresse,* both for the standard in Groves or hedges, & will mount to a considerable stature provided the ground about his rote be well cultivated & loosned. *Yuf* will be formed and spread **[page 102]** into most beautifull hedges; and be shaped into any forme of *Topiary* worke; and so with *Box* of all the tonsile shrubs the most susciptible of formes, and usefull, were it not much impeached by the rankenesse of its smell. Ivy must be perpetually supported, but is of incomparable use and ornament, conducted by pillars, and sustain upon *Cupolas* of yron rodds, or the bigger sort of Wyre to an excessive height: And most of these forenamed trees, shrubbs, etc may be either planted at 3 yeares groth, or to be sure, sowen within a foote of the Palisades, carefully {shaded} weeded, and thinned {at first} where they rise too thick and confusedly; But above all, let the Gardiner be carefull not to suffer his young plants to gett head over hastily, till they are sufficiently furnished at the foote, which is the grace of these ever–greene ~~hedges~~ operations. This also we thinke fit to caution, that he at no hand admitt of any plant which sheads its leafe, to be mixed with his perenniall verdures; because it would be a very greate deformation to the rest, make a gapp, and looke like a patch ill sorted in a new and fresh garment. We advertise againe that it is a grosse mistake of divers, & a tradition ill understood, that the *Cypresse* is never to be cutt, but keepe them poled, and bound up, which heates and destroyes the tree; whereas they may be clipped, topped, & moderately cutt into any shape, and are better maintained without a stake (which is a very considerable charge {& trouble} where groves of them are planted) by shortning at *Spring,* and *Autumne* the middle branches, and clipping the collateral, circling some very extravagant parts with a wyre if neede be, from 3 foote to 3 foote; and thus they will thrive, and grow furnished to the foote, which is most gracious, and aspire to a greate height; ~~though~~ especially if the place where they grow be anything secured from the Northern and Eastern winds: For so you shall observe, that in Gardens they flourish exceedingly, till they come to peepe above the Walles; and verily 15. and 20 foote yea ten, is {a} very gracefull and sufficient {height} for the *poynts, internodiums* and heads of *Terraces,*

Parterrs, Beds, etc: for *Palisad hedges* 12 is competent, and to sustaine them well either of *Cypresse, Granade, Alaternus, Jessamine, Roses, Rosemary* etc: unlesse **[page 103]** they be planted by dubble rowes, it will be requisite to supporte them, and to keepe the more tender branches in order by passing a wyre along at every 3 foote, as you perceive there is occasion. Two foote of *Granatts* make incomparable hedges; of which there is one in the *Thuilleries* at *Paris* of a very greate length: To entertaine them well rather prune ~~then en~~ {& cut} then clip them, taking away all the superfluous wood before they be plashed & sometymes in ~~the~~ very sharp winters they must be covered with hurdles made of matts, like other tender shrubbs. Finally there may temporary & most beautifull palisade walkes, *Cabinets* & other *Relievos* be made of the *Virginian Ivy*, with divers sorts of *Gourds* & *Calibasses*, which with their umbrageous leaves & goodly fruite will twine, & climb & circle about the frames making a wonderfull & glorious effect. {The statues proper for groves are more especially {Orpheus} Pans, Fawns & Satyrs all the Sylvernia numina:}

And thus have we finished what we thought necessary to the direction of planting artificiall *Groves, Walkes*, & other *Relievos* of that nature, **[text to bottom of page crossed out]** for so we propose to distinguish betweene those stately & majesticall shades of huge Oakes & other goodly trees ~~crowning the~~ adorning our *Elysium* & crowning the brows of lofty hills, such as were never prophaned by the inhumanity of edge tooles; woods that none know the ~~planting~~ {setting} of, like the goodly *Cedars* of Libanus *Arbores dei* ~~& take~~ according to the Hebrew, and such as are {as much}[15] to be preferred before {all} the little trifling plantations of the lesser inclosures, as they exceede them in stature and the most venerable Antiquity. ~~Neither~~ let it {not then} seeme tedious or impertinent to the present discourse, if to reinforce our esteeme of these goodly ~~Groves & venerable~~ shades, we deduce things from their originall, and historise a little concerning *Groves*, the choycest & most sacred of all the *Hortulan* delights. {~~as we are able to make out the very first enclosures, comprehending mountain & fountaine, as of a peculiar sanctity, & the old sense~~}

To take it {then} in order. The name of Lucus Quintilian & others, derive, *quod parum luceat* because of its thicknesse. {~~for that a mi~~}

nullo penetrabilis astro.

where Apuleius used *Lucum sublucidum*, & the *Poets sublectris umbra*: others have taken it for light in the *Masculine*, because there they first kindle fires by what accident unknowne

Seu coeli fulmine misso,
Sive quod inter se bellum silvestre gerentes,
Hostibus intulerant ignem formidinis ergo
etc: [1244–1246]
Whither it were
By lightning sent from heaven, or else there
The Savage Men in mutuall warrs, and fight

---

15. **[Margin note]** 103. psal: 6

Had set the woods on fire, their foes t'affright
Or whether the trees set fire of{n} themselves
Mutua dum inter se rami; stirpesque teruntur.
Whilst clashing boughs thwarting each other frett.

Luc: L: 5.

or haply to {burne their} sacrifice, whence the *Comoedian*, cum primo Lucu ibi hinc.
Terent: Adelph: [5.3.55] {but the poet speaking of Juno says: ~~we will leave it to the gramarians~~

    Gratæ Lucinæ: dedit hæc tibi nomina lucus
{whilst as if she had imposd the name} ~~The poet speaking of Juno &~~ {the} ~~Lupercal was sacred to Pan and there Romulus & Remus sucked the wolf:~~
~~But~~} then againe *Luce* differed from *Nemora* by the silent, private & more sollemne Religion *Sylva* in *Cicero* is used for *Hortus*, but it is to signifie such a Grove as we have already described, adorn'd with statues, and other curiosities; or, as *Asconius* interprets it, *Viridarium*. ~~Then againe Nemus & Sylva differ~~; but ~~we will contract these~~ {why doe we multiplie} Criticisms.

    {In Summ} *Luci* were manes *consiti & numquam celui*, so *Cic: de leg* and were venerable for ~~their~~ amtiquity of their groth: **[page 104 crossed out to end of page]** hence *Quintilian* calls them *Sacros ex vetustate* {But you shall have it sumarily [xx] ~~For~~ certaine it is that such were consecrate to pious uses, and that not onely by superstitious persons to the *Gods* and *Heroes*: but the *Patriarchs* themselves did *ab initio* (as 'tis presum'd) retire to such places to compose their meditations, and celebrate their sacred mysteries, both of prayer and sacrifices; following the traditions of the *Gomerites*, the *Nephews of Noah*, who first inhabited *Galatia* after the Deluge where 'tis sayd the Druyds (whose very name imports an Oake) did derive their originall: for without doubt ~~it was from them that~~ *Abraham* did but imitate what the children of God had practised before him, when he planted himselfe at the *Quercetum* of [16]*Mambre*: Gen: 13., {~~& spent afterward constructing built a chapell in honor of the 3 Angels that appeard to this Patriarch~~} but more expressely when removing thence after he had confirm'd the league with *Abimelch* 21. Gen, and settled his abode at Barsheba, he design'd a certaine place for Gods divine service: And there the text says. *he planted a Grove and called upon the name of the Lord* etc: that is, saith *Card. Cajetan*,[xxi] he ~~errected~~ founded a Chapell for himselfe & his Family: {~~To this Grotius~~ **[continued in margin]** ~~upon the woods, (Subter quercum 24 Jos: 26 illam~~} We reade likewise of the Oake or Tuffet of Trees when Abraham came to מורה אלון Elon moreh *ad Con vallem illustrium*; but whither that were such a Grove, in which the *High-priest* reposited the stone after his exhortation 24 Jos: 26 we dare not determine. Under an *Oake* says the text, it grew neere the sanctuary, & probably it was as also that which *Jacob* the grandchild of *Abraham* consecrated by the buriall of his beloved *Rebecca* 35 Gen: *Sacra Nemora*; for tis evident by the Context that God appeared there againe to him.[17] And here because we have mentioned *Rebecca*

---

16. **[Margin note]** Euseb: Eccles: hist: L: 1: c. 18.

17. **[Margin note]** and Grotius is positive upon that word (subter quercum) illam ipsam (says he) cuius mersio Gen.: 35. 4. in historia Jacobi et Judd. 9 . 6. ~~Jo l~~ & adds Is locus honorem Jacobi diu pro templo fuit.

the learned we cannot lett passe, what the Learned observe, concerning the custome for the prophets & inspired of old to sleepe upon the boughs of Trees *ad consulendum Deum.* to aske advise of God: The *Laurell* and *Agnus Castus* (trees which did greately compose the phansy, and facilitate true visions as 'twas believ'd) for the Laurell is held particularly efficacious πρòς τοùς Ἐνθουσιασμοùς as ({Hesiod} T̶h̶i̶o̶c̶r̶i̶t̶u̶s̶ has it, to inspire a poetic furie) And such a tradition then goes of *Rebecca* in imitation of her Father in Law; the instance is [18]recited out of an antient *Ecclesiasticall hist* by *Abulensis*, and that hence the *Delphic Tripos, Dodonæan* Oracle in *Epire* & such other might receive their originall, for *Sathan* was allways Gods Ape, instituting his *Groves, Altars, Sacrifices* & many other sacred rites of the people of God: For even o̶f̶ {at} this Decubation upon boughs *Juvenal* seemes to hint: Sat: 6 [543–545]

> *Arcanum Judæa tremens mendicat in aurem*
> *Interpres Legum Solymarum et magna Sacerdos*
> *Arboris ac summi fida internuntia coeli*

Meaning by the Interpreter *Moses*, and p̶e̶r̶ ̶t̶a̶b̶u̶ by the Tree, the [19]Oracle of God: & *Claudius* expresses the manner 26.[18–19]

> *Cæso Tomini Jovis augure luco*
> *Arbore præsaga tabulas animasse loquaces*

For the Delphic Oracle (as Di[o]dor[us]: Sic[ulus]: L: 16 tells us) was first made o̶f̶ *e Lauri ramis* & The *folia aduertis in specus modum* etc[.] But we hasten, all this being to shew onely h̶o̶w̶ {where} the *Gentiles* first derived their superstitions, & that it was from the people of God that they received these antient Traditions.

[page 104a crossed out to end of page] For, *Hi fuere* (says Pliny speaking of Groves) *quondam* [20] *Numinum templa, priscoque ritu Simplici̶o̶r̶a̶ ꝼ{ j}ura, etiam nunc deo præcellentem Arborem dicant: nec magis, auro fulgentia atque ebore simulachra, quam lucos, et in ijs silentia ipsa adoramus* etc: where he reckons up particular[.] And the *Chaldean Theologues* & other Estern people did much resort to these places,[21] retaining (as we shewd but now), divers of their Rites & some opinions, agreeable to the primitive truth, how ever vitiated by the deceipt of {that great fantic} *Sathan*, who converted all into superstition.[xxii] For when they were afterwards consecrated by *Faunus*, he set up his Oracles openly in the Groves, and the Heathen *Oratories* were called *Fana*, whence that of *Plautus. In duo luco Fanoque esse*, became a proverb (says *Donatus*) importing the being in anothers power & disposall; for they were of old *Asyla* also, & had the privileges of *Sanctuaries*, as appears out of Livy, where, whosoever fled to them had protection, & here Ovid

---

18. **[Margin note]** Hieron: in Tradit: Heb: 3. Reg. c. 4.
19. **[Margin note]** in panagyr:
20. **[Margin note]** L.12. c. 1. [12.2]
21. **[Margin note]** especialy the Persians who as Pliny: L: 16 c: 43. used the Oake in all their mysterious rights. **[Insertion indicated but not present]**

Romulus ut Saxo Lucum circumdedit alto,
Quilibet huc dixit, confuge, tutus eris.
Fastor. [3.431–432]

{We also reade of the *Nemorale Templum* of the suburban Diana etc, that is the Diana Aricina.[xxiii] The Mysteries which the famous *Druids* performed in their[22] groves & under trees, we may reade at large out of {Cæsar &} *Pliny*[23] {Strabo, Diodorus} *Amianus Marcellinus* & divers others[xxiv] nor are they at this[24] present ceased, for the *Indian Brachmans*, descend from[25] the old Gymnosophists extreamely devoted to the Woods: *Pythagoras*[26] 'tis believed instituted his silent & *Monasticall* Colledges[27] from this sect of Philosophers, & learned from them much of that which he afterwards taught his Schollars: All which we[28] have produced onely to shew, how reverent an estemation the Antients universally had of Groves, and good reason

Habitarunt Dij quoque Syluis.[xxv]
Virg. [*Eclog.* 2.60]

To whom as we shew'd they were perpetually consecrated; for their age and perenniall viridity says *Diodorus*, or for that the use of Trees, had bin taught them by the Gods, or some famous persons whom, for their worth & saience they esteemed as Gods, not to trouble our selves much with the conceite of those who would have men to spring {from them[xxvi] ~~yet~~ {Hence} the poets included a dryad ~~in~~ or Nymph in every tree, whose tuition they had {& who lived & dyed with the tree, but} the Hamadryadi ~~but~~ remov'd upon occasion from place to place & were immortal[.][29] Here {infra} we must therefore mention the Dodonean or Vocal Forest neere Chaonia, whose Temple is ~~fa~~ celebrated by Pliny; & the miraculous fountain by Lucretius:[30]} **[page 105 crossed out to end of page]** out of Trees, according to that of Papinius [Statius *Theb* 4.280–281]

---

22. **[Margin note]** Com lib: 5.
23. **[Margin note]** Pli: L: 16.
24. **[Margin note]** Pli: L: 16.
25. **[Margin note]** Stra: Geo L: 4; Dio: Ser: L: 5.
26. **[Margin note]** Mela:
27. **[Margin note]** Apul: L: 1.
28. **[Margin note]** Lucan: [indecipherable] L: 2.
29. **[Insertion on bottom of page]** And here I might inlarge **[insertion indicated but not present]** with strange stories of their breaking out & appearing to men, & interceeding for the {standing &} life of a tree, when they have ben cutting or destroying woods, or some eminent ~~tree~~ antient tree of which you may see the poet Callimachus Hymn: in delum, Pausanias in Phoc: & Arcad: & the fam'd story of Panabius related by Apollonius in c 2: Argonaut: who tell of the Aparition of severall such Nymphs on such occasions, & of the terrible disasters insewed those who destroyed these trees etc:
30. **[Margin note]** Plin: L: 2: c. 103 Lucretius: L: 6:

> ac populus umbrosa creauit
> Fraxinus et foeta viridis puer excidit orno.

or the ~~fabulous~~ conversions of Ovid, the *Vocall Forest* & other fictions: {But to proceede with the reverred account the Antients had of them.}

The *Minturrensian* Grove was esteem'd ~~so~~ venerable that no stranger might be admitted into it, and the greate *Xerxes* himselfe when he passed through *Archaia* would
not touch a Grove which was dedicated to *Jupiter*, commanding his Army to doe it no
violence. The like they did when the *Persians* were put to flight by *Pausanias*; though
they might have sav'd their lives by it as appeares by the story: *Hercules* would not so
much as tast the waters of the *Ægerian* Groves after he slewe *Cacus* though extreamely
thursty: heare the *Priest* speaking

> *Puniceo canas stamine vincta comas*
> *parce oculis hospes lucoque abscede verendo*
> *cede agedum, et tuta limina lingue fuga*
> *Interdicta viris metuenda lege piatur*
> *Di tibi dent alios fontes*
>   Propert: L. 4. [8.52–55, 59]

Nor in such places durst they hunt, unlesse it were to kill something for a Sacrifice as
Avianus tells us; whence *Strabo* reports that {in the *Æolian* Grove dedicated to Diana}
the beasts were so tame that the *Wolves* & *Staggs* fed together like lambs, and would
follow a man licking his hands as he walked without any feare: Such a Grove was also
the *Cretonian*, in which Livy writes there was a spatious field ~~full peopled~~ stored with
all sorts of wild Beasts ~~who fed together~~ situate in the very middle of the wood: {But
{~~we also speake of~~} ~~Diana had likewise the suburbanæ templum Nemorale Dianæ, or~~
~~the Diana~~} There were a world of Groves sacred to *Jupiter*, ~~and~~ *Juno*, & to *Apollo*, especially that which was called *Epidaphnes*, neere the *Syrian Antioch* which was a most incomparable pleasant one, full of Fountaines and rare statues, admirably planted. There
was to be seene the *Laurell*, which had bin his beloved *Daphne*: And in the navell of it,
was his *Temple* and *Asylum*, where afterwards *Cosroes*, and *Julian* did sacrifice ~~at~~ {upon}
severall occasions, as *Eusebius* the *Ecclesiasticall* {historian} ~~writer~~ reports; but ~~h~~ could
obtaine no answer of the *Oracle*, because the holy *Babylas* lay buried neere the place;
for which respect it was reputed so reverent ~~as pe~~ that there is an expresse Title in co
Justin: *lod: de Cupressis ex luco Daphnes non excidendis, vel venundandis*, that none should
dare either to fell, or sell any of the Trees about it, & which *decree* the Emp: Arcadius
did afterwards confirme.[31]

Besides these, famous were the Groves of *Minerva*, **[page 106]** *Isis, Latona, Cybele,
Osiris, Æsculepius,* & *Diana,* especially the Aricine, in which there was a goodly Temple,

---

31. **[Insertion on separate piece of paper]** & here we may againe note how
sacred these places were for Burial; for besides that of Rebecca already ~~examined~~ mentioned; we reade they secretly buried the greatest persons in them, ~~This is meant~~
{& this} I suppose the text meanes, ~~when the~~ C[h]ro: 10.12 when the valiant men of
Jabesh interred the bones of Saule & Jonathan under the Oake there for that was a
speciall tree as we observe

erected in the middest of an Iland having a vast lake about it, and a huge Mount ~~&~~
~~Grotto~~ and *Grotto*, full of streames which trickled out of the Rock decored with divers
statues: In this glomy place it was that *Numa pompillius* so often conversed with ~~Diana~~
~~the Godesse~~, {his Regina} as *Minos* did in the Cave of *Jupiter* by whose pretended in-
spiration they made the people believe they received new laws, doing in the meane
tyme what they pleased, a policy derived ~~from thence~~ {to} *Mahomet* {thence} downe
to the present ~~Rebells~~ {age} & ~~Late~~ Impostors who have cheated the {silly} people of
~~this~~ {our} ~~Age~~ miserable Nation.

To these we might add the Groves of *Vulcan, Venus, Cupid, Mars, Bellona, Bacchus,* ~~Pan~~, *Sylvanus,* the *Lucus Camoemarum* & that at *Helium,* famous for the statue
of *E{u}phemes,* the Nurse of the Muses. {not forgetting the *Lupurcal* sacred to *Pan* &
amenable for the festum of Romulus & Rhemus.} That of *Vulcan* was guarded by a
dog that was used to bite all prophane persons who offered to enter, but allway[s]
wagged his tayle & fawned upon honest men. {The Pinea Silva of which Virg: a: 9:
was dedicated to the Mother of the Gods, & 'twas much used in Groves.} *Venus* has
many Groves in *Ægypt,* & in the *Gridian* Iland was one which had the renowned statue
~~made~~ of that Godesse cutt by *Praxiteles*; Another ~~at~~ in *Pontus* where the Golden Fleece
hung. Neptune had ~~a~~ Groves much celebrated in Greece, especially the *Helicean*: There
were likewise the Groves of *Ceres, Proserpine, Pluto, Vesta, Castor & Pollux.* In that of
Pluto 'twas that *Pericles* saw his fortunate vision: The Famous *Feranian*: and the *Mons
Parnassus* were set about with incomparable Groves, described by Hor: od: 1 [30–32]

> *ille gelidum nemus*
> *Nympharumque leves, cum Satyris chori*
> *Secernunt populo.* {& that of Virgil: Nostra nec erubuit

Sylvas habitare Thalia: Ec [2.6]} & hence Petrarch Sylva placet Musis, urbs est inimica
poetis Lucum Cambænis sacravit Numas,[xxvii] & they are more expressely the ornaments of Paradise then the flowry walkes. The very shade of Trees create a muse [xxviii]
And ~~others~~ {such} were the *Lebadian* Groves, the *Arsiroan, Paphian, Seronian* and a world
of other dedicated to all the Deities, as you may reade in *Pausanius, Arrianus, Livie,
Lucian* and other historians to omitt the poets; But besides those that were consecrated to the *Gods,* some were likewise dedicated to *Men* {etc}, especiall to *Hercules,*
and *Achilles, Bellerophon, Aglaura, Hector, Alexander* the *Greate,* & severall others of the
Heroes, some of which thought it honoure to derive their names of Trees; so, *Silvius,*
the posthumous son of *Æneas,* the *Alban* princes, *Stolon, Laura, Daphnis,* etc, Countrys,
Regions, & Cittys as *Cyparissa* in *Greece, Cerasus* in *Pontus, Laurentium* in *Italy, Myrrhi-
nus* in *Africa,* Ports, Mountaines And **[page 107]** eminent places, {as the} *Viminalis,
Nevia, Æsculetum,* etc.[32] But ~~I~~ {we} quitt these profaner Instances. The thing which we
would mainely drive at ~~is~~ {being} to shew how these ~~pleasures~~ {ornaments} as they
become Hortulane, have bin {of old, & may yet be} improved to holy & sacred uses.[33]

---

32. **[Margin note]** Se: L: 3. c. 2.

33. **[Margin note]** and that they were sacred to devotion the very name denotes
פרדס [Hebrew, pardes] a Sanctimony Apud Naharvalos (says Tacitus) antiquæ religionis
lucus ostenditur. Anal: 1.

~~And we~~ For our owne part we find it by experience, & professe it that there is nothing strikes a more awfull {& sollemne} reverence into us, then the gloomy umbrage of some majesticall groves ~~of goodly & tall trees~~ of goodly & tall trees, ~~as we sayd of the *Platanus*~~ {Such as the oake, elme, etc}

quæ præbet latas arbor spatiantibus umbras.
                    Ovid. [*Remedia* 85]

extreamely apt to compose the mind, & infuse into it a kind of naturall Devotion, disposing to prayer, and profound meditation; For on this account were those antient *Oratories* and *Proseuchæ* built in Groves ~~even amon~~ not onely amongst the *Gentiles* as we {have} already touch't; but amongst the people of *God* himself. The *Jewes* as *Scaliger* well observes in *fragment: Berosc*,[34] and Such was that of the Fountaine *ad portam Caperam*, of which *Cic: de Nat: deorum*, & that of Juvenal

Nunc sacri fontis nemus
    {Se 9 verses} [3.13]

{And the tyme was when men had honor according to their forwardnesse of reducing the wood, to the house of God: Psal: 74: 5.

At nunc discanti cessant sacraria lucis
Aurum omnes victa iam pietate colune Propert: L: 3. c: 11

They came afterwards indeed to be abused to superstition for in the end of Isaiah, *exprobatur Hebræis quod in Opisthonais Idolorum horti essent in quorum medio februabantur*: & they were interdicted by 16 Deut: 21. 6 Judic: 26. 2. Chron: 33. 3 ~~and they~~ {being} forbidden to be planted neere the *Temple at Jerusalem* for that very reason: {& an impure grove on M: Libanus dedicated to Venus was by a decree of Constantin destroyed as Euseb: tells us.} But the *Feasts of Tabernacles* were celebrated with Trees and temporary Groves, & are so to this day amongst the moderne Jewes. ~~But~~ That the Antients, especially the *Germans & Romans* had no other Temples at first, as *Tacitus* writes: ~~And~~ there is {somewhere} extant an Inscription

P. CORFIDIO. SIGNINO. POMARIO. A. PROSEUCHA.

And that made it Sacriledge to violate the least Tree about them. ~~For~~ {Add to this that} in Groves they formerly made their Sepulchers, & in the famous *Hyrretian* was the ~~Tomb of~~ Monument *Daiphon*, *Ariadnes* Tomb was in the *Amathusian* Grove in *Creete* for they thought that the spirits & Ghosts of Men delighted to walke & appeare in such {gloomy} places: we have noted before where the *Martyr Babylus* was interred & it was in a Garden that our B: Saviour himselfe **[page 108]** consecrated that Sepulcher in which never man lay but that *The anthropos* the God man *Christ Jesus* & we do here

---

34. **[Margin note]** hence that of Philo speaking of one who πάσας Ιουδαίων προσευχὰς ἐδενδροτέμεσε that had cutt downe all the trees about it. Such a place the Satyrist means when he says in qua te quæro proseuctia [Juvenal 3.296] **[Insertion indicated but not present]**

avouch, & for many other weighty reasons, which we could produce that there are none so fitt places to bury in, then in our Groves & Gardens, where our Graves may be ~~perpetually flourish~~ decked with {vegetan &} fragrant flowers perpetually ~~Greenes~~ verdures, & perenniall plants the most naturall *Hieroglyphicks* of our future Resurrection and Immortalitie; besides what they will conduce to meditateon & the taking of our minds from dwelling too intensely upon other more vaine objects: And here we might worthily declaime against our Custome of interring our dead in the body of our churches, as both ~~very~~ undecent, ~~& very~~ unhealthy, and a moral presumption; but we referr it to {what we have sayd in lib: 3: c. 3.} some more able pen, & for that [35]it is ~~no part of~~ a digression from this Institution.

[36]For these severall respects Groves were ever had in greate reputation, 'twas observed by the Antients, that the Gods did never suffer him to escape Punishment that violated Groves: Pompeius says it was a Capitall delict: consult Pluto in Pericles, & Cicero {sharply} ~~reports~~{roves} that *G. Gabinius* for robbing them in Greece. What became of *Agamoemnons* Army for spoyling the Grove at *Aulis*? The Plague which followed could {by} ~~no oth~~ no other meanes be appeased, but {by} the Sacrifice of his onely Daughter *Iphigenia*: The like fate had the *Cleomenes* & the *Amazons* who could not, with all their force make the *Axes* enter, but {that} they still rebounded back & wounded the hewers; the other dyed Madd. whenc *Tamessæus genius aderit*, became a proverb when any man was grievously afflicted, because those who destroyed that Grove were so sorely punishd for it: *Lucan* L: 3. [429–431] speaking of the Groves which *Cæsar* commanded to be cut downe neere *Massilia* says he commanded indeede

> Sed fortes tremuere manus motique verenda
> Majestati loci, si robora sacra ferrent
> In sua credebant redituras membra secures.

Till the {bold} *Emperour* himselfe set to ~~a~~ his hand & felled the first Tree before the souldiers; how ~~sadly~~ {pathetically} dos the *Poet* [Lucan] expresse the sad regrett of the *Gaules* at the action, exclaiming at it as a greate piece of impiety

> quis enim læsos impune putaret
> esse Deos?
> [447–448]

[Page 109] {But it was a noble & worthy example when that ~~Ge~~ {famous} Generall Marques Spinola commanded his Army not to touch the grove of trees belonging to the P[rince]: of Orange at the Seige of Breda, it may be he had reade the misfortune which befell the ridder of them} And Appian records that when *Mithridates* intended[37]

---

35. **[Margin note]** vide: B: Hallwill[?] [Perhaps Thomas Howell, bishop of Bristol]
36. **[Margin note]** twas held inhuman in Charles the French K: that {ano 729} when he entered the Prisone & had slaine the Captaine, he cutt down the Groves.
37. **[Margin note]** Traitor trees for Treason cut downe at a yard high about ther seate in France as the greate affront etc. cf.

to cutt downe a Grove neere *Patara* a citty of Lycia, to make warlike Engines with the timber; being strangely terrified in a dreame, he desisted from his resolution {~~not to passe over in silence~~} & spared it: we heartily wish the like might {have} taken effect with all {the} sacriligious Purchasers of the Yron Age amongst us, especiall such as have devowerd {the Sacred} Royall & Ecclesiasticall ~~Proprieties~~{atrimony} & made such prodigious havoc ~~especially~~ of those goodly {Groves &} woods to satisfie their impious {& hellish} avarice, which ~~were~~ {being once} the glory and ornament of this Nation. ~~& were~~ {were certainely} reserved for repaire of our ~~Wooden~~ Oaken–Wales the ~~glory~~ {boast} & safeguard of this {noble} Iland, ~~in case~~ when necessity and ~~the~~ some imminent danger should threaten it; & not to be devoured by these insatiable Cormorants, who ~~have eaten up~~ to the eternall ~~scandall~~ {reproch} of Posterities & {sainted to} the Christian name, have swallowed Gods owne Inheritance but whose {sons &} Nephews must certainely disgorge it againe and with it all the rest which they might otherwise have hapily enjoyed. The Church Lands Impropriated are like the Eagles Feathers amongst other plumage, & the Moth {is surely} gotten into ~~a mo~~ {their} Garments, Infallible Devowerers. *Expertis credite o quotquot Sacrum patrimonium per fas nefasque devorastis* ~~And so we leave~~ {dismisse} ~~you to your doomes~~. But leaving this to their proper {Scorpions & Eresicthanian fate} ~~But~~ Besides the uses of Piety ~~formerarily~~ specified recited. The *Athenians* were wont to consult of the gravest matters & publique concernements in their Groves: Famous for these meetings was the *Ceraunian*; and at Rome the *Lucus Petrilinus* and the *Ferentine* where was held the greate assembly after the defeat of the *Gaules* by *M. Populio*: for it was supposed that in such holy Places, they would faithfully and religiously observe what {ever} should be concluded amongst them.[xxix] {Thus {you see why ~~I am~~} Sum Nemorum studiosus &}[38] Truely we have inlarged upon this Subject; but what more pleasant, or more ~~worthy~~ delightfull & worthy our reccommendation, then the preservation and culture of Trees

> Seris ~~fatura~~ {factura} nepotibus umbram
>   [*Geor.* 2.58]

that shade to our grandchildren give. And afforde so sweete and agreeable refreshment to our Industrious Gardiner

> Cum post labores sub platani cubat
> Virentis umbra
> When he his weary limbs has layed
> Under the florid platans shade
>   Claud: [11.18]

Or some other goodly Tree, such a one as so strangely inamoured the greate *Xerxes* in *Lydia*, **[page 110]** that it made him stop his march and stay an entire Day under {the shade of} it, pitching his numerous Camp round about it, & decking it with

---

38. **[Margin note]** Met 7: cf.

Jewells, as if it had bin his Empresse {or his shrine},³⁹ & it seemes it was so ~~goodly~~ majesticall a Tree, that the wise *Socrates* was want [*sic*] to sweare by it;⁴⁰ I have read of another Platanus {to their reproch: Pliny **[continued in margin]** says they were of such as chiefly grew in our Gardens ~~for it~~ as Cypresse, Lotus, Cedar etc as Pausanius has curiously observed For ex quo in ligno we know not fit Moenia} besides that at *Veliternus* called the voluptuous Tree, for its beauty & shadow which had boughes which spreaded 80 foote at a side; what then may we imagine of those stately *King palmes* & other {prodigious} Trees which in the *West Indies & Barbadas* are reported to be no lesse then 300 foote in height, & every way proportionable for shade & magnificence.ˣˣˣ

{But} We will conclude this Chapter, after all that has bin sayd to prove the amoenities, and sacred uses of Groves with the two elegant Descriptions of *Lucan* and *Papinius*, speaking of the feasts which they did there usually celebrate {& bespeaking ther venerablenesse}

> Sylva capax ævi validaque incurva Senecta
> solibus; haud illam brumæ minuere, Notusve
> Jus habet, aut Crætica Boreas impactus ab ursa
> Subter opaca quies, vacuusque; silentia servat
> Horror et exclusæ pallet mala Lucis imago
> Nec caret umbra deo nemori Latonia cultrix
> additur; hanc piceæ, cedrique, et robore in omni
> Effictam, sanctis, occultat Sylva tenebris.
> [Statius, *Theb.* 4.419, 421–427]

> Illis et volucres metuunt insistere ramis
> Et lustris recubare feræ: nec ventus in illas
> Incubuit Sylvas, excussaque nubibus atris
> Fulgura: non ullis frondem præbentibus auris,
> Arboribus Suus horror inest: tum plurima nigris
> Fontibus unda cadit, similacraque, moesta deorum
> Arte carent cæsisque, extant in formia truncis
> Ipse situs putrique; facit jam robore pallos
> Attonitos — etc.
> [Lucan *Pharsaleae*: 3.407–15]

---

39. **[Margin note]** for indeede by early Idolatry they made the gods of the very trees, ~~so~~ which the prophet cf so eloquently describes

40. **[Two insertions indicated, only the first of which is present, located elsewhere on page 110 of the manuscript, and transcribed as follows]** Such a Platane tree was that which invited Ciceros Friends, whom he introduces in his de Oratore; & such another there is now at Basil in Switzerland in the place before St Peters Church where in the middle of a fresh Grove stands a stately spreading Platanus under which was a murmuring Fountaine capable to refresh, shade & delight some hundreds at once, then which nothing can be more usefull in Summer.

[page 111]

~~And~~ With aboundance more which one could add upon this ~~delicious~~ {incomparable} subject, Since with the Poet we professe ~~that~~ {it} that amongst all the hortulane delights

> *Nobis placeant ante omnium Sylvæ.*
> Groves above all ~~do please us most~~ {affect us most}.
>   Virg. [*Eclog.* 2.62]

Here inserte the Plotts of Groves & {other} Relievos.

¹Of Transplanting

Having {then} carefully set out and drawne our Plotts which shall be destinated for the Groves and severall Relievos, according to the Rules layd downe in the former chapter; We thinke it necessary to say something {here} by way of Appendice concerning Transplanting itselfe: For by this tyme we presume the Seminary (which in the fourth chapter of this Booke we have prepared) may be ready to ~~furnish~~ {supplie us} with Such Trees and plants as we design'd for ~~trans~~ the furniture and ornament of our Elysium. Supposing then our Nurserie capable to send forth colonies for this worke: Such trees as are of two yeares groth (after their sowing) may be transplanted {~~some stocke for fruite a set to be inoculated~~} into such places about your Garden where you desire they should stand for good & all.

But you must take speciall care that in removing these tender *Imps*, they be not rudely plucked up, before the ground about the rootes be sufficiently loosned, for feare least you over streine and violate them: When you have taken out a convenient number for that days Transplanting (if it were neglected in the Nursery at their first pricking into line) you may shorten the Master downeright roote, cutting it off with a very keene knife; also you may clense the roote of the fibrous & stringy perplexities, which the Cypresse especially and some other plants have entangled about their feete.

Your Plot is well prepared to receive these strangers if the yeare before it hath bin well husbanded conformable to the precepts which are given, and that it be of something a better mould then the place from thenc they come: But the stations to receive them were better be made in Rills or Fosses, then in pitts & holes; for the more easier expansion of their rootes, and greater facility of planting: The Depth and breadth must be regulated **[page 112]** according to the nature and proportion of the Plant. two foote broad and 1 1/2 deepe, is sufficient for most plants, where the ground has bin universally trenched and made loose; for where in any other parte we speake of greater allowances, it is to be understood of the sides of Walkes, where the ground is hard, and hath not bin opened: In this worke let the severall moulds be layed asunder as has formerly bin directed, so as the most rich and airy may be

---

1. **[Insertion on separate piece of paper]** ~~Since all trees & plants whatsoever suffer & require transplanting in their severall Seasons~~ This worke was thought so sacred & so necessary for the melioration & civilizing of Trees & fruits, that the Antients thought fit to put it under the patronage of a Deity: when they made Vertumnus preside over all that in the field was turn'd or ~~Transplanted~~ transported to another place: But we do not intend to sacrifice to him here, but give {our Gardner} such ~~rules~~ farther ~~orders~~ {precepts} about this affaire as we omitted in the foregoing period:

Having then carefully set out —

turned in next to the rootes; and thus you may set your Trees at convenient distances for your designe, so as not to bury the stem further then it was before, and finishing the rill or pitt, with the last which was dug out, making the surface about the bottome of the plant a little hollow, by pressing gently & fixing the Tree, for the better reception of the water and raine which now it will often thirst after. Mr Sharrock, to whose judgment and experience we ~~allways~~ subscribe, advises that the rootes of Trees be so planted, as that they may run shallow neere the surface, provided they be frequently moystned and refreshed the first yeare; and dos worthily reprove the profound interring of trees under a thick clay or Gravell, having observed that for many yeares together they have not shot a span in length; whereas, others set {shallower} in the same places did mightily spread & thrive; nor dos the digging so deepe, and putting good mould at the bottome & sides, contribute much to their improvement: since you will find them to thrive no longer then 'till the rootes are arrived to the sayd rock or clay; But this, in general; (& especially Ortchard fruits which stand best above this mould.} for there are some particular Trees, which insinuate with ease, and flourish best in the very rock it selfe; of which sort there are Firrs, and severall other Trees & shrubbs.

There be some who plant the rootes of Trees upon the very surface itselfe, covering it with a load of mould; and it may be convenient for marshy ground, and especially for Fruite Trees, whose rootes have bin prepared for Spreading as we have taught in the Chap: of Seminaries. {but then order it so as the water may not run from it by a banke or trenche about it:

²In the trimming of rootes, as we but now directed, there are some which will not so well beare the pruning; and those are such as have large pith, such as the Wallnutt {& Almond} which not onely abhorrs the knife, but indeede succeedes not so well in transplanting, as where it comes up from the *Nut*, & is never removed; The like may be sayd of the *Asp* {Birch} and some few more which indure not the topping of their heads: Such Trees therefore ought in cases of necessitie be transplanted with as much earth adhering to the rootes as can be convey'd with them. {& by all means preserve walnut rootes from cutting or bruises} Most sorts of *Perenniall Greenes* thrive best where being sowne they are suffered to stand to maturity, **[page 113]** if those which grew to neere about them were timely thinned as we have shewed: But if they be removed at one yeare & a halfe or two yeares groth in a moyst & benigne season, they will shoote a maine: Such as are the most impatient of Transplantation are generally the *Cedars & Pines*; and therefore we advise them to be removed with earth and all, and for that purpose to sow & set the kirnells & nutts at the greater distance in your Seminary, that so you may with ease take them up without the least disorder, at any fitting tyme of the yeare, especially if the earth be moyst, or frozen, provided you have begun to undermine them before it be too hard for the Spade to enter, and that you plant them in the same posture ~~whereoff more anon:~~

This being of wonderfull concernement, for when the south or west side of the Tree comes to be expos'd to the north or East, it frequently kills & sterves [starves]

---

2. **[Margin note]** for pruning rootes let this be the rule: large heads must of large rootes smal rootes a smale head tis better to leave a smalle head a large roote then a smale roote & large head.

it, so true is that ~~a teneris assuescere~~ {rule of costume}, even in the education of Plants, {as well as of children}, so the Poet advises our Gardiner

> Quin etiam Cæli regione in cortice signant
> Ut quo quæque malo steterit, qua parte calores
> Restituant: Adeo in teneris conscuescere multum est.
> [Geor. 2.269–71]
> That he to plant it as it was do marke
> The Card'nall poynts upon the tender barke
> To know how every Tree did grow.

Pliny neglects indeede this curiosity, but it is of greate concernement, and the cutting of any tree in an open airy place, will by the circles, evidently discover the manifest operation of the warmer aspects, by the dilatation of its veines and that in *Brazill*, and the like exotick woods we find these ~~circles~~ {rings} or graines exactly equall and the circles concentrall, proceedes from the eternally equall illustration of the Sun in the *Torrid Zone* where these trees flourish; & there onely it matters not indeede how they are planted but with us tis to be duly observed. {We will say nothing here of those exact Astrologiall Gardiners who counsell us to transplant all sorts of trees & flowers in the very uniforme posture of the heavens in which they were first sowne.}

But to returne, if in difficult removalls, the Earth be not sufficiently tenacious, bestow a good watering the night before: But to be secure of your choycest plants & such as are removed with so greate difficulty {as the Pine & some others}: Set every kirnell in an Earthen pott which hath no bottome, but a board or moveable tyle; and thus, your plant being a handfull high, at the first hard frost which comes, hold the pott a while in a vessell of hott–water and it **[page 114]** shall slip out with earth and all into your hands so as to be transplanted in the holes which you have before prepared to receive it, without the least shaking or disorder: and this is of all other the most infallible way: when it thawes, remember to establish the ~~tree~~ plant by closing the commissures of the earths together.

But there may be some occasion happen that you would remove a greate, and almost, full grown Tree, for the adornement of some particular place, & the raritie of the plant: In such cases there is this expedient. A little before the hardest frosts surprise you, make a square Trench about a Tree at such distance from the stem, as you judge ~~his principle~~ {sufficient for the} rootes ~~may may extend~~, dig it of competent depth, then ~~either~~ case this weighty clod with fower plankes, fitted and fastned to one another with such skrues as joyners use about their bedsteddles; thus let things remaine till the next hard frost, then you may undermine the rootes with safty, till you can place blocks, and quarters of wood to beare it up, and so convey it upon a Trundle to the place where you will ~~trans~~plant: But if the earth be so heavy as not to be removed ~~wit~~ by the strength of mens armes alone, you must then raise it with a moveable Crane, or pully hanging betweene three strong & talle limbs, fastning the cables to the under quarters which beare the earth upon the rollers, & so you may with ease set the whole clod upon the Trundle to be conveyed, and replanted where you please, being perpendicularly set into the place which you have prepared to receive it by help of the same Instrument. And by this meanes you may Transplant Trees of wonderfull stature without danger, and many times without cutting of the head, if it be not extraordinary till: Of all the dry Trees, the Elme will suffer to be removed when he is as big as ones middle, and will thrive well enough being plentifully watered.

Touching the Season of Transplanting, the antient præcept of Hesiod about the eight day of the moone is stil observed: This for Trees of Boscage: But Fruite trees should be planted in the Fall: {& the sooner, the better} And at the first approach of Winter or Autumne rather as soone as ever the leafe begins to fall, and never deferring it, as many do, till the trees are quite bald. But this is to be understood of the hardyer sort; for not onely the choycer plants herbs and such as are set of slips should be reserved for the spring; but for the most part all sorts of evergreenes, at least immediately after St Bartholomew: we know how greate the variety of mens opinions is concerning the planting of these tender plants, most of our Gardiners are for an early Autumne; but we, governed by much experience, and **[page 115]** no smale loss of ~~plants~~ thousands of Ever–greenes, that the approching winter dos for the most part prevent their taking roote sufficient to establish ~~them~~ & maintaine them through the rigourous colds, which for so many moneths seizes upon them: So that doubtlesse, the Spring is the best season for those plants, and that not too early neither; for though after February the frosts are not so considerable; yet the Northern & Easterly winds (which we affirme to be much more noxious to plants & flowers then the severest cold of the Winter) are bitter enemies to these new inhabitants, and therefore, unlesse you have extraordinary securitie, from the invasion of these blasts, Let March be well ~~spent~~ {forward} before you remove your Ever–greenes, and being transplanted, give them shade for some dayes, and frequent refreshments with insolated ~~& imbibed~~ water, the foote of each plant encompassed with a little earth & cow–dung well matured, as for flowers, and layed somewhat hollow like a bason, covered with some brakes of fearne to keepe it coole, and retaine the moysture: In the light and dryer Soyle you may set them somewhat deeper {& earlier **[continued in margin]** in very humid ground after Xmas may suffice:}, then in the moyst & heavy and there be some who reccommend the ashes of wheate straw & beach chippes burnt in the pitt or fosse, and plentifully intermix't with excellent mould & dung; and it is excellent for Oranges, Granads and for such curiosities as are commonly set in cases and Pensile Gardens. {In transplanting or removing any rooted plants or flo: it may sometimes be dun even in Summer ~~after~~ {in the} evening heate is over & then watered & shaded: The Imbrex extractum is for this but be sure to do it deepe enough, for if the least fiber breake the sap running out indangers the plant[3]}

---

3. **[Insertion on separate piece of paper]** Mr: du Song (that admirable Mechanitus) assured me he removed trees of vast & prodigious groth even at Midsomer, for the P: Elector at Heidelburg by filling the hole with good mould which he ~~beate~~ mingled with water & ~~ma~~ beate into a very pap, in which he plunged his rootes, with strange successe, & without slagging up a leafe: & this I conceive very likely:

In very hott & sandy ground, I advise always to power to the rootes a very moyst rich papp, & then fill up the ~~hole~~ pitt with the sand, it will {seldom or} never faile

In moyst ground where men are to plant very shallow, some fling in a well burned Spruce faggot into the bottom, & lay earth on that, upon which they plant with successe: & it is good doubtlesse to drain the moisture

But it sometymes falls out, that the Season may be spent either before men begin to plant, or (having very many to remove) before they have finished, to anticipate this accident, Let your trees be taken up a fortnight before *All hollars tyde*, trim, cutt off, and quicken the master, and fibrous rootes, Thus prepared set them in some moyst pit, 40, 50, & 100 in loose bundles, together covering and filling the rootes with mould which must be kept very fresh; and thus by the Spring, they will not onely be perfectly recovered of their wounds, but be also ready to ~~cheque and~~ shoote and immediately to take roote where soever you transplant them; whereas being trimmed at Spring, they seldom recover, and very often pine and dwindle away: {The same is also eminently seene in graffs when they are inserted after long spring.} But this is best practicable in dry Trees.

Nor do all Trees suffer {universall} peregrination, *Seleucus* tried all meanes possible to transplant the *Nardus, Amomum* ~~and~~ {in} *Assyria*; but it would not be; Nor could Mithridates for his life raise *Myrtil or Lawrell* about the *Cimmerian Bosphorus*, though the place produce other exelent trees. The *Cherry* thrives not about *Rome*, nor the *Peach* or *Almond* about *Tusculum*, though one may see whole woods of them a little farther at *Anxur* [Antium?]. The *Corke* is every where in *Italy*, hardly to be met with in *France*, so true is that saying, *Non omnis fert omnia Tellus*. **[page 116]** but the causes of this we are chiefly to impute to the varietie of aire, winds, reverberations etc more then to the earth and the soyle.[4] {I will here add one note that the rarest & most hardiest of our perenniall greenes, the holly, should be planted in a moyst **[continued into margin]** Season & a light ground be it stones, or Gravell, or Sand {which is hott}, but it thrives not in rich ground, nor by any meanes in clay, weeping & cold places[.][5] Concerning the figures and distances of Trees, we referr

---

4. **[Insertion on separate piece of paper]** Scaliger mentions some plants {amongst us} that will not admitt removing. As the Iris, the Crocus {Fenegreeke} that the Cornal tree degenerates ~~to which he~~ & then cites Aristotle: {1: poet} Quosdam homines fer vos natis but this is not literaly so; for ~~many~~ {most} even of these plants will both more increase & become better:

5. **[Insertion on separate piece of paper]**
i General rules may be Trees may be older than shrubbs, shrubs than plants, ere they are remov'd: for Trees at 4: shrubbs at 2, & plants at one year old are commonly fittest
ii Frequent transplanting is amongst the causes of retardation:
ii Fruite too neere planted hinders fructification:
iv Transplanting magnifies & multiplies {best} Fruites & flo: & plants:
v Tender Trees transplant neerer the Spring, hardier neere Winter: of the first sort are Walnuts, Figs, peaches, Abricotts, Mulbers, & generally the more pitthy: of the 2d sort: Forest trees, pears, apples, ordinary cherrys, plums, etc: The Autumn Moneths cont: from mid Sept: Octob: Novemb: ~~Rose & other Frutices~~ Vernal: Mid feb: Mar:

Shrubbs as Roses, Corinths, Rasberies etc: do best in Autumn: Evergreenes in Early Spring, or end of August: as raines ~~com~~ & Season invite: Flo: {especially bulbs} take up about end of July: replant end of Septr: cutt off their fibers, keepe them dry & airy, & so you may keepe them out a full yeare if you please: but indeede Bulbs indicat best themselves when they should be transplanted by putting forth as they lye

our Gardiner to what the learned *Browne* has written of the *Quincunx* of *Cyrus* and to what we ~~have~~ say~~ed~~ in the foregoing {& future} Chapters; for such as are to be applied to *Palisads*, walles & other Relievos ought to be in even lines at {neere} a foote distance; ~~su~~ from the worke, & at such spaces from one another as their species require: Those which we plant in the open field, for ~~Groves and~~ Walkes, Avenues etc so as the aire {& Son} may best visite them, especially if ~~Fruite~~ standards of Fruite;[6] but

---

naked **[continued on verso]** Squammous & ~~tubers~~ {Fibrous} rootes as Lillys, Violets, Strawberys etc: transplant when they begin to drye the stemms towards Autumn: Tuberous in Autumn, or Early Spring:

For the lunations {remove} Trees & shrubbs from the full to the new moone, especiall the {first} Full before {& after} Mich: But herbes & Flo: from the Increase

Weather, rather moist than dry: tepid than hott, evening than ~~noone~~ {morning}, but trees rather in the morning: Water after planting: Herbes {& Fruits} with impregnad water, Flo: with insolated: but for Flo: See more peculiarly all the necessary rules in c: 16. In ~~pre~~ removing be carefull to bruise no roote, quicken them that are; let no rootes lye unburied: let your rootes be covered in transplanting: Trees, especially fruite, first with naturall earth, then rotten compost, & so 5. 3. 5. that no dung touch stemm or roote ~~but by~~ before thus qualified: keepe the surface about trees stirr'd, & cleane, & ceald:

6. **[Margin note]** Apples {& peares {which}} would never be lesse then 12 foote, cherrys 18 & Wall trees as much: Aspect South East: (1)

[Continued as insertion on separate piece of paper] Touching rules for the transplanting of Fruite trees: Some stocks raised even of Kernells may be fit in two years for Inoculation; & within two more to graff on, & within a yeare of that to be removed where they are to stand: {Especialy, peaches} which may be don about Septr: {& therefore never buy Peaches out of Nursery above a years budd, or that has bin headed above once for if they **[continued in margin]** stand longer, they head them for fresh so as to deceive the customer & then being transplanted they perish with the Gumme:} **[end]**

One of the best markes for the season of removing of graffed Trees is their ceasing to grow, & the closing of their top branches & that no more small leaves appeare: when you draw them strip of the leaves, for the aire & sunn exhaust them, then trim (as you are taught the intangled rootes & top roote with some of the branches if or 3 or 4 yeare groth: but if the plant be very small spare them more; I need not tell you how the holes are to be made, so as to set them shallow, & fling in the best (i) the upmost mould you tooke up) upon them, & then securing them against winds & Cattell etc:

Also choose ever fayre weather to transplant & remove in, & never when raining: Cutt not the greate rootes too short, & not slanting, but that it may stand the better & not be subject to penetrat: especially peares: standard fruite trees may be headd at 6 foote, cutting off all the small twiggs bearers & others, but in this worke **[continued on verso]** let the largenesse of the roote much govern, for a good roote will beare a better head: But for Walls & hedges cut them the shorter to make them furnish below, without which they are worth nothing: Peaches especially must be kept {this} low, because they grow bare in the middle so soone: in placing the rootes

in Groves and Boscage we have already given our reasons for a promiscuous order, and such as may most approch nature herselfe, whose workes are most delightfull for being irregular, and therefore in these plantations we take the Liberty to depart from the Laws of *Solon*, who we reade made ordinances concerning the very distances of Trees, and so did the *Romans, Theodosius*, and others, which had their *Sanctions* in the *Senat*, as is to be seene in the *Institutions of Justinian, Cod: Tit. de Æquæduct*: ~~and~~ in *Junius Frontonius* etc but not greatly materiall to our designes. And thus we conclude this Chapter being onely a supplement of those which went before, where we have

---

spread them handsomely {as much from the wall as possible} & set no trees neerer than a foote from the wall & in planting lift it up now & then to shute the mould about the rootes, where should be flung some very rich earth of the melow kind; if fruite trees: & plant as shallow as possible that the influences may penetrate, for when you see trees grow yellow 'tis an indication they are too deeply buried: & tis better to lay an heape above about the rootes for 2 or 3 foote, then to set the stemm deepe in the older earth, or to cover it about ~~March~~ with mungy stuff to protect it from heate in June, also frequent digging, & by degrees taking away those heapes of earth when you see the Tree strong is as good: Above all plant not the dwarfs too low, & be carefull you cover not the graff, for then it puts forth roote & turns wild: We have spoken how to plant in very moist earth, even on the surface: or in case you plant in holes or trenches, put stones etc under to suck away the humidity: In securing Trees by thorns, tis good to keepe the thorns from grating the rind with straw or hay for the galling sometymes kills them: Some do this for 3 or 4 yeares even when no cattell come, if they transplant out of ~~cold warme~~ {shady} & cold goves & expose them to the Sun, which over drys them: Keepe your fruites thus in standars not to have a head above 18 inches for **[continued as insertion on another piece of paper]** for the first year by pinching off the budds, but afterwards let it rest for 3 yeares & then in March disbranch the weake & bare, & stubbs close; but for Dwarfs & hedges let them run at liberty till first yeare, unlesse they shoote extraordinarily, & then stop them to fortifie & furnish the foote: & for such {& for dwarfs} give the Earth 3 or 4 halfe choppings with the spade in March, Octob: May, July: & so must you be sure to do to trees that are in fields & pastures for 4 or 5 foote compasse: Flouers & rootes do ill neere the rootes of trees, strawberys excepted, if not too neere.

Beech {Birch} & Oake {etc} would not be {Aprill} headed in Transplanting but very little, as we have sayd but left at least 3 foote in head, & you neede not stirr the earth soo, but a little at top, & make a trench for the water to sinke to the rootes: Cutt not the roote of Pines & Firrs, but very warily, & in March or when ~~(being well taken)~~ you prune rub the wound with ~~hogs~~ cow dung: to hinder the bleeding:

But it is not universaly agreed amongst Gardners whither {with us} the heads of evergreenes ought to be diminished or not; though in {hotter Countrys as} Italy they for most part use it; reguarding the austerity of our Climate above thus; & the Reason is evident for over much cutting would with them quite dry them & prevent even the saps intercourse: but in Engl: cutt off the head of an Orange tree {at Transplanting} & it shall hardly ever rise againe ~~being dra~~ but when an Ever greene has sprung & taken **[continued on verso]** fast roote, if any of the ~~to~~ head dye, cutt him boldly:

amply touched the particularrs omitted here; and do expressely referr what remaines concerning the Transplanting of some other rare Plants, Flowers etc to their proper {& peculiar} Chapters, ending with that considerable saying of *Pliny*

[7]*Omnia autem Translata meliora, grandioraque fiunt.*

[Page 117]

---

7. **[Margin note]** Nat: hist: L: 19. c12 [60]

{Improve this Chap by Ramelli Cause etc:}^{xxxi}

Of Fountaines, Cascad's, Rivulets, {Canales} Piscina's, and Water–workes.

{Dulcior iniquo nihil est clutior horto: Hor: Serm: Sat: 14 & therefore tis}

It is no wonder that *Varro* in the very entrie of his worke dos *Lympham precari* And that *Homer* was so carefull to place his two Fountaines in the Gardens of Alcinous. Since amongst all the embellishments, serving for use as well as ornament {of our Elysium} Ἄριστὸν μὲν ὕδορ — there is none comparable to Water, and of that especially which proceedes from the Living Fountaine, to refresh and irrigate the thirsty plants, to dispose and elevate into Fountaines, Girandolas, Cascade{'}s, Piscinas, and {other} innumerable pleasant and magnificent diversions.¹ So that if this sole ingredient be wanting, all other cost upon a Garden is to little purpose, as still deprived of that Spirit which can alone give it life, and most contribute to its perfection: {not altogether to omitt the use of & delight of melancholy of the murmuring Fountaine}

Be it therefore the principall care of our industrious Gardiner so to situate himselfe as that he may obtaine plenty of this liquid christall, gliding from its naturall sourse; seing that which is forced, stagnat or collectitious, be the Engine, or Receptacle never so perfect for being often out of order, expensive, unwholesome, & wanting the vivacity of the {its} naturall origine are little to be esteemed, and therefore hardly worthy to be spoken of.²

---

1. **[Insertion on separate piece of paper]** amongst which these melancholy murmurs are none of the least charming, as oft as they reconcile our weary Gardner to his repose with their levi susurro as the poet sweetly expresses it. [Virg. *Eclog.* 1.55]

2. **[Insertion on separate piece of paper]**

I do not here pretend to discourse of the Original of Fountaines {nor will I trouble my reader with the various opines of Philosophers} (in which of all that I have read our Country man Tho: Lydiat has best satisfied) (after which our learned countryman Tho: Lydiat {& others more modern} has written) onely in briefe I {somewhat favaour} take yield to the opinion most who derive them from the Raine which sinks into the Earth till it encounter some layer of Sand, clay, or stone rock etc whose impenetrable bottome is capable to retaine it, & then not able to penetrate farther, it rises & seekes passage through the next crany which it either finds or makes, if perpendicular building up, if in veines serpenting through them as in rivelettes & streames, & then often failing of such fountaines in dry Summers, & before the fall of æquinoxiall showers dos greatly establish. I then proceede to the Search But these for being detected neede no artifice for the delivering the of them; It is when they

~~In search of this~~, there can then be never applied to greate Industrie, in case it be not found bubling up, or running in some eminent place, higher then the situation and Area of your Garden. For this purpose *Vitruvius* prescribes that³ ~~the~~ the skillfull *Aquilegus* rising early before the the [*sic*] Sunn, should walke forth about the Moneths of *August* ~~and~~ *September, and October*, and prostrating his body on the ground, looke all about the Country, and where he perceives a mist or vapour arising, There to digg, for that in a drye and thirsty place, this seldome appeares: Likewise, that he well examine and consider the Soile, whither it be chalk~~y~~, Sand, gravell, ~~Rock or~~ loame {or} bogg~~y~~, ~~whither~~ {or} Mountain{e}~~ous~~, and rock~~y~~; Whither the{re} ~~place~~ be any place which produce Rushes, Willows, Alders, Reedes, and the like plants,⁴ ~~which are~~ never spontaneous growers, but where they have water to friend; {may the raile leade up to these tryalls} but above all (~~says some~~ {affirmes} an Author) where the *Argentina* or the wild Tansy grows,⁵ Pliny says *Tussilago*, the *Chrysanthemon* etc and there to open the ground, by digging 3. or. 4 foote about and 5 foote at least profound, with hope of probable successe; And, though at first there be little appearance, yet, he bids us not be despond; but to lay a quantity of Wooll in the middle of the pitt, covering it over with a bason, or some vessell which may protect it from the **[page 118]** Dew, for if we find it well charged with moysture the next morning we may hope with confidence to recover the Spring: But we passe over these and multitude of other experiments, which may be read at large in *Pliny, loco cito,* ⁶In *Constantine* de Agric, ~~L: 2: c. 4~~ *Cassiodorus*, and the famous⁷ *Receipt* of the *Gothick Theodoric*, where to the rest he adds the swarming of Gnatts, and that as the height is of the vapour, so is the depth of the Source which together with my Ld: Bacons artificiall collection ⁸in manner of a Fontinell or Issue, we reccomend to your triall, though not without suspicion of the fraudulency of ~~many~~ {divers of these prescriptions} because one fortunat invention, dos so richly commute for so {many} cheape and cheape Experiments.⁹ But we

---

do not so evidently breake out & redound, that will become our search, & for this then can never be too greate industry applied:

3. **[Margin note]** L. 8. c. 1.

4. **[Insertion on facing page]** Kercher dos solemly affirme how he detected a latent sourse of water by the magnetisme of an Alder rod, which he ~~made~~ so contriv'd as to make it play (like a touch'd needle) upon the point of another stick, & which he conceives wrought the effect by the aquous steames of ~~kin~~ affinity to the moysture; This is to be tryd in the forenoone whilst the vapors are strong & copious ~~& which he~~ & that which confirmd him in this conjecture was the effect which a vessell of warme water had upon his divinatory instrument: But these things I do not confidently rely on, but to tempt men not to resist all sortes of tryals to find out so necessary a treasure: ~~besides~~ {add to this} the plants below needed for being never spontaneous

5. **[Margin note]** L: 25. c 6.

6. **[Margin note]** L: 2. c. 4 . 5 Variar: L: 3

7. **[Margin note]** ad Apronianum.

8. **[Margin note]** Nat: hist. cent: 1: exp: 25:

9. **[Insertion on separate piece of paper]**

We must be advisd in our surveying of grounds, to have especiall reqard to the

will suppose the Spring {to be already} found and plentifully suppling our desires, either in the Garden, or at some convenient distance from it (which will extreamely contract {and facilitate} the expences of conducting it), and then the next thing will be the *Libration* of it: *Librare {autem} aquam non aliud est, quam conferre altitudinem Loci, unde concipitur aqua, cum loco quo deducenda est.*[10] For we must know, that we can raise the water no higher than the head of the ~~Fountaine~~ {source}, and indeede hardly to that altitude. Let therefore, our *Hydroscope* provide him a Levell with a *Dioptra* or by an ordinary *Quadrant*, calculate the height, that so he may accommodate his Fountaine beneath, and proceede with confidence in ~~his~~ {the} rest of this worke. For the current if the water lye high, the descent will be more violent or easie; and so smale a matter sets it running; that an Inch declivity in 5 or 600 foote is sufficient; especially provided it be {from} a plentifull and exuberant originall; for that will not onely add to its pace, but carry it in a lesser bore; then if the water be sluggish and of {too insensible} ~~smale~~ declension.(1) [xxxii]

~~The water thus liberated, a Cisterne must next be sunke into it, and it~~ {which} may be made of lead, or stone layd with *Plaster of Tarris*, well–beaten and made up with lime,[11] unlesse it may be hewn out of the living rock, which for being most naturall, is best of all: or else you may build dubble wales of chalke, ramming of clay very well betweene them. This don, cover your Conservatory, that neither mudd, or any other ordure, (frequently accompanye the Land slowls) have any entrance, doe stop the pipes, or disturb the water; but let there be some smale overtures on the sides thereoff, that at competent heights, the ~~sun may~~ {raies} of the Sunn may sometymes {visite &} illustrate it, which do greately digest and purifie the water and therefore we say, do not totally imprison your cisterne as many ~~do~~ use, unlesse you place it at 30. or 40 foote distance from the Source, which is **[page 119]** very commendable where the descent is not too rapid & violent. Now it dos oftentymes happen that Waters are found in severall places neere to one another, capable, being united, to supply the defects of a single head. In this case it will be expedient by channells to derive them

---

sides of hills & all declivities, & ~~Spe~~ search whither any weeping, or the foresaid ~~indications~~ {signals} in the least betray themselves & so open their sides, & neere the foote of them, which may be don with the least change (though in this so necessary & usefull an ornament (we must not talke of changes) they may be lead, or steaned so as to hinder their wast, & to indicat the pulses of springs in their severall seasons both of the day & yeare; These observations are of Philosophical importance; & the greate cephalic Arteries of the Earth may by this meanes be opned: & three or foure of these lowest conduites may convey a streame when smallest the others as many & as minute as you see good; & these channells would be so close as to spend only by their single orifices or cocke ~~where by lead or other melted~~ {one over another in severall tubular partitions may} descend on each side alternately into one ~~basen, or~~ {common} Receptacle: by by [*sic*] this also may you {happly} ~~perceive~~ {guesse} what changes of increase or decrease the water of your spring holds with that of the Sea fluxes; & then a good Thermometer may try both its strength & quality

10. **[Margin note]** Philander.

11. **[Margin note]** or even Sand if very fine, & beaten well with strong new Ale–mort, which is an excellent cement.

Figure 23. Parts of a cistern illustrated in text at page 119. A larger, more detailed drawing is inserted on a folio sheet facing page 119 (see Fig. 24).

to the cisterne, and if, as frequently they run profoundly, by flinging stones, flints and other solid rubbish into the channells to make it {the water} rise, as the {wise &} thirsty Crow did in the Apologue. But in this worke, there must {be} greate caution, not to force {constraine} the water over much, {in} with hopes to advance it by the {fitt} weight and reinforcement {pressure}, least it find out some chinke or {casme} cha{sm}nnell in the lead, and so you loose it by clandestine and seacret diversions; all which yet may yet in this case {also} be prevented, by a leaden Cisterne, the common {amplitude} content {for example} whereoff {for instance} use to be {being at} about 12 foote square, and seaven foote depth, will be sufficiently competent capacity.

When the Cisterne is thus accommodated, the next worke will be to *gage* it, and that is dun by appling of severall pieces of pipes to the lowermost edge {margent} of it; if the water passes through without overflowing the brimns, or {too} sensibly sinking, it is of a just bore for your purpose, if it over exceede this, enlarge the diameter of the pipe; for, so much and no more may may you receive of the water, which likewise should not run into the Cisterne immediately out of the Earth, but let {untill} it {have} first passed through a trough or channell cut in stone, which may convey it into the pipe that delivers it into the Regard or Cisterne, & before which there must be an Apor{o}n of lead or copper peirced full of holes as big as the topp of your finger; and another would be also fitted to the bottome {naithermost} pipe which stands perpendicular, which & is likewise pierced perforated all about, but with lesser {smaller} holes {overtures}, and all this, to preserve both the Cisterne, and Conduct pipes from ordure and other accidentall stoppings, for which reasons it would be frequently visited, a stop–cock being fitted to the pipe delivering it out of the stone channell; that so you may at pleasure let it forth {exhaust it}; and another at the bottome Convey pipe, to intercept the water upon any occasion of mending or reforming the branches, fountaines, and conveyances, in the interim, that the Wast pipes, discharges the Cisterne, which being placed at the very margent of it, and comming out through the wall of the Conservatory. But we will present it in figure.

[illustrations, see Figs. 23 and 24]
[Page 120]

Concerning the pipes themselves, they may be used, made of three Sorts, of Lead, Earth, or Wood; but the best of these materialls is the first, somewhat chargeable indeede but most usefull {durable} and lesse troublesome: The second is best for health, and the last is esteemed the worst of the three, being very subject to decay, imbibes externall moysture, and sometymes affecting the transient water {for alder makes it red}. They are commonly made of Alder, Oake or Elme, and of this last most{re} frequently then of any the rest: Every {Each} piece consisting of 8. or. 10

foote length and a foote in diameter must be bored with an Auger, and the extreamities ferulled with yron, and fitted to embouch one within the other. It is sayd, that in
these the water is not so ~~subject~~ obnoxious to the frosts. {& I am of opinion that there
might a mixture **[continued in margin]** of rosin be devisd which might long preserve them, if lined with it as Canns are:} Touching Leaden pipes we shall neede say
but little, they are the most ordinary, and it belongus to the Plumber, both to make
and lay them; nor is their the least difficulty in the worke. But for those of Earth,
seing they are lesse vulgar, and may be of good use in many places, where nor lead
no any of those forementioned woods are to be easily procured; we think it will not
be amiss to speake briefly of them.

[12]These pipes are made of strong potters clay, {such as Jugg-potts are, if it may be

---

12. **[Margin note]** {Cast} Leade pipes found out in H[enry]: 8: tyme were beate
round & sothered: but the clay had agary fistules & canales of old we reade in Jul.
Cupitus in Maximo et Balbino Anguis & Plin: Jun: L: 5 Epist. 6. Aquaducts were
the sulci publici Impp: Theod: et Valint: L: 6. c. de Aquaduct: 5. sid: Apoll: carm 22.
& in Frontorius, that they were many of lead: particularly ad Thomas: Se Claud de
Apon: Baln:
[Insertion on separate piece of paper]
    devehit exceptum nativo spuma meatu,
      In patulas plumbi labitur inde vias:
          [49.55–56]

*Figure 24. Full-page plan for parts of a cistern
inserted at page 119.*

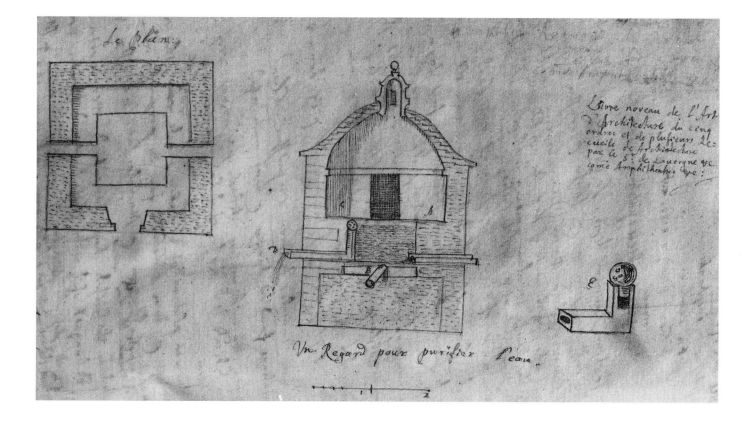

had} well baked and glazed. The length shall be a foote & halfe, {or 2 foote} The thicknesse ~~an~~ neere an Inch, and the diameter of the bore proportionable to your water: And these must be so contrived in their ~~making~~ {forming} as that every pipe may shoulder and mutually embouch into each other: They are commonly made round, though in some antient ruines, they have bin often found square without. Your pipes thus prepared, let the trench to lay them in be of two foote in widenesse, and of {3 or} fower {in} deep{th}; and for the better Security of all this, let there be a foote square lined with brick ~~made~~ in the middle of this trench ~~with brick~~ made in forme of a close gutter; ~~and~~ In this channell lay your pipes, buried about with mortar, and then covered above with the ~~brick~~ bricks which are to close up the ~~gutter~~ the receptacle: Or you may ~~witho~~ lay them without more adoe in the earth onely, especially {if of Jugg–pott clay &} in places where there passes no Cartes, nor heavy burthens over: but in all cases one may lay the bottome with brick, or some flatt stone, to preserve the pipes from the equall or accidentall pressure of the {superior} earth ~~itselfe~~: But since these pipes of Earth besides their insertion into one another as we describ'd, must be cemented, and that not above 4. or 5 can be well cemented together so as to be transplanted and layed, because of turning them aboute to powre & applie it, being hott {upon} all the joyn[nts] **[page 121]** junctures of the pipes: and that, when a competent number of them are thus fastned, they cannot be united to the rest in the Trench, without a hott Cement for the first, and ~~after~~ {a} cold one for the last, we will here instruct you how to make and employ them both.

& ~~pamper~~ Papin: L 1. fil: 3. & others so likewise were celebrated those of wood also, as appears ex Ænigmate 72. Cælij dym posij

> Truncum terra leget, latitant in cespite lymphæ,
> Alveus est modicus, qui ripas non habet ullas,
> In ligno vehitur medio, quod ligna vehebat: but I dwell to long:

Speake also of the Earthern pipes laid by the Romans some found in the mines of Lond after the fire: how embouched by juxtaposition onely not embouched, & the difficulty of cementing eases by a short & wider pipe slipping over it with a hole or tunnell to poure the cement in, a clout or paper onely wraped about the commissures to keepe the cement from running between them

[illustration, see Fig. 25]

not that you must have such a slipping pipe to every commissur:
heating the slipping box with coales about it, the cement melting, you may slip it farther, & upon any occasion repaire a broken pipe.
c.d, the 2 pipes
a their joyning
b where the mealted cement is put in that fills & closes the commissure:

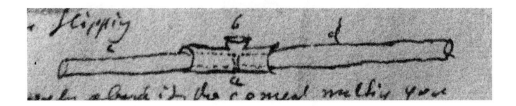

Figure 25. Connecting water pipes made of earth, illustrated in an insertion at page 120.

Take flints, pibbles, glasse, scales of Yron, *ana*, tyle shards & broken panns, as much as of all the rest, pouder, & passe all these mixed together through a fine sieve, and then ~~mingle~~ blend them with a dubble weight of Rozin mealted with a little nutt-oyle {for a neede linseede} q. s. the pouder putt in by degrees and continually kept in motion with an yron spatula till it become like bird lime & draws into threids: but it is then fittly qualified for your use, when dropping two or three drops thereoff into a dish of water, it become well tempered & ~~manageable~~ tractable: Take it therefor {now} from the Fire, and powre it into some old yron pott, having a little warme water at the bottome, to hinder it from sticking and ~~preserve it for your use~~ thus have you the hott ~~Vernich~~ {Cement}, which, when you will use, you may breake with an hammer proportionally as much as will suffice to fill a good Laddle, by which, being mealted, you may powre it about the joynts of the pipes, and when it is cold (which wil immediately be) it will become as hard as a stone. When thus you have fitted a competent number, you may carry and place them in the gutter or channell which you had before prepar'd; and then with the same Cemment accommodate as many more, joyning them to the former with this Cement following.

Take the forementioned powders *in specie*, proportion & temper them with nutt-oyle, but very thinnly, and so mingle it by degrees, continually stirring it with a wodden stick; ~~lastly~~ {then} in this strew some store of Thrumms or flocks of hempe, such as the ~~mari~~ shipwrights use for *Ockam* cutt very short, & ~~Lastly~~ add a little deare-suett or the like, being very smale shread & ~~mi~~ blended exceedingly with the rest, Lastly with the pouder of new unfleked Lime, bolted, & made exquisitely fine, temper all these by degrees with the rest, and beate it, 'till it do clamme no more, either to the earthen Vessele, in which it was made, to the spatula or {to} your hands, but become in the consistence of a past. With this Cement fix your former layers of pipes, at those joynts where you could not come to cement, with the hott, because of thir posture, and that by appling it to the joynts & commissures with your hands and fingers: ~~And~~ This in a short tyme will also become exceeding hard, and thus you may ~~continue~~ proceede with the rest of your layers, till all is finished.

[Page 122] But if your sourse be very far remote from your Garden, it will be requisite at {every} two or three hundred foote space to build another smaler repository or Servile Cisterne, but it shall not neede be above 3 or 4 foote Square; because they are of greate use in detecting the faults of any unsound pipes, beginning the examen at that which lies neerest the maine source, or capital cisterne, and so save you the opening of ~~so~~ much ground; which, if you be uncertaine where to apply the cure, you must of necessity breake up. It is also necessary sometimes in long tracts, to leave now and then a vent (as in the midway betwixt these ~~heads~~ receptacles) to give course to the water, the mistake of which smale Philosophy, did of late cost the *Genoves's* an immense summ, after they had built a famous *Aquæduct*, 'till a poore man discover'd the seacret, and shewed them the cause of the stop, & retrogradation of the Water. This vent is made with a stone bored & errected in perpendicular to receive the ~~mouth~~ {orifice} of it in this manner, and somewhat like the tunnell of a Chimny to be stopped with a plug, and opened upon occasion. **[illustration, see Fig. 26]**

We have bin the more particular and industrious to describe the fabrick and manner ~~of~~ of laying these earthen pipes, to gratifie such as are not willing to goe to the charge of leade: But to proceede, In laying what pipes so ever be carefull to leade them by the directest course; for if there be any considerable flexures, sharp and frequent angles, the water is apt to regurgitate and many tymes breakes out: But in such

Figure 26. Air vent in an aqueduct, illustrated in text at page 122.

cases, or being to passe some greate Vallie or River, ~~'tis~~ it will be necessary to convey your pipes upon a channell of Masons worke of stone or brick errected of a convenient altitude; but this is a chargeable and expensive transportation, fit for princes & greate persons to undertake, & {such} have bin hereto fore ~~the~~ at the common charge of whole states. ~~among~~ & it is esteemed amongst the most magnificent of publique structures, as is ~~se~~ yet to be seene in ~~the~~ many places of Italy; where we have traveled ~~more~~ days journeys by these ~~stately~~ {noble} conveyances; & which though built for the publique service; yet such a prospect had they of old to the incouragement of Gardens, that even some private person might ~~dra~~ lay a pipe into the{ir} Garden, ~~for~~ {as} ~~the~~ we find it provided by an expresse Law *de Aquaduct: Sub: J: Front*: Or lastly this convenience may be supplied by raising a banke of Earth, and interring your pipes in it according to the former præcautions.

And now though we have made so little esteeme of forced and unnaturall Waters at the introduction of this Chapter, yet to the end that there may be nothing defective to accomplish this Argument {& render it universall **[page 123]** And for the benefit of such as being in low, or ~~drye~~ {thirsty} places have not those wished for conveniencys of water & rising fountaines, we will speake a word or two concerning artificiall elevations. Forced waters are such as are raised out of standing or running waters which ~~are below~~ breake out, or lye beneath the {levell of the} Garden, & the places where we would dispose {of} them. And the onely way to raise these waters is by the help of Engines, Compressions, Siphons, Suctions, Wheeles, Contrpoises, Syringes ~~etc.~~ & the like *hydraulique* inventions.[13] If, of necessity, you are to raise it out

---

13. **[Insertion on separate piece of paper]** It shall suffice to ~~list~~ {give} some generall hints of both the antient & modern Engines or Gins; In order to which ~~take~~ & for conduct to such as shall set about the excogitation of new ones, This may go for an universall precept That they endeavor after a just proportion ~~tw~~ betweene power & tyme, for if we faile in either of these, our labor is to no purpose, ~~&~~ what is gained by one, being lost in the other; This only unobserved, ~~hath~~ has ~~ben~~ deceived many: It is onely the irreconcileablenesse of these (weight onely added), which has frustrated so many hopfull attempts towards the perpetuall motion, as Antients call it. But to come to particulars

One of the most ~~famous~~ antient, & indeed favorable & admirable for raising water by rather a seeming than direct forme has ben the Archimedan screw, this will

of Wells, Let them be Sunke in places that are remote from Sinkes, Stables, Dunghills, and other noysome places, steaned with chalke, as far as the water rises, and making them of such a depth after you are arrived at the Spring, ~~that~~ to prevent their being suddainely exhausted or dring up in Summer; And for this efect those who are very curious, & consult all advantages, advise us to begin the worke when the Suun is in the East of *Virgo*, before the *Autumnall Æquinox*, viz, about the beginning of *September*; for then, through the ~~drinesse~~ {Siccity} of the Summer the bowels of the Earth is comonly at the driest. As for the former, so they be large enough, it signifies not ~~of what~~ whither round or Square.

~~If in this worke you obviat a Rock or encounter some {such} other difficulty {acident}, by meanes whereoff you cannot hope for Water without excessive difficulty~~

If in this worke you meete with a{n} ~~rock~~ impenetrable rock, or encounter ~~any~~ {some} such other accident by meanes whereoff you cannot hope for water; to obviate this difficulty; ~~They do~~ in {many } ~~places~~ {parts} beyond the Seas in hott Countrys, & especially in *Venice*, where being seated in the very bosome of Neptune, they are totaly deprived of these conveniences, they serve themselves of cisterns & conservatorys in which ~~the~~ to retain a very greate quantity of Raine Watters sufficient to supplie {their oeconomie} & all ~~uses~~ manner of uses. Now to make such a Conservatory; ~~looke out~~ if it be for the ornament of your Garden, looke out the highest eminency of Ground neere to it; else, if it must be elevated above Your ~~ground~~ area, the re-

---

both so let the water to considerable heighth, but may also be redoubled story & story, taking the water from one to another to greate purpose, in raising or evacuating it

2 The old buckett gin of wood, or leather {(with chaines)} accommodable for almost all water, by living or dead force, or by the ~~sev~~ New–Castle ~~Gin~~ or Scotch Gin, received into the Cisterne by the yron grapple, & this is likewise performable with the treading wheele {for man or beast} very practicable for Gardens:

3. There are likewise other open Ladles & Tankards of use in Tide waters & Rivers for drawing or slowing:

4: Succking pumps & chaine pumps are very familiar & usefull, especially if the bucckett goe deepe, which will to a greate height, & with more ease

5 By force & weights perpendicularly falling into wooden Tubes & urging the water up, then gin performed by beasts but with vast paenes, & unconstant

[Continued on verso]

6 By the double rope through groove–Wheeles, which raise water to vast heights & do greate execution but they are also unconstant & not lasting

7 But [i.e., By] the supplement of poles diversly contrived

8 By the Ciphon which every Virtue uses, & will operat to a considerable height with few precautions as to the proportion & first setting on worke, which must be a force beyond suction:

9 By Cogg–mills under & (which is best) over shaft & by an insirting of all expedients of which Authors are full, ~~& the tipes to be seene in Ramelli & others~~ In all which Operations (especially wheele {& cogg} worke) let the materialls be {specially} good, the Circles large, the shaftes strong etc: & ever remember the rule, that the more simple they be, the more naturall & most likely to succeede: who has a desire to see ~~that~~ Type & figure may be satisfied in Ramelli & others.

ceptacle should be built of {free}stone, flint, ~~chalke~~, or brick, and well lined with a coate of plaster of *Tarris*; unlesse you will bestowe a Cisterne of Leade, which is best, & most permanent: but if to avoyd that charge you desire to make some other shift, lay the bottome of your Reserve very thick, ~~I~~ wee would have it at the least 3 foote, nor {much} lesse the sides; & for the proportion or content it is ~~done~~ {calculated} by ~~making a~~ computation{ing} how much your Fountaine will exhaust in a days ~~running~~ playing, & so to adjust your Cisterne that it may serve 3 or 4 moneths running during which tyme, in England, you will seldome faile of fresh & ample supplies: A conserve of 30 foote square and 12 foote in height, will containe such a **[page 124]** quantity of water, as being well husbanded, will serve the playing of an ordinary fountaine a very greate while: but then (I say) it must be ~~carefully~~ frugally employd: The frost will be apt to make the plaster scale in such places as are not covered with water; but if it be tempered with linseede oyle, it is ~~made~~ {renderd} almost impenetrable; or if the Receptacle be so placed as to be easily covered with earth the freshnesse of that would rarely suite with the {cold} cement which we formerly spake of; or else the Wales superinduced with this following composition. Rx smiths dust and scales, Glasse, pibbles, ana, ~~as mu~~ of Tile dust as much as of all the rest: pulverise these ingredients very finely, & mix it {thinnly} with excellent vinegar; then strew it by degrees with Lime slecked without water, & made into a most impalpable pouder: stirr all these till it become of sufficient consistence: ~~Then~~ {lastly} add the glaire of Eggs well beaten immediately before you applye it, ~~in~~ incorporated by degrees, & with this masse incrust the Walls of your Reserve ~~about~~ to the thicknesse of {halfe} an Inch; ~~but first it will be requisite~~ If the Walles be wrought rough it is so much the better, & the application would be made whilst they are yet greene, for the union will be stronger. And this composition dos very much resemble that famous Cement which dos yet remaine upon the Walles of the *Centi Camarelli*, which the Emp: *Nero* built neere *Naples*, for conservatories of water. The Cistern thus prepared, the Water is to be conveyed into it. by Troughs of wood or leaden Conducts from the Eaves of the Houses, that the raines which descend about the Spring & Autumne may ~~replenish your Cister~~ fall into it;

But ~~these~~ Conveiance~~s~~ which immediatly delivers it into the Reserve, must have a ~~gutter~~ grate or Aprone of Leade to keepe out the Ordure, & therefore in greate & violent showers it should be tended, & carefully clensed, or at the least diverted for a while, till the Roofes of the houses be well {& sufficiently} washed.

Last of all let your Cisterne be covered, for else the raines falling into it immediately will continually trouble the waters, which 'till it repose will not recover its former purity; but otherwise, the matter is not of so greate importance. And thus may you sinke a Cisterne in the Earth, or with lesse cost, and more Ingenuity as {the} *Signior Manfredo Balbani* invented for a Gentleman at *Paris* ~~after an excellent~~ certainely a most happy & effectuall expedient as well for the purifing of waters, as the retention: We will here describe the ~~manner~~ Operation. let there be a square Fosse of 30 foote diameter and 18 foote deepe; at six foote from one of the **[page 125]** sides of the Square of this vast trench, sinke the Earth 4 foote deeper then the greate Fosse; at the bottome whereoff lay a layer of excellent clay, tempered so as to make Tyles, and upon that halfe a foote thick of Sand, steene this second Cisterne with flat stones, or with chalke {a foote thick} without mortar {in a} round ~~about~~ {forme} 4 or 5 foote diameter: The bottome of the greater pitt, is likewise layd with rammed clay to retaine the water, and over that a bed of Sand, yet so as not to touch the sides by a foote: in which intervall errect a Wall or Contre–banke of Clay ~~well wrought~~ a full foote {in} thicknesse, well & closely wrought & layd by hand, clapping it on in balles, & managing it dextrously: All these three workes (viz the steening of the Inward Cisterne, the Walles of clay & the sand) must be wrought equaly & together, til they be brought up to the brims of the grand Fosse, & then you shall finish the Cisterne part with ~~S~~ a Coping of Square stone ~~& n~~ layd in Mortar and ~~neately~~ {artificially} wrought. The Reserve thus fitted, convey the Raine by Trough, as in the former; but it must be brought onely into the outward Fosse where it may ~~run~~ {dissembogue} into the Sand, through which it percolates into the Inward Cisterne, the steaning whereoff was for this cause set without mortar: We had almost forgotten to ~~direct~~ {advertise} you that some piles are to be droven in at the bottome of our Cisterne {upon which you may place a wooden grate or lattice} to keepe the Vessells, which are let downe to draw it, from taking up, or stirring the Sand which we ordered to be layd upon the clay:

And thus a ~~Cisterne~~ Reserve may be sunke within the earth of admirable use, & litle cost, both for the ~~preserv~~ retaining & defecating of Waters. To all these, the application of pipes for the ~~convenience~~ Supplie of Fountaines is to be, as we have already shewed in the former instances; And for other Machines, ~~Engines~~ {Divices} & Forces either accommodable to this, or any other, you are to consult the skillfull Engineere, & such Modells as are already detected to be most practicable: ~~And wee~~ And to conclude this Article, we have at the foote of this Chapter, ~~described~~ {reppresented} (amongst the rest of the Figures) the construction of an Engine suitable for this effect, the ~~figure~~ {members} whereoff ~~is~~ {are} so perspicuous, as there neede nothing be added to render it more demonstrable, but that the same may be imitated & refin'd upon by the ingenious & skillfull Gardiner: So that now whither by Art or Nature your water be raised and conducted to the place where you desire it, Touching the Fountaines themselves (as usually we call those pleasant diversions, & spouting of the water in Gardens of pleasure) the principall parts of them consist in these two things, the *Bassin*, and the *Gyrandola*. That we call the Basson, **[page 126]** which is the common Receptacle of the Water, that issues & falls from the statues, figures, spouts & other devices, placed in, or about ~~the~~ it, and is for that reason to be made either of Lead, ~~brasse~~, {copper} or ~~stone~~ Marble, in such forme & shape as may best containe the water, for which the directions & instructions prescribed before concerning cisterns & conserves are here very practicable.

We do not pretend to define the exact proportion or diameter of these Bassins, because they are to answer to the figures & other ornaments which you will bestow: But for a generall ~~rule~~ {instance}, those which are of 30 & 40 foote over, are ~~ver~~ exceeding noble and gracefull, & do become a Parterr of a large area: The least would be of 10 or 12: but there are those which do farr exceed these proportions, as that in the *Palais Cardinal* at *Paris*, capable to receive a pretty Boate, & that which was design'd for the Lower part of the Garden of *Luxembourg* which is about 200 foote diameter. Touching the depth of ~~And as to the Basin, so are the statues & Figures left to the fancy~~ Such Receptacles as are to serve the discharge of Fountaine waters, we would not alow them above five foote at the most; not onely for that it is ~~of~~ competent but because it is much more beautifull & pleasant to to ~~see~~ {behold} the pibbled ~~or~~ paved {or inlayd with Pietra Commessa & Emblematique worke usual in Italy} bottome refract {& play} through the cleere & chrystall streame, then when the ground of it is darke & impervious through excessive depth, which {would} better becomes ~~the Piscena~~ {a fish} pond or Piscina then a Fountaine.

Now though we commonly find the circular to be the most usuall forme of *Bassins*, as indeede the most capacious & commendable; yet our Workeman is not herein obliged to any particular, but may varie according to his pleasure; ~~nor is it materiall, whither~~ but we do not so much approve of ascending to Fountaines by stepps; nor is there any ~~way~~[?] so gracefull, as ~~these~~ where the Bassine lies almost levell with the superficies of the Garden or Ground, especially neere the Parterr, because the elevation is unnaturall, and nothing so agreable to the eye. We do not speake here of such as are contrived in Grotts & Rocks, and other naturall or artificiall inequalities of Ground. It is in the very navill of the Bassin that the master pipe of the fountaine is to be placed, which is the pipe that communicates with the originall Cisterne or Conservatory **[page 127]** whereof we have spoken & therefore to be well cemented and fixed in the stone worke, {or metal} and to appeare so much above the surface of the Gage, destin'd for the height of the Water as may serve to carry it into the statue or Figure to be placed there.

Now as the Bassine, so are the statues also and other ornaments referred to the fantsy and judgement of the Architect: Sr: H: Wotton advises[xxxiii] that the designe be proper & ~~by no meanes~~ {relative} ~~averse~~ as he illustrates it in the Fountaine which is {placed} at the lower end of the long Walke at *Pratoline* (a delicious Villa belonging to the *Duke of Tuscany*) where the statue cutt by the famous *Michael Angelo*, reppresents a Woman wringing a Cloath, out of which there runns plentifull streames of water into the subjacent Lavor or Bassine; ~~something that a naturall de~~ and certainely the more naturall the designe be it is the better for ~~so~~ {here} the statuary may introduce Whales, Syrens, {Sea Monsters} Delphines, Tritons, {Glaucus} The Nymphs, and River Gods, water fowle, ~~Rock worke~~ Sedges, Shells, ~~and~~ {Mascks} Rock worke and Rustick order of Architecture, disposing the Water through their mouthes, breasts, eyes & other overtures, or else in Girandolas, perpendicularr, oblique, canopies & innumerable other devises; yet always designing the middle for the highest & most conspicuous. But we will conclude this particular with an Idea, as to this purpose of {well} fitting our ornaments ~~with~~ taken out of the accomplish'd Sr Phil: Sidny. ~~where describing a very fine Garden~~ {who thus describes it}[xxxiv]

In the middest of all the place was a faire Pond, whose shaking Christall was a perfect mirrour to all the other beauties; So that it bare shew of two gardens; one in deede, the other in shadowe; and in one of the thicketts was a fine Fountaine made thus. A Naked *Venus* of White Marble, wherein the Graver had used such cunning, that the naturall blue veines of the marble were framed in fit places to set forth the beautifull veines of her body. At her breast she had her babe *Æneas*, who seemed (having begun to Suck) to leave that, to looke upon her faire eyes which smiled at the Babes folly, meanewhile the breast was running etc.

There must to the pipe which supplies the Girandolas and other issues of the Fontaine, be fitted a stop–cock of brasse and that should be placed in some convenient corner neere the Bassin as much out of sight as may be and passing through a frame of stone worke, covered with the same to be taken up & removed by a ring of yron upon any occasion when the Fontaine ~~will shut or set it a playing~~ with the yron key which is made to turne it will set it a playing, or shut it, as in tyme of impetuous winds, and when there is necessity of empting the Bassine: And for this purpose **[page 128]** it ought to have a pipe in the bottome which may ~~convey~~ voyde the water either when there is occasion to clense the Bassine, or repaire any fault in the Fountaine, by this meanes to convey it into some empty place, or some other Fountaine situated in a lower ground, and such a one may ~~be fed~~ by these superioure waters be continually ~~be~~ fed by the Wastpipe, which is also another necessary member of the Fountaine, to be placed in the worke of the Bassine and accommodated to the just altitude that you will have the water to stand, be it 3. 4. or 5 foote, for thus the superfluous water discharged will maintaine some lesser Fountaine as we sayd, and preserve the Greater from overflowing.

The Statues and Figures applicable to this Ornament are cutt, or cast of severall materialls, ~~Brasse~~ {Copper}, Lead, Marble, etc, other stones being for the most part spongy & penetrable, weare off with tyme, and contracting mose & other filth contaminate the water & are not fitt for this purpose.

By *Cascads* we understand all sorts of falls and præcipitations of water from Cliffs, Rocks, Stepps, ~~&~~ inequalities naturall or artificiall; Also from one Bassin or Concha into another, Instances whereof we have eminently in the naturall & horrid Falls of the *River at Tivoli*, and that of *Frascati* so magnificently reinforced by all that Cost can possibly contribute to them: But {as} it is most artificiall, In the greate *Cardinalls* Villa at *Ruelle* {& Vaux le Vicount the surintendants house neere Milan} where the *Cascade* is composed ~~{by a}~~ of Bassins & stepps continuing in a very large series from the topp of the hill to the head of the long Walke where the waters rise in ~~that~~ {a} *Canopy Fountaine*, and ~~after~~ glide along in a Silent Streame or Rivlett to the distant Grotto. And these are ornaments of wonderfull delight in Gardens, ~~the spa~~ caused by the foaming, sparkling and rebounding of the Watter, especially if the falls be naturall, which are infinitely to be preferred before the Artificiall {how costly soever}; but where there is not this accession, and {that} the water be in aboundance (for these kind of Fountaines do exceedingly wast it), let the worke be contrivd to resemble nature as much as possible.

[Page 129] Rivulets and streames are the lowest, though not the least of the liquid ornaments of Gardens, and are rather to be admitted then the larger Waters, unlesse where some goodly River may be brought to passe by and wash the farthest ~~end~~ {extreame or foote} of our *Elysium*. The plott sweetely declining from the North; and so as to descend by staires and degrees to it, and view it from a parapett wall ballustraded and addorn'd with statues & Vasas: Such a noble situation has the *Villa of President de Maisons* neere *St Germaines en Lay* where the River *Seine* supplies an ample *Naumachia* {by} cutting the bankes like a Harbour or Bay into {a part of} the Garden {itselfe}, capable of containing divers Vessells of good burthen, and fitted for such Triumphs and Navall encounters as ~~usually give~~ {may when} the Owner pleases give a magnificent divertisement & entertainement to the Spectators. We would be the more particular in this to reccommend the many incomparable advantages which our admirable River of *Thames* affords of this nature in severall places above *London* on the North side, & where the situation is generally so apt for this, and all other {Ornaments} perfective of Gardens of Pleasure and noble Seates that there were nothing more desirable then that Gentlemen & such as delight in Gardens ~~understood it better~~ did cultivate and understand it better.

Where these magnificences are not to be hoped for, let the Rivulets in Gardens be narrow & shallow, ~~two~~ {3} or ~~3~~ {4} yards broad, and 3. or 4. foote deepe will be sufficient; and if it must be *steand* to preserve the bankes, let it be don as naturall as may be, and so cutt, as not to glide altogether in a straite line, but in frequent meanders & serpentings so as now & then to forme *Ilands & Peninsuls* an example whereoff we have {in the vineyard} at *Hatfeild* in *Hartford–shire*: But it is necessary that whereever these are introduced in Gardens, ~~that~~ the Watter be very pure, and that the bed be layd with the finest & brightest Sand or Gravell, that there be some naturall or artificiall damms to breake the waters, incite agreable murmurs & interrupt the silence;[14] that it be furnished with Trouts & other fishes such as delight in in [*sic*] cleane & limpid streames, and may be se~~a~~ene to play, leape, & shoote up and downe the Waters.

[Page 130] The last of the watry ornaments which we admitt in Gardens are *stagna* or *Piscinas*, {& *Natatories*}, which indeede ~~my~~ {The} L Bacon would have {utterly} Vanished as altogether insalubrous; but if they may be taken into the grand inclosure of our ~~Elysium~~ {Garden} towards the farther and most remote parts from the Mansion {& be fed with the living follower} we ~~too~~ looke on them (in defect of the *Naumachia* formerly described) as greately contributing to the perfection and accomplishment of our *Elysium*. {& imitating those *Roman* magnificences, as may be seene in *Varro*, & the descriptions [continued in margin] of *Lucullus* Gardens whereoff hereafter more at large.} We designe therefore a *Piscina* to be of such a capacity as may serve not onely to keepe a good quantity of Carps, Tench, Trowts, Pike, or other fish, but for to saile and row about with a Pleasure Boate built of some antique shape, or Pinnace like, with a Cabine ~~and other conveniencys fitt for the diversion of Ladys~~ gunns, sailes, streamers, and other ornaments fit for the divertisements of Ladys, and entertainements upon the Watter, then which there is nothing more agreable in the Summer and {during the} hott weather. And thus a Vinary of 2 or 3 Akers may be made with much more facillity if the situation of the place incline to it; But if it must be dug by hand, the Earth to be voyded may be disposed for the raising of Mounts, Tarraces, Bankes, and other artificiall Relievos about the Garden.[15] Now to the expedition of this ornament the naturall Vally dos easily contribute, or if ~~it be~~ there be a depressure open at one end, a *Bay* may be raised either by errecting dubble walles of stone, and ramming good clay betweene them, or else by making of two bankes of square Turfe, ramming the vacuum betweene them with clay as before; but in this worke you must remember to place the Sward & grassy part outmost, and that they be built sufficiently slanting for the better establishment: finally that there be

14. [Margin note] & which by the various heights of the falls may be turnd to a kind of musicall & grave harmony:

15. [Margin note] And such were the expenses of Lucullus in these pleasures that he dug through whole Mountaines to let in the Sea in to his Piscinas which did ebb flow & reciprocate with the ~~Sea it~~ ocean itselfe so that ipse Neptuno non cederet de pisatu says an Author * but of this we shall speake more amply in another chap:
* [Insertion on separate piece of paper] For Columella thus directs our choyce L: 8. c. 16 as if the land were not sufficient for the pleasure & Contemplation of our Elysium, without bringing the Ocean also into it; but rather ~~becau~~ for that indeed Fresh water fish were so little esteemed amongst the Epulos: & therefore to excell, he would have us before we begin the worke ~~of Piscinas~~ Naturam loci contemplari, quo piscinas facere constituerit, non enim omnibus: littoribus omne genus piscium haberi potest: The limous & muddy regions producing the flatter etc

accommodated a sluce to clense and sew the Pond, with a grate of wood to let out the wast, as in other stews and *Vivaries*. There is of this nature a noble *Piscina* in the [16]Gardens of *Fontaine Beleau* a palace belonging to the *French king* where is a Vivary of neere an English mile in length, having two pretty Fountaines rising out of it in forme of a Flower *de lis* ~~Seeming to~~ and adorned with a very stately walke of Trees about it then which nothing can be more pleasant. {Or as his Majesty has to greatest perfection, equald it in his **[continued in margin]** chapelle at St: James & Hampton Court which is 100 foote broad}

Let the depth of our Piscina be so contrived ~~being~~ **[page 131]** as declining with an easie gradation one of the sides may serve for a bathing place in the heate of Summer, and for this ~~cause~~ effect that the ~~bed~~ bottome be layed with the finest sand, or Gravell unlesse the bed be naturally so, which is a greate perfection. For the rest 8 or 10 foote deepe will be sufficient in the middle itselfe. {& if the length be much, 100 foote broad is competent:} The Ld: Bacon would have this Bathing place so railed and cancelld from the the [*sic*] rest of the Piscina as neither fish nor mudd may gett in for 4 yards about; to this we add, that there be a Tent or Tabernacle spread partly on the dry Carpet, and partly on the Water, that the Ladys may goe in privatly & bath themselves; or else that a room be built for the purpose having a slip advancing a competent depth into the poole, and accommodated with a chimny and other conveniences of Warmth suitable to their tender bodys {by} no {meanes} to be exposd to the aire or view during this healthfull and refreshing exercise. (1)[17]

And even such ample Piscinas as these have we many times beheld invironed some with Fountaines, Bassines & Cascads falling into them; Some encompassed with goodly walkes of Trees, some that had Ilands and artificiall *Rocks, Nidaries, Decoies* and receptacles for Wild fowle which would be calld and summond about you flying in

---

16. **[Margin note]** Versaille cf
17. **[Insertion on separate piece of paper]**
In Italy (not to speake of Turkey & the more Eastern parts of Asia) they have ben at infinite expense in these Conveniences: That famous architect Leone Leoni made a prodigious Fountaine for the Bathes of Signor Adamo Centurioni: & for Sigr: Gio: Bap: Grimaldi in Bisagno, consisting of a round basin in which 8 or 10 persons might very commodiously wash themselves; it has 4 marble Monsters adorning it, which vomite warme water from ~~a~~ Caliduct, & there are 4 Froggs sitting on their heads which cast out cold to mix with it: The Sponda or brim of the Bath has ~~below~~ beneath a margent broade enough for two people to passe in brest: The invioring Wall is Octangular with as many Nices, capable for one man to bath in, & they are each filled with two spouts, one of warme, the other of cold, which issue out of the hornes of a Mascharane above them; The whole room is covered with a Volto of rare Architecture, in the middest whereoff there hangs a large Chrystall Spheare that holds a lampe, which at night illustrates the whole Bath like the Sun in his Meridean: To this joyns an Anti–Chamber to uncloth & dresse in which is richly adornd with Sculpture: And this shall suffice for an Artificiall example, though I could produce many more, & exceedingly dilate upon the Antiquity & use of this refreshing Subject; ~~but of~~ for that it was an usual appendix even to the noblest Gardens Se our description of the Junior Plinys: Lib: 3. c: 9 of this {our} Hortulan labour:

the air, & swiming in the Water upon the Sound of a horne or other Signall to our no smale admiration and divertisement:

To conclude the inventions & varieties of {these} Water workes are almost innumerable, for to instance in some that we have seene, and upon which our {ingenious} Gardiner may easily refine, it were not possible to comprehend them all in this Chapter. Thus a pipe ~~couched~~ {layd} about the whole square of the Garden, did by many smale & imperceptible overtures or pipes couched crosse one another, send up {by degrees} a growing hedge of Water in forme of a Lattice or Palisade, of a competent ~~hight~~ height, neere them; & this was all the fence which that Garden or parterr had, and to which the entry was an Arch of water resembling a Portico. Varieties of shapes, as of Glasses blowne are effected by sundry ~~sundry~~ formes of Socketts ~~made~~ {contrivd} of brasse, which applied to the Dug or pipe of the Fountaine spread & distend the water into Canopies, Umbrellas, Cupps, Bells, Dishes, starrs, Crownes, and the like: Balls are made to play uncessantly, by so inclosing **[page 132]** of a lusty *Getto* or spout of water at the very Issue with a cradle of wire or brasse, that a Cymbale of the same mettall made hollow and light, may continually be tossed and borne up into the ayre upon the summit & watry wings of the *Girandola*: and when by any accident it falls ~~off~~ a side, lighting into the foresayd Cradle meeting againe with the *getto*, it will immediately rise againe & be kept up in perpetuall motion. Thus we have beheld Crownes, balls and Crosses throwne up & playing in the aire {& water} *tanquam Ludibria Elementorum*. There are likewise wayes of contriving seacret pipes to lie so as may wett the {gazing} Spectators, underneath, behind, in front and at every side according as the Fontaneere is pleased to turne & governe these clandestine ~~issues~~ & prepostrous showres: By water may also be reppresented, *Raine-bowes*, {Halos} *Stormes, raine Thunder* and other artificiall *Meteors*. The pipes & forces so disposd as to breake & scatter the water into such a deaw as the Sun darting on it refract a perfect *Iris*. {The Eye ~~obverted~~ of the Spectator obverted to the ~~light leaves~~ light} And thus the wind & Aire forceably expelled out of an empty pipe, by the suddaine & impetuous entrie of water will ~~imitate~~ {resemble} Thunder, Stormes, & the roring of the Sea to admiration, {&} which ~~may be for~~ {we have seene} followed with a dismall showre made to fall downe steeming from Grott or Canopie in which were couched innumerable {smale} pipes inserted into frequent branches of greater, & precipitating into a large bassine, as is to be seene at *Frascati* in *Italy* & other places.[18] But we

---

18. **[Insertion on separate piece of paper]**
~~For~~ The Naides ~~& Nymphs~~ Pegasis. Hesione mounted on Wales, Sea horses etc: ~~are proper Ornaments for these Works~~ Levi volitantem flumine corrum. Catells are proper & aposite in these workes: So the figures of ~~Ite~~ Juturna & Nymphs dedicated to piscinas, lakes & Rivers whenc the poet celebrates

Diva deus fluviorum as Maro: in 12 & these Annæ perennæ
streames that allways run, such as that Blandisiam neere the citty Regilla divinely celebrated by Horas

O fons Blandusiæ, splendidior vitro, Dulci digne mero,
non sine floribus, cras donaberis hœdo.

for **[continued on verso]** they used chiefly to sacrifice a Kid to the Nymph of which see an Inscription mentioned somewhere by ~~Phr~~ Pighius.

should never make an end of describing these varieties ~~tha~~ did we pretend to persue all that might be introduc't to inlarge & illustrate this argument; and therefore we referr our Reader to ~~de~~ what we shall ~~di~~ farther remarke {in cap: 12} in the History of Gardens {cap: 7; b: 3} concerning these ornaments, and to those publicque pieces exposed to the view of every Traveller in the streetes of *Florence*, where the Fountaine of the Grand *Piazza* is compos'd of 4 *Parian* Marble statues, and 8 of brasse reppresenting *Neptune* & his watry family of a *Collossian* magnitude governing 4 Sea-horses, which do all powre their streames into a Bassine or Lavor of a wonderfull dimension.^{xxxv} The {very} streetes of *Rome* are {plentifully} furnished with these magnificent publique workes, ~~the~~ {&} in which is to be seene whatsoever is rare & admirable in Sculpture & Architecture: of this kind is that exuberant **[page 133]** & pearly Canopie of Water before the *Vaticane*, That at the Entrance of the *Palazzo Barberini*, for the ~~hei~~ excessive height of the *Girandola*: The *Aquæducts of Augustus* reedified by *Paulus quintus*, brought 35 miles in *Arcads* to the Citty, and discharging itselfe into divers vast Lavors out of the mouths of Swanns & Dragons, & which being situate upon a very conspicuous eminence, affords so glorious a Spectacle in divers places, of the Citty when the Sun darts vigorously upon it. The Fountaine *delle Therme* or *Fons Felix* the ~~basso~~ {*mezzo*} *relievos* whereof is *Moses* striking of the Rock (all of white Marble) & giving passage to the water into three ample subjacent Bassines: The *Aqua Claudia* which cost neere 8 millions of Crownes: But above all, the late stupendious ~~worke~~ Moles erected by the munificence of *Innocentius decimus* where in the *Piazza Navona* there is a Rock, Grotto, & Fountaine adornd with {rare} statues, and that famous *Obeliske* erected by *Cavalier Bernino* with ~~infinite~~ art & industry not to be described in a lesser volume then the learned *Kirkerius* has set forth in his *Ægyptian Oedipus*, and which dos undoubtedly exceede all the publique Fountaines in the World: We might add to these that of the *Parthenopea & Syrens* in the vast *Concha* of Brasse neere the *Neapolitan* Mole, The Fountaine of Neptune in the *Piazza* of *Boulognia* {~~or abundant~~} with innumerable others, {the Fountaines in the Garden of P: Andrea Doria ex abundanti} but these shall suffice. {I will onely give you here the names of some}[19]

The River gods enter into these ornaments most naturaly, Oceanus, Thetys, & Amphitrides, & the Nereides, Nilus, Tiber, why not Tane & Isis cumbent on the greate Amphore & Jars, the heads & bodys ~~shra~~ cro[w]nd & incrusted in sedges etc: And yet I cannot say but that sometimes the Antients departed from these so apposite designs for governmnt of Fountaines, as out of the mouths of Beasts, especially the Lyon because by the benefit of that Constellation the Ægyptians believed their River of Nilus was supplied, & it was a symbol **[continued on separate piece of paper]** symbol of their inundation: & therefore we to this day figure the tops of our leaden spouts with them, and head ~~the~~ our Modiliums with their fore parts, as by many examples out of the Greeke & Roman Architects: Se Plut di Issod: & Osir: & our learned Dr: Brown in his Vulg Errors: cf. [Sir Thomas Browne, 1605–1682, *Pseudodoxia epidemica*, London, 1646.]

19. **[Insertion on separate piece of paper]** Some of the ~~most famous~~ Masters most fam'd for the designe {invention} & performances in these Workes as it concernes the Statuary, which with those enumerated in Cap: X: where we speake of statues, may suffice for a rich & plentifull tast:

Renound for these workes were Camillo Graffico of Friuli, at first by profession a Graver ~~in Coppr~~, but excelled in ~~making~~ {casting} Fountaines of ~~Brasse~~ {Copper} for Gardens, & contriv'd some with that rare art, as to maintain a jetto in manner of a perpetuall manner without wasting the water ~~adorning~~ & some of his designes he adornd with exquisite Architecture:

Next him Giovanni Maggi a Painter of Rome, was excellent: And Bramante, who contriv'd that wonderfull Fountaine before the Vatican: Frances Giovanni Angelo who contriv'd & made that stupendious Fountaine in the piazza of Mesina in Sicilie before the Domo where you se 4 Rivers pouring their streames into a Basin of 102 palmes circumference *

Of later days John de Bologna has left incomparable workes {both in France & Italy} & so has Fanelli with us in England, as may be seene in what stands in his Maj: Garden at H: Court:

But of these & of ~~their~~ {more} admirable workes yet extant you have them at large in Lib: 3: cap: 9 to which I referr you.

* {it is octagonal & full of excellent Bass relievos} The rest of the Figures about it are Europa, Pegasus, Icarus, Jason, Narcissus, Diana, Acheon, etc: 8 Marine monsters lying upon Cubes, Nilus, Tiber, Hebrus, Cumanus are the 4 Rivers, with severall Nymphs ~~&~~ which all make 17 gettos of water, besides the Fishers, Sirens, 4 Tritons, Scylla & Carybdes, 4 Dolphins, 4 ~~Boys~~ Cupids on as many Sea–horse, Orion etc: all figures exceeding the life & indeed for art, cost & magnificent above description: And neerer the Sea there is also another not much inferior to this: I am the more acurate in describing it {~~not onely~~ as well to assist our workmans inventions as} to shew how other Countrys out do us in publique workes, in which they are {more} sumptuously liberal, & it is a just reproch of our northern ~~dul~~ stupidity & avarice when such an inconsiderable Towne as Viterbo in Italy can shew a publique fountain that cost more art & mony than all the Fountains this day in England, & such Elegances do {~~greatly~~} not only contribute to pomp & shew, & to celebrate {& encourage} Workmen, but the very sight of them has some effect upon the manners & comity of {the} men who behold them, & dos sweeten & enliven their spirits: as do large streetes, uniforme buildings, ~~&~~ greate & stately Palaces & ~~well~~ Churches decently adorn'd, & I wonder how great persons who enjoy them can be wicked, & do unworthy things in them.

verte **[not continued on verso]**

CHAP. X.

Of Rocks, Grots, Crypta's, Mounts, Precipices, Porticos, Ventiducts.

[1]There {Nor} is {there} certainely {any}nothing more agreable then after the Eye has bin entertaind with the pleasure & refreshments of Verdures, {the fragrant} Flowers, {the christall Fountaines} and other delicious and sense-ravishing objects, to be unexpectedly surprised with the con horror and confusion of naturall or artificiall *Rocks, Grotts, Caverns, Mounts & Precipices* well reppresented; when besides that they most naturally suite with the *Waters & Fountaines*, which have bin the subject of **[page 134]** our former discourse; so do they greately contribute to the pleasure and divertisement of Gardens & may be reckned (in our esteeme) amongst the most desirable of all the hortulane varieties; For what can be more sweete and refreshing then

cum post labores sub platani voles
Virentis umbra quam gelido SPECU
Torrentem fallere Syrium,
Et membra Somno fessa resolueris.
          Claudian: [11.18–21]
              Then in coole Grotts
T'avoyde the Dogstarrs sulthry aire
And wearied limbs, with slepe repaire.

---

1. **[Insertion on separate piece of paper; first paragraph crossed out]** As the World would {be no more} neither be beautifull nor {so} usefull with out the varietys of the glabrous & uneven surfaces, Hills, rocks, Cliffs, & Valleys {as well to the view of the beholder as their naturall productions} than a face without a Nose {forehead} Eyes & {sweete &} cheekes dimpled cheekes, some more eminent, others more depressd, no more would a Garden

'Twas the insolent {impious} Alphonsus (not worthy the name of a Prince) whom Roderigo of Toledo L: 4. c. 6. tells us belch'd forth that blasphemy, of his being able to have bothered the frame of the world, which had the almight form'd to his insolent fancy, it would have ben no more the world, that is beautifull; for so it signifies; & a face without a nose would have ben as taking, as the universe without Hills, Rocks, Mountains, & comely environings, whose various ascents, lofty tops, & sweete declivitys, give ornament & use: It is in imitation of this that a skillfull Gardner should mingle his relievos, & designe the for variety, for {as} all things do not grow & prosper in these places, so most of his hortulan furniture delights in severall situations. Nor is there certainly a nicety more agreable.

And in the heate of Summer {*Sub cavis estivos æstus vitare sub umbra Tibullus*}[xxxvi] ~~to~~ {by} ~~retire~~ {retiring} into those gloomie fresh and silent ~~Recessements~~ Recesses, especially if they be such as well ressemble the naturall, like those which one may behold in the Hermetages de *St Maurin* neere *Riez* in *France*, where amidst those holy Solitudes, a man may see *Gamah'es* reppresenting whatever figure you will imagine, some pendant at a prodigious height, some at the side, ~~some~~ {others} like to *statues* fix't in their *Niches*, ~~as if Nature had for~~ in summ so strangely full of varieties, ~~as if~~ as if Nature had forgotten nothing, to render the place full of ~~Prodigious~~ {prodigie} not to mention the ~~prodigious~~ {exuberant} Sources of Water, which gush out in many places and make an agreable horror echoing {& rebounding} againe from one Cliffe to the other. [2]*Ortelius* speaks of a desert in *Tartarie* where the naturall Rocks appeare like *Camells, sheepe, men*, and other *Animalls* and pretend that it is but a *metamorphosis* of about 300 yeares ~~past~~ {standing} but be that *penes Authores*,[3] There is nothing ~~to be~~ more to be desired then that ~~if we have not the we might find~~ in the place where we ~~could have~~ {affect} this ornament; we might find the naturall Rock {of} such {a rare place} ~~as th~~ as that which incited the most illustrious *Cardinell of Ferrara* to begin [4]his incomparable Garden at *Tivoli*, where, the River *Ariene* in a furious *Cascade* precipitating from the adjacent montaines of *Latium*, has made within the entrails & cavities of the banke, stupendious Rocks, incrusting them (by processe of tyme) with a naturall *Tartar* or *Lapidescent* juice congealed into wonderfull varieties; so as an ordinary {fancy} ~~imagination~~ may almost call anything to his imagination, so prodigious are the extuberances & irregularities. These, we say, where they may be encountred, are

---

2. **[Margin note]** In Tab: ~~Georg:~~ Sciograph: Russie

3. **[Insertion on separate piece of paper]** Such are those natural representations of the rocke at Panormus {& Messina} in Sicily, & those mentioned by Pausanias neere Olympus where whole armys of souldiers seeme to stand, & the like are to be found in the stones of Bellonius, Olaus Magnus & {of} Kircher of the B: Virgin's figure in a rocke ~~at~~ at Chili in the West Indias, ~~to which the use solem procession~~ not (as he says) anything miraculous, but fortuitous, yet which they have ~~well~~ gained much credit ~~by & ta by~~ by taking that advantage of the credulous people:

{all which art is able to accomplish by the rules of parastatic optics as Scotti demonstrates in his Magia pas: 1. L: 4: to which I referr the curious:}

There are admirable compelations for workes of this nature made by the water of of [*sic*] the river Elsa in Tuscany which are transparant & seeme (Some of them) to be of marble, vitriol, Alum, etc: & such materials are also found about the mount Morello ther 8 miles of Florence of which the noble Fountaines were made for ~~the~~ Duke Cosimo in **[continued on verso]** his sumptuous Gardens dell Olmo a Castello, the rustique of which was made by the famous Sculptor Tribolo {before mention'd} & they are suspended in the work by vines, leaded over to preserve them from rust, & branches of Yron so as they seeme to imped, & threaten to fall, & these are very proper for the hiding & covering small pipes ~~with im~~ when we will immitate showers & naturall distillations; for the water gliding along the sides of these rugged pieces, seeme to sweate & drop out of it:

Such another place was that

4. **[Margin note]** Se: L: 3. c. 9.

above all other to be preferred, Notwithstanding, the defect thereoff may be well supplied by Rocks made artificially, which therefore we would not have built so smale, & trifling & stiff & regular as we usually find them even in greate mens Gardens; but of a good height, & in proper & naturall places, **[page 135]** especially where the water may fall in the naturall *Cascade* in which case, the under worke would be made of Flint, or some other rugged stone, Layed with Mosse, and not, (as some) with brick & Tarris, much lesse with other mortar; because it will not be so easie to form into such irregularities, as with the forementioned materialls, nor so apt for the fastning of protuberances & other ~~pendencys~~ {extravagances} as upon such a craggy & uneven surface without greate wast of Cement & wire, which yet may both be applied, when imminent & pendulous stones {as we noted} are to be placed, and for the application of shells, ~~etc.~~ and such other naturall ornaments & varieties incident unto it: {When spongy stones are to be had it is best, but they may be well conterfited with stucco & plaster in moulds, others cutt in stone mixing them **[continued in margin]** with shells, & forming nices, festoons, frezes, etc: Also may glazed brick be used, & the refuse of glasse workes & furnaces:} The chiefe materialls ~~to be used~~ {applicable} on these Workes are the hard hony-comb millstone, Sea Rock, Talkes of all Colours, Coarse Coralls, black, white, red, petrified Issickles of which there is a sort in Ireland which is yellow & transparant like Amber: The petrification of our knarsburow in *Yorke-Shire*, & *Oky-hole in Summersetshire*, in the Peake & divers other places: All the varieties of *Marcasites & Media Mineralia* as for the Mineralls themselves, *Vitriolique* stones, *Thunderbolt Iron-Cinders* etc, they would be used lesse frequently; {& where they may lye dry} because they are not onely ~~obnoxious~~ Subject to contract rust, but many ti[m]es contaminate {and affect} the waters: Above all ~~for~~ the grosser materialls, the *Spars of Lead, serpentines*, Course Amethists & Crystalls, most sorts of variegated marbles & Achats, the drosse which is found at the bottome of the Crucibles, wherein ~~Glasse is melted~~ the Glassemen mealt their metall, {~~is excellent~~} transparant pibbles etc are most excellent ingredients, and indeede whatsoever is irregular and best resists the continuall tricklings, & cadence of waterrs, & penetration of Frosts.

Of the first & grossest of these materialls should the ground of your Rocks be composed, wrought in with Flint, Sea-Rock; Millstone etc, and afterwards inriched with *Conchiliage, Corrall, Flags, Sedge, Ivy* and other accidents frequently adhearing to them, such as are the *Spongg Stone, the pumex*, all sorts of *Conchæ Lævigatoriæ* brought out of *Turkie* and *Ægypt*: The *Umbilicus* or *Sea beane* which are of sundry unfractuous formes, & beautifully spotted; The *Nerita* or *Zigornet*, all the kinds of the *Murex & Bucina*, which are those vast wreathed Trumpet shells, called by some the *Musick shells*, & such as the *Paynters* put into the hands & mouthes of *Tritons* Sea monsters & others of ~~the Retinues~~ *Neptunes* retinue: The *Strombus, Turbines, The pentadactyle purple* full of wonderfull extuberances, and that sort which the *Italians* (from its resemblance) call Porcellani with all other retorted shells: **[page 136]** Add to these *Oyster-shells* of all sorts whereoff some are very rare & {that} ~~are~~ come from the *Indies*; Oysters of the *Ægean Sea* and *Propontis*: The *Limp*, the *Donax* or *Dactylus* of both Sexes; ~~Cockleshells~~, {~~pecten or~~} *Esc{h}allops*, or *Pilgrims* shells the best whereof are to be found about ~~Malta~~ the Shores of *Malta*, & the *Pecten* of which a world are gathered about *St Michaels* on the coasts of *Bretagne*: Also the Chama of greate varietie worne likewise by the{se} devout ~~Pilgrims~~: {Travellors} The greater & lesser *Tellinæ*, and all the *Margaritiferæ Conchæ* which are transported from the *Indies* and lined with *mother of pearle*, & sometymes with embossements of pearly substance of which sort are the *Pinns*, the *Mytulus*,

& some kinds of Mussles, the largest whereoff are found in fresh waters: The *Glans or Calognone*, & above all the rest accommodate to this worke, the *Patella*, greate, & smale, which is that broad shell resembling a spoone having 5 holes next to the Scroule edge, & is lined with a faire *Mother of Pearle*, cutt into divers formes by the Artist & frequently found in the inlayings of *Cabinetts*, roofes of chambers, and other curious workes etc: With these may be numbred the *Nautile shells* of all sorts some of which are prodigiously greate and elegantly gilded within: The *Cancellus* and *Locustary* Fishes: Many of the *Succuses ex aquis stillantibus*, *Pseudo-corralls* and *Finngons corralls* ~~as we sayd~~ {before mentioned}, The *Sprites*, *Ostracites*, *Ostracomorph's*, *Chirites*, Pyramidal *stelechites* & of various shapes. The *Pyrites* very extravagant, the *Malta Glissopetra's*, the severall *Osteoceli*, The ~~Tyburtine~~ *Spongites*, & *pumices* such as the *Tyburtine* are ~~the~~ All sorts of *Lithophytons*, and *petrified* Branches, *Sea Fann*, *Peucites*, *Astroites*, the severall *Fluors*, *Iris*, *Molybdoides*, *Siderammonites*, and thousands more to be [5]mett withall amongst the curious amassers of shells, & in which there is so greate a variety that we have knowne a Collection of them valued at a thousand pounds.[6] ~~all~~ All these, we ~~say~~ {affirme}, enter well into Rockeworke; being naturally placed & with judgment; and are fastned with the ~~former mentioned~~ Cement mentioned in the ~~last~~ {former} Chapter; with the addition onely of some course shells broken to ~~powder~~ {dust}, & mingled with the grosser powder of the *Oare* of lead; which is ~~much better~~ {as ~~good~~ good} to strew upon the *Cement* {& plaster} of Rock-worke, ~~then~~ {as} either the *black Indian* Sand, or the dust of *stibium*, by some used with greate danger, as imparting an Emetique {& ill} qualitie to the Water:[7] The coarse & naturall Corralls of **[page 137]** all sorts may be procured at reasonable rates; or for a neede, may be conterfeitted, ~~by~~ either by ~~dipping~~ {plunging all over **[continued in margin]** & referring none of the wood ~~to appeare~~ uncovered:} the extravagant branches of the white-thorne, (~~when~~ {after} the barke is peeled & the wood exquisitely dried in the smoke)[8] in a composition made of hard wax, Such as is brought in flatt pieces out of the *Indies* rarely coloured. {or in a composition} {or} Another sort of Artificiall Corrall ~~is made~~ {compos'd} with the shavings of {goates} hornes made into powder & steeped in strong lie, made of Ash-wood ashes 15 days together: Then[9] take{n} ~~it~~ out and colour{'d} ~~it~~ with *vermillion* disolved in water: {& mingld with the lie} Set ~~it~~ {this} over a gentle fire 'till it become thick and of a consistency to be made into what forme you please, for so it will abide being drye: {polish it with steele} But for that we have reason to suspect either of

---

5. **[Margin note]** No place so many materialls for Rocks, Shells etc: as in the Antille Ilands: See: Hist: Nat: et moral des Iles Antilles, c: 19: Art 10. [Cesar de Rochefort, d. 1690, *Histoire naturelle et morale des iles Antilles de l'Amerique enrichie de plusieurs belles figures des raretez les plus considerables qui y sont d'ecrites avec vn vocabulaire caraibe*, Rotterdam, 1681.]

6. **[Margin note]** For, nusquam magis luxuriarita Natura, quam in genere Concharum. Plin: L: 9: c. 33.

7. **[Insertion on separate piece of paper]** Or there is a more course & ordinary Cement made with new bees wax a qr of a pound: a pound of Rosin, Burgundy pitch half a gr: mixed with a competent quantity of tyle dust exquisitely powdred:

8. **[Margin note]** ~~& then dipd them in boyling oyle: then~~ {prime them} ~~primed:~~

9. **[Margin note]** but first dip the branches in boyling oyle & let them be prim'd

these receipts when the frosts and the water shall come to invade it: {powerfully} It
will prove the most infallible way to cast leade into the shape of branches, & to painte
them over with red: These, though they are not so polite as the other; yet being con-
tinnually wett they appear so, ~~and they~~ remaine forever, & are easily refreshed: {but
if with the red Indian varnish, it is incomparable} for places drye & less obnoxious to
the weather the former ~~will~~ dos exceede it; but the naturall has no comparison. *Ivy,
Sedge, Flaggs* artificiall *Weedes & shrubbs* to twine about, {dangle}, & emerge out of
some places of the rock is very naturall, and many of these will grow being planted,
& in tyme of themselves, or else may be dissembld & imitated, by cutting, or casting *Lead* or *Laten* ~~in such~~ to resemble such plants, ~~&~~ colouring them greene in oyle;
Sampier seedes frequently sprinkled in the chinkes of your rockworke, where there is
mosse, mortar or Earth will take hold & produce not onely a most naturall & agreable
verdure; but serve you also with an excellent Salad, as we have {thus} often ~~planted~~
{raised} it: {also Trickmadane} But the principall arte in this Worke is to build your
Rock hollow, obscure, protuberant, craggy, in the most rustick, unconstrained & extravagant order (if so we may call this dissorderly worke) and the most approaching
to the Naturall: ~~And therefore~~ {I}it is {therefore} utterly an errour, where we find
them made with an affected uniformity as sometimes we ~~do~~ see them; costly indeede,
but ungracefull: We may also people ~~our~~ Rocks with ~~Beasts~~, *Fowle, Conies, Capricornes,
Goates* {& rapitary beasts, with} *Hermites, Satyres,* {Masceras} *Shepheards,* **[continued
in margin]** {rustic workes river gods Antiqs etc} and with divers *Machines* or *Mills*
made to move by the ingenious placing of {tinn} wheels, painted, & turned by some
seacret pipes of waters; ~~And~~ The *Figures* above named may be **[page 138]** formed of
Potters earth, well moulded and baked;[10] but if the statues must be larger, of stone or
Mettal: By these motions, histories, {Andromedas} and *sceanes* may be reppresented as
we shall shew hereafter when we come to speake of other *hidraulique* inventions *cap:12*:
or as you may learne from the very *diagramms* themselves of *Heron in Lib: Spiritalium*
published a little after the decease of *Commandinus* by his son-in-law *Valerius Spacio-
lus* & dedicated to the *Cardinall Rovuerius* with this instance as to our argument. *Hinc*
(says he) *ediscere poteris multa quibus amoenissimi illi horti tui Urbani et Foro sempronienses
multo jucundiores et ornationes firi poterunt* etc. But this shall sufice.

Grotts are invented to reppresent *Dens* and *Caves*, and they are also either
{N}~~n~~aturall or Artificiall; both of them made by hollowing some banke of stone or
hard Sand; or else they may be built by the *Architect* with stone, brick, Flint and such
materialls, with an entry of *Rustique worke*, of the *Tuscan* or *Dorick* order: Some affect
to have the inside wrought as before we ~~taught~~ {shewed} of Rocks; we for our part
choose to have them without much of that; both are Commendable; seing the bleeding forth of Water is exceeding naturall; and so {is} ~~are~~ the growing of some verdure, ornaments of statues decently placed: Others are inriched with roofes of *Mosaic
worke*, {used for that & for paving of Fountaines etc.:[11]} ~~which is made by sticking into~~

---

10. **[Margin note]** or of plaster, grossly embossd, & clad or ~~seald with~~ armed
over with pieces of white marble shells, pibbles which is lasting & proper.

11. **[Insertion on separate piece of paper]** Musaec or Mosaic:
But in Mosaic worke there needs great mastry to conduct those smale pieces
so united that at a little distance they appeare like the best {& most exquisite} pic-

the Cement {or into a good plaster no thicker layd then to fasten then even stones}
smale square pieces of various coloured pibbles, Glasse,[12] shells etc, and {which} from
{w}hence {it derives its} has the name of *Grotesco*: In these may be made {contrivd}
Niches to fit in *Fountaines*, artificiall *Raines* etc: In some they {floores} are paved with
various colourd marbles, pibbles and furnished with Tables of stone to collation upon
in the heate of Summer & are built with aboundance of Cost & magnificency; but
nothing to be compared with the naturall and lesse uniforme: {Antra were conse-

---

ture: I say he that undertakes needes practice, Judgment, & desire: & therefore his
cartunes must be large that he workes by, else confusion will follow: {The Greekes
& Esterlings were the first that touch it} Famus for them was old Giotto, & of later
time Domenico del Ghirlandaio of later times {& some more modern as we see by
what they have performed in St Peters in the Cupula & altar pieces at St Michaels
etc:} The matter is made of ordinary glasse, colourd of all sorts of colours at the in
the furnace & when tis {the marle} soft & {well} melted anealed {seasoned} they take
it out of the cruett & put it on a smooth marble with a long yron spoone, & then
rolle it with another piece of marble upon it, & make rolls about the bignesse of a 3d
part of a fingers height {thicknesse}, then they square them, & cutt them in pieces
{with a hot yron} & fitt them with the cutting Emrie & with these of all pieces of all
colours they fill boxes, as the printers do th with their letters, & work off {compose}
as dextrously; some of these they gild, as commonly for the ground, & it dos most
richly b the rest of the worke being extreamely glowing and magnificent: & then
they doe with gomm water: & then covering the pieces so gilt with a thin piece of
glasse, heate it in the them on a fire pan or plate in a furnace 'till the g thin glasse be
red hott, this incorporates the gold so on the heads of the pieces masar mater, that it
comes exceeding faire & is for ever, then they cutt away the superfluous thin glasse
fit for the worke: note that the {designe is calked on the} skreen or plaster & then a
day 2 or 3 daies after when it is in good temper, they worke one it with the pieces:
The plaster may be made of marble pouder stone pouder of free stone, lime, beaten
brick dust, gumm tragath & white of egg: & so they keepe it moist & so set in the
pieces according to the designe & Cartune, the evene the better none has written so
much of this that we know of unlesse it be G: Vasari,

Pietro Commesse for irevelation of Walls, & pavements especially the bottome
of Fontaines which refracting then the christall water makes an admirable effect, & is
infinite last durable: & one sort of them is by ingraving the stones & filling the hollows up with a mixture of pitch & Asphaltum, & then polishing all the surfaces that
advance when tis cold; this is likewise don in plaster, St Laurence library in Florence
is of this, but the most excellent & durable is when the commesse is stone in stone,
as wood is inlayd on Walnutt usually:

cf your list of stones & marbles for this purpose: & that rare Florenttine M[aste]r:
of your tyme that made your Cabinett: more of these works Se in L: 3. c.9. **[margin
note]** A course sort is made of shells, course stain'd, glazd Earth, marble cut in peeces,
pibbs of divers colors, stuck only in plaster of paris so deepe as onely to containe them
with an even surface

12. **[Margin note]** Course small glazd earthen wax purposly and marble

crated to the **[continued in margin]** Nymphs, especialy to the Naides, because of the water in them; See Porphyry, de Antro Nymph:}[13]

The statues {& figures} of *Shepheards, Satyrs, Lyons, Wolves, Serpents* and other *Troglodites*, enter well into these ornaments, and may be in this case, ~~put~~ {layd} ~~into~~ their naturall colours, which were {a barbarisme} otherwise insupportable. Amongst other varieties of this nature, we once observed a dry *Grott* artificially made with the extravagant & vast rootes of Trees, which had bin grubbed **[page 139]** up, congested and heaped one upon another, like the mountaines which the *Gyants* would have sealed heaven withall in the *Poet*, these were fastned in many places with wyres & yron worke, & it was so covered with the naturall Ivy twining about it; that in ~~our lives~~ we never beheld a more delightfull spectacle: This kind of dry Grott ~~is~~ {were} very practicable where store of wood is, and may be of excellent use in the hott weather; being not so apt to strike a damp, as other subterranean Caverns are. But if *Grotts* may be made to wind or circle into various *Meanders & Dædales*, as in such places where they have a propitious banke {or quarie} (like that on which {The Towne of} *Notingham* is built) they are without comparison preferrable to all others, ~~I read~~ as most ~~disposed~~ {fitt} for retirement & {holy} solitude, to which a lampe hanging in the farthest & darkest part, will ~~greately~~ {much} contribute, as greately disposed{ing} ~~for~~ {to} devotion & profound contemplation: For ~~thus~~ {so} the holy *Hermites* lived in {the} tymes of Persecution, and the ~~the~~ subterranean *Catacumbs* are thus described by {the learned} *Bossius & Paulus Aring*{h}*ius*: Thus they heretofore made *Labyrinths* in the Mountaines, {as} at the foote of *Ida* in *Crete*, cutt out of the maine rock, ~~&~~ which was ~~made of~~ contrived so intricate; that an antient Inhabitant of a Village neere it, ~~that~~ who ~~was~~ {had} usd to shew it to strangers no lesse then twenty years, ~~was~~ lost himselfe & was never more heard of.[14]

Crypta (for the *Anthrum* or *Grotto* was none of the Moderne Crypta) are onely artificiall Passages under Ground, such as the *Catacumbæ* but now mentioned, and where a Concave being dug very farr into the Bowells of the Earth, and made narrower at the top then the bottome, and so arched either with the naturall Rock or steaned ~~with~~ by Masons worke, and to descend into by passages or stepps, may be ~~seene~~ {discovered} the starrs even at noone day: {heare we} *Lucretius* ~~gives~~ thus *Philosophise* upon ~~it~~ {the reason:}

---

13. **[Margin note]** περά του έν Οδυσσεια τον νυμφον ὑντρον

14. **[Insertion on separate piece of paper]** In France are divers wonderfull Grotts, amongst which famous is that of St Maurin where the stones are so figured, as they represent few one can imagine of extravagant & horrid; nay, besides the menacing & pendulous Stones, some of these seeme to represent even statues in the niches: Such another is the Autounoires neere Aaxem where all the Gamaches are hollow, which shews them to have ben but the concretions of {the} lapidescent ~~med~~ water; ~~&~~ {but} Ortelius speakes of the occidental parts of Tartary, affirmes that some of these rocks retaine the shape of men, camels, sheepe etc. which the inhabitans the above believe to have ben produc'd by a real metamorphosis. **[Margin note]** In Tab Sciograph Russ:]

E tenebris autem, quæ sunt in luce, tuemur:
Propterea, quia cum propior caliginis aer
Ater init oculos prior, et possidit apertos;
Insequitur candens confestin lucidus aer.
Qui quasi purgat eos ac nigras discutit umbras
Aeris illius: nam multis partibus hic est
Mobilior, multisque minutior, et mage pollens.
Qui simul atque vias oculorum luce replevit;
Atque patefecit, quas ante obsiderat ater;
Continuo rerum Simulacra ad aperta sequuntur;

[Page 140]

Quæ sita sunt in luce, lacessuntque ut videamus
Quod contra facere in tenebris e luce nequimus;
Propterea, quia posterior caliginis aer
Crassior insequitur; qui cuncta foramina complet:
Obsiditque vias oculorum, ne simulacra
Possint vallarum rerum confecta moveri.

                              Lucret:L:4. [337–352]

But from the darke, we spie things in the light
Since when the neere dul aire invades our sight
And dos our open Eyes possesse, bright aire
Forthwith ensues, and purges them as 'twere
And the first Aires darke shades discusse: For this
Then it by many parts more mobile is,
Minute, and smothe, which when it fills with light
All the Eyes Wayes, ~~and open~~ disclosing what the Night
And darke had stopt, immediately insue
The Images of things to open view:
Discovering those things i'th light, which we
Out of the light in darknesse cannot see:
Because the later aire o'th' darke place will
Pursue us thicker, which all pores dos fill
And to the ~~avenues~~ {passage} of our eyes deprive
That Figures can no way to them arive.

And for this learned and ingenious Speculation did the famous Astronomer *Ticho Brache* make *Crypta* in his nobel Gardens at *Vranaberge* {with greate cost}, in which to observe even the diurnal revolution of the Constellations & Celestiall bodys, ~~turning~~ converting this ornament into a profound & usefull pleasure: How they may farther be improved for ~~the~~ congelation and many other Philosophicall Experiments, let the Lord Bacon informe you in his *Idea* of *Solomans* house, ~~And~~ such as are exercised in Chymicall operations.

[15]*Mounts* are the the [*sic*] highest & most aspiring Relievos of Gardens, whither raysd by Art or Nature, and would best be situated towards the remoter parts, as from whence

---

15. **[Margin note]** illa naturæ dona sunt, nec ubique extrui possunt:

to take a universall {vista &} prospect not onely of the Gardens, but of the whole
Conutry. For so the Windsoria Tempe, & that rich & ravishing ~~prospect~~ {Surveie} ~~of~~
over the Thames & the Metropolis which crownes it are beheld from ~~the Eminences
of~~ the Castle, ~~and~~ hills & other eminences about Windsor & Greenewich, then which
no part of the **[page 141]** World, I dare avouch (not excepting the so much celebrated Constantinople {itselfe}) can ~~rep~~present us with a more ~~rich,~~ {magnificent}
various and distinct prospect; Since ~~not~~ the ~~lesse, but the pleasure of the Eye~~ pleasure
of the Eye is not altogether in the Lontanance {distance}, & losse of its object; but
in the diversity and notices of it, & which {transcend} in the former instances ~~are
most transcendent~~. Mounts then cannot be ~~raised~~ {elevated} to high: As for the shape
whither round square or bicepitous & resembling Parnassas Let the Gardner please
his fantsy: But in our conceite A mount raised with the perfect dimensions of the
Greater Ægyptian Pyramid {exactly} described by the Learned [16]Mr: Greaves; would
repprefent to our imagination one of the most sollemne and prodigious Monuments
that the ~~World~~ {earth} has standing upon her {ample} boosome; & it may be so ~~made
to~~ {contrivd} ascend{ing} by degrees to accurate resemblance, the Entrailes ~~left~~ made
hollow for the best & most naturall of conservatories for shade & astiration, & in
summe for a thousand diversions and experiments. Such as are Verrucous and round,
are to be ascended by a winding ~~& limacious~~ circle or spirall passage of two yards
broad, ~~yet so as the~~ easie, and with a moderate acclivity; of which sort we remember
to have seene one in the Gardens belonging to the right honourable the Ld: Seymor
neere the Towne of Marlborough, which is sayd to be a mile from the ~~botto~~ foote to
the summit: where the area would be flatt & sufficiently spatious {either} for a smale
Coronarie Garden & a Speculatory {~~& Mathematicall~~} Towre built Fortresse like with
battlements where {amongst other Mathematicall Engines} two or three smale pieces
may be mounted to be shott off upon Triumphs & Sollemnitys, or else, a peruq of
Trees be planted, such as are ~~ever greene~~ the pine, firr & other perenniall Greenes, {&
~~such~~ plants & simple) lovers of prowde & loftie situations:
But there is incredible paines & cost required for the raising of these Eminencys &
therefore not to be rashly undertaken; but where there is much rubbish & earth to
be ~~taken~~ {~~recei~~ furnished} from other places, either for the sinking of Wells, ~~Gro~~
Ponds, hollowing of Grotts, & Caverns, and the like these workes ~~will rise~~ do suddainely swell, ~~and~~ may be ~~finished~~ perfected with success and {at} reasonable charges.
{Though historys informe us, that the Chinese spare no cost **[continued in margin]**
for the raising these artificiall eminences, for which end they bring from far stupendious morsels of Rocke, & other materialls, as with wonder & delights both Alvarez
Semede, & the more accurate Dutch Authors describe it: Se: L: 3. c: 9:} If one of
the sides of a mount, cast into some other method for the ascent, & lesse regular, be
cutt downe in perpendicular, so as to forme a natural cliff & precipice, respecting ~~the~~
gloome part of the Garden, it will extreamely affect the eye of the beholder, after it
has been sated with the softer and more luxurious objects of flowers & fields: **[page**

---

16. **[Margin note]** Each side of the greate Pyr: was 693 foote, 494 high measurd
by a perpendicular, but the former 693 as it ascends inclining so as the whole area of
the Base contains 400249 foote square or 11 akers of ground, each degree without
4 foote hight & 3 breadth compassing it round in a levell.

142] We would therefore have these made prominent, ~~and~~ horrid & cliffie with now and then a ~~cleft~~ rift {or chasma {naturally form'd}} for the inviting of birds, {migratory fowle} the production of {shrubbs &} simples such as the Sampier {& Caper} above all affect; & if this be ~~made~~ {composd} of some chalky materiall {with frequent veines of some course murasite etc} it will strike a wonderfull Light when the Sunn beames dart upon it, & prove none of the least of the Hortulan varieties; There may likewise Grotts & Caves ~~to~~ be contrived within these as in the former; But if {the} Rock be naturall & that a living Spring plentifully gush out of any superiour part so as to fall into ~~an~~ artlesse Cascades, there can be nothing added to the perfection of these ornaments. {The Statues ornamental for the severall particulars of this Chap: are the Nariades, Hydriades, & Water Nymphs, the Oreades, and the Mountain Deities:} And thus we have gon through the most solid, and grosser {& loftier} Relievos of our Elysium, the worke of {many} hands more then of the head: But where the skill of the *Architect* is indeede principally required about our Gardens of Pleasure ~~cannot more~~ {is most} appeare{ant in} then in the magnificent & ~~loftie~~ {superb} structures of Porticos, {& Peristyles Xisti, Cryptas, Porticos} which being ~~made~~ {erected} at the Vestibule or entrance of the Garden, adjoyning to the back Front, or ~~against some~~ before some Pinacotheca or chimelium ~~of Rarities whereoff~~ some of the roomes would be destind for retirement, Librarys, Repositorys of Rarities etc: {These} doe make an admirable effect, & cannot indeede be well dispensed withall: For here are the choycest statues, Urnes, Vasas, Inscriptions & other Marmora to be placed partly in Niches, & partly on their Pedistalls; And here may the Lord of our Elysium {share their ~~Gestations~~ Walkes discourses Collation & take the aire, {or walke (in covert) ~~when the Sun & the heate~~} at such tymes & Seasons as either the Sun or the Raine forbids him a freer enjoyment:[17] We would not therefore have our Portico of lesse then long,   broad   high.[xxxvii] The materialls of Marble, ~~or~~ Freestone or brick: ~~Sr~~ Sr ~~Hen: Wotten instructs you how to mould them: and truly~~, but then, we would ~~have~~ {order} the projectures and Ornaments {to be} of Freestone, especially if the Columnes ~~be~~ {are} of Brick, as Sr H Wotten ~~th~~ instructs us how to mould them, after the example of the Atrium Græcum at Venice: for the adornements of these aerie structures should be with all that ~~the~~ {our} Architect can decently introduce by the most luxurious of his Orders; so that as within & on the blind Walle it be fitted for ~~statues~~ Nices, the smaler Fountaines falling into convenient Vasas; so should the Front & ends be inriched with all the magnificence that may be: The Floore may be paved with marbles of severall colours {Emblematic worke} or ~~inlayed with~~ Pietra Comessa, which is an inlaying so calld by the Italians, reppresenting **[page 143]** flowers, birds, Landskips & severall other {inlayd} Workes in their naturall colours; & with this also they often incrust the very Wales, a rich & expensive, but very glorious & permanent decoration: The Volto or rooffe may be painted *a Fresca* by some able hand. We have had a *Pierce*[xxxviii] in England not inferiour to some of best Italians for this kind

---

17. **[Margin note]** These were also cald & they used to be carried in to them in little Sedans or rather open chayres when we are to take the ayre & that these were some of them disjoynd from the house & planted about with trees especially the Platanus etc: & much used in magnificent Gardens we may reade in the descriptions of the younger Pliny Thuscia & his Villa at Nomentanum

of worke, wherein either ~~historie~~ some apposite historie, fiction or Grotesque may properly enter{taine the Spectators}:

And here ~~I~~ {we} may not forgett a very noble Instance of such a Portico or rather Peristyle (because of its ~~situation~~ application) contrived by ~~my~~ {our} late & worthy kindsman Geo: Evelyn, in the Gardens of our most honourd Brother at Wotton in Surrey, abating onely some mistake in the order and the ornament about the trabeation; for certainely, if ever, here it is that the *Corinthian* and *Composite* are most naturall and agreable as being the most adornd with foliage in the Capitalls and Freeses; where Festoons & Frutages are ~~the~~ more proper then Metope, Triglyphs, Skulls of beasts & sacrificing instruments. Let the cover of our Portico be flatt, balustraded at the sides, with Pedistalls at convenient distances for statues; or the Front of this Battlement may be broaken by some smale projection, with a Tympanum for two Cambent figures if you thinke good. Examples whereoff we have aboundance in ~~Palladio~~ Andrea Palladio & other Masters. And to these we might add the description of the Ægyptian Entertaining Room, which the Interpreters of Vitruvius describe, but because it is don so exactly by the ~~forementioned~~ {accomplished} Sr H: Wotton in the first part of his Elements, we purposely forbeare it, & referr the Reader; ~~because~~ since the Overture at the topp may haply be thought not so well to compart with the Climate of our Country: If Musique roomes be designed, they would be so contrived by the Archment above, that the ~~focus~~ Focuses of the reflected Angles below, may entertaine the Auditors with varieties of Sound & Ecchos, and the filling up of the Walles of such ~~places~~ fabriques, may be ~~by~~ with broaken and whole earthen vessels as it is in that of the Garden of Sigr Cornare in Padoa cf {the description of which we thinke is extant in Paladio: without tormenting our selves ~~with~~ about the Vitruvian text de vasis Echeis ~~ab~~ which has made a greate deale of noise amongst the learned to little purpose:}

[**Page 144**] And here ~~I~~ {we} cannot omitt a curiosity of a fountaine which in a certaine Musique Roome, falling into so agreable a murmure as {sweetely} accompanied the consert; it {~~rise rose~~ ascends} into a round Bassine which stood {in the middle} table high, but in such a Calme {& even Surface there); that the Parts ~~of~~ being reversly pricked, and pinn'd up at a just distance ~~one~~ {upon} a frame that was made over it, gave every Musitian his lesson in the Water, as in a cleare & christall mirrour. ~~It was a singularity~~ But of these more hereafter. ~~Lastly, though in this Region of ours~~ Lastly, though in this Region of ours we seldome want more then {very} ~~moderat~~ {temperate} ventilations; yet for the novelty diversion & ~~some~~ in some seasons the ~~use~~ {benefits} of it, when the aire of our very Gardens is anithing ~~intemperate~~ immoderate, hott, or stagnate, it is corrigible & {wonderfully} attempered by the invention of artificiall *Ventiducts*. They are made by collecting the aire in Earthen pipes of ~~the~~ {a} larger size then usually for water, or other camerated channells, tunnelled some what largely & of that shape above where they receive ~~this aire~~ & draw in the{is} ~~ayre~~ {spirit}, & are best to be placed where they may respect some Vallie or contracted place exposd to the winds {or so} ~~as~~ as *Gassendus*[xxxix] describes them in the life of {the noble} Pherustius *per Canaleis ac tubulos* brought *e criptis* ~~fro~~ *domum usque* from farr, *per meatum subterraneum* & then distributed in the Roomes, where at pleasure you may refresh the aire in Summer; Such as are now {above all usd in *Languedoc* & about Montpelier in their houses and} extant comming from the mountaines neere Vincentia in Italy, & these with a stop cock may be {graduated &} governd {& opned & playd with} at ~~pleasure~~ like water, or as the Antient Romans did their *Caliducts*,

which was the introduction {but} of a hotter Vapour[18] ~~from boiling Iland~~ {But} it is
by ~~these~~{is} {kinds of} invention (though feasible also with an Organ billowes) that
a ball may be tossed & made to play aloft in the aire, no vissible body touching it, if
the issue be made in the middle or {floore} ~~bottome~~ of the ~~floore~~ {Roome}, & some
what concave, like that which we described of the dauncing of Symbols upon the
Water Jettos in the foregoing chapter: ~~an~~ pretty example of ~~this~~ {which} we have beheld in the ~~tripudiating~~ {tripudiating} ball. In the **[page 145]** The Musique roome at
Frascati, at which the lesse perspicacious Travellor is wonderfully astonished. {I sayd
the organ breath dos this, as hereafter we describe it from the **[continued in margin]**
rarefaction of the Water & compression of the airs; but the other is safer & far more
naturall.} And thus we have ~~don with~~ finisht what we had to say concerning Mounts,
Prospects, Præcipices, Grotts, etc, to which we might add Pythian Vaults, Legislative
mountaines, Hills of Blessing & Cursing for to ~~these~~ {Such} uses were these ~~places~~
{solitarie} & reverent places consecrated of old, as greately contributing to the ~~raising~~
{inciting} of ~~our~~ devotion, contemplative & Philosophicall Enthusiasme: {~~but of this~~
~~in its due place~~} ~~In solitudine puriar cælum, apertius, familiarior as The Learned Dr:~~
~~Casaubon shewes us, out of that Epist. of Hippocrates to Philopoemon shewes us; and~~
~~that such~~ {these}[xl] {as} places {that} have allways bin affected by such as have attained
to that sublimity of mind as to be superiour to all worldly cares that they might not
be obnoxious to impertinent disturbances:[19] **[Text crossed out from here to *]** For
as often as the mind, interrupted in its operations by severall objects, would have the
body to be still, presently it betakes it selfe unto these Retirements, where nothing
can molest it, & where all disturbances are excluded & dare not approch for reverence of those that inhabite there: For there inhabite the Artes, {the Virtues, Gods,
& Daimons, Angels, Counsells, & deities yea} the wide and ample Firmament itselfe,
with all its varieties of Starrs & Planets of ~~sever~~ various motions, by which it is so
beautifully decked and adorned; & indeede whatsoever can dispose the curiositie for
the Speculation of Nature & her incomparable workes, Such affections as are better
felt then expressed: Hence that of the *Orator* in his booke of *divination, Nullos nemora,*
Sylvæque multos omnes aut maria commovent, quorum furibunda, mens videt ante multa quæ
futura sunt. {Upon this account it is we shall here after shew how}* The sight of vast
objects, as Rocks, & Mounts ~~and~~ willd Prospects, and the attent consideration of some
naturall object in a Solitary place, ~~Especially if an Eccho by joynd,~~ dos dispose some
men to Ecstasie, transporting their thoughts beyond {the} ordinary limits, & raises
strong affections in them: And for this cause doubtlesse did so many Prophets & holy
men retire to them {as ~~Elias & others~~} *quam in solitudine purior cœlum apertius familiarior*

---

18. **[Insertion on separate piece of paper]** But my Ld: Bacon seemes to commend rather the couching of pot shards & fictile vessells in the Water (as they practise
about Gaza) to collect the wind from the top, & passe it downwards in spouts as it
were ~~rath~~ than these Italian pennings ~~of the winds~~, & reverberations of the winds,
But it is etc:

19. **[Margin note]** We may say of these elevated places as the Panegyrist of the
remote birth of Constantine Sacratiora sunt profecto mediterraneis loca vicinia cælo,
et inde proprius a Dijs mittitur (I will say) Hortulanus ubi terra finitur. These places
being neerer the heavens, & so more sacred then they are lands end as it were.

deus {as} ~~says~~ *Origen* {says}:[20] And such as these were ~~the~~ {other} mountains {of Judah} ~~Carmell~~ nemorus & full of odoriferous shrubs celebrated by the frequency of the prophet{s} ~~Elias~~. But none so famous as that of *Olivet*, called in Scripture *Mons Sancta*[.] For here the holy David fling from his rebell Sonn, went up barefoote, weeping, & worshiping God; & there the Son of David did use often to retire to his devotive pernoctations, here he left the last impressions of his blessed ~~feete~~ {foot stepps} in memory whereoff our British Helena ~~built~~ {erected} her yet extant Oratorie **[page 146]** And here 'tis like{ly} he will first appeare againe, & leade us from this terrestriall {~~Paradise~~ Elysium} to his heavenly ~~Elysium~~ {Paradise}. {The Pierion Mountaine gave name to the Thutes for its amoenity.} Of Horeb we have seene exact descriptions, and the very landskipp has something of majestie & horror in it. It seenes to have three conspicuous tops, & in the middle was the Law giver, to be ascended by no lesse then 11000 stepps of stone from the Monastry of the Greeke *Colojeros* which ~~stands~~ (is seated} at the foote of it.

Mount Tabor is ~~a~~ most incomparably fitted for these retirements, & is {naturally} ~~as~~ round as if it were cast up by ~~And & was~~ heretofore everywhere invested with delicious trees, shrubs, & ~~flowers~~ the most fragrant flowers, which were allways coverd with a sweete deaw that distilld upon them, & these ~~so in~~ nemorous places so haunted by birds, and beasts, ~~ut totus hic mons pascendis oculis~~ as ~~if~~ the whole mountaine seemed to be dedicated to the pleasing of the senses: So ~~fit~~ {sweete} a place it ~~seemes~~

---

20. **[Insertion on separate piece of paper]** Some portions of the Earth were affected with divine honour. The Cappadocians, & the Daci, ~~as we find~~ esteem Mountains for Gods, as is to be seen out of Strabo & Max. Tyrius. Of ~~Tabor the~~ M: Carmel thus Tacitus. 2. Hist [2.78] Est Judæam inter Syriamque, Carmelus. ita vocant montem deumque . nec simulacrum deo, aut templum: sic tradidere majores: aram tantum et reverentiam. ~~for such~~ To the same purpose also: Suet: in Vesp: c. 5 & {but} what is antienter then all this is Scylax Caryandensis *Κάρμηλος ὄρος ἱερὸν Διὸς*. The mount Carmel, the Temple of Jupiter It signifies a Temple & the Seate of God; nay a God ~~{him}selfe~~ itselfe; from the genius of the place, & happly twas so because of Elias the Thisbites Schoole & habitata Amc: of which: Se John the patriarch of Hierusalem of the institution of the first Munks:

[Insertion on another piece of paper] Maimonides in his book de Idololatria shewes ~~what~~ that they first put the Gods sub arboribus: maius in lucis quam in templis says his Interpreter Vossius. ~~after them~~ as the antient Germans long observed it:

& Loca edita were {as we sayd} the first area as he thought & {before} the artificiall, & tis plain in Herodotus: L. 1. c: 131.

that the Persians temples a long time had neither statues temples nor altars: *νομίζουσι Διὶ μὲν ἐπὶ τὰ ὑψηλότατα τῶν ὀυρειων ἀναβαίνοντες θυσίος ἔρδειν [ἔρδειν]* because they usd to have their sacrifices & devotions on the tops of mountains: & these the Greeks calld ~~them~~ the ~~old~~ tops of hills *βωμοὺς* ~~because~~ as suggesting such places even by nature herselfe destin'd to the divine culture, & the Americans say Acosta held them in greate veneration. **[Continuation indicated but not present]**

[Margin note] Grotius upon 3. Reg: 3. 23. They cald the Gods of Israel Dij montium, {~~ὀρεβατω~~} *ὀρεβατώ* by which name the Greeks cald Pan, & say {because} heathen heard that God gave the law on a mountain.

appeares ~~it was~~ {to have bin} that our Saviour chose it above all the hills of *Judah* to make a heaven upon Earth on, when his countenance became more restilgent[?] then the Sun upon it, & when he so ravished st Peter, that he would willingly never have descended from it: There is now a most sweete & delicious Garden planted upon the very place as we have read, full of fountaines and walld about, to which they resort with greate devotion.[21]

---

21. **[Insertion on separate piece of paper]** And that we may {~~give~~} say something of Caves, the ~~example~~ **[Margin note]** Se: Pom: Mela: cf **[end]** {description} of that {humble} Vorage nere the citty Corycus ~~is almost incredible~~ {not far from Cilicia & the promontory of Sarpedon} will furnish us with an instance of what nature has made in that kind, the most stupendious; ~~for opening~~ it enters at the ~~jawes~~ {Summite} of a mountain descending {no lesse than} a mile & quarter, where it enlarges itselfe into a {Spacious} Valley which is on every side beautified with trees & flowers, most pleasant to behold, & the ~~des~~ foresayd descent to this being wonderfully uneven, is yet adorn'd & shaded with covert, & ever & anon ~~breaks out~~ breaking out with ~~noble~~ {naturall} cascades of water which thunder amongst the prominent rocks & huge stones; being come to the ~~foot~~ botome of this {Crypta}, there opneth another hollow Grott into which being {a little} entered, there is a sound as it were of confused musique, but as the Traveler proceedes forwards to the more obscure part, he finds a passage without end, ~~descends~~ sinking as into some {profound} Mine, at the botome whereoff rises up ~~an~~ mighty ~~river~~ sourse which ~~running~~ {after it has run} a smale way, sinkes downe againe into the Ground, which swallows it up making a horrible roaring, & neere this are {frequent} other Caverns which even affright the Spectators so that few dare penetrate into them; ~~ye~~ yet are the places esteemed holy, the habitation of Daimons & Gods of old; for the naturall arching, & pendulous stones at so prodigious a height, the Echos, & Sounds caused by the winds, & waters, render it so majesticall & great that no man beholds it without ~~won~~ some wonderfull ~~chan~~ ectasie, & {even} changes in himselfe. {but describe Cliffden:}

To come neerer home, wonderfull for the effects is that at Bracciano in Italy, calld the Sasso ~~about 20 mile from~~ {not far ~~neere~~ from} Rome in which whoever incommoded with frigid & cold disease ~~such as~~ the Paralisis, Leprosy, Venetian hues, Arthriticall Dropsy, etc: goes naked in, ~~lyes~~ lying upon his belly holding his breath (as much as may at best) & ~~making~~ {discovering} no ~~sigh~~ Signes of life or motion, is immediately invirond with multitudes of Serpents, who creepe out of ~~their~~ severall crevices of rocke, & ~~these~~ licke, & sucke, {& draw} out all the malignity of the disseased body to a perfect cure: The Country men who will shew Travellors this experiment, usually goe {stript} in for a {smale} piece of monie, & they tell us a tale of a chiefe Serpent who has a crowne on his head that comes out first, the rest following him as their Basilisk or king: Such as desire the effects perfectly, use to take opium that they may lie the stiller & be without fright: the best Season for the Cure is in May: {A coach-Man of} the Cardinal of Valencia was of late years cured of the F: pox & Goute of which he was miserably tormented in this ~~Cave~~ Grotto: but of this, as also of the reason of this cure Se: Tho: Rautheline: Hist: cent: II. Hist: 47. and as ~~I~~ {we} remember Kircher speakes of it in his Magnes: & attributes it to the sweate which the Subterranean hott vapour (which is Sulphureous) of the ~~Earth~~ Earth ~~causes~~

We the more readily give instances of these, not onely to refresh the Reader, but because we would ~~wil~~ reccommend the shape of them to the imitation of our very Gardner, & that in raising even at these which are made by hand, we might strive to ressemble them: for even that also will be found extreamely to highten & exhalt our contemplations: Nor ~~are their~~ is *Europ* destitute of such vast & goodly objects: we have travelled the *Apenines* & *Aspiring Alps* & can well remember the affections & rapture extraordinary which then possessd us: The *Mons Serratus* seemes to penetrate the skies, & the hills about it ~~seeme~~ to be so disposd, as if ~~nature had intended~~ {they did reverence} ~~them~~ to this {superb} pinacle, ~~& nature~~ such a religious horror it strikes into the spectator: for here ~~the it~~ {they} sometimes runs along like a vast wall, with the apparition of frequent Towers, prominent and goodly Castles, {& pendulous clifts} {which with} a certain trembling surprises at the sight of the huge prominences which seeme ready to ~~fall~~ {precipitate} upon the ~~climbing~~ {culminating} Travellor, yet so ~~are~~ has nature decor{ate}d the passages with all that {Art or} human industry can wish, even for **[page 147]** of the hortulan delights, naturall fountains, stupendous Cascades, profound Grotts, {lowd} Echos, Trees, flowers, & hearbs of all sorts, that which with the cheerfull warbling of the birds, the murmour of the Waters ~~&~~ the gratefull shades of the umbrage Trees & goodly prospect oer Land & Sea, the place of all others under heaven seemes to have bin intended ~~to~~ for an Idea of what we would describe in this present Chapter, so that we shall not neede to ~~speake~~ {discorse} of the flowry *Athos*, nor the delicious *Paneia*: The *Spelunca Adami* where he did his pennance, nor the caves of *Macpela* celebrated for the Sepultures of the Patriarchs; or those {other} of the *Trachoritiall* region; though to passe all these we might bring noble descriptions even out of our owne Iland the Elysium of Greate Britane, especially about *Wales* & *Derbyshire*; because we have ~~don~~ sayd enough to shew what they are ~~we meane~~ we ~~meane~~ intend in this chapter, & what their effects & what they signifie to contemplation & devotion: ~~And so~~ {Let us hear} that Lover of the Mountaines ~~Veni di Libano~~ speaking to ~~the Sponsa~~ {Holy Church} *Veni de Libano Sponsa mea, veni de Libano, veni coronaberis de capite Amana, de vertice Sanir et Hermon, de cubilibus*

{produces}, which causes sleepe, & that stillnesse invites out the Serpents who never leave licking till all the sweats be off, then when the patient wakes or moves, they retire into their cranies: verte

[continued on verso] But before I conclude this period I should thinke that Snow pitts & Conserves of Ice might most aptly come into even the necessary ~~orname~~ accomplishments of Gardens, ~~not onely as they~~ because they contribute to so many Philosophicall aydes of cooling of wines & beverage, but ~~also~~ of fruite in Summer & preserve of Flowers in beauty; ~~by them We have already described~~ The noble Mr: Royle has honored my description of the making of them in his incomparable Hist: of Cold p: 408: to which I onely add, that a pumpe may fitly be placed beneath neere the entry to exhaust any admitted water which may rest at the bottom, unlesse ~~it can be~~ the pit can be sunke so as to make a draine: & what I shall add of ~~Ornament~~ {decorum}, how in stead of straw & thatch, it may be covered with Turfe upon an Arch of brick ~~or flint~~ layd in tarris, on which a mound of good thicknesse may be raised, & on that I would have Cypresse planted to preserve it from the Sun, & for a speciall ornament, & to convert a rude deformity into shade & beauty:

Leonum, de montibus pardorum. For [22] tis observed by the {late B: of Down & Conner} ~~Devout learned & my most Reverend friend Dr. Taylor that accomplished~~ Father of the *Grand Exemplar*, {whilst he lived} {our} worthiest Friend, that our B: Saviour affected the mountaines more then all the places of the Earth, {besides} that the Arke ~~rested~~ {reposd} on a Mountain after the Flood: ~~Gen: 8: 4~~ On a Mountaine Abraham [23] was to offer his Son: On a Mountaine ~~he~~ {God} appeared to Moses, On a Mountaine {he} received the Law, On a Mountaine he shewd him the Land of Promise, On a *Mountaine, he ravished Eliah*: On a Mountaine he commanded the Temple to be built: On a Mountaine Christ resisted the noblest Temptation: On a Mountaine he made his blessed Sermon: On a Mountaine he passed nights in prayer: To a Mountaine he fled when they would have made him King: On a Mountaine he was Transfigured, On a Mountaine he finished our Redemtion & died for us, From a Mountaine he Ascended and over A mountaine it is likely ~~we sh~~ he will ~~come~~ {appeare} againe to judge both the quick & the dead: So that well with holy David may our devout Gardiner exclaim, I lift up my eyes unto the hills, from whenc cometh my Salvation. ~~For~~ His Sepulcher was **[page 148]** in a ~~Rock~~ Grott, & that Grott was in a Garden, to which our Saviour did so frequently resort; & as if he would consecrate both the place & the profession above all others, he chose {there} to ~~be seene~~ appeare first in the forme of a Gardiner, & to sanctifie those ~~places~~ retirements with his glorious ~~body~~ presence. And this shall suffice to shew the use of inclosed Mountaines, & Solitary Recesses for ~~devotion~~ contemplation, Devotion, ~~inspiration~~ {Enthusiasme}, Rapture, Divine {Inspiration} and Legislative informations, for Cursing, & Blessing, Oratories, & Altars: {& for the fixing of those in our imagination} for there they had their Adyta & Antra where the inspirations came both to Gods, eminent ~~people~~ {prophets} of old, to the Sibylls {according to their measure of light} & to others: To such places did the Patriarchs, Prophets, & our B: Saviour retire for the exercise of the sublimest ~~devotion~~ & most seraphique devotion: It was haply commanded *them*; & never prohibited Christians that we can learne; {if it be true [24]} Sure we are the holy Hermites chose such places in the primitive ardours, & they are spirituall helps, diffused in the very frame of nature, & of the Creation, & to last as long as the very mountaines themselves: Poets, Orators, and men of the most heavenly and divine Geniuses find in themselves (at lucid intervalls) some raptures & even inspirations, elevation{ing} {them} like the Philosse mentioned in *Eunapius*, that he was taller in this study in tyme of speculation than at other tymes and so scholar ~~& contemplative men~~ holy & contemplative men are even above the drynesse of their owne reasons & narrower intellect at ~~other~~

---

22. **[Margin note]** Cant: cf.

23. **[Margin note]** 4 Gen: 8. c.22.2. 31 Exod: 18. 19 Exod 11. Rex 19.9. 4 Mat: 8. 5 Mat: 1. 14 Mat: 23. 6: John: 15. 17: Mat: 1. 19 Jo: 17. 1 Acts: 9. Psal: 121: 1.

24. **[Insertion on separate piece of paper]** They were not to set up altars on Mountains nor plant Groves neere them, ne passiva (to use Ter[t]ull[ian's] phrase) et voluptuosa religio, aut uniatem veræ religionis enerbat, as B[eatus]: Rhenum [Rhenannus] explaine it: in lib: advers: potest: Yet **[continued on verso]** where there is now no feare of the returne of these Superstitions, & that our B: S: has sanctified them & that holy Hermites etc:

{such} {those} Seasons, {& raises us to highest conceptions} so as they may even say {cogitante calescimus illo}

> *Est deus in nobis, sunt et commercia coeli*
> *Sedibus æthereis Spiritus ille venit*
> *Mens congesta deo*

[25]And now let any grave Divine that has conversd with Antiquitie {but} ~~tell~~ {informe} us {in} what age these holy inspirations and the benefit of Sacred Retirements to Mountaines, Caves, Deserts, {And the like} forsooke the ~~Earth~~ Church of Christ, who himselfe; as well as St Paule went into the Wildernesse immediately after their Baptisme to conflict with the ~~greatest~~ {most dreadfull} adversarie of Mankind & of Gardens ~~who~~ {because} he ~~raised~~ {made} him ~~out~~ loose Paradise, and the {innocent} delights of what this chapter has {so} ~~celebrated~~ much celebrated.

[Page 149] {Here place the Iconismes
    Improve this Chap: by Dr Plots descript of Echos: etc}[xli]

---

25. **[Margin note]** For so the Holy Hilarie: contra Auzentium. when as yet the Church of Christ had but a few corruptions appearing: Montes mihi et Sylvæ, et lacus etc sunt Iutiores: In illis enim prophetæ aut manentes, aut demersi Dei spiritu prophetabant; for what a sweete & safe retreate have they afforded Eliah & to as many others as they have protected from ~~tyme to tyme~~ the rage of Tyrants, and the heate of persecutions, from the temptations of the world, & from the ~~meatus~~ {impertinences} of life.

CHAP: XI

Of statues, {Payntings}, Columns, Dyals, Perspectives, Pots, {Urns} Jarrs, Vasas and other Ornaments:

As a Garden without Water hath no life, as depriv'd of its radicall humor; so without *Sculpture*, it has no action; for by this it is that we reppresent the figures of ~~Men~~ those {greate} Heros, & Genious's that have so well deserv'd of Gardens, & so much celebrated by the Antients, affording an ornament not onely of exceeding pleasure to the eye, but to the intellect it selfe, and the furniture of the most profitable discourses, whilst we behold our *Elysium* ~~inri breathing &~~ inriched & (as it were) breathing with the statues of those Gallant & illustrious Persons, whose actions have filled our Histories with the most glorious ~~act~~ actions instances, & whose inventions & industries have stored our Gardens with the ~~best~~ {noblest} of her diversions:[1]

And what can more aptly refresh our memories of them, then their lively reppresentations! ~~It was for this reason that~~ {For which} {It was for this} {reason {that} the *Ægyptians*} ~~we~~ first, & then the *Greekes* & *Romans* decreed them, placing {them} not onely in their Gardens; but likewise in the Market{s} ~~places~~ {piazzas} & highways; ~~&~~ {nor with lesse gratitude} ~~we~~ would {we} have the statues of our most famous Gardners ~~in pictures or plaster~~ {statue} to adorne the *Pinacothecæ* {Repositories} & *Porticos* with some of their Elegies ~~in short~~: {& to preserve their memories} As {did} that ~~noble illu~~ noble *Genious* & *Virtuoso, Paulus Jonius* ~~to adorne~~ {embelish} ~~his Gardens neere the Lago di Coma~~ who by Friends & Letters to the greatest persons then in Europe obtained the true pictures {& statues} of the most illustrious men ~~to adorne his~~ {which he placed in} {to embelish his Galleries &} Ga~~lleries~~{rdens neere the Lago di Como.} ~~non enim poenis tantum deterrent a flagitijs, sed~~

But to institue our *Gardner,* ~~Statues were first made of Wood~~ {& discourse a little of the} materialls & their progresse: *Statues* were made first of {Clay}, Wood, ~~then of~~ Ivory, ~~clay~~ stone, & divers Metalls: Those which ~~made~~ {them} ~~of wood~~ carved them of wood, were called *desectores*, of Clay *Fictores*, of stone & Metalls onely *Marmoraries & Sculptores*, all of them by the common appellation Statuarij: But of all these ~~we~~ preferrable for our Gardens: **[page 150]** we make use onely of the two last; for

---

I. **[Insertion on separate piece of paper]** And for this reason statues were ~~the esteem~~ accounted so essentiall, that a Garden was not esteemed compleate without them: This is that which the Orator means 4: Officium: when he ~~tells us~~ mentions Pythium Canio vendidisse Hortus instructor; for so we gather from the same phrase in the Younger Pliny speaking of the prodigious expense of Domitius Tullus ~~upon~~ {to adorne} his Gardens. Plin: Epist: L: 8: Rufino.

being the most naturall & durable; however, such as are form'd of Plastique{er} worke (of all {certainely} the most antient, & there calld *Sculpturæ matrem*) are not totaly to be rejected, where they may be preserved from the weather, & other violences; nay even ²exposd, being well layd in oyle, Purpurine, (ressembling brasse) & other or *stone-colour* & often refreshed, they have bin knowne to continue 40, 50 yeares or longer; & is indeede a cheape piece of magnificency; being well moulded from antient & excellent things, which are infinitely {render them in our opinion} preferrable to those even of the most lasting & costly materialls, cutt by the same Workemen of our tymes:

There is of late an invention of superinducing a thin Epidermis or Cuticle of Leade upon these Statues of Plaster; which is don by washing the Moulds with molten leade, as the Ladys doe their moulds of Wax Worke, & then filling the Core with Plaster to make it sollid³ The frequent use of these dos indeede sooner impaire the moulds; but the service of it upon the statues so polite & permanent is {dos} infinitely payd reccompense the decay of trifling moulds: But {Yet} for the other of bare plaster, *Diabetes* of old expos'd them to the weather; such was that *Jupiter* placed in the *Capital* by *Tarquinius*, the *Fictile Hercules*, & the *Quadrigæ*, & many others:

But of *Statues* we are to understand that there are fowre kinds; the *Pariles*, *Magna's*, *Majores*, & *Maxima's*: The first were form'd of just proportion, & were made in memory {& for monuments} of wise, learned, & good men: The 2d Sort had neere a Sesquialteral proportion, & were neere {almost} halfe as big more, & therefore calld Ag *Augustæ*, dedicated to Emper Emperours & Kings: The *Majores* were a degree bigger & reppresented a dubble proportion to the life, devoted to the *Heros* & *demi-Gods*; but the greatest of All all were three times as big as the life, consecrated to the *Gods* alone & were either from their inward inanitie or from the Author denominated Colossus's, {and} afterwards grew to so prodigious & mad an excesse & as that of Neros, & that at *Rhodes*, the fall whereoff caused an Earth quake & the broaken pieces loaded 900 Camells, which yet were but some fragments of it, please a thousand {that remained} many hundred years after its ruine {overthrow}. Such {now} as were lesse & shorter (then what we have enumerated) then their due proportion, were the *Signæ*, *Trunc's* and *Busts*, which were {they did} frequently formed of Wax & lesse durable materialls, & for that reason, more carefully preserved {in the drie Galleries & *Atrias*} & places not so obnoxious as the Gardens {open aire} **[page 151]** as the open aire of our Gardens.

Touching the Posture of statues, it is erect, flexid, Cumbent, & various as that of mens; but the upright, & cumbent as most majesticall, So & applicants; so most in use; the one for *Niches* & *Pedistals*; the other for the adornement of *Arches*, *Tympanas* {projectures,} & *Pediments* of buildings, as occasion requires, all of them exceedingly gracefull. The places The places or stations (for a *stando statuæ*) are at the enterances of Walkes Gardens, & *Walkes* {as the ostiarie statue & terminus}, The ascent of

---

2. **[Margin note]** cf. how doe by the statuarys[?] by Northumberland house so as to indure the winter[?] & even lasting in all weather:

3. **[Margin note]** & burning {not sothering} as they sett it on the joynts with exceeding hott leade to consolidate such parts as are necessarily to be set on, as Armes etc: the yron pin usd as in marble

Steppes {upon *Meniana & Scamilla*}; the topps of *Balustrads & Corniches*, which, {if ~~very~~ of considerable altitude,} ought to be made some what inclining for an indispensible reason in Perspective, least approching, they too much foreshorten & therefore also should statues be chosen of such magnitude & proportion (amongst those we have ~~discoursed of~~ {recited}) as may at any reasonable distance appear *Parilia* ~~& not too much contracted~~ {& as they do in the Basse relievos} {up}on the Historicall *Columne of Trajan* in *Rome* to this day; & not too much contracted by the common mistake. Also in the Ni~~ches~~{ces} of *Porticos*, {*Faciatas*}, *Walls*, & {on} some ground *Pedistalls*; *Heads & Busts* betweene the *Flower-pots Vasas*, & huge *Amphoras* produce a most magnificent effect. We have seene Ni~~ches~~{ces}, ~~cutt~~ made & cutt out of the ever-greene hedges & *Palisades*, which have wonderfully become *Statues*; but we do by no meanes approve of {these} Figures to be {framd} ~~made~~ (but very sparingly) of those ~~materialls~~ weake & dissorderly materialls; for reasons already discussed in the *Topiary* workes. Cap:7: Lastly, ~~&~~ {but} principaly, statues have place in & about Fountaines & Water Workes, where they are ~~reppresented~~ {exposd} in all imaginable postures; but not without ~~choice~~ {judicious} delection & choice of the ~~Fig~~ Reppresentation, ~~such~~ none more becomming {upon} those occasions, then such as are proper & relative, ~~such~~ as the *Nymphs, River-Gods, & Watery Deities*; {&} as S^r: H: Wotton handsomly instances in ~~his~~ the *Lawndresse* of *M: Angelo*, of which we have already spoken.[4]

What ornament Statues add to Groves, Grotts, & {silent} ~~Solitudes~~ {recesses} in which[5] {what they contribute to their solitude} {also} *Sphinxes, Harpaies,* ~~Satyrs~~, *Lyons, Goates,* {*Shepeheards*}, *Satyrs,* {*Eremites*} etc: we have likewise shewed in that which went before, and therefore ~~leave~~ {reccommend} such as desire farther instruction in this admirable Arte, to the ~~learned~~ {large} discourses in *Plinie* of old, & of late to *Pompenius Gauricus* the *Neopolitane,* {the} Commentaries of *Ludovicus de Montjosius, Leon Baptista de Alberti,* whom indeede I should have celebrated with the first **[page 152]** {But not onely statues, but even huge Colossus ~~stood~~ {were brought} into Gardens (as that of Nero in the Marian Garden[)]} & so *Obelisks, Pyramids, & Columns* ~~add pleasure~~ {afford} also an extraordinary Ornament to our Gardens, and may, amongst other Antiquities, have place also amongst the *Statues,* ~~as~~ egregious examples whereoff we find, in the *Medicæan* Gardens & those of *Mathæi* at *Rome.* [6]*Ferrarius* describes a *Columne* of Flowers which we referr to a more apposite place; But the~~se~~ two *Metae's* Sudantes {in} the wreaths whereoff the water perpetually descends at *Frascati* are worthy our [7]admiration. {And this ~~Movable~~ furniture was & is esteemd so sacred & genial to the places where they were once ~~pla~~ set, that they often prohibited their removal out of the Gardens, as we learn in Tacitus, & even now at Rome the statues seldome are alienated, but with the sale of the Garden.

---

4. **[Margin note]** Cap: 9:

5. **[Margin note]** Some of them may be made to speake or sing by passing a long pipe of lead through their bodys to the mouth, the other extreame conveyed under ground to some seacret place where the lead orifice being made somewhat open like a tunnel one may speake or sing **[continued in margin of page 152]** sing or whisper to the affright & amusement of the ignorant

6. **[Margin note]** ~~Se Flora~~ vide: L: 3: c. 2.

7. **[Margin note]** Se: cap: lib: 3: c: 7:

And here we should conclude what we have ~~fu~~ to say ~~concerning~~ {of} {about} {of} statues, for the {peopling &} adornement of our *Elysium*. ~~but it will~~ {did it not first} concerne us to speake a word or two concerning the Reppresentations themselves; since (as we ~~sayd~~ affirmed) all are not to be admitted promiscuously; nor indeede (amongst Christians) all that we find they did of old, entertaine in their Gardens.⁸ ~~*Puta* was the statue for the earthly Planett, Pomona for Fruite, Segesta & the Tutalinæ, the Nodini Lactueinæ, Patalena, Hostilinæ, Volatrinæ, Sinensis, Devorronæ, Robij, Liber, Ceres, Vesta, & the minor~~ *Apollo, Liber, Ceres,*⁹ *Vesta*, the obscene *Priapus*, & *Flora*, &¹⁰ *Venus* {Pomona} ~~Pato~~ {Rubiga}, etc ˣˡⁱⁱ these were the *Tutelar Gods* of Gardens, To these were added the *minor Deities Puta, Rusina, Nodæa* {Runinas}, *Patalena, Hostilina, Runeina, Spinensis, Segesta*; The *Tutulinæ, Nodini, Lactucinæ, Volatrina, Devorronæ,* & ~~{besides the statues of Amphyra Mercurie}~~ & as none of the least meritorius *Stercoraties* that invented & improved the dunging of Grounds & composts:

Nec cultor nemorum reticebere Mænalide Pan,

Pan must not be forgotten, ~~Pan~~ *Pan omnium custos*: Geor: [1.17] For —— *Habitarunt dij quoque Sylvas*: Virg: [*Eclog.* 2.60] Especially {Orpheus} *Sylvanus, Faunus, Ilithia,* ~~etc.~~ wth others: ~~These had all of them place in the Gardens of old~~ Besides the Statues of *Amphyra, Mercurie, Argus, Eæho, Narcissus, Syrinus, Arion,* {the} *Sirens,* & *Naides*, proper for Fountaines, ~~&~~ relating to Sound & *Hydraulique* inventions.

These all had places in the Gardens of old, and may safely for the most part, be {~~modestly~~} introduced into our *Elysium*, with such applications & cautions as we shall hereafter ~~shew~~ declare: In the meane tyme, that to shew how the Antients, did not ~~place~~ {admitt} into their Gardens *Priapus* & other obscene *Scar-crows*, out of any immodest principle **[page 153]** as divers ~~learned~~ (even amongst the learned) we find to have conceived; we will here presume to make some ~~reflexions~~ enquirie concerning the reason, {& occasion} ~~of fixing~~ why that *Statue* was so much celebrated in *Gardens*, & the *Mythologie* is this. *Priapus* signified the *Solarie* virtue, *et Hortis præesse dicitur, propter eorum fecunditatem* {Priapus} (says Isodor} {was faind} &¹¹ {to præside in Gardens because of their fertility} naturally it is the Sun itselfe, as {~~is~~} easily deducible from the supposed hymns of Orphæus. [Hymn 5]

---

8. **[Margin note]** Alcamenes ~~was the first I reade of~~ plac'd his famous Venus which he made in his Garden at Athens, & after that they invited more of their Deities thither, & then came in place Venus, Mercury, Harpocrates & of the heros Hercules, Achilles etc

9. **[Margin note]** which indeede I should have nam'd first because ~~it was~~ the first statue of brasse which ever the Romans dedicated was to this Hortulan Godesse.

10. **[Margin note]** All the Deæ Matres Asta{r}te, Natura Tellus, All Garden Genij long since celebrated even in this Brittain of ours as Mr: [John] Selden shews us out of an Inscription in Sir R: Cottons Garden: See his Dijs Syr: Sintag 2. c. 2. & Terras was thought to be the Mother of all the rest namely of the Gods Lucret: L: 2. & the antient Idol worshipers confounded her with heaven not knowing which was first which we do.

11. **[Margin note]** vide Isodor: Orig: L: 8: c. 11.

καὶ κόσμον
λαμπρὸν ἄγων φάως ἁγνὸν ἀφ' ὅυ σε φάνητα κικλήσκω
Ή δὲ Πρίηπον ἄνακτα

~~per mundum~~
~~Emicantem ducens lucem, à parte phaneta voco~~
~~Atque Priapum regem~~
That round this Ball
Carriest the glorious light, where I thee Call
Phanest, and King Priapus.

For *Priap* is certainely the same that *Horus* in *Ægypt*, that is *Sol*, of which ~~an~~ {pregnant} instance out of *Suidas* puts all out of question. τὸ ἄγαλμα τοῦ Πριάπου etc etc. The *Ægyptians* (sayth he) calld *Priapus Horus*, & carved him like a man holding a Scepter in his right hand, to [12]denote his regiment over Land & Sea; & in his left, τὸ ἀιδδῖον, because he sowes the Earth with Seedes: Winged, to shew the celeritie of his motion, ~~& with~~ The Circles of the Disch indicat his rotunditie; to conclude τουῦτον [?] τω ἤλιο δοξάζουσι, he is the very same with *Sol* {himselfe}; some attribute all this to *Pan* as *Pharnatus* & others; ~~but~~ {which} we passe ~~them~~ over expressly to avoyde ~~the impertinency~~ prolixitie: But after *Priapus* is thus decried, ~~it will &~~ {& in some sort} defended; it will haply be objected that *Flora* was realy a lewd ~~slutt~~ {strumpet} & so by no means fitting to be admitted into our Gardens:

    Lactanties ~~was~~ ('tis confessed) is extreamely bitter on this subject: *Just: L: 1: c: 10*[.] She had (says he) amassed greate riches by her prostitute life, & afterwards upon bequeathing her wealth to the *Roman People*, they out of gratitude celebrated their *Floralia* in memorie of her; and to acquitt her of the ignomonie, faind her to be the *Godesse* of *Flowers*, & to præside in our *Coronarie Gardens*: And after this Sorte, many grave Authors goe away with it, & pay them selves as with the veritie: But let us see what **[page 154]** (amongst others) The learned ~~learned~~ *Vossius* says to this: *L: 1: de Orig: et progressus Idololat Vellem Lactantius* ~~(says he)~~ *addidisset suamne de isto conjecturam adduxisset; an alios secutus sit auctores sane non arbitror, ullam fuisse ejus nominis me retricem, quæ sua legerit P: Romano.* ~~He~~ I wish (says he) *Lactantius* had added, whither it were his owne conjecture; or that he had ~~foll~~ taken up the opinion {from} ~~of~~ some other Author; truely I do not believe, that there ~~ever~~ {ever} was a Lewd woman of her name, who gave her estate in that manner to the Romans; Thus, *Vossius*: For the *Floræ Sacra* were in the time of *Romulus* himselfe, introduced by K: *Tatius*: & *M: Varro de L-L.* confirmes it also, for the word is *Sabine*, of whom they received that Deity. And the *Floralia* themselves celebrated first: *A: V: C: L > XIII. C . Claudio Centhone, & M: Sempronio Tuditano Coss*: not ~~for~~ in memory of *Flora* The ~~whores~~ {famous strumpets} Legacy: *Sed ex pecunia multaticia eorum, qui peculatus damnati forent, qui* ~~puq~~ *publicum P. Romani agrum occupassent*: And ~~'tis~~ {this is} confirmed, {by} the *Medaills* or *Coynes* then stamped by the *Ædiles*, in which ~~the~~ was *Roma* at one side, & {on} the *Reverse* the figure of a Ram or Sheepe: the ~~figure~~ {Symboll} of the *Mulct* or *Peculatus*; & {so} the crime being *à pecude, pecunia* came in time to be the {common} name for mony. The *Inscription* about it was. M . POBLICIUS . MALLEOLUS, & ~~here was~~ {thus have we} the institution [13] of the

---

12. **[Margin note]** Se more of him in Stephanus & Suidus etc:
13. **[Margin note]** the day was 4: Cal: May

Floralia, & the {true} reason of it not every yeare celebrated neither, 'till it had bin afterwards decreed *A . A. V. C. L > L XXX L postumio Albinos & M. Popillio Lænate Coss*: upon ~~occasion~~ emergency of a very intemperate Spring, & barren yeare ensuing, that the Flowers, ~~blo~~ & Trees, might prosper by the propitiousnesse of that Goddesse, & so [14]~~tis~~ {I se it} celebrated by the Poet in his *5: Fastor*:[15] But we spare our Reader.[16]

---

14. **[Margin note]** Ovid:

15. **[Insertion on separate piece of paper]** where we have not the least mention of her levity but her unwilling rape by Zephyr recounted by her selfe as the ingenious poet brings her in [Ovid: *Metamorphoses* 5.183–327]

     *   Dum loquitur vernas efflat ab ore rosas

While from her lipps She vernal roses breathed:

Chlori, eram quæ Flora Vocor etc: ~~35 Verses~~

De quorum per me Sanguine etc: 35 verses, & then a little

after, she declares her dominion

Forsitan in teneris tantum mea regna corones

esse putes to Talia dicentem etc. ——— 14 verse

So also how solemly ~~celebrated~~ {instituted} first in Aprill

convenere patres, et si bene floreat annus: 4 verses

& after in May

Mater ades florum ludis celebranda jocosis etc: 4 verses

*Englished by Gower p: 107: etc: [John Gower, fl. 1640.]

16. **[Insertion on separate piece of paper]** Pomona who presides over fruite we learn out Varro & Festus: she ~~had~~ was in such veneration that she had a peculiar Flamen who was cald Romonalis

Vertumnus was another that may have place here, & is described by Propertius L: 4: to be the deity *ad omnes figuras ac formas opportunus*: Ovid tells us he was Thuscan prince that first taught us skill in vines & orchard fruite & therefore his feast was celebrated in October: I say nothing of ~~Si~~ Seia, Segesta, Tutilina, Robigus & many more which you may have out of prophan Authors {Pliny: Macrobius} & St Aug: de Civit Dei ~~L: 4 de: iv: etc: but~~ {onely} ~~let~~ may not passe by Bonus eventus or these ~~image~~ {state} ~~se~~ Plin 35: says Ephranor made holding a dish in his right hand & the head of a poppy in the left: & ~~our~~ because our Master Varro is so devout to him & he begins nothing without particular invocate: Such another statue did the famous Praxiteles place in the Capital & indeede there remaine as yet some ruines of a temple so dedicated at Rome twixt the Minerva & St Eustachius

To these add Pilumnus & {his brother} Picumnus of whom Servias 6: Æned: the stercoration deities, some will have them the same with Sterculius, which was the surname of Saturne: St ~~Macro~~ {Macrobius L: 1. Saturn: c. 7:} & for our Bees fate we add Mellona, out of Arnobius:

& Terminus for safeguard so established by N: Pompilius: that men might not contest above the limits: ~~Se Dionysius: L: 4.~~ This stout God would not even give place to Jupiter as we may se in {Livy} Dionysius, Ovid, Augustin etc: & the witty Enigma in Agellius. L. 12 c. 6: Semel, minusæ, an bis minus sit etc: **[insertion on verso]** Terminus: his statue emerged out of square stone {or stump of wood} crowned {& anoynted} Se Arnob: cont: Gent: L: 1. & Min: Felix: Cl: Alex: L: 7: strom: in protrept:

~~But~~ {And} if these instances be not {yet} sufficient to wipe of the reproch, {from our chast goddesse} & vindicate {her dominium &} the use of these ~~statues~~ antient reppresentations, we shall not impugne: But concurr with those who shall {rather} reccommend {to our Gardners} the introduction of the statues of the *Patri-archs,* ~~*Adam,*~~ *Kings,* and *Heros* which we find in the sacred stories, such as *Adam, Noah, Abraham,* ~~(for he~~ *Jacob* (for they ~~in~~ made **[page 154a]** planted Groves):[17] {Also} *Solomon, Nabal, Susanna,* {*St Paulinus*} etc: and in the prophane, The most morall & {famous} ~~excellent~~ *Zoroaster, Ossyris,* {*Semiramis*} *Hesiod,* {*Thalia*}, *Democritus, Epicurus, Xenophon, Hieron, Philomet, Agathocles, Menander, Aristomenes, Crates, Lysimachus, Cyrus, Aristophanes, Dionysius, Mensorates,* {*Aristotle*}, *Varro, Cato the Censor, Tremellius, Virgil,* {*Mecoenus*}, *Seneca, Pliny, Theophrastus, Fabricius, Curius Dentatus, Quintus Cincinnatus, Furius Antinus, Cicero, Lucullus,* {*Dioscoridus*}. And of later times, *Constantinus Pogona-tus,* ~~Higin~~[18] ~~Cornelius Celsus,~~ *Matthiolus, Hippolito d'Este,* Petro Aldobrandino, not to omitt our *Parkinson, Johnson* & *Gerhard, Clusius, Taber[nae] Montanus, Lobel,*[19] & sundry others which we might enumerate, worthy of eternal memorie both for their writings, ~~& aff~~ inventions, & ~~affections~~ to Gardens, whose statues may aboundantly, & with better reason, supplie the ornament {of} ~~with~~ those fained and impure Dieties which did formerly ~~decore~~ {prophane} the Gardens of the superstitious *Ethnicks*: abating onely, that for their exquisite workemanship sake ~~& Art~~ even some of those also may be ~~warily~~ judiciously exposed, ~~or cons~~ in our ~~Gardens~~ *Elysium* {inserted either in the Wales, or erected in solitary places} or conserved amongst the *Marmora* and things of Art in the *Peristyles* {*Atrias*} & *Galleries* destind for Collections of that nature; where likewise *Urnes, Sepulchers,* {*Sarcafas*}, *Altars,* ~~and Ins~~ {*Mezzo*}, *Basse Relievos* & *Inscriptions* have their due places, & are of extraordinary use & benefit for Learned men & Antiquaries; a noble *Specimen* whereoff we have in the *Marmora Arundeliana* collected by *Mr. Selden,* out of the learned and reverend Wales of the Gardens ~~of~~ at *Arundel house* in *London;*[20] & in those of *Bossius* at *Rome:*

Lucian: Apul: L: 1. Floridor: & seculus Flacc: de conditionibus Agrarum & innumerable poets: There were also some Trees calld Arbores terminales of which Ammicus Marcus: T: 18: {Paulus} & the Lawyers: **[end insertion]**

But above all Pan must **[continued on verso]** not be omitted because he is all Nature ~~it~~{her}self, the World, & first & most antient of the Arcadian deities: & his proper place is ~~Woods~~ Groves, with him we joyne Sylvanus: etc: * but enough of this.
* so cald for haunting Woods, his statue held a Cypresse in one of the hands whose culture tis sayd he ~~faind~~ taught: as Martianus Capella L: 5 de Nupt. Merc: et Philolog:

17. **[Margin note]** And {with} reason since Cedrenus affirms that Geruch, the Gr: father of Abraham πρῶτος τους πραξαντάς τὶ ἀνδρεῖον ἀρετῆς καὶ μνήμης ἄξιον ἀνδριᾶσι στηλῶν ἐτίμησε. To be the first that honourd with a statue such as had don any memorable & noble action: This he had out of Euseb: Chron Epiphasis Theophrastus

18. **[Margin note]** Epiphan: l: 1.

19. **[Margin note]** & above all our Cowley then whom none has better deserved of our profession, for the everlasting dignity he has don it.

20. **[Margin note]** at my instance given & transferred to Oxon by the illustrious Sr: H: Howard of Norfolk.

We ~~named~~ {mentioned} *Urnes* & Sepulchers in our Gardens; since there ~~did~~ they did antiently interr their dead; that where they most delighted themselves, ~~wh~~ being alive, there they might also be buried; & supposed their ghosts might sometimes ~~de~~ refresh themselves in them, as in *Elysian* fields: *Strabo* relates, that in *Alexanderia* there were many such Gardens: *Cyrus* was so buried, out of whose monument *Alexander* ~~commanded~~ drew forth an immense treasure; we have in that *Author* the description of his Tomb: So was the Sepulcher of *Belus* in his *Babylonian* Garden; *Sergius Galbus*, *Antoninus Pius*, *Adrian* ~~at Rome~~ were also interred in their Gardens at *Rome* & {the delicious} *Baiæ*; Indeede what were these magnificent *Mausoleas* but *Pensil Gardens*, planted with Cypresse, ~~& other~~ & innumerable *Statues*, *Urnes*, *Obelisks*, *Pillars*, & *Inscriptions*, ~~of which~~ whence that of *Juvenal*:

[Page 155]

> *Contentus famæ, jaceat Lucanus in Hortis*
> *Marmoreis* [Satires 7.79–80]

And for these, celebrated were the Gardens of *Salust*, & many others: But this we have already ~~read~~ given some accompt in our ~~Chapter~~ {discourse} of Groves Chap: 7: {& shall say more L: 3: c: 8 & 9} And we did ~~aledge~~ for what use full, & politique reasons {statues w} ~~& in what relation to the advancement~~ *statues* were thus sprinkled as it were ~~in~~ {about} all their places of diversion, or necessary Convention; & that in such aboundance, as that in *Athens* & *Rome*, *Pliny* records of his Age, ~~that~~ there were almost as many *Statues* as living men; {that thus were in that little Ille **[continued in margin]** Rhodes above 30000 but those of Olympia & Delphos more The Corinthium innumerable:} ~~like~~ a noble contention (says Sr: H: Wotten) in poynt of fertility twixt *Art* & *Nature*; & not onely arguing an infinite ~~ab~~ plenty of *Artists*, & *Materials*; but likewise of magnificent & Majesticall ~~designes~~ {thoughts} even in the commoner persons of those Ages: besides the relation, those ~~noble~~ {glorious} Monuments and Memories of well deserving ~~&~~ & meritorious persons, had to nobler designes; not as a bare & transitory entertainement of the Eyes {onely}, or gentle deception of the tyme; but as it had a seacret & powerfull influence even to{wards} the advancement of *Monarchy*, by their continnuall reppresentations of {great &} vertuous Examples; so as in that poynt, Art became a piece of State; ~~A~~ The same may be applied {also} to the encouragement of Industrious & Ingenious men, when they shall behold the honour which is don to such as by their Art & Science had obliged the World: For thus were the Effigies of Greate & excellent persons us'd to be plac't both in the Gardens [21] & houses, *in prima ædium parte: ut eorum virtutes posteri non solum legerent; sed etiam imitarentur:* ~~but Salust above all~~ Let us ~~have the incom~~ {joyne that golden} ~~parable~~ {period of} Salust [*Bellum Jugurthinum* 4.5–6] upon this {to this} instance: *In prologo sæpe audivi* {says he} *Q: Maximum, P: Scipionem, præterea Civitatis vestræ, præclaros viros solitos ita dicere; eum Majorum Imagines intuerentur, vehementissime sibi Animum ad Virtutem accendi, scilicet non ceram illam, neque Figuram, tantam vim in se habere; sed memoria rerum gestarum eam flammam egregiis viris in pecctore crescere, neque prius sedari, quam virtus eorum famam atque gloriam adæquaverit.* That he had frequently heard that *Q: Maximus*, & the

---

21. **[Margin note]** Se Valer: Max: L: 5. c: 8: Exemp: 3:

greate *Scipio* were wont to say, ~~that~~ when they beheld at any tyme the Images & statues of their Ancestors, that their **[page 156]** very soules were as it were inflam'd ~~to~~
with Courage & virtuous desires; not that these waxen figurines had so powerfull a
charme in them; but the memorie of their famous Exploits it was, which kindled that
zeale in their breasts, & which could not be extinguished 'till by their owne Virtue &
imitation, they had equalizd both their Fame & Glorie; ~~We made~~ How strong a passion ~~it raised~~ the sight of ~~Young~~ *Alexanders* statue {alone} incited in *Julius Cæsar* when
it made him shed teares for anguish or ambition, that ~~so young a man should~~ {such
a stripling in} comparison to his yeares should have so early exceeded his conquests,
{having subdued the whole world, ere he had conqu[ere]d a province:} we may reade
in ~~Authors such as~~ those who ~~write~~ describe his life; & doubtlesse, there is nothing
dos more stimulate a noble & generous spirit, then a virtuous emulation: & for this
reason, *Sr: Tho: More* allowed the use of statues also, in that ~~perfect~~ most ingenious *Idea*
of his *Republique*, where otherwise, we shall find he ~~admitted little~~ {was very sparing}
of {pompous &} unnecessary expenses: ~~Non where~~ {When} discoursing of rewards
& punishments, ~~he says~~, *Non poenis* (~~says~~ he says) *tantum deterrent, à flagitijs; sed propo-
sitis quoque honoribus ad virtutes irritant,* ~~*Deoque*~~ {*ideaque*} *statuas, viris insignibus, et de Rep:
præclare meritis, in Foro collocant in rerum, bene gestarum memoriam, simul ut ipsorum posteris,
majorum suorum gloria calcax, et incitamentum ad virtutem sit:* And ~~thus~~ {therefore} of old,
they {never} decreed *statues*, but to such as had don some ~~worthy~~ {signal} exploits, or
invented some usefull thing; for so they {dignified &} made them Noblemen as the
Æmilij & others; ~~But if~~ For {breaking them {againe} in pieces when by any vile action
or Treason, they deserved so ill of their Country} after all this, if men degenerate from
their industrious Ancestors

> *stemmata quid faciunt? quid prodest, Pontice, longo*
> *sanguine censeri, pictosque ostendere vultus*
> *Majorum, et stantes in Curribus Æmilianos*
> *Et Curios jam dimidios, nasumque minorem*
> *Corvini, et Galbam auriculis nasoque carentem?*
>
> *Tota licet Veteres exornent undique ceræ*
> *Atria. Nobilitas sola est, atque, unica Virtus:*
> > *Juvenal: Sat: 8*: [1–5; 19–20]
>
>   What is't our Ancestors to show,
> In paint or statue! The *Æmilij* plac't
> Intire in charriots, *Curij* to the Wast:

[Page 157]

> *Corvini*, that by th' shoulders lesse appeares;
> And *Galba* wanting both his nose & ears!

{And after:}

> The house why do so many Gen'ralls fill
> Breathing in Marble?

Fill all thy Courts with old Wax ~~Images~~ {Imagrie}
[22] *Virtu's the true & sole Nobilitie:*

And which may serve for a just represe of those who with *Damasippas* do *insanire veteres statuas emando*: as some ill advis'd, & passionat *Antiquaries* have don, to the prejudice of their Fortunes, and reputations in that particular, ~~who~~ running all over the world, ~~&~~ & compassing land & sea, to feede this Vanity. And so much shall suffice to have bin spoken concerning *Statues* etc: as they relate to our *Elysium*. {& to *Gardens*, in which we conceive it a very greate mistake of my L: Bacon, when discoursing upon this subiect he thinkes they do nothing conduce either to their pleasure & amenity: but we have aluded instances sufficient to consult it[.]}[23]

Dyalls are an ornament of necessary use in our Gardens, and such we have frequently seene planted in the Parters & Traile worke; but then the *Circles Lines & Hovers* should be kept very low, that they may not shade the ground to much when the sun is past the *Meridian* at any {considerable} distance: Such a *Dyal* we have seene at *Frascati*, which is ~~ple~~ of Myrtil; but in all that we have hitherto observed, the *Style* or *Index* for being very ~~large~~ long, & made of ~~two~~ one quarter, of wood {& as our to sustaine it} has {to much} the resemblance of a strapado post or Gibbett, so that we could wish that this ~~neces~~ requisite member of it might be contrived into some *statue* in a bending & ~~stoopi~~ inclining posture, resembling the famous *Gladiator*, who might hold ~~an Instr~~ Sword, or ~~staff~~ Speare, so as to indicate the howers, instead of the ordinary ~~Style~~ {gnomon}: And thus a *Horizontal-Dyall* might very nobly become a Parter, being reguarded from the superiour roomes of the Palace or Mansion: {But we reade of a Dyal in Campo **[continued in margin]** Martio of unequal Houers whose style was an obelisk of 115 palms high erected by Augustus afterward flung down by the barbarous Gothes you may see the construction of it in Kirkers Obelisc Pamphilius}[xliii] *Dyals*, which are contrived in stone worke, of several aspects & Faces, Concave, Convex, declining, inclining, {verticall cf} etc: are a noble & gracefull ornament; being made of goodly & large dimensions, as in which to contrive The

---

22. **[Margin note]** {Sr: R:} Stapilton: [Sir Robert Stapylton]

23. **[Insertion on separate piece of paper]** But besides Statues paintings {Signor Verrio Windsor Gardens etc:} have ben in use in Gardens, especially in dry porticos: The most antient piece now in the world is in that of Aldobradu at Rome don in Water a fresca which is a piece of learned use, describing the old Roman manner & rites in the Marriages: upon which severall critics have discoursed, & it gives greate light to their conjectures: But it is especially in use & (in my judgement) most commendable for perspective to enlarge narrow viewes etc as we shall give frequent examp: in the last chaps of this worke:

The Archbishop of Cypresse caused the Walkes of his Gardens in Rome to be so painted with Satyrs, Faunes, Baccanti {Grotesco & other wild things} etc: by that greate Mr: Perino del Vaga, adorning it with divers poses, ~~especially in his Lodges~~ But I like better that of Primaticcia in the Gallery ~~of the Garden~~ at F: Bleau, which is the story of Ulysses's Father planting & working in his Garden, & which is more apposite & chast: this is rarely graven in F by Van Thulden. Arch at Ruel:

Babylonian & Easterne houers, signes, & in summ a projection of the whole Spheare with divers other singularities; & such a Dyall may be placed on a *Pedistall*, & many tymes supplie the ~~pl~~ defect of a Fountaine where water is not to be had:[24] Such as are ~~made of~~ {drawne on} Brasses, are the most vulgar & of those the *dubble Horizontal*, (invented by Mr *Oughtread*) is the most accomplished & universall; but then would we have it described ~~in~~ {on} a plate **[page 158]** of two foote diameter, as is that made by Mr: ~~Greatorex~~ {Alen} in the Garden at Grays–Inn. {But since we lately spoake of statues, what a raritie was that reported by *Hieronomus Rubeus* made by *Severinus Boetius* at *Ravenna* that it turned about with the sun & was indicative of the hour by a magnall & spontaneous motion.} {But} Suppose ~~yet~~ that some crosse Allees ~~with Indi~~ might {in the bordures} be ~~ordered~~ contrived, & furnished, with certaine ~~peculiar &~~ *Indicative* & peculiar plants to the use of *dyalling*; yet so, as the Phantsy be neither too faint, nor too open, would it not appeare a singular invention, more apposite then the former, & a moderne Elegancy[.]

Now by *Indicative–plants* we meane such as may be[25] observed to marke the Weather, & the time of the Day, by their *matutine, meridional,* & *Evening* ~~shutt~~ {postures} openings, dilations, obsequiousnesse, & closings: (for ~~such are noted~~ some of these are noted by my *L: Bacon* to direct the Husbandmen) Thus we will suppose {that} to a dozen of Cypresse trees, or more humble shrubbs, clipped into round bosses or bowles, a *Large Lupine*, or *Heliotrope* should be the *Gnomon*: which in rainy or clowdy seasons, will aspect the true place of the Sun (or very neere it) sufficient to resemble a *Dyall*. & resolve us in the degrees & temper of the ~~weather~~ {aire}, & many other Philosophicall Speculations:[26] For 'tis from here, that our Gardner may prognosticate the Season of the yeare, & that with very great probability, {~~as~~}{taking in} his ~~very~~ Flowers, {~~especially the~~} {most} ~~Indicative plants &~~ plants & fruite; especialy the most Indicative; as by their aboundant ~~flowering~~ {blossoming} & leaving a ~~hard~~ {severe} winter: by the budding of the {wise} Mulbery, the cold {to be} past; & as by ~~some~~ {others} 'tis remarked, that the leaves of the *Ash, Poplar* & {~~divers~~ some} other Trees, turne the very day of the *Solstice*. {Such as are the sallow}[27] Several other curiosities

---

24. **[Margin note]** mention his Majesty's at White hall where is no fountaine

25. **[Margin note]** Vide Kerke Magnes 731 and 750

26. **[Insertion on separate piece of paper incorrectly noted for insertion on page 157]** And if these hortulane miracles be deceiptfully related; tis disingenuous that such learned persons should so considerably relate them:

27. **[Insertion on separate piece of paper]** ~~Plants convertible at the Solstice ipsa die Solstitij;~~ are the Sallow, white poplar, elme, tilia, olive in which observe the tropical harmony, & visible sympathy, when you shall find the face of the leafe turn'd ~~with its~~ to say nothing of the Cicory, malow, calendula, Lotus pratensis, heliotrop, thithymal, helioscop: & all solseques: ~~Lunaria that~~ the Lunaria which observes the moone

Most perspicuous is the Sympathetique dial of the Egyptians only observed by the {mystic} Philosophers which they used in their mistic consultations, viz Lotus aquatica a palustrall plant which at Son rising it rises out of the deepe water & follows the Sunn to the meridian where it seemes to stand, inclining with the Sun againe till it

of this nature may be attempted for the indication of Houers & Seasons by *indicative-plants*; {of which see our Chap: of stupendious plants & particular the **[continued in margin]** hist of the sensitive} Thus ~~we have read~~ Gassendus tells[28] us that ~~the Jesuite Linus filled a glas Phiall of Water of that temper, ut internataret medius globulus cum descriptis circum horis 24, quæ ad pisciculum seu indicem fixum allabentes ex ordine horas diei con notarent, tamquam globulo Cæli motum exactissime~~ *Athanasius Kirkir* sowed the seedes of a certaine Sunflower, *fragmente suberco*, in a fragment of Corke, which did like the Flower itselfe convert towards the Sun, & being placed in a ~~vessell~~ {bowle} of water, ~~the howers being~~ designed & poynted at the houers, which were noted in the Vessell, with ~~an~~ {~~its~~} {an} index {which was fixt in it.} But {on these} we enlarge no farther in this place; because the *Mural* & other sorts of shadows of this nature are {indeede} innumerable; & for ~~that~~ that, we ~~shall~~ {may} have **[page 159]** occasion to ~~disco~~ {speake} ~~inlarge~~ more on this subject when in the next Chapter we ~~shall~~ come to discourse of *Hidrauliq* Inventions, & *Automotes*.

We are now to ~~speake~~ {say} something concerning *Perspective* as it relates to Gardens, & ~~its~~ {the} extraordinary {& stupendious} effects {of it,} for the amplifing of contracted & straitned places; to the comprehension whereoff, we shall not oblige our Workeman to passe through all the *præcognita's* & Rules, which the exquisite *Masters* of this rare *Arte* deliver: & of which their methods are various; but so far as may serve to furnish him with what may bee {of} use~~full upon in~~ {to} his profession, & upon which he may refine & improve, as ~~his tyme and ingenuitie furnishes~~ he is furnished with tyme, & ingenuitie. The places where *Perspectives* are {the} most naturall & ~~may be erected~~ {properly} & properly erected ~~are~~ {be} at the ~~&~~ {entrances} of short Walkes, & *Nil Ultras*; whether {so} affected or ~~so~~ by accident, ~~of~~ {by reason of} a dead Wall, ~~etc.~~ {or} house ~~etc.~~ {interposing}; For ~~Pe in such a pl~~ upon such an obstacle, *Perspective* ~~do~~ can do wonders, & is able to give the Eye a {Lyncean} passage {even} through a stone wall; by seemingly protracting the walke *a perte de vue* {& to losse of object,} as the *French* say; And this {is effected} by *Arches, Peristyles,* ~~well~~ *Palisade*, hedges, {trees} ~~distant~~ *Landskips*, & well discernible distances; so as to ~~deceive~~ {impose} even {upon} the most skillfull in the Art himselfe, who before {were} not premonished of the deception: {This I remember **[continued in margin]** succeeded so well in an instance at Paris that an Architect dwelling in the Rue Tarane near the horse Iland with my F[ather] in L[aw] Sir R: Brown his Majesty's Resident with the F[rench] King having nothing but a dead wall ~~in a Court~~ at the end of the entry of his little house which (when the door was open) might be seene: caused a Garden to be so rarely paintd & dressed in perspective that everybody stopd as they passd by to look on it & divers considerable desire to go into his Garden:} {Perspectives} ~~They~~ are usually painted in Italy & ~~where &~~ {in the} Southern Countrys, where the aire is more benigne a'*Fresca*; but in our Climate, they will require ~~oy~~ to be {well} layd in oyle, and ~~is~~ {are} truely an Ornament so ravishing & pleasant, that they are in nothing in-

---

~~sub~~ ever submerges againe going deepe as the Sun goes farther under the Earth: Se: Arte Magister L: 3: par: 5. c. 4:

28. **[Margin note]** in vita Piereskij. [Gassendi, *The Mirrour of the true nobility*. The lined-through information is repeated at page 195 of the manuscript.]

feriour to the noblest & most august ~~magnificence~~ of the *hortulane* magnificences: for by these are reppresented *Triumphal Arches, Temples, Aquæducts, Statues, Amphitheaters,* & & in summ, whatsoever may tempt & divertise the eye of the Spectator: And by this pleasant deception, we have ~~beheld~~ {admir'd} a very smale garden {of} not 50 foote Square, seeming as if it had bin an enclosure of many miles; & {but} what appeared ~~very~~ {most} extraordinary {was} a very short streame of Water, which, after it had not {really} ~~passed~~ {run} above 40 foote, ~~so~~ {the Aspect so} well reppresented (where it sunke at the foote of the wall, & had {there} a clandestine passage made for it) as if it were a continued **[page 160]** streame for a long course: The *Triumphal Arch* of *Constantine* in the *Cardinals Villa* at *Ruell* ~~in France~~ neere France {painted with just dimension} is a noble Instance of the wonderfull effects of *Perspective*, where they Eye (otherwise bounded by a dead wall) ~~passes through the overtures~~ after it has bin entertained with the historical ~~sta~~ *Relievos,* & Architecture of the piece, passes through the Overtures & Arches ~~t~~ into a most delightfull prospect, which is terminated with a far distant horizon:[29]

Nor may we here forgett ~~a well painted Ruine,~~ {another stately instance}, which we have somewhere ~~beheld~~ {observed} in a Garden abroad, of no ordinary invention: where at the extreame of an ~~Garden~~ {ample} Walke, ~~with~~ stoode a very high wall of stone; ~~well painted~~ on which was painted onely a Skie wth Clowdes; before this wall was erected another wall ~~of~~ or skreene of stone of equal height {& convenient distance} whereon the *Ruine* of a *Roman Antiquitie* was painted; which having severall openings, as Windoes, arches, & breaches cut & abated in the stone worke, did, as the Spectators walked or changed their steps, reppresent the motions, or rack of the Clowdes, seeming to flye before the wind: as ~~it~~ we familiarly behold it
For

> *Raraque per Cælum cum venti nubila portant*
> *Tempore nocturno; tum splendida signa videntur*
> *Labier adversum nimbos, atque ire superne*
> *Longe aliam in partem quam quo ratione feruntur*
>   Lucret: L: 4 [443–447]
> When through the Aire Winds cary in the night
> Thin Clouds; the bright starrs seeme to glide & goe
> 'Gainst them, in Course oppos'd to what they doe
> By Nature: {or as} ~~when~~

> *Qua vehimur navi, fertur, cum stare videtur;*
> *Quæ manet in statione, ea præter creditur ire,*
> *Et fugere ad puppim Colles, campique Volamus*
> *Quos agimus præter navim, velisque volamus.*
>   [Lucretius, *De Rerum natura* 4.388–391]
> Ships with transport us move, when fix't they seeme,
> And those at Anker, under Saile we deeme,
> And ~~to~~ {towards} the Barke, Hills, & Fields seeme to flie,
> Where as, in truth, we Saile & passe them bye.

---

29. **[Margin note]** birds fly against the well desembled skye:

[Page 161]

But let us now instruct our Gardiner in the Practick:

{Here consult Bernard Lamy Translated into English, printed 1702: you have in your library at Wotton. Pag 122 123 etc.}

[illustration, see Fig. 27]

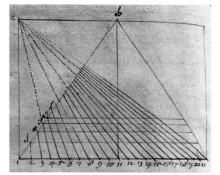

Figure 27. Perspective grid for plotting wall murals, illustrated in text at page 161.

Let therefore a ~~Perpendicular~~ ground line be drawne (which will be the foote of the wall, even with the Walke or Area: (note that the wall is to be first well prepared, ~~primed~~ politely plastred, & primed) divide that line into indifinite parts; then note the ~~horizontal~~ poynt principal {three times} ~~so high as 'tis from the center (a) of the wall~~ {or horizon} ~~to the ground line, as at what height you thinke good, not commonly not exceeding 6 or 7 foote: as suppose at (b) & at 3 of those divisions~~ a 3d{d} {equal} part of the ground line, as suppose b: {~~errected~~ on a perpendicular errected at the middle of the ground line} to this draw all the concurrent lines, 1.2.3.4.5.6 etc: ~~as farr as you will have the extent of your perspective extend which we suppose to be that of your walke~~: then determine the height of your eye, or poynt of distance, which we ~~set~~ {place} upon the perpendicular c.1, erected at the end of the ground line, which is likewise a 3d part {there} of; ~~the ground line~~, Thither draw all the diagonals 2c.3c.4c.5c. etc: ~~So~~ {to} the utmost of your ~~di~~ ground divisions ~~cutt~~ {cutting} the whole table as it were into two Triangles: Now these diagonals do by their intersections, direct all the termes of distances by adding the paralells d.e.f.g. etc: & so is our Area prepard to ~~pur~~ continue the walke upon: ~~Now there remaines the collaterall erection of~~

[Page 162] Now for the erection of the Colaterall ~~Wales~~ lines, directing how the uprights are to be elevated, whither we designe them for Trees, hedges, statues, Wales, Arches, so as they may seeme to continue the palisades, hedges or other ornaments ~~of Walkes~~ for the protracting of the light: Our Gardiner is first to consider how many feete or divisions in height or breadth. his upright shall ~~be allowed~~ {have} & at what distance placed: this resolved: Let him take so many ~~parallels~~ {squares} of that ground line amongst the Parallels ({with his compasse} ~~of sl~~ in the ~~sloping scale~~ {parallels}, ~~which his compasse~~) where he designes {the foundation of} ~~his upright and erect it~~ his upright & measure it proportionally to the altitude he determines: For example our Walke or ally is protracted 9 feete in length The ~~Tower~~ {pillar} which we will erect one foote square at the Pedistall & 5 foote high, the next shall be 4 foote distant of the same dimensions, ~~as the~~ On the other side we have ~~planted~~ {a range of} trees, the better to demonstrate the contraction; & which would terminate in a Cone if the {~~Regi if~~} Scale or Geometricall area be ~~set~~ {planted} with them till they encounter: Now the Covering or arching of these ~~is very~~ {uprights} ~~obvious~~ for the reppresenting of close walkes, Galleries & porticos, is very obvious, having respect to the former rules, & their respective intercalumniations, models, heights & proportions: The minuter ornaments, as corniches, projectures & other members {~~whereoff are~~} to be plotted by a ~~divid~~ scale divided on a foote of that paralell, upon which the upright is ~~rai~~ elevated, Se the Iconisme:

[illustration, see Fig. 28]

{The ~~Hypothesis~~ {Cause} ~~directing~~ {producing} all these contrivances results from these Hypotheses from which anything of this nature may be fram'd, namely, because ~~That~~ equal intervals in the same plane & right line do appeare unequal ~~the~~ by which the spaces most remote from the eye appeare lesse than those which are neerer, & that whereever the eye be placed. After the same sort the remote parts of any plane

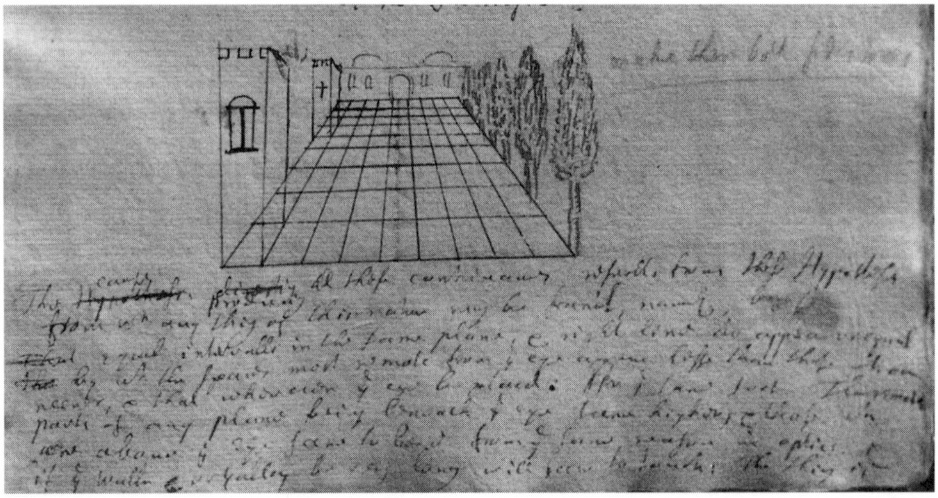

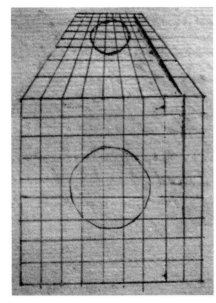

Figure 28. Illustration of a wall mural using a perspectival grid in text at page 162.

being beneath the eye seeme higher, & those which are above the eye seeme to bend from the same reason in optics: & if the Walke & or Gallery be very long will seeme to touch: The thing is **[page 163]** so very plaine that I shall neede give no scheme. ~~I shall onely here take a welcome occasion to celebrate that excellent~~ If a Walke be very short, the trees {or hedges} would be kept at gradual heights for which Cypresse makes the best effect, & the ground or *area* would be made to slope or ascend a little, & in **[continued in margin]** all such acclivities especialy if there be any buildings at the end of it, the lines would be so drawn as to see through the little perspective; of this that incomparable genius & my most honored Friend, Dr: Wren gave ~~an instance~~ a delightsome instance in D: Wilkins (now the R[ev]: D[octor]: of Rippon) Garden in Oxford, a person not so namd by me without infinite respect:) it was a close cradle walke short but much protracted by Art here the ground rises & the sides or poling were contracted, at the extreame ~~places~~ was plac'd a looking glass set so declining as to take in the skie, having a landskip paintd under it, which made a wonderfull effect.}

But if occasion require some round figure, as where the Columne is without a Plinth; As for Alters, ~~pe~~ some fashion'd Pedistalls, Touers {Circling {publique} building} & or the like: Then must our ~~Ga~~ ingenious Gardiner plott ~~a~~ his ~~feete~~ {divisions} of the ~~fling~~ {~~paralell~~} Scale or Area {ground line} first into exact Geometricall feete, of equal sides; ~~then then divide~~ which is don by dividing the square into so many equal parts or feete, as your ground line contained, & then having decribed the *peripherie* of ~~req~~ {the} Circle to what dimension ~~I please~~ he pleases, ~~let~~ & ~~also~~ acurately observing what lines it ~~cutts~~ {intersects}; let him draw the same by hand, upon the Area, or ~~flying Scale~~ {Paralells}, ~~divided~~ projected as in our ~~Second Example~~ {foregoing} Diagramm; or according to this Example: & thus having {established} the foundation of his worke, erect the upright by the precedent Rules:
[illustration, see Fig. 29]

{And here I will oblige the ingenious Gardner with some no vulgar Directions & precious seacretts, how if his spirit lead him to it, he may himselfe prepare his walls, designe, & paint them, at least direct the workeman & be satisifed when it is well: We have already shew'd that these exposd Workes were by the Antients, ~~& yet are in Italy~~ (for the antientest painting now extant in the World is of this sort) & yet in Italy used: Revived about an age since by that incomparable paynter Titian & his

Figure 29. Grid for plotting rectangular objects on a wall mural, illustrated in text at page 163.

master Georgione who left divers rare things, which we have beheld with admiration {as well} for the ~~goodlinesse of the designe~~ {freshnesse} durablenesse of the worke & exposd as it has been now so many yeares to all assaults of the weather, as for the goodlinesse of the designe in which these Mastrs: excell'd. The addresse of this worke consists in a steadinesse of draght, quicknesse of hand and ~~Finaly~~ fancy, for it is to be don when the Walle & plaster is moist & fresco as they}[30]

---

30. **[Continued on separate piece of paper]** tearme it, & must therefore be quite finish'd at first even the very day tis begun, else it never succeeds as it should but will prove full of spotts, whither by reason of the aire, heate or cold, & therefore it must continualy be kept moyst; nor ought it to be touch'd over or heightnd when dry, for if then any size, goom, glare or oyle come over it, it will grow black & rusty immediately: For the effect you must ~~choose~~ {use} Colours which are compounded of Earth, & by no means of minerals, & thus if the ~~workman~~ {Artist} be able, & can finish whilst the ground is as we sayd moist, his work will appeare to his greate satisfaction {lasting} glorious & vivid; but as we sayd it requires skill and dexterity, a steady judgment & in Summ is the utmost perfection & difficulty of a painter; & it is a noble manner of worke as becoming the better & more glorious by the ayre {which purges it} & not much impaired either by raine & etc: {as may be seene by that rare worke of Antonio Virizano at Rome which he never repaird or touchd some}

Somewhat of this we may behold in his Majestys: Privy Chamber at White hall, being the worke of the Incomparable Holben; but that for being within dores, dos not so fully reach our instance. And yet if you will imitate this, & paint in Oyle, let a dry Wall be well oyld over with boyld oyle 2 or 3 tymes till it will drink no more, then prime it; & then designe your work, tempering your colours with a little vernish: But there is yet another way by making your plaster with that of Paris, & oyld over as above, with a mixture of greek pitch, mastic, & grasse vernishd boyld together, ~~priming it~~ {plaster it} over with a large brush, & lastly smoothing it with a hot trowell: This will stop the most rugged surfaces of walls, supposing the ground to be ~~brick or~~ stone {or brick}, as commonly Garden walls are with us: Then prime it as above, & worke upon it: There are many walls of Gardens, & even houses & intire streetes in Italy thus painted.
Or Thus:

Let a ruged wall be plastred with good lime, ~~broken~~ brick dust, & sand & so let it dry; Then worke it over againe with Lime brick dust & scales of Iron {of} each a 3d part incorporated with glare of Eggs well beaten ~~{which}~~ & linseede oyle; this plaster is incomparable: & when layd on, ~~smooth~~ {floate} it perpetualy with the Trowell till it will worke no longer, so that you shall have it close exactly without the least cracks, & very polite[.]
[Insertion continued on separate piece of paper] There is also a slighter manner of worke that the Italians name as Graffito, which is a kind of Charo scuro, ~~as we~~ used likewise in Gardens, as we have seene in those of San Stefano del Bufalo neere the Fontana di Trevi at Rome which is incomparably don by the hand of those greate masters Polydoro & Maturino, especially in the Parnassus, & the Grotescos in which the first has performed miracles: But Geo: Vasari **[end]** But Geo: Vasari **[continued on verso]** Vasari has taught us to work after another manner on these walles, by razing

[Page 164] [31] Finaly, amongst *Statues, Perspectives,* & other Ornaments, ~~suiting~~ exceedingly usefull; ~~in Gardens~~ {our Elysium} *Pots, Vasas,* & the {Urns, Jarrs or} Greate *Amphoras* may be ranged: for they likewise stood in Gardens; And the *Excussores* & *Figulæ,* who carved repair'd, & formed these Vessels, were formerly reckned amongst the *Statuaries.* The first of these may be employed for the {Sowing}, Setting in & preserving of the choycest Flowers; especialy the *Carnation, Auriculas, Amaranths, Anemonies* etc; & for some shrubbs, & plants of the rarest ~~sort~~ {kinds}: & therefore to be made of various sizes, depths, & diameters; frequently & commodiously enough ~~made~~ moulded ~~by our the potter~~ of common potters Earth; but always pierced at the bottome, for the passage of superfluous showers; which, would other wise, overwash ~~&~~ ~~sta~~ {rott} & sterve the rootes they contained:[32] some of these of a larger size, we ~~have~~

---

the designe with a poynt of yron, not much unlike to Engraving upon Vernish on Copper plates for A Fortis: & it is by first coating the wall with plaster made ~~ordi~~ of ordinary mortar is mixed with burnt straw, which tinges it with a middle obscurity blackish: This dry they {lay} ~~coate~~ it over a 3d tyme with a white plaster, & so worke with the poynt or style upon it, & it renders a very pretty effect provided the workeman be an able designer, as I have seen in many places in Italy; & especially ~~for~~ becoming Grotescos & resemble the large Cartoons of brasse Cutts at a distance;

The ~~Fi~~ paintings which best become Ciaro Scuro are large Figures {Prophane} Stories, Arches, Porticos, {Huge Cornices} Nices, statues like contrfeited Brasse, & Copper Columns, Obeliskes; Ruines & ~~Canals~~ Gardens:

Grotesco on the Contrary is of {a} lesser & more running fancy & is a licentious kind of painting, antique, & extravagant, without rule or sense, mixing all sorts of chimæras, & the more ~~nonsensicall~~ (cappricious} the better, as an horse to have the leg of a bird, a man a serpents tayle, an Elephant to hang in a Cobweb; & an Ox or Lyon to have the hind legs end in leaves or flowrs {etc. or else Emblems, Rebus's & devises} & it dos aptly in Frezes, Roofs, {Fretts, Cartouzes, Spandrells. etc} & volts of Galleries, peristyles, & porticos: In this you may also countersett Medalions, relievos, ~~&~~ Camei & Intaglios: Some we have seene preserved with admirable successe in plaster Embosd & relievo: whereoff an noble example still remains about the house at Nun–such in Surry, which tis pitty should so decay as comparable to any I know extant & certainly don by some rare Italian Master: ~~I wish~~ which makes me wish his Majesty: would sometimes thinke of ~~remo~~ preserving, or else removing & putting into some other place, they would ~~nobly~~ magnificently become some palace or Gallery where they might stand dry, though they have now I believe encountred ~~ther~~ all weather of this Climate near 100 years[.] For other worke we have had a Pierce [Edward Pierce/Pearce] {& [William?] Lightfoot} as able as the best, as we now have Fuller, Streeter & others of our own Countrymen, comparable to any abroad had they as great incouragement. Mr: [Thomas] Povey [ca. 1615–ca. 1702] has in L[incoln's]: in[n] fields a rare perspect enlay about either the guise we mention these workes for, the worke of Mr: Streter [Robert Streater, 1624–1680.]

31. **[Separate piece of paper illustrating urns inserted at page 164; see Fig. 30]**

32. **[Margin note]** but the best course to preserve your choyce Flo: potts is to

Figure 30 (facing page). More illustrations of urns and vases, continued on verso of piece of paper inserted at page 164.

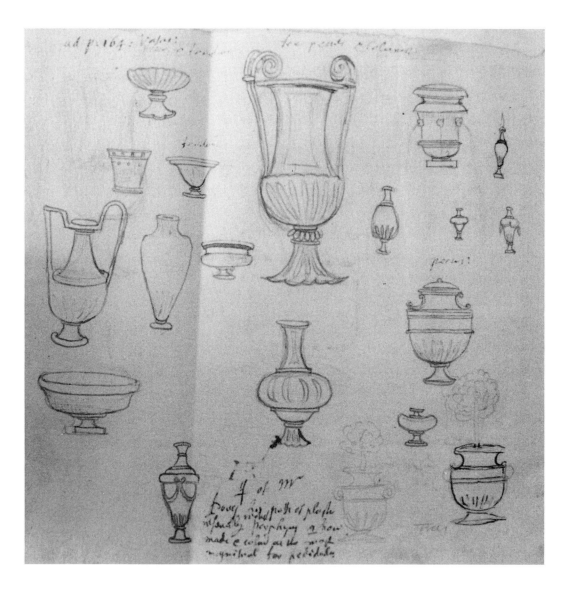

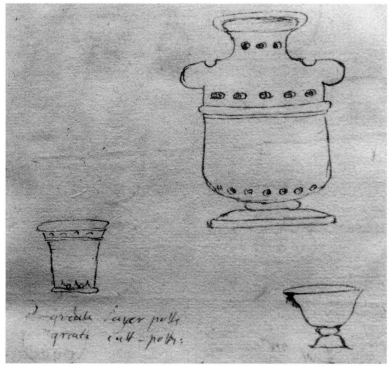

seene would have contrived to open at the sides, with such dores as are made for the Mouths & *registers* of Earthen *portatile Furnaces*; such as the *Chymists* ~~some~~ often use, & to be fixed wth a Circle of wyre, convenient for the renovation of exhausted mould, to the immense refreshment, & improvement of the plant, without the least disorder or perill to the roote; but {more} of this {in due place} hereafter.[33] ~~when we come~~ *Carnation potts*, made large & full of {sloping} holes, as wide as ones finger; at inch distance or more, & in every of these holes hysop or Tyme planted, & kept {evenly} cliped, ~~still~~ in ~~ſo~~ shape of the ~~pott~~ {Vessell} is a very pretty ornament, & seemes to be a ~~Vessell made~~ pott composed of herbs; & {whilst} for a greater accession the middle may be planted with some Lilly, ~~Gi~~ Carnation, or other ~~Superiour~~ {more lofty & glorious} plant: And in this manner our {curious} *Gardner* may ~~have~~ {contrive} *Pyramids, Columns,* ~~&~~ {or} any other Figure of Man or Beast, formed of Potters clay, & backed hollow, ~~perf~~ which, perforated at convenient distances, may be treated like the Potts; onely in scorching weather, they will require to be removed, or ~~ta~~ obumbrated with some Canvasse Tent, or skreene a little moystned, or they may be translated a while into the porticos ~~etc.~~ & ~~are~~ {being} **[page 165]** being very agreable ornaments *pro tempore*.

We speake nothing here of the particular formes of these potts; men are to please their phantsies ~~but the mos~~ though we should affect the most antique: & such as we have described in Iconisme ~~And these britt Vessells may be~~[34] But these materialls are so fragile, that to have them cast in *Lead*, with their *frutiges, relievos,* {*Escutchions, Cyphers*} & other ornaments, were infinitely preferable to those of Earth; and after those such as are ~~made~~ {carved out} of hewen stone; But these for being commonely {bigger &} of lesse moderne shape, may be reckned amongst the Vasas; which were frequently ~~hew~~ cutt out of Porphyrie {Oriental Alabaster} ~~it selfe~~, & other rich {& lasting} materialls, with exquisite workemanship, ~~and~~ for the adornement as well of Gardens, as the ~~most~~ furniture of their Houses: For of those we have oftentimes beheld ~~pro Lavors~~ *Vasas, Urnes, Lavors,* & *Amphoras* of Prodigious capacity, & admirable arte, placed, as the rest, on *Pedistalls,* & Antique supporters about the~~ir~~ *Roman Gardens,* & in their ~~Porticos,~~{*Atrias*} & Cimel~~y~~{i}ums: And what a noble & grand effect, those goodly *Amphoras,* or *Jarrs,* (Though but of simple ~~Earth~~ {clay}), cause, in that {spacious} area before the Villa of *Pr: Ludovisio,* ~~Every~~ {The} Traviler may observe: we have some in our ~~famous~~ {richer} Oyle shopps, ~~much~~ resembling them {in shape}

---

place an ordinary flower pot filld with earth & wherein your flo: grow within the greater one, so as it be even at the orifice:

33. **[Margin note]** L: 2: c: 16. L: 3. c: 1.

34. **[Insertion on separate piece of paper]**

Yet for a moderat proportion ~~let th~~ & generall rule, they ought to be as broad at the Orifice as they are in height, two inches lesse at bottome (I speake for ordering ~~of~~ Carnation potts, etc) so as inverting ~~it~~ the whole masse of earth may come out intire upon occasion, & let there be holes at the bottom of sufficient widenesse that the water may have convenient passage for which reason pibbles are better to strew & keepe the mould from clodding, thus tyle shards or oyster shells with which Gardners usually cover them. but in filling these potts with mould, be sure to let it exceed the brimms thereoff by an inch, in reguard of its sinking etc:

& not much inferiour. [35]And all these {fictilia} ~~airie vessells~~ may be painted & layd in oyle, of stone, ~~Colour~~, lead, bronz'd, or any other colour; some bestow the cost to gild them; but we, for our parts, do not affect it, unlesse it be universall, & all over the pott, which were an excessive charge:

We might here say something of Cases, but it is not {so} materiall; only such as are furnished wth ~~the~~ *Oranges, Myrtills, Span: Jessamine,* the choycer evergreenes {~~plants~~} & shrubs, ought to be framed of excellent {3 Inch} planke, well seasoned, & pitched within, and **[page 166]** by no meanes so square as we usualy see them; but contracted more {naturaly} at the top: They may be {also}[36] painted white or Greene, with festoones, ~~devises~~ Armories, Cyphers, & other ~~ornaments~~ devises, & {as} being none of the least {of hortulan} ornaments: some ~~ro~~[37] affect them round, not wee; ~~yet are they most~~ both are removed by rings, handles, ~~&~~ Barrs, & are to be pierced at the bottomes, for the {same} reason ~~given~~ as the ~~po~~ Flower potts: ~~Lastly,~~ {to conclude}

~~But~~ *Potts* {& *Vasas*} ~~so~~ made {use of} ~~as~~ to preserve flowers not growing, & to be placed upon solemne tymes and entertainements, either abroad, or within; by ~~potts~~ {these} & etc: meaning such as are by some named *bough-potts,* ~~us'd to~~ {set} usually {set} in Windoes stands, Chimnies, & Tables; together with *flowry Columnes* & ~~other curiosities~~ inventions of this ~~nature~~ {kind,} we expressly reserve to describe in chap: 2d: L: 2: when we shall come to treate of *Chapletts,* {*Garlands*} & *Festoones,* & other ornaments of this nature. ~~Lastly To conclude~~ Lastly, The proper places for these ornaments of Potts, {*Vasas* etc:} ~~is~~ {are} at the sides of *Alles* & Gardens; Springling some about the *parterr* {& *Trayle worke*} as the designe invites: ~~Also~~ But for the larger *Vasas;* upon *Pedistalls,* of stone, ~~& the~~ betweene the ~~ranks~~ {files} of the *Statues,* Upon *Balustrades,* & the Ascent of stepps, & {generally on all elevated places} whereever we find them Gracefull: *Amphoras* {~~Urnes~~} & the greater *Lavors,* about the *Fountaines,* & in such places as they may ~~serve~~ {be used} for reserves of Water, {imbibitions} & *Insolations.* {Here place the Iconisme} I thinke fit now to conclude this Chapter with the Names of such Workemen as have excelled in their calcographicall descriptions ~~of~~ both of Gardens & their Ornaments, because their labours may be not of delight onely, but of great use to affect our Inventions for Fountaines, Parterrs, Statues, Flowers, Water workes etc, the subjects of the ~~fore~~ many of the foregoing chapters:}[38]

[Page 167]

---

35. **[Margin note]** blacke lead dos very well being layd in oyle upon them, or but rubbed: cf

36. **[Margin note]** vides: c: 1 L: 2: num: 46. also: c: 14:

37. **[Margin note]** Some of these may be made to open at sides like the Flo: pots before described, with hinges & bolts: {to visite the rootes}

38. **[Insertion on separate piece of paper]** Gardens & Fountains divers M[a]st[e]rs have set forth worke in Taille doe: as Jaques Boisseau by Van Lachen, Jo: Guera: Cort[?] after Francis Floris: Fr[ancesco?] Primaticio Abbot of St Martie: Daniel Rabel: Isaac de Cause ~~that large Cutt of the Heidelburg gardn:~~ Jo: Vredon of Friseland: Jag: Mathan [Jacob Matham?] after Sebastian Vranck: Jasp[?] Isaac. Jaques, Noel, Claud & Andrew Mollet for Parteres & broderie. Francis Corduba at Rome, Solomon de Caus Architect at Frankfurt. Mario Kartaro: Michel L'asne [Lasne] after Alexander Francine, Jaq: Cal[l]ot: Justus Sadeler C. Van Mander Hans Fridman [Vredeman de]

Vries Theodor Galle, Adrian de Vries of the Hague Architect & Sculptor: Jo: d'Ach, one of the Emperor's painters: Lucas Kilian after Francis Aspruck of Bruxelles: P: Perret: G: Baussonnet: Edme Moreau, Jo: Stradan, Cl: Goyrand, Fra Corduba, Fra: Fanelli a Florentine Sculptor of his Ma[jes]tie: Char: {1st} 2d: of Engl: Domenico Parasacchi of Rome: Jo: Maggi Roman painter & Architect J: de Francine, Abraham Bosse, Jac: Androvet de Cerceau, L: Gautier, Aug: Carrach [Carracci], Crispine de Passe, Jo: Bologna the greate statuary famous for Fountains: Tho: Lauretus Panormitanus Architect: [Henri] Mauperche in all above 412 pieces of Gardens & Fountains etc:

CHAP: XII

Of artificial Echo's, Musick,
& Hydraulick motions.

It has been rightly observed that a Garden hath of all other diversions the prerogative alone of gratifing the senses virtuously; The tinctures of its flowers ~~shames~~ are able to make all the most beautifull colours of the painter to blush for shame, ~~Let him~~ {dare he} produce his *Virmilion* & his *Ceruse* before the Rose or the Commonest *Lilly*, when yet Solomon in all his glory, was not cloathed like any of these? What artificial perfume, or most precious extract will compare with the Redolency of the purple Violet, the Orange, the Gesamine, & the precious Nard! and dos not the productions of {its} fruite entertaine the most ~~luxurious~~ {curious} {~~& disti~~} palat with the rich Melon & the jucey Grape, ~~not to mention~~ the nectarine, Abricot, Cherry & a thousand varieties more, not to mention here, that ~~Regal~~ ¹Imperial pine, reported by all that have tasted it, to resemble the gusto of whatsoever the most ~~stall~~ luxurious or distinguishing *Epicure* can summon to his wanton imagination: And when the *Poets* would describe the utmost delight of the touch, they present us with a Prospect of the *Golden Age*, when ~~the~~ the whole world was but one Garden, ~~where we see~~ in which we see the tendernesse of the Grasse & flowry bankes invites every body to lye downe, and enjoy the easinesse of those soft & fragrant beds whilst the murmuring of the {christall} streames, & the warbling of the musicall birds, charm'd them to repose, as if this last ~~alone~~ were alone able, to vanquish, & captivate all the rest ~~of~~ {of} the senses; especialy, where their naturall & rurall aires are exhalted by the ravishing accents of Vocal or Instrumentall Consorts, reduplicated by the undulation of Echos repercussing the voyce, & repeating the notes, which ~~happen from the~~ is the effect of reverberation & intervall & renders ~~the~~ a place (by we know not what kind of ~~magick~~ {charme}) seeme the more ~~sollemne &~~ majesticall. {& solemne, & fit for contemplation,} It is for these reasons that we seeke for them in our Elysium & to render it accomplished; but since in all Gardens they are not to be found, especially in the flatt; or is ~~at all~~ {indeede} anything considerable, where the Reflection comming direct, renders, but *one* for *one*, **[page 168]** and that the situation of hills, rocks, ~~caves~~, woods, building & grotts of hollow flexuous & camerated ~~places~~ places, retorts, ~~& in~~ the voyces & sounds from one to another by more frequent ~~undulations~~ repetitions & undulations; Like the Catoptricks ~~of~~ described by ~~Lucretius~~ {the Poet}, & the operations of ~~Gla~~ *Speculary* reflections {For saxa sonunt {varij} offensa resultat Imago: Virg: [*Geor.* 4.50]} which multiplie by succession.

---

1. **[Margin note]** See Liggon hist: Barbados: [Richard Ligon, *A True & Exact History of the Island of Barbados . . .* , London, 1657.]

Sex etiam aut septem loca
Lucret: L: 4:

As we reade of the *Heptaphonos* {Olympian portico} neere Athens, the Echo at *Pavia*, which renders ~~the~~ to 13 {the bridg at Charentan} & that of *Syracuse* in[2] *Sicilia*, which is sayd to repeate a song consisting of ten Heroick verses, or a whole lesson playd on the Lute exactly answering to every shade & softest relish; with others which we could enumerate: Since these effects (we say) are not to be hoped for, in many Gardens, which but for this onely wanted nothing of perfection; we shall heere endeavour, to instruct you how to produce an *Artificial Echo*, and by an innocent ~~kind of~~ magick & without superstition, to raise up {& deprehend} that vocal {& fugitive} Nymph, ~~&~~, to consult her oracles at pleasure, ~~& deprehend that fugitive~~ {accompanie that solitude} & decorate your Garden.

Those who have written of this *Anacampticke* Geometrie, have ~~furnished~~ set downe ~~many~~ rudiments, which consist of many propositions, problems, & Hypotheses conducing to this wonderfull doctrine of *Echosophy*; as amongst others, ~~Blun~~ the learned *Bluncanus* & the later *Kerkeres* ~~to whome we have~~ {acknowledge} ~~infinite obligation~~, and had rather[3] referr our curious ~~Artist~~ Gardiner, then trouble him with their definitions of a *Sound*, with the *Objects*, *Medias* & other *Postulatus*, that we may hasten to demonstration, & to the practique how our *Echotect* is to proceede in his worke. {to find out this Hermitesse, or rather oracle of the woods, & rocks, this citizen of the shade, ~~this mother & daughter~~ the mother & daughter of nothing, vox et prætera nihil} First then let there be erected a smoth & solid Wall of stone or brick of competent height; then retiring from it in a direct line, & sometimes againe, approching to it (for there is no mathematicall & ~~definite~~ {certaine} distance to be otherwise defin'd) ~~'till examining you at the last~~ {when} by examining the severall steps of your motion, you ~~have~~ {shall} find the perfect reddition of a syllable or word; & at that fix a marke, & measure the ~~space~~ intervall; after this ~~retrograde~~{ceede} againe & againe, till you find more syllables, **[page 169]** there likewise ~~place~~ {set} a marke ~~& do as before~~ & so at every *polysyllable* observing punctualy the distance: For thus you shall find upon experiment, that the spaces by which one syllable is augmented are not equal, but diminish, the reason of it proceeding from the faintnesse & languor of the Voice, weakned, & now tired by the variety of the distances: so that the proportions being altogether uncertaine, ~~may in some part~~ *mechanicaly* explored ~~will~~ {may} ~~sometimes~~ {probably} resemble this Accoumpt

Monosyllable ——— 100	foote	
Dissyllab: ——— 190	"	
Trisyllab: ——— 270	"	
Tetrasyllab: ——— 350	"	
Pentasyllab: ——— 430	"	
Hectasyllab: ——— 515	"	
Heptasyllab: ——— 600	"	

---

2. **[Margin note]** that in Scotland se Sir R: Murays designe

3. **[Margin note]** L: 2: Musurgiæ. [Kircher, *Musurgia universalis sive ars magna consoni I dissoni*, Rome, 1650.]

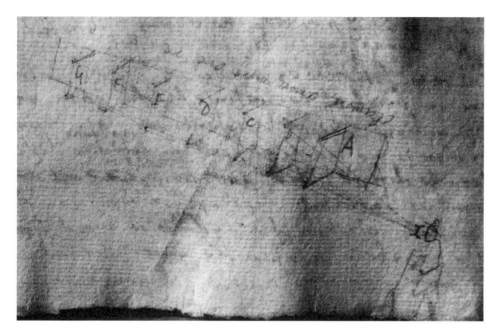

Figure 31. Faint pencil rendering of an echo chamber at Athens in text at page 169.

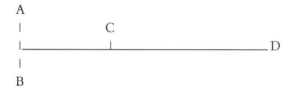

Let the wall be (for instance) AB, & let the *Echomitre* receede from it continualy pronouncing ~~some~~ *Arma virumque cano* etc some lofty sounding word or verse; 'till the
Echo {make} answer which we expect ~~to be~~ at ~~th~~ C. where {the marke} is to be set;
& ~~thus~~ {so} continue still retroceeding. In this manner let there a wall be built containing 7 Buttresses, at such distance from each other as the voice X is from the first
Buttresse A, & let the superficies of every Buttresse be parallel & perpendicular to the
Voice or station X: We say, the voice X incident on the 7 walles A.B.C.D.E.F.G. will
be seaven tymes rendered, & so you have made a *Heptaphone Echo* like that of Athens

The Ichonisme

[illustration, see Fig. 31]

[Page 170]

In like manner may you erect a *Polyphon* Circle: ~~Thus~~ {v.g.} Let the *Phonocamptic* points A.B.C.D.E.F.G.H.I.K.L.M. be so dispos'd that the lines AB . AC . AD . etc.
may be drawn from the Vocal Center A. We affirme, that from the point G. the lines
GB. GC. GD. GE. GF. GH. GI. & GL. being marked, will assigne the site or station
of the *Phonocamptick* objects; because by the *16 Element: {Euclid} L: 4*, The Angles in a
semicircle being right, the lines drawn from G to the sonorus lines (drawne from A)
shall be perpindicular: And therefore the Voice incident from A on the object B. dos
againe reflect the Voice ~~from~~ {to} A; & the lines GD. EF. HI. KL ~~retort the voice~~
~~to A~~ being perpendicular to the sonorus described from A, the Echos founded on
them, dos likewise repercusse the Voice to A; Now {as} the lines from A are unequaly
protracted longer & ~~large~~ {shorter} so ~~the~~ are the responses more ~~remissely~~ faint &
remisse in their returns, repeating yet, as often as there are objects, or points in the

Figure 32. Faint pencil drawing of a "polyphone" echo chamber in text at page 170.

Circle: But, if these points be so disposed in both the Semicircle, as to be æquidistant from A, the voice will answer in equal & just tyme, & {be} reverberated ~~dubly as stron~~ {will dubble} the force. And this *Consectarie* proves how easily ~~a~~ *Polyphone Echo*{s} {& *super-reflections*} may be made in a Circular Walle, & ~~will~~ {dos} also present us with those admirable ~~pro~~ kinds and proprieties of ~~motion~~ the motion {& undulations} of the figure, expressing the Languor {& decaidance} of the Sound: For the *Anacamptick* spaces GP. PO. ON. being unequall decrease proportionably ~~to~~ {as} the quantity of the line of action AG abbreveats; so that the Intervalls PG. is to PO. & OP. to ON ~~so are~~ as the *phonocamptic* objects are to the distances which repeates[4] the *Echos*:

The Ichonisme:

[illustration, see Fig. 32]
[Page 171]
~~And this~~

    But we will conclude what we have sayd with a *Diagramm* of that *Artificiall Echo* (to give our Gardiner a Garden Instance) which we find erected at the ends of the long Walke of the *Thuilleries* in Paris, where without much stresse of the voice maine-taines an Heroick Verse very well; for which it rarely suites with the *Serenades* of those beautifull Ladys ~~which~~ that frequent it, such Evenings as ~~these Gardens~~ that *Elysium* sparkles with the beauties of that illustrious Court. And by this, ~~such that~~ such as are affected with Musique & Solitude, may even in flat & levell places (like that) where nature affords no assistances, erect an *Artificiall Echo*.

[illustration, see Fig. 33]
A.B.C the wall of 15 foote high with the angles D.E.F: the *Focuses* ~~the~~ where they speake or sing {~~from the benches to the trees I to H~~} EF for the *Singers* & D for the *Auditors* being benches: GG. part of the Wall which encloses the *Thuilleries* Garden. H the Entrance into the *Echo* planted with double ranges of lime trees, round the Circle: I The long walke of the Garden planted with Elmes described cap: 6. etc:

---

4. **[Margin note]** Se Kerker: Tom: 2: p: 264.

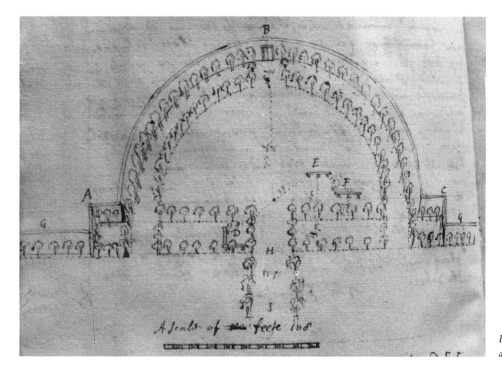

Figure 33. Example of an artificial echo chamber at the Tuileries, illustrated in text at page 171.

[**Page 172**] Just as we were finishing this discourse & meditating what farther ornament we might of this kind introduce into our *Gardens* a most civil lettr comes to our hands from the learned *Dr: Browne* of *Norwich*, wherein amongst other particulars relating to Hortulane amœnities, he touches upon *Whispering-places*, which since they also relate to the voice, to some of the foregoing remarkes concerning *Echo*, & must needes be a most divertissant variety, we will heere subjoyne the description[.]

Draw over an Arch of an *Elleipticall* forme, made of a line of a d{o}uble center, denoting the two *Focusses* of the *Elleipsis*, ~~F~~ & you have a place {so} qualified, ~~for whispering~~. For in the longest diameter of an *Elleipsis*, there are two poynts, equidistant from the center which are tearmed *Foci*, from one whereof if lines be drawne unto the Circumference, so ~~posited~~ {disposed} ~~flecting~~ that the *Angle* of *Reflection* be equall unto that of *Incidence*; they will all revert unto the other *Focus's* by the multiplicitie & union of the & so the sound or voice be strongly conveied unto him, whose Eare lyes at it; And if we whisper at one *Focus*, the Vocall *Raies* which are carried to the Circumference of the *Elleipsis*, being by reflection all united at the other *Focus*, by the ~~multi~~ frequency & union of these reflected *raies*, the voyce will be distinctly heard at that part; not easily in the middle, {as} unto which a direct & single ~~raie~~ {beame} onely ariveth. The mysterie of this phœnomenon may be thus ~~expl~~ illustrated.
The Ichonisme

[**illustration, see Fig. 34**]

[5]A.B. are the *Focuses* {(where Cupid speakes & the Lady listens)} the rest of the Lettrs: denote the Angles of ~~Imi~~ reflection upon the *Elleipticall Arch*.[6]

{Other wayes of finding out the focus {is don} by the projection of the light from

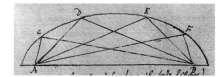

Figure 34. Schematic for an echo arch and angles of reflection in text at page 172.

---

5. [**Margin note**] Let the Sculpture draw a figure a Lady & a Cupid, one standing at one Focus, & the other listening & appling his care at the other.

6. [**Margin note**] cf this in our Register at: R: Society

Sphericall {concave} glasses, & likewise by parabolical & eliptical as may be learned out of those who have written of ~~Cap~~ Catophical Echos: of which Scotti gives a very large catalogue:}

[Page 173] And Instances of such {acustic machines &} places there are many yet extant as in our *Cathedral* of *Glocester* ~~knowne by enough~~ famous over *England*, in St *Peters Church* at *Rome*, in the Palace of *Heidelberg*, in the Physicke Garden of *Montpellier*, & divers more, yea very frequent, whither by designe or accident in many ordinary places in Italy: And here we might mention, as also notably relating to sound & to the Eare those *Bosca de verita*'s {such as the one the Duke of Tuscany has} contrived in some advantagious ~~places~~ {corners} so as to heare all that is whispered or spoken in places of encounter, & where people are usualy found to stand & discourse in private; but for that these may administer to greate impertinences & be of dangerous consequences, we passe them over as also divers other *Acousticall* and Auditorie Instruments, *parabolically* or *Elliptically* contrived to the greate advantage of hearing, to be ~~seene in~~ {gathered out of} the Workes of *Bettinus* {& others}:[xliv] For much after this figure was formed that remarkable horne of *Alexander the greate* ~~of~~ containing 5 cubites {in} diameter, the blast & sound holes being at the extreames thereoff & the noise ~~there~~ {or Halus} ~~off~~ to be heard over all the camp, & {of} no lesse then 100 furlongs; {as} ~~See the Figure of it in~~ *Kerkerus* {has exhibited the figure in} his boke *de luce et umbra*[xlv] ~~onely and he shall suffice~~ {But that which is more wonderfull is what *Borell*[xlvi] relates of an Elme that in the yeare 1653 at a place calld Caumont [continued in margin] neere Tolouse uttered a voice like {to} a mans as those of the Oracular *Dodona* to the amazement of all the country, but it proved at last to be the effect of Echo, through the hollownesse of the trees, which the people ~~at first~~ a long tyme did not perceive, & many such miracles their are produced by Echo, as the dauncing of waters & *vibration* of the very earth at the pronouncing of certaine words & syllables more apt to breake & repercusse the aire then other.

And may this suffice our Gardiner to ~~have~~ {be} spoaken concerning *Whispering places*, *Sounds*, & *Echos* {of} which ~~if it~~ with the *Artist* in the *Poet*, we have ~~adventur'd to painte~~ in our severall *Diagramms* adventurd to paint, ~~(that we have prevented the censure) thus *Ausonius*~~ & perhaps {with better successe} prevented the censure of *Ausonius* [Epigram 32]

Vane, quid affectas Faciem mihi ponere Pictor,
  Ignotamque oculis sollicitare deam?
Aeris et lingua sum Filia mater inanis
  Indicij, Vocemque sine mente gero;
Extremos pereunte modos a fine reducens
  Ludificata sequor verba aliena meis
Auribus in vestris habito penetrabilis Echo
  Et si vis similem pingere pinge Sonum

Vaine Painter! why to draw dost thou delight
A Godesse Face, conceald from humane sight?
I am the Daughter but of Tongue & Aire
Mother of Judgment vaine; a mind I beare
without a voice; & with faint accents play
Repeating the last words which others say:

[Page 174]

I, Echo, in the Eares meanders dwell,
Paint then a Sound, if thou wilt paint Me well.

For to what purpose serves our Echo & the artificiall or natural fabricke we have ~~described~~ {erected}, unlesse ~~we provide it~~ amongst other varieties, & to entertaine the {vocal} Nymph, we accompanie her with Musick, and furnish our *Elysium* ~~with~~ as *Pythagoras* has the Heavens {over it} with {its} harmonical proportions: And if ~~it~~ {that} be true ~~that~~ {when} *Quintilian* writes, *Inst: Lib: 1. c. 18* citing *Timayes* for the first author *Musick*, affirming it to be the most antient of all the sciences and that *Strabo* tells us that *Philosophy* & *Musique* signified for[7] so long a time the same thing: How can our Gardiner be ignorant of it, to accomplish ~~the~~ {his} Character: 'Twas not then for nothing that the divine *Plato* held the soule it {selfe} to consist of Harmony, and that all the world was made by ~~it~~ & subsisted of it; Nor ~~that~~ as to our reguard, that we find *Pan* to be the inventor of the pipe, *Apollo* of the Harp, *Zephyre* of the Flute etc all of them ~~Gar~~ *Hortulan Dieties* ~~& return to~~ We will therefore say no more to ~~introduce~~ demonstrate the absolute necessitie of introducing Musique into our Gardens, which ~~accompanied~~ in consort with the Voice or it selfe, may upon all occasions give us the diversion of a pleasure so ~~divi-celestial~~ {divine} & abstracted, ~~and at with the fountaines whilst the~~ & greatly conduci~~ve~~{ng} to extasy & the most heavenly raptures, whilst ~~the Fountaines & waters seeme to dance, and~~ {our soules being drawne as it were out of our bodys} the Waters seeme to dance out of the Fountaines, ~~&~~ the Flowers & trees, to ~~move~~ {nodd} & keepe tyme, ~~& to be moved out of the~~ {& like the wales of Thebes} at the touch of *Amphion*, to be moved out of their places.

And this we will effect, by instructing our docill Gardiner, how he may himselfe make & contrive these wonderfull *Automats*, {& compose these *irrigua carmina*} which at present so celebrate the Gardens of the greatest Princes; and in particular, as in most ~~present~~ perfection at present, those of Frascati, Tivoli, & many other famous Gardens of the most illustrious persons of the World. And because of all ~~the~~ expedients for these Effects, the *Hydraulique*[8] have bin ever {The most} esteemed, & do so naturally ~~agree~~ {accord} with fountaines, & the motions created by them, it will be very requisite that our Gardiner ~~to~~ turn a little back, & {refresh} ~~informe himselfe of~~ his memorie with **[page 175]** some rules & præcognit's, ~~which are~~ set downe in cap: 9th: where we have discoursed at large, concerning Fountaines & Waterworkes: For in ~~Summ~~ {briefe} there we learne that there are 4 principle things conducing to the motion of Hydraulique & pneumatique ~~in effects~~ inventions, by which we move & governe our water engines & *Automata*, viz, ~~the~~ the attractive force, 2ly {by} the expulsive, 3ly {by the} rarefactive, & lastly, by the natural gravity of the waters itselfe.

Now of all these, as it relates to our present designe, {&} the ~~effecting of~~ pretence of this ~~remainder~~ Chapter, the *Expulsive principle*, ~~by~~ (which ~~bodily~~ {to avoide} {the} penetration {of dimensions} dos miracles) will be the most usefull for our Gardiner to

---

7. **[Margin note]** Georg: L: 10
8. **[Margin note]** long since invented, as we find by Pliny, Athænaes [Athenaeus], Sueton, Vitruvius, etc:

informe himselfe in {& of} such experiments as best demonstrate the effects of compression. For example, ~~we would~~ & ~~for~~ the use of our hydraulique=Organ, {chirping of birds, motion of Images} Ventiduct, or ~~any~~ {some} other invention, we would produce a perpetual wind: The Figure ~~unde~~ beneath is rendred so perspicuous by the Sculptor, as to neede no other description, then that the {overshot} wheele O, being turnd about by the overshooting streame K circumvolves the incurrated Axis EK, which is inserted into the walle at M, upon the ~~in~~ crooke whereoff goes a rod of yron LK, which by the wooden beame A.B.L librating upon the post RD, fixed in the walle drawes up the Billowes H.I. by the two rodds fitted with rings to the{ir} handles ~~of~~ & to the ~~sayd~~ beame above sayd: The billows ~~have for their~~ thus expanded, have for their depressure, either of them a sufficient weight of leade; And this is one way ~~for the~~ {of} animation, from these mixt ⁹motions of wind & water.

     [Page 176] But quitting these more vulgar inventions {~~the~~ to be seene in every forge:} most expeditious, & in our conceite ingenious, are those *Eolique* vaults, & chambers, which onely with the ~~fall~~ {precipitation} of water alone produce wind sufficient for all our motions of this kind: And such ~~are~~ was that, which ~~the industrious Kirker~~ {was not long since} ~~did himselfe lately~~ invent{ed} for *Pope Innocent* the Xth in the *Quirinal* Gardens at *Rome*, which here (together with the Hydraulique Organ animated by it) we describe.

The Fabrique of the Hydraulic Automat or Autophône Organe.

     There are 3 principal members that appertaine to the construction of this Instrument: 1, The *Æolique* or *Wind-Chamber*¹⁰ 2, An ordinary *Organ*; and 3ly The *Phonotactic Cylinder*: The *Wind Chamber*, is a hollow ovall place built of brick or stone of competent thicknesse, the height whereoff ~~is~~ shall be 5 foote, the breadth 3 1/2, as in the *Ichonisme* V X V Z. Then you shall place the two *Diaphragmes* or partitions XY pierced through with holes like a Cullander; & these are made ~~t~~ on purpose to hinder the mounting of the water, & for passage of the aire: Then let there be three pipes, viz, Z.R.T.S. fitted to the *Wind chamber*, the upmost whereoff curved as YZ, or otherwise contorted somewhat resembling ¹¹ the ~~pip~~ worme of a *Refrigeratory* or {hott} still {that the aire may through so long a passage, & by the interposition of the two Midriffes, become the more defecated {of all aquæus atomes that might otherwise injure the pipes & sound} & aire} A second pipe ~~must be~~ of a reasonable good boare, ~~must be placed wth its stop-cock~~ T.S. with its stop-cock to let in the water into the *Wind-chamber*, when you please to make the ~~Water~~ *Organ* play, & this pipe must be let in towards the inferiour part of the *Chamber*, ~~The third V.Z to be placed~~ that the aire excited ~~through~~ {by} the impetuosity of the Water, ~~be~~ {&} pressed out (to avoide *Vacuum*) through the *midriffs*, may be conversd into the *Organ Windbox* by the crooked

---

     9. **[Margin note]** Se Kirk [Kircher]: fig: iiii . v.

     10. **[Margin note]** Vitruvius: L: 9: c: 13: ~~notes the inventi~~ speaks of the construction of such a kind of organ; but it is not perfectly described by his commentators:

     11. **[Margin note]** this pipe where it is fixed to the wind chamb: may be made ample, like an Urne or tunnell.

pipe VZ above described: Lastly, the Pipe R, inserted at the botome of the *Wind-chamber*, to let out the water, which turnes the Cogged *Wheele* M.Q.N., a as that by its *axis* OP, turnes the *Vertebra* L. which *Vertebra* circumvolves with it the *Cylinder* H.K: ~~Now the Cylinder must be care~~ exactly placed under the *Keyes* and *Cyphers* of the *Organ* EF; And thus the *Cylinder* fitted ~~& inserted &~~ {with its Teeth} harmonicaly inserted (as we shall {hereafter} shew) lifts up the *Spatulas* or *Tongues* fastned to the Wyres 1.2.3.4.5. etc ~~the wires moving~~ {& moving upon the rod AB.} and this deppresses & ~~gives~~ moves the *Keyes* EF, to which the *Cyphers* are ~~fastned~~ {tyed} {tyed} {tied} with a smale thread or wire, which ~~depresses~~ opning the holes of the *wind-box* animats the pipes, & so the desired effects suceede:

Now it ought to be one of the most principale cares of the Workeman that the Cylinder be not whirled about with too viollent a motion, but equally proportionable: & this will {much} consist in the ordering **[page 177]** of the *Vertebra*, for the more teeth or barrs that has, the swifter will be the motion of the *Cylinder*: {to conceive this the fuller} ~~But~~ See this in the subsequent fig: where L. the *Vertebra* circumvolved by the {water} Wheele NQN ~~and~~ catching{es} into the teeth of the ~~head~~ {plate O} ~~of the cylinder O~~ annexed to the *Cylinder* HK: but, to be sure in this considerable particular it were good to consult the *Clock-makers*, who are best skilled in determining this difficulty & adjusting varietie of tynes to their wheeles.

The Ichonisme.

[12][illustration, see Fig. 35]

To Delineat the Phonotactique Cylinder harmonically.

The Phonotactique *Cylinder* may have a double configuration, either by {making it of} an oblong figure; or like a drum, or rather resembling the Roller of a Garden: The more [13] *Columnary* will serve for the shorter Tunes, of 15, 20: or 30 *Sembriefs*, the bigger & more compasse *Cylinder* for the longer Tunes; in briefe it must be of the full length of the keyes, under which it is placed, and ought to be divided into as many circulary lines as there are keys, exactly corresponding: for Example; Make a *Cylinder* of either capacity, ~~or forme~~ and of such an amplitude or compasse, as may suffice to receive **[page 178]** a *Tune* of 13 *Sembriefs* or full measures, and of that length, that beneath the *Abacus* it may be equally divided into 36 lines answering to the whole length of the keys: divide it therefore downewards into 36 circling spaces, exactly as we sayd, ~~answ~~ {opposite} ~~ering~~ to the keyes, and then againe into 13 oblong spaces, from one base of the *Cylinder* to the other; Then compose a song of 3. or 4. parts; but not exceeding 13 measures, and accordingly resolve them into their due measures, or Tymes, distinguished by lines, adding the numbers to their front, as in the Table following, where you have set a simple song, expressed in the larger notes for from simple it will be facile to proceede to the more buisie & quick:

The Abacus or Table of the Organ-keyes

[illustration, see Fig. 36]

---

12. **[Margin note]** note that this organ should be set in a very dry part of the Grott; The wind chamber & wheele may be exposd & conceald. yet if the ~~vault~~ wind chamber were in a dry place so much the better:

13. **[Margin note]** The Popes Organ being of 8 foote diameter contains a Symphony of 6 voices

Figure 35 (overleaf, left). Illustration of a phonotactic cylinder in text at page 177.

Figure 36 (overleaf, right). "The Abacus or Table of the Organ-keyes," illustrated at page 178.

of the Vertebra, for the more teeth or cam that has, the swifter
will be the motion of the Cylinder: to conceive this the better, in the subsequent
fig: where L the Vertebra circumvalued by the wheeles M Q N.
cal may indte the teeth of the *plate* O annexed
to the Cylinder H K: but, to be sure in this considerable particular
it were good to consult the *Clock maker*, who are best skilld
in determining this difficulty & adjusting varietie of tynes to their
wheeles.

The Jettonisme.

note ye the Organ
should ye set in
a very dry part
of ye Grott: the
wind chamber
e wheeles may be
made of ... concealed
... it is ...
... were in
a dry place so
move the bellows

To delineat the Phonotactiq Cylinder
harmonically.

The Phonotactiq Cylinder may have a double configuration, either by an oblong figure; or like a drum,
or rather resembling the Roller of a garden: the more
Columnary will serve for the shorter tunes, & ye largest
the honey Organ *Semibrief*, the bigger & more compass Cylinder, for the
being of 8 foot longer grunds; in briefe it must be of the full length of the
diameter containing keys, vnder which it is placed, and ought to be divided into
a Symphony of 6 as many circulary lines, as there are keys, exactly corres-
voices. ponding: for example:

Make a Cylinder of either capacity, forme and of
such an amplitude or compass, as may suffice to receive

a space of 13 sembriefs or full measures, and of if length, that
beneath the Abacus it may be equaly diuided into 36 linke
answering to the whole length of the keys. diuide it therefore
downewards into 36 circling spaces, exactly as we said, into the keyes,
and then againe into 13 oblong spaces, from
one base of the Cylinder to the other. Then compose a song
of 3. or 4 parts; but not exceeding 13 measures, and
accordingly resolue them into their due measure or
Tymes, distinguished by lines, adding the numbers to their
front, as in the Table following, where you haue set a
simple Song, expressed in the largest notes; for from simple
it will be facile to proceede to the more busie & quick.

The Abacus or Table of the Organ keyes

The Measure or Tyme.

The Columne or Interstices of the Keyes.

Here haue you the phonotactic Cylinder harmonicaly diuided, and
the composition following disposed in it; which, you are to note,
may be either transferred imediately vpon the Cylinder (thus diuided) or you may delineat it vpon paper (as we haue don) first
and afterwards transpose it on the Cylinder is is made of wood.
and indeede this we comend as the safest course: past therefore so many
sheetes of paper together as may precisely fit the compasse & magnitude of the conuex superficies both in length & breadth, which

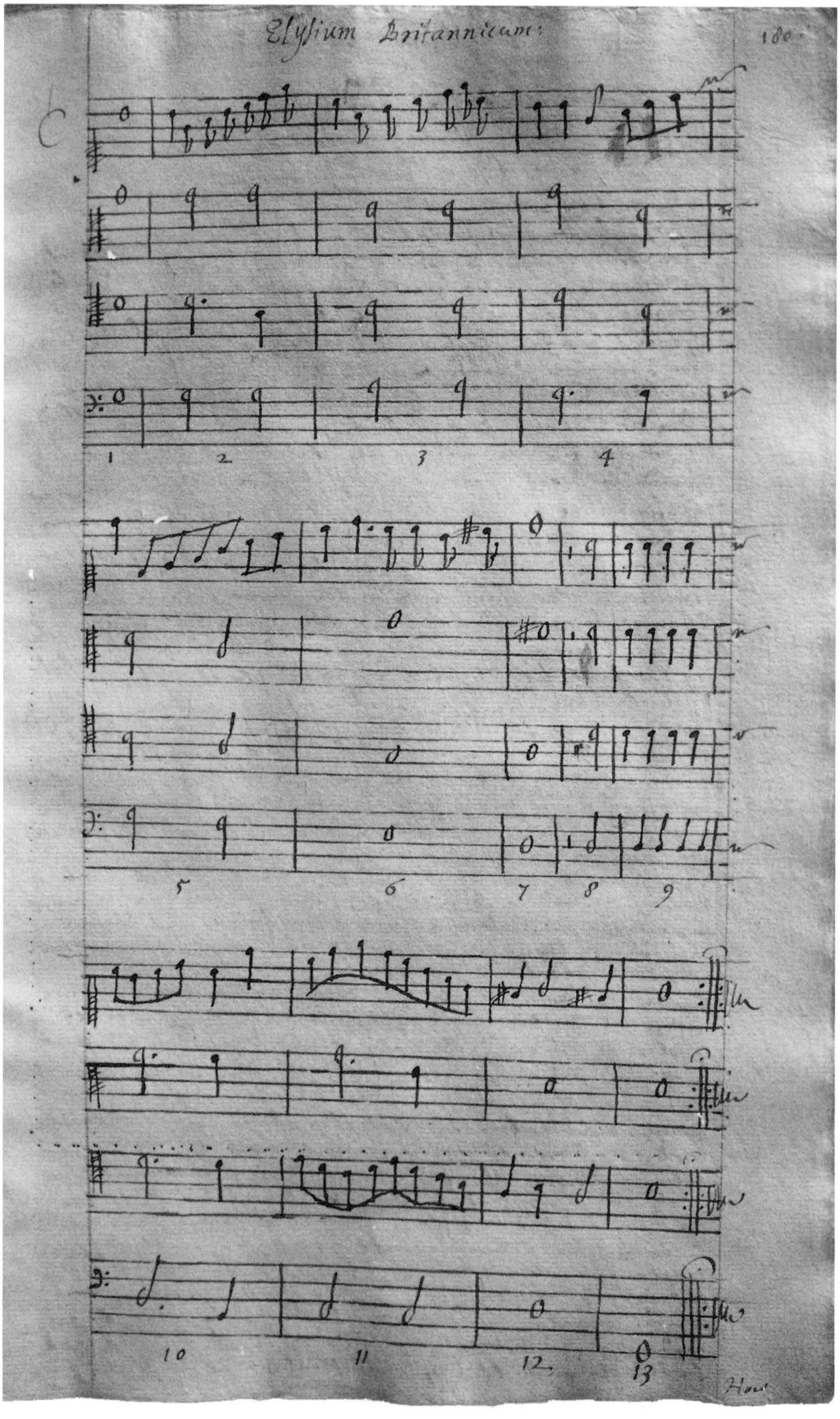
Elysium Britannicum:
180
1 2 3 4
5 6 7 8 9
10 11 12 13

Figure 37. The music for Evelyn's composition on the Phonotactic cylinder on page 180.

The Columns or interstices of the Keyes:

Here have you the *Phonotactic Cylinder* harmonicaly divided, and the Composition following disposed in it; which, you are to note, may be either transferred immediately upon the *Cylinder* (thus divided) or you may delineat it upon paper (as we have don)[.] first and afterwards transpose it on the *Cylinder* which is made of wood: and indeede this we commend as the safest course: past therefore so many sheetes of paper to gether, as may precisely fit the compasse & magnitude of ~~the~~ {its} convex superficies, both in length & breadth, which is **[page 179]** easily don by a just measure V.G. suppose the oblong side of the papers to be A.B.C.D (as in the Ichonisme) commensurate to the Cylinder etc:

Now to transferr the *Parts* or *Song* upon it, worke thus. first, Divide the sides AD. & BC. which correspond to the length, into 36 equal parts (or into so many as there be keys to your Organ) and draw from each poynt of the division of the sides AD parallel lines, to the side BC (that is from *base* to *base* of the *Cylinder*) these shall forme the spaces betweene which the *Teeth* or *peggs* are to be fixed in the Wood, or body of the *Cylinder*, correspondng to the notes of the severall parts of your *Composition* (and are {frequently} marked p {amongst} our divisions, by those *short black perpendiculars*, being ~~the~~ for the notes of the following *Tablature*) This don, divide the side AB into 13 equal–parts, and draw Parallel lines to the opposite side DC. from each poynt of the former division, the line somewhat more plaine & full: For every one of these Intervalls do referr to one Measure, *Tactus* or *Sembriefe*, as the collateral figures indicate. But because this were too large for the minor *notes*, Every of these spaces of *Tyme* are to be divided into two equal parts, for the *Minims*; then againe into 4 for Crotchets, yea into 8 . 16 . 32 & more, in case the *Song*, require it, as that it be full of *Quavers*, *Semiquavers*, or, yet lesser notes, quick & *Cromatique*; Seing those numbers & divisions will but serve to time these notes, according the vulgar estimation.

These therefore must be equal parts; We have here divided every Tactus but into 4 onely, as serving for the composition following, & already marked in their due places: each whereoff we do yet in our mind subdivide into *two* more, for the lesser notes, & this purposely for the avoyding of confusion, which must needes have hapned, should we have described them all by lines in so streite a *scheme*; & after this sort, may the mind multiplie them, as occasion & the minor notes do require. The Composition follows:

[Page 180]
[illustration, see Fig. 37]
[Page 181]

How to transfer the ~~Composition~~ {Song} upon the Phonotactic
Cylinder, harmonicaly divided, Serving for a General Example.

The ~~Cylinder~~ {*Quadrant* or Table} thus prepared, and your Composition ~~eh~~ made choice of, to transfer it upon your divisions (as before described) do this: Begin at the first *Note* of the Base, which in the foregoing *Tableture*, being in *G Sol re ut* & a *Sembrief* correspondent to a full Measure, Seeke in the front of the *Quadrant* (for so we name the ~~cartaceous~~ {paper} *Cylinder*) amongst the *Keys*; for the letter G. or .g. then betweene the Parallels which comprehend the first *Tactus*, draw a {short} black perpindicular; yet so as it do not quite fill the intire space; that is, not ~~to~~ touch the line assigned the second space of the 2d Measure or *Tactus*: For since the first line of the 2d Intervall constitutes the beginning of the 2d *Tactus* (for distinction sake) the Period of the first measure ought not præcisely to reach so farr; but remaine a little short of it; as the ~~figure~~ scheme demonstrates. ~~it~~ Againe, seing in the *Base*, the notes of the 2d *Tyme* or *Tactus* are two *Minims*, æquivalent to a full *Measure*, and possessing the same key *G Sol re ut* or (g) placed under G or .g. twixt the space assigned to the 2d *measure*: you must determine them, beginning that *Note* from the first line of the 2d Tactus, to the 2d smaler parallels, with halfe of the succeeding space; & then in like manner from the 3d line 'twixt the same space {in the Columne} corresponding to G. or .g. to the 4th smaler parallel line & one halfe as before. Thus shall you have finished two *Measures* or *Times*.

Now since the *Notes* of the 3d *Measure* in the *Base* are likewise *Minims* placed in *A la mi re*, search for (a) in the front & amongst the scale of Keyes in your *Quadrant*, and ~~there~~ in that Columne, 'twixt the space of the 3d *Tactus*, determine two like short perpindiculars as before. Againe the *Notes* of the 4th *Tactus* of the same *Base*, are a *minime* with a *poynt of Augmentation*, & a *Crochett* in *G sol re ut*, draw your black perpendicular 'twixt that 4th space or *Tactus*, just as you wrought before. The *Notes* of the 5t *Tactus* being also in (G or g) is a *Minime*, place therefore the *black perpendicular* in the 5t measure under the *Columne* of (Gg.) as you are taught: And seing the following *Note* is also of the same nature, &, ~~in the same~~ *Time* onely 'tis placed in (F fa ut) cliff; Search the *Front* for the key f, and in the space of that 5t *Tactus* situate the Saide *Note* in Columne as before, & protracting the *black perpendicular* from the 3d to the fourth {line or} parallel ~~or line~~ with the moity of the next: The 2d note is a *Sembriefe* in *E la mi*, ranging with the 6t *Tactus*, determine the *perpendicular* for it twixt the *Columne* E of yr *Quadrant*, from the first line of that *Measure* to the fourth *Para* **[page 182]** *parallel* & halfe the space. In like sort, the 7th being in *D Sol re* a *Sembriefe*, must be determined in the seaventh space of the 7th *Tactus*, in *Colomne* D. drawing also the *black perpendicular* from the {first} line to the 4th, with a halfe space, as before. The *Note* of the 8 Tactus being a *Minim Rest*, you shall quite omitt the *perpendicular* containing that ~~measure~~ {Tyme}, in the space of the 8th ~~Tyme~~ {Measure}; but the ensuing *Note* being a *Minim*, & placed in *D Sol re*, you shall there draw the *black perpendicular* betweene the middle space of that *Tactus*, from the 3d slender *Parallel* to the 4th with halfe a {succeeding} space. The next, & 9th being in the same key, containes 4 *Crochetts*, to be determined as you see, 'twixt the interval of the 9th *Measure* under *Columne* D, upon their respective lines, & reaching but to halfe ~~a~~ spaces. Moreover, seing the space of the 10th *Tactus* containes a *Minime* with a *poynt* in the same key, & a Crochett in *Bi mi*, transferr them (as you find it) 'twixt congruous spaces of the 10 *Measure* in your *Quadrant*. The Notes of the 11th *Tactus* are two *Minimes* in *C. fa. ut*. Of the 12th a *Sembrief* in *D Sol re* And finally, of the 13th, the same in *Gam ut*, all which you must transpose ~~in~~ {to} their appropriat {s}p~~l~~aces, designed for them in your *Quadrant* or *Cylinder*, producing onely this ~~las~~ ultimate *Note* somewhat longer as the close of that part; & so have you finished the *Base* of your Composition:

After the same manner it is (proportionably) that you are to proceede with the *Altus*, *Tenor*, ~~&~~ *Cantus* & the rest of the *parts*, if more there be; but for that the *Cantus* is indeede frequently more minute & swift then the rest; we thinke expedient to describe briefly, how our ingenious *Gardiner* may transfir them on his *Quadrant*. Know therefore, that all *Sembriefe* notes (as we ~~sayd~~ {observed}) employ neere an entire space or Measure in the *Quadrant*; {neere, we say}; because it ought not intirely to possesse it, that a beginning may be reserved for ~~the~~ *Note*{s} of the 2d *Tactus*. The *Minime* takes up almost the moitie of the space of one *Measure*: The *Crochett* neere a 4th part. A

Quaver almost an 8th & *Semiquaver* about a 16th, & so proceeding after this computation. These *notions* established; whenever you ~~meete with~~ find that the highest *Voice* of the *Part* is expressed in *Clauses* that are very swift: Thus you shall insert them in the *Quadrant.* Suppose (as in our foregoing *Song*) the first note of the *Cantus* being a *Sembriefe* be placed in *b fa b mi*; seeke for the utmost key (b) in the front of your *Quadrant*, and in the first, ~~and in the first~~ space of the *Columne* (b) answering to the first *Tactus*, inscribe the *black perpendicular*, competent to a *Sembrief*, as formerly you were instructed in placing the *Base*: But the *Notes* of the 2d *Tactus*, **[page 183]** consisting partly of *Crochetts*, partly *Quavers* ~~placed in~~ situated in severall keys; you shall determine the ~~blake~~ {short} perpendiculars, which correspond to the *Crotchet* for the same *note* in the space of the 2d measure, directly under the *Columne* (b) ~~that it~~ {yet} so as it [14]take {not} up a full 4th part of that space, commencing from the first line: But seing the first *quaver* is in *g sol re ut* sharp, have recourse to the *Columne* under ♯ g & there draw the *perpendicular* to neere an 8th part of the space, or intervall of the second *Measure*; beginning at the 2d line. The other *Quaver* in *a la mi re* referr by assigning the *black perpendicular* in columne (a) in the ~~measure~~ {space} of the 2d *Tactus*, possessing neere an 8th part of that intervall, ~~be~~ & beginning after the preceeding 8th part of the space; that is, from the meddle of the smale intervall, ~~or line~~, succeeding the first grosser line deputed for the space of the 2d *Measure* or *Tactus*. And after this sort you are to proceede in placing ~~the~~ other *quavers*, as well in this first, as in the rest of the *Measures*; ever remembring to place the *short perpendicular* of the sequent note, in ~~the~~ {a} more inferiour space then the præceedent, till you have ~~duely~~ {exactly} inserted all the *Notes* into their ~~proper places~~ {proper places &} due positions.

How to transferr Syncopated Tunes in (b) flatt, and Semitones upon the Phonotactic Cylinder

Though our studious Gardner may with a little meditation, collect this from what has bin demonstrated in the former Examples; we will yet add this smale instance to facilitate the operation, & finish this period.

[15][illustration, see Fig. 38]
We will likewise suppose this Serap of three parts to illustrate what we have to say ~~&~~ ~~referr~~ in reference to this portion of our *Quadrant.*

Cantus [illustration, see Fig. 39]
[Page 184] Begin the Song, as you were shewed in the former example, viz: Supposing that the *Cantus* have in the first place a *Rest*, leave it out, & ~~omitt it~~ marke it not in its place ~~of the~~ upon the *Cylinder* or *Quadrant*; but if the *note* following prove a *minime* in *di la sol re* (as in our *Cantus*) note it with a short *perpendicular* in the *Columne* d, of the quantity of halfe a *Measure* after the first space; and so is it *Sincopated* according to your desire. The *note* following being a *Crochet* to ~~make~~ {compleate} the *Tyme*, & placed in *C Sol fa ut*, bound with the first *note* of the 2d *Tactus*, which is also a *Crochet*, you may determine in the *Colomne* C, so as the first *note* take up the whole space from

---

14. **[Margin note]** If this do not precisely answer to the spaces in our Quadrant: the errour may be in drawing the lines ~~of~~ sufficient{ly} capable

15. **[Margin note]** Note that we have here only taken in the first and 2d Measure or Tactus of a Quadrant; as sufficing for our demonstration

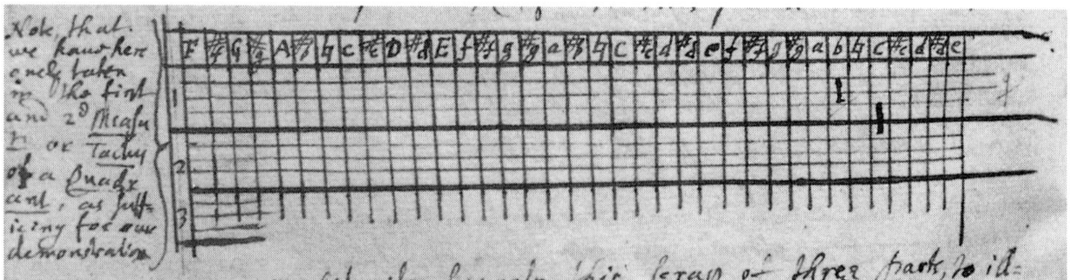

Figure 38. "How to transfer syncopated tunes in (b) flatt, and Semitones upon the Phonotactic Cylinder," illustrated in text at page 183.

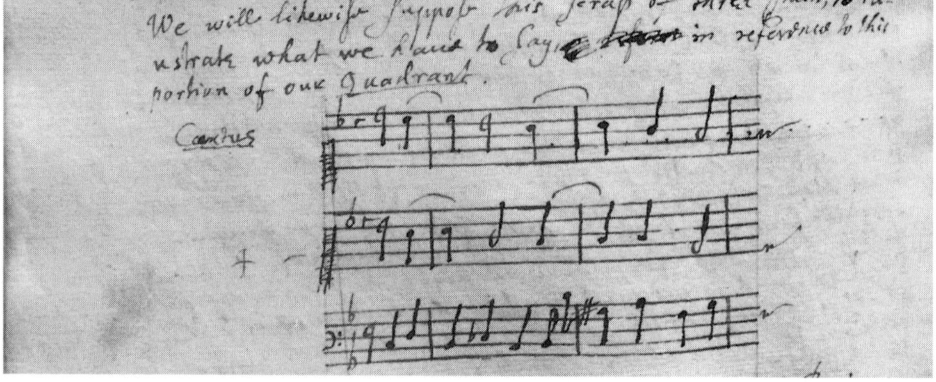

Figure 39. Part of the syncopated music for the cylinder, illustrated in text at page 183.

the 4th to the 5th {grosser} line, which beginns the 2d *Tactus* or Measure: & protracting the black *perpendicular* to a 3d part of the first space of the foresaid 2d *Tactus*. And after this manner are you to proceede with all *Sincopated*, ~~and~~ *driven notes*, & the like.

We have already shewed how to insert into the *Cylinder Notes* of the least & most minute Value, however divided & broaken, so as no *Trillo* of the *Voice* {whatsoever} shall be capable of ~~following~~ {accompaning} them: And it is don (as we sayd) by dividing each *Measure* or *Tactus* of the *Quadrant*, and so consequently, of the *Cylinder* into 32 equal spaces for the *Semiquavers*; because they require that number to make up their proportion, or one *Minime*: If quavers onely, 16 will be sufficient; If semi-semiquavers (as we may find in some ~~compositions~~ parts) & which performe those nimble effects which we mentiond; then of necessity must you divide each *Measure* of your *Quadrant* into 64 lines, and this division made to proceede as before. The thing is so easie to comprehend, that it were superfluous to exhibit any figure: For thus may be transferred *Triples*, *Sesqualteras* and the like proportions of *Tyme*; all *Cromatic* and *Enharmonicall Clausula's* how difficult, & perplext soever.

How to fitt the Teeth or Peggs into the Cylinder

The Paper *Quadrant* thus *divided*, *noted*, and prepared, transfirr upon the *Cylinder*; ~~or else~~ by either taking of the severall *notes & perpendiculars*, & rightly placing them upon it; or, (with more expedition) by accurately ~~past~~ appling, & pasting the Paper it selfe about it; which don, fix into the wood *Teeth* of *yron* well filed, & polite, in the places of the paper ~~Cylinder~~ *Quadrant*, which are marked for the respective *Notes*: So as a *Sembriefe* ~~note perpendicular~~ {note} have a *Tooth* or *Pegg* of such a length as the short *Perpendicular* expressing it, requires. The same to be observed ~~proportionably~~ of all the rest, according to these proportions. **[page 185]** where the length and bredth of the *Teeth* for the severall notes are ~~d~~ adjusted.

[illustration, see Fig. 40]

Figure 40. Illustration of "how to fit teeth or peggs into the [phonotactic] cylinder" at page 185.

Note that all the *Teeth* ought to be of the same height, that is, equaly projecting out of the wood, or *Cylinder*: for in the accuratenesse of this, chiefly consists the perfection of the whole harmony. And these accommodated, exactly, oppos'd to the keyes, and fitted against the *Tongues* as has bin taught, upon the motion of the *Cylinder* produce the effect desired. ~~Last of all~~ Thus the immovable *Teeth* are to be fixed; but a *Cylinder* may be fitted so as to move, take out, & change the Teeth at pleasure, ~~pl~~ to place other in their stead ~~which the immoveable are not capable of~~: and so a new *Composition* may at any tyme be applied; which a *Cylinder* ~~Fu~~ already furnished with the immoveable is not capable of.

For example of this: Divide a *Cylinder* into 24 *Measures*, each of these {full} divide againe into 8 equal spaces, as we noted for *Quavers*; you shall bore holes, at every point of these divisions; so as being ~~prepared~~ {furnished} with a greate number {of} *Teeth* (as the *Printers* box is with Letters) for all sorts of *Notes*, which you may keepe in a divided Drawer contrived some where about the *Organ*, you may insert ~~then~~ a new *Composition* or Tunes at pleasure in your *Cylinder* which, the more large & ample it is, will be so much the better for our purpose.

How to transferr more Tunes ~~then are~~ upon the Same Cylinder ~~at~~

But since there is nothing more tedious & unpleasant, then still to heare the same thing over, how excellent so ever the *Composition* be; & that variety is the thing which we would seeke {for} in all our diversions; & especialy in this nature; ~~mo~~ were it not most desirable, will some say, that more then one song might be transferred upon the same *Cylinder*. {We answer that} ~~And~~ so, there may, provided that ~~your Cylinder~~ it be of a very large size; and, that the *Columns* or spaces **[page 186]** corresponding to the keyes of the *Organ* be likewise ~~ample~~ of sufficient amplitude. We will exhibit an example in the following *Ichonisme*. Suppose that the spaces of the sayd *Columne* be in breadth as AB. BY. YZ. etc: and that each of them were divided into eight equal parts or intervalls: We then affirme, that eight different *Tunes* may be transferred on the {same} *Cylinder*; since the spaces of each of the keyes are equaly divided, as we have supposed; and the particular yron *Tongues* or *Spatulas* (which are those which are elevated by the *Teeth* } to depresse the *Organ keyes*) fitted to their respective *Cyphers* so ~~as to~~ placed, as to play freely upon the *peggs* or *Teeth* of the *Cylinder*, answering the spaces AB. or else be ~~any~~ applied to any of the foresayd 8 *Parts*. For this effect, must the *Axis* of the *Cylinder* be somewhat long, and prominent in both extreames, and the extant part thereoff, divided into so many equal parts or *Notches*, as the space of a key is divided: But the figure will be our best Demonstration.

The Ichonisme

[illustration, see Fig. 41]

Let the spaces AB. BY. YZ. be the Interstices to be divided ~~in~~ each into 8 equal parts. c. d. e. f. g. h. i k. described about the whole *Cylinder*, and answering to the

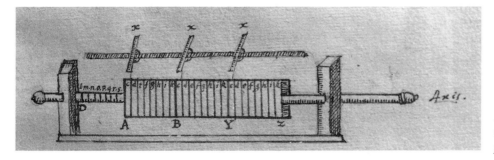

Figure 41. Illustration of "how to transfer more tunes upon the same cylinder" in text at page 186.

this {common} signed *keyes* ♭. C.D. (note that in this ~~Cylind~~ narrow Figure, we can onely expresse the three eight part spaces in lieu of 36, which each of them ought to comprehend) Now seing every space of the 8 parts stand but to one of the 36 keyes (i) {to} one of the *Tongues* & Cyphers, which here we have noted by the letter x.x.x, it will follow, that the handle, or prominent *Axis* of the *Cylinder* placed & resting on the uttermost *notch* or ring .L. at the edge of the hole ~~which is~~ through which ~~it passes~~ the axis passes in the post .D. will by moving the whole *Cylinder* to which it is fixed, promote the *Tongues* x.x.x. to all the octopartite spaces of the *Cylinder*, {as here} immediately on the key .c. Urge againe the Axis to .m. & the {foresaid} *yron Tongue* will remove from .c. to .d; & so of consequence it will follow, that the second *Tune* or *Song* will come in place; Thus againe thru it to re, the **[page 187]** *Tongues* will passe to e, and the 3d *Tune* or Composition ~~of 8 parts~~ succeede: In this sort all the rest .o.p.q.r.s. even to eight *Tunes* may be described and fitted to the same *Cylinder*. And thus much shall suffice for the *Hydrauliq Organ* & *Phonotactic Cylinder*.

[16] The *Alexandria Heron* in his Booke of *Spiritalls* especialy in the 14. 15. 16. 28. 30. 36. 40. 43. 44. 49. 54. & 75t *diagrams*, has accomodated these inventions to the counterfeiting the various ~~voices~~ chirpings of birds, foule, & the motion of several Images: It were tedious to describe them {all} in this chapter already ~~of~~ {increasd to beyond} a just length; We will therefore comprehend all in some {few} general & practicable ~~Methods~~ {Instances} ~~and~~ because they are indeede varieties extreamely suitable to our former designes, and none of the least of the *Hortulan* ~~pleasures~~ accomplishments, ~~pleasant~~ {which} ~~& that a Garde~~ our Grotts, & Fountaines ~~be~~ {are} furnished with all sorts of Hydraulique motions, ~~and Automates~~ ingenious, & stupendious Automats, & that in a ~~place~~ Mysterie we have so highly celebrated there be nothing deficient, which or Art, or Nature can contribute to it.

Of Hydraulique Atomats

[17] You have in the succeeding *Ichonisme* An *Hidraulique Organ*, together with a whole consort of other Instruments, The motion & chirpings of *Birds*, *Satyres* & other {vocal} *Creatures*, after a wonderfull manner, contrived in a *Grotto*, shewing how such Instruments ought naturaly be seated in your Garden: And the description is so perspicuous that we shall not tire our ~~gardi~~ Reader with more discourse, then may suffice to shew how necessary it is, in these Inventions, to give some motion to the living creatures which upon these occasions we introduce, that they may the ~~more lively~~ {better} imitate nature, & appeare the more *magicall*. Also, to shew what Communication the *Wind Chamber* A, has to the severall *Instruments*, turning both the *Cylinder* E.P. & animating the *wind box* of the *Organ* P.B. with the rest of the motions. Of the *Birds*, the *Cookow* being the first figure in the *Grotto*, pearches upon the *Wind box* PB. & is made to moove ~~mouth~~ bill & taile by meanes of the *Lever* or spring (aby) ~~which is~~ fastned to the Wyre, ~~&~~ which is immediately tied to the *Cypher* I at which tyme the two pipes seacretly contrived in the *Wind box*, & distant a *3d minor*, two other wyres, fastned to the Organ keys ~~a~~ (rt) and to the lowermost *Cyphers* of the *Cylnder* HK upon the *Axis* (OP) exhibit the sound of that ridiculous note, *c, Sol, fa, ut,* & *Alamire*, thus:

---

16. **[Margin note]** cf Kirker concerning p: 310: 334: Fig: 1. [Kircher, *Musurgia universalis*]

17. **[Margin note]** Kirker: p: 343.

Figure 42. Illustration of a bar of music in text at page 187.

[illustration, see Fig. 42]

Now to transfer this on the *Phonotactic Cylinder*, **[page 188]** describe {the} 3 Circles (do,ko,tu) in the first whereoff (do) being before divided, fix the *peggs* or *Teeth* so as to lift up the *Cyphers* IHK. The first I {shall} moves the Bird, & {while} HK depresses the *Keyes* of the *Organ* & lets in the wind: The Teeth, thus alternately planted in the *Cylinder* through that whole circle.^{xlvii}

After the same sort dos the *Cock* both clap his wings & crowe, The *Teeth* inserted in the 4 next Circles: And so the *Satyre*; For thus the *Cylinder* being of competent length, the *Consort* & *motions* may be exceedingly varied; either & that, either by Animating **[page 189]** Such *Calles* as usualy are brought from *Nurnberg*, made by *Nicholas Kren* (a set whereoff we have long had by us) or else by imersing of pipes in the Water, to expresse the warbling of Birds, as the *Nightingalle* & others; for which purpose we have in theis po Fig {Ichonisme} placed the Vessell ✛ That Figure on the right hand, reppresents another *Cylinder* of a smaler size, & a set of *Pipes* correspondent to it, which being incamerated in some other part of the Grotto, ingeniously contrived, may Echo to the *Satyre* & the rest: The thing is facile fro to comprehend, from the *Picture*, & from what went before.

To conclude, you have here a reppresentation of many other *Automates*, as in the *Pythagoricall Smyths*, the *Daunce* of the young men, & the to which a little *Cupid* placed in the middle of the Consort, keepes *Tyme* in *triple proportion* & to 8 voices, so to be disposd, & applied on the *Phonotactic Cylinder* as you have bin taught. It is facile to understand how the armes & joynts of the laborious *Cyclops*, & the statue of the *Cupid* are lifted up & moved: The pin (e) being pulled downe by the Wyre for this purpose consisting of some ponderous matter. The rest of the figures being made of wood, are painted. The *Anvile* must be made hollow & resounding; & if you would have the heads or other parts either of *these* or the *dauncers*, to moove with their bodys, it is effected by appendages of leaden pipes within the cavitie of their bodyes breasts, after the manner that puppets of wax are made for children.

And so have we don with the chiefe {of our} *Musicall automats*, for the better accomplishment whereoff we our *Gardner* is reccommended to the *Instrument* makers & to the profound *Musitians*: And for the Harmony {composition} itselfe, such truely we esteeme the most proper, harmonious, & best sorting with the sollemne murmur of the water, & Solitude of the place, which is grave & lesse *Chromatic*, in the *Lydian*, *Dorique* and *Phrygian* moodes.

The Ichonisme^{xlviii}

[Page 190]

The Ichonisme:^{18, xlix}

[Page 191]

---

18. **[Margin note]** Ichon: Kirker: p: 347: fig 22.

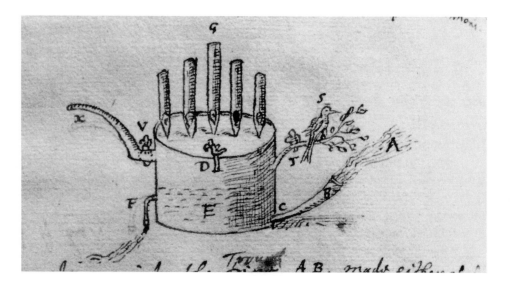

Figure 43. A hydraulic automaton for the animation of birds, illustrated at page 191.

How to build another Sort of Windchest for the Animation of Birds.

The figures & I~~ch~~onismes following, we have added to the foregoing *ex abundanti*, and because that being lesse expensive, & very ingenious{ly} ~~inventions~~ {ordered}, they may haply ~~be~~ {prove} acceptable, to such as delight in these inventions.

[illustration, see Fig. 43]

[19]Convey a streame into the ~~Pipe~~ {Trough} AB. made either of Lead or of 4 boards of some convenient length, (for the longer, the more brisk & violent the wind) & let it end in a Pyramidal pipe B.C. which must enter the side of the Vessell ~~at ee~~ {(ED) at (C)} neere the bottome: Let there be at the opposite side a short *Siphon* fixed at F. or else a *Cock* that ~~as~~ {neere as} much water may be voided there at, as comes in at (C) upon the head of this vessell place what pipes you please, so as may best accomodate what the *Verse* of your birds to be animated, with the cock (D) at the edge, & ~~an~~ {two} others at the botome of the pipe, VX .T. S. & so let the pipe passe the body of the Birds. Then opening the Trough A. & the water entring the pipe BC, into the Vessell ED. The stop cock at V, being ~~open~~ also turned, the aire will ~~then~~ immediately be forced through the channell or pipe VX, & the mouth of that passage serve for an Artificiall Ventiduct, sufficient either to refrigerate a roome in Summer, or to animate any other Bird, blow the Fire, turne any Image or wheele, made light & fitt for ~~it~~ the force of it, & very proper to be placed in a Grott, or Rock worke, such materialls being compos'd of thin boards, {or} *lattons*, whilst nothing seemingly dos touch it, to the greate admiration of the Spectators. And if you open the Cock T. the bird .S. is set a singing, open D. and the *Organ* plaies, & is {becoming} an Instrument of wonderfull varietie. And here I will not conceale, how profitably & usefully these Æolique chambers may be improved, especially those camerated with brick or stone, mentiond in the foregoing Ichonismes; for the use of Smiths, & principaly of Forges & Furnaces, which are constrain'd to make use of Bellows which are very chargeable, & often out of order all which may be remedied by this invention, where

---

19. **[Margin note]** Schotti p: 237.

there is **[page 192]** plenty of water to ~~effect~~ produce the effect: **[illustration, see Fig. 44]**[20]

A Watchman ~~blowing~~ {Sounding} a Trumpet for example by expulsion

Erect a Tower, divide it into two parts or roomes exactly[21] close A.B.C.D. EFG.H. and derive a *Siphon* from the cover of the inferiour Vessell EH. to the bottome of the {Vessell} B & leaving at C: Make also another *Siphon* KL to begin from the cover of the lower Vessell & to passe by the ~~middle~~ {corner} of the upper {viz, through the middle of the pillar secretly} and so through the body and mouth of the Speculator or Watchman, & there sothered to the Trumpet. Then fill the Superiour Vessell with Water, and shut it exactly, but keepe the Inferiour empty: If then you shall turne the cock .C. the water descending into the Lower Vessell, and protruding the air, & expelling it by the *Siphon* KL. will animate the Trumpet. And thus you may apply any other statue, bird, or the like:

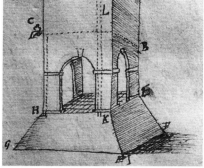

Figure 44. Illustration of a "Watchman Sounding a Trumpet" in text at page 192.

Of ~~Hydraulic~~ {Water} Dyalls ~~by~~ {for Example of} Attraction
[illustration, see Fig. 45][22]

Fill a large Glasse of water, made in shape of a Column, & applie to it a *Siphon* inverted (as in the Figure ~~it~~ is expressed) so as being boid–up with a Corke it may rise and fall, denoting the Howers to be inscribed upon the Glasse:

The Vessell is ABOD. the Siphon KLM. the water conveyed into the Vessell every day, is to be let out at ~~the~~ of the *Siphon* at the osculum K. will marke the hower on the side of the Glasse AO. note that one ~~end~~ {extreame} of the Siphon must ~~pa~~ be fastned to the Corke E through which it is to passe, a little advancing into the water.
[Page 193]

How to erect an Hydrolage or water dyall ~~shewing~~ giving notice of the hower by the Sound of a Trumpet for {an} example of Rerifaction.
The ~~Ichonisme~~:

[23]**[illustration, see Fig. 46]** The Figure of the Siphon ~~curved~~ pipes, & severall Receptacles, are very perspicuously described in {the} *Ichonisme*. This onely shall suffice to explaine what may appeare most difficult: That the passage letting in the curved *Siphon* through the *diaphragma* or partition N. must be carefully sothered; then upon the upper cover of the second chamber cutt a Round hole some what large, & sother or cement exactly to it a Concave Glasse made in forme of a *Cupola*, viz: L O M, or it may be wrought of very thin copper plate: Then let a smale pipe passe from the lower receptacle K into I, where it must be fitted with a *Vulvulus* to open at the orifice whilst

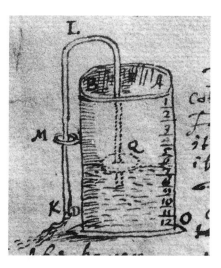

Figure 45. Illustration of a "Water Dyall" in text at page 192.

Figures 46 & 47 (overleaf). Illustration of "a Hydrolage or water dyall giving notice of the hower by the sound of a trumpet" (above) and "other water dyalls" (below) in text at page 193.

---

20. **[Margin note to right of illustration]** note that the pipe KL should goe more perpendicular & upright & the right foote & thigh of the ~~trumpe~~ {statue} advance neerer the center, that the pipe may passe directly to the mouth of the Trumpet; all which the Sculptor must reforme:

21. **[Margin note]** Schotti p: 207 clos: I. Icon: 10.

22. **[Margin note]** vary the shape

23. **[Margin note]** Schotti: p: 251. examine it. This Receptacle or chamber BDNQ must be much bigger then that on which the cupola stands:

How to erect an Hydrologe or water Dyall, giving notice of the hower by the sound of a Trumpet: for an example of Rarifaction.

The Schronisme:

The Receptacle or chamber BONQ must be much bigger then that on which the cupola stands:

The Figure of the Siphon, curved pipes, & severall Receptacles, are very perspicuously described in Schonisme: it shall onely suffice to explaine what appeare most difficult:

That the passage letting in the curved Siphon through the Diaphragma or partition N, must be carefully sothered: then vpon the vpper cover of the second chamber cutt a round hole some what large, & sother or cement exactly to it a Concave Glasse, made in forme of a Cupola, viz: L O M, or it may be wrought of very thin copper plate: Then let a smale pipe passe from the lower receptacle K into I, where it must be fitted with a Valvulus to open at the orifice whilst the other mouth determines in the water. This don, Fill the bigger Receptacle wth water to a 3d, and expose the whole Machine to the Sun, and when any side of the Cupola or Copper Hemisphere shall grow hott, the water wch is thereby rarified in the large chamber, will repell the it selfe by the Siphon G N H. The Cock Q. is for the drawing forth of the water out of the large chamber C out of the lesser by the Siphon K J. But this effect would follow were there no water in either, by the virtue of Rarifaction. And to reinforce the operation, Let burning glasses be so placed in an æquatour, as to passe like an Arch ouer the Hemisphere & so disposed for distance, that euery hower the sun being oppos'd to one of them, the rarifaction may be more vigorous.

Other water Dyalls more facill

Prepare a Vessell of competent capacity, AB. Fit a cock at C wth an orifice so smale as to discharge the water but once in 12 howers. To the side of this Vessell fix a narrow pillaster of wood, divided into 12 points or howers as you see them equally marked: In the middle part of this pillaster, in a smale narrow groove fix a tube or pipe of glasse, reaching from D to E, and marked on ouer Fig: wth pointed lead: this must be open at the extreames E. in this pipe put in a stile or Index of yron or wyre, painted wth blacke or some or marcable colour, & fasten the lower part of this style in a hollow thin Brazen base, F: the water (vpon turning of the cock) sinkes at C with the other mouth determines in the water. This don, Fill the bigger Receptacle with water to a 3d, and expose the whole *Machine* to the Sunn, and when any side of the *Cupola*, or Copper *Hemisphere* shall grow hott, the Water which ~~ra~~ {is} thereby rarified in the large chamber, will expell ~~the~~ it selfe by the *Siphon* G N H. The cock Q. is for the drawing forth of the water out of the large chamber, & out of the lesser by the Siphon KI. But this effect would follow were there no water in either ~~by~~ {from} the virtue of Rarifaction. And to reinforce the operation, Let *Burning glaces* be so placed in an *æquatuor*, ~~so~~ as to passe like an Arch over the *Hemisphere* & so disposed for distance, that every hower the sun ~~may~~ being oppos'd to one of them, the ~~Effect may~~ rarifaction may be more vigorous.

[24]*Other Water Dyalls more facille*

[illustration, see Fig. 47] Prepare a *Vessell* of competent capacity, AB. Fit a cock at C. with an orifice so smale, as to discharge the water but once in 12 *howers*, to the side of this Vessell fix a {narrow} pillaster of wood {painted white} divided into 12 points, or howers, as you see them ~~exactly~~ marked: In the middle part of this pillaster in a smale narrow ~~furrough~~ fur{r}ow, fix a tube or pipe of glasse, reaching from D. to E. and marked on our Fig: with pointed lines: this must be open at the extreame E. in this pipe put in a *style* or *Index* of yron or wyre, painted ~~with some~~ with black or some remarcable colour, & fasten the lower part of this *style* in the hollow thin brazen ~~po~~ box F: This ~~don~~ as the water (upon turning of the cock) sinkes at .C. **[page 194]** will abase the floting style, which you will find to descend from hower to hower. Note that the Vessell must be daily ~~rew filled~~ replenished: But seing (as we have taught in cap: 9) {that} there passes ~~out~~ more water out in the first hower then the 2d, more in the 2d, then the 3d, & so proportionably from hower to hower the water spends faster: The divisions of the howers must of necessity be also unequall: To effect this therefore, you shall marke the points by some exact Dyall: Yet with all this, it will not goe at all tymes perfectly: because the very temper of the *Aire* will at some seasons, much governe the descent of the Water, to which it has so neere an affinitie: notwithstanding, this smale difficulty ought not discourage our ingenious Gardiner because it will come so neere the hower, & is so pretty an ornament. This dyall we have much reformed from that of *Bettinus & Schotti*.   Another.

[illustration, see Fig. 48] [25]

Prepare a Vessell capable of containing a sufficient quantity of Water, ABGC. fit to it a Cock at G. with such an orifice as in the former; Fill this Vessell with water, & place a Man whose feete shall be fastned to ~~an artifici~~ little boate (for the more ornament) fastned so with a smale string as may direct it to the middle of the Vessell: Let this man hold a stile in his hand poynting to the howers (which are you see marked on a board fixed to the Vessell EA)[.] Then either turning up an howerglasse, or exactly reguarding a Sun dyall, let out the water by the cock G. & {at} every hower sinking of the boate observe at what part of the board EA, the stile held in the mans hand, dos poynt, there marke the hower (1) & this doe 'till you have noted all the 12

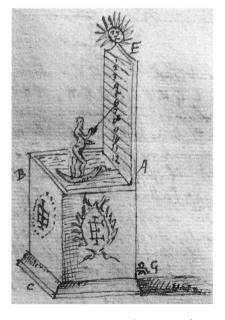

Figure 48. An automaton with a man in a boat marking time as water drops, illustrated in text at page 194.

---

24. **[Margin note]** Schotti p: 263.

25. **[Margin note]** vary the shape. cf Mr: [Ralph d. 1717?] Greatorex's Water Dyall

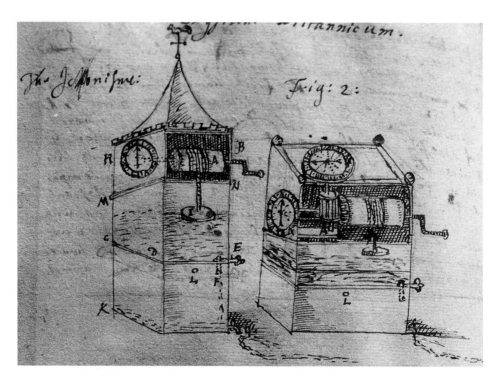

Figure 49. Another complicated water "dyall" or clock, illustrated in text at page 195.

howers. Thus have you a perfect Water dyall, & which, according to the amplitude & the time that you set it running, ~~you~~ may be made of Astronomicall, Italian or Babylonian accoumpt   Another

[Page 195]

The Ichonisme: **[illustration, see Fig. 49]**

[26]Frame an oblong Vessell A B G K . divide it into 3 chambers or ~~ap~~{com}partiments, C G K E . C D E M, H B M N. fitt a Cock at the bottome of the lowest cisterne: G. and a {short} pipe at the bottome of the middle Vessell: so as to run into the Vessell beneath: F. let this pipe have its stop cock at E. In the upmost roome separated likewise from the rest if you please let there be a Cylinder A, which by a line fastned at one of the extreames to an hollow box of Copper, filled {& poised} with a competent weight of leade, may turne it about and consequently move the Index H to a *Horary Circle* placed without: as the water in the middle receptacle sinkes: the Cock E being opned: ~~that the water may sinke~~ into the lower vessell from whenc it is drawne, & refunded into the middle againe daily, or else let to run quite out, & ~~fresh~~ the vessell supplied with fresh. This horary Circle is againe noted by a glasse or Sun Dyal, as the former; and the Line to be daily wound up so as the floate may continualy swimm above the water: And thus may you contrive the Horari Circle to be Horizontal, by adding onely a vertebra as in fig: 2: A: Note that there must be a smale hole, ~~at a~~ L. in the lower vessell for the aire, that the water may descend out of middlemost. {And much after this} ~~Thus we~~ manner was made that *Ship Hydroscope*, invented by that famous French *Mathematician Orontius Finæus* [Oronce Fine] for ~~one of the~~ *Francis the first*. ~~And thus~~ *Gassendus* tells us in *vita Peireskij* of one *Linus a Jesuite*

---

26. **[Margin note]** Schotti: p: 271.

that filled a glasse with water of that temper, ut *internataret medius globulus cum descriptis circum horis 24, quæ ad pisciculum, seu indicem fixum allabentes ex ordine horas diei connotarent tamquam globulo coeli motum exactissime imitante* so as a Globe described with ~~the~~ a horary circle, swamm in the middle of it, which orderly ~~turning to~~ **[page 196]** [27] turning about to a fish fixed in some part of the vessell, ~~shewed~~ pointed the howers of the day, ~~as if it had bin~~ most exactly immitating the motion of the very heavens & celestiall orbs themselves: But till we can be so fortunat as to find out what that water was & the ~~tem~~ happy temper of it, we must content our selves with the Dyals which we have described.

The Statue of Memnon.

[illustration, see Fig. 50]

But before we {altogether} shut up this chapter, and that the effect to be produc't proceedes likewise from the virtue of Rerefaction, we could not let passe to say something of the so much celebrated statue of *Memnon*, which is reported to have spoaken, & uttered a voice like a man, so soone as the Sun arose & darted his rayes upon it. This statue was erected at *Thebes* in *Egypt* & {was} extreamely magnified by Pliny, Philostratus, Pausanius, Lucian, {Tacitus} Strabo, {~~Tacitus~~} who writes to have seene it, & others; For it was esteemed {as} one of the Worlds wonders; & continued above a thousand yeares. *Kirker* in his 2d *Tome* Ægypt: Oedip: par: 2. classe 8, where he discourses de Mechan. Ægypt: c: 13. Set: 1. pragmatia 1. has thus described it:[1] Let the base {or pedistall} of the statue ~~be~~ AB{C}D {be} made hollow, & divided by a partition EF in two contiguations; Let the sides G F D exposed to the Sun rising be made of a thin ~~brasse~~ {copper} plate, as easily to conceive the heate: Let a hole be made in the **[page 197]** partition EF to which let the mouth of the crooked pipe or *Siphon* R be fastned, passing into the {nether} ~~lower~~most hollow: {~~Then~~} ~~In the upp~~ then in the roome above, viz, AB.EF place a wheele, ~~made~~ frame'd of some thin & delicate materiall, easily moveable, ~~inserted~~ the axis sustained by the sides of the box: Let this wheele be made with thinn, flatt Coggs, ~~somewhat flatt~~ & ~~the~~ let the coggs be penn'd with ~~the~~ pieces of quills, ~~like to~~ as the Instrument makers penn the jacks of virginalls: Then ~~extend~~ {take} certaine wyre strings, fastning them upon the bridges NP, ~~& extended to~~ on the {in}side of the {box or} hollow AE. which is exposed to the west, & extended {them} to the opposite bridges, on the inside of the same ~~hollow~~ box GB.F.{D} ~~east~~ East ward: & ~~tune~~ {accord} these wyre strings to the tune of some song, as they tune an *Irish harpe*; placing them so, that ~~when~~ {as} the wheele turnes, the quills of the Coggs may {touch &} play on them: The Instrument thus

---

27. **[Insertion on separate piece of paper without indication of where the inserted information is to be placed on page 196]** Here we might mention the antient invention ~~or~~ or kind of Teraphin, in the shape of a man divided into 24 circles to which an Index pointed as ~~Abr~~ R: Abra Ezra in Gen: 31 describes it ~~being~~ {which some thinke to be} a sort of Mathematicall Instrument by which Laban was want to divine and therefore (as he says) stolen away by his daughter to prevent his discovering of their flight: {but} Wartius in Schema Hieroglyph: concludes it to be such a kind of thermometer, as Horus Apollo describes to arayd the Water by the pudendum of a Cynocephalus: of which see also Macrobius where you may find more of these ὡδρομεδρουτα Idols for we shall not trouble our Gardiner with other Instances:

Figure 50. Illustration of "The Statue of Memnon" water "dyall" in text at page 196.

fitted, when the Sun shall come to ~~beate~~ {dart his beames} vigorously upon the side ~~B~~ G {B} F {D} expos'd (as we advised) to the East, & that the plate GBF~~D~~D begins throughly to heate {& rarifie} the aire, which the Night before had bin condensed within through cold; ~~I~~ {We} say that the *aire* thus *rarified*, finding ~~not~~ the receptacle too streight ~~fo~~ to contain it, will ~~pass~~ issue ~~out~~ {out} with such impetuosity at the pipe R into the box or chamber ABEF, ~~so~~ as to turne the wheele, ~~which~~ whose coggs are therefore adjusted exactly against the orifice of the {fore sayd} pipe; & ~~set the~~ cause the Musique to play; which, that it may {be} the better ~~be~~ heard, ~~there~~ ought to have sound holes made upon the cover of the Receptacle. But, if you would animate the *Statue* above, ressembling it in some sort to the Famous *Memnon* from whom this ~~prett~~ ingenious invention is denominated; place another pipe {Siphon} from the bottome of that chamber, which may terminate at the mouth of the *Image*, & in which {such} a pipe is to be fitted, as may ~~resemble~~ {counterfeit} the voice of a man (for such we have often heard} & the effect desired will ensue: The same rarifaction of the aire, ~~will~~ may also serve to make artificiall Eyes & hands to moove; And [28]Birds furnished with proper calls & whistles, will be heard to sing, to move their tailes, heads & clap their wings; & that either by disposing of the passages of the {issuing} aire,

---

28. **[Margin note]** ~~Se: p: Schotti 241~~

or by contriving[29] {in} other ~~wheeles &~~ partitions some wheeles, which may cause
what motions you desire:[30] But we passe from those to an Instance or two more, &
so finish what we have to say concerning *Automata*.

[Page 198] *How to contrive a Thermoscope or whe{a}ther–Glasse for a Garden*

This being also ~~made b~~ caused through Rarifaction, we have thought fit to allow
it place in this Chapter. Make a *Siphon* or *Tube* of Glasse straight or *Tortuous* like to
some winding *Stalke* or *Convolvolus*; Let the superiour part ~~be made~~ of this ~~Glasse~~
brittle plant be made with a round protuberous head, A, a little open at top & per-
vious to the *Aer*; let the other extreame or roote be fixed to the bott{le} or Vessell B,
which Vessell or Bottle must be filled with water to a 3d: so as no aer may passe; but
becomming rarified through change & ~~heate~~ {ambient} warmth of ~~th a~~ it propell the
water up into the Tube or pipe; ~~whilst~~ {till} being condensed by the vicisitude of the
weather & cold, it sinke & returne againe to its former tenor: These Instruments are
most certaine & usefull in the Summer, Spring and Atumne, because in winter the
glasse is obnoxious to the Frost. Note, that if you stop ~~up~~ the hole of the globe A. the
effect will ~~be con~~ prove contrarie. We have severall formes of these Weather–glasses,
placed artificially in Rock–worke, the water for better distinction ~~coloured~~ {tinged}
greene: & therefore we will pursue it no farther, then to let our *Gardiner* know that
even ~~from~~ {by} this common invention, he may not onely decorate his Garden with
an ingenious variety; but become very knowing in the judgment & disposition of
the Aer.

[illustration, see Fig. 51] [31,32]

Figure 51. A thermoscope or weather glass for the garden, illustrated in text at page 198.

To this we were adding the description of *Versatile Cocks* which indicate {the}
severall quarters of the Winds; but because they are so frequently knowne, we
~~thought~~{inke} their omission no defect, {~~and~~ or their mention any levity} after we
shall advertise our Gardiner that the higher {& more exposd} they are placed, the
better; **[page 199]** and that of all the Inventions of this Nature, those seeme the most
curious & usefull, which (like that in his *Maties* {withdrawing rome to} Bed chamber
at *White hall*, made for K: James when that Blessed ~~Son~~ *Martyr* his son was in Spaine)
~~coming~~ having its shaft so long as to reach into some Banquetting roome, or Grotto
roofe, ~~may~~ dos poynt by an Index to every Rhomb of the Compasse, which is described
upon a board, & verticaly placed; or {so} ~~such as~~ {the} Invention may be ~~contrived~~
{refined} {inlarged} that ~~the~~ a ~~wheele~~ {vertebra} contrived ~~at~~ now the foote of the
shaft, or any other part ~~which th~~ {may} move~~ing~~ a smale {jack} ~~wheele clock~~ wheele
made like a clock wheele fixed at ~~the end extream~~ one end of another yron rod, that
will turne an Index, Muraly ~~exposed~~, placed, & exposed ~~like~~ abroad, ~~like~~ upon the

---

29. **[Margin note]** &: fig: M: concerning the tong M & this wheele

30. **[Margin note]** But concerning the more prodigious animation of statues &
rendering them vocal, se the whole processe & fabric described by Scotti in his Magia
Phonotectonica: par: 2: L: 3 etc:

31. **[Margin note]** Schotti: 231.

32. **[Note to side of illustration]** Improve this by the R: Society. Put in an
Higroscop or Barometer: for the ayres gravitation, & that for the wind out of Mr:
Hooke

out wales ~~of a bu~~ & cheveron of a Building like the dyall of a ~~Clock~~ Towne Clock, & so may be seene all over the Garden, ~~without~~ as well as in the Roome.

But these Inventions, are endlesse, & so would be ~~our~~ {this} chapter, did we pretend to pursue the subject {~~still~~} of *Hydraulique* & other *Automata*, and not rather intend the instruction of our Gardiner, how by these few Instances, {most divertisant} usefull, & facile, he may ~~refi~~ improve the Hortulane Ornaments, and refine upon what has bin sayd. For as these ~~motions~~ {motions} are endlesse, {in number} so would some make them perpetuall, ~~in~~ And it may possibly ~~be~~ be objected by some, as a defect, that we have spoken nothing of them either in chap the 9th where we treated of Water works & Fountains, nor in this present discourse: But ~~the~~ we shall easily support it, since being not fully convinced of the possibility of the Thing, we leave it to the profounder Artists, & to those who shall square the Circle having (for our owne part) promised our Gardiner, to deliver (as neere as may be) none but solid, and unsophisticated experiments: whilst {yet} to satiate the ~~&~~ thirst of those {more} curious persons, we recommend them the Writings of *Bettinus, Grunbergius, Matinus, Kirkir, Finugius, Drebell, Boekler, Harstorffer, Schoti,* {etc}; not forgetting our Countriman *Flud.* and ~~referr respite~~ for the present silence ~~our Argu~~ any ~~oth~~ farther Arguments why we thinke it amongst the Impossibils, till we come to see & to know more of that *Soul & Body*, even that *Miracle* which Becker ~~has produc't promisd~~ pretends to, and, as 'tis reported, {has} produc't {lately} at *Ments* in *Germanie*. Our most ingenious Mr. Dymocks has invented **[page 200]** such rare & admirable assistances, for the raising {of} Water, & improvement of Motions; that there is nothing of this nature which {modestly speaking} we may not ~~hope~~ promise our selves to derive from his industrious Elucubrations.

CHAP: XIII

Of Aviaries, Apiaries, Vivaries, Insects, etc [1]

And where could this chapter have bin more appositely placed then after our discourse
of Artificiall musique to introduce the naturall,

> *Nam liquidas auium voces imitarier ore*
> *Ante fuit multo quam lævia carmina cantu*
> *Concelebrare, homines possent aurisque iuvare*
> *Et Zephyri cava per calamorum sibila primum*
> ~~For men did with their mouths first imitate~~
> *Agrestis docuere cavas inflare cicutas*
> ~~The warbling Birds, 'ere they could celebrate~~
> *Inde minutatim auleis didicere querellas*
> ~~Sweete verses in their songs, & charme the ears~~
> *Tibia quos fundit digitis pulsata canentum*
> *Avia per nemora ac silvas saltusque reperta*
> *Per loca pastorum deserta, atque otia dia.*
> Lucret. L. 5 [1379–1387]

> For men did with their mouths first imitate
> The warbling Birds, 'ere they could celebrate
> Sweete verses in their songs, & charme the ears
> And the agretic Pipe, the Zephyre neere
> The first which taught to blow when they inspir'd
> The hollow Reedes: Then (by degrees acquitted)
> Melodious complaints the Flute ~~pourd~~ {breath'd} out
> Touch't by the quavering fingers all about
> The pleasant groves, the plaines where shepheards graze
> Their bleating Flocks, with leasure crowned laies.

For by the Method of the Poet, Musique it seemes {immediately} succeeded Gardning, ~~& perhaps~~ of which he spake {but} just before, and perhaps, gave occasion ~~the~~
to the witty St. Amant to bring ~~in~~ Apollo {in} to his Banquet, who after the eating of ~~an excellent~~ {goodly} Melon, made the first Lute, by stringing the rind & he
concluded the Collation with straine as delicious {to the ear} as the fruite was to the

---

1. **[Margin note]** Se Rusdens Improvements for Bees. [Moses Rusden, *A Further
Improvement of Bees*, London, 1679.] & Dr. Listers De [lue] venera etc. for the Chapter
[Martin Lister, 1638?-1712, *Sex exercitationes medicinales*, . . . , London, 1694].

t̶a̶s̶t̶ palat: But whither this divine Art was taught by birds or Angels, there is nothing certainely more agreable then the chirping of these winged choristers, the cherefull inhabitants of our Gardens and Groves, where if the place or the climat prove so u̶n̶h̶i̶ unhospitable as t̶o̶ not to invite their spontaneous frequenting; T̶h̶e̶ ̶G̶a̶r̶d̶i̶n̶ our Elysium cannot be without their company though it be at the price of their liberty: For doubtlesse amongst the v̶a̶r̶i̶o̶u̶s̶ innumerable **[page 201]** ornaments of our Gardens, none is more to be valued then the Volarie, none more divertissant affording so much profet in the contemplation of their nature as put the Greate Alexander to a considerable charge for his M[aste]r: Aristotle & to much pleasure in the harmony of their delicious warblings. {For} here the Nightingall G̶a̶r̶r̶u̶l̶o̶s̶

> Garrulos fudit melos
> Nec tamen interea raucæ tua cura palumbes
> Nec gemere aeria cessabit turtur ab ulmo
> > Ecl: 2 [1.57–58]

> A̶p̶e̶s̶ ̶i̶t̶e̶m̶ ̶s̶u̶s̶u̶r̶r̶o̶ ̶m̶u̶r̶m̶u̶r̶a̶n̶t̶,̶ ̶g̶r̶a̶t̶æ̶ ̶l̶e̶v̶i̶
> > C̶u̶m̶ ̶s̶u̶m̶m̶a̶ ̶f̶l̶o̶r̶u̶m̶,̶ ̶v̶e̶l̶ ̶n̶o̶v̶o̶s̶ ̶r̶o̶r̶e̶s̶ ̶l̶e̶g̶u̶n̶t̶.̶
> > > Hor: Eph:

We would therefore so plan t̶h̶e̶ {our} Aviarie in some part of the Garden, as the singing of the birds might resound even to the house, & be the oftner visited; I̶ {We} say within hearing because the distanter places will likely be peopled by such as a̶r̶e̶ n̶a̶t̶u̶r̶a̶l̶y̶ are wild, & naturally seeke the solitude, whilst those of the Volarie once circurated & accostom'd to this retirement sing, c̶u̶p̶p̶l̶e̶ make love, cupple, multiplie, & do all other actions proper to them with the same freedome as those which are loose. Touching the forme & e̶x̶t̶e̶n̶t̶ {capacity} of the Aviary, as they signified[2] in *Varro*, all sorts of places & coups, *quæ intra parietes Villæ solent pasci*, in which were so many thousands of Thrushes, quailes, & other fowle {for the table}:[3] they must {needs} be of a̶ vast amplitude: it would even amaze one to consider their excesse in that kind, but we have nothing to say concerning them; I̶t̶ ̶s̶h̶a̶l̶l̶ so nor a̶r̶e̶ were they for pleasure so much as profit: It shall suffice that ours be built in forme of a Bird Cage, o̶f̶ neither too little, nor to large; for that at P̶e̶ *Genoa* in the Garden of *Andrea Doria* {wherein are huge trees} is too vast, and my Ld: *Verulams* designe little lesse u̶n̶l̶e̶ except we thinke fit to preserve the greater sort of fowle in them such as Cranes, {Bustars}, peacocks, pheasants etc amongst the S̶i̶n̶g̶i̶ Canorus {& smaler} birds which we do not altogether disapprove, in which case, it may take up the whole length of the flanke of some particular Garden: b̶u̶t̶ be it 2 or 300 foote long, & of c̶o̶m̶p̶e̶ {proportionable} t̶e̶n̶t̶ breadth & height: But if the designe be lesse august, & yet very well suting with the pleasure & use of them, An Aviary of 60 foote long, 15 broade & 30 high will be sufficient to hold 500 smale **[page 202]** Birds together with T̶u̶r̶ a competent number of Turtles [turtle doves], Quailes, Partridg & Pheasant, for the furniture of the Area, when the rest of the {family} more nimble & v̶o̶l̶a̶t̶i̶l̶e̶ {volatile} f̶a̶m̶i̶l̶y̶ chants it in the Aer: And e̶v̶e̶n̶ if an Aviary of these dimensions do neither camport with every mans

---

2. **[Margin note]** See: R: R: L: 3. c. 3.

3. **[Margin note]** where the doores should be low & windos few:

occasion, cages of 20 & 30 foote in length will hold birds enough to make the Welkin ring with their musique, for it is incredible to believe {what} a concert 50 or 60 birds will produce, being well sorted & chosen. But concerning the fabrick they may be built of all shapes, there be some affect the round; but it will be difficult to support the Cupola, if the designe be large; ~~Some~~ others the Square, but we would choose the oblong as the most convenient forme; & that not wyred or reticulated all about to the very bottom; as some we find ~~to~~ be made, it being too cold & defencelesse; It will suffice that the two {long~~est~~{er}} sides be Wyred, & both the ends closed especialy the North, & if but one of the sides be wired, as we frequently see them, it is best of all, because there is nothing more pernicious to birds then the through light which both makes them extreamly wild, and render it excessive cold in winter, & when sharp winds blow through it. Besides in this side Wall, as well as at the ends, are the holes {& recesses} to be made, compitently wide & deepe for them to ~~make~~ build their neasts in, as wherein ~~they will~~ you will find them to delight & breede more, then in those artificiall ones made up with broome twiggs, heath or like materialls, especially, if ~~during th~~ against that season you cover them with boughs of holly or the like to preserve them from the common & naked exposure during their sitting: Let there be at the ends, or at least at ~~the~~ one, a chamber for the safer retreat in the cold of winter, stormy weather, & built with that care that no mouse or vermine may get in; for they are cruel enemies to our birds; & therefore it were best to lay the foundation & build all the walls of {round} stone or brick, & in such case after 15 foote the side wall may suffer the rest to be wired to the roofe; but there would be a lower wall of about 4 foote from ground all about, upon which to lay the sleepers ~~&~~ {&} errect the punchions which beare the plates, & sustaines the Roofe:

The punchions may stand four foote asunder, & at every halfe foote. The dubble twhart wyres, to strengthn the upright which we approve much before the ordinary nettworke, such as they use before glasse windows to preserve them from stones: Let the Cover be partly of Leade layd upon curved Rafters archwise, & in this frame **[page 203]** fram a Cupola at every 10 foote, unlesse you will make them very ample & then fewer will serve, ~~as is a~~ whereoff some would be also covered at the top, & some ~~naked~~ wyred onely, that the birds may sit & weather themselves, which they above al things affect, & is extreamely necessary for them; but then must these be contrived with {out} ledges & with yron worke onely; for if they ~~settle~~ chance to settle upon the sides & be invited from the perches that ought to hang in the middle; they will be miserably exposd to the hauke; & it is for this reason we do by no meanes approve those Aviaries which are made swelling with the yron worke at the sides, where even the sharpest spikes (frequently sett about it) {we find} ~~is~~ not sufficient to guard them from those harpayes in the days, ~~&~~ the catts & Owles in the night.

The Wires would be placed at ~~the~~ {such} distance as that 25 might furnish a foote, which is at somewhat lesse then halfe inch asunder; bound with the twhart ones at every halfe foote upward: {But the sizes take more exactly thus **[continued in margin]** If in meshes take the Flemish course fine of 14 meshes in the foote: If of skreene worke (i) strait wyre then it must be Flemish *Reuen* so called: The first will stand you in 7d per foote the other 20d} There must also be hung in severall places of the roofe (besides the Cupolas) perches for the birds to sit on; some fixed in the punchions & walls, others hanging loose & swinging ressembling the ~~bra~~ motion of the branches when the wind plaies upon the trees. These may hang loose upon swivills of wyre to keepe them from breaking & falling downe being over agitated by contrary motions

Figure 52. Illustration of a seed trough in text at page 204.

& impetuous stormes: but such as are made of wyre contrived into ~~rings~~ a multitude of rings in manner of a wildernesse or Labyrinth, are at no hand to be forgotten; for the birds greatly delight to ~~follow~~ {pursue} & chace one another through these & rest on them in the night as upon the other perches.

Of necessity should there be a shallow Fountaine under the middle Cupola, as well to refresh the Birds, as to wash the Aviarie, for which end it is requisite, that ~~it~~ {the floore} be either paved with tyles or Marble; leaving a yard or two foote voyde, & unpaved for a margent of Earth in which the Birds may {pick} ~~dry~~ {scrape} & baske themselves, & the Earth should be now & then renewed for it will else be trodden hard & stenched with their dung: At either end of the Aviary, a yard or two distant from the walls & under cover, let the seede troughs be placed, so ~~made~~ contrived that the seede may fall into them **[page 204]** as fast as they eate it: which it will do if the box containing it be made in fashion of a Mill–hopper: & so covered as neither the birds, nor their ordure can get in: for this purpose, & for prevention of mice, let this box be supported on a single short pillar of 2 foote high: in this manner,
[illustration, see Fig. 52] [4]
and the troughs likewise have lids full of holes {& a square pearche about them} to keepe the birds from getting into the meale ~~&~~ {fowling &} scattering more then they eate: lastly there ought to be a porch & the entry into ~~it~~ the Aviary ~~made~~ secured with ~~a~~ double doores {~~the inmost of which must be~~} made to fall of ~~the it~~ {them}selves, that, whiles he that has care of the Birds enters into one, the other may close ~~aga~~ at his back. All things in this order, the Paynter may ~~colour~~ {lay} the wire and all the timber worke is in a greene colour, reppresenting boscage, Landskip & skie upon the dead wales & ceeling within.

Those who desire to keepe curious Birds, Nightingalls & such as appeare in the Summer onely, must add a stove to attemper the aire in Winter, with curtaines made of oyled canvasse {greene Tarpaulins} to draw before the wires, & had neede have a man continually attending upon them which were a subjection so greate, that we shall rather reccomend the keeping of such Birds in cages apart, & within the ~~the~~ man-

---

4. **[Margin note]** Sr: J: Shaws better, & for neasts put the materials in netts [Sir John Shaw, ca.1615–1680.]

sion house, not onely to avoyde the impertinence, but because they seldome Feede in common & that their meale is different; but if there be any {whose} for curiosity and overcomes this trouble, such birds may be put into the Aviary at seasonable tymes, and taken out againe when the weather grows intemperate, that is from Aprill to September, provided that they be duely fed with such foode as they require: In the meane tymes we rather advise our Gardiner to people his Aviary with such onely as will feede in common upon such seedes, graine & berries as are easily procured, such as hemp, Canarr [Canary seed], Millet, paris, Rape whole oats, etc. Hawes hawes etc. holy berys, etc of which store may be provided at reasonable charges: Bird Birds of this kind & for the most part indigene & the natural inhabitants of our Climate are the Linnet, Greene bird finch, Bullfinch, Goldfinch, chaffinch. Reede Sparrow (which setts all the rest asinging with his querulous note) **[page 205]** The Skie Larke, Wood-larke, Yellow–hamer, Bunting, Thrush, black–bird, Redbreast, Sparrow, etc & of the outlandish, hardy, & facily kept with the rest, The Canary Bird, Virginian Nightingall, & some others. Pheasant, Partrig, Quaile, Turtledove never to be forgotten, All these will agree well together, are {cantatrices} birds of note &, allways chirping, being kept in heart, often clensed & refreshed with greenes & medicall plants to be frequently scattered amongst them by the Gardiner, such as are Cicory, Beetes, Mercurie, Thistle & Plantane Seedes Groundsell etc

Let there be also set a trough of smale Gravell {dry morter & dust} & now & then a fresh turfe: In Cuppling tyme make provision of Mosse, bents, short straws, feathers, the short currings of horses & cattell, with other materialls for the building of their neasts, {which should be hung up in purse netts to keepe from scattering & blowing about, the birds will pick it out easily. When they begin to lay, it will be convenient to cover the Fountaine with a wodden lid, bored full of holes that so their heads onely may come to the water, & they kept from bathing as at other tymes which dos but chill their eggs.

Some fit them with artificial neasts made as we sayd of twiggs, broome, birch & heath; & some of these may be stuck up, together with flatt basketts woven of oate straw for the Turtles, and Receptacles apart below furnished with wheate streames etc, for the greater Birds, & which seldom pearch aloft, such as partrig, Quaile, Pheasant etc: & which for this reason, were happly better reserved in the Vivarie from the smaler birds, because they are given to scrape & fowle {stench} the Aviary more in a day, then the lesser birds will do in a weeke. However the qua especialy the Pheasant; as for the Quails, & beautifull Spanish Partrige, they may be kept without difficulty. We have already sayd how necessary it will be in tyme of breeding, to shade the eaves alcoves & Nestling places with greene boughs, brought in monethly, & stuck into the Earth so as they may seeme to grow for in these the birds will frequently make their nests, & they are a greate protection to them at all tymes, serving them both for shadow & repose: we say stuck into the Earth, because it is impossible to make them prosper by planting the living shrubbs, for the continuall dunging of the birds upon them, & picking of the **[page 206]** birds so soone as any appeares, dos so burne & spoyle them that they never arive to perfection; but are immediatly killed:[5] Such

---

5. **[Margin note]** Besides Varro says that if birds see greene trees, it makes them pine, & therefore banishes them from Aviaries, his words are: quod earum aspectus

boughs therefore are fittest for this {supply} whose leaves are ~~hardy~~ the most hardy, & difficult of quitting the twiggs; Such as are chiefly the Evergreenes, especially the Hollys, Giniper {Laurell} etc, in which they will exceedingly delight themselves:

It is very true, that in that {goodly} Volarie mentiond to be in the Garden of ~~the~~ P: Doria at Genoa, there [are] trees, which both grow & thrive as in the woods themselves; but then we must consider, that they were come to perfection, being little inferiour to some of our tallest Elmes & Oakes, before they were inclosed; & that the whole Aviary is made of yron worke, wyred without any ~~extra~~ dead–wall or extraordinary shelter. The climate & place not requiring it; besides it ~~if~~ is of that amplitude as to keepe in it Peacocks, bustars, Cranes & all sorts of greater fowle, which are not birds of prey.

The best season for peopling your Aviarie, will be about the beginning of February, before cuppling tyme, & care must be taken that they be well mixed, that the Cocks be not over many for the henns; for if there be any defect in this particular, there will be continuall warrs, & hostilities committed, & seldome do the breede successfully; but such as want Wives & Mates will certainly ~~pull in pieces~~ invade their Neighbours propriety, pull in pieces & disperse the neasts of such as are cuppled. There is special care to be taken from Mid–June, 'till mid September: for then the Birds begin to be sick of their feathers, & sing but little; especialy if the season prove very hott & faint; ply them therefore now with verdure, & medical hearbs, & keepe the Cage fresh & shady. To this add the Seedes of Melons or Gourds squeezed in ~~water~~ a trough of water till it become a kind of emulsion, also Succory, beetes, chick–weede; ~~dry sand~~ now and then likewise it will be profitable to put some sugar {licoris} & saffron into their water ~~to~~ especialy when the weather is cold & untowards, or that you perceive your birds to droope & looke ill: also meale & Earth wormes, Ants & ~~Flies~~ Caterpillars, with now & then some figgs, both dry & newly gathered are as ~~perf~~ convenient for them, as for the Nightingalls & other choyser birds which feede on Past or hearb.

[Page 207] And thus we have don with Aviaries in which we have bin the more accurate & prolix because we have ~~ever~~ {ever} esteemed it amongst the Sweetest varieties & ornaments of our Elysium, & in which we have taken wonderfull delight, as often as we diverted our selves either in contemplating their natures, or admiring their songs: For what can compare to ~~this~~eir extraordinary & inimitable musique ~~of birds~~ the warbling of the smaler birds, chanting their Motetts, in ~~consort~~ {harmony} with the thrush & Turtles accompanied with the murmuring fountaines;[6] especially if the Nightingall who is a {alone a} concert of himselfe shall strike ~~&~~ in & mingle her sweete & ravishing note with the next: *Tanta vox tam parvo in corpusculo, tam pertinax spiritus; deinde in una perfecta musicæ scientia modulatus editur sonus: Et nunc continuo spiritu trahitur in longum, nunc variatur inflexo, nunc distinguitur conciso, copulatur intacto: promittitur revocato, infuscatur ex inopinato etc* and then againe, *~~Medita{n}tur~~ Meditantur*

---

marcescere facit volucres in clusas but thats because they cannot come at them & he meanes it I suppose of Fowle whom he would have fatted in the darke. [*De Re Rustica* 3.5.3]

6. **[Margin note]** as the witty author of the poem intitled philomela (by most imputed to Ovid) has reckond them up: Dulcis amica venit etc.

aliæ juveniores, versusque quos imitentur, accipiunt. Audit discipula intentione magna et reddit, vicibusque reticens, Intelligitur emendatæ correctio, et in docente quædam reprehensio etc:[li]

[7]Thus Pliny: And is there anything more stupendious that from so narrow a throat & feeble a breast such long & continued notes should sally fourth, so artificially inflected, divided, & broken into varieties? Sometymes warbling so softly as ~~hardly to~~ scarsly to be heard; anon exhalted to such a pitch, as to emulate even the most shrill & resounding of Instruments: sometymes by plaine & grave notes, sharp, & sincopated, & minute; then quavering with such zinzillations & trilles as are altogether miraculous & inimitable.[8] Add to this that ~~she~~ he sings for 15 dayes & nights almost without ceasing; & therefore truly ~~called~~ was this bird above all others called φιλειμέλες: ~~If~~ But if either that wonderfull dialogue betweene two Nightingalls, recited[9] by *Conradus Gesner* be true, or the Contention

[Page 208]
With the Lutinist so sweetly sung by *Famianus Strada*[10]
who ~~will~~ {would} not stand amazed ~~at the adventure~~ Let us heare the Adventure

> *Jam Sol à medio pronus deflexerat orbe*
> *Mitius è radijs vibrans crinalibus ignem*
> *Cum Fidicen propter Tiberina fluenta sonanti*
> *Lenibat plectro curas æstumque levabat*
> *Ilice defensus nigra scenaque virenti*
> *Audijt hunc hospes Sylvæ Philomela propinquæ*
> *Musa loci nemoris siren innoxia siren*
> *et prope succedens stetit abdita frondibus alte*
> *Accipiens sonitum, secumque remurmurat, et quos*
> *Ille modos variat digitis, hæc gutture reddit*
> *sensit se fidicen Philomena imitante referri*
> *Et placuit ludum volucri dare, plenius ergo*
> *Explorat citharum, tentamentumque futuræ*
> *Impulsu pernice fides: Nec segnius illa*
> *mille per excurrens variæ discrimina vocis*
> *venturi specimen præfert argutula cantus.*
> *Tunc Fidicen per fila movens trepidantia dextram,*
> *Nunc contemnenti similis diverberat ungue*
> *Depectitque pari chordas et simplice ductu:*
> *Nunc carptim replicat digitisque micantibus urget*

---

7. **[Margin note]** Nat: hist: L: 10; c: 24. [43]

8. **[Margin note on page 208]** As Sigr Jo Caprasio ~~tryd~~ {adduced} even with his quarter notes but was foild and could not come near those admired fugas of one of those {naturall} choristers. as Mr: Ligon tells us

9. **[Margin note]** In: 3: hist: Aviam Epist: [Conrad Gesner, *Historiae animalium . . .*, Frankfurt, 1617.]

10. **[Margin note]** Proles Lib: 2: 6: poet. academ. 20 Claudiam Stylus. [Famiano Strada, 1572–1649, *Stradae Romani e Societate Jesu Eloquentia bipartita . . .*, Oxford, 1662, or edition unidentified.]

Fila minutatem celerique repercutit ictu.
Mox silet. Illa modis totidem respondet, et artem
Arte refert. Nunc ceu rudis aut incerta canendi
Proijcit in longum, nulloque plicatile flexu
Carmen init, simili serie, iugique tenore
præbet iter liquidum labenti è pectore voci:
Nunc cæsim variat, modulisque canora minutis
Delibrat vocem, tremuloque reciprocat ore.
Miratur Fidicen parvis è faucibus ire
Tam varium, tam dulce melos: majoraque tentans
Alternat mira arte fides: dum torquet acutas,
Inciditque; graves operoso verbere pulsat,
permiscetque simul certantia rauca sonoris
Ceu resides in bella viros clangore lacessat.
Hoc etiam Philomela canit dumque ore liquenti
Vibrat acuta sonum, modulisque interplicat aquis;
Ex inopinato gravis intonat, et, leve murmur
Turbinat introrsus, alternantique sonore
Clarat, et infuscat, ceu Martia classica pulset.
Scilicet erubuit Fidicen iraque calente,
Aut non hoc, inquit, referes Citharistria sylvæ
Aut fracta cedam cithara. Nec plura loquutus
Non imitabilibus plectrum concentibus urget.
Namque manu per fila volat, simul hos, simul illos
Explorat numeros, chordaque laborat in omni,
Et strepit, et tinnit, crescitque superbius, et se
Multiplicat relegens, plenoque choreumate plaudit

[Page 209]

Tum stetit expectans si quid paret amula contra
Illa autem, quamquam vox dudum exercita fauces
Asperat impatiens vinci simul advocat omnes
Nequicquam vires: Nam dum discrimina tanta
Reddere tot fidium nativa et simplice tentat
Voce canaliculisque imitari grandia parvis;
Impar magnanimis ausis, imparque dolori
Deficit, et vitam summo in certamine linguens
Victoris cadit in plectru, par nacta sepulcrum
USQUE adeo et tenues animas ferit æmula virtus
                    which is thus rendered.
11

Now Westward *Sol* had spent the richest beames
Of Noons high glory, when hard by the streams
of *Tiber* on the sceane of a greene plat,

---

11. **[Margin note]** Mr: Crashaw. [Richard Crashaw, 1613?-1649, *Steps to the Temple Sacred Poems, with Other Delights of the Muses*, London, 1646.]

Under protection of an Oake, there sate
A sweete Lutes–Master: in whose gentle aires
he lost the dayes heate, & his owne hot cares
Close in the covert of the leaves there stood
A Nightingale, come from the neighbouring wood:
(The sweete inhabitant of each glad Tree,
Their muse, their Syren, harmelesse Syren she)
There stoode she listning, and did entertaine
The Musicks soft report; and mould the same
In her owne murmures, that what ever mood
His curious fingers lent, her voice made good:
The man perceiv'd his Rivall, & her Art,
Dispos'd to give the light–foot Lady, sport
Awakes his Lute, and 'gainst the fight to come
Informes it, in a sweete *Præludium*
Of closer straines, and 'ere the warr begin
He lightly skirmishes on every string
Charg'd with a flying touch: and streightway she
carves out her dainty voyce as readily;
Into a thousand sweete distinguish'd Tones
And reckons up in soft divisions
Quick volumes of wild Notes; to let him know
By that shrill tast, she could do something too.
His nimble hands instinct then taught each string
A capring cheerfullnesse; and made them sing
To their owne dance, now negligently rash
He throwes his Arme, and with a long drawne dash
Blends all together, then distinctly tripps
From this to that; then quick returning skipps
And snatches this againe, and pauses there.
She measures every measure, every where,
Meetes art with art, sometimes as if in doubt,
Not perfect yet, & fearing to be out

[Page 210]

Trayles her plaine ditty in one long spun note
Through the sleeke passage of her open throat,
A cleare unwrinckled song; then doth she point it
With tender accents, and severely joynt it
By short diminitives, that being rear'd
In controverting warbles evenly shar'd
With her sweete selfe she wrangles. He amaz'd
That from so small a channell should be rais'd
The torrent of a voyce, whose melody
Could mealt into such sweete variety,
Straines higher yet; that tickled with rare art
The tatling strings (each breathing in his part)
Most kindly do fall out; the grumbling Base
In surly groans disdaines the Trebles grace;

The high perch'd Treble chirps at this, & chides
Untill his finger (Moderator) hides
And closes the Sweete quarrell, rowsing all
Hoarce, shrill, at once; as when the Trumpets call
Hot *Mars* to th' Harvest of Deaths field, & woo
Mens hearts into their hands: This lesson too
She gives him back; her supple Breast thrills out
Sharpe Aires, and staggers in a warbling doubt
of dallying Sweetenesse, hovers o'r her skill
And folds in wav'd notes with a trembling bill
The plyant series of her slippery song;
When starts she suddenly into a Throng
Of short thick sobs whose thundring vollies float
And roule themselves over her lubrick throat
In panting murmurs still'd out of her Breast
That ever bubbling spring, the sugar'd Nest
Of her delicious Soule, that there dos lye
Bathing in streames of liquid Melodie
Musicks best Seed–plot, where in ripen'd Aires
A Golden–headed Harvest fairely reares
His hony–dropping tops, plow'd by her breath
Which there reciprocally laboureth
In that Sweete Soyle it seemes a holy–quire
Founded to th' Name of greate Apollo's Lyre,
Whose silver roofe rings with the sprightly notes
Of Sweete–lipp'd Angell–imps, that swill their throats
In creame of Morning Helicon, and then
Preferre soft Anthems to the eares of men,
To woo them from their beds, still murmuring
That men can sleepe while they their Mattens sing:
(Most divine service) whose so early lay,
Prevents the Eye lidds of the blushing day!

[Page 211]

There you might heare her kindle her soft voyce,
In the close murmur of a sparkling noyse,
And lay the ground–work of her hopefull song,
Still keeping in the forward streame, so long
Till a sweete Whirle–wind (striving to get out)
Heaves her soft Bosome, wanders round about
And makes a pretty Earthquake in her Breast
Till the fledg'd Notes at length forsake their Nest,
Fluttering in wanton shoales, and to the sky
Wing'd with their owne wild Echo's pratling fly,
She opes the Flood–gate, and lets loose a Tide
Of streaming Sweetenesse, which in state doth ride
On the wav'd back of every swelling straine,
Rising and falling in a pompous traine
And while she thus discharges a shrill peale

Of flashing Aires, she qualifies their Zeale
With the coole Epode of a graver Note,
Thus high, thus low, as if her silver throat
Would reach the brasen voyce of war's hoarce bird
Her little soule is ravisht: and so pour'd
Into loose extasies, that she is plac't
Above herselfe, Musicks *Enthusiast*.
Shame now and anger mixt a double staine
In the Musitians face; yet once againe
(Mistresse) I come; now reach a straine my Lute
Above her mock, or be forever mute.
Or tune a song of victory to me,
Or to myselfe, singe thyne owne Obsequie:
So said, his hands sprightly as fire he flings
And with a quavering coynesse tasts the strings.
The Sweet lip't sisters musically frighted
Singing their feares are fearefully delighted,
Trembling as when Appollo's golden haires
Are fan'd and frizled, in the wanton ayres
Of his own breath: which marryed to his Lyre
Doth tune the *Spheares*, and make heavens selfe looke higher.
From this to that, from that to this, he flyes,
Feeles Musicks pulse in all her Arteries,
Caught in a net which there *Apollo* spreads,
His fingers struggle with the vocall threads,
Following those little rills, he sinkes into
A Sea of *Helicon*; his hand does goe
Those parts of Sweetnesse which with *Nectar* drop
Softer than that which parts in Hebes cup.
The humorous strings expound his learned touch,
By various Glosses; now they seeme to grutch

[Page 212]

And murmur in a buzzing dinne, then gingle
In shrill tongu'd accents: striving to be single
Every smooth turne, every delicious stroake
Gives life to some new Grace;[lii] thus, bravely thus
(Fraught with a fury so harmonious)
The Lutes light Genius now dos proudly rise,
Hear'd on the ~~fingers~~ Surges of Swolne Rapsodyes,
Whose flourish (Meteor like) doth curle the aire.
With flash of high-born fancyes: here and there
Dancing in lofty measures, and anon
Creepes on the soft touch of a tender tone:
Whose trembling murmurs melting in wild aires
Runs to & fro, complaining his sweet cares
Because those precious mysteries that dwell
In musick's ravish't Soule he dares not tell,
But whisper to the world: thus doe they vary

Each string his Note, as if they meant to carry
Their Masters blest Soule (Snatcht out at his Eares
By a strong Extasy) through all the Spheares
Of Musicks heaven; and seat it there on high
In the Empyræum of pure Harmony.
At length (after so long, so loud a strife
Of all the strings, still breathing the best life
Of blest variety attending on
His fingers fairest revolution
In many a sweet rise, many as sweet {a} fall)
A full–mouth *Diapason* swallowes all.
This don he lists what she would say to this,
And she, although her Breath's late exercise
Had dealt too roughly with her tender throate,
Yet summons all her sweet powers for a Noate
Alas! in vaine! for while (sweete Soule) she tryes
To measure all these wild diversities
Of chatt'ring strings, by the small size of one
Poor simple voyce, rais'd in a naturall Tone;
She failes, and failing grieves; & grieving dyes:
She dyes: and leaves her life the Victors prise,
Falling upon his Lute; O fit to have
(That liv'd so sweetly) dead, so sweete a Grave!

And thus the *Duell* ended, nor did she certainely deserve a lesse glorious Monument, then one of her noble progenitors which it seemes lay ~~buried~~ enshrined in a ~~famous~~ {curious} Urne of white Marble, all covered with Mosse, and {which (as we were one day walking in that delicious Villa)} we found amongst other Antiquities about the ~~Villa~~ Gardens of *Signior Jacomo Bossio* without the *porta del populo* at *Rome* very neere the bankes of *Tyber,* ~~as one day we were walking in that delicious Villa~~ {where this combate was fought and this inscription extant.}

[Page 213]

DIS AVIBUS

LUSCINIAE . PHILUMENAE.

EX . AVIARIO . DOMITIORUM . SELECTAE.

VERSICOLORI . PULCERRIMAE.

CANTRICI . SUAVISS.

OMNIBUS . GRATIIS . AD . DIGITUM . PIPILLANTI.

IN . POCULO . MURRHINO . CAPUT . ABLVENTI.

INFELICITER . SUMMERSAE.

HEU . MISELLA . AVICULA.

HINC . INDE . VOLITABAS.

TOTA . GARULA . TOTA . FSTIVA.

LATITAS . MODO.

INTER . DULLA . LEPTUNIS . LOCULAMENTA.

IMPLUMIS . FRIGIDULA . CLAUSIS . OCELLIS.

LUCINIA . PHILUMENA.

DELICIAE . SUAE.

QUAM . IN SINU . PASTILLIS . ALEBAT.

IN . PROPRIO . CUBICULO.

ALUMNAE . KARISS . LACRUMANS . POS.

HAVAE . AVIS . IUCUNDISSIMA.

QUAE . MIHI . VOLANS . OBVIA.

BLANDO . PERSONANS . ROSTELLO.

SALVE . TOTIES . CECINISTI.

CAVE . AVIS . AVIA . AVERNA.

VALE . ET . VOLA . PER . ELISIUM.

IN . CAVEA . PICTA . SALTANS . QUAE . DULCE . CANEBAT.

MUTA . TENEBROSA . NUNC . IACET . IN . CAVEA.

{Like to this was the learned Sparrow of Susanna Bartoletta celebrated by Barlæus Miscell. L: 1.~~And this was~~ The forme & ornament of the Urne,}[12] **[illustration, see Fig. 53]**

Figure 53. Illustration of a ceremonial urn containing the remains of a songbird in text at page 213.

[Page 214] *Salve toties cecinisti*: For it was no such unusuall thing to have a *Nightingall* taught to speake in those dayes since without going to the *Apologue, Jo: Grammaticus* in his Commentaries upon *Hesiod* speakes of their wonderfull docility, & we reade that *Drusus & Britannicus* the two sons of *Claudius* had *Nightingalls* that could speake {both} *Greeke & Latine.* {& of later times as Aldrovandus mentions in his 18 booke ornithologie} Though in truth it be somewhat admirable, & very rare that any Birds but such as are πλατύγλωσσα & have broad & thick tongues should ~~come~~ {arive} to that perfection: ~~and~~ For *Papinius* ~~(Syl L: 2)~~ who~~e~~{n} ~~seemes to~~ {he} reckon up ~~all~~ {most many of} the Vocall Birds ~~says nothing of~~ {dos not omitt} the *Nightingal*

Plangat phœbeius ales

Auditasque memor penitus dimittere voces

Sturnus, et Aonio versæ certamine picæ

Quique refert iungens iterata vocabula perdix

Et quæ bistonio quæritur soror orba cubili

Ferte simul gemitus

Syl: L: 2. [4.17–22]

For such a Partrige {it ~~happens~~ appeares} had *Agrippina* the wife of Claudius and *Plutarch* speakes much of their loquacity, especialy[13] in *Laconia*, as also *Athenæus*: But we insist ~~to~~ {no} longer on these, ~~and~~ least haply we ourselves be thought ἐκ περδίκισαι as the proverb is. {Yet he that would reade wonders of this kind, let him consult Aldrovadus, Pausanias in Arcad. Oppianus, Majolus, Greg: Tolosanus.[14] Onely concerning

---

12. **[Margin note]** It was about the capacity of a Gallon

13. **[Margin note]** Plut. in Sympos. In digno Soph

14. **[Insertion on separate piece of paper]** Birds, ad: p: 214. Pliny: L: 10: c: 40 & 43 {& Solinus c: 55.} where he speakes of their salutations of the Emperor: Ælian: L: 13: c: 18. confirm'd by the poet Martial, Persius, Statius, etc: Scaliger, Cardan, who in his varieties L: 15 C: 82. tells us of a Parret he knew of could sing all the ~~notes in the Musique Scales or~~ Gamut or Musique Scales: & Andrew Thenet in his univer-

the antiquity of Aviaries besides the former Inscription, which seemes to have bin in *Domitians* tyme, *Varro* tells us that *M: Lælius, Strabo,* a *Roman* knight of *Brundusium* was the first who built them: And *Alexander* the Greate had them *Voluptatis gratia* & such the former Author calls the *Ornithanes,* to distinguish them from *Vivaries*; and describes that of *Lucullus* at his Gardens in *Tuscalano*; where neere the ~~Flavius~~ {Rivers} Casinus & ~~the river~~ Virius ~~which w~~ were those three famous Aviaries built with ranges of *Corinthian Columns,* the passage twixt them into the Court being 48 foote, & these were furnished with all sorts of shrubbs & singing birds innumerable; ~~But we~~ For after a subdial walke of 450 foote long & 10 broad upon the brinke of the Rivers, (which were walld up breast high) The two *Aviaries* had an ~~passage~~ alley betweene them which entred into a Square of 72 foote long, ~~& out of~~ This Court had on either hand two *Piscenas* oblong of forme towards the Portico, & from this by a narrow *Isthmus* was a **[page 215]** passage to a round Iland, wherin was built a house of pleasure coverd with a Tholus or Cupola upon like pillars, ~~without all this~~ the water compassing it comming through arches & channells, for the ducks & water foule to swimm out &

---

sal Cosmography tells us of greate wonders of the Indian birds: Hen: 2d of France greately delights in these curiosities {as divers of the Fr: Kings have been especially **[continued in margin]** Lewes the 13 father of the present Monarch who ~~is sayd~~ (besides his vast expenses about them) is sayd to have made Luinas a Duke for his addepts in birds, & teaching sparrows to hauke at Butterflies} & had some that could recite ~~wh~~ intire Psalmes of David such a ~~one~~ {Bird} as that of Cardinal Ascanius whom Rhodiginus L: 3: C: 23, says could repeate all the Articles of the Creede distinctly: & those who would be furnished with more of these examples may have them out of the fore-cited ~~Pliny~~ Authors to whom we may add Plutarch, Macrobius, Stotlerus, upon ~~Proclus~~ the Sphere of Proclus. P: Gregorius, {&} Cæsar Mancini: ~~who has als~~ which last has published an expresse treatise of the very art of Teaching Birds to speak & singe as well as to feede & keepe them: etc:

And here something might ~~appositely be said considered~~ be sayd of the greate disputes that have ben amongst the Philosophers & Witts about the loquacity of Birds & to which some have attributed judgment & raciocination as well as words, for to this sense Porphyrie L: 3: de sacrific: when he recounts how Melampus Thyritius, Apollonius & others perfectly understood their language asserting that they discoursd to one another very intelligible: you may see the passage in Philostratus in the life of Thianeus citing Melampus the physitian & others: & Pliny says as much of Democritus: Theophrastus wrot a booke how to learne this language, if at least there be such a piece of his extant, as I have read there is in the Vatican. But it is thought to be magicaly effected, & perhaps so it was don by that Ericus mentiond by Olaus Magnus in his Septentrion history L: 3: C: 15. & I remember Cornelius Agrippa tells a pretty story of a friend of his who knew the mind as well as any of the Antients; but I referr the more ample consideration of these particulars, as likewise ~~that~~ what might farther be sayd concerning the reason & understanding to what Plato, Aristotle, Cicero, {Tertullian}, Luctantius, {S: Augustine} ~~Simplicius~~ Albertus Magnus, Stapulensis, Pius Mirandola ~~and a volume more cited by~~ besides the poets {Aratus}, Lucretius, Virgil & a volume more cited by the learned Duret in his History of Languages: c: 89:

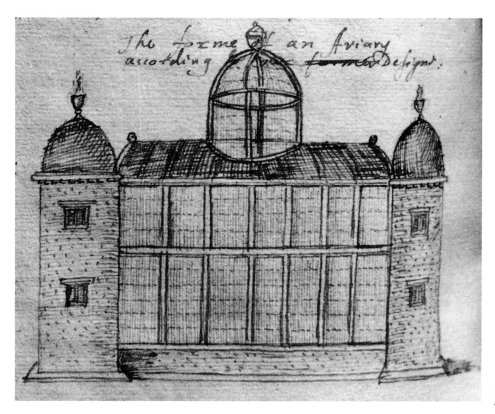

Figure 54. Illustration of an aviary based on a classical description from Varro in text at page 215.

in; & the Walke ~~or Falowe~~ about it raild in with ~~ma~~ parapet of Marble, was encircled with a sumptious *Theatridium* covered with nett to keepe Singing Birds in: Under the Cupola or banquetting roome was a conceited table so contrived as to turne about & serve any dish the guest pleased, without Servers to attend on them; & from under it two spouts of water, which upon the turning of ~~th~~ a cock gave them either ~~hot~~ {warme} or cold water: but what was most admirable was the workemanship ~~& art of~~ {of} the Cupola, which by the motion of its artificiall hemispheare shewed ~~what~~ the hower of the day & night: It had also a Circle that divided the quarters of the wind, indicated by a Fane, as it is most elegantly described by our Master Varro L. R. R: c: 5. and ~~in~~ more at large in our Chapter of the most Famous Gardens Antient & Moderne, which is the 7th of our last booke, whither we referr the Reader.

The forme of an Aviary according to our ~~former~~ Designe

[illustration, see Fig. 54]

[15,16]Vivaries {A Gellius} defines thus: *Vivaria sunt quæ* παραδείσου *Græci appellunt*: Some have conceiv'd it ~~as~~ an errour in the *Amanuensis* and that it should be read *Viridaria*: but it is evident that the whole ~~discourse~~ chapter treates of *Vivaries* only: Or as others **[page 216]** *Vivaria sunt loca septa, in quibus feræ vivæ aluntur nempe inter arbores et herbas.* Vivaries were by the Greekes calld *Paradises*; and are {greene & shady} places inclosed where wild beasts are kept. Some will have them to signise parkes & huge Forrests. Such a one as *Asaph* was chiefe Raunger of to the greate *Artaxerxes* 2: *Nehe-*

---

15. **[Margin note]** folg pattern by Sr: j: Shaws: Speake of wyre tunnells
16. **[Margin note]** Noct: Att: L: 2: c: 20:

miah 8 Sylvarum præfectus, the word is פרדס [Hebrew, pardes] and they were kept like Paradises full of all sorts of Pleasures and Living creatures, so as we picture it in that of *Adams* where the wild beasts, the flowres, & the fruite trees stand thick about him: But the more moderne, & approching our designe were invented by *Fulvius Hirpinus*, And *Alexander* the greate had goodly ones for his ~~Ma~~ learned *Præceptor, Aristotle,* {and the Emperour *Montezuma* in Mexico exceeding as we reade of} furnished with all sort of wild beasts & fowle that by diligent observations the natures of them might be found out: and in imitation of this *Fredrick* the greate duke of Urbin was at vast expenses; we do not meane here the *Leporaria, & Roboraria* which *Polydor Virgil* cele-brates our Country for, as being indeede fuller of Parkes then any in *Europe* or the World besides; but lesser enclosiures to be contrived in some remoter part of our *Elysium* with Wales {partitions} & accommodations sutable to their natures: {as his Majesties at St James}: That worthy Embassador *Geslin Busbequius* made places pur-posely for this contemplation, during his Solitary residency at *Constantinople* wherein he kept severall sorts of wild beasts & Fowle, insomuch as his dwelling resembled another *Noahs Arke* as himselfe expresses it in Epist: 3: for having beheld the docility of the Elephant & read of their dauncing on the Ropp in *Seneca* & that they had (if we ~~believe~~ {accept} {believe} Pliny) bin taught to understand the Greeke *Alphabet*; he was ~~re~~ {incited} ~~solutely~~ {by a laudable curiositie} to inquire into their natures {farther} & see by {his owne} experience how far the antient Naturalists were to be credited:[17] And truely it is admirable what he there affirmes upon his owne knowl-edge, concerning the love of a Lynx to one of his attendants; and that of a Crane to the Spanish Slave {the inhospitable disposition of the clergy} with the strang arts by which the Turkes Cicurat & Familiarize, ~~even Loyans~~ Beares, Wolves, Leopards, & even ~~Lyons~~ the fiercest Loyons & panthers[18]

---

17. **[Margin note]** that the Ibis taught Clyster the dove chastity, the storke piety, ravens justice, etc: & that there was almost no virtue where beasts did not exceede men. **[Continued on separate piece of paper]** And in sagacity doubtlesse they do, & are therefore usefull to our Gardner for Birds præsage many things, as the ayres temper etc. & changes: Their bringing up their young is publique, so are most long-ing to men; & to their parents. but not because they fly neere heaven therefore (as the heathren thought) are they so sagacious: piety, providence education etc: but from another indication impressed in their severall natures etc. **[continued on separate piece of paper]** for which the poet:

Haud equidem credo quia sit divinitus ille
Ingeniu, aut rerum fato prudentia major,
Verum ubi tempestas, et cœli nobilis humor
Mutavere vices, et Juppiter humidus Austris
Denset: erant quæ rara modo, et qui a densa relaxat
vertuntur species animorum pectora motus
Nunc alios, alios dum nubila ventus agebat
Concipiunt: hinc illa avium concentus in agris
Et lætæ pecudes, et ovantes gutture Corvi

Virg: G. [1.415–423]

18. **[Margin note, which is crossed out]** It seemes this was no new thing:

The Ichneumon, Camozzis, Capricorne, Marts & Zibelenes porcupines,[19] Tortoises, Foxes, & Apes, Eagles, Ostriches, Ravens, {storkes} Cranes, & other sorts of exotick creatures {divers of which} may be kept in these inclosures, & such a one we have formerly seene 'twixt the Garden & Parke of *Bruxells*; But the Squirell is for the Groves, & The Tortoise, {of which I wonder we do not keepe {more} for breede in our woods & meadows} Olive, & Lapwing etc may be permitted even in our Gardens of Pleasure with much **[page 217]** more indulgence, though lesse ornament then the Peacock, who envies there should be any place Flowers, besides what {doe} grow in here stately {& magnificent} trayne.

We might in this place likewise speake of the late subterranean warren by which as our ~~Garden~~ {plantation} {Elysium} is situated ~~we may~~ the Gardiner may reape an underground profit & have the pleasure of a rare & most ingenious invention without prejudice: Especially if the underlayer be sandy & a {bed} gravell above it, Thus: Dig a ~~Square~~ pitt ~~10~~ {5} or ~~12~~ {6} foote deepe[20] 14 Square, & let it be walled ~~&~~ or steaned in manner of a Cellar, onely towards the foundation of the wales leave overtures, somewhat resembling large gutter holes, at which the Conies may begin to dig their berrys & draw forth the soyle. To these holes are fitted {4} bords which run in the groves wrought in as many pieces of timber fixed to the Corners of the Pitt: These boards being drawne up a competent height above the holes hang by lines united to one line which passes over ~~th~~ {a} pully pendant in the middle of the roofe: yet so, as by the slipping of a button, the boards fall suddainely downe & cover the holes like a trap: By this meanes (observing when the Conys come forth to feede) they are caught at pleasure, & are reported to be altogether as sweete {fatt} & excellent, as any that have the liberty of the upper warren.[21] The pitt thus prepared, you must erect a frame of Timber of a competent height 6. or 7. foote is sufficient above ground, which may be wyred or lathed to ~~keepe~~ defend it from the Vermine; & then making a dore to one side & a ladder to descend into it, tyle it over with a roofe as this segment reppresents it.

[illustration, see Fig. 55]
[Legend to left of illustration]
A.B.C.D. The height of the Wall or Pitt.
1 The holes:
2 The board
3 The posts in which the boards slide over the holes;
4 The pully with the line fastned ~~with~~ by a button to the board:

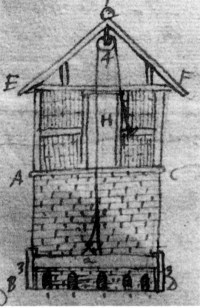

Figure 55. A rabbit warren, illustrated in text at page 217.

Varro speakes of it: L: 3. C: 13. Quintus Orphea vocari jussit qui cum eo venisset cum stola et cithara et cantare.

19. **[Insertion on separate piece of paper]** The wood Tortoise that breede in Languedoc might haply be made harbour in ours also: they are rare meate, we have eaten them at Rome, the wood would be in the meadow for food & I am persuaded that they might breed well in Eng. even such as are brought from Virginia etc. & kept in our Gardens

20. **[Margin note]** not above because they would have as much sun as may be

21. **[Margin note]** Some {rabitts} have weighed 7.1/2. & are better in tast then the wild as I am credibly informd:

EA.CF.G the height of the Frame {wired with wyre} above Ground
H The doore to descend into the pit.
[Legend to right of illustration]
~~1 The holes~~
~~2 The Trap board~~
~~3 The boards posts in which the boards run~~

Enquire of Co: Geo: Tuke how this is made for Dimension keeping food etc:
[Page 218] Some breede the Rabetts in Hutches, & when they are fitt to weane, let them run in the subterranean Warren 'till they are {& of bignesse &} ready to {be} eaten: Others, make one Warren for the breeders, & another for the ~~young ones~~ starters: some to hinder their dangerous undermining when their berrys are conceived to be large enough, do ~~cutt~~ chop off the first joynt of one of their fore feete:[22] this will hinder their digging, but not their breeding:

Note that the Bucks must be chayned like Beares to a stake, that they do not molest the does whilst they {are nurses &} give suck. Two are sufficient for a Warren, & the Does will come to them as they require their company: ~~Feede the~~ Bran, Chalke, Clover grasse with some hay & a little greene, according ~~to~~ as the weather & season prooves will be their constant Foode: ~~But~~ you must also allow them water:

Clense them once a weeke for they will have drawne forth a tun of ~~excellent compost~~ earth within that space which with their ordure ~~ma~~ will be most excellent compost: And this shall suffice to have bin spoaken of subterranean Warrens, after we have cautiond our Gardiner not to sinke ~~it~~ his pitt too neere the Dwelling House, least he ~~neede a Legion to~~ endanger the foundation; ~~& hazard the ruine~~ or if his ~~Garden~~ {ground} be not lined with a gravell ~~above the earth beneath the~~ over their heades ~~leas~~ which will hinder & {repell} their mounting, hazard his Garden: like the *Baleares* who we reade were a people so infested with Conies, that ~~that~~ they were forced to ~~sen~~ desire a Band of Souldiers from *Augustus* to destroy them.

We have already sayd that Fish ponds are comprehended ~~in the Vi~~ in the Vivaria,[23] & to reforme the common ~~Errour~~ {mistake}: It is evident they are delighted

---

22. **[Margin note]** middle claw at least & seare it.

23. **[Insertion on separate piece of paper]** Varro discorses of two kinds of Piscinas of sweete & salt waters to the latter Neptune affords supplys, but these it seemes were made with that cost ~~at~~ that they doe magis ad oculos pertinere quam ad vesicam et potius marsipium domini exinanire, quam implere. [*De Re Rustica* 3.17. 2] Hir[t]ius amongst others was vastly expensive in these shews & spent 12000 Sestertices in feeding them & gave ~~for a present~~ {lent} once to Cæsar 2000 Lamprys, which made Varro say wittily comparing the meterranean [*sic*] as fresh water – shews with these quam nostra piscina plebeia recte dicitur dulcis et illa amara. besides some they had divided as painters how to keepe the colour {even} in Boxes as tuum quos proinde ut sacri sint ac sanctiores: ~~like those~~ sed hos pisces nemo cocus in jus vocare audit. Q Hortensius had wonderfull rare piscinas at Baia which he tooke greate delight to feede himselfe & had many attendants on them & grew so fond of them that you should as soon have gott one of his Coach mules as a Mullet of him, & if a fish had bin sicke, there was more adoe then if one of his servants were dying for they tem-

with the voice & {affect} Musique, we all know the story of *Arion* sung so sweetely
by *Ovid*, & 'tis reported that Lucullus had Lamprys which would come ~~bei~~ to hand
being called by their names, Varro says to the Greeke pipe, ad extremum²⁴ lithes, atq
a{o}ram.²⁵,²⁶,ˡⁱⁱⁱ ~~Sed nemo hos pisces nemo coquus in jus vocare audit~~ ˡⁱᵛ {And thus the
same author relates how they cicurate ~~beasts~~ wild beasts: c: 13 *Quintus Orphea vocari
jussit, qui cum eo venisset cum stola et cithara, et cantare esset jussus, buccinas inflavit, ubi tanta
circumfluxerit nos cervorum, aprorum et cæterarum quadripedum multitudo, ut non minus for-
mosum mihi visum fit spectaculum, quam in circu Maximum Ædilium etc}* ˡᵛ In the greate
piscinas are {kept} *Swans* & all other Water fowle; but they must have a *Nidarie* in
some solitary part of it, coverd over & often clensed. We have seene one built {~~in
an Iland~~} of rock worke of a stupendious height, which was full of Cavernes both

---

pered the very water, & tooke greate care ~~it were not too cold for the drinkes~~ they
might not drinke it too cold.

[Continued on separate sheet of paper] M: Lucullus was ~~even sick till~~ despised for
not having so good ponds: but Lu: Lucullus dug through mountaines to let in rivers
of salt water to feede his piscina which ebbd & floud like the sea itselfe; ut ipse Neptuno non cederet de piscatu: & some of his most beloved ones he had fresher places
for when it was held weake & (as Graziers do) chargd as 'twere the pasture & shelter
etc: Se Varro: R[e]: R[ustica]: L: 3. c. 17

24. **[Margin note]** RR: L: 3. c: 17

25. **[Insertion on separate piece of paper]** If so the Fishes here though we
know not by what organ. In Cæsars piscina, they heard & came ad nomen, & this
Lucian affirmes in Serm de Syria dea [45] ὖτοι δὲ καὶ ὀνομάτα ἔκουσι καὶ ἔρχονται
καλεόμενοι that they have names, & come when calld whence Cicero: ad Epist: ad
Atticum: Nostri autem principes digito se cœlum putant attingere si muti barbati in
piscinis sint, qui ad manum accedant: alij autem negligant. **[Insertion continues on
separate piece of paper]** The Roman men *per luxuriem* in fishes that fresh fish was
[indecipherable]. They made canals to let in the Sea Water [indecipherable] into the
Gardens, especially Phillipus, Hortensius, Lucullus, etc. Se: Varro: L: 3: de R. R: c: 3
& Pliny says, they had pensile vivaries as well as Gardens. Plin: L: 9: c: 56 & some fish
they lovd so well that they ~~mourned solumly for their deaths &~~ hung jewells in their
gills: ~~sed nihil~~ {& gave immense prices for them}[.] They ~~These things may be true~~
So Antonio Drusa in his Villa etc. **[Insertion on a separate piece of paper]** Vedius
Pollio the Gule was so cruell {~~& inhuman~~} (we cannot properly say inhuman} that
he fed some of his Lampreys with slaves, ~~as effecting to tast even mans flesh in them~~
causing them immediately to be drest that he might tast the mens flesh in them. **[end
insertion]** gave 8000 crownes for a lamprey: & what was the mad lux of Hortensius
& Apicius in there kind: etc: so true is it that in these pleasures may be so great sin, if
not well usd: but what says St. Ambrose: L: 5 Hexam: c. 1 sed nihil creatora deliquit:
alimenta dedit, non vitia præscripsit.

26. **[Insertion on separate piece of paper]** But more memorable is that which
is repeated of Plinys Dolphin cald Siman or more lately of the American Manati recorded by P: Martyn, but most admirable of the Xiphia or sword fish which the
Mamertines can take no other wayes so effectual, as with a song & certaine words
which they use, the story whereoff you have at large in Tho: Fazellus & Kerker:

below & above growne over with sedge & ~~weedes~~ flaggs & shaded with a Circle of lofty trees, **[page 219]** which for being built in an Iland & extreamely Stored with all sorts of Foule was one of the most pleasant Vivaries that could be fancied. The Swan had neede be well kept, for he is a greate devourer: They hatch but once a year, & lay commonly not above 3 eggs. There is a sort of them which have one of their feete shaped somewhat like an Eagle, with which he ~~Lea~~ seizeth his prey, whilst ~~with~~ the other (being flatt & filmy) helps him to swimm & row about: It is of old {we learne} that this bird was highly ~~honoured~~ {celebrated} & for his voice, & ~~for that reason~~ consecrated to Apollo for his gift of divination & melodious singing his owne *Requiem*, as foreseeing {be like} the ~~good good~~ hapinesse of being delivered from a painefull ~~life~~ vaine & uncertaine life: Whither or no this be literaly true, some may doubt, because it has bin so rarely heard: But if ~~we may~~ our owne Father oblege the credite with strangers, that none who had the honour to know so excellent modest & incomparable a person would refuse him. It is ~~to be~~ an undoubted veritie which once he related to us; That being a young man, & walking at the head of a Pond neere his house where were Swanns, he heard upon the suddaine & most ravishing note, ~~after~~ which being ended with an extraordinary fluttring & beating of the water immediatly, one of the Swans expires in the middle of the Vivarie, & was anon borne by the streame to the bankes of the pond. A rare event, & mostly our Testimony. ~~His Majesty's~~ And here we [27]

Finaly the *Hernorie* may be an acceptable accession to the perfection of these de-

---

27. [Insertion on separate piece of paper]

And here we may not without ingratitude conceile what the skill & industry of our worthy friend Hadrian May Esqr: has producd of these noble diversions in the Enclosure & Vivare of his Majesty: at St James, where ~~wishing the noise of so greate a citty & almat~~ in the middle of a Greate & populous Citty, there is to be seene not onely a parke ~~ful~~ stored with ~~deare, Antelops~~ staggs & deare of all sorts, some brought from the farthest Indies, ~~Elkes~~ Antelops, Elkes & other strange Creatures, but likewise Vivars of Fish & Foule, duckes, teals, Widgeons, Broad Geese, Spanish ~~Gees~~ Solan & broad Geese, Stork, hearn, Pelicans, & innumerable sorts of other rarity, brought from all parts of the universe: It is admirable I say to behold how familiar they are & what ~~his art~~ {the Effects} of {his} Cicuration is, when ~~at no~~ the wildest Creatures come to his hand & his wistle: Here are Eagles, Ravens, Coruts, Chughes, Starlings, Pigeons, doves, & all that the Arke almost contained of rare & divertisant; to them are large piscinas, chanells, Decoys, Thicketts of Copps wood, tall & lofty trees for the Birds & beasts, & Sedges, Ozyr hops, & ~~pens~~ & ~~ful~~ covers of Furres etc for the foule to breed & shelter in: They have also places planked, & dry banke of Sand for them to sitt on (which foule must have) & {wicker} basketts made like fish potts open onely at one end, to lay & hatch in; These are supported a foote above water with poles & fitted with straw, which both protect & shelter them: In Summ you have here at large what I would suggest & {for} ~~paradise &~~ magnificence & usefullnesse beyond all that I pretend to describe upon the subject, & which I have therefore touched, that posterity may have a record of his Ma[jes]ty: greate mind & in which he incites the great Alexander, & gratifies Philosophers & contemplative Spirits ~~for~~ in the knowledge of Nature;

lights: And it is made (say some) by shuting up a Hern–shaw neere the place under huge & lofty trees that stand about Waterrs & ~~Marshy places~~ & {vast} Piscinas: The crye of the young *Herne*, attracting others, who finding the place apt for foode & shelter, will haunt it, & breede in the Trees: Others ~~in~~ keepe them in Coupes 30 foote high: We might here enlarge concerning ~~Decoys~~ *Eiries* for *Haukes*, how by Turning out [blank space] The Lord of our *Elysium* might furnish himself with ~~the~~ [blank space] but then his woods must be very large, his Warrens dove houses & Neighbours ~~provisions~~ {poultry} at their mercy; which when the person ~~be~~ {is} not absolute, ~~&~~ {or} very mercifull is both clamorous & chargeable: And therefore ~~it~~ **[page 220]** ~~will better become~~ {let} the Forrests & Woods of Iceland & Norway supplie this pleasure[.]

To conclude Decoys suite better with our Water²⁸ Vivaries, then either of the former, but for that the is not propper for places too far removde from the Sea, & that we suppose to have largely spoken on these subjects of ~~Vivaries~~, we shall forbeare any farther discourse concerning them, then that they are pleasures mixed with extraordinary profit & is a contemplation worthy of admiration {(if that be true we are made believers)} to consider how they are ~~educated~~ {cicurated} reclaim'd, chastiz'd sent abroad & educated to entice & deceive their fellow Ducks & Foule from all quarters to their perdition: {if at least it be not a tradition, for in truth there is no such description: most foule will do it: if fed & kept constantly fed at a place:} But because neither the morall, nor the example is so beneficiall, we pursue it no farther at present {, though we could wish our Villa furnished with one of these also, as we enlarge the designe in the 9th chap. of the 3d booke.}

ˡᵛⁱ*Apiaries* are the next, & we define them to be places wherein Bees are kept, not relating to the Hive onely; but to the area or enclosure where they stand; for of old tyme they ~~had~~ destin'd whole Gardens and ample plotts of ground to this purpose; & so *A Gellius* describes them *in quibus siti sunt Alvei Apium. Noct: Att*: L: 2. c. 20. But, *Varro* lesse corruptly μελισσῶνας or *mellaria*; and such a one doubtlesse was that which the two *Spanish* soldiers did so thrive upon, that they yearly received *dena millia sextertia ex melle*, which as the accoumpt then went, amounted to above fowre score pound a yeare sterling,²⁹ a pretty income for one bare aker of ground, & which besides, had a country house in it, & a garden, as our Master describes it de R. Rustica: L: 3. c. 16. And such a place truely we would recommend to be somewhere seated ~~in~~ {about} our *Elysium*. ~~The~~{ An} ornament {that} cannot be dispensed withall, and the Bee itselfe of such use for contemplation and diversion, that there is not any which merits more esteeme or reccommends it selfe with more solid advantage

Apes item susurro murmurant, gratæ levi
Cum Summa Florum, vel novos rores ligunt.
Hor: Eph:ˡᵛⁱⁱ

Their very murmurs are agreable and exceedingly charming, and if they rob our Flowers, it is but to gratifie us with their Hony & that delicious Elixir which these

28. **[Margin note]** describe it a little from St. James
29. **[Margin note]** Scaliger says that he knew one that made 2000 livres yearly which is 200 of our money

industrious chymists extract, ~~a panacea~~ no imaginary *Panacea*, but the richest most elaborat and admirable that nature produces, or arte can shew, & then which, nothing dos more certainely **[page 221]** contribute to the hapinesse of our *Gardiner*: For the famous *Pollio* being asked by *Augustus* how he came to that greate & vigorous old age, answered *Intus mulso foris oleo*, both of them the products of our Gardens, & ~~it was ever impu~~ the wonderfull longevitie of the Inhabitants of the Iland *Corsica* was ever imputed διὰ τὸ μέλιτι ἀεὶ χρῆθε to their perpetuall use of hony: But I should fill a Volume, not a Chapter onely to pursue this subject through all its varieties, & ~~weary~~ {tire} our Reader with what may better be collected from the writings of so many considerable Authors, as have ~~treated~~ dipped their pens in hony, & treated of this sweete & profitable ~~creature~~ {confection}. If we will contemplat, the *Bee* is a rare *Architect*, forming her hexangular cell for every foote or Angle; They have a Citty, King, Empire, Society, They prey not on flesh, fat or blood but on the sweetest flowers, yet so feede on them as not to deface either their beauty, ~~or~~ rifle ~~their~~ or discompose their chast folds:[30] Idleness they abhorr, & when any difference arises, Musique reconciles them againe, & therefore they are the *Muses* birds ~~& dedicated to~~ {prophetic &} auspicious to Poets & eloquent men, {Plato, Pindar} *Virgil*, & St *Ambrose*, & divers other persons are instances of this assertion: Add to {it} ~~this~~ that they ~~traine~~ institute martialy & live as in a well ~~disci~~ ordered camp, keeping exact discipline, send out Colonies, march under their leaders at the sound of the Trumpet & are of all the ~~entoma~~ ~~workes of Nature~~ Creatures, the most affected to Monarchy, & the most Loyall, ~~&~~ reading a Lecture of obedience to Rebells in every {mans} Garden: Solomon knew it ~~when~~ well & sends us to the Bee, *Vade ad Apem et disce quomodo operationem venerabilem facit*. How venerably & mysteriously the workes, for so reades the *Septuagint*. The *Ant* indeede for ~~others~~ {themselves}, but the Bee for others *Sic vos non vobis —*, so far excells their Government that of the Republique, & so ought we ~~direct all~~ direct all our labours for the publique benefit: And all these considered in this one creature is indeede stupendious, ~~in search~~ & indeede of so profound contemplation[31] that *Pliny* tells of one *Aristomacus Solanensis* who spent {no lesse then} 60 yeares in ~~studying~~ {admiring} their natures. [32]For of all the Living creatures Ἡ μέλιττα ζώων ἔσι σοφωτάτη καὶ ἐυμηχαγωτάτη καὶ συνεγγυς ἀνθρωπῳ κατὰ τὸ συνέτον {etc} The Bee is the wisest, the most artificial & approching neerest to the understanding of men, So *Didymus*[33] long since[34] **[page 222]** Let then this suffice for the {use &} dignitie of this profitable Insect which we will yet reinforce by instructing our Gardner, how he may best convert this so much celebrated creature into one of the rarest & most considerable Ornament of our Elysium: And that shall be by

---

30. **[Margin note]** Scaliger affirmes that they smell an Injurious person farr off, & will be sure to sting one that has newly polluted himselfe: Castæ apes.

31. **[Margin note]** Se also Plin: L: 11: Nat. Hist c. 5.

32. **[Margin note]** Geogra: Lib: 15

33. **[Margin note]** ~~& which I would parallel with as much out of~~

34. **[Margin note]** and he that desires to see more instances of the prudent œconomie of this divine Insect may consult the learnd Jo: Loccenius: Respublica apium where in an expresse political treatise he has at large compared the regiment of Bees with that of Civil Empire.

prescribing some few directions, in what is least knowne save amongst the curious, & how he may frame a Philosophicall Apiarie, ~~so as to~~ for Speculation, together with some briefe observations touching their Government.

The Place destin'd for the Apiarie shall have a Southern or ~~Oriental~~ {Western} aspect, The Hives framed of well seasoned Waine–Scott or Clapp–board, like Boxes of what shape you please, But the *Hexangular* seemes to be the most agreable because it resembles the forme of their cells, Let these Boxes be of capacity to containe about [35] three pecks, and so exquisitely dovetayld & joynd that the weather may by no meanes seperate or pierce them, to which purpose they may be layed in oyle with a white colour, and paynted with floures, Emblemes etc for the greater ornament. Of these you shall provide store made exactly of the same shape, with a flatt bottome or lid, which yet shall be so fitted as ~~not~~ that ~~1~~ {2} parts thereoff be separate from {sides of} the box almost halfe an Inch, For ~~this~~ a reason to be hereafter shewed: and these spaces shall also have covers ~~over to draw~~ running in two groves to be drawne over them by wires at pleasure. The dores for the Bees to enter shall be made at the lower edge of the Hive, with little sliders {of wood} to open & shutt at pleasure. But the upper part of the box must advance above the lid a full Inch, to be sloped away convexedly. The Bottomes concavely that ~~by the me~~ being thus prepared they may mutually fitt, and applied fast & close to one another where you will ~~set~~ {connect} two or three one upon another interchangeably. Lastly For the side opposite to the ~~hole~~ quarter where the holes or dores are, let there be a Window to open with hinges with lock & key. This may be about 4 Inches broad & five high within which fix a piece of ~~musco~~ Normandy glasse, {exquisitely} cemented to looke in upon occasion:[36] All this don, mealt ~~some~~ {store of} Rosin & a little Benzoin & storax in a well glazed pott, & with a large brush of hogs haire anoynt it all over withinside, as they rosine their Canns for Beere, & this will [37] long preserve your hives, & is far better then the matting of them which some use {which rott & are a shelter for the mothes}. Now there must be a **[page 223]** cover which may be removed at any tyme, taken off, & set upon the upmost hive. This should be made of a good thicknesse & ~~well~~ with a concave Ledge to fitt the ~~hi~~ convex of the hive, & to defend it from the the [*sic*] Raine & other accidents of the weather, for which purpose let it be made of a pyramidall forme, & to project 3 Inches at least, that the raine which dropps down may not wash the stoole which is therefore not to be [38]above 2 Inches broader then the Circumference of the Hive, & to be supported on a single pedistall of two foote high. But you may ~~forme~~ {contrive} the Cover of what forme you will, & so as may most adorne your Apiarie for such we have made to resemble Palaces, Towers & fortresses, or the hives may be placed under coverts of stone worke with a Dome or Cupola supported with ~~pi Cor~~ Fower Corinthian pillars with Architrave & freezes, statues & busts, as you will have it more or lesse magnificent.

[illustration, see Fig. 56]
The description of a Transparant Bee–hive

---

35. **[Margin note]** content
36. **[Margin note]** window
37. **[Margin note]** Lining with wax & Rosin
38. **[Margin note]** Stoole

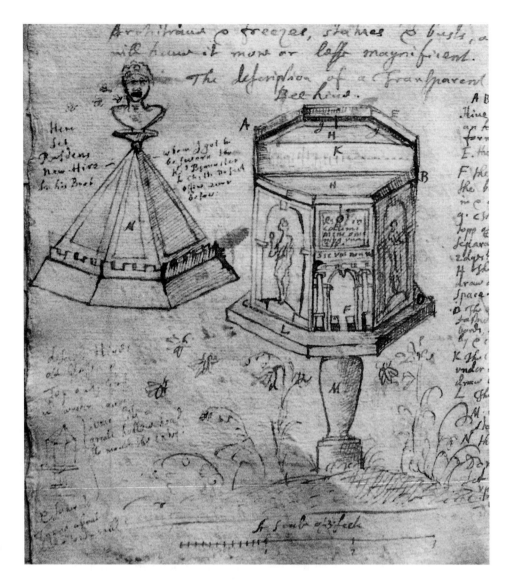

Figure 56. A transparent beehive, illustrated in text at page 223.

[Legend to right of illustration]

ABCD the Hive or Box an ~~hexog~~ octoganl Forme.

E The convex lidd

F The Doares for the Bees to go in & out

G The lid or topp of the hive separated from the edges by a space:

H The boards to draw over the space.

~~O~~I The string or wire fastned to the draw boards to draw them by & close the spaces.

K The Twhart pieces under which the draw boards run.

L The stoole:

M The pedistall

N The Roote or Dome to be set over the upmost hive.[39,lviii]

---

39. **[Margin note]** Here set Rusden's new Hive – Se his Book

Whom I got to be sworn the K' Bemaster to Ch: II: No such office before: Describe

[Page 224] The hive thus prepared you shall people it with a lusty Swarme {or metro-politane stock} early in May, & when that is well furnished (which will be quickly if the season be any thing favourable) Set it upon another empty hive, emboxing the concave ledge of the bottome, on the sharpe or convex edge of the others topp, shut-ting now the holes of the uppermost, that their intercourse may be onely by the dores of the neithermost; & wh But note, that the draw boards H, must be pulled {set} open, that the bees may freely descend & worke in the lower hive. Which, being like-wise full, (to be seene from tyme to time, through the window described) drawing those sliding bords closse to the edges by the wire (o). The uppermost hive shall be taken away, and another empty one placed beneath, to be governed as before, & so they shall neither cast, nor be destroyed till the stock be quite antiquated; There are who make 3 hives succeede one another in this method by setting a 3d under the two first, (being filled) & when the whole body of the Bees is fully gon downe into the third or lowest box, then (and not before) may the first or upper hive be taken away from tyme to tyme as often as the lower shall be filled, & a new empty one put under. Others thinke best, to place the empty hive nithermost, when that which receedes to it, be {is} almost full, shutting all the dores of the lowermost, that the bees entring by those of the uppermost may both finish their worke there &⁴⁰ then descende into the empty one, by which meanes the heavy loaden, instead of painfull carring up their burthen, may worke downewards with more ease. Hives of this kind we have may have 2. or 3 windoes to command a full view of their workes, but two will be sufficient, because they do not so much delight in the coldnesse of the glasse, & {too greate} intromission of light: {distracts them}

There are many other curious wayes of hiving these laborious & admirable creatures besides the ordinary which I expressly forbeare to describe, & the rather because {for that} since those vulgar ones are come in use, the antient government of them with-out killing them is for the most part lost in all Europe, {for in Italy **[continued in margin]** has laws ben made that none should kill the bees but uppon urgent cause.} The Housewife cruelly destroying them to take their Hony; And therefore we do ear-nestly reccommend to our ingenious Gardners the practise of the former invention, as that which we find published by our worthy friend Mr: Hartlib, in his Common Wealth **[page 225]** of Bees. The invention it seemes of one Dr: Browne a Divine. For since Bees are found never to leave their place of Breeding, but for want of roome⁴¹ or some filthy annoiance, & that in their doings working they move downewards, that the trunkes of hollow Trees, wherein they most naturaly inhabite are round, He advises to make their Hives of that⁴² shape, as of empty caske well seasoned with ca-narie or Malaga {Raisins or Figgs}, & of the proportion of a bushell. The breadth to

---

Hives of Glasse, & top only glasse with wooden cover some like a greate hollow head the mouth the entry: & some to turne about like wind-mills:

40. **[Margin note]** nota or if the cover be not made to remove a Cupola may be contrived & louer holes at side, so as to go in at the top like pigeons into a Dove house: or into the mouth of a bust as in our designe, the tongue out for the settle

41. **[Margin note]** for in Magdalen {C[hrist].C[hurch].} Coll & other places they have haunted the same ceeling above 100 yeares:

42. **[Margin note]** Shape of Hives & Content

be a 3d part more then the height: at the upper part of this Vessell viz at C. should be made a round hole D. 3 inches wide & above the lowermost hoops (which should be of yron) six in all, shall be bored the holes of unequall size for ~~bees o~~ the greater & lesser bees: Note that the lowest hoope must be sett an inch from the end of the Vessell, & that place F. covered with a thin circle of yron, to ~~stand~~ {project} ~~out~~ an Inch beyond the ~~end~~ {extreame}, as ~~the hoop~~ to clap on like a box lid, upon another hive. Note that both in these & other hives, there are to be placed convenient sup-porters, ~~which~~ for the Combs, which may be made of stickes to be let in, & rest upon holes made in the sides thereoff from stage to stage. To each hive sett two handles for the more ~~easie~~ {commodious} ~~removing~~ lifting up & removing them: For the greate hole D, fitt a cover of lead, with a handle to take it up by. The Hives ~~thus~~ prepared place them thus:

It is supposd you have one old hive furnished with a lusty colonie, which we will imagine to be A. Take B. one of your new hives, & fasten them together, leaving the hole D at the top open, then cut away the skirts of A. to the very combs, & set it upon D within the compasse of the hoope E. Then lay a false bottome with a hole in it, upon the top of the lower hive making it fast, to prevent the cleaving of the combs of the two hives together: Thus when the Bees are {all} descended into the lower hive B, (which will be when the old is quite full) you may take away the uppermost, and set on the cover H. upon the hole in the lower hive B. & then place another new hive {under it} & a false bottome upon it ~~{as before) under it~~ & when the upmost is also full, & the Bees descended into the 3d hive B.B. take it away as you did the former: ~~See~~ The Figure expresses it to the life.

[Page 226] [43][illustration, see Fig. 57]
[Legend to right of illustration]

A.   The first upper hive,
B.   The 2d or first lower hive:
BB. The third, or 2d lower hive:
G.   The handles:
H.   The Cover for the greate hole in upper hive.
I   The mouthes or dores ~~of the~~ for the entrie of the Bees.
D   The greate hole in the upper bottome:
E   The hoops:
C   The upper bottome.

But if this {seeme to} be a more ~~vl~~ vulgar & lesse polite hive then what we for-merly described, we present you here with another, which is a Dutch invention & very rare. By which expedient the weakning of stocks by swarming is prevented; Drones uselesse, the young Bees (in other hives idle 'till a new Colony goe forth) em-ployed, provision plentifull; the Bees preservd, & hony taken without detriment to them, their Labour rendred far more easie, then by the usuall inventions: These Hives did {not} stand upright, but lay along upon a horse as Barells do in a Cellar, Thus: In a Sweete Garret under the roofe were placed two poles or railes so neere the roofe that the Bees could creepe in & out under the tiles. The close end of the Hive was

---

43. **[Margin note to left of insertion]** make it another shape as pyram[i]dal

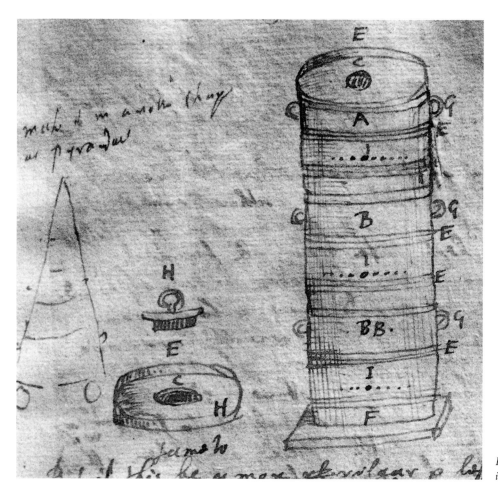

Figure 57. A vertical segmented beehive, illustrated in text at page 226.

contiguous to the {very} tiles. In the upper part of each hive was cutt a hole for their intercourse: The wide end commonly stands clapt downe upon a planke, or a botome made of straw, pinn'd to it on every side with wodden teeth: by which meane were upon occasion joyned straw hoopes of any breadth for the lengthning of the hives if neede required, by which meanes a hive extending to 2 or 3 yards in length the Bees never swarmed. The hives as they lye separated:

[illustration, see Fig. 58a]

The Hives upon the horse closed & pinned together:

[illustration, see Fig. 58b]

[Page 227] It is a common Hive layd along upon one side, in the upper part whereof is cutt a round or square hole, through which the Bees passe & repasse marked C. Turne this hole rather upward, for the more facile descent of the Bees when ladned, & that it may the better be applied to the wall or ceiling of the roofe, where the overture is made for their comming in, or rather joyne it to the upright wall of a garrett, ~~or~~ chamber or closett, Thus they may be kept safe from all Accidents & the lower this roome be, the better because of winds & stormy weather. We would have a low roome purposely built in our Elysium, neere the Coronarie Garden, or some other convenient place: {made warme neate & close with Glasse windows to open & shutt at pleasure & in this **[continued in margin]** ~~this then may be fed during winter with & other tymes of unseasonable weather sticking up fresh bowghs & flowers that in~~

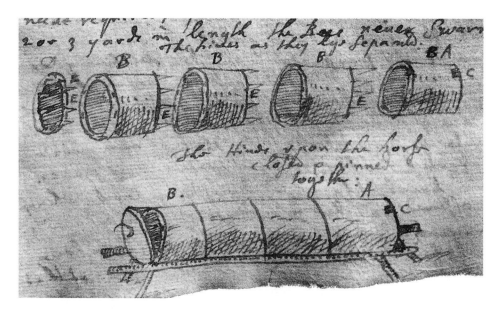

Figure 58. A horizontal segmented beehive with the segments separated and closed, illustrated in text at page 226.

~~swarmming time they may settle on them~~} The open end is shutt with a botome of straw as you see reppresented in D. which not subject to swell with {~~or loosen~~} the weather or loosen, is easily applied, or taken off at pleasure, better then if it were of wood. When the Bees have neere filled the hives, take off the lid D. & add a prolonger, like the other hive save that it hath no head, such as are shewed by the letters B. & then close it as before with the straw doore: And when you will take some Hony from the Bees, smoake them with linnen Raggs, by pulling away the Dore (D) by which meanes the Bees crowding towards the mother Hive A. you may take away as many prolongers as you thinke fitt, & putt a fresh one in its place, cloosing it up with the lid as before. But to returne to our transparent Hives, the {late} inventor ~~of them~~ or reviver of them (~~was~~ For even Pliny [44] is not silent concerning them) was Mr: Mewe of Eastlington in Glocestershire, the happy product of his exile or Eclipse during our unnaturall Wars; His ~~letter to~~ owne description is as follows:

The Invention is a fancy that suits with the nature of that creature, they are much taken with their Grandur, & double their taske with delight. I tooke 14 quarts out of one of the transparent Hives, double their quantitie of others: etc: I can take a strict account of their workes & thereby guesse how the rest prosper. Every time I view them, I have *aliquid novi* (something new) which must needes be more pleasing then the sight of a Fountaine which affords but water, running in the same manner. This hony diversly placed with diversity of Combs: whereof I have observed six filled in 6 dayes of so many quarts. I first intended it for an Hyeroglip[h]ick of Labour upon which a Gentleman bestowed a statue of **[page 228]** that forme to crowne it, which yielding in time to the injuries of the weather, now leaves at the botome of the pedistall this Inscription. Non amissus, sed submissus: & has instead thereoff erected at the top 3 Trygonal dyals, over them 3 weather–glasses, with a Clepsydra to show the hour

---

44. **[Margin note]** Here see Dr. Plotts Nat. Hist. of Oxfordshire for the first inventor: & Floods late patent & little book:

when the sun shines not, over that a clock [i.e., cock]^{lix} that will speake the winds seat at Mid–night, with this ~~Inscription~~ Saphique:

> Has Apes durus Labor hic Coronans
> Occidit, Sole, et Borea Maligno
> Quos Vigil Gallus capit et superstes
> > Clepsidra Monstrat.
> Labour held this, 'til storm'd alas
> By Weather, Wind, & Sun he was;
> All which are Watcht, as here they passe
> By Diall, Weather–Cock & Glasse.

I like them well that view *Magnalia dei in Minimis*: If every man of my ability, through the land cherished so many Hives as I doe it would be in the Commonwealths way 300000 *per annum*, which is lost by negligence, or ignorance of the use of that creature

Another extract from the same:

When I saw God make good his Threate (*Salvam Cingula Regum*) and breake the Reines of Government I observed that this pretty Bird was true to that Government wherin God & Nature had set it to Serve. etc: I never kept 20 stalls, & usualy take but half, yet do I value my wax and Hony worth 20 nobles at the least: Now if he that is valued but as the tenth part of a Parish, at most, can make so much, what may the rest? What may the Country [i.e., County]^{lx} what may the Nation! Had we a hundred hives for one, when there are store of Oakes & Maples, the place cannot be over stored; So that if there were a statute for Parish Bees, as well as Parish Butts, and Parochial Apiaries designed for those places, where observed best to thrive I know not why a Parish may not make as much Hony (as a Gent: in *Norfolk*) viz: 300lb *de claro per annum* {(to which we add) and yield a considerable subsidie to the prince himselfe, as certaine provinces in France are said to doe where the King has an antient droict upon the very bees which their Laws tearme the Aurislages}

As for my transparent Hives I have but two etc. They serve onely to give me an account of the daily income, and a diary of their Negotiations, whereby, if I spend half an houer after dinner or supper, I know what hath bin don that day, can shew my **[page 229]** can shew my friends the Queens Cells, and sometymes her person with her Retinue: She afforded me 14 quarts in one yeare and if the rest afford 10 a piece, I thinke it a fair gain. There is not an Hive to be seene about my house, ~~nor~~ etc. My Apiary consists of a row of little Houses, two stories high two foote a part, which I find as cheape at seaven years end as straw *Hacles*, & far more handsome. ~~where~~ Where I have Bay–windowes, I have a set of unseene stalls, whose room is handsomely spar'd; and their company very harmonious, especialy for those that lodge in their Chambers, whether they would wake or sleep, in so much as I have heard some say (that have lodged there) they would give twenty pound to have & heare the like at home. So much the most ingenious Mr: Mewe's.

Vincenzo Tanara in his *Oeconomia del Cittadino in Villa* has {best} described the *Italian* forme of Hives: They make them 2 foote long 8 Inches diameter: The holes in the middle bored obliquely because of the wind, and no bigger then to receive one Bee at a tyme: At the top, is a cover fastned with wooden pins, to take off, the joynts & comissures closed with lime and cow dung. They frequently set their weake hives in the Wine–Cellar where they will maintaine themselves with the sent of the Wine, 'till the Spring: ~~And thus~~ They drive them by setting an empty Hive upon the full, taking off the top cover which was for this cause loosely staied with pinns (as we sayd) then they stop their holes with dittany, so as they may have aire, but not come forth, then lifting up the under hive Smoake them a little up into the Empty, this don, they draw a board betweene to hinder their returning 'till they have gelt them as much as they please: This they do twise a yeare 1 in *June* 20 daies after their swarming, leaving a 5t part of their goods: and then removing the board, suffer them to descend againe: And this opportunity they take to clense them of mothes & ordure, sprinkling them with wine. But you are to be carefull that in cutting the Combs (which they do with a hooke made of this forme[)] [lxi] you dissorder nor bruise those which you spare. Secondly, in the beginning of *October*; but then they **[page 230]** leave halfe for {hyemnation &} their winter provision: some stopp the hole above with a corke, or leaden weight, but the very best way were with a lid fastned with hinges & to be locked to the hive.

There are some which (as we sayd) have whole roomes {with glasse windows} set about with hives, which they lock up, & release at pleasure, by this meanes he preserved them from all accidents of weather, & by sticking up fresh bowes, & slinging flowers, & sweete compositions feedes them when they are not disposed to goe abroad: upon these boughs they also many times hang their swarmes[.] It is sayd that Apiaries should be placed *ubi pabulum* [45] *sit frequens et aqua pura.* The Cythisus, Baulme, {Time}, Rosemarie, Woodbind, and generally the blossomes of Trees do greately contribute to their thriving, as being fuller of that mel–deaw {Cæli sudoris} & fermenting it better for the melification, then other floweres & plants: But above all the Oake, maple, & willow are greately sought after, as also the pine, & all resinous trees, so as they nowhere prosper better then neere the woods & even in the midst of them, peopling the hollow trees of the coldest tracts & countries, witnesse *Russia, Moscovia* & other of the Northern ~~coun~~ climes from where that prodigious plentie of wax & hony is dispenced through all Europe: {for as for those who conceive they cannot prosper without abundance of flouers & {plenty of} provision: Palladio, an old Gardner, will **[continued in margin]** tell us ~~it~~ an over fruitfull yeare destroys them, nam si nimis floribus annus exuberat, dum solam curam gerendi mellis exercent, de prole nihil cogitant.} For their ~~Winter~~ provision & in hard weather, & ~~tedi~~ tedious winters they may be fed with compositions made of Molasses, Refuse Sugar, Sweete wort, {&} tosts {dipped} & Ale, Milke Barley meale, Figgs, Raisins, Ani–seede & sweete fennell: but care must be had that there lye stalkes & branches [46] of Fennell, or the like, to preserve them from inviscating in these liquors, & so their troughs of water should be prepared shallow, & cleane, with, now and then a handfull of Bai–Salt lying about the Stalks: Also, water {whereoff that of raine is to be preferred as most impregnate} & hony made tepid & sprinkled amongst the combs, a pint at a time is profitable,

---

45. **[Margin note]** above all English Aniseed sowd in the full in Feb cover it with littier: & when they sow themselves sow againe which is best: rich soile is best

46. **[Margin note]** also some hony or a pint of Molasses, 3 parts of raine water & meale: note it must be the first Molasses so calld & not what the sugar ~~refiners~~ refiners leave out refuse hony is better with aniseed & meale beaten; it is good to lay flowers of malt or corne for them in wet seasons

especialy for the first Swarme: for the 2d, & 3d, prepare a Mulsum of eight parts of water, to one of hony, boild to a quart, & served in {slitt} Canes, or hollow troughs, & ~~mixed with~~ {full of} straws {for them to settle on}. The perfumes which delight & profit them are made of cow dung, {galbanum} Storax, Benzoine etc: but with greate prudence & not above 2 minutes at a time; But ~~for~~ {to summ up all these by} more general Rules take notice of this following Kalendar; as where we shall endeavour to describe all the chiefe particulars concerning their government.

In *March* your Bees begin to breede, & to sit: {it is a dangerous moneth for robbing, therefore close the wiccketts evening & morning, & clome them well.} In Aprill they hatch; & therefore in these 2 moneths may **[page 231]** be served, especially if the weather be hard & unseasonable {now you may a little enlarge ther issue} In *May* {give them full liberty for} they come abroad & are not fully provided 'till mid May; at which tyme they frequently swarme & those are ever the best because In *June* they are in their strength & prime for then there is greate plenty of flowers, & hony deaws: Then likewise they swarme; For being too full & numerous, they ~~they~~ send forth new *Colonies*: but first they who are ~~to goe in~~ {designe for} the expedition resort together about the Hive 'till their King having found {fit} a place for their *Rendezvous* ~~pitches~~ {first lights} himselfe, then immediately followed with innumerable numbers pitching their camp round about their ~~King~~ {Royal General} they hang together till certaine Scouts which before they had sent forth, tanquam *exploratores*, bring them tidings of a ~~fitting place to live in~~ {convenient quarterr}, which notice he gives them by a certaine touch which he ~~gives~~ {imparts} to the out guards, that by a ~~certaine~~ kind of shivering motion communicates it to the whole swarme {& center bees} in a moment at which ~~marke~~ (signal) they ~~fly on seperate~~ {dissolve the populus & moving Cone}, & fly immediately to the place their King leading them in front. In this interim therefore they are carefully to be hived: that is brushed into a well prepared hive. ~~and knitt up into a sheete {which were spread under them before} 'till they are well settled, & that towards the evening they may be placed on the Stoole where they are to abide~~ which you ~~We do not trouble our Gardner with~~ shall set upon a propp on a sheete that the stragling Bees may enter. Sometimes you may cutt downe the bough on which the Cone hangs, the varieties of accidents & cases are infinite, but being now entered, knitt up the sheete, & cary them gently to their stoole in the evening a little before sunset. If they lye out the next day or two, it is a signe they are underhived, in which case you shall enlarge it with a circle well closed & supported.

The prognostications of their swarming are taken from a noise which some Eminent Bees make, 2 or 3 nights before, resembling that of a Trumpet:[47] *Mr: Butler* has contrived this *Melisso melos* into a ~~Song~~ ditty of 4 parts, & shewes how if the Art of musique were quite lost, it might againe be recovered by the Muses Birds: There is likewise a certaine humour which you shall find about the skirts of the stoole below. There may be above 30000 in a busy swarme. ~~In July the stalls are full of hony~~ If the hives stand too hott {this moneth} shade them with boughs etc. Seaven or 8 daies after Midsomer, stop their swarming and set them up to be taken, that is enlarge the hive; and if for all this they swarme, ~~kno~~ after they are hived, knock them out upon

---

47. **[Margin note]** . . . et vox auditur fractos sonitus imitata Tubarum: Virg: [*Geor:* 4.72]

a table set even with the stoole, that they may enter againe into their old hive. **[Page 232]** But if you will dubble a Swarme, prepare an empty hive binding two thwhart sticks half an Inch Square that may lye parrallell {upon the mouth there} then reverting the old hive well fixed with stakes or a frame made purposely to hold it in that posture; set the empty hive upon it, into which they will ascend, worke & breede. By the end of August you may take away the old one, & place the new upon its stoole: To effect this the better, you must cloame the edges where the two hives meet upon the sticks, all but a place for the doore: do this about 10 at night, & so let them stand till the end of the Dog daies. Then in a faire calme morning, very early, shut up all the rest of the ~~dores~~ {stalls} in your Apiarie, and when the Sun is half an hour risen, parte the new combs which m[a]y by this tyme be contiguous to the old with a sharp wyre flatted, & so separate the two hives, placing the upmost upon a stoole.

In *July* the stalls are full of hony, kill therefore the drones, especially of those you intend to take: & about mid *July* ~~set~~ streighten the dore or passage, to prevent robbing: {And yet I remember Columella L: 9: de R.R: L: 15 is not for a total extermination even of those laizy & predatitious Bees, *ne apes inertia laborent* **[continued in margin]** least the labourious Bees should grow idle; for says he it makes them the more industrious to recruite & so sayd Aristotle κεφηνες ἐργατικωτερας ποιουσι, τας μελιττας [48] That the drones render them but the more labour, but this is to be understood of a few. & the fewer the better.} In August, the most breede of Bees is past; continue your hostillity against the wasps who now infest them; keepe therefore the passage very streight: And {to} those stalls which are not furnished within a handfull of the stoole, if you will keepe them, apply a fals botome with a hole for their descent to keepe them warme, or else abate the Skirt of the Hive, least the cold in such a vacuum endanger them. Now also you may let downe your raised stalls, which are not wrought ~~tow~~ to the margent. Now likewise take your light stalls & such as have bin to weake for the robbers. In the end of this moneth, kill or drive your Bees for *vindemiation*. In *September* Bees have don gathering, stop them close & halfe shut the doores, especially morning & evening when you may keepe them quite shutt. In *October*, examine in what state they ~~b~~ are, if spoiled by robbers, & continue the same care: dressing, clensing & perfuming your hives etc: In November stop them close up, & let none stirr out unlesse the weather grow extraordinary faire, in such case, about mid day you may give them a little liberty to recreate themselves; ~~Or~~ If the season be very sharp, you may house your Skepps, till the end of Jan: that they begin to murmure: but let the place be darke, close & quiet. In December do as in the former moneth. **[Page 233]** In *Jan* turne up your hives, & comfort them with a little luke warme wort sprinkled upon them; also a composition of water & hony: but let this be don suddainely: In *February* halfe open the wiccketts, or before if the weather prove inviting; then also clense them well scraping the stooles, if neede requires, & cloame them anew. And now you may remove the false botomes of your over–hived swarmes, & the false skirts or circles of the under–hived: Also you shall now feede your weake stalls, or drive them where store of provision is; by setting a well furnished hive upon the mouthe of the weaker, fastning the hives ~~as~~ and wind-

---

48. **[Margin note]** Aristotle, Hist. Anim. [627 b 9. Smith, *Bees*, p. 38, noted that Evelyn misspelled the first word.]

ing a long Towell about the brimms, to keepe them from going out: then clapping
the lower hive cause them to ascend.

And by this *Cycle* ~~y~~[ou] our Gardiner may governe his Apiarie from moneth to
moneth: we have but a word or two to add touching *Vindemiation*: If {upon tryall in
Aug: & *Sept*:} a swarme exceed not 10 or 12 pound weight the hives deducted, it will
not be worth keeping. If it poise 15 pound it may thrive with carefull feeding: But
those of 20. 30. or 40 pound weight are to be esteemed, & without reproach. You may
commence your *Vindemiation* from the expiration of the Dog daies, or {almost} end
of Aug: till mid September: Those of 3. 4. or 5. yeares take, especially the last, & all
poore stalles, & all of 3 yeares & upward which have missed swarming: Generally, take
the best & the worst. In forraine parts {where they spare the Apes emeritæ for their
good service} they *Vindemiate* by Exsection or Castration about *Autumne* {without
killing out right} but for many reasons this mercy proves to be a fruitelesse cruelty
at last. and therefore our housewifes rather smother them then reduce them to these
necessities. If you will remove your Bees from one place to another let the weather be
serene, in *Autumne* or *Spring*, & that in the Evenings an hower before sun set: The best
manner of carring them is by tying the hives in a sheete, & bearing them one a Coal-
staffe twixt two men. And of old we learne that they used to transplant their whole
Apiaries as the Tartars do their heards of Cattell caring their hives from place to place
according to the season & for the benefit of the flowers: Thus they **[page 234]** traveld
with them from *Athens* to *Negropont*, & to the *Cyclades* Ilands, & in *Italy* they usd to go
downe the *Po* with them ~~in~~ {by} *Boates* full, ankering at certaine places till the vessell
beginning to sinke to a certaine gage~~d~~, they by it knew how full they were, & then
caring them back to their home tooke the honys: We are told they use this costome
still about *Holland* & *Zeland* in the season that the Turneps are in flower and we have
known a Bee Mr: in our owne Country that was wont to place his hives in Fields of
Buckwheate for this purpose, to his very greate advantage. The Enemies of Bees are
very many, & some sicknesses they are also obnoxious too, especially the rotts, & the
flux: The vermine which haunt them must be taken, Their maladies are discovered
best by their lookes & mortalitie, & {much} remedied by the perfumes of Galbanum
& ox dung: {~~of~~ But of this, see Columella: L: 9: c. 13.} If (as sometimes) they fight,
fling dust amongst them, Sweete water, or Beere which will make them all smell alike
& reconcile them; {The punctures & stinging of Bees is cured by their own huny, by
juice of Malows, by cow dung mixed with vinegar:} And ~~this~~ may {this} suffice to be
sayd concerning Bees, whereoff choyce would be made of those who are of bright
browne, smooth & of a middling size to people our Apiarie, which being well defended from the Northern & Eastern aspects, and exposed to the South with a poynt
or two of the west shall then be situated in their due position for health & safty. The
stooles should stand a little shelving for the better conveyance of the raine, and if they
be placed in rowes, let them be 2 foote distant, & 5 foote betweene the streetes, and
so a plott of 50 or 60 foote square will containe halfe a dozen ranges commodiously,
& that without eclipsing one another, if the ground be made with a smale declivity,
no stoole exceeding another in the height of the pedistall: But then they should be
fixed in the *Q[u]incunx* order for the freer enjoyment of the son: {having the Specu-
latoria & Hive Royal placed in front for ornament & inspection.} But let the rest of
the ground be an area of turfe finely kept, or of wild time, and the bordures planted
with such flowers as the chiefly affect, and if the stalls be many, they will richly deserve the inspection of an under Gardiner, ~~whose~~ who ought to be a neate fellow,

and have his lodge neere to the Apiarie: We do not trouble our Reader with the Philosophy of their production, nor enter into the discourse of æquivocall & anomolous Generations, because of swelling this Chapter, whereof this is but a section; & for that we have something farther to say concerning insects; **[page 235]** This onely ~~we thinke good not to omitt~~ {may not be omitted} that {those of} the {blood} Royall ~~rare~~ are found to be a brede by themselves as immixed as the *Persian Magi*, nor passe they through those various ~~tr~~ & stupendious transmigrations that the vulgarr & their other subjects doe. For so it was fit, that the *Amazonian* race of Melessa should be preserved incontaminate, whom the wiser Heathren ravish'd with the contemplation of their workes, made more antient then Jupiter himselfe, for the Phryonides {'tis sayd} nursed him up with {their} hony.

And here we might compile a just volume to record but halfe of that which has bin sayd, by the Eloquent & the Naturalists touching their admirable Government: St: Ambrose,[49] Basile, and divers of the Fathers have written copiously on the subject, but let us heare the incomparable poet, summe all up in this of his Georgicks, to recommend the prince of Virtues, their Loyaltie to their Sovraine:

> Præterea Regem non sic Ægyptus et ingens
> Lydia, nec populi Parthorum aut Medus Hydaspes
> Observant: rege incolumi mens omnibus una est
> Amisso rupere fidem; constructaque mella
> Diripuere ipsæ, et crates solvere favorum;
> Ille operum custos illum admirantur; et omnes
> Circumstant fremitu de[n]so, stipantque frequentes,
> Et sæpe attollunt humeris, et corpora bello
> Objectant pulchramque petunt per vulnera mortem.
>   [*Geor.* 4.210–218][lxii]

And as to their Œconomie:

> Quod superest, ubi pulsam hyemem Sol aureus egit
> Sub terras, coelumque æstiva luce reclusit;
> Illæ continuo saltus silvasque peragrant,
> Purpureosque metunt flores, et flumina libant
> Summa leves. Hinc nescio qua dulcedine lætæ
> Progeniem nidosque fovent, hinc arte recentes
> Excudunt ceras: et mella tenacia fingunt.
>   [*Geor.* 4.51–57]

[Page 236][lxiii]

Or let us heare *Du Bartas*[50]
For, if old times admire *Calicrates*

---

49. **[Margin note]** In He{x}am: Aristot: Plin:
50. **[Margin note]** 5. day

For Ivori Emmets; and Mermecides
For framing of a rigged ship so small
That with her wings a Bee can hide it all;
Admire we then th' all wise omnipotence
which doth within so ~~stout and~~ narrow space dispence,
So stiff a sting, so stout & valiant hart,
So loud a Voyce, so prudent wit, and Art
Their well rul'd State my soule so much admir's,
That, durst I loose the rains of my desir's
I gladly could digress from my designe
To sing a while their Sacred discipline

For all this being no other then what ~~all~~ that{ose} {who} contemplate this admirable creature {universaly} subscribe to.

Esse Apibus partem divinæ mentis et haustus Æthereos dicere[51]
[*Geor.* 4.220–221]

We come next to {~~discourse~~ treat of} the Silke=worme, for we may ~~not~~ {by no meanes} passe him ~~bye~~ {over} without injure & imperfection; Since 'tis observable that after plants, *Solomon* the most wise upon Earth, discoursed likewise *de reptilibus*; in which it cannot[52] be imagined that he {should} omit~~ted~~ thi{e}s{e} stupendious Insects, nor may we forgett to speake something concerning ~~it~~ {them} seing we both find & ~~feede~~ {nourish} them in our ~~Gardiner~~ Elysium, which as it feedes our Gardiner, with the delicious *Nectar* of the Bee, so it cloathes him {likewise} with the soft & richest spoyles of this ~~Silke worme~~ {profitable} Creature, ~~so as even Solomon in all his glorie~~ We neede not here inquire into their travells as how from *Persia* they were {first} presented to *Justinianus* above 1000 yeares agoe, {~~for none of the old Authors of husbandry say anything of them~~} & from thence came over the mountaines & {passed} the Sea to our more Northern Countries; It shall suffice us to know that they were the product of our Plants, & brought {in} the Mulbery tree along with them to ~~the pla~~ adorne our ~~Gardens~~ {Alies & Groves, that they have produced severall acts of Counsell, bin encouraged, & favoured by the greatest kings & princes; {is numbered amongst the most considerable merchandise enriching whole countries} & is therefore amongst the innumerable sorts of Insects, the noblest & most usefull.}

[Page 237][53] The Silke Worme is the pleasure & contemplation of ~~six~~ {Nine}

---

51. **[Insertion on separate piece of paper]** consult Dr Lister & others for Insects: & reforme as you find occasion; Speake of Mr: Martials etc

52. **[Margin note]** 1 Reg: a: 33

53. **[Insertion on separate piece of paper]** The silkworm is the wondrement & miracle of Nature, & astonishment of ~~mortals~~ {the world}, the Type ~~of~~ & Emblem of Immortality: For it passes Seaven stupendous changes, from a graine no bigger then a mustard seed to a Worme of 24 leggs, which changes its hue & skin 4 times, buries itselfe in its owne winding shroud made of one intir thrid, in that it becomes an husky beane, sleeps in it without light, foode, or ayre; ~~then~~ slips that skin, pierces

weekes but the emolument of the whole yeare: And therefore are during that period to be sedulously attended: But the greatest difficulty is in procuring stoore of mulbery leaves early, that their Eggs may disclose ~~by~~ betimes, and {the wormes} accomplish their worke before the Solstice if possible, & to prevent their sicknesses, & the inconvenience of ill seasons: But since It would employ a Volume to discourse of all these in particular, take these short observations, & consult ~~with~~ at your seasons, those who have written expresselly:

Set out, in some convenient quarter of your Garden a Plantation of Mulbery trees. The White are best: Let the Earth be well dressed, layd out into beds of 4 foote large, & in [54]rills of ~~3~~ {2} fingers deepe, 8 inches distant. Water these beds well, & 3 or 4 houers after that refreshing, sow the trenches with the Seedes {(outlandish, over ripens rot)} very thicke: but first we advise you to macerate the Seedes in water a day & night, then mixing it with sand make it through drie: being sowen, cover the trenches with a fine rake: This may best be don in Aprill, May, June, July, or August, In the New Moone, but the best is {that of} Aprill: We reccommend their sowing thus in smale rills, for their better Weeding: because being scattered at randome, it indangers their extirpation: 3 or 4 dayes after the Seede is sowed, let it be well refreshed againe; but gently, least too violent a shoure beate it out of the ground; to prevent ~~th~~ which some use to lay a wispe of straw along every trench, & water it through that strainer; When the young Trees appeare a little strong, they may rest the winter; and after one yeare be transplanted the roote & top cutt & trimmed so as not above 3 inches stand above ground; & thus they may be ~~planted~~ set with a dibber at 3 foote distance either in March or Aprill, in some other bed of the Nurserie: ~~Being~~ two years passed, cleanse them carefully from their Succkers, & when they are of competent groth, remove them {into a dryish Soyle} where you will have them remaine, planted at 18 foote asunder:[55] after this you have no more to doe save now & then to water them well the first yeare, & within two after {though if 6 or 8 yeares old better} you may gather leaves for your Wormes: ~~And thus you~~ {which if they happen to prevent your Trees, lettuc ~~& nettles~~ will a while support them: In Syria Bellonius[lxiv] says for a neede **[continued in margin]** they will feed on the Fig {rose elme best} leaf & the Nettle but these do not spin yet with lettuce a long while, & spinn if at last fed with Mulbery leaves:} But there is choyce to be made of the Eggs, for in some Countries they produce less hardy Wormes, & not so proper for our Climate for which those of Calabria {& Spanish & of Bolognia} are esteemed the best: Being stored with Eggs ~~Spre~~ {about the tyme of the budding of the M: leaves} let them lye thin in shallow drawers, lined with Chamlett {or Say & a thin layer of cotton wool & on that} putting

---

its way without any gnawing, comes forth a butter fl[y] of 4 wings engenders, ~~dyes~~ produces, & dyes, & yet in its Seed never dyes, the heate {& the Sun} raises another like the first & if there be any Phœnix in nature, there is no other then this, nothing more admirable

The silke worme is the pleasure

54. **[Margin note]** See for this what we have more at large sayd in our Sylva, chap: 9:

55. **[Margin note]** Some recommend graffing {on the stalke} also to make them excellent & lasting. 5 large Trees will nourish an ownce of seede:

a paper full of holes **[page 238]** [56] upon them, and on the paper some of the tenderest Mulbery leaves place your box upon {or in} a bed, with the Curtaines drawne {in a

---

56. [Insertion on separate piece of paper without indication of where the inserted information is to be placed on page 238] tis not amisse to have the worme disclose early as soone as the leaves come out, & that they disclose together & not one after another, that their mutations may not confound you, cost more trouble & leaves because they stench one another: some sprinkle the eggs with generous wine & dry it off before the fire or Sunn, but with grate caution: Aprill is the ordinary season of the ~~des~~ hatching new moone best: but the very best season is to strive to produce them just when your trees begin to leafe generaly, & not when one or two forwards trees leafe:

Some cover the box of seede to disclose ~~un~~ twixt 2 warme pillows & a blangett a little warmd in the Sunn or at fire: Some put it in bed with them all night, & leave it in their place the next morning, & some ~~la~~ have layne in bed till all were hatched, which is commonly 3 days

Keepe them warme 3 or 4 days after the first birth, Those that disclose not in 4 ~~or 5~~ {6} days: cast away for they never come to good:

Some ladys hatch them in their bosoms in taffata baggs & tis very naturall; & when ready to disclose, as is to be seen by their colour, put them in a warm box as before:

Every sicknesse they sleepe 4 days, then they eate 8 dayes then sicker againe to the last & 4th change, & then there is no more rule for their foode to be observed:

When you change the leaves, take up the old ones with a bodkin of film & then lay fresh, & so change them; & sometimes clense & warme {& dry} the drawer or shelves, for they must by little & little accostome to the ayre whilst young, & not at once or suddainly.

Those that disclose at a time, should be seperated & kept together apart from the others, that they may learne better how to governe them in sicknesse without confusion; or else by observation putt all the sick together.

~~Although~~ After the 2 first sicknesses or changes give them food twise a day, after the 3d 3 tymes, & 4th as much as they will eate (1) **[insertion on another piece of paper]** if cracking the seede {be new &} under your ~~ha~~ nails it crackle & cast out humour, 'tis a marke ~~of gr~~ they are fecund, the best is smalest, {of} gray dust, yet lucid; & not so easily blown away, for it may be moyst within, yet sterved {& infecund}; & made of Flye which are the males: & yet for all this unlesse you have a faithfull ~~co~~ correspondent on the place you may be cheated with seede that has all the faire marke of good, & be still naught, for there is greate deceit in this, & though they disclose, yet they come to nothing & make no good silk: therefore much care ought to be above this as the very principle: **[end insertion] [Continued on verso]** 4 or 5 tymes in 24 howers at an equal distance of time as you can; & in their last foode the leaves of the black mul: is best, as being strong & substantiall, that are fresh, greene, and healthy, not over moyst, & therefore new sprung leaves are not the good, but indanger the bursting by their surfeiting on them:

Note that worms that dispatch the worke in 5 or six weekes, are much the best; & therefore early hatched to be preservd: Other accidental sicknesse comes by ill smells,

very warm roome} & every two houers visite them; [57]{but such} as they ~~hatch~~ {disclose} you shall find them creeping through the holes, & adhe10ring to the leaves, &

---

ill foode, want of care, & over much heate, but cold seldome hurts them and therefore an encouragement to us: Every day open one of the windows ~~for~~ for ayre strongly revives them[.]

Sometymes they forsake the foode, & then they wont change; but if they still refuse, stirr them no more till they fall to it The muske coloured {& gray} are not to be thought sicke, but are often best: those that stray after the 3d sicknesse seldom come to good

The last 12 days they commonly have a string of glue or silk at their mouthes: & defile the leaves with it, which often deceves ~~men~~ the unexperienced keeper, who takes them off putting them too soone to spinn, whereas tis a sicknesse, & for want of ayre which you should then give them more frequently: but the best signes for spinning is when they quitt the green & yellow circles & become of a ruddy & flesh colour toward the tayle, & that they cling to ones fingers & prick a little with their feete, & feele soft, yet firme.

Nothing better then the peelings of Oziers scattered amongst some sticke that may keepe them hollow, because they are weake of themselves or else better, putt them thin twixt the hollow, that the arches ~~make~~ of other Spriggs make in the shelves as we have shewed

When a Caban or arch is full enough, take away the superfluous that you find at bottom on the leaves, & transport them to other seede cabans or arbors: do this the 4 day after ~~they they~~ their fellows are mounted, because you will not be able to distinguish of their worke, & so will run many inconveniences of piercing; & besides the stench of meale hurts those that worke who would have made again **[insertion continued on separate piece of paper]** Such as you find after all the changes {of place} & care will not work put them in houses of paper & they will commonly worke there, or else on peelings of Ozier confusedly[?] layd in some ~~dish~~ wodden dish or box; but of these reserve none for seede: & such as in the Arches of branches do not spin, put also in these places or hoods of paper ~~as~~

Before you put them in the Oven etc: peele off all the loose slezy stuff that adhears to the codds, as much as your fingers can gett off for it but ~~hinders~~ burnes, & hinders your drawing off: **[on same piece of paper but noted: "p: 248"]** Furnace 2 foote high: so built as the smoke & heate incomode not the workman, the basin proportionable so as he may sit on a stoole by it & neath all & approach his reeled frame **[illustration, see Fig. 59]** he that assists the Winder must be carefull to stirr the codds, & keepe the Silk & files from any ordure huskes or impediment of ill codds which may interup or breake the threid, & such he must take out, & purge of what hinders, & if any prove to be neverso little pierce it, take it out altogether, for twill never turne with the rest; such will also sucke in water & sinke & be heavy, & some have rotten wormes in them: One may wind of about 3 pounds of silke in one day: in winding stop now & then to clense the skaines of any ordure, which do with a needle before it be cold & too fast glued on: what cannot be well wound off in scaine, reserve for binders to tie the skaine in 3 or 4 places as you take it off the Reele

57. **[Margin note]** but such as disclose not in 2 or 3 days, reject for they will come to late & are worth little.

Figure 59. Illustration of a "furnace" to heat silkworm cods as they are wound off in an insertion at page 238.

then by degrees you may accostome them to the aire removing them upon sheets of paper⁵⁸ {but at every removal laying fresh leaves}⁵⁹ when they are a little growne & require more roome, afterwards {being past their 3d sicknesse} you may bring them into the place or upper Cabinet {opning {all} to the N & South for airing & comforting them if neede require} {for they must not be kept too} destind for them, & there lay them upon shelves {or in bundles of oziers} which being ranged as for bookes in a Library {yet so as one may passe twixt the wall & them} should be made to draw out & put in, that so they may the better be ordered & clensed: if there be a Curtaine or Valans before⁶⁰ it will be the better {let them be while they loose the colour:} for the season may be {prove} so unkind as to require it, & some do add a stove to attemper the aire in moist weather; {& when they are sick, & therefore chose a temperate place & dry roome}⁶¹ but great care must be taken not to keepe them too hott in on such cases occasions; {nor to lay them too close, or over many on a shelfe} sometimes they burne perfumes also of storax, Benzoine, Cedar etc; {strewing the floor with sweete herbs} rubbing the shelves with Sp: of Wine; {& sprinkling them sometimes with strong wine or vinegar on a hot pan for perfume} but this is

---

58. **[Margin note]** which will keepe them from stain[i]ng anything you lay them on:

59. **[Insertion on separate piece of paper]** I heard of some who have successfully turnd their Wormes forth to Ex the Mulbery trees, exposed both to the cold & moisture of the ayre & yet don well, nay better then those which were more tenderly kept, but I cannot be too bold in reccommending it. **[Insertion continued on another piece of paper]** but thus they do indeede in the southern parts of Europe: Spaine, Italy, {&} Sicily & setting up temporary stages {in tents & reede hutts} for them even in the Mulbery groves; & thus persue without any meanes as extraordinary care upon the very ground; etc. **[Original insertion continues]** It were convenient to have so many M: trees as that you might now & then spare some trees once in 3 yeares from disleav gathering to make it last the longer:

To clip off the leaves (as in some parts of Spaine) is best **[continued on verso]** to let them fall in a sheete under the tree. Never be sure quite to strip a tree, ere you give over; & then yearly prune where any {twigs} are broken or hurte; sometimes by this meanes trees have twise leaved in the same year:

Every 10 or 12 yeares tis good to lop {some of} your trees: provide leaves for wet season keeping them in a dry ayry roome, & oft turnd, or best on the boughs from your lopps, which may be latter end of May, which in the trees will not much hurt it; gather the leaves with as little touching {& as clearly} as may be: give the tendrest to the young ones.

60. **[Margin note]** let the shelves be 18 inches asunder & & so as they still diminish to the ceiling **[continued on separate piece of paper]** ceiling that the louerm[o]st being broader may receive any falling worme when they wander towards the edges as sometimes they do. Firr is the best for this:

Be sure to make the roome so as no vermin may enter: they hate {{poultry} sparros or other birds, great noise} tobacco smoke: & stinkes: The roome & shelves made clean often & so edges[?] changed, & therefore to be made to slip in & out: do this every 4 days

61. **[Margin note]** the windows with a paper chassis & through light best

to prevent their Sickenesses of which they have fower the first 12 daies: and then at
the end of every weeke they are indispos'd 2. or 3. dayes {& the heads grow white &
swell & thus seeme shorter} at which tyme you must feede them very temperately,
augmenting their proportion as they grow in vigour after every ~~si~~ maladie:[62] It is the
changing of the Silkewormes *Sloughs* {& quality of seasons & foode} which causes
the~~iri~~s sicknesse in them, & then they eat little or nothing but lye as dead; therefore
detract of their foode, & see that the leaves be {young} very cleane & drie {above
all to chase away the Ants, for nothing sooner destroys them}: about the 3d day they
begin to recover & then you may feede them with more libertie; {~~yet still but twise~~
~~a day~~}; but still with moderation; Morning & Evening; till towards their[63] last sicknesse & afterwards 3, or 4 tymes, or more if their stomacks require it, & that they
hast to finish: but in thus changing their leaves, ~~& removing the Wormes~~ {give them
ayre, or warmth as they neede; sometymes **[continued in margin]** to expose the
shelfe in the ayre if temperate halfe an houer before sunrise}, handle them as little
as possible, but remove them rather upon the leaves with all tendernesse {every 3 or
4 dayes unlesse in time of their sicknesse for then they are not to be handled; & every
time you change **[continued in margin]** them, lay some new leaves upon those you
take away that such worms as ~~you~~ lay here may come forth upon them; this especially
when they are young} When they begin to spue,[64] you shall gradualy detract of their
allowance, & when they totaly reject their foode, which will be when they appeare
diaphonous & translucid like the ripest grape {or amber, or greenish}, it will be time
to provide for their working by making them Arbours, sticking up {withred & dry
& sweete tops oziers best of all peeled} twiggs & branches of Lavender, {Chestnutt,
lime, vine cuttings} Genista, birch {but they love it not so well as ~~other~~} rosemary
or shelve {in arches,} betweene the Shelves {arch wise} (which are for that purpose[)]
set 18 Inches one above another {& 2 foote broad}. Upon these you must transport
your wormes {but lay not the sick & ill coloured with the healthy for fear of infec-
tion} every Colour apartt as the yellow, Orange, reddish, white Greenish to be easily
known by their hue: {with a few leaves if they will eat upon paper} In three daies they
will have finished {absolved} their *Pensum* {viz [65]} & after ~~three~~ {11 days} more you
may take off the Codds gently without bruising, reserving some of the fairest {& best
coloured} for breede: Two hundred Wormes will produce an Ounce of Seede ~~males~~
~~& females~~ {of both Sexes within a weeke after:} **[Page 239]** [66]The Males you shall

---

62. **[Margin note]** Some are curious about the quantity of the leaves, 20 will
maintain a worme during his whole course so as the calculation is easily made.

63. **[Margin note]** they very {spotted} & yellow with sicknesse have the plage,
cast them away.

64. **[Margin note]** which some affirme to be from certaine mammalæ not from
their mouths

65. **[Insertion on separate piece of paper]** The 1 day they make onely a thin
web, the 2d they form their Thecas or cases within the webb & involve themselves all
over with silke: The 3d you see them no longer but with the same cord or thred they
afterwards continue so to thicken their bottom, yet with that subtilnesse, as it has ben
computed one bottome has containd ~~thred~~ a thrid which would reach 6 English miles.

66. **[Insertion on separate piece of paper]** 8 days at farthest after the Wormes

~~know~~ distinguish by the longnesse of their bottomes, the Femals are more orbicular:[67] And having made your provision passe a Needle & Thread through a little of the more sleazy part of the Silke so as by no meanes to pierce the whole Cod, {much lesse the Theca or Case} stringing them male & Female interchangeably, & so hang them up like Festoones in a dry, but fresh, chamber neere the Wales having a table underneath that so as they come forth {which they do by moistning the end of the cod with a liqur, & boring with their bill, but do not gnaw} they may lite upon it {or be put gently on it} encounter ~~&~~ engender {& die}[68] ~~But~~ For this purpose let the table be covered with a piece of chamblett, & a ~~piece also~~ {part thereoff} pinnd to the Wall[69] within one fortnight they will {come forth a white butterflie &} have stored

---

have finished the ~~codds~~ silken Urnes or Sepulchers, choose out the best coloured, hardest

Tis believed they neither breath within {when like huskes} nor without the codds when Flyes as having no lungs which is miraculous

The femals are whiter {& bigger behind} then the Males

The Males perpetuall move their wings till fastned to the Femalls:

67. **[Margin note]** it is also seene by ther Aurelias or Chrysalis within these codds: let the cods you reserve be such as rattle & are not rotten.

68. **[Margin note]** but let them not engender above 9 or 10 houers, which may be from morning (when usualy the come out) till evening, longer coition dos hurt, & these take off the malles & fling them away, one femal will emitt 300 graines of seeds; others die in casting it

69. **[Insertion on separate piece of paper]** & indeed they purge out several liquours before the seede falls. when they will first hang & then on the where the femal sometymes purges before coition ~~But~~ {but for Seede} best of all upon lattices or matts made of rushes filed together with a threid, which drying, or passing them through your fingers they will drop off with greate ease without brushing than from paper ~~at~~ or chamlett; seperating the rushes that were ~~found tacked~~ taked together: & drawing each rush through your fingers gently:

The femals being impregnated ~~put~~ take off from the ~~first~~ {second} place {~~or raising pindery~~} & putt them on the rush matt. You ought to watch them, & helpe them to stouter males if any fall of before the tyme for they ought engender 9 or 10 houers: The Seede changes from white to greenish reddish & lastly grayish; if white at last good for nothing: tis good to change Seede now & then as each 3d yeare and **[continued on verso]** And this may be don if it succeede which it is confidently reported, ~~happens~~ to be thus producd:

Feede a Cow grate of Calfe & neere her calving, & at beginning of spring let her feede only on Mulbery leaves till she Caves, continue it then also 8 days, then cause the Calf as well as the Cow to feed on the same foode for some days without other foode whatsoever: then kill the Calfe being well fed with these leaves & full of milke of his mother, chop him in pieces, flesh, skin, entrælls, leggs, hooves, blood, bons pell mell, & put it in a wooden trough, set on the top of an roofe, or other part extreamly exposed to the Sun, & thus being rotten will (as sayd) produce silke wormes, which gathered on ~~Mould~~ Mulbery leaves will be of a most generous kind, & neede not be renewed above once in 10 or 12 yeares **[illustration, see Fig. 60]**

Figure 60. Insertion at page 239 with illustrations showing generation of silkworms through a "curious" experiment.

you with Eggs {one femalle will lay 500 at a time} which when a little brown you may scrape carefully off with a knife {or better a thin piece of gold} & reserve them in a lined box {kept dry, not cold, wett, or hott, but amongst **[continued in margin]** dry linnen or a chest of clothes:} till the next season of hatching: {some rather stay till spring before they scrape the old} Such as are dubble bottomes may best be reserved for breede; because they are difficult to extricate when they come to be wound off: and these pierced codds should be layed apart to be carded & spun, & to serve for the making of flowers in *Nunns* worke, because they yield no intire *skaine*. The Idle & the Laisy Wormes which you find do not climb, put in capps or pyramids of paper to worke in, & such as fall, raise up & replace: The rest of the Codds, being gathered from their twiggs put into a *Basin*, & draw to their Silke immediately, for then it {more} kindly quitts, then when older & drier; for their Silke is but a fine tenacious Gumme which in time grows obstinate, & is with greater difficulty wound off: But if you have many, & the time prevent you you must expose the rest either in the hott Sun upon ~~some pavements~~ {a sheete} 2. or 3. dayes, {as many houres at a tyme} or in a warme {2 houres after the bread is out} Oven halfe an hower: but be very careful that by either of these expedients you burne not the codds, & therefore visite them frequently, & turne them gently; for if you bruise them, now, they ~~east~~ glue so fast together ~~that~~ within as spoiles the bottomes: In the Oven you must lay them upon boards or peeles {or wicker hurdles} to keepe them from the hearth, & now & then open one or two {Aurelias} to see if they be perfectly dead.[70] This don, sort them according to their finesse & colour, so have you them ready to wind off[71] ~~which is don by a wheele, & taking the ends of 5 ten or 15 bottomes lying in a basin {or pan} of water mixed with a little gumm drag; let this {when it is} heated on a portable furnace till it bubbles a little & is more seething~~ which you shall thus doe:

[72]Place a large basin or pan full of faire water upon a smale portable furnace {or one built of brick} or over a Trevett, and when it begins to ~~simper &~~ have a Scumm upon it, & pearles[73] before boyling cast in the bottomes, which you shall remove & agitate up & downe with a smale broome or thin whisk, & if they come not off handsomely increase the **[page 240]** fire a little, otherwise slaken it some what, & thus the threids[74] will adhere to the twiggs, which draw out with your fingers the

---

70. **[Margin note]** or to be more sure wrap them in an hott blangett after they come out of the oven that they awake not too suddainely & some returne againe

71. **[Insertion on separate piece of paper]** but another more accurate & sure way is to fill a Coppr ~~of kettle~~ or Furnace with water halfe full, & to fit a Wooden cover bored full of holes so as to be let down into the copr that it cover, but do not touch the water by 3 inches on this lay a {~~thin~~} carpet of any thin woolen cloth. on this lay your bottomes ~~or Wormes~~ stirring them frequently, ~~&~~ but with care, & when you cease stirring them, still cover the ~~upmost~~ mouth of the Furnace or Coppr, ~~til~~ this certainly smothers them without any danger, then take them out & spred them in a ~~dr~~ row to dry: Thus your silk will loose none of its glosses.

72. **[Margin note]** Some change the water if they do many:

73. **[Margin note]** have also cold water by to attemper over heated:

74. **[Margin note]** clense your Waters from time to time of the worme that fall to the bottom:

length of halfe a yard or more, till all the grossest of the Cods be ~~wound~~ wond off, which you shall cutt away & lay apart holding with one hand {in} ~~all~~ the ~~while~~ meane time, all the threids⁷⁵ of your botomes ~~&~~ joyned & united, as 5. 10. or 15 according to the silke you desire to make, *Organcin, Verone* etc & passe it first through a wire ring appoynted to ranke the ~~threads~~ clue which {ring} is fastned to the fore part of the frame that containes the Reele, & crossing it on the bobbins which⁷⁶ twist it, & then againe through the Lincet ring ~~fastnd~~ it upon the Reele & wind it off {swiftly, the sooner the better} & so continue your threid by putting in the like number of bottomes till⁷⁷ all be wound off & your skeane finished: Some use to put gum Arab: in the water; but it may be let alone & the silke the better: {Your pierced bottomes should be warded, then put in hot water with a little sope ~~to make a~~ first dissolved in it, then boyle them a 1/4 of an houre, then wash them againe in cleane water, dry them, **[continued in margin]** then beate them with a mallet on a ~~stone~~ block, then pull them in pieces & opend as well & so spun on a distaff:⁷⁸ etc. some only cutt them open with sizars & pull & spin them:} And lesse ~~I~~ {we} ~~was~~ere not willing to say concerning this noble & profitable creature; but ~~have give this~~ have presented our Gardiner with this Compendious discourse how he may governe the Silke worme, & derive a most considerable profit ~~from this creature~~ for a little industrie: Besides the Speculation is so fruitefull, as we know not if in all the operations & ~~wonders~~ {miracles} of Nature there be any thing more stupendious, whilst it passes through so many strange metamorphoses, weaving its owne Sepulcher, & then ~~rising~~ {emerging} againe out of its silken urne, a perfect embleme of our ⁷⁹Resurrection {upon which St *Basil* so eloquently discursed of them}: So that when we have {then} contemplated the many wonders & excellences of this Creature, it has amaz'd us, that it lay so long neglected & so little celebrated by the Antients: *Virgil* indeede semes to speake of the rich fleeces which the *Ethiopian* Forrests & those of *Seres* produced

Quid nemora Æthiopum molli canentia lana?
Velleraque ut folijs depectant tenuia Seres?
Geor: 1: [120–121]

But some have doubted whither this were our Silke: The first mention of it in Italy was in the tyme of ~~A~~ *Octavius*, & that they had bin found (by *Pamphyllia* the daughter of *Latous* in the Iland of *Coos*, as now that goodly race of Wormes in *Virginia*,

---

75. **[Margin note]** for ribun 8, for Velvett, stuff etc: 12: all which will not be bigger than an haire.
76. **[Margin note]** you will find that you have hold of all the bottoms by this motion:
77. **[Margin note]** Set the draught of the Reele etc.
78. **[Insertion on separate piece of paper between pages 237 and 238]** Others take all the slezy parts, pierced & confusd codds that will not wind off well, & macerate them in ~~water~~ a basin of {cleere} water 3 days, changing the water eac[h] day, then boyle them in a cleere {ash} lie which has ben strained for halfe an houre, then wash them well at a cleere running spring & being dry the women can order them like ~~len~~ flax to the distaff & spin them:
79. **[Margin note]** Hexam: hom: 8:

upon other trees besides the Mulbery: We reade likewise of the *Assyrian Bombyx*, {in *Martial*, *Propertius*, & *Ulpian* the La[w]yer} but neither of this do writers agree, nor anywhere direct us ~~what~~ how to manage their workes; & it was a long tyme after sold for its weight in gold in Aurelian & the later Emperours tyme which made even the modester princes refuse to weare a thing so precious, nor would K: Hen: 2d of France for that cause ever weare a paire of Silke stockings; but it afterwards came to **[page 241]** be in such plenty, ~~that for~~ that not onely princes, ~~but their clergy~~ {likewise} ~~araid themselves in Silke as it was~~ but their Nobles likewise arrai'd themselves in Silke; And when from the greate *Cardinal Wolsey* our countriman (who was the first of the Church men that ~~wore it~~ {used it} so far indulged himselfe) wore it, it was commonly {which laudably let others define} assumed by the rest of the cleargy, & then by the Seculars even to the most inferiours; {wormes were cloathed with wormes,} so as now there is nothing more common: But, as we sayd, it was long e're it spread so in our Northern parts, & travaild as far as the Iles of *Taprobane* to *Seres* or *Catthaia* {wherein some of those countries **[continued in margin]** the inhabitants eate them being in the cods & cast away the silke:} & from thence to *Constantinople* whither it was brought & presented by 2 Monkes to *Justinian* the Emp: A: {o Christi} 526 & afterwards the manufacture of it {in these parts} was discoverd by two prisoners who ~~fled from~~ {were carried to} *Panorme* in Sicily in the reigne of the *Emp*: Conrade, & so in the tyme of *Charles* ~~octavus~~ the 8 in France who brought it from Naples 1480 into Provence, Toures {in which many poor townes are become exceedingly peopled & rich} nay of late into Paris & Normandy itself; & that to so strange & immense an inriching those provinces, that we infinitely wonder at our remessnesse in England, ~~where this goodly Treasure~~ {& that after all the injunctions &} care which his Matie: K: James {has} set forth {& bestowed **[continued in margin]** in the 6th yeare of his comming to the Crowne} to reccommend it, we should neglect so certaine a Treasure, there being nothing which may reasonably discourage us, & would set so many thousands on worke, augment the glory [80] of our Nation, & tend to so publique an Emolument. But we must finish, having something more to say of Insects in generall before we conclude this Chapter: For to ~~For what can be m~~ treate of them in particular would tyre our Gardiner, there being as many sorts of Insects as of Plants.[81] The Caterpillers of various colours producing as greate a diversity of ~~Buterflies~~ {Papilliars}, longer, shorter, rough, smooth some ~~fatter~~ furnished with innumerable feete: Of Cantharides there are above 35 sorts, of Scarabæus's 40: of Erucke as many, of Flyes 70, of Buterflies above an hundred as we have seene them curiously ~~collected~~ variegated like so many precious Tulips, & with infinite industrie, & educated through all their circles, & collected by *Mons: Morin* that rare Florist of *Paris*, who preserved & kept them ranged in ~~boxes~~ {flatt drawe} flatt & shallow draw boxes furnishing a Cabinett with such flies as drew the greatest princes of Europe to visite & admire [82] them.

---

80. **[Margin note]** Consult Malpigius

81. **[Margin note]** Those we define Insects which are such as have not their vital power in one part more then another, they are Entoma or so calld from their Incisures.

82. **[Margin note]** The like I am told one Mr. Martial has of our owne country:

And most of these {volatile flowers for so we may call them:} are produced of Eggs {~~in spring {of deaw & leaves} & especialy the Eastern wind~~} & are to be treated like the Silke worme {& may be fed} ~~or~~ under a Melon bell, with such leaves {& flowers} as you find them upon: Others are thought to spring from æquivocall {& anomalous} generation, by moyst & warme corruptions {& fermentations etc} of plants, assisted by that *Lentor* & deaw which is in them, especialy in the *Spring* {if East blow} & *Autumne* **[page 242]** and sometimes in the very *Winter* {itselfe} if the South wind spire long; nay out of the mudd, & severall soyles which {they} are all spirited according {as} ~~to~~ their materiall qualities fabricate to themselves such {& such} a domicile: *Aldrovandus* relates that digging under a certaine Oake ~~towards~~ at the East side, he found imperfect Grasshoppers very pale & white, & without wings & as not yet come to their perfect shape; It would therefore be examined how varieties may be produced out of mucilagines, made ~~of~~ {by} putrifing hearbes, flo: fruits, & berrys, the wodds & barke, & by evaporating their juices to a thick consistence, setting & covering it in some moist place:[83] For besides that they feede upon them {& that every plant has a peculiar animal} Insects ~~ha~~ retaine a wonderfull affinity to plants, partly in that being cutt & divided, they yet live, and the reason is because their life ~~be~~ {resides} not (as in other animals) in the heart; but but [sic] is equaly dispersed through the whole body; so that though it retaine but one actual principle, it has many potentiall; Now, that they live not so long as plants after their seperation, is for that plants have still the same stomac & mouth remaining which the other are deprived of, ~~as Cæl: Rhodig~~[84] Now for their time of pregnancy *Insecta pariunt haut ita multo post coitum,* ~~especially~~ the Silke worme immediately after, the Cicindela, the day after: as Scal: {Cæsar has shewed} in 4. *Theophrasti de Causis plantarum*: And as their gestation is short, so their lives are not long, some ~~have seene their~~ finish their whole course in one day, And *Aristotle* says there be few that live above one yeare: Some Insects chew with their teeth, some suck, others have a straiter intestine, others are fractuous, & if they have neither heart nor liver, yet have they all some ~~oth~~ part analogicall to them: Againe some are sanquivorus, carnivorous, & most feede onely upon herbs & seedes; but for a general rule, what *Aristotle* affirmes L: I. Polit: c: 10 is for most part true in the nutrition of Insects Παντί ἐξ [']οῦ γίνεται τροφή τὸ λεπὸμενον ἔοι, Unicuique residuum ejus, ex quo nascitur, e pro nutrimento: that commonly they feede on what produces them; yet 'tis observ'd that the *Culices* bred of the *Caprificus* flie to the leafe for foode, not to the fruite, whose juice it seemes is too crude. ~~And it is another observation that those living of Insects the Males are the least~~ If that observation hold, that those living creatures are produced of the putrifaction of those Animals which usualy fed on them, as serpents of the storke, Spiders of henns, Froggs of Ducks etc: it will be of good use, to raise experiments upon; if that at least be true, which *Jo: Poppus a German Chymist* affirmes: But then these putrifactions must be accelerated by buring (as we sayd) in dung, or some moist & warme place: So universal & omnipresent (as we may say) is this Animal Spirit, & so unwilling, without such a processe to quitt

---

83. **[Margin note]** & there is a way how to medicate a plant whilst growing, so as it may produce severall sorts of Insects if Kirkir say true in his Magnitisme Plantarum.

84. **[Margin note]** Cæl: Rhod: L: 21. Ant: lect: c. 1 in T. Aquin:

matter; ~~& yet~~ & which rather then it will doe it is brought to some living creatures of another kind, as we see it in these Insects.[85]

[Page 243] To hasten, for we desire chiefly to speake onely of the Vegetable Insects: Some are *Arbores, Fruticarij; Leguminarij, Frumentarij, Herbarij* etc: of which are the *Ligniperdes, Ænxile, Thripes, Cussi, Teredines* & the damn'd Termites that devouers to the very heart of our plants & trees: Also the *Raucæ, Syrons, Mites,* & *Acarus* of which there are some so smale & crile, as neither to be felt or injured by pressing him betweene your fingers: yet so powerfull is even this despicable nothing that he will pierce the hardest & thickest barrills head, whenc they used to call him Διὸς τὰμιον or *Jovis promum.* But were this possible *nisi Jovis ei aliquid inesset, aut divinæ virtutis* as one says. *Ringelbergius* reports that the gentle which we find in moist Summers in the Philbert, being nourished with sheepes milke[86] will grow as large as Serpents, & *Cardan* ~~shewes us~~ {describes} the manner how to give them suck: It were good to trye how Insects might be augmented; but our attempt on scorpions in Italy which we ~~pre~~ kept in glasses, & fed with spiders etc succeeded not. The rich & so much valued *Cocci* are wormes gathered from the *Ilix* {*Ficus Indica*} and some other trees about June: {More of as rich a nature might be found out, & will if men be industrious} The Curculio is found in meale & a sort of them in your hott beds, both of them for the Nightingals: Violets have a small black & very swift Insect frequenting them: & the very *Suggar Cane* (which some report resists all putrifaction) is not without a worme which feedes upon the juice of it.

The *Asphodel* is food for the hop-worme: In the Rose and other Flowers the greene Beetle is well knowne; But the Papilion layes eggs of severall colours, which they fix upon the leaves of Cabbages & especialy the Mallow, som bigger, some lesser, yellow, bleu, black, white, greenish: & of these ripened by the Sun, are hatched Cater-

---

85. [Insertion on separate piece of paper] But there are yet more noble considerations ~~about~~ {to be derived} from the ~~natural~~ contemplation of Insects, as particularly the nature {& original} of vivification {& figuration} better (as my Ld: Bacon Cent: 7) detected in small than greater things, & more perfect etc; but I referr you to his Lep: & to your choice, whither you will so readily assent to their æquivocal generations: though divers experiments mention'd in a lettr: to Mr: Hartlib, in his Commonwealth of Bees, which is both very philosophical & very rational, are the best Instances of it that I know: His precept ~~for this generation~~ or Encheiria for their Generation is thus: Vegetables of tincture are either Herbs, Wood, Fruite or Berries etc: for Herbs, dry them, or steem them, & let them dry till no juice will run from them (this is the Sun or like heate) if dryed, infuse them in {warme} water 24 h: evaporat it to a Syrup put this masse in a wooden vessell with straw at botom, to keepe it loose; set the vessell in a {shady} pit of earth, put above it wett leaves, or like mungy stuff, over it a board, & on that straw: This will produce first a shelly husky worme, then a fly of the tincture of the Cement

Of Berries, stampe & boyle, & evaporate & use as the other woods {pulverised} infuse in water, & boyle out the tincture, evaporate etc: This hint I thought fitt to ~~set do~~ mention for encouragement:

86. [Margin note] 7: de rerum var:

pillers, which excluded in 14 daies produce Butterflies of the colour of the Eggs, but now & then miraculously variegated: They are of severall classes: Some (as the *Phalænas*[)] are Noctivolant & flye about onely in the Evening; some in the day, the glory of whose colours mocks the skill of the painter to imitate; they are incomparable to behold, & may be termed the flying flowers of our *Elysium*. {Dr Flacourt Hist: Madagascar. p. 143.[lxv] describes the Papillion which make a sort of excellent sugar in the pleasure gardens of these **[continued in margin]** these Ilands they call it *Tabarir* not that described by P̶y̶ *Paludanus* but the *Tantelle Sacondre* from the name of the Buterfly which formes it: for it ingenders in the rind of the *Mambu* like a black flie at first, the extreames of whose wings be white. & the flye resemble a flower stuck upon the barke of the tree which after one moneth turns into a Butterflye, some of which are red, others greene, yellow etc: which in a little tyme eate up all the leaves of the tree, & afterwards convert into this sugar, or rather hony which becomes hard like S: candy, excellent souveraigne for the Cough & all pulmonique affections} *Erukes* are pennate Insects, feede both on leaves flo: & fruites a very astute & subtile animal, & the greatest enemies of Gardens: {they have sometymes bin seene to have the l̶o̶w̶e̶r̶ p̶a̶r̶t̶ hind part like a spider} The *Cantharides* we frequently find upon our Ashen {Fig, {pine} wild brier} trees, and *Sycomores* & which falling downe do oftentymes raise blisters upon the skin. {This incomparable Dragon flie: of both sexes:}

But to be more particular we may not passe over **[page 244]** these stupendious productions without a little contemplating their admirable natures, being truely *magnalia Dei in minimis* and not imperfect Creatures (as some would have them) since they want nothing to the p̶e̶r̶f̶e̶c̶t̶i̶o̶n̶ {consummation} of their Natures: and a Man is perfect, though he have no wings, & be not an *Angel*: Insects are as gemmes to huge stones, m̶i̶r̶a̶c̶l̶ *miracula in nodo*, and that made St Aug: preserve a silly[87] Fly before the *Sun*, because it exercis'd vital acts which that {g̶l̶o̶r̶i̶o̶u̶s̶} planet did not; & though happly some what of that value may be abated, & especialy by our Gardiner who is so much a friend to that glorious starr, the end being so much superiour to the forme; yet are Insects infinitely worthy our consideration {as in which the nature of vivification & figuration is best inquired into} and have bin the subject of many admirable discourses of the greatest Philosophers: *Non laborat in maximis Deus* says st *Ambrose, non fastidit in minimis*.[88] and *Pliny* calls Insects, *Immensæ subtilitatis animalia*:[89] and that nature is in nothing more specious & approching[90] to miracle, *In magnis siquidem corporibus, aut certe majoribus facilis officina sequaci materia fuit, In his tam parvis atque tam nullis, quæ ratio. quanta vis, quam inextricabilis perfectio!* u̶b̶i̶ ̶t̶o̶t̶ ̶s̶e̶n̶s̶u̶s̶ ̶c̶o̶l̶l̶o̶c̶a̶v̶i̶t̶ as he instances in the *Gnatt*, for so he goes on *Ubi tot sensus collocavit in culice ubi visum in eo prætendit? ubi gustatum applicavit ubi odoratum inseruit? ubi truculentam illam, et portione maximam vocem ingeneravit? qua subtilitate pennas annexuit? prælongavit pedum crura?* etc: & thus concludes, *Turrigeros Elephantorum miramur humeros, Taurorumque colla, et truces in sublime jactus, tigrium rapinas, leonum jubas*; Let others admire the Towerbearing *Ele-*

---

87. **[Margin note]** L: de duabus animis: c. 4.
88. **[Margin note]** L: 1: Hexam: c. 11.
89. **[Margin note]** L: 11: c. 1.
90. **[Margin note]** c: 2.

phant, the strong necks of *Bulls*, the cruell *Tiger* & crest of the fierce *Lyon*, *cum rerum natura, nusquam magis, quam in minimis tota sit.* Nature is no where more compleate and truely stupendious then in the least of ~~th~~ all her productions.

We will begin with the *Flye* & the *Gnatt*, which are able[91] to pierce the skin of an *Elephant* and to make a Lyon run madd, for so they ~~cha~~ have preserved some countries from being destroyed by them, as others they have caused to be abandoned, ~~as~~ *Pausanias* relates it of a Citty in *Africa*: They combated the Tyrant of Ægypt, ~~and~~ one of them was enough to kill a *Pope*, & the numbers of them which darkned the very Sun {so} filled the ~~wayes~~ {roades} with their slaine betweene the Monasteries of *Sion* & *Shene* in our deare Country of *Surry*, that they were faine to sweepe them into heapes to cleare the wayes; but it ~~presa~~ was held to presage the dissolution of *Abyes* {& droven} which shortly succeeded: It is wonderfull to observe how their Armies flie in Phalanxes & other Martial figures, & out of which forme as not one of them is seene to breake his ranke; so nothing can discompose their order, but as swiftly as thought they unite together againe: Now that so smale a body should utter Such {a} Sound, & have the strength to pierce the ~~Skin~~ Skin, & suck the blood, when as **[page 245]** yet *rostelli cernie nequit exilitas.* ~~it~~ {The instrument} is hardly be perceived ~~says~~ {as} Pliny {has it} who would not admire, & be ready to breake out with *Heraclides* upon the like occasion ἐνθαδ γὰς καὶ θεόι God him selfe is amongst them! The Fly {which some affirme not to be a race that continues their owne species but are still producing new kinds as the deaw, raines & severall **[continued in margin]** seasons are qualified} is a bold & nimble Insect, nothing is able to affright, or cicurate this {giddy} creature, but still it returnes where it is beaten off, & therefore it is observ'd that *Homer* chose rather to compare his *Hero* to a Fly then to a Lyon, or a Beare: {but we will be sparing in his Encomium, because Lucian has **[continued in margin]** bin intemperate, & if *Beelzebub* ~~is~~ be their leader & the God of *Ekron* their prince *Ælian* is revenged on them.} their long motion after the head is serene, & reviving in warme ashes, perswaded some that their Soules were immortal: For as to their structure, it is so admirable that some have written whole volu{m}es of ~~them~~ it, as in particular *Johannes Hodierna* in his treatise intituled *L' occhia della Mosca* {printed in *Palermo 1644*} ~~being~~ containing onely the *Anatomie* of the eye of Insect Animals onely, where in pag: 6, he calculates a Table of all the Speciall Species of those Animals, & shewes how this Insect, having neither neck, nor motion of the Eye, yet sees every way without any turning either {of} the head or body, and indeede the demonstration is evident & stupendious which a good *Microscope* will present you, without which, the pleasure & contemplation of Insects will prove greately deffective: But we give instance in the head of a Fly which it thus augments. {reforme this out of Mr: Hoock: Micrographia:} **[illustration, see Fig. 61]**[92]

A.B reppresents the Head, Eye brows, the Braine, and *proboscis*, by which it sucks the blood, or rather conveys that into ~~its~~ his mouth, which with one of the fore feete is ~~put into~~ taken up, as we do with our hands: C. is the whole *Orb* of the *Eye*, pulld out

---

91. **[Margin note]** ~~of which there are in the Philo~~

92. **[Margin note at side of illustration]** The muske fly in shape of a Smale Bee {gliding often} upon the dandelion has the perfect sent of muske; Se of this Mr: Hooke Micrography:

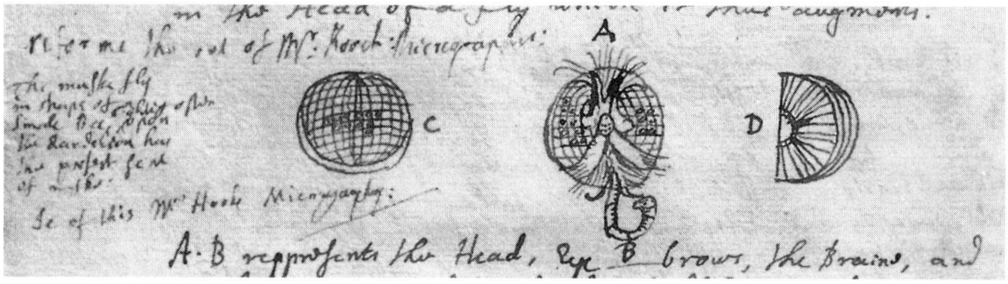

Figure 61. Illustrations of a microscopic view of a fly's eye, based on Robert Hooke's Micrographia, *in text at page 245.*

& freed from the rest of the head, in the *cornea* whereoff (o stupendious & altogether admirable) may be numbered above 3000 squares or fibrous decussations, in each whereoff is a perfect ball ~~which~~ resembling a rich embrodery of pearles, which hath nerves leading to the braine, as may be seene by the section D: where the ~~pyramidal~~ {poynted} triangular Muscles being of a *christaline humour*, ~~have~~ {extend} their in the superficies of the *Cornea* resembling the forme of pyramids which terminate on the skin of the Uvea that takes up the center of the Eye, in the interiour whereoff (as in a gloabe) the *Cenbrosa Substantia* is contained. The fruite of the Mulbery (of which this Insect is very licorish) dos extreamely resemble this description, as well in fabrick as substance, & so dos the strabery: The multicuspid Tongue of the fly was first[93] observed by the diligent Peireskij; and a world of other particularities more, which without the ayde of the Microscope **[page 246]** could not be detected: but we must not play *Domitian* {too long}[94]

But though *Arachne* be not ~~bread~~ {the offspring} of our plants, yet we often meete with their ~~toyles~~ {webbs} in our Gardens, & especialy amongst the Orange & Limmon trees, where they make and display their {geometricall}[lxvi] Toyles to catch the Flyes that are greedy of those sweete Flowers; and it is incredible with what skill and arte they weave their netts, which they make with a tenacious substance spun from their owne bowells: ~~and~~ It would amaze one to consider how they will draw a cord or line crosse a channell of Water, yea over a River, and yet it has neither wings nor can it walke upon that fluid element, as the Water spider dos, who is no spinster: {But} there is in their worke great varietie, for some make a finer threid then others, & differ in the radius, *pecten, stamen*, & closenesse of the webb, which like the purest & transparant lawne has a glossinesse & rare vernish upon it that inviscats the {unfortunate} flies so as they are fataly intangled, before the spider moves out of her {silken} canopie where she has a receptacle curiously arched {& tapastryed} above her, & from where she takes an intire view of all that passes; so as I doubt not but it was this admirable creature, which first taught foulers both how to make their netts, & to catch with them. ~~Well therefore did Solomon~~ In the night they worke & repaire their netts which had bin broaken in the day; but these prey on nothing but what offends them & vex ~~mankind~~ {our Gardens}: There is a sort, which let themselves downe from the

---

93. **[Margin note]** Vita: peir: L: 4: [Gassendi, *Mirrour*]

94. **[Margin note]** You may by an exact Microscope detect the compages {& conjunctions} of the smale bones even in the limbs of a Bee, all the curious commissures of the joynts: the smale nailes & claws of the feete The incomparable variety of colours in the wing, curiously miniatured, the distinction of the teeth, proboscis, brows, eyes, haires etc: cf: your Jesuits dedicated to Urban 8.

branches of trees to kill {the} serpents which lurkes amongst the Flowers beneath; for they are at deadly enmitie, & ~~it~~ is it not admirable that so trifling an Insectile, which has hardly any skin at all, but is a living lump of glue should encounter & vanquish so formidable an antagonist? But so it {has sometimes} challenged the Toade to single Duel, and overcome him for all his plantane, the storie is so frequent that *Erasmus* tells us of a sleepy *Monke* that was delivered from a Toade which was crawling into his mouth, by {such} a generous & hospitable Spider.

But of all the kinds of this Insect, there is none has afforded us more divertisement, then the *Venatores*, which are a sort of the *Lupi*, who have their dens in {the} rugged walles of our Gardens, a smale browne spider delicately spotted, whose hinter legs are some what longer then the rest: Such a one we did frequently observe at *Rome* which esping a Flye at 3 or 4 yards distance upon the Balconie where we stood, would not ~~come~~ {make} directly to her, but crawled **[page 247]** under the raile, 'till being arived to her antipodes it would steale up, seldom missing its aime; but if it chanced to want anything of being perfectly opposite, would ~~immediately~~ at the first peepe immediately slide downe againe, 'till taking better notice it came the next tyme exactly upon the flyes back, which if it happned not to be within a competent leape, then would this Insect moove so softly, as the shade of the *gnomon* seemed not to be more imperceptible, unlesse the Flye moved, and then would the Spider in the same proportion, keeping that just tyme with her motion, as if one soule had animated them both; & whither it were forwards, backwards, or to either side, without at all turning her body, like a well mannag'd horse, but if the capricious flye took wing & ~~skipt~~ {pitcht} upon another place behind the ~~Spider~~ {Hunter}, then would the Spider turne its body so swiftly about, as thought it selfe cannot be more speedy, by which meanes he always kept the head towards her{is} prey, in appearance as fixt & immoveavble as if it were a naile droven into the post, 'till by that indiscernable motion being ~~gotten~~ arriv'd within compasse, ~~she~~ made a fatal leape {swift as lightning} upon the Flye, ~~swift as lightning~~ catching her in the poule, where it never quitted hold, till his belly was full, & then carryed the remainder home: We have beheld them ~~di~~ instructing their young ones how to hunt, which they would sometimes discipline for not well observing: But if any of themselves had missed a leape, they would run away ~~as a sham~~ & hide themselves as asham'd, & haply not be seene abroad in 3. or 4. houres after. Truely so stupendious {& wonderfull} has ~~their intuition contemplation~~ {sagacity of this Insect} appeared, that the very contemplation has filled us with amazement; nor doe wee thinke that there is in any chase whatsoever, more cunning observed, or variety of stratageme: some of these we have found in our owne Garden, when the Weather was very hott, but they are nothing so given to hunt, as those in Italy:[95] We might here add, how long some spiders watch for a prey, what hapens at home, how celebrated for ~~the~~ conjugal love, in every thing an Embleme of Oeconomique prudence, For so *Aristotle* calls it a most wise creature: *Nascitur Aranea cum libro, lege* et lucerna, It is borne with a Booke, a ~~Law~~ Rule, & a Lamp: Their Geometricall toyles, concentration of the severall radiuses, **[page 248]**

---

95. **[Margin note]** and in this if we have appeared prolix it has not bin without designe of amplifing the hist: of Insects which we wonder how it could escape their observation ~~of this &~~ whatsoever yet taken in so many other trifles in comparison:

the exact diminution of the distances of the threids as they approch the common internodium, is altogether admirable; so that well dos Solomon celebrate this Insect amongst the fowre, and reccommend them to the Palaces of Kings, as examples of ~~Labour~~ {Industry}, Ingenuity, ~~parsimony~~ {Frugality} & other princly virtues: And for this cause Mouffet[lxvii] makes a formal declaration against the Broome, that destructive instrument which Sweepes them away & at once spoil~~inge~~s them both of their labours & their lives: We wil not here inlarge to the Fiction how ~~poore~~ *Arachne* became metamorphos'd, & came to be so hospitably entertaind in the Cottages of poore men; because we pretend truth & usefull information onely: This onely we add, that it is a mistake that men hold them generaly venemous, we reade of many who have eaten them with~~out~~ appetite, besides the wench who was presented to *Alexander*: They are medicine to birds, & the delight of henns & monkyes; and if any of them be poyson they are such as reside in darke Cellars, moist and filthy places such as *Glauber* has experienced, which abounding with an inexhaustible glue & slimy mucilage, make a web of that amplitude in so short a tyme, that comparing it to the bagg from whence it proceedes, can hardly be assigned to any physicall or naturall cause.

There are Spiders in Hispaniola as bigg as Tenis balles, and those in Brasile have clawes like great birds which make excellent tooth–pickers, as we can shew: {Some {are} of admirable colours, & in the *Bermudas* there are that spin a silke nothing inferior to the worme. **[continued in margin]** gloves have ben knitt of ther silke, & considring the quantity they make in a yeare, how hardy they are I wonder it is not improved:} Some are armed with Teeth, & others sting, Some have 4 {others 8. eyes} eyes, [*sic*] & there are many of various colours, curiously dappled, & transparant.[96] But there is none has bin more admired for the {prodigious} Effects, then the *Tarantula* a sort of *Phalangium* frequently found in the fields & Gardens of *Calabria Apulia*: There are some of an ash colour ~~others black~~ with black & white spots, some with red & greene; They take their name from the citty Tarento, & though there are of them in other places, as in *Sicily*, & about *Rome* yet none but those around Apulia have those dispositions, so much admired, The Gardners are frequently ~~stung~~ {bitten} with them in the 3 summer Monethes, & the veneme is ~~su~~ of that nature that it ~~immediately~~ seises the heart, producing effects of strange variety, for some run about, some laugh, others crye, some roare {out} aloude, then sleepe, & some there be who cannot put their eyes together; ~~in~~ {in} most of them it excite vomitings, some daunce perpetually, then sweate, are strangely perplex't with feare & goe trembling, in Summ, it initiates the symptombs of all sorts of madnesse, according to the quality of the poyson, & the constitution of the Patient: **[page 249]** It seemes at first it resembles onely a Sea–bite, but after a yeares revolution (for it will lurke long in the body) fermented by the heate of the Sun, & season, at the sound of certaine {Musicall} Instruments, & particular compositions, you shall see both men & women, ~~otherwise~~ at other tymes very modest & sober suddainely to flie out into such gestures, grimaces & extrav{a}gencies, as if Bedlam were broken loose, & that they were all demonaicks: By the first two monethes, the malignity begins to appeare, by the parties losse of appetite, {atrophie},

---

96. **[Margin note]** Some that make webbs will catch a Sparrow: they make women vailes with them they will wash pure white. In the W: Indies are some spiders whose bite is madnesse, they are skiny & resemble a thistle

& feavorish disposition; for which they take the common Antedotes & cordials, but it is generaly found that there is never happens a perfect cure, unlesse Musique be an {chiefe} Ingredient & the composition of that too, correspondent proportionable to the qualitie of the poyson, which by a miraculous kind of consent, provoakes the Patien, will he nill he, to daunce & skip about, till the whole po virus of the infection be exhausted transpired by a universall sweate, which renders him so faint, that he falls downe as dead upon the ground, 'till he be revived by taking pouring a little wine into his mouth, which so soone as he has receivd, & is come to himselfe, again he falls a dauncing againe & so continues in this humour for 2 or 3 dayes successively: & sometimes the venome is so irradicated & seizd of the total habite, that for divers yeares he falls to his periodicall dauncing {& folly} at the sound of such Musick, till the whole {total} force of the poyson be exhausted. We will not trouble our reader with the various & ridiculous gestures which they expresse in this exercise, onely their passionat love to certaine colours during this distemper, is not to be passed by, for with some they are so strangly {& vehemently} affected as their is nothing is able to expresse how they will worship & kneele downe to red or yellow cloth, flattring, kissing & embracing, sighing, & even weeping over it as if they desired to become metamorphosed into {one with} it of which the poore Capution recited b mentiond by Athanasius Kerkir is a prodigious instance: Others there are who expresse the same affections for a we some shining & bright weapon, and will use a naked sword with the same fondnesse, & such strange gesticulations, as if some new enthusiasme had possessd them, & that it were a creature capable of all demonstrations of endearenesses: Others doate upon some certaine tree, as if they desired to be metamorphos'd into them: some delight as much in water & the greene sedges, {dapp{bb}ling} fancing themselves to be {some} foule: Some againe become Mimickes & will act the pomp & gravity of the Spanyard imaging themselves some King or greate one, & lastly others there be who sit weeping, deploring & wringing their hands, & some that prostrate themselves upon the ground beating their breasts, {distorting} & taring themselves like the most miserable of Epilepticks & Lunaticks: **[page 250]** But amidst all these effects & symptombs so extraordinary{vagancys} & dreadfull, as they are excited; so are the likewise as suddainly & strangely compos'd & dissolved, upon the hearing of certaine Musicall touches & harmonious tunes; so as they will start out of one of their fitts into a calme & extraordinary astonishment, daunce, sing, & be infinitely pleasd;

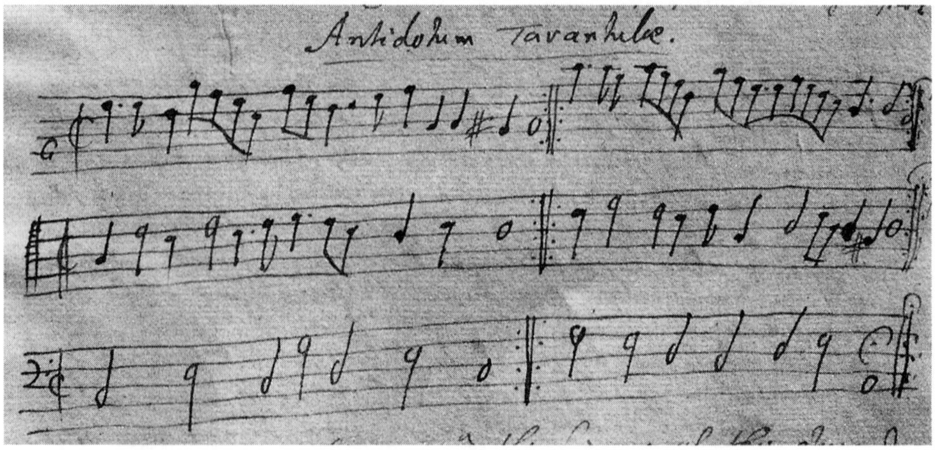

Figure 62. Music for "Antidotum Tarantula," illustrated at page 250.

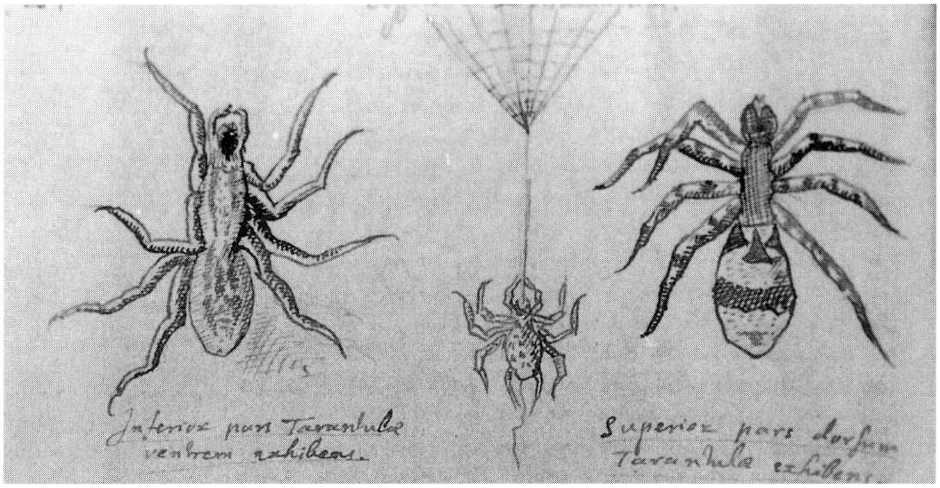

Figure 63. Illustration of the tarantula spider in text at page 251.

whilst the musique strikes their eare with an amicable ~~harmo~~ consert; but if either out of ignorance, or studiously sometimes, the Musitian put in a discord, you shall perceive ~~them~~ the patient grow mad againe, & by the gesture of his ~~bo eyes~~ hands, torsion of his eyes, & actions of his whole body expresse the intollerable injurie ~~of th you~~ {he} hath don him, & torment that he indures.

And though they are various modulation & songs according to the divers quality of the poyson, by which they are cured; yet are they more frequently pleasd with one tune above all the rest, & that goes by the name of the *Turkish aire*, & the people themselves have {as it were naturaly} strange dispositions to Musique {in} general~~y~~ & will upon the suddaine sing or play extemporary giggs extreamely appropriated to the passion & affection of the patient ~~&~~ which likewise they expresse in certaine ditties as this

Non fu Taranta, na fu la Tarantella
Ma fu lo vino della garratella
Dove te mozico? dill'amata dove fu,
Ohime si fuste gamma, ohime mamma fu
Twas nor ~~the Wine~~ Taranta, nor yet the Tarantella
But 'twas the Wine ~~of~~ out of the greate Botella
When did it bite, say when my ~~deare~~ love say where:
Was it the leg, Oh me, oh me, my deare!

Those which are ~~bitt~~ affected with greene, are cured with songs ~~made~~ composd in praise of Gardens, flowers, & {the} glorious objects of the inamelled fields: Those that love the redd, with the martial musique, Iambicks, dithyrambicks & bacchicall ~~musi~~ {tunes} {in} {phrian & Hypodorian moodes} & so of the rest: But we will instance in a Famous *Tarantella*, for so they call the Tunes proper for those affects:

      Antidotum Tarantulæ   **[illustration, see Fig. 62]**
and now we will give you the figure of this stupendious Insect:
[Page 251] [illustration, see Fig. 63]
Musica sola mei superet medicina veneni
    We could heare relate the story of an {certaine} incredulous Spaniard who to convince himselfe of the verity of these effects ~~foolehardily~~ tooke two Tarantulas into

his hands, and provoking them, was bitten by them both; but such the Insects being of contrary tempers, such contrary ~~effects fol~~ symptoms followed, that there could be no musique found to aswage them both; but that whilst one played or sung & {seemed to} appease ~~one~~ one {kind} the other was so offended & tormented, that finding no remedy to compose them both, the man died miserably, & was a sad example of his temerity & foolehardinesse: Other wonderfull instances we could add, of cures as strange; but because we have already exceeded the limites of our chapter, ~~after~~ we hasten: The reason of the patients dancing that's bitten by this Insect, seemes to proceede from the impulsion of the aire by the chords of the Musical Instrument, & this, after the same sort as ~~the Tarantula it selfe is stirred~~ {themselves are} concerned: For so the harmony delighting the eare, passes to the very animal spirits which ~~indiv~~ informe that organ, & this aire so moved, wafts those various tremblings into the senses, affecting the fantsy with these motions, & mooving the spirits in the braine hence diffused into the nerves & muscles of the whole body & so meetes with a thin & acrimonious humour, the vehicle of this poyson, which ~~fe~~ disperses & ferments it, inciting that pruriency & itch, which causes the patient to daunce that he may quiet & allay it, & this putts him into {such} a sweate ~~which~~ cures it by transpiration, ~~&~~ during the Parasysme. This is now evident, by the dauncing of the patient at certaine Tunes onely: ~~for the~~ As the effect is melancholick, more sprightly & fantastick: For it is observed, by a noble Experiment, that the same Tune which makes the person bitten daunce, makes the Insect also itselfe skip & leape about, like a dauncer upon the Ropes, observing the just cadences of the musique, after a most **[page 252]** wonderfull manner: And this is so usuall, that there are divers *Musitians* stipendiated by the State in those Parts who upon enquiring in what Garden, field, or place, the patient was bitten, with his colour & some other questions, will play a Tune ~~immediately~~ {extemporary} that will set him a skipping & give him immediate ease; for belike the study the care, & are very cunning at it. As for the Colours ~~which we doubt not~~ which recreates them, we doubt not of their like magnetisme affecting the fantsy & sympathizing with it; for we know how gratefull some are above others, how lyons & Turky cocks ~~are~~ grow furious at the red, how our eyes are delighted with blew & greene & the middle colours which by a certain titellation workes upon them, & then for sounds how our very Teeth are set on edge at some.[97] whilst the diapason, Diaperte, ~~&~~ fourth & thirds compose us againe & make their owne unisones to tremble.[lxviii] But hitherto shall suffice to have bin spoken concerning this stupendious Insect. {though much more might be added to confirme the prodigious effects of Musique not onely to the healing of sicke, but its effects on the healthy & well, if we may credite what the Musitian Timotheus wroght on Alexander the greate, & Agamemnon's Harper on Clitemnestra etc.} Of the Scarabes there are innumerable sorts, some of the *Canthari* breede of their owne putrefaction, & as the Phenix have no females; we have read of a Scarabe which fought with an Eagle: {for they are arm'd & goe in Troopes their murmurs ressemble a drumm, & some princes had them borne in their standards.}

The Ant is infinitely noxious to our Gardens, yet a wonderfull Insect, & one of

---

97. **[Margin note]** as he that could not hold his water if he heard a Bagpipe

those to whom the wise king sends [98] us for Instruction: ~~They have a probe to explore the way~~ {Their Industry, Justice, love & regimen} is admirable, & the consideration made Cleranthes attribute Reaso[n] to mute Animals: They explore their way by a Probe & make the most ruggd pathes, nay stones & rocks, to become smooth & easy by their often tracking: contemplate this Insect so smale, that he has a head, eyes, braine, mouth, tongue, teeth, palat, throate, brest, ribbs, lungs, belly, stomack, womb, etc:[99] &[100] other similar & dissimilar parts, what a burthen one of them will carry far exceeding their owne bulke & weight.

> *Corpora vidisti; mores quos ante gerebant*
> *Nunc audi: parcum genus e patiensque labori*
> *Quæsitique tenax et quod quæsita reservet.*
>   [Ovid *Meta.* 7.655–657]   4: Ænead: cf.

To altogether stupendious to consider their subterranean passages, so elegantly contrived, inflexed, tortuous & onfracted to fortifie the accesse, this they mine with their {fore} feete & ~~fli~~ cast out with their hindmost, fastning their contignations & covering their cavernous roomes with sticks leaves & strawes: Then they cast up a mount for the enjoyment of the freer ~~ayre~~ aire & to preserve their workes from the wind & raine: Within are three conspicuous vaults or Chambers, the greater & more spacious for publique conventions, & another beneath where their wives lay their eggs & breede, the lowest {& safest} to be the magazine of their provisions & to keepe their stoore; because being lesse profound it would be **[page 253]** subject to the Frosts: The rodes & extreames of their mount are Catatumbed for ~~their~~ Sepulture of their deade whom the very sollemnly ~~interr~~ inhume: They live under a *Democraty*, & observe Lawes; for some preside over the workes, some are about the stores, & some are leaders in Martial Discipline: They gather in of all sorts of graine which others dispense; ~~They are~~ There are some Archetects onely, others pioners, & taskemasters, If any faint in the way there are helpers, & some going before bring ~~dimensions~~ directions how they are to ~~turne~~ governe their burthens, so as if a beame a sticke or straw being too long, is turned endwise a yard before the doore, or else broaken shorter & fitted for the overture, the ~~cond~~ inspection whereoff has very often {even} amaz'd us. When they goe forth to forage, some climb up to bite of the spike, ~~which~~ {while} those ~~which are~~ that are below watch for the falling of the corne, take it out & clense it of the huske, carry it home, & there, least it should sprout, being layd in the magazine, bite of the germinating poynt; & sometimes, if they find it requisite, they will spread it before the sun, & aire to drie & ventilate it. The worke also in the bright of the Moone, but not in darke night: In summ their assiduity is so indicible that it

---

98. **[Margin note]** Ants in the Philippic Ilands 6 ~~inches~~ {fingers} long & a finger brode:

99. **[Margin note]** which puts me in mind of the contest of St. Basil who alayed the pride of a pert Philippe who pretended he could define every attribute of the deity by 27 questions concerning the body of an ant.

100. **[Margin note]** Ælian: 6: Hist: Anal: c: 1.

exceedes all description; so that we no more wonder at those who have affirmed that they possesse but one soule amongst so many Myriads, seing all their actions are directed to the same common end: Liggon in his Hist: of the Barbados: speakes of such miraculous effects of their industry, courage, & sagacity as were almost incredible; as how suggar being put in a box in the middst of a basin of water, they will crawle ~~on~~ about by the Ceeling of the roome, & let themselves downe by a line {contexed} of their owne bodys, perpendicular to the prey, & divers the like stratagemms. Concerning their Militia what [101] Æneas Sylvius relates happned Bononia is admirable, & that at Upsaal, recited by *Olaus* the Bishop: where they buried their owne slaine, letting their enemies bodys lye rotting in the field: It was certainely from all these virtues, & incomparable Instincts, that the Father of the *Myrmidos* produc't itselfe, & hence they fain'd that *Jupiter* himself was changg'd into a Pisonire to beguile the Mother of the Graces, for a lesse hypocrisie could not have ~~deceived~~ violated *Eurymedusa*, henc *Jupiter Formicareus*. Their presaging of change of weather, knowne by their care, running & generall dispatch etc. & for all these perfections they of old sacrificed them to the Gods, as one of the most pure & acceptable: ~~and If~~ And if they be the plague & common robbers of our Gardens, ~~for Pliny calls them~~ *Pestes Arborum* as *Pliny* calls them, yet do they not more harme by their depredations, then good by their instruction, silent, & moral examples, ~~& teach since our~~ inciting ~~our~~ {the lesse industrious} Gardiner to Labour & watch against them: And therefore wittily did the antients expresse it by an Embleme of an Emett, holding 3 spikes of corne in her mouth: ~~Their~~ {Nor are their} wonderfull effects in Medicine to be slighted; but we ~~will not~~ {may not so farr} exceede.

[**Page 254**] The Grass–hopper are an armed insect *a tout piece*, they goe forth in ~~troopes~~ companies, & follow their generall, especialy a sort of Locusts by which whole Countries as well as Gardens have bin devoured. It was one of the plagues of Ægypt, ~~We reade~~ We reade of a sort of them more humane, & so intelligent, as being asked of an {erring} Traviler the way to the next Towne, will by stretching out one of his legs direct the passenger & seldome deceive him. It is an Insect much delighted in its owne singing, uttering a sound, by shaking & stirring that dry gristly skin, & the power of a certaine Spirit comprehended in that *diazoma* [102] as *Aristotle* calls it, which it moves sometimes inwardly, sometimes outwardly, by which it renders the sound more or lesse shrill, elevated or depressed, which thing we have also observed in the *Virginian* Rattle Snake: {They sing most when men are in the field, & love it better then their meate, 'tis pretty to consider how when a man is neere, they will sing as if very farr off, & when he is at a distance, in so loude a note as if he were just by one:} Some make a murmure or bomb like Bees; & generaly they are great lovers of musique. ~~which~~ not to mention that kind Insect which skipt upon *Eunomius's* lute, when contending for the prize with *Ariston*, he supplied the place of a broaken string, by which the victory was obtained: The story is recited as a verity both by *Solinus* & *Strabo*: A kind of these *Grillos* the antient *Greekes* as now the Italians do keepe in Cages, & are much pleasd with their dry tone & jarring song.

The *Cicindela* or *Laciola* is a wonderfull flie, resembling sparkes in the aire, we

---

101. [**Margin note**] L: de Europa c. 50:
102. [**Margin note**] περὶ ζωες καὶ θανατου

once betweene *Bolognia* & *Ferrara* upon the River of *Po* thought the aire had bin on
fire for so the learned *Carthusian Reischius* contends that they are {indeede}. The *Glow-
worme* is {lies like} a terrestriall starr amongst our flo: & under our Garden hedges {in
the hot sommer monethes}: In the *West-Indies* the [103] *Cucuios* {or Igniclures are} of of
the bignesse, as to give light by which one may write & reade, they illuminate the
way for Travellors, and some worke by them in their houses if we may credit *Oviedo*.
And here we might mention the malicious & implacable *Chego*, neere as smale as a
Mite, who is able to produce a Gangreene where it bites. The *Lizard* is a pretty Animal, variously coloured, greate lovers of men & Musique, they inhabite our Gardens,
& pursue the flies which they catch by darting forth their tongue at a distance with
incredible swiftnesse; They can very much inliven or obscure thee hue of their scaly
skin, as they are pleasd or out of humour: I ha We have taken one on our Garden not
much inferiour in bignesse & beauty to those of *France* or *Italy*[.] The *Waspe* & *Crabron*
build admirable combs, in Trees if their King be slaine, otherwise {their caleptra is}
in the Earth, they live on fruites & sweete things, & will hauke for *flies* very pleasantly: But the *Hornet* is a bigger sort, his sting is able to inflict a Feavor, & I have read
{of one} which kild **[page 255]** a Sparrow, in the midst of all the streets at Peter-
barrow before many witnesses; & we reade how they drove out whole Nations in the
Scriptures.

Wormes there are of severall sorts, their dilation & contraction, like the *Proboscis* of the *Elephant* is very strange, & so is their obstinat adhesion, when they are in
coition but what we most admire is how they corrode the very {entrails of a} flint
as we have often found, without do being able to discover where it gott in, unlesse
whilst the stone was in its softer rudiments. *Olaus Magnus* speakes of an Earth worme
40 cubites found in the coasts of Norway, that was 40 cubites long, *Pliny* of much
longer about *Ganges* There is a {smale red} worme in the very Snow, {if it lye {con-
tinue} long upon the Earth. Nay my Ld: Bacon speakes of one that is borne in the
very fire}[.] The Snaile is well knowne, and worthily chased out of our Gardens for
the Spoile they make of our fruite, but i & slow & laizy pace; Ferrarius tells the Metamorphosis of an Idle Gardner into Limax with much aggravation. but though it be
slow of pace, it has a greate stroake with the mouth, & is a vast devourer: We have
dissected them & found their rews of teeth, which we reserve in papers to shew, &
you may sometimes heare them crackle as they feede: There are severall kinds of these
Some carry their houses on their backs, others are without shells, & lastly gad abroad:
{That they beare their eyes in their hornes like the Crab, which they can shrink in &
withdrawe is conspicuous.}

Who dos not admire the pretty spotted *Lady-Cow* the Nimble Tiquett or Cabbage Flea and the lordly the fraile Ἐφήμερον or diary fly what being {is} borne
with the sunrise, dyes at his setting, & is a perfect brevi embleme of the vanity &
brevity of life: These are bred in the Autumne from the huskes of rotten grapes: {etc}
But wonderfull stories have ben recorded of Flyes, Lastly, since we mentioned the
Mite, & Syron which we have seene to move so nimbly, & have {making} the same
use of its snoute which in a cheeze, as the hog dos in the Earth, It we had rather give

---

103. **[Margin note]** They catch them & put them into their chambers to hawke
for gnatts for they prey on them as long as is one left;

~~you~~ our Gardiner the description of him in picture as it was accurately taken by a learned Gentleman a friend [104] of ours & presented to his *Electoral Highnesse* then make a ~~more~~ description which can no way reach the perfection of the original, & the~~at~~ rather that our wonder may be the greater, when we behold such a variety of parts in so minute an atome, so ~~smale crile~~ smale an Insect [105] ~~such~~ so crile a nothing, ~~or as Tertullian expresses it unius~~ {& which Tertullian Unius puncti animal.}

[Page 256]

> Nunc age jam deinceps cunctarum exordia rerum,
> Qualia sunt; et quam longe distantia formis
> Percipe multigenis quam sint variata Figuris etc.
>
> Lucret: L: 2. [333–335]

For so the poet, when he speakes of the formes of his Atomes, though in reguard of their ~~nicitie~~ wonderfull minutenesse, they seemed to be all of a shape: And thus ~~so~~ are divers Insects so smale, as not to be perceivd by the acutest eye, hardly by the best *Microscope*; But as Plutarch upon another occasion Χῄριαθα λόγῳ θεώρητα [lxix] to be discerned by the Mind onely: And this resemblance & uniformity of some Insects ~~it was~~ as they are superficially looked upon yet so disforme & unlike being put into ~~the Microscope~~ that Instrument gave me first the curiosity of examining some of the smaler kinds of Seedes, which ~~outwar~~ appeard smooth, round & perfectly uniforme, whereas in truth, they were in themselves prodigiously unlike, rugged ~~of~~ & of the most ~~glabrous~~ {unequall} superficies: So strange a hebitude is in our senses, compared to the subtilty of Nature {&} so truely is that {saying of one} *Ubi nostra Industria subtilitasque desinit, inde incipere industriam subtilitatemque Naturæ*: Nature having formed in one Graine of *Millet* Seede more distinct parts {the bulke considered} then a man can destinguish in the globe of the whole Universe itselfe: For what wonder would it raise, to behold the many angles, faces, & varieties which in a good Microscope are reppresented in this ~~seemingly~~ speciously smooth, round & polite ~~Seede~~ graine! and then, if it be contused, how much more various {are} the bruised & dispersed parts: But of this Speculation more hereafter, whilst we returne to our Insects, & contemplate that incomparable Atome, the *Cyron*, hardly to be discerned by the most *Lyncæan* eye, whilst yet it containes bones, snout & proboscis, by which it perforates the skin & sucks our blood; his joynts feete, tayle, {& very} haire, & {then} to consider what lurkes within, as of necessity, for the ~~rest~~ {furniture} of its vital functions, stomack, Intestines, liver, heart, braine, veines, ~~vital f~~ arteries, nerves, muscles, fibers, & innumerable other parts or members at least analogicall & without which it could have neither sense nor motion {much lesse imagination}; add to this, these not onely confusedly, but beautifully ordered & disposed {that they have voluntary motion & therefore imagination & that determinate & not at random}, a speculation able to confound the proudest Atheist, & abase the sublimest thoughts, how smale soever the Instance, & the smaler, with the greater power & Counsell, & to crye out with *Galen*,

---

104. **[Margin note]** ~~Mr: Wren~~ Mr Hook
105. **[Margin note]** de Anima c. 10:

Compone hic Canticum in creatoris laudem[106] when he beheld things lesse surprising: For if that Sculptor was admired who carved the story of the fall of *Phæton* in a smale ring, so as every part of the harnasse of the ~~chariot~~ {horses} was to be discerned: or the charriot made by *Myrmicides* which a fly could cover with its wings, & the ship, which a Bee could hide **[page 257]** with how much more stupor & admiration shall we looke upon the workes of God in these severall Instances, and ~~be~~ encourage our Gardiner {to} philosophise, study & learne out their natures; it is certainly one of the greatest antidotes against Atheisme, & it is thought that the ~~learned knowing~~ {greate Father} *Tertullian* had never bin a *Heretick* had he bin a better Naturalist. For next to man there is nothing ~~more divine then Insects~~ in which the divine omnipotency is more conspicuous: & therefore let none any more admire the huge ~~Co~~ Rhodian Colosse, the ~~Elephant~~ Pyramids, & Amphitheaters, the workes of mens hands, when the wisest of kings celebrated the hysope upon the Wall, & sends us to the ~~very In~~ Smalest Insects to learne wisdome & ~~virtue~~ {prudence for}, ~~& whose structure is so admirable~~ for the loftiest of those structures are not to be named with the least flye or gnatt, whose ~~parts~~ contexture is so admirable, made with such art, indeed with such instinct, {repaired} & nourished wihithout [*sic*] the least labour: {& yet what wonder, Ex pauescis in minimis lauda magnum qui fecit in cælo Angelum, fecit in terra Vermiculum: S: Aug: in psal: 148.} Moreover, how stupendious is the consideration of the vital Spirit in some Insects, which is sometimes compelled to desert as it were the Organs, making them cease from all operations, whilst it selfe ~~concenters~~ {retires} in the centrall parts so close, & in such a poynt, that for many daies, nay moneths, ~~yea~~ {&} yeares, it lies as it were a sleepe & plainely dead, & yet awakens againe at last, diffusing itselfe through all the members, & exercising its former vitall operations: For so we find it in Flies, Spiders, Froggs, etc ~~other In~~ the like not to mention Swallows, Nightingalls, Tortoises, or the Inhabitants of ~~the~~ some Northern parts, because this last is a mistake.[107]

{And if we will argue from their worth} He ~~therefore~~ that contemplates the Bee, the Silkeworme, & the Cochinell, & that which makes our Gummlug, besides ~~the~~ what others contribute to ~~Me~~ the *dispensatory*, will not despise Insects & ~~the~~ even these productions of our Gardens.[108] And then for their fortitude & other considerations, How even these despicable things can when ~~God~~ {Heaven} pleases confound

---

106. **[Margin note]** de usu part: 17:

107. **[Insertion on separate piece of paper]** The Natur of Vivification (says me L: Verulam Cent: 7: ex. 625) {as the very nature indeed of all things} is commonly better perceived in small than in greate; & in imperfect then in perfect; & in parte than in whole: whenc he inferrs that the nature of vivification is best enquired in such Creatures; ~~& derives these~~ when he derives these {fruitfull} contemplations the disclosing ~~of~~ the original of Vivification, {&} Figuration, & divers things in the nature of more perfect Creatures, & lastly in traducing by way of operation some operations in the Insects to worke effects upon perfect Creatures

108. **[Insertion on separate piece of paper]** Some thinke even Medicines transcending even the Chymists; for every plant which retaines a medicinal Virtue, is also sublim'd up into this living quintessence.

the power of the greatest {potentate}; God himself calls them his Army, & by divers of them he chastiz'd *Pharo* {in *Egypt*} & has since brought them upon other Countrys, as sometimes even our Neighbour Kingdomes, France, Germany, Spaine etc: Italy has often bin infested from Africa, when after the devastations they have made of the fruites, their stinke alone has cause a plague in which 800000 men & catell perished, & in 1478 about the Venetian territories about 30000 died of the famine: In Syria of old, & of late in the Iland of *Palma* they have bin forced to march out in military order against them {the locusts}; *Hercules* was almost slaine with flyes alone, as he went to sacrifice to the *Devil* their prince & *Genius*; And Sap **[page 258]** we reade that *Sapor* the K of *Persia*, was compelld to raise the seige of *Nisibis* because of Hornets & horseflies which infested his Camp; for it seemes that some have vanquished their k enemyes by slinging hives of Bees amongst their rankes & Squadrons: So as there it appeares, there is nothing so trifling & little, which God cannot arme to overthrow & confound us when we displease him: of all men therefore it behoves our Gardiners to be {as} pious and religious persons, that none of these plagues so fatall to his labours destroy the workes of his hands: I wi {In Summ} we will conclude this discourse with what *Seneca* has sayd of them c: 33. de *vita Beata* of Nature {& applie it to *Insects*} *Perditura e fructum sui si tam magna, tam præclara, tam subtiliter excogitata, tam nitida, et in uno genere formosa, solitudini ostenderet: Scias illam Spectari voluisse, non tantum aspici.*

Therefore it were worth the Industry of our Gardiner to study wayes of preserving them being dead that he may make a collection of them, to be kept {reserved} in boxes as one of the rarest Cabinet pieces; for this he may effect by medicating & embalming their bodies with a composition of Myrrhe & el campher water, in which is infused a little Aloes, which being also by filling their skins with lyme, & in strewing pepper amongst them & rubbing the boxes with oyle of Spike: {but first bruise the head a little} & being Thus dried, pierce them through with a pin, & stick them upon a thin sheete of virgins wax, which is layed even {superinduced} on the bottome of a shallow drawer & {for} thus you may [109] makeing such an embrodery with Buterflies alone as will at once both delight & amaze you: The rest may be ranged in classes in other boxes, as we have seene them to many hundreds in number. There is a Seacret how by a composition wherin Cypresse Terpentine is [110] the chiefe Ingredient, to embalme any Insect, yet so as the matter being hard becomming hard & translucid you may behold the Insect as in the p flyes in the purest amber & as that Lizard to be {which we have} seene amongst the rare collections of *Sigr: Rugin:* an *Illustrisso:* of *Venice*; this is an immortale way of preserving them from putrifaction; but I {we} have it *sub sigillo* & {therefore} may not prophane it.

[Page 259]

---

109. **[Margin note]** take them up & consider them at pleasure
110. **[Margin note]** Se Mr Boyles receipt in his Essays, publishd 1663.

Of Verdures, Perennial-greenes,
and perpetuall Springs.
{How they are to be propagated & Governd}

After that which has already bin spoken in Chap: 4: 7: & 8 concerning the raising
{planting} and propagating of ever Greenes and the planting of them into Groves, we
have little more in this place to add: For that we call *perpetuum Ver* which the ancients
one sort of {*Viretum* and} *Viridarium*[1] *locus arborum viriditate naturali amoenus* or *vin-
darium* ἀλόη etc: and hence *Viridarij Serui* are by *Ulpian* the Lawyer such as had charge
of these places particularly, though likewise they were appellative is common to other
Gardiners. And Viretum such a place shall in our designe be planted in the next division to the Parterr, and object from the house 'twixt it and the grove of the taler
& winter trees,[2] for so we {best} distinguish betweene the deciduous, & ever-greene
leaved, because of the freshnesse & agreablenesse of it to the eye in the horrid Season
of Winter {for, *confusis oculis prosunt virentia*} and conveniency of it for warmth;
since being perpetualy clad with leaves, it defends both our Gardens and the dwelling
from the penetration of the winds, and extreamities of the weather: And verily, an
ingenious Gardiner may so invirone his Enclosures and Avenues with Verdures, that
they shall seeme to be placed in one of the Summer Ilands, and to enjoy an eternal
Spring, when all the rest of the Country is bare & naked; & for which reguard we
pronounce it a most sweete & incomparable part of the Hortulane amoenitie, and
to our particular inclination, the most agreable: For Nature having sited {scituated}
our Country in the Sententrion *Climates*, where the Sunn is lesse friendly & benigne
then in other Tracts; there can nothing more reccommend our Industrie, then to advance it by *Arte* & {For} truely, it is so eminently effected by the plentifull propagation of Verdures, and such as will very gratefully answer our expectations & paines;
that upon every gentle emission of that glorious planet, or lesse rigour of the cold,
an English Garden, even in the midst of Winter, shall appeare little inferiour to the
Italian, where the Seasons are more kind benigne, and the gardens almost perpetually florid: so that, if all the avirons [environs] of a Dwelling were planted both with
the taller, & lower sort of Evergreenes, even for some miles about, it can hardly be
imagined, how infinintely delightfull the place would be appeare {prove} {and} how
it would even strike and surprise the Winter Spectator, who might imagine himselfe, by a pleasant {kind of} deception to **[page 260]** be transported into some new
or inchanted Country; Such as they report the Iland *Tilo* in the *Arabic Sea*, & some

---

1. **[Margin note]** Sueton in Tiber: Plin: L: 8: c. 22. Onom:
2. **[Margin note]** as at Wimbledon

others in the W: Indies, In *Æthiopia*, also neere Memphis, and the *Tempe* of the *Afric Hammon* so celebrated by the *Poets* for its *perpetuum Ver*, those *Fortunatorum nemora* etc: ~~amoe~~{rd}a ——— *amoena virecta* as *Virgil* ~~calls~~ {tearmes} them[3] and especialy ~~since there~~ if the ~~plantation~~ {plot} be large and the plantation *ad simulacrum naturalis defesti*, for which my *Ld: Verulam* destines at least a third part of the whole Enclosure; and that there is such choyce to be had of greenes for all purposes; As the lofty *Cedar, Pines* and *Firrs* for the taller wood, and of old celebrated for its magnificent shade about a Seate, as *Xenophanes* has it

’εις στεφάνους
‘εσᾶσι δ ἐλάται πυκινὸν περὶ δωμᾶ
The ~~*Abies*~~ {Firrs} ~~stand~~ like Crownes about
The goodly ~~House~~ {Mansion} ~~doe~~ stand

Not to omitt the *Laurell*, which in standards comes to be a beautifull & prodigious Tree,

Brumaque illæsa Cupressus,   Statius

{The *Cypresse*} heretofore thought so delicate a tree, that it was seldom seene out of Princes Gardens, where as, even upon *Ida* in *Creete* ~~all are~~ {perpetualy} covered with Snow, they ~~grow~~ {thrive} plentifully;[4] and so the Cedar {Terpentine Tree} & divers others:[5] *vide adenta* ~~sup~~ {in} *papra et regione* Of the more inferiour sort, *Bayes,*

---

3. **[Margin note]** 6 Æne: [638]

4. **[Margin note]** yet it thrives not in starving grounds that are apt to be wett or full of springs, but will grow in dry hot grounds

5. **[Insertion on separate piece of paper]** nor doe we doubt but that in tyme, by costume, & culture we might bring *Oranges, Limons,* and divers other plants, which now we esteeme so rare & delicate, to grow more familiarly in *England* and endure our *Climat*: We remember to have seene a *Myrtil* {in *Sussex*} that ~~was~~ being planted against a Southe wall, had never bin housed in above 30 yeares {but then {so undid} ~~cutt~~ them cloase to the ground} and we have kept orang trees with very little care abroad all the Winter; for it is certaine they will become very hardy, by being accostumed to a lesse nice education; We reade that the *Persica* was at first thought so ~~deli~~ tender a Tree, as that it would onely ~~gro~~ thrive in *Persia*; & even in *Galens* tyme it grew no neerer then *Ægypt*, of all the *Roman* dominions, then into Asia, Greece, but was not seene in the *Roman Gardens* ~~till~~ till above 30 yeares before *Pliny*~~s tyme;~~ ~~and now they flourish every where~~ {where as now there is no tree more universal} as *Columella*. L: 2.

Exiguo properat mitescere Persica malo,
Tempestiva mardent, quæ maxima Gallia donat
Frigoribus pigro veniunt Asiatica fœtu.

And the same may be affirmed of divers other perigrine trees: especialy the *Evergreenes*: {For} *Josephus* says, that *Saloman* was the first that planted {even} the *Cædar* in *India*; we had first the *Myrtil* out of Greece, & the *Cypresse,* ~~out of~~ {from} *Creete* &

~~Yufe~~ {*Yough*}, *Arbutus, Alaternus, Celastrus* etc: For hedges, far exceeding all kind of growing fences whatever, the *Agrifolium, Pericanth,* etc so ~~easily~~ {facily} reaised [*sic*] of Seedes, & berries, hasty producers {of long continuance} and easily govern'd: to this we add their errect posture and universal sweetenesse, and indeede whatsoever may reccommend them to our industrie & care: We shall therefore neede add no more to this Chapter, then to send our Reader back to what we have already sayd in Chap: 7, where we have expressely treated of Groves, and particularly of Perenniall greenes, & where we have likewise given a Catalogue of all the sorts applicable to this purpose ~~So as we thinke~~ {conceive} ~~the recapitulation altogether superfluous Such as the We~~ {with some repitition} ~~may be supplied by this enticing Catalgoue:~~ ˡˣˣ[**page 261**] etc ~~and~~ {with} divers more which we have already enumerated[.] The manner of elevating and governing ~~whereoff~~ {thereat} together with their proper places, we have handled at large in the chapter forgoing; So as the recapitulation would now appeare superfluous:⁶ But ~~by~~ with these Ingredients, & with this furniture might that *Ver perpetuum* be perfectly accomplished, observd at by my *Ld: Bacon*, where he reckons {them} ~~up, what of~~ {confusedly}⁷ promiscuously; together, with what ~~flowers~~ shrubbs, plants & flowers are in prime every moneth in the yeare; & which ~~li~~ likewise may be interspersed amongst them, especially such as prosper in ~~such~~ {those} shady places, an accoumpt whereoff we have largely ~~given~~ {exhibited} in the formerly cited⁸ Chapters:

Now then let us but imagine the beauty, ~~&~~ verdure, {& variety} which all these must needes produce; the hardy at all tymes, the tender and more choyce in their seasons, ~~& being ranged~~ sometymes in the *Conservatory*, other whiles under the por-

---

which in our remembrance was esteemed so rare a Tree, as we noted {before}; and 'tis likely that at first, they would onely grow in hot Regions. It was the 680 yeare V.C. that *Lucullus* brought *Cheries* into *Italy* out of ~~Greece~~ {*Pontus*}, which a little after travaild ~~into~~ {as far as} *Britanie* as *Athenæus* notes: L: 2. And no doubt but many Indian trees, as well as Plants would thrive amongst us, which as yet are mere strangers: *Olives, Capers, Pistacias,* some sorts of the *Palme,* as well as *Madder, Licoris,* yea *Ginger* which ~~I~~ we heare has bin ~~pl~~ successfully planted: But some indeed there are which we shall never obtaine, nor will {they} be made to travell, whatever industry we bestowe; such as the *Syrian Balsam,* the *Arabian Myrrh* & ~~the Thus~~

  Solis est Thurea Virga Sabetis Sola nigrum
   Geor: 2 [116–117]

 Fert Hebenum Speaking of *India*: ~~which~~ so genial an affection {it seemes} they retaine to their owne Country; yet we have seene a smale *Cinnamon* tree & other very great rarities of that kind; but we will passe them over.

 6. **[Insertion on separate piece of paper]**
Observe onely that I have frequently numbered the species, which if with an adjunct nominated shewes it to be the more rare & fitt for our purpose if with an astrisc; a stranger with us, but prompting to experiments: as for such as require the favour of the Greene-house, & so are onely to be set out in potts & cases, consult the following {Calendar} Chapter: & the 23.

 7. **[Margin note]** Essayes: Ess: 44.

 8. **[Margin note]** 7: Cap: l: 1.

tico's & peristyles, ~~wh~~ in both which they may be transported in their cases, & orderly ranged so as to forme most delicious groves, even in the very middest of the Winter: But the ~~next~~ following Chapter will instruct us {yet} farther, and illustrate what is {here} yet deficient.

[Page 262]

CHAP. XV.

Of Orangeries, {*Oporothecas*} and Conservatories of rare Plants & Fruites {With the manner of raising them:}

It was for the care of these golden fruits that the Daughters of *Atlas* committed them to the custody of the Dragon, and which invited *Hercules* to that memorable combate and expedition: It was for this that the *Jewes* report our first Parents sold their immortality; but whither we may in that give them credite, when so greate a person as their *Rabbi Solomon* tels us it is a seacret {to be} reserved for the comming of *Eliah*, we will not persist in the meane time it is generaly held to be the Tree under which they us'd to ~~keepe their~~ {celebrate} *Tabernacular anniversaries* about *September*, dressing up & adorning their Booths more with the leaves of this golden Tree, then any other, and indeede it is so beautifull that it has well deserved that splendid Epithete, and the care which we shall take in this chapter to reccommend the culture & preserving of it to our Industrious Gardiner: we meane the *Orange & Limmon*, which are doubtlesse the most worthy ~~&~~ of all other Trees, which in these parts of Europ we are ~~best~~ blest with all, and that render our *Elysium*, one of its noblest decorations. In the remoter parts of *Italy*, about *Rhegium*, the air is so clement & propitious, that they frequently inviron their Gardens with hedges in *Palisads & Contrespaliers* of the goodly *Citron*, as familiarly as we doe ours with Codlings; The like about *Genoa*; and neere *Valentia* in *Spaine*, they have bin planted & maintaind in forme of a spacious ~~chape~~ {Cathedrall} ~~church~~ with its chapells, cloisters, Altars, the stales for the *Canons* etc: after an admirable order of Architecture, cutt & maintaine: But though the more southern parts of Italy (whither first *Palladius* brought them, & thenc transferred into Spaine as *N: Monardus*[lxxi] tells us) abound in these blessed Trees, yet even almost all other parts of that Country enjoy them with our greate industry, especialy the most maritime; ~~for even~~ whi~~ch~~ere they flourish more apparently, as extreamely affecting ~~that~~ the ~~salt~~ {Spanish} aire ~~of~~ that proceedes from the Seas: ~~For we have beheld the water both at Genoa & Rome &~~ And hence it is that these Fruits about *Genoa*, & *Nice*, the *Barbados*, & *Bermudas* (which exceede all our *European* trees) is so excellent, as more abounding with {th}at vegetable Sature so propitious to them. **[Page 263]**

But as to the care for the conserving of such as adorne our *European* Gardens, we have ~~seene~~ {observed} their Walles both in *Genoa* and Rome covered against the invasions of the *Tramontane* winds, & injuries {even} of those gentler winters; nor about *Madrid* in *Spaine* are they preserved with lesse caution; since (as we have formerly touched) not so much the frosts, as those winds which hisse & come off from the Serry [Sierra] mountaines it is, that is so noxious to them, & which in those parts, we have felt more keene & penetrating then in ~~the~~ {our} *Elysium* of great *Britaine*. With good reason dos it therefore stand that we should provide for these inconveniencies with us, which ~~both~~ are so much reinforced by the frosts which likewise invade our Gardens:

But before we proceede to the errection of our *Conservatory* the common receptacle of all our tender & delicate plants, to supplie what may seeme defective in *Chap: 4* (where we discoursed of *Seminaries*) we shall here endeavor to prescribe some directions how these rarer sort of plants are to be govern'd and cultivated in our Country; exemplifing in the *Citron, Orange, Limmom* and some others the most choyce and delicious of our *Elysium*. We commence with the *Citron*, a stranger as yet to our Climate; yet such as might be produced with successe, and doubtlesse brought to some maturitie by the industrie of our Gardiner. It takes pleasure in a light and easie Soyle, mingled with sheepes dung, & made very fine: here we *Pontanus*

> *Nec mihi displiceat, Salebrosi glarea ruris*
> *Quæque sola tenui graciles imitatur arenas*
> *Si modo sæpe fimo spargas, si pronior unda*
> *Dilvat ipsa super lætusque instillet et imber.*
> *de Hort: Hesper: L: 1.*[lxxii]

And here we might much enlarge, by taking in the directions of *Theophrastus, Palladius* and other of the Antients upon this subject, did we not rather studdy brevity, and to informe our Gardiner in true experiments, Then to multiplie them out of bookes, composed for Countries {& Climates} so much different from ours. The Earth therefore thus prepared, and put into a fitting case in the *Seminarie*: choose Seedes which are ripe and large & **[page 264]** and after ~~it~~ {they} has{ve} bin washed cleane, & a little wiped by gentle pressing ~~it~~ {them} betweene some linnen cloath; prick them an Inch or somewhat more deepe into the Earth, about the end of March[1] or beginning of September, if the weather be mild, a day or two before the Full: Place your pot or case in a South aspect, well defended from the *North & East* and keepe the Earth allways fresh, with water well qualified: {earth them up as they rise to establish them:} Then after two yeares you may transplant them into larger vessells by themselves, {clense them of their under branches **[continued in margin]** & budds {& thornes} that they may com straite, smooth & ~~full~~ tall} and in 10. or 12 yeares (if they be let alone) they will produce a wild & sower fruite: But if you have them perfect, & usefull you shall at fower yeares groth (the stock being about a finger thick[)] graffe them by approch, or (which is best) Inoculate them. The ~~othe~~ one from *May* to *August*, the other from *May* to the end of *october* in the waine of the *Moone*. We doubt not but even the Buds may (for ~~a made~~ to have excellent, & varietie) be had even from *Genoa* itselfe by some very speedy passage, being tenderly wrapped in some[2] moist ~~Mosse~~ handfulls of Mosse, and enclosed in a box lined with a case of clay tempered with hony: or, for a neede make use of such as ~~the~~ {any ~~more~~ lesse remote} curious Gardens ~~of our owne Country~~ afford, ~~Such as are at Pensherst, Bedington~~ etc. The Bud, or Graffe thus lodged and taken, ~~defend~~ sedulously defend from impetuous winds &

---

1. **[Margin note]** or sow them & sift over them:

2. **[Margin note]** choose a bud from a round not a square branch or twig for then it will not fitt your stock:

raines, and governe as in other cases where you Inoculate fruite trees. But they are also propagated by *Layers* in *July* to mid *August*; and even by cuttings in *Italy*, as other perennial greenes are, ~~as~~ {&} as *Pontanus* instructs us.

> *Tum fragmenta lege, et ramos secerne valentes,*
> *Obliquosque infige solo, tamen ut capite extent:*
> *Stipitis aut truncum gladioque et falce dolatum*
> *Infode, et in tenui nudatum contege sulco*
> *Continuo ingentem vicino ex omne paludum*
> *Elice, diluvioque comas immerge Salubri*:
>
> Hesp: L: 2. [p. 151][lxxiii]

Nay this worke may be attempted from *March* till *August*, the tender twiggs of about 2 foote in length being couched along, & covered with the mould, within one halfe foote; **[Page 265]** And so, after two yeares transplanted either into cases or large Potts, or in the ground itselfe immediately, provided it be against a Wall, as other choyce fruite is treated: with this onely difference, that the whole[3] tree be covered & defended in Winter from the cold and inhospitable seasons. That the Potts, and cases be accommodated with ~~a~~ {plentifull} hole{s} ~~or two~~ {as} we have formerly cautioned: Then lay a layer of {the biggest} gravell, or {the core of lime siftings brick batts} ~~tyle shards~~, brush of old broome, or the like to keepe the botome holow, that the Water may [4]freely passe: upon this ~~stratum~~ a *stratum* of compost fatt, rott, & well qualified, of about halfe foote deepe: then as much excellent lite mould, made a little capped upon which to spread the rootes of your plant: unlesse you can remove the Tree, Earth and all, which is best: {Set so shallow as some of the roote even appeare.} The plant thus placed, fill the rest with {naturall cleane} Earth, within halfe a foote of the brim; lastly, cover it with fatt soyle, yet so, as it touch not the Stemme, to burne it by any [5]accident; Then watering it ~~plentifully~~ {sparingly the first yeare}, set it in the shade for twenty daies {till it begin to to [*sic*] stirr: If you are so happy as to plant in the ground immediately let it be very exquisitely prepared, by opening the holes the yeare before, and furnishing them with excellent mould as before you are taught, watering it 8 or 10 daies after: The stocks to be transplanted would be 3 yeares groth, of the best kind, & ready inoculated, of 2. or 3 foote in height & a finger thick, the rootes trimmed within halfe a foote of the stemm, embaulmed with loame, or covered with clay, that boald over with mosse, they may be sent you in barills; for thus defended they will last 3. or 4 Monethes and may be now & then watered if neede require:[6] but before they are barill'd up, the wounds & amputations

---

3. **[Margin note]** This transplanting which is out of the Conserve is not safe till about May: nor removing till August, & then laying is also proper

4. **[Margin note]** tis good to mingle these sticks short broken with the Earth within 3 or 4 inch of the top of the base to preserve the Earth from clogging which rotts the fibers be sure not to set too deepe:

5. **[Margin note]** Such as we have from Paris etc do best with us: or rarely Flanders Ghent the fairest that ever I saw

6. **[Margin note]** or put as many as you can well thrust in the barill or case, the

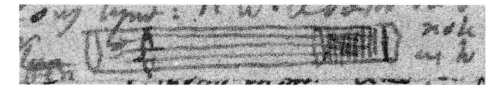

Figure 64. Illustration of a "box" to transport tender seedlings and buds in an insertion at page 265.

would be covered with wax: And their former position carefully marked with read oaker, or some other distinction[7] When you receive your plants, wash off the clay, and plant them at the very first opportunity, as you are instructed: The best season will be[8] *September* in the old *Moone*. When they have taken a little hold of the ground

---

rootes a little trimmed, & letting the earth hold about the fibers; then sift dry earth over them, & put dry {sweete} straw & stop them very close, for wett mosse, earth, or waste rotts them: They bring their Oranges etc now from Genoa with heads & all, the fruite & leaves on them, in barills the rootes onely secured with dry straw which is best because you ~~can ruine~~ still may then bring in the kind

7. **[Insertion on separate piece of paper]** There is another rare way of transporting ~~your~~ {the budds of the} tendrest & choicest plants which is to shut them up in tin boxes made round; big enough to contain two or three ~~plants~~ {twiggs}, the ~~rootes~~ {ends} stuck in moist clay & so seperated with peggs of wood or a partition that it cannot fall from them, & so shou[l]d the heads likewise, & then the lid made very close to the Canon; thus they will be preserved as fresh as may possibly be imagnd a very long tyme: it will better be seene in this figure **[illustration, see Fig. 64]** note that you must cut the heads so short as to be 6 inches shorter then the Cannon ~~lay this in water all the nights & as lon often~~ **[continued on verso]** lay this box in water a nights and as often as you can in the dayes whilst it is in comming.

[illustration, see Fig. 65]

a　　The sticks crosse that go in stiff to keepe the twigs asunder from twisting: both at top & bottom:

b　　The clay from the bottom to the the [*sic*] peggs or sticks:

c　　the Cyons or twiggs. The lid of the Canon: note that you fill it clay at bottom 2 inches above the peggs; & cutt your Cyons like a pen thrusting them down to the bottom: in the clay:

8. **[Margin note]** rather Aprill with us: for this is Ferrarius. If they be newly come from abroad, well water them a moneth or 6 weekes in the greene house exposing them not above one houer in the morning sunn sometimes in the first yeare. **[Continued on separate piece of paper]** If the Trees lose their leaves after first planting tis a good signe & that the roote is taken; if the leaves crumble & stay on tis an ill signe & that the rootes perish:

Figure 65. Another illustration of a "box" for transplanting tender seedlings and buds on verso of insertion at page 265.

spread and governe the branches as you doe your Abricotts & Nectarines against the
wall, that they may receive all the advantages of Support & reflection. The *Italians* do
about *Autumne* stirr & dresse the Earth about the rootes, neere halfe a foote deepe,
& for 4. or 5 foote compasse, pruning off the farther stragling rootes, and then they
mellow it with some soyle, which they lett lye & consume till the spring, when they
rake it all even againe; but with us this opening **[page 266]** must be much abated,
least we chill them imprudently, Thus also they serve their potts & cases {more fre-
quently} bearing the earth, within a little of the roote, & replenishing them with
excellent mould; because in cases & potts the raines & waterings do wonderfully exhaust the virtue of the mould: and it were good that our Gardiner did repeate it also
in *May*, & *August*, & ~~to~~ lay hoggs bristles, old shoe leather about the rootes, covering them with earth, & keeping them moist both winter & sommer with insolated
water, which every 4th or 5t day may be powered upon them in moderate quanti-
tye, ~~morning &~~ {in the Summer} Evenings, & winter mornings for they do this even
during all *January*, {but we are to be more sparing lest we rott them.} It is not to be
concealed that they esteeme the ordure which is taken out of *Privies* above all for the
lætation of these plants; but it had neede be well mingled & dulcified by being exposed to the aire before application. The branches would be kept pruned, for a foote
above ground, & then {the moone decreasing} display them like a fan {in Spring &
Autumne as you would for Wall fruite.} if you remove cutt away all the dry twiggs
{& pare the rootes **[continued in margin]** which ought to be don every 2. or 3
yeares to those which stand in cases about the end of September, but with its masse
of earth about him of which take off halfe & add fresh: if it be too hevy, suspend the
tree with a cord & pully till you have don just over the case, & so may you with ease
let it downe when you have finished, but bind something about its neck to keepe the
rope from galling: If you perceive an unthriving part, turne that the next yeare to
the Sunn.};[9] otherwise being now arived to competent stature, ~~prune them but~~ {be}
sparing in amputations: With us the fruite will not ripen ~~(as~~ from the Blossome (as
in other places it dos) till the second yeare or more: They Flower about the end of
June, knott in *October* & become as big as pidgeons Eggs, grow yellow & perfect the
third Sommer for so this *Eliphantique partus* takes time to mature its productions. We
have bin the more accurate in our instructions about the government of this Tree;
because, we suppose it is yet much a stranger in our Countrie; though elevated with
as greate facilitie as *Oranges* & other choyce fruites: & so it is, in some parts of *Flanders*,

---

9. **[Continued on separate piece of paper]** They monethly stirr the Earth at
toppe of the Cases in Italy & strew some rich soile amongst it: These they never water
if raine comes unlesse the leaves crumple: But such as stand without in plaine Earth,
they water thus in Sommer 2 a weeke: The[y] have Earth potts a foote deepe & as
wide, & the sides of these are pierced with {one line of} holes 5 or 6 in the rank
{line} ~~To~~ {About a foote from the stem of} every plant, they interr 2 of these potts,
the range of holes next the plant, the pot sunke in the earth, within an inch of the
brim: These they fill with water & cover them from ordure, this affording a leasurly
humictation (for which effect the holes are very small) wonderfully make it produce
greate & large fruite, & may be a good expedient for other trees: let the water be
impregned with pigeon dung & insolated: ~~Transport this rath~~

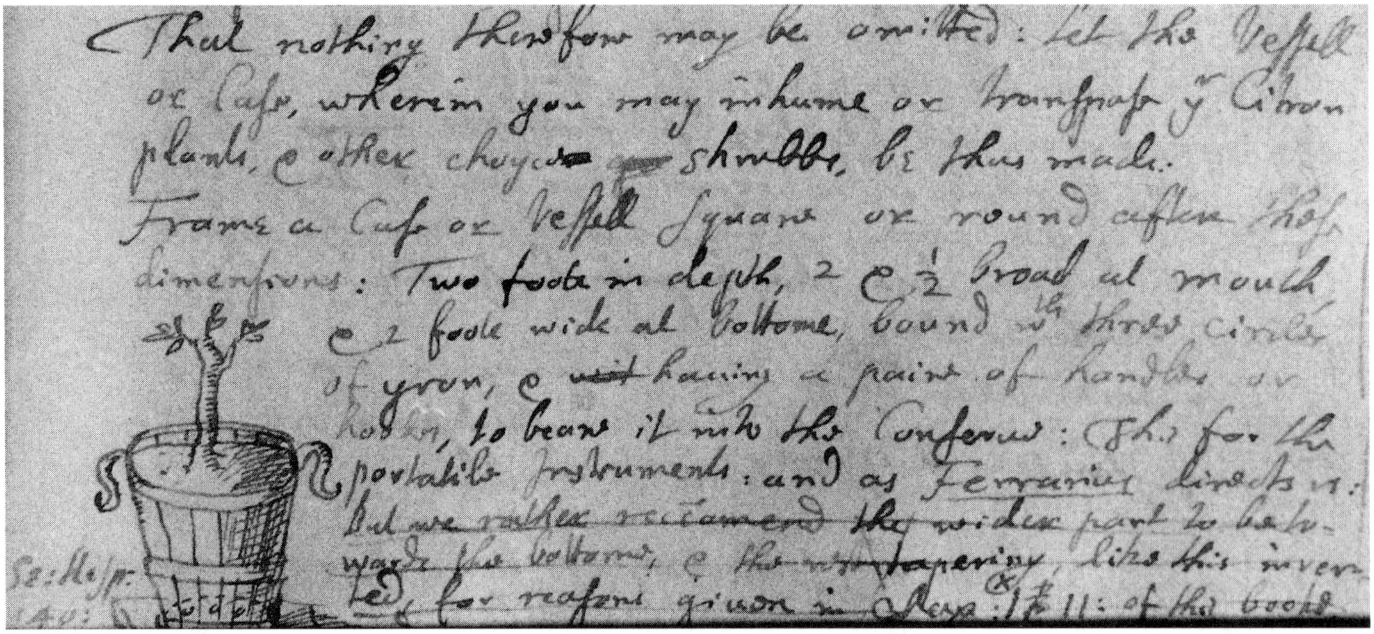
That nothing therefore may be omitted: let the Vessell or Case, wherein you may inhume or transpose yr Citron plants, & other choyce ~~gre~~ shrubbs, be thus made.
Frame a Case or Vessell square or round after these dimensions: Two foote in depth, 2 & 1/2 broad at mouth & 2 foote wide at bottome, bound wth three circles of yron, & ~~wit~~ having a paire of handles or hookes, to beare it into the Conserve: This for the portatile Instruments: and as Ferrarius directs us: ~~But we rather reccommend the wider part to be towards the bottome, & the rest tapering, like this inverted, for reasons given in Chap: I & 11: of this booke~~

Figure 66. A case or vessel to "inhume or transpose your Citron plants," illustrated in text (bottom, left) at page 266.

particularly in the Gardens of *Monsr: de Blasere* at *Gendt*: which being so little remote from these quarters should mithinkes be a greate encouragement to us. That nothing therefore may be omitted: Let the Vessell or Case, wherein you may inhume or transpose your Citron plants, & other ~~gre~~ choyce shrubbs be thus made: Frame a Case or Vessell square or round after these dimensions: Two foote in depth, 2 & 1/2 broad at mouth,[10] & 2 foote wide at bottome, bound with three circles of yron, & ~~wit~~ having a paire of handles or hookes, to beare it into the Conserve: This for the portatile Instruments: and as *Ferrarius* directs us: ~~But we rather reccommend the wider part to be towards the bottome, & the rest tapering like this inverted, for reasons given in Chap: 1 & 11: of this booke;~~

[illustration, see Fig. 66] [Page 267] The fruite being ripe, let them not hang till they rott & impaire, but taking them just at their turning perfect their full maturity in fresh & dry straw, if neede require: The Sorts of Citron are {chiefly} three: 1 the Vulgar, 2 the Sweete, ~~and~~ 3 the Multiforme, & which for its beautifull extravagence ~~wh~~ we doe here represent in figure:[11]

For *Limons* the same directions will serve from which the *Antients* did not (that we find) distinguish them: But of these {there} are very greate Varieties. as 1 the *Vulgar*; 2 *Ligustic*, 3 *St Remus* 4 *Liguriæ Ceriscus* 5 *Pusilla pila* 6 *Caieton* 7 *Amalphitane* 8 The Smale *Limon* of *Calabria* 9 *Lim: a Rive* 10 *Lim: Lauræ* 11 The *Incomparable* 12 The *Imperiale* 13 The *Sweete Limon* 14 The *Lim: Spadifora* or *peare limon* 15 The *Rhegio Limon* 16 Lim: Racemosus 17 The *Striated Limons* of severall sorts. 18 The *Shardonian Lim* 19 The *Rosolin* 20 The *Sbardonian lim* 21 The *Barbados*: 22 The *Scabious lim* 23 The *Lim:*

10. **[Margin note]** num: 46

11. **[Margin note]** v: Hesp: p: Cit: 77. [Evelyn refers to a figure in Giovanni Battista Ferrari, 1584–1655, *Hesperides, sive, De malorum aureorum cultura et usu libri quattuor*, Rome, 1646.]

Citatus, whereoff some *tamquam in utero matris* 25 The Wild *Citratus* 26 The *Ponzinus* of 4 severall kinds. 27 The *Spongy Limon* 28 *Pomum Paradisi* 29 The *Pome Adams* of various Sorts. 30 The Lumia of 5 sorts. 31 The *Lima* of 5 sorts where of there is one called the *monstrosa* & is exposed in this figure:[12]

We may farther observe for the propagation of this plant, that the *Limon* is not altogether so tender & delicate as the *Citron*; notwithstanding it is seldome raised of Seedes, or succeedes so well; for, besides that some have no seede at all, they come not up so ~~well~~ {freely}; & therefore the best way to worke upon this ~~plant~~ tree is by Inoculating it into an *Orange* stock: They do also thrive best against the Wall; however they may be kept in Cases & removed into the *Conserve*: In the Warmer *Climes* they forme them into *Espaliers* ~~& Palisade hedges~~ {& Palisades}, clipping them into beautifull thick hedges; once in 10 dayes irrigated; & if two woody, pruned, but this sparingly, especialy of the greater branches; ~~because~~ least they run into gumm, & bleede to their prejudice. In *Florence* they ~~dung~~ {soile} them twise a yeare, *Spring* & *Autumne* with a compost made with Pidgeons or sheepes dung: {treating them ~~so~~ as the *Citrons*} and so they ripen about *November*. Concerning *Oranges*, the propagation & government of them is now become more familiar amongst our **[page 268]** Gardiners of note. We have heard they were first brought into ~~our Country~~ England, & Planted at *Bedington* in our deare Country of *Surry* by that worthy lover of all *Hortulane* amenities. *Sr: Nicholas Carew* {about the R: of Q: Eliz} where they yet remaine planted in the Earth, almost as faire trees as you shall see in any part of South *France*, not excepting *Province* itselfe, & very full bearers: But into *Europ* they were first ~~imported~~ {translated} out of the *Iland* of *Cyprus* {or rather Carthage} & called *Malam punica* {as well as *Granades*}. They Flower about *May* & fall wonderfully, & therefore are to be diligently gathered for the composition of Water, & many excellent perfurmes, wherein they are {precious} ingredients, before they perish: and also the immature Fruites, to be treated as we shall shew hereafter: ~~They~~ For it is two yeares before they[13] arive to maturitie, & by that ~~spa~~ intervall the trees become so charged, that no lesse then 4000 *Oranges* have at *St Remie* neare *Genoa* bin gathered from one tree, and yet produce them with so little detriment to the stock, that the tree will last 200 yeares.

> *æternum genus, immortalis origo*
> *Et Species æterna quidem. Stirps Citria longum*
> *Ipsa manet, Sæcla exuperans, et jungere sæclis*
> *Sæcla parans: Trunco Extincto mox surgit et alter.*
> *Inde alter: Victrixque diu sua robora servat*
> Pontanus: [*De Hort. Hesp.* 1.147]

Of these we have seene above 12 foote high betweene *Rome* and *Naples* & almost excorticated through age, yet burthened with an ~~numerous~~ {innumerable} progenie. They are likewise of various kinds. 1. The *Vulgar.* 2 The *Orange without pepins* of 3 sorts: 3 The *Crisp leaved Or:* 4 The *dubble flowered Orange.* 5 The *Stellatum:* 6 The Rosy Orange. 7 The *Virgutum or slushed* Orange: 8 The *Striatum.* 9 The *Greate bellied or Foeti-*

---

12. **[Margin note]** vide: fig: 337. Hesp: [Ferrari, *Hesperides*]
13. **[Margin note]** c: 3. L: 3.

ferrum 10 The *Hermaphrodite* 11 The *Callous* 12 The *Horned Orange* 13 The *Crooked Or:*
14 The *Citratum.* 15 The *Olysipon or Lisbo Orange* 16 The Philippine of 5 sorts. 17 The
China Or:[14] 18 The *Sweete rind Or* 19 The *Gigantine* whose figure we here exhibit[15] as
it gro{e}wes at *Naples* in the Garden of the *Marquesse de Cardenas* few yeares since.[16]
{Now for as much as the China Orange has so mightily obtained of late yeares tho
now a pure dignity, but to infinite improvement motivated in the barbd etc, I will
relate how it first came into Europ as I heard it from the mouth of that noble person
el conde de Cardel Mellian etc} Now the *Orange* tree is not so impatient of Cold &
the mutations of the aire & soile as many curious plants are, but is denison'd in our
Country with lesse care & stirr **[page 269]** then usualy we imagine (we have in the
former chapter spoken somewhat to this poynt) provided we cocker him not over
indulgently at first: They are elevated by seedes in good mould, such as we prescribed
for the *Citron*; but they produce onely wild and agrest fruite, ~~unless~~ & that not till
12. or 15. yeares unlesse they be timely Innocullated, or graffed by approch; by both
which expedients they come to perfection; ~~being~~ the stock being 3. or 4. yeares groth:
Neither are they ~~min~~ multiplied of cuttings as the *Citrons* are; but they may be gov-

---

14. **[Margin note]** ~~here insert the Count de Cardelle Melian storys~~

15. **[Margin note]** V. Hesp: 439. [Ferrari, *Hesperides*]

16. **[Insertion on separate piece of paper]** They do in Italy innoculate them
upon a wild ~~sort~~ {stock} cald the Adamo, which {raised by Seedes} they purge of all
the small twigs, ~~leave~~ budds & spines chosing the even & straite, plant them after
2 yeares at more distance in rich earth exposd to the Sunn. & being about the bignesse
of ones finger then they innoculate in the season of innoculating ~~which the Italians
expresse~~ ~~{that is as the}~~ {as the Italians expresse it} quando L'albero va in amore, when
the Tree is in love: & they hold that what you innoculate should be from a worse into
a better, & not (as in other fruits) a better into a worse: for example The Limon in
the Citron, not e contra: but both do well in the Adamo, & ordinary Orange; & the
reason is because they ~~trim~~ {hold the} stock inriches it, & therefore they also bare the
stock of leaves & branches that it may enjoy the whole juice:

But I have found a very exquisite way of propagating these fruites by layers; Thus
choose a branch of any bearing tree Orange, Lemon or Citron; & without cutting it
from the trunk, in a fitting place wrap a piece of leather of the bredth of your finger
about it, & marke out the bark with your your [*sic*] knife as deepe as the wood, then
taking off your leather peele out the barke & immediately ~~put~~ {apply} your leather
in the void or peeled place which bind fast on with waxed pack-threid: then lay your
branch thus ~~fit~~ prepared through a large layer pott with **[continued on verso]** excellent earth, & set upon this a vessell or glasse of insolatd water which with a tong
may continually drop (but very easily) upon the earth, suppling it when empty, as also
the holow with fresh earth which that dropping causes, & at end of 6 moneths it will
strike rootes, ~~which~~ & then ~~cutt~~ seperating it from the mother you may plant it in
good earth, & it will produce fruite in a ~~moneth~~ yeare after: The S[e]ason to lay is in
march that it may be redy in September, or vice versa: but if thus it be not taken, let
it alone till March following, which is the more certaine. By this way of stilicidium I
have knowne small Twigs of Citron & limons with their leafe onely which leafe has
ben interrd to a third part with the twig that bore it.

ernd well in cases, or planted neere the Wall (not displai'd & nailed) in plaine Earth 10 foote a sunder and 5 {or 6} foote from the ~~Wall~~ Foundation: Such a Wall would be 17 or 18 foote high, built against a southern aspect; and at 12 foote distance would we have a range of Pilars {or pilasters} 14 foote in height, & 7 foote ~~the inter~~ the *Inter-columnations*, over these an Architrave, to support the *Cheverons* or *Rafters* upon which to lay the boards, which are to be wrought so as to lap a little over each other to keepe out the aire & so to be fastned at the extreames upon pinns that they may be taken off & removed at pleasure: so in like manner, let the Pilasters stand tennon'd in Socketts & Mortices made ~~of~~ {in} stone, ~~ev~~ almost even with the *area* of the Walke to be taken away & removed with the reste of this wooden tabernacle when the Season invites: but in the interim to be shutt up with dores at every Intervall, in which dores there should be overtures made like windoes, & covered with Canvasse, oyled paper, Cloth, ~~or~~ Glasse or Matt [17] according ~~to the~~ as the weather requires. For thus they shall stand in a Conserve without being at all removed & disturbed, may be ~~ventilated~~ {aired} & refreshed with the naturall showers & ventilations, and when the spring is entered, the {whole} contigration removed, you have your Orange Grove in its genuine perfection; for so according to the breadth & amplitude of the Conserve may you multiplie the ranges of trees as you please: Such a ~~Plantation~~ {*Cedrarie*} ~~of~~ as this, we once saw in a Curious Garden at *Vincenza*, ~~which~~ where the trees were all arched over in manner of a ~~Cradle~~ {Galery}, the {pendulous} fruite adorning the florid roofe, for neere a thousand paces, & which we beheld with a ravishing admiration. {Cf how treated at Versailes:} You may for prevention of all accidents, build & place stones at every 6t or 8th tree, and lay a Coverlett of reede or matt, made into moveable pannells, ~~where the roofe~~ under neath the roofe withinside, before you clap on the boards: Amongst these you may also ~~place~~ {set} your Cases, for some would be to remove, to ~~set in the~~ place in the *Porticos* **[page 270]** *Halls* & Romes [*sic*] of entertainement, when they are full & proude of their flowers to perfume the aire, & for their beauty: But for these effects, the *Dwarfe* ~~tr~~ Trees doe best, & such as we have out of *China* & the *Indies*. These cases would be dressed with the compost before mentioned, about *Autumne*, lightly stirring the mould about them, & adding frequent irrigation; afterwards it will be sufficient to give them drinke once a moneth & more sparingly about *Aprill* & *May*; for then they begin to flower, & too much moysture renders the blossomes extreamely caduc & deciduous before the fruit be well knitt; but by this we intend the hand refreshings, not the *Celestiall*; For at other times, *Orange trees* should {not} be kept {over} moyst ~~even in the midst of Winter~~ unlesse the Season be ~~extrea~~ {very dry} ~~the most vigorous~~; then not till the frost be ~~over~~ {well} spent. They would not be pruned above once in three yeares; neither do they it oftner in *Italy*, unlesse some dead branch require it: {The Season {for Citrons} is Aprill before they spring, else let it alone till next yeare, wax what you cutt, let them not run up to high:} Two gatherings are made of this golden Fruite, the one, when they are ripe, another, whilst they are yet greene, immature & very smale, as being {then} fittest for condiments when they are gathered 6 moneths before they be ripe. After a yeares hanging, they ~~loose~~ {impaire} of their goodnesse: But thus governd, the Orange is of all {other} trees the perfectest Emblem of a good man, according ~~to~~ {as} the Psalmist describeth him,

---

17. **[Margin note]** to slide & run {a side} like the french Chassess or frames

quod fructum suum dabit in tempore suo, et folium ejus non defluet:
                                                         1: Psal: 3.4.

for it is never without {ripe} Fruite upon it, and would have avoided the malediction of the *Fig tree*.[18]

After this manner are other choyce shrubbs, perennial greenes, & precious plants to be treated, as the *Persian*, {American} *Gessamine* {*Myrtils*} ~~& Olive~~, *Pistacios*, {*Granads*} *Dates* {etc} for some of which Capps may be framed of straw, or reedes, the Earth covered with[19] *Alga-marina* ~~and~~ {mosse} *Woad* etc: With this note, that what ever comes to be surprized with frost, is not hastily to be ~~re-thawed~~ {~~covered~~} {recovered} by ~~art~~ an artificiall thaw; for that infallibly kills it, not to be covered with reaking dung & litter, which burnes & suffocates; but by a very gratuall ~~heate~~ warmth, or else to abide 'till the frost breakes of itselfe: Unthrashed Barly straw is excellent to cover {with} in winter, and so is Mosse; {Alga-marina, gourd leaves dryd} but chiefly for things that are housed; for being exposd, it is apt to become musty. Also saw dust may be sparsed amongst Tulips, ~~at the beginning of Spring & Auriculus do best abroad all winter~~. Note that the Plant *Aloes* must not have a drop of water during the whole winter, to which in Summer you can hardly give enough.[20] **[Page 271]**

But to proceede with farther directions how he is to house and conserve these rare & Tender Plants against the injuries & rigours of the Weather; to which divers

---

18. **[Insertion on separate piece of paper]** When you set your Oranges in your house which should be about {Mich: or} mid October or as the season invites winds ~~in which~~ the dry berries & the trees dry, stirr the uper mould & cast some horse dung {I like it best when so consum'd as to seift} on it, the Italians use mules as the hotter, yet so as by no meanes to let it touch the stem, & this indeed they do ~~be~~ some time before inclosure that the raines may moisten the plant & wash in the dung: Leave the windoes of your Conserve open some time, that your trees passe not to hastily into extreame: note that if your Orangery be infested with mice or ratts, they will both gnaw your trees, & stench the aire mortaly. ~~These rule~~ {Water moderatly in Winter & not till after frosts; ayre your plants as often as you can. These rules are for all housed plants except Aloes}. They take both fruite & flowers from the Citrons & most tender fruite before they shutt them up: Some cover the Espaliers & wall fruite with Matts made fast to the walls above which on a suddaine they can {furle &} roll up with pullys like a saile & give them the sun, letting them downe againe, & closing the bottom with weights: Others make cases for the standard trees as we do hackles for bee hives & cloth the stemms with long straw onely

19. **[Margin note]** Se cap: 1. num: 49.

20. **[Insertion on separate piece of paper]** This plant so delicate with us, as ~~seld~~ hardly escaping a winter without rotting; growes in the Iland of Jarsey (as also do, severall other rarities) as in its naturall soile; so as I am assured, that in Gardens where there have ben plants at one corner, they have by some seacret running of the fibers under ground come up at a greate distance of them selves, as if the ground had naturaly produced them; happly they would prosper better with us the neerer the Sea: upon this occasion I thinke fit to advise, that our Gardner be tender of housing his Sedum for keeping them close they suffocate & rott sooner then abroad.

of them are exceedingly obnoxious in these *Septentrion* parts, especialy the Citron whereoff we have so largely spoaken. {for Δένδρες μὲν χειμὼν φοβερον κακὸν as Theocritus truely:} In some Countries they house them out of a contrary respect, and {as much} to defend them against the ardours of the Sunn {for shade & estivation} as we from the exertions of the cold & rigours of the Winter: {We reade of a nation (~~amongst~~ whom Alexander conquered) that were constantly wont yearely to burie their fruite bearing trees under the ground to defend them from winter: doubtlesse it was in caves and} For this effect *Caves* naturall or artificialy made within the bowels of the Earth, are preferrable to all other, as needing neither stove, or other ~~vapours~~ calidaries; but then they must not be used whilst they be newly made, nor should they be lined with wales, which ~~too~~ are too moyst, {contract mustinesse} & condense the vapours, which sometimes kills & destroys the plants: {And in our Country where the ayre is moist unlesse in very rocky or sandy hills hardly to be avoided: ~~we reade of a nation yet that were wont constantly to~~} But if the Conserve be to be built, we would not assigne lesse then ~~40 or~~ 50 {or 60} foote for ~~that~~ it: Let it therefore be designed of an oblong forme, of breadth as you will have it more or lesse capacious & magnificent: The height 24 foote {which if for cold may be reduced to halfe}; ~~th~~ with a front at south consisting of a range of ~~Pillars~~ *Colomns* of the wreathed forme & adorned with foliage & *Corinthian* Capitals: Over these may be layd the Architrave of the same order, & upon that, the Rafters, & cover as you are taught[21] unlesse you will have it permanent, (as one indeede our Elysium should ~~have~~ be furnished withall) in which case if the whole structure be of stone {or brick which is best} & arched above, it will be the more stately & magnificent: Such a Conserve did *Salomon* {*de*} *Cause* erect for the *Electors* Incomparable Gardens at *Heidelburge*, & we expresse in the following *Ichonisme*[22] But even let such a Portico have the Intercolumniations ~~ef~~ {at} the South moveable, that it may be the more usefull in ~~the~~ Summer, for to walk in during the excessive heate, & for the greater ornament of the Garden. The Conserve at *Frascati* in *Italy* built in ~~the~~ *Aldobrandinis Villa* is one of the most august & illustrious examples which we can propose for {our} Imitation. It is above 200 foote[23] in length, 30 broade, & 35 in height, all built of hewen stone, & with exact Symmetrie. The Windoes {in dubble rows are above another} cancelled with green barrs, besides they

---

21. **[Insertion on separate piece of paper]** or more commodiously after these dimensions
D: Chaur[?] [Sir John Shaw?]: Greene house
20 yards long:
6 y: broad: {too much}
11 foote high
Windows 2 y brod: & up to the top:
2 foote from the ground
Dore the same widnesse: to the top
Hole for fire 1 y: long: 2 foote
broad: 2 f: deepe:
There are 2 of these under the middle peece within on the doore sides.

22. **[Margin note]** Se: Caus: L: 2: prob: 27.

23. **[Margin note]** above (15) foote too broad for our country:

have shutters of wood, so as the aire & [24]Sun is intromitted & excluded at pleasure,
below, or above: Hither the rarest of the trees are brought into their Winter quarters, & for Hybernation, which are every yeare new **[page 272]** planted as it were in
the ground; a fosse being cutt about the *Ides* of *November* {a yard deepe}; the severall
Trees taken out of their cases with ~~rootes~~ {mould} & all their fibrous rootes somewhat
pared away: Thus ranged the Earth is flung in, & the *area* levelled: It usualy containes
three rowes, which forme an incomparable wood of *Perenniall-greenes*, the choycest
that Nature affordes, & then which, nothing can be more agreable to contemplate at
that season: The two walkes, or passages are 5 foote wide, the tallest are planted in
the middle, & the rest are ranged as they best correspond with one another, & thus
they remaine ~~for~~ during 6 monethes, 'till *Aprill*, when they are (with the same care &
Industrie) taken up & replaced in their cases {& stations} as before: The Conservatory
is so singular, that we could not omitt to present you with the perspective of it.[25]
But, though (as we sayd) this be very magnificent, & for the variety & structure of it
highly worthy the imitation; yet[26] the event dos prove, that it is nothing so natural
& genuine to the plants, which by this meanes being twise removed, are extreamely
prejudiced: And therefore do we much rather {re}commend those temporary Conservatories ~~mentioned~~ {for shade & æstivation} before mentioned, & that of the D: of
Parmas which being built of Timber is covered with boards, and of that capacity, as to
contain severall ranges of Trees, as in an *Ortchard* in the *Quincunx* order. {~~& may also
upon stresse of excessive heate be~~ but the *Ichonisme* will more perfectly describe it.[27]

　　We omitted to advise that a Windoe may be made both at East & West End, {but
to be glazd} very usefull in calme & serene seasons; for at such tymes, the rising Sunn
is very propitious to our Trees. And if (for the comprehending greater store of plants,
especially such as are set in Flower Potts etc) there be benches & shelves *Theatricaly*
placed in degrees one above another, it will be ~~very~~ {exceedingly} convenient: yet so,
as the Gardiner may walke betweene, & about the ranges of the greater Cases: In the
æquinoxial raines if the weather ~~be~~ {prove} seasonable the covering of our moveable
Conserves would be taken away, & when the weather is very propitious & warme
the side shuttings, for the admission of the Sunn & aire: And now for the warming
of your Conserves, the opinions of Gardiners are very differing: ~~for air raine~~ In most,
there are {calidaries &} stoves provided at competent distances, as every 20 foote; &
some in Italy have a fountaine betweene every stove, which playes all the Summer, &
is infinite **[page 273]** infinitely ravishing: We for our owne part would be as sparing
of artificiall warmth as might be {& a well made Repository will not neede it} and
when necessary urged their use; have a large Pan of Coales throughly kindled, & free
of the least Smoake or *nidorous* smell before it were ~~carried~~ {set} in; and then placing
it upon a *Hand-barrow*, have two men carrie it gently about the Conservatory, & betweene [28]the Ranges for an hower at a tyme, & then set it downe, at one extreame,

---

　　24. **[Margin note]** glasse & shades better
　　25. **[Margin note]** v. Hesp. p: 457. [Ferrari, *Hesperides*]
　　26. **[Margin note]** A Conserve of boards ~~lined~~ pitched {& rosind} & lined with
mosse would be very warm.
　　27. **[Margin note]** v. Hesp: p: 462. [Ferrari, *Hesperides*]
　　28. **[Margin note]** Cf: Mr Hook Exp: that ayre is burnt up too much by fire

~~some~~ distant from any tree[29] {for the stove frequently kills the plant that is placd next unto it, & fire & **[continued in margin]** too much heate devoures the naturall life of the ayre}: This don constantly morning & evening, whilst the rigour of the season continues, you will {it} find preferable to all stoves, or artificiall warmings whatsoever: But it will the lesse neede this also if the windoes be well guarded, & closely matted, {with deep bed {stead} matt nailed like tapestry about **[continued in margin]** all the roome, a foote base of deale at bottom & if straw longways under the matt or reede tis the better & culing also reeds which the moisture & frosts will not abide on as upon harder substances} the chinkes of the boards loamed over; especially during the {cold} night, for at other tymes, in the day, whilst the Sun shines, & the winds are at pea~~se~~{ce}, you may ~~Su~~ afford the free aire & Sunn even all winter long; being carefull to shut them up early in the Evenings, & when the Sun inclines to the west: & not open them {~~againe~~} till he visites them againe the next morning: {& thus We know no plant so tender but will abide even the sharpest winter with{out} more adoe:} Moreover you are to take this caution, that in applying the stove, or pan, you strive onely {moderately} to temper, not to heate the aire: for so it keepe {the} water (whereoff a pan full should {be} always placed in the Conserve) from an Icy *pelicule* you neede not feare the tenderest & nicest of your plants. {Though to be more Accurate & compleat, let such a Roome be furnished with such a sealed & graduated Thermometer whose liquor is Sp: of wine **[continued in margin]** This, together with those we have descoursed in the 5. Chap of the 1 Book will be of secure use for the exact knowledge how to govern the stoves etc placed for the {just} attemperm[e]nt of the ayre at all seasons & the best are to be had of our operation of the R.S.}[30]}

 Lastly concerning the precise period for the howsing & carring in your {choyce} Plants & Cases; it cannot be reduced to so certaine {a} rule; because of the uncertaintie of the Season: ~~it selfe~~ And it seemes that our Gardiner neede not be too hasty; since in *Florence* itselfe, they usualy suffer them to indure one or two smale Frosts, the better to fortifie & harden them, e're they remove them ~~into the Conserve; & then they~~ nor yet, are they brought into the Conserve, 'till they have passed some tyme under some lee South Wall, or Portico, from whence they passe into the ~~Store~~ House, but are not totaly imprisoned 'till about *December*; which for us, were too late, by at the least two moneths, & for that there sometymes happens a tirrible frost upon the suddaine, without any previous more gentle, ~~by which we may take warning~~ {admonition}; & therefore, let our *Gardiner* proceede with caution & greate prudence upon this re-

---

 29. **[Margin note]** or make the fire in a pitt sunk 2 foote in the ground {under the} opposed wall of your ~~trees~~ ranges; that it may rather ~~heate~~ warme the ayre upwards & cast it immediately from the coales:

 30. **[Continued on separate piece of paper]** And now I ~~spe mention~~ {speake} Water, some hold that the very placing of Vessells of Water neere tender plants dos avert ~~the frost~~ effects of the frost from them, & by similitude attract the cold to itself; but there being little reason for it we onely mention it

 Tall trees, & warme inclosures are to be reckned amongst the best & most naturall protections of ordinary tender things abroad; as I have found by Myrtils etc: planted in warme thicketts etc. where the wind & frost did not so fiercely penetrate:

marke, and begin to house some of his more tender plants by mid-*October*; but **[page 274]** yet permitting the Windoes to ~~be~~ {stand} open, at least: so long as the weather is anything tollerable; for to imprison them altogether, at once, would ~~extreamely~~ {wonderfully} prejudice them, which as all other things, cannot safely passe from one extreame to another: But if the weather become misty, & that foggs infest the aire, then guard even all the overtures, as sedulously as from the Frosts, for there is nothing more noysome & poysonous to your plants: yet for this, shutters {& sliding chases} of {glass &} oyled paper, Canvasse or the like would be most proper; for even the light dos rejoice them, as long as they may safely enjoy it. ~~And~~ Remember that the plants be drie, & not wett {nor dusty}[31] when first you cary them into the conserve; for ~~that~~ {being wett it} will contract a mouldinesse upon them, which will indanger their lives: Therefore let the remove be upon a very faire {& serene} day; ~~caring~~ bearing them in gently ~~upon~~ {by} {their} barrs & handles, & the potts & lesser Vasas, upon the Hand=barraw betweene two {or rolling ~~the at~~ Truckle if too heavy: c: n: 72. L: 2: C: 1} for feare of concussion. You are to Earth up your choyce *Gilly flowers* before Winter, & may cover them with empty potts that are either bottom-lesse, or having an ample overture at the {inverted} topp: *Auriculus* will abide the ~~ha~~ severest frosts without removing: {if it raine much cover your choyce ones with Glasse} but for more particular directions consult ~~cap~~ our *Kalendarium Hortense*: {where you have a list of all such as require Hyemation in the Conservatory:}[32] The Spring approching give your Conservatory aire & openings by the same ~~degree~~ gradation as you did

---

31. **[Insertion on separate piece of paper]** The preserving of Fruites after the naturall season was ever esteemd a greate & princely ~~dai~~ rarity, so we reade of the perfecting Domitian {Suetonius} with Abricots in September, though it be much controverted & believed to have ben a certaine Tuber. Sir Richard Browne **[insertion indicated but not present]**

32. **[Insertion on separate piece of paper]** Some plants require lesse care as Cistus, young Arbutus Seedlings, Ilix, Geranium, Flos Cardinale, Marum Syriacum: Marocoh etc: which after michaelmas & when frosts begin to be had, may be plungd with their potts in Earth, under sunny walls, & coverd with {perforated} bell-Glasses, dry mosse about them & under the glasse; but now & then take all off, & shew them the ayre, & ~~gla~~ continue till Aprill: If ~~trees be~~ seedlings as young Arbutus, Ilex etc be too tall for the glasses, beehives or hackles {& pyramids} made of reede {or raisin trailes which is best & closed} more coverlits will be best; with {dry cleane} straw ~~ato~~ about the plant; & thus I have seene goodly headed Orange trees secur'd abroad all winter without more trouble: **[Insertion indicated but not present]** Etc:

What ever you find frozen hard abroad {as forgotten to be set in in tyme} never carry in to those artificialy, but let it alone to resolve of itselfe; & neither touch or breath on them or else heape earth up to the bowgs of any tender plant abroad, cover that earth with dung, & then dung with ~~wheate~~ cleane wheate straw, or else then bury the whole plant, it infallibly preserves it: Thus for Myrtils, Oranges & dwarfe varieties, which you would keepe abroad: straw itselfe readily & thick flung on & then covered with a sheete of canvas, & then fastned that the winds disturb it not is as good as any: {dry leaves of gourds are particularly good to cover with, but algamarina incomparable the best of all:}

the shutting up & confinement: ~~of your plants~~ ever remembring to avoyd extreames, & observing the different hardinesses {& educations} of the Plants; ~~If~~ But their utmost ³³ exposure & intire liberty would not universally be granted, till *Aprill* be well entered; & then, if not before Earth up {change} & cherish ~~the~~ your cases, whose exhausted ~~mould~~ & resty mould would now be refreshed exposing them now and then, even during *March* (when the Season is mild,) & the winds ~~at peace~~ {tranquill} to the Æquinoxiall showers, which will exceedingly impregnat & improve them.³⁴ At the end of the {large} *Conservatory* The *Oporotheca* may be made & built like a little Cabinett, well wainscotted & secured from the mice & other Vermine, having onely a Windoe towards the North;³⁵ let it be {furnished &} fitted with shelves ³⁶ & Drawers; A Table, Basketts & other conveniences for the laying up and conserving {of fruites} your Bulbous & other rootes, taken from time to time of the *Coronary Garden*, {& out of the Ortchard:} {Note if both fruite & flower should be gathered at noone {the wind not South} about the new ³⁷ of the Moone in a {dry &} faire day {at noone} & with a soft hand ³⁸ ³⁹ in basketts lind with cotton ⁴⁰}

[Page 275]

---

33. **[Margin note]** Then also brush off the dust & water a little to wash them: Do it in the morning:

34. **[Insertion on separate piece of paper]** But what if for the more naturall conservation of perennial greenes, a Gaden [*sic*] might be so contrived in some hapy spot of it at least & as opportunity may afford ~~whe It~~ as to adventure the choycest plantation of them abroad all the yeare. This is a seacret, but it is to be observed that where you find small chrystall currents & streames runing merrily & reaking (so as we shall see in some parts of that sweete {reaking} river Micham in Surry) you shall seldom ~~see~~ find the Snow to lye a moment unmealted; nor dos the hardest frost concerne the bankes {& ~~meadows~~} about them, but the herbs are even greene & tender: Now such a smoking streame by a sufficient declivity falling brightly into a levell & running into a kind of maze {or spiral line} ~~would doubtlesse~~ with walkes & bankes of 12 or 14 foote wide or wider, would probably, I conceive undoubtedly, ~~pro~~ be very safe for the protection of Myrtils & almost all our tender Greenes, & also draw forth their fragrancys upon all occasions; and I should wish a diversion at the head of such a spring, or at least at command; that this refreshment might be at ~~comm~~ call in some seasons: I conceive ~~it is~~ this warme exalation ~~which~~ {would} preserve the ayre from the keenest impressions of the Winter; & I have observed such places very healthfull, & we have many of them in divers sweete Vales all over England which immediately dissolve the frosts by their ~~heate~~ steames at a competent distance; & a friend of ours has by his Thermometer (which we therefore reccommend to our Gardner to apply that so he may find out how far this influence reaches) measured {the ~~ayre~~ benigne breath of} some ~~of~~ such ~~places~~ {springs} to exceede the warmth of Aprill itselfe:

35. **[Margin note]** Some say west

36. **[Margin note]** as Varro bidds us

37. **[Margin note]** L: Bacon says for keeping best at a decrease: Ex: 626

38. **[Insertion on separate piece of paper]** Our mention~~ing~~ of the glazing ~~of the glazing~~ the Conservatory, recalls to mind what we have ~~heard~~ {reade} of the ~~ol~~ antient Romans practise to preserve some of their rarest shrubbs; & it were worth

a critical Gardners enquiry what fruite trees they were which the Romans received from Cilicia that were so carefully housed even in the clime of Italy? Whither a kind of Zizipha (Iujub) or palmittost and what that speculary stone was wherewithall they enclosed these delights: I do take it for Ising-glasse (though Pancirolla c. 6. say hodie non reperiuntur Speculares) that qualitye of dull light of a dull light of being proper for Windows (as by us still used in shipps, & before pictures) & of divisibility into exceeding thin slivers or flakes of pellucid matter cuncurring all in them both: But for this they used them as we gather from Mart: & Plin:

Poma quod hiberna maturescentia capsa, [*Epigrams* 11.8] where we have the origine of the french chasse, shrine etc

Pallida ne cilicum etc so Mart: L: 8: Ep 14:

Qui Corcyræ vidit pomaria regis etc: ep: 65

'Tis also named Lapis Selenites, Aphroselemus, Arabicus, Sphangites, Speculum Asini, Glacies Mariæ, Se Junius, & if it were not our Muscovy-glasse we are yet to seeke; but doubtlesse our Ising-glasse would do the feate for many purposes both of hyemation, & divers experiments of acceleration: that they had covered walkes of them I have else where noted: Cap: 7.

39. **[Insertion on separate piece of paper]** Walnutts, Filberts etc: kept in ~~Earth~~ earthen potts & ~~po~~ buried; or mingled with dry sand keepes them fresh either to sow or eate.

Greene Figgs to be kept long fresh in greene Gourds stopped: & set in a coole place. These Conserves ~~are mentiond also~~ were cald Opora from ther Autumnal uses Et varios ponit fœtus Autumnus. Virg: Geor: 2. [521]

The {knavish} jeast in Aristophanes shewes its ~~to be~~ {to be} ~~an Ambiguous tearme~~ {antient Signification};

They cald the Fruiterers of old Oporones, which ~~we tearm~~ the Latins tearmd pomarij: They should be built in sweete & airy places which we do not well observe, & commonly destine some obscure corner for the conserve; where as the Romans as Varro shews us, were so curious of them, that they {often} paved them with marble for coolenesse ~~bu~~ & built them towds the north (as we sayd) where there is least {subject to} change & for this Vitruvius also proposes such ~~places~~ situations for ~~them~~ {gathered} fruite, quæ sit a solis cursu aversa. {but the Window may in dry & serene days be opnd sometymes:}

Some put the fruite on lattices {shelves}, so Palladius proscribes, having first dry straw ~~under them~~ or dryd nutt leaves: under them; so also ranged as not to touch but that ayre may flow about them; also every sort apart

Some putt their ~~choicest in large Chests, closed the all~~ on places plastred over with loame & straw & so closd as no ayre can approch them: {during frosts} Barly straw {is best} ~~chaff, & even in~~ some cover the fruite {with matts some} in chaff, & even in the barly itselfe; some in {hay, flower, chalke **[continued in margin]** lime Ashes hanged in smoke covrd with Crabbs, onions some closd up in wax: nay clay as cotonea cf} sand as we shewed, but so as not to touch in any of these **[insertion on separate piece of paper]** also freed from their leaves, & sometymes turnd. Of all which my Ld: Bacon renders this accpt: Cent: 4: Exp: 318: ad: 323.

That in wax {after a moneth} was as greene as at first puting in; but it may tast of the wax: That in smoke wrinkling, dry, soft, yellow: etc: Those in lime & Ashes well mature sweete & yellow, for a smothering heate neither liquifiing nor aresting is best, & truest maturation, therefore this is a usefull experiment: Apples coverd with Crabbs & onions were well matur'd: Those in hay & straw ripen by ~~a knowne~~ {an} experiment known by every boy; but that in straw more: In close boxes they also ripen from the expulsion of ayres; & all these compar'd with other apples of the same kind that lay of themselves, were more sweete & mellow etc: {Cf of preserving in vaccum} In: Ex: 625 etc: he commends vessells filled with fine sand, powdred chalke, meale of fower, dust of Oake wood, or in the Mill etc:

Pepins should be gatherd in the full after Michaelmas to ~~pr~~ keepe them without wrinkles: So onion seede, & other seeds which you would keepe full & plump:

Carrot rootes {Parsnips, Turneps} etc in the sand .S.S.S. cutting off the topps close to the roote, & some of **[continued on verso]** of the small ends of the rootes this don in Octob: or Nov: dry season: & about ~~the~~ Christmas ~~when~~ {if} the ~~tyme is~~ {weather be} open & not frosty, unpacke them againe, & if you will then keepe them longer, pare off the new shooting at top of the roote, & lay them againe as before **[end insertion]** Some have them in Cypresse & Cædar chests, which will certainely give them both smell & tast of wood; some wrap them in dry & sweete mosse & so put them in ~~potts~~ Vessells of Earth: Quinces in ~~wood~~ {cotton} also in ~~ba~~ hampers of chestnutt {well} luted: Varro commends such made of vine twiggs for apples, & that they should be layd in fig leaves si[n]gly:

Sorbe do well in Myrtil leaves & branches which give them a pleasing ~~odor & tast~~ relish. ~~Vines are~~ Grapes are to be hung up in the ceiling {(not opening to north or east) if a warm roome} & then you should wax or pitch the stalke, & so your choyce peares, ~~of the~~ to which happly the Epigramm aludes

Non pyra, quæ lenta pendent religata genista:
{wrap grapes in a paper close & they will hang on the tree very long, & good} but for that the talke of besmaring the twiggs of the trees with the juice of the greene Satyrij, or the touch of ~~green~~ a Lizard; believe it who have tryd: Some pott grapes in stone potts covering them with sand; The antients were wont to make much adoe to preserve the pomegranads, trying many experiments, winding them over with yarns {or threids} & then plunging them in melted gypsum & so letting them hang on the trees, also by ~~putting~~ {hanging} them in new potts exceedingly close, {as in latons well sotherd potts will do well} or pitchd vessells as Varro but we refer these to another place where we ~~expresse~~ treate of conservatories upon another occasion: L: 3. C. 1.

The Medlar must {not} be gathered ~~unripe~~ as long as they will well hang, they {& sorbs} may be kept in fictole vessells, close covered, & putt 2 foote under ground, cherys before sun rising, & some ~~str~~ comend strewing penyroyl under them & S. S. S. & over all hony to exclude all ayre: {I wonder Laurenbergius should mention mercury & Aquafortis for this use} Apples newly covered sprinkled with old wine is sayd will preserve them from wrinkles; & some string them in chapletts & hang {Fruite put into blown bladders (says Cardan, or Aristotle rather) but ~~tis not good~~ tis an error for the ayre will soon corrupt:}

Grapes hung in an empty vessell well stopped, set the vessell in a dry, not moist place, (as we shewed) large cluster by cluster in a very warm roome[.] Some say better in a vessell halfe full of wine, but not to touch the wine:

Thus by putting the stalke into the pith of elder, the elder not touching the fruite others putting the fruit into empty bottles, well stopt, & let down in a well under water **[continued in margin]** or dry grapes {Figgs, cherys, etc} in the stove till the faint water be spent & so keepe for your table all the yeare: they will plump againe in warme water; but gather them at full, very ripe, or so gathered & hung up especially with a little of the old wood to them & hang up {in a warme chamber}; they keepe to almost Easter.

40. **[Insertion on separate piece of paper]** Let the windoes open a moneth, if weake invite the sweate, then shut them, till all is spent, & put no more in till the roome be very cleare, & dry & sweete: let the roome be where it may not freeze, nor be too warme, & when you feare frost cover your frute with straw & upon that {a} wet sheete, closing well the windoes, & touch nothing till the thaw be well past:

CHAP. XVI.

[1]Of Coronary Gardens, Flowers, & rare Plants; how they are to be propagated, governed, and improved; together, with a Catalogue of the Choycest Trees shrubs, plants, Flowers; {with a touch of their Virtues} and how the Gardiner is to keepe his Register [lxxiv]

{For} It is then that Nature rides in Triumph, and gives our *Elysium* the greatest ornament it is capable of, ~~in~~ {or} that indeede the ~~Terrestriall~~ {Earthly} Paradise can boast
{againe} of its ~~perfections~~ {existance} {after all the recherches had bin made for it}
when she paints and enamells her Parterrs Beds, & Embossements with that varietie
of Flowers which then enrich our Coronary Gardens, when escaping from the severest captivity of the hard winter. ~~her~~ She seemes to smile & rejoice at their liberty:
It is a kind of Resurrection from the dead, & the noblest argument of its veracity,
that so many ~~th~~ myriads of seedes {so long} mortified under the asperity of that cold
season, & sowne in dishonour, should now at the sound of the genial Zephyre, rise
up as from their Vrnes & funerals, ~~producing~~ to behold againe that glorious planet
the fountaine of their life & ~~varieties~~ perfection, producing ten thousand varieties, &
glorious beauties perfuming the aire, & ravishing all the senses. So that if at any tyme
the skies fall, & that there is truely a heaven upon earth, it is when these terrestriall
constellations ~~inlighten~~ {illuminate} & adorne it. {in a seasonable Spring

    [2]O ver! o pulchræ ductor pulcherrima gentis
     O Florum Zerxei innumerabilium!}

We have already ~~speaking~~ {spoakin} concerning disposing & plotting of the Ground,
assigned the *Serraglio* for the purpose of our Coronary Garden, {to} be at one of the
Flankes of the Mantion: And in Cap: 10: L: 1· of the mould & soyle the most naturall & productive: [3]And in what went before something in generall serving ~~for~~ {to}

---

   1. **[Margin note]** In the Chap: before you begin to transcribe any flo: Consult
your insertions, & set ~~each~~ Latin names below each flo & plant Alphabeticaly: you
may have them in Rea, etc: Dr: Morison, Cowley
   2. **[Margin note]** Cowley: L: 3. Flora. cap: 3. L: 2.
   3. **[Margin note]** Cap: 4: L: 2.

the raising of Nursery for the furniture of this {sweet} plantation: All which we shall
therefore passe over unrepeated; with this {~~direction~~} onely addition by way of direction, that ~~being~~ having made your Garden fit for their reception, & they of strength
sufficient disposed now to flower; they be transplanted into convenient Beds, Bordures & Compartiments, after moyst and temperat seasons refreshed & shaded for
some daies, till having taken some hold of their new habitation, they now begin to
errect themselves and promise a future selfe preservation. [4]We have likewise in our
chap: of parterrs & Compartiments spoaken somewhat of the formes, dimensions &
qualities of the Beds & Bordures proper for Flowers & *Coronary Gardens*: So as to be
more briefe in what the following particulars may seeme to require. But, because we
pretend **[page 276]** in this present chapter to give the most perfect accomplishment
we are able to the Argument, something more particular must be described.

We have already {likewise} desired that the limites of the *Coronary Garden*
{might} comprehend an entire Flanke of the Mansion, & be subjacent to the ~~lower~~
{collaterall} roomes upon an equal area, & so as to be beheld from all the roomes of
{state} Entertainement, both above & beneath ~~of all~~ that side: ~~If~~ For Example that
the *Parlours* & *Withdrawing* Roomes have easie passage into them, but if this Flanke
be not of a considerable ~~length~~ extent, in such case, our Gardiner is not to confine
himselfe but may amplie fix it discreetely; ~~yet~~ giveing it either square, oblong, or
what other figure best sorts with his fansy: The magnificence of the Owner. Yet, still,
with this Caution, that even herein he exceed not to monstrositie; because of the
immense Subjection, & continual Labour; & for that there would as few under Gardiners & assistants be employed as may be with convenience, least the opportunitie,
& the tempting delices of the flowry furniture, sparkling, like so many gemms in
their eyes, ~~tem~~ from ~~so many~~ *Argus's* transforme them to {so many} *Briarius's*, & you
be risked of the most precious treasure, which the Earth can shew upon all her faire
& spacious bosome: ~~And~~ to this add, that in a *Coronary Garden*, the beds should alwayes be maintained so richly furnished, as that nothing of Earth appeare naked &
which were not perpetually covered with their Enamell, which since ~~to~~ a plott too
immense cannot hope to obtaine, unlesse what is very vulgar be introduced; it ~~will~~
dos argue that there be a mediocrity in the extent & such, {~~in which~~} as the Master
himselfe may take the greatest pleasure to cultivat with his owne hands, be he Prince
or Subject: for even to this was the onely Monarch of all the World destined ~~in~~ before he lost that Innocency. which bereav'd him of so sweete an Employment, & for
which Kings have often {ex}changed their Scepters.

It would seeme but impertinent to ~~bid~~ {advise} our Gardiner {with Columella
& Cato} {to} have a care not to ~~place~~ {situate} his Coronary Garden neere stables
or Barnes, because the chaffe ~~that flies~~ & Atomes of the Straw ~~flies~~ {are dispersed}
from such places, which perforating the flowers with their acute angles are noxious
to Flowers, burning and discolouring them though aplied to the ground in {fitting}
season, it preserves from the Frosts. In Summ, a cleane & open aire is the best which
may be found one the East part of the house, and for a neede on the West, in case the
other be accidentaly over much exposed to the intemperance of that Quarter. Touching the Contrivement of the Ground, it should be exquisitely picked and clensed for
the sharpenesse of stones do many times {mortally} wound the rootes which grow

---

4. **[Margin note]** Cap: 5. L. 2.

amongst them: But for[5] the forme ~~of the~~ & disposition of the Beds, they may be either mixed with parterrs, & Traile-worke & Compartiments {& Grasse plotts}, or be so marshald by themselves as to be brought to an agreable worke: Though (To speake our owne sense) we do least of all affect the planting of Flo: in the Compartiments {or in the knotts}; but all other Intermixtures is gracefull, & if the choyce be well made, extreamely agreable:

[**Page 277**] Let then your Coronary Garden consist {of} Carpet, Environed with bordures, & in some places with larger beds contrived into some decent ~~worke~~ & angular workes with now & then a branch of the Parter for the greater variety, a *specimen* whereoff we have exhibited at the conclusion of this Chapter. These Bordures shall be three ~~& 1/2~~ foote wide {at least}, about the whole Enclosure, next the foote of the Wall; reserved for the taler Flowers & rarer plants: To this succeedes a proportionable Walke, according to the rules [6]given in Chap: 6: and a convenient Fountaine well inriched to Spring up in the Navil of all this Garden, to which the Crosse walkes (which compose the Quarters & {*area coronales*}) may tend. The Beds (~~are~~ {which} made to resemble Embrodered Cushions for thence *Pulvini*) may be 3 f: & 1/2 or 4 foote broade, giving somewhat above a 4th ~~fo~~ to the Path, or Water table, & layed with a decent not excessive swelling; ~~one~~ {8 inches} ~~foote~~ in the middle being sufficient, & then ~~rising~~ declining to within ~~4~~{3} inches of the Walke or Edg, & which may either [7]be determin'd with Spanish Pinke, {Thrift} ~~Frith~~ Box, or best of all with 2 or 3 Inch planke, pitched within & layd in oyle without paintd white, but concerning this consult our 5 Chap:[8] {Sr: F: Bacon speakes of *cumulous* bankes for flo: to be raised in some places for variety, And some such would be contrivd to be carpeted with Cammomile Violets etc:} Now as the environing bordures serve for the taler flo: so these beds for the more humble & lower: The *Coronary Garden* admitting the *Verticulate, Umbeliserat, Corymbiserat, Capitate, Campaniforme, papiforme*, some *Gigantine*, some of the Ordinary stature, Even to the dwarfish {groveling} & abortive, ~~ex Fungus and Mosses~~ so greate is its variety, & so agreable the effect being judiciously disposed & gradulately ranged with dubble & triple orders of Beds & Bordures. Thus if the dubble-stock {~~Irises~~} ~~Calcedoines~~ & Lilies, {Cro: Imperials, Turke-caps} grow next the Walles, let the *Tulip* succeede; with the *Iris, Calcedone, Narcissus, Carnations, Larkes heele* in their *Series* for so likewise they (for the most part) ~~they~~ flower one after another whilst the middle is reserved for the *Primroses, Crocus, Anemonies,* {Ranunculus} *Auriculus* {*Epaticas*, Gentianelles, Hyacinths} and all these interspersed with others, that the Beds appeare furnished at all Seasons, & for which purpose, we referr [9]you to the last Chapter of this second Booke. And here, such as are ~~very~~ {extreamely}

---

5. [**Margin note**] yet some round stones it may be better, for it keepes the ~~soile~~ mould looser & moister, & hinders binding in some grounds:

6. [**Margin note**] Lib: 2.

7. [**Margin note**] Klinker or Flanders brick with Tarre superior to all

8. [**Insertion on separate piece of paper**] But in Italy & hott Countries they frequently make the bedds without rising because it better preserves the moisture & indeede in hott places tis advisable for many other regards, provided they be well & handsomely distinguished by smale edgings of either plants, Klinker, or {some} tonsile plant; since they will only neede stirring, & preserve their forme very elegantly

9. [**Margin note**] C: 21. L: 2.

~~Curious~~ {nice}, have searched into the mysterie how even the very colours may be sorted into the most striking & surprising beauty, & how medled into such shades & alleys, as may best ~~illu~~ set off & illustrate the rest: For to that laudable Curiosity was Sr H: Fanshaw arived as it is recorded by that mirour of all politenesse & order Sr: H: Wotten: for it seemes he so ~~diligently~~ {precisely} observed {& examined} the tinctures & seasons of the Flowers, as at their ~~setting the~~ comming up & blowing; the most inward (which were coevous) were always somewhat darker then the outmost, & so served them for a kind of gentle adumbration, like a piece not of nature but of the most exquisite Art: And to the encouragement of this elegancy, so rich and bountifull has Nature bin, as that from *Christmas* to *Midsomer*, & thenc to **[page 278]** Christmas againe our Coronary Garden may be furnished with flowers suitable to this designe. Of the taler sort of flo: are the *Heliotrops, Holyhocks, Amaranths, Affricane, Lady-bower, Roses,* ~~*Syringa*~~, *French Marigold, Batchelour-buttons, Lichnis, Snapdragon, Stock Gilly-flo: Wale-flo:, Turks-cap, Calcedons, Iris, Larkes heele, Crowne-Imperial, Daffodiles, Lupines, Convolulous,* [*Convolvulus*] *Columbines, Dubble Poppies, Lilys, Marvel of Peru, Campanellas, Digitals, Gladiolus,* ~~etc.~~ *Nasturtium Indicum, Datura;* And if for the heads of bordures, & other remoter parts you think fit to admitt the *Amomum Plinij, Miserion, Laurus tine,* ~~*Laur: Lose*~~ {*Oleander Laur*} *Cerasus, Syringa, Jasmines, Periclymenas* etc: {Some in cases, & ~~others~~ {some} in the ground removeable}

For the middling sort & of lesser stature, *Tulips, Phalangium, Lichnis Constantinop:* ~~*sow-bread*~~ {*cyclamen*}, *Bulbous Violets* ~~*Hepatica*~~, *Star-flower, Crow foote,* ~~*Sow-bread*~~ {*Speculum venus*}, *Cyclamen, Martagon, Fritillaria, Hyacinth, None-such, Rose-Campion, Winter-Wolfe bane, Bee-flo:, Snow flo:, Carnations, Corne flo:, Sweete William, Peony,* etc.

For the lower & innermost beds, *Anemones, Ranunculus, Vernal Safron,* {*Hepatica*}, *Crocus, Auriculus, Primrose, Bellis,* & {~~*Epatica*~~, *sedums*} some of the Mosse etc: All which may be yet more equaly & accurately ranged ~~are~~ {though we} somewhat promiscuously & without respect had to their Colours. ~~because~~ to avoyde prolixitie & to reserve ~~some~~ for our industrious Gardiner.

But before we begin this worke, a special inspection is to be had of the mould, for not that which is the most rich & luxurious will be proper for a *Coronary Garden;* But such as is of a fine, quick, & friable ~~temper~~ {quality} ~~well~~ {yet} apt to be moyst; & such may be composed of loame, cowdung, {or lime & dung} & Sand, proportionably mixed & exceedingly stirred and matured till it be well incorporated, that nothing of the dung, or ponderous domineere: Therefore should it be 2 or 3 yeares exposed, dulcified & evaporated; or to come neer the ~~matt~~ seacret, that a 4th part of the soyle {first dried to powder} be mingled with a 3d of mould, sifted exceedingly fine; For herein the rules of *Columella* egregiously faile: There are some so curious about this particular alone, as to prescribe a peculiar soile for every plant, & which they pretend to compose by reducing the plant to incineration, & then mixing it with the mould. Others set *Tulips* in that which rather incline to a sandy: The *Anemonies* in Earth ~~ma made with~~ mixed with the rotten part of hollow & {of the} old willow trees {& leaves}; which truely we find to be excellent for most flowers, provided it be {sweete} well consumed & incorporated with some ligature that may mainetaine a {fitting} moysture: In Summ, ~~our~~ the Mould of our Coronary Garden ought to consist of an ~~light~~ Earth neither too light, nor heavy, fatt, or leane in extreames for the general: for the excesse of the latter spends the plant, more in luxurious leaves, then in ~~beautifull~~ lovely flowers; & being too meagure, it sterves them for want of nouriture & body, whereas, that which consists of a just & right temperament **[page 279]** restraines the premature luxurie & produces the Flowers in their just proportion, and due Season. That we therefore pronounce the best mould for our flowry bedds, which sitts easiest about the rootes, rendring a facile passage to the tender ~~roo~~ stemns & sproutes, receives the raines & celestial Influences without ingratitude. [10]In a Word, such as *Cato* calls *Tenerrima*, {such as is the first spit deepe under rich pasture where cattle are tetherd} & if this be renewed every 3d or 4th yeare it will [be] much the better: But this we would have done yeare by yeare successively, now one bed, now another, to avoyd disturbing the whole garden at once, & discomposing the order.[11] The Garden, thus plotted and prepared, sow such flo: as you will raise of seedes {during the} Spring & Autumne *Equinox*, or by the begining of Octob: at farthest; The Earth being moderately moyst, & the weather mild, & Moone increasing: But ~~being~~ when rootes are committed to the ground, let it be rather dry, receiving the moysture by degrees. Let your rootes, bulbous or other, be clensed of their disorderly fibers, pulling off the old, dry, & shrivel'd skins. Halfe a foote of sifted mould will suffice for the sowing of ~~smale~~ the smale & minuter seedes: provided it be in Potts, or Cases: & if the seedes are not exeeding ~~erile~~ smale, they may be sowne in rills or even lines, one by one at convenient distance, or else scattered thick by sifting mould over them, & gently clapping it downe with the back of your Spade to settle them the better. {In Autumne towards the approch of winter you may sift or lay a little mature & well ~~disposd~~ qualified Soile to keepe them warme & after 3 yeares take them out of the cases; if of a **[continued in margin]** fitting groth, letting the rest alone from yeare to yeare.} Those beds which have the greatest benefit of shade, reserve for the vernal Season, & keepe them moyst; So likewise must you the rest, shading them a little: and note, that all Seedes may (for the most part) be macerated in water wherein a smale quantitie of *Niter* has bin dissolved, a day or longer, according to their severall hardnesses & drinesse: Being come up, & appearing you shall extirpate the wild & degenerate, reserving onely the most likely: But of these more ~~particularly~~ in what followes. For we are now come to speake of Flowers in particular, in which yet, it is not to be expected we should importune our Gardiner either with their accurate descriptions, or ~~multitudes~~ {varieties}, which are as the starrs in Heaven for multitude: {& were but to deflower the Herballs of **[continued in margin]** which our Nation is better stored then any of Europ:} our intention being onely to give instance in some of the most rare, and such as are frequently cultivated, and adorne the most illustrious

---

10. **[Margin note]** de R. R. c. 15

11. **[Insertion on separate piece of paper]** & ~~in~~ {let} this worke be don in a dry season {taking up} those first, which blew first as {the smallest} Narcissus, & do it with care that you wound not the bulbs or rootes for which cause when you have stirrd the mould, take them up with a large wodden spoone, & your left hand to assist it, that none of them escape, which are to be ~~put t~~ spread in a dry roome, & {then} the rarest kinds, as Giunchilias etc: rapped in papers till you set them, & not till then seperating the offspring: But Anemones would anualy be taken up, as being more obnoxious to putrefaction by long standing: Ranunclus sooner even so soone as the leaves are drye; & would be preserved in dry sand in boxes[.] Other rootes may be planted as soone as taken out & that the mould is refreshed: all these about Autumn, but of these more particulars anon:

Gardens with their beauties, {&} by which, this Chapter will (we hope) want nothing which ~~can~~ may contribute to ~~t~~ its accommplishment. But first we are to understand a Plant to be a mixt Body, of a middle nature, & consisting of severall parts, may be divided into Perfect and the Imperfect; {of a} Woody, or more soft & tender substance: The Woody are of 6 sorts: 1 *Fibrous*, 2 *Ligamentous*, 3 *Bulbous*, 4 *Tuberous*, 5 *Carnous*, 6 *Joyntie*. Of these, some are Trees, as the *Oake, Pine, Cypresse*, etc: Some Bushes, as the *Box, Cytisus*, {*Myrtil*}, *Jasmine*, etc. Some Shrubbs, as the *Clematis, Hysop, Arbrotanum* etc: 1 The *Fibrous* are such as have their rootes thin, small & stringy ~~lik~~ resembling little threads: Such as the *Cyanus, Hepatica*, etc. {These may be **[continued in margin]** if they retaine the fibers & let stand in the ground longest without removing:} **[page 280]** 2 The *Ligamentous* whose rootes ~~are~~ consist of a grosser Substance, like to {~~th~~} ~~smaler~~ cords or ligaments, shorter & longer, such as the *Asphodells, Ranunculus*. 3 The *Bulbous* have fibrous rootes or ligaments joyned to the Onion-like {& globous} rootes ~~circumvolved &~~ compasd & circumvolved with ~~smale~~ {thin &} skins {as the *Tulip* etc} some onely excepted which are invested with scales, as *Hyacinths*, {*Lillys*}, *Iris*, etc. 4 The *Tuberus* have fibers also with ligaments like the other, a little ~~round globous~~ {round}, browne & roussett of colour for the most part, without either skin or scale {considerable &} emitting severall stalkes ~~upon~~ {from} the same roote in which it differs from the *Bulbus* ~~whi~~ that has but one, as the *Anemonie, Serpentaria* etc. 5 The *Carnous* or fleshy have their rootes long round and sharp, out of which grow some few fibers, ~~like the~~ most conspicuous in the *Reddish, Malow* etc. 6 Lastly the *Joyntie* have also fibrous, ~~&~~ thick ~~rootes~~ and extravagant rootes, consisting of severall smalle joynted parts, & such as usualy grow even with the ground, as the *Chameiris* etc. These we denominate in perfect plants {& Anomolous} which result rather from putrefaction {or rather very minute scales} that{n} any other way of propagation, & which neither produce flowers nor beare {conspicuous} Seedes, ~~so as~~ of which ranke are divers *Mosses, Funguses, Coralls*, ~~&~~ *Sponges* etc. Now rootes of all sorts should be planted for the most part at a span distant, none neerer then the span of 4 fingers: Or else they may be set in potts & Cases, whereof the first may be sunke into the beds to the brimm, and ranged at pleasure, & as they best become their stations; but the spaces & Intervalls may be filled with other Flowers to hide that *vacu~~um~~* {*ities*}: But in the naked Beds they are to be ranged as before we shewed, & that without detriment one to another: ~~and yet it hath bin~~ unlesse experience demonstrat the prejudice; for it has bin observed by some, that the *Ranunculus*, dos scorch ~~the~~ {depredate} & impaire the *Anemonie*,[12] and that the *Spanish Nar[c]issus* and the Tulip are inhospitable plants *inimica inter se*, and affecting to dwell by themselves, & for which cause once would assigne the more curious to Beds aparte: which that it may be don in order & exact method. The *French* have invented a Frame of Wood ~~made~~ contrived like a *lattice*, every square of competent dimension, this they presse edgewise upon the Bed, & where the impression remaines, there make the holes: Others being ~~framed~~ formed of flatt ~~teeth~~ & blount teeth in manner of a rake, yet so redubled as to stand in the *Quincunx*, make severall holes at once: But of these, See Chap: 1: num:[13] 22· 23. *Bulbous* Rootes (which truely are commonly the most rare of the *Coronary Garden*) should

---

12. **[Margin note]** the reason Se: Lo: Bacon cent: 5. nat hist:
13. **[Margin note]** L: 2:

be set somewhat deeper then other, especially the *Narcissus & Exoticks*: over all these strew fine, sifted mould till the Holes become even with the Beds: Other rootes, as the *Tuberous* etc: are better to be spread in a smale & shallow fosse, made halfe a foote wide; or else they may be ranged **[page 281]** ~~with~~ {by} the line, & Planted with the *dibber*, & without more trouble then marking their Spaces with the Compasse: Such as you dispose in Potts may be covered with 4 or 5 fingers over, a little ~~em~~ rising in the middle, but by no meanes plunge them in hastily, least you breake & impaire the brittle rootes. Lastly, shade them sometime till the leaves begin to appeare, and re-member to keepe the bottomes of the potts a little hollow,[14] setting them upon stone or pedistall that the water may enjoy a freer passage. {But if any impetuous stormes surprise your potts ~~when the flo: is spent~~ and too much drench them as often hap-pens both in spring & Summer: either cary them into coverts or prevent it by leaving them upon their sides: But when the Flower is spent, least the rootes burne. Set them in shady places, both pots & cases, as in some Portico etc: where yet they may enjoy the aire.} You may plant your rootes in *September* generaly after a convenient raine; yet not whilst the ground is oversobby & untractable for feare they rott, before they roote: In excessive dry Seasons you may irrigate them a little weekely, & that whilst yet in flower; but then are they to be placed in the shade: nor may you breake of the leaves & stalkes, least you too much exhaust the spirits. {But if you be minded to leave the roote in the ground longer then the yeare above September you may discover them without loosing the onion & with a decoction of *Lupines* (so as to hinder their sprouting) mixed with **[continued in margin]** the earth you tooke out with some fresh mould added[.] cover your rootes againe & the surface of the bed with a little fine mould moderatly soiled[.] This is excellent for the rootes & greatly improves the Gilyflo:} The curious φώτοφιλοι are very accurate in the election of their Seedes that it be the ofspring of the strongest, fairest & most ilustrious Plants, seing *Forte creantur fortibus et bonis.*

Therefore to preserve that which is finest & most volatile, Spread a Cloath under the flower, such as the *viola Peruviana, Nasturtium Indicum* etc, for as long as it sticks, it is immature, & so soone as 'tis ripe it falles & looses, so the *Rosemarie* etc: Some againe is to be gathered before it be altogether ripe, & finish its maturitye being hanged up in the conserve. To have Seede then which is excellent & genial, bare the stalkes of all superfluous huskes, & when they seeme to be surcharged, that the remainder may be perfect indeede: & then gather it, when the Pods begin to gape: & to speake for their delivery. But some advise that the pods of the *Gily-flo:* should stand till the end of October, and then onely to cutt the *Spindles* & hang them up till the Spring: Re-member that your gathering Season be dry, & esteeme that for your choycest Seede, which resides at the bottome, is most ponderous & solid, ~~wh~~ which ~~se~~ reserve carefuly in Boxes apart [15]as you are taught cap: 4: *Bulbous* & some other rootes may likewise be propagated by *Offsetts & Appendices*, after the Mother Roote has layn interred 3· or 4 yeares:[16] and these are produced in greater aboundance if the bottome & *Fibrous*

---

14. **[Margin note]** Strewing gravely pibbles underneth rather then oyster shells which flatt:

15. **[Margin note]** Lib: 2.

16. **[Margin note]** for the longer the more you will have, but the oftner you

part of the roote be slightly vulnerated with your naile, a little dust {or Sand} strewd upon the wound: {this may be prevented if you goe so deepe as to put your hand under:} But since this may indanger it, spare your choycest: {About mid June you may uncover any Bulbus roote, & take the offsett, the roote removed **[continued in margin]** & cover againe with fresh earth:} By about mid-*July*, or *St James tyde* you may take up your Onions, & separate their *Offsetts*, clensed {the fibrous strings cutt off} & kept in some fresh, yet dry place, & not in boxes, but rather {hang them up} in bushells, to prevent their moulding: Do this immediately ~~by no~~ {at no hand} leaving them alnight abroad, for the Raine & the deaw will corrupt them: but before you thus basket them, let them be spread on the floore 2· or 3· dayes, to aire, & sweate. Some preserve them in fine Sand, & it is allowable provided it be not moyst: **[page 282]** they will themselves discover best when it is time to put them againe in the Ground; For then you shall perceive them to germinate & put forth: But if they are sent you from far distant places, committ them not immediately to the Earth, though the Season invite, till you have ~~sprea~~ exposed them 2 or 3 dayes upon a table, & that they are refreshed: {If you find any perished rootes, *ense residendum* cutt it out to the quick, & cast sand on it **[continued in margin]** Bulbous rootes that are carnous and soft would be coverd with sand or a little moyst earth; such as the Fritellaria least, they shrivell & chap: {Bulbous rootes generally should have their earth and bed renewed every 3d yeare or 4th: laying the best & richest beneath & the naturals immediately about them.}} Other rootes may be replanted as soon as they are taken up as the *Gilflo*: etc, & that twise every yeare at *Autumne* & *Spring*: ~~And these rules may suffice for all the Generall, we descend now to the particulars:~~ Lastly, Flowers are also propagated by Purchase, gift, & Exchange; which, that you may the better secure, if the Season be not proper for Transplantation; ~~pre~~ thus prevent the deceipt thus: Cutt two pieces of a Card into competent squares (or rather a little oblong,[)] & about halfe inch in breadth, & joyning the pieces together, passe a needle & thread through them at two places; So as opening & separating the parts of the cardes, the stalke may be comprehended betweene them: but first you must seale with Spanish wax the uttmost part of the threid, ~~drawne~~ for that purpose drawne close to the outmost Card, then lay the Cards gently about the stalke, and drawing the two ends of the threid tye them very close with a dubble knott, which cutt off as close as possibly you can: But this *Ichonisme* will best expresse it.

[illustration, see Fig. 67]

And these Rules may suffice for the Generall, we descend now to the Particulars. And first of the *Tulip*; because it is the pearle of our *Coronary Garden*, a compendium of all that is rare & lively, & absolutely ~~greatest~~ {the most stupendious} ornament of the terrestrial Paradise, created there before the Sun it selfe to whom yet, she has ~~bin~~ since bin so much obliged for her beauty & perfections: {Here review & insert Sr T: Hanmers paper: of Tulip}[lxxv]

Tulipa

---

take up the fairer your flower. And generally most rootes whose stalkes & leaves dye & dwindle in the Summer are to be taken up: præcox Bulbous as the Narcissus should be taken up somewhat earlier then the rest because the showers in Aug ~~inda~~ sometymes indanger them:

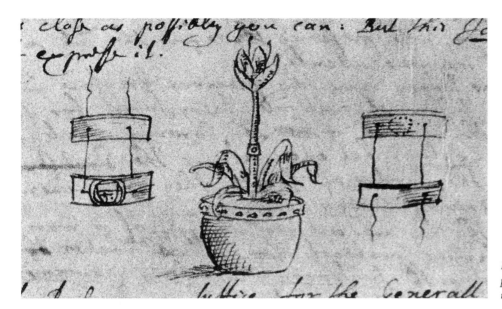

Figure 67. Illustration of a method of tagging a plant obtained out of transplanting season, illustrated in text at page 282.

The *Tulip* is ~~certainely~~ {undoubtedly} the most considerable of Flowers, for even in all the workes of Nature, has the divine Providence established a certaine order of Superioritie: And therefore well do the rest of the Flowry people, Salute the *Tulip* for their prince & Supreame ~~fig~~ since even *Saloman* in all his glory was not cloathed like one of them. To begin then with its Pedigree, as it may be derived from Authors, *Clusius* brings it from the antient *Geles*, but this ~~is an~~ originall as uncertaine as the Country it selfe, **[page 284; page 283 et seq. misnumbered by Evelyn]** we do decline: unlesse as *Berosus* the~~y~~ {Inhabitants} descended from *Sem* the son of *Noah*, whose offspring inhabited *Panonia* & the bankes of *Danubius*, whither it is possible some of these rare flowers might have bin transported; but this cannot be ~~proved~~ averred from their spontaneous & indigene productions, at present, which furnish onely a bastard kind, or rather a Narcissus, ~~as we shall shew more perfectly: so that it is most probable that the Tulip, which we heare meane was~~ Such as *Delcampius*, who favours this opinion, speakes of in *Thrace*, which he names the *Autumnal*, or that of *Persia*. [17]*Monsr: de la Brosse* affirmes that the *Flemings* first brought this precious jewell out of the *Levant*: and there are indeede a vulgar sort: But to be briefe, We cannot find that this ~~br~~ right excellent {& Royall} Tulip appeared in *Europe* 'till about the yeare 1530, which is some 160 yeares since when it was first brought by *Don Lopez Sampayo, Vice-Roy* of the *Eastern Indies* into Portugal as one of the most precious commodities: *Edovardo Barbarossa* a *Portugal Pirate* tells us in his treatise of the *Indies* that they were first ~~se~~ taken notice of in the Ile of *Zeilan*[18] neere *Cape Comorin* and the

---

17. **[Insertion on separate piece of paper]** And surely ~~'tis~~ {Persia is} most likely to have ben ~~its~~ {the} mother of this rare flour: Susa, urbis nota per Historicas et poetas says Grotius, sic dicta ob amœnitatem ex nomine Lilij; quod שושן [Hebrew, shoshan] *Μσα*, as Athenæus notes, whence *Μᾰσινον μύρον* or *χρῖσμα* the famous oyle of lillys, as Theophrastus, Dioscordes, & our Author or 1 Nehem: But whats this to the Tulip? ~~treating~~ hearing the subsequent relation

18. **[Margin note]** & no marvell for ~~it~~ this Iland is thought by some to be the

Golfe of *Bengala*, places well knowne to our Contrimen for ~~an~~ the most pleasant & smiling of the World, & where these, & all other flowers grow in their perfection. And these it seemes were presented to the King, who preferred them before the Gold & the pearles with which they were attended.

And now no sooner came this precious treasure into *Europe* but it was suddainely cultivated, being sought for farr & neere by the Curious of ~~Cor~~ the *Coronary Gardens*: For not onely in *Zeilan*, but even al over the ~~East Indies~~ *Oriental Indies* & the borders of *Ganges* they grow, even to the very confines of *China*. Those of the Levant are (as we sayd) of a more vulgare sort: Busbequius speakes of them, & ~~we~~ {the *French*} recken ~~of~~ them {usualy} of 5 ~~so~~ kinds: as *Boulonnois, Bombia'n, Pergamen: Cretan,* and *Narbonian,* ~~but ther~~ all of them *precoce* & single & nor ~~char~~ variable or indeede comparable to the other, which are sayd in their owne Country to retaine what crownes all perfection, that they cast ~~an~~ {rare} agreable odor which in our colder & lesse benigne Climate degenerates; or is at least hardly discernable in the *Brancion, Aubepine* & *Yellow-Pallot,* which are not altogether inodorus. {Johnson tells us that the rootes preserved in sugar or otherwise dressed become good nourishing meate} Concerning their sorts, they are ~~innumerable, but~~ vulgarly distinguished by *Præcoce* ~~Medi~~ & *Serotim* to some have added the *Medional*. The first of these are wonderfully faire & various, {though lowest in stalke} flourishing about 3 weekes or moneth in perfection before the other: {& are commonly Edgers} The Serotine and Medionall are frequently {Edgers} red & tipt with yellow, or yellow adornd with red, whereoff the best ~~have~~ beare their Crowne in the middle which is perfectly round.

[Page 285] Now Tulips are divers of them raised of Seede, which comes with infinite varietie of Colours, & so as nor art can Imitate, nor truely wordes expresse, especially when Science is applied to the natural production. Another sort of Tulips we ~~ae~~ esteeme the *Panaches* or striped, of which the first and least are the *Paltots* red & yellow, white & red; These ~~are~~ afford 2 classes ~~one~~ whereoff one is more variegated then the other. Likewise is there a second species of *Panaches* which are named the *Morillion,* which is also of two kinds: A 3d sort, ~~na~~ cal'd *Achates,* which likewise are two, the first consisting of two colours onely, the 2d of three & more, very distinct & rare. But the fourth sort of *Panaches* is yet superiour to all the rest, & that we call the *Marquetine,* & consisting sometimes of 4. or .5 distinct colours, ~~& in~~ which is that which the Curious so much search & study, their markes & tinctures being so admirably sorted, & hemmed in as it were with a narrow border or threid, like an imbrodery of silke. There are besides these other sorts of *Tulips* as the *Monster* which is indeede a bold, & rarely coloured Flower, also the *Jaspes,* the markes of whose stone it much resembles, And some that are dubble having to the number of 20 leaves: but we have ~~named~~ {noted} the best. Concerning the Name. The *Turkes* who esteeme no ornament comparable to that of Flowers, have this in veneration above all others, for which reason they adorne their *Turbans* with them when they would appeare in most Splendour: & hence it is, that they have given that name to the Tulip, as the most capital flower: For the word is a compound of *Tul* which imports head, & *Ban,* which signifies a ligature: as who should say [19] Head Band, so that ~~for Euphonia~~ the (p) being

---

old paradise & there is a mount in it that they call Adams hill upon the summit which they shew the vestige of his feete: The Ile is neere etc

19. **[Margin note]** Cf: Co: [Christopher?] Wase:

put for (rb) the result wil be *Tul{i}pan*, {which} *an* ~~are~~ omitted (for the *Euphonia*) we pronounce *Tulip*: But as {for} other particular names and appellations *Gardiners* upon their severall trialls, & fortunate improvements, have gratified their fansys, imposing such as seemed best to accord with the Colours, so as to agree in a certitude from ~~th~~ what we find in our Catalogues, were altogether impossible: For some are for places & some for men, The *Hollander* much affect the giving them the names of their Generals, The French of their Gardiners, & Princes, others of ~~places &~~ kingdoms, as the *Polonoise*{*ian*}, which Ao: *1646* was so much prised in *Holand, Flanders & France*: Some of the *Ladys*, The *Turks* of their *Mistresses*, some of *Painters*, of *Gemms*, Verdures, & whatsoever we ~~esteeme~~ {accoumpt} most estimable in the universe; so that we affirme, it is almost impossible to fix them, or transmitt an universall Catalogue. **[page 286]** Now it is not the quantity of the Colour which renders a Tulip famous, so much as the quality, vivacity, & agreable mixture & position of them, & in the *botomes, strakes* & forme, & of which in Summ, these are the *Transcendents*. That the Colours be 1 even layd, 2 splendid, 3 as perfect & distinct within as without, 4 well placed, that one kill not {& obscure} the other, but add luster rather to it, like a good piece of painting; 5 That the Panashed be long, commencing from the very bottome of the flower, & extending to the brims in forme of a shell: 6: That, if spotted, they pierce the leaves of the flower, 7 & be well seperated from the dashes. 8 that the bottomes be of a celestial azure, 9 the Crownes black in appearance, but darke blew in effect. {To which I joyne **[continued in margin]** an excellent note of Mr: Rea: that the Tamis remaine without change as by which the flo: may be knowne through all the mutations of it as a certaine rule in most of the best flo:} These, & these onely are the most exact & remarkable Characteristicks of ~~an~~ perfect & most accomplished Tulip, {10} adding lastly that the forme be of a reasonable proportion, the ~~leaves~~ {flowers} rather long then short, & the leaves a little reversed & some what *campaniforme* not too globous: finaly that it be borne upon an errect & stately stalke. For thus they adorne our Coronary Gardens with an ~~unimaginable luster~~ {with their majesticke heads}

pinguuntque terras gemmeis honoribus   Maro:

But it is affirmed that there is no tulip which preserves his Colour perfect above one yeare, & that sometimes a rascaly ~~Tulip~~ roote produces a gallant flower, though it survive not long after it. These & the like, we referr ~~fo~~ to the erroneous & at least if by this they intend such as are duly taken out of the ground, which dos rather improve then impaire the flowers: but as for the Seede indeede it never produces that which is exactly alike, but ~~yet~~ peoples our Gardens with incomparable variety. The method is as follows: [20]Choose such Seede as is ripe ~~that~~ {from lusty stalkes} which you shall best discover when the topps do of themselves open & are ready to sow it {as about July} & then laying it a day to dry in the *Conserve*: ~~and~~ Now the Flowers which are observed to produce the best Seede are the Crimson, which hath a little darkish purple violet, or lively incarnadine, that are large at the bottome, blew or white, or ~~a~~ consisting {rather} of a mixture of those two colours together, ~~& that the~~ having the Crowne or

---

20. **[Margin note]** Some advise to ~~let~~ {plant} such as you will retaine the seede of in ~~the~~ sunny exposure, halfe a foote deepe placd to prevent the hasty parching of the rootes ere the seede be mature.

head a little blew or {&} violet-browne The Widdows also produce very faire & good flo: & so dos the white *Serotine*: but note that the *præcox* Tulip Seedes dos frequently bring the *Serotine*. & the *Serotine* the *præcox vice versa*: but here we meane the purple præcox, or purple with white edges, plentifully ~~spe~~ maculated & blew-bottomed, or else the total {& virgin} white, which some do most of all approve having a black or violet fond: {Of the *Medias* the lighter sort, & such as are spotted, blew-botomed or purple such as are some Holias & cloth of silver: excellent. **[Continued in margin]** generaly the more beautiful the better: but merly red & yellow mixtures not good} The Mould shall be naturally good, ~~&~~ {or} if it want inriching let it be pre-par'd a yeare or two before, ~~for~~ to prevent the worme & therefore let it have a quarter part at least of Sand, for a two fatt earth is by no meanes proper; but if it be over dry, a little loame may be admitted, all of them exceedingly well **[page 287]** stirred, & mixed together, & if there be occasion to dresse with compost, that it be well dul-cified & aired before it be applied, & that the more stinking & heady be altogether abhorred, especially *stircus humanum*; for though it dos indeede wonderfully advance the groth of ~~the~~ all Flowers, yet it infects them with so tetrous & ill a sent, as is not to be indured: From the ~~end of~~ commencement of *September* to the end of *October*,[21] the *moone* in full you may {either plant the rootes or} fall to sowing of your Seede, {very thinly that none touch one another; & clensed of the huske} either in cases, or the open bed; but the mould would not ~~be~~ cover them above a finger thick, {for deepe sowing certainely ruines them:} which must be finely sifted over them. Thus committed to the Earth they will begin to peepe ~~in~~ {about} March following, bring-ing first a blade not much unlike a leeke or smale spine of Grasse, the *onion* no biger then a pea, & so increasing yearly: Some of them have produced flo: in 3· or 4 yeares some not till 7 or 8. They must be kept accurately weeded, {& refreshed} & if any shall ~~at~~ happen to rise out of the ground in *June* or *July*, when the leaves are dry sift some good mould over them, else they are in danger of perishing: for ~~which time~~ at this season there are some who advise us to take them up, {the 2d yeare} & clens-ing the *onions* to replant them immediately {in earth varied & refreshed with new} though some not till the middle of *October*. [22]{& thus to do yearly till they flower

---

21. **[Margin note]** all which tyme the seeds onely remaine in pod though gath-ered in August

22. **[Margin note]** every tyme altering the distance, ~~Also~~ & when they flo: re-taine the purple black & best bottoms separated from the vulgar **[continued on separate piece of paper]** It is a good note of Mr Rea, that those young seedling ~~Tul~~ flo: though they come first up but of one colour, yet if some be either brimstone, Haire, Dove, Gredelin, Isabela, Chammay, or any other light or strange Col:, they are to be esteemed: & the males & Selfe-Colours (as he calls them) whose bottoms {begin to} run up into the leaves with well marked colours; not onely their seedes, but their seedlings may produce good flo: etc yearly removing them into different soiles, fresh & variously compounded, sometymes richer, sometimes poorer: the same observe for offsetts: For other rules & Experiments of variation Se: what we have sayd in our Para-graph of ~~Colour~~ Transmutation & Colour: L: 3: c: 1. & for the cure of their infirmities to its proper place: c: 72.

* Tis sayd of the Tulip that the most vulgar of them, the grave before {the bulb}

each tyme at greater distance: **[continued in margin]** noting that none come to beare till they shall force a double leafe.} Now of such as you ~~sowe~~ produce from seede hardly one will resemble the other, which diversitie how it proceedes from the various effects & operations of the Sunn, ~~&~~ Elementarie vertues, & unequal perfection of the Seede in the same *Tulip* shall be handled more at large in Cap: 1. Lib: 3· where we come to examine the abstruce nature of Colours *ex professo*. {The leaves of the præcoce (whilst young) may be discovered from the *Medias* by their leaves standing above ground shewing the small foote stalke, the older do not appeare wholy out of the earth.} Those heads which you do not reserve for Seede, may be pulld, or cutt off {when the flo is fallen} rather that the rootes & *Onions* may increase & amplifie, an indication whereof is the dwindling and shrinking of the Stalke; but when that {sufficiently} appeares, {as commonly about mid-Summer} the ground dry, & the day faire take up your *Onions*, from 7 to eight in the morning, & againe from five in the afternoone, that they be not exposed to the excessive ardours, {or winds} & in doing this worke diligently observe their *Tallies* & committ them to your Register, to avoide confusion when you fall to replanting: {no[w] also separat the looser offsetts} In which interim let them dry {on a table} in the Conserve, & {& for 20 days} sweat out their superfluous humidity {gently}, turning them time after time & peeling the skins from the wounded, {secure them in boxes, & now & **[continued in margin]** then visite them & wipe off the moulding with a dry woollen cotton osburgs:} or else suddainely buring it againe which is the best expedient. Some that are very curious, wrapp up every roote in a particular {dry} paper with the earth adhering to it; ~~and at the tyme of~~ And without dispute it is necessary that they be taken up, & to begin this worke in Season, as about the end of June etc. for if the Autumne prove any thing more wett then ordinary, the[y] are in danger **[page 288]** of perishing, ~~&~~ becomming rotten; & of many other accidents, Especially of plunging themselves so deepe, as hardly to be recovered againe: Besides this, they frequently degenerate {& too much spend themselves in offsetts.} When you will replant your *Tulips* againe let their Beds be new made, ~~&~~ turned, ~~&~~ well-stirred & something varied, {& refreshed} sifted curiously from all {sharp} stones, which many times impeade & wound them in their growing[23] {but note that removes **[continued in margin]** after they have taken roote & shot forth their fibers is dangerous from September to flowering be past, but both in flowers & after (unlesse very) young, you may take them out at pleasure:} The Beds in this frame, & of about ~~2~~ {3} foote & halfe broad, will suffice for 5 {or 6} rankes at 5 Inches Intervall every way, & the holes of the same depth; but the ~~dubble flat~~ Dibber must be made flatt at the topps & not poynted, because of leaving a vacuum, & hindring the earth to sitt close about the rootes. Some that are exact set their best in cases & others pave the beds at bottome; but then let the tiles be so layed that the water may draine away. When you replant your rootes remember to clense

---

~~it~~ naturaly dies (as all this have their stated period) it presents the Owner with admirable variegation; ~~as~~ {& that} all others never so rarely variegated turne of simple Colour before their roote perish: a patient Gardner may observe the event:
* if not already

23. **[Margin note]** best composition is a natural light sandy mould, if too poore mixed with well consumed cow dung perfectly fine & sifted:

the *Onions* of their shriveled & moulded skins, & to pare away {& quicken} the dry fibers at the bottome. But if you leave any in the earth without taking out {which ought not be above 2 years} forgett not to cover them with mould in convenient tyme.[24] Such as you intend to practise upon for the transformation of the Colours, should have their bed apart, & never [25]be suffered to produce offsetts: but of this ~~in cap:~~ hereafter. And as you plant be very mindfull to prick in your *Labells* two inches from the hole, letting about as much appeare out of Ground: making that the most remarkable either in bignesse or shape, which is destind to the head of every Ranke; so as you may say, the 2d, or 3d of such or such a file, & this to be diligently referred to the Register, as you shall anon be instructed: ~~Also~~ taking notice also of the wounded & infirme: {when flowering time approches spread your pavilions over them both to secure them from ~~cold~~ {haile} & nipping nights & scorching days ~~as~~ giving them sun with great discretion & showers as they shall need: ~~after flowering crop off the seede podds of such as you spare not for seed, to maintain the roots in more vigor:~~} The last manner of propagation is by *Off-setts* & *Appendices* which ~~onely never~~ {seldom} varie from their Mothers & Originals, as the Seedes doe; ~~This therefore is the best~~ {unlesse the fault be} very much in the mould, & other like accident as it lately happned to a certaine *Gentleman* who had purchased some rare *Onions* of the famous *Morine* the Elder, at *Paris*: For being put into his bed in his Garden at *Blois*, they came ~~to be~~ up very common flowers, which filled the *Gentleman* with such indignation at *Morine*, that he complaind of the cheate to all who came into his Garden: *Morine* hearing of this, at the next opportunity affirmed the *Onions* to be right, & they ~~had done him no wrong~~ were the same which he saw in flower: withall demanding into what Earth he had ~~set~~ put them; The Gentleman replies, into the best and richest he could make: and th~~ere~~{us} says *Morine* you degenerated your flower, plant them next in ordinary {light} mould, with a mixture of Sand, & expect the product, which he immediately essaied, & found them the next revolution of flowers, as faire & **[page 289]** and perfect as their mothers, whose off spring they truely were. This is a very famous, & true story, ~~&~~ of excellent use, & greately inlightning.

To returne then to our Off-setts, Reserve 2· or 3 beds especially for them, {especially for the widdows which not seldom produce variety:} planting them in a closer order, for these are your Nurseries, & suppletories for the furnishing of such places, as in your beds may not succeede:[26] It shall be necessary to replant these also (in case you take them up) by the end of *August* because they are yet but feeble, or within a fortnight after they have bin out of the ground: But if you resolve to continue them two yeares, let them be carefully covered & weeded. If you would convey a Tulip farr, or remove it at an unseasonable tyme, being taken up as you are taught: {Reserving} Set it in a coole place & plunge it into dry Sand: Or they may be sent in boxes, being severally wrapped up in paper, & sealed up, to preserve them from bruising, & imposture, stuffing the vacuities with mosse that is very drie, & the whole box covered with a Cere-cloth, to defend it from any accidental moysture. Other brittle Rootes,

---

24. **[Margin note]** some in planting mix the colours, others study more accurate composition for lights & shades: others each sort apart

25. **[Margin note]** L: 3. c. 1.

26. **[Margin note]** this with the extracting imbrex: cap: 1. num. 25.

as *Anemonies* etc may be layed in Cotton, & then involud ~~with~~ in paper, those which are more fibrous amongst mosse moistned in a little hony, which will preserve them very ~~moist~~ {fresh}, & yet resist putrifaction; but if the journey be not very long, a little moistned will do well enough. For such plants as you convey in Cuttings, or very feeble rootes, which are obnoxious to drouth, stick them in a little fresh Clay, that has bin temperd with hony involuing the whole packett in fresh mosse as before; but let all Seedes be conveyed as dry & secure as possibly may be. These directions shall suffice to convey your *Onions* even from the very *Indies*.

And now that so renownd and rare a Flower should not be prophan'd or despised, such has bin the reverence {& esteetion} which the *Flemings* & the *Holanders* pay to it, that in the yeare 1637 they had a consultation of making the Tulip a staple commodity, and to commerce with it as ~~for~~ {amongst} *Diamonds* & *Pearles*, & this they had doubt-lesse effected had not the *states-General* by {out of} a politique maxime defended, so as to interdict their publique vendition; & turning the designe to exchange for the most part. The *Virtuosi* & *Life-habbers* in *Flanders* to doe ~~it honour~~ this princely Flower honour, errected a *Confraternitie*, choosing *St* **[page 290]** Dorothy for their *Flora* & *Patronesse*, & when at any time they came to Paragone, & compare these beauties, had a *Syndic* for their *Judge* in all Controversies that might arise in *troque* or otherwise from whom, collegued with fowre whom they called *Notables*, there was no *Appeale*: & this *Confraternity* is yet in high reputation, as consisting of persons of the most noble & agreeable conversation. The Holanders, with lesse ceremonie, have (when their *Tulips* are in perfection,) an Annuall *Festivitie*, where they elect one of the Company to be Judge for the ensuing yeare {, & celebrate their *Floralia* according to their naturall *Genius*[27,28]} What concernes the Disseases of this precious Flower, we referr to its

---

27. **[Margin note]** yet Barlæus has given the flower such an elergy as may ~~justly make all claims to the perfection of~~ be admired Se his Elegiar: L: 3: [Caspar von Baerle, *Poematum pars II, elegiarum et miscellaneorum carminum*, Amsterdam, 1646.]

28. **[Insertion on separate piece of paper]** And it is not for nothing that the flower has above all others ben had in such esteeme, if indeede it were the ~~Sole-marium?~~ Lilly which our B: S: preserved before the Glory of the wisest & most glori-ous King: ~~Certaine it is that~~ The learned indeed observe that under the word Lilly both Greeks & Latins (& therefore more necessarily the Hebrew in which language Mathews Gospell was {first} written) dos containe all kind of beautifull flowers: Thus Virgil: Ecl: 2.[465–467]

Tibi lilia plenis
Ecce ferunt Nymphæ calathis
Manibus dute lilia plenis. & then the Greek their
κρίνον λείριον λίριον as Eustach: Hesych: Suid: Etymol: & Pollux upon Homer & Theoc: Eidyll 19:
Ἢ ποτ ἐκ λειμῶνος ἐυπνέα λείρια κέρτα

And that the Hebrews did not abound with distinctive appellations, may appear by Canticles c. 4. & 5 where some translate Lips like lilies, whereas they rather re-semble roses than lillys: The like Hosea 14. 5. 6. So the Word λευκοιον & Viola do passe for all kinds of beautifull flowers: But somebody (says my Author) borrows novum catoptri genus quod res minnitas ante oculos positos grandescere facit. Hence he jus-

proper *Chapter*, but the Catalogue will follow ~~in the at the end of~~ {before we finish}
this, & at the head of the rest which are most worthy of it. And thus we have don
with the *Tulip* which we have therefore described the more accurately, that such as
have abilities, & are at full leasure, may accomplish the *Coronarie Garden* with all that
may appeare deficient in this chapter & because it would require a volume bigger
then this designe, to descend to all the particulars in the rest: but we would have it
~~don~~ {effected} by an experienced hand & ingenuous spirit. ~~We~~ {We} proceede then
next ~~to~~ {in order more alphabeticall}[29]

The *Crowne Imperial*;[30] whose originall seemes to be neere the Tulip, for we find
them naturaly in Persia not far distant from the Indies, ~~& t~~{w}here he is calld in *Lat:
Lilium Persicum*, though *Byzantium*, ~~also challenge it~~. both common and dubble, loves
a natural fat Soile, rather then artificial. 'Tis propagated by Seedes {ripe endure} or
Bulbs, sowing about *September*: {some think better about mid Sommer or as soone as
ripe} but they will not attaine their perfection till 6 or 7 yeares after: [31]The rootes
would be {yearely} taken out of the Earth about St James-tide and may within a
moneth be replanted, the hole which you find in them a little stopped with a vine
leafe to keepe out the raine from immediately dropping into it. Set it 4 finders [*sic*]
and two spans distant.[32] The ~~Smell~~{ent} of this plant (the roote especially) dos so re-

---

tifies our Saviours comparison of the Tulip with Salomon. *Si per id contemplentur
stamina illa exilia itemque filamenta et fissuras lilij fatebitur nullam humanas {lingua}
illam elegantium illud miraculum efferre ac satis prædicat posse.*

To which may be added two helps: 1 that the lilly of Palestine is sayd to be a
Tulip, which cals back that first sentence; by others to have 30 or 40 flowers in eodem
Thyrso which increaseth the beauty. 2dly, the august ornament of that age in the Eastern parts was to be in white & bright apparell, as neerest the appearance of Angels[.]
Hence tis proposed that the naturall choyce of beautyfull colours is by comparing
the simple colours & mixed with the parallel simple strokes & concerts in Musique;
& every vulgar painter knows, that as in Musique, there are unpleasant discords, but
some by speedy changes sweetned into harmony, So there are some tawdry colours
that may be fringed into beauty, {&} the holy Text will give much authenticall luster to this argument. The choyce of some fansys of eminent **[continued on verso]**
Genius's, & the National peculiarities must be allowed some place in this subject: All
the Esterlings generally affecting raiments & ornaments of Oriental Colours, & would
never have cloathed their men of Sanctity as we do in sullen black like messengers of
darknesse rather then light; but in brighter Colours & more tulip or lilly like: & our
Saviour himself we see allways so painted by them, & Josephs Coate was gay; & ~~all~~
both ~~Turks, Chinese~~ the Tyrians & Assyrians wore {purple &} Scarlet of old ~~&~~ as the
Turkes & Chinese do at present all the most splendid & cheerfull: But let this suffice
What concernes the disseases etc:

29. **[Margin note]** Insert the next page. [See Appendix 8: "Translating of that
part of Morines catalogue . . ."]

30. **[Insertion on separate piece of paper]** is of 4 or 5 Sorts, but the double
& the yellow are the onely rare:

31. **[Margin note]** Cro: Imperial

32. **[Insertion on separate piece of paper]** {Set the offsetts or tubers in a bed

semble the Fox, that it were not possible to distinguish them: nor do we thinke it lesse effectual. {The Hollanders mention using them against all Historicall ~~deseases~~ affects but it dropps a Natur:

[33,34] *Crocus*: came first out of the Easter countries, we derive the name in English from the Arabians: It is of severall kinds & many delicate Colours, both the proper Crocus & the *Colchicum* {~~of~~ & which are above 20 kinds vernal & Autumnall:} ~~The~~ It is indeede commonly purple, ~~&~~ yellow, & whitish blew. Some are double floured & rarely streaked {& chiquerd:} the lesser *mountaine* has a various coloured flower, *Greek, Assyrian, Constantinopolitan, Portugal, Chio, Naples,* & twise flowering:[35] The Cordiall & exhilerating effects are well knowne together with its usefull tincture: They would all be planted 3 fingers deepe & as farr a sunder, being best raised ~~of~~ {by} offsetts: {of which they are wonderfully fertile} but in planting, remember to put the smale eminency which appeares at the side downe wards.[36] The Soile would

---

apart till the 2d yeare, & then plant them among the Tulips where they succeede & will then flower}

Cro: Imperiall

Were this flower as ~~sweete in~~ odorous for smell as glorious for shape & shew

Ad nimium fælix, omnique ex parte beata,

Ni gravis ornatum deduoraret odor.

Cowley 3: L: Flo:

For the sent of this plant: {Some for a year or two have ben sayd to produce above 60 flowers on a stalke,}

~~The plant it amongst the Tulips which succeede them:~~

33. **[Insertion on separate piece of paper]** Colchicum or Meadow Saffron, of which are severall, the double is the best & above all the Agrippina for its delicate strates: There is likewise ~~the~~ other variegated sorts, & the freckled {of Chio which is tender & must be garded from cold & wett, & placed in hott places}, the darke purple, the Versicolor, double purple, & others: plant them in Autume, & are to be taken up when leaves dry: for they loose their fibers,

34. **[Insertion on separate piece of paper]** They love an airy {moyst} place, good ~~earth~~ mould {set} 4 fingers deepe & as far asunder distant & neede not be taken out but for increase: sown they produce varietys with Tulip patience the strip'd vernal yeild best seede, also the greate purple, neapolitan bleu a large flo: strip'd purple, yellow strip'd, flame-coloured, etc: besides the Seedes {in Septr & every 2d yeare removed {to greate distance in light ground & rich:}} the offsetts give variety many tymes

35. **[Insertion on separate piece of paper]** There is besides these the Imperiall, {Regal &} Episcopal, the large white, Mæsiacus, Small ~~purple~~ {& greater} & greatest purple; the purple striped, large yellow, ~~&~~ yellow striped, & Jute: but the rarest & best are the Greate yellow, ~~the plumatus~~ {both} & both the plumatis & they may all be raised of seed with variety of the Mæsiac, & purple flam'd: & for loosing their fibers take up when the leaves turne till Autume

36. **[Margin note]** they do properly best amongst the Tulips: if it were not for the stragly & intangling rashe leavs for which some plant them by the ditch ~~&~~ in ranges mingled as the Colours best sett off

see page 297 **[continued at top of page 297]**
[Page 291]
{Here insert what you found proper
out of Sr: T: Hanmers notes at}^{lxxvi}

Anemone, then which there is nothing beares more varietie of Flowers being raised of
Seedes: Take therefore that of the ~~broadest leaved~~ {latifolian}, & of them the dubble
Orang tawny, {purple pine sky colour} especially the whitish & pale coloured Single or
dubble ^{lxxvii} if they produce Seede: Some most commend the single narrow leaved; Let
it be gatherd ripe, {about May} that is when the *Lanaginous* plush begins to rise of it
selfe at the bottome {& ere the wind blows it away}: Lay it then carefully up for 10 or
12 daies, then rubbing it with a litle dry & soft Sand or earth separate it fully from the
downe: This don, attend not the Spring, but sow it within a moneth of its maturitie,
~~which~~ in potts or cases filled with excellent light mould such as the rotten willow
trees afford in their hollow trunkes, mixed & sifted as we have shewed. In the Earth
scatter your Seedes, {~~not to thick~~ reasonable thick} covering them about {a quarter
of} an Inch deepe, & gently watering it, {with your Aspergating or wett broome}
least you beate them forth, for they must be kept a little moist till they peepe, ~~gi~~ & be
shewed to the Son, 2·or 3 howers {morning} comforting the tender rootes by fresh
mould, {about a moneth after their appearing, gently & often waterd.} till they are
somewhat fortified & about an Inch out of the ground; & therefore in winter, house,
or preserve them from the cold {~~by straw or fearne cast loose over them~~} when their
leaves, wax dry, till Aug: or Sept following, ~~&~~ by which tyme they may be fit to be
planted in your beds: or else {loosely} covering them with straw or ferne, {born on
sticks not to touch the plant} which is as effectual. They beare the 2d or 3d yeare after
sowing, ~~being~~ & then may be transplanted in a well prepared earth ~~not over~~ {moder-
ately} rich,³⁷ b {&} ~~wel~~ expos'd to the Sun, {~~in an airy place:~~} plant them 3 find{g}ers
deepe, at a span distance, watring them at first peeping if the drouth be greate, but
not in Aprill, nor after flowering: {yet at spring:} And in the planting they should
be dextrously handled & not squeezed downe but handsomely spread that the earth
~~ma~~ sit easily about them, their sprouts, being upermost: Let the aspect (as we said)
be airie & ~~well exposd~~ {but yet some shade} otherwise they degenerate & become
abortive, spending all in the {greene} leaves: If the Winter happen to be very moyst,
they be best in large potts, {& so do very young ones} because the water passes more
freely: Some plant them monethly to have flowers often {successively & late, as I have
experimented even in the middle of winter}; but they are short lived, being made too
luxurious: Some would be cutt cloose to the ground, especialy if ~~the~~ you perceive
they degenerate, this likewise corrects their over floridnesse: Every two {or 3} yeares
you may do well to take them out of the ~~earth~~ beds, {not oftner: (yet some are for
every **[continued in margin]** year) & truly in our climat to prevent the snows &
cold thawes a caution not amisse: ~~remember~~ Gardners will, I believe, not soone forget the yeare 1662. However had they bin coverd with 3 or 4 fingers of fine earth, it
had sav'd many thousand lives, & tis good to secure them so before the cold wether:}

---

37. **[Margin note]** or the rich earth layd under & over not next them {such
as is foderd earth under turfe} mixt with sand loame neates dung & lime ashes well
consum'd & mixed.

replanting in Autumn; & removing such as you set in potts into shady places, but in {liberal} ~~a faire aire~~ as airy as you can find ~~whe~~ the flo: being past: & being carefull to preserve them from over much raine: A weeke after you take them up (which may be about mid-July) separate with a knife the young rootes by the parts where they easiest ~~divide~~ sunder, & keepe them {not to} dry {nor too moist}; but if in doing this you indanger their much wounding let them remaine longer cutting out the perished parts which you find in any: & abducing the Cicatrice with a terpentine & wax plaster when it is perfectly drie. When you thus take them up spread them in ~~the~~ {a} dry ~~shade~~ roome for {8 or} ~~to drie~~ 8 or 10 dayes {others put them in sand} and then you may box them up, but plant the smale ones immediately in a vase {4 or} 5 or 6 fingers deepe, & cover them with another empty vessell from the raines: planting the rest about *October* following when the ground is moist & in best temper: This especially **[page 292]** for the Tenuifolia: The Latifolia would rather be exposd to the Sun in Winter, at 3 fingers under earth: which the dubble yellow requires should be somewhat fatter then the rest. But to have them produce flowers where they are {much} infested with Sea-coale smoake is impossible, especially in London unlesse they be planted in the hot bed about mid *January* when the aire is lesse poysonous both to men and this delicate Flower.[38] They came to us first from the Levant.

---

38. **[Insertion on separate piece of paper]** We have indeede sayd September is the best season both for these & Ranunculus, but experience shewes how often they miscarry unlesse the ayre & soile be extreamely agreable, & the winter very favourable both as to cold & raines & therefore about Lond, & {all} inclement places so by situation, or other accident, I hold Jan: to be fittest, & thus you must proceede, raise an hott bed, take then a light sandy loamy Earth not two light; or what is taken out of pastures under the ~~horses~~ turfe immediately (good for all Bulbes & Tuberous rootes which affect not dung) {which cankers them} but naturaly sweete rich Earth) with this earth cover your hott bed 4 inch deepe, on that plant your rootes 5 inch distant, then cover them 2 inch deepe with the same earth; if you thinke it not rich enough strew {rotten} soile upon it that the raines may wash in the vertue: in 9 or 10 days they will roote: whereas being planted in the ordinary way the dry rootes suck in the moysture {so fast} till they burst, & rott {without} ~~without~~ rooting for till they roote, they never shoote upwards; & if they chance to beare ~~the~~ flo: the first yeare, in the next they commonly perish: Therefore in such ~~occasions~~ {places} take them up as soon as don flowering & that the leaves begin to wither, dry & keepe them till next season of planting: in Summ, whenever you find they do not well being planted in Sept: treate them thus: The rule in Jan: is a sure way provided you ~~give~~ allow them fresh earth next the roote, & make the bed 6 or 7 days before you plant that the heate be well qualified: in places where good {naturall} earth is not to be had[,] get the lightest you can, mingle it with cifted {hollow} willow Earth, rotten wood ~~over~~ {amongst} your naturall earth and a little well consum'd neates dung to wash in ~~over~~ {over} all, or in defect horse dung, to make the strike well betimes verte

[Continued on verso] If you plant in Septr: in the open beds, I advise you to therm in hard frosts, as they do in France, but in Eng. you must be sure to give them ayre frequently, else mustynesse destroys them, therefore in wett weather especially expose them all days to the aire, provided it {actually} raine not, & in hard frosts once

{Note that in case a sharp winter much prejudice them, cutt off their first springs to the ground, & they may recover & beare:}[39]

Amaranthus[40]

The *Flower-Gentle* {The noblest of all Annuals} *Heli{o}chrysum:*[41]

> *immortalisque Amaranthe*
> *Et quos milli parit dives natura colores*

whose rutilant & glowing nitor seemes to inflame the Coronary bordures, are best raised by Seedes in the hott bed {springing in a weeke} being an Annuall plant, though it oftentimes sowing it selfe, springs with lesse curiosity if the yeare be favourable: They are best sowen {thinly} in potts {in March} ~~pl~~ of sifted ~~mould~~ {earth}, & placed in the hott bed: but let the mould be thinly sifted over them, & the seedes as thinly

---

a day; & after a ~~thaw~~ {long frost} let a good shower or two wash them at the thaw if it comes to ~~settled~~ settle the Earth, which the frost has made spongy; & then beware of suddaine or long covering: ~~But th~~ Now your planting in Jan: frees you of all that trouble & danger, & the heate of the bed preserves them from frost, without any covering, & the plants peepe not till warmer weather, but if you cover they will come up in a fortnight & be in danger, especially the bed cooling: for all tender plants require moysture & warmth etc

39. **[Insertion on separate piece of paper]** To all these observations we may add that for greate variety the tenuisell simple flo: produces admirable ~~diss~~ flo:: nay sometimes double flo: from whose seede spring the Hermaphrodites etc:

The beds to plant {well} growne rootes in would be of a good depth: the Latifolias would be planted at least a moneth before the other; such whose leaves you find grow suddainely yellow, likely have lost their fibers, & will soone lose themselves unlesse taken up: The broad head rootes should not be separated till they are ready to part of themselves: The more ordinary Flo: may be kept out of ground till almost March: & then some advise to macerate them in warme water 24 houres:

The most rare which one would be stoard with are the Latifolia flo: pleno coccinio variegata & the purpurea: of the tenuifolia the {double} Scarlet: purple, & bleu: also the tenuifolia flo: plane amarantine variegated of Paris, also the Bel–Zizwaire, most tender, & therefore to be looked after with greate care as all the striped must be; to these add the Bel–Rigate, Orlates, Diavolus, Cajetan & Italian flowers, Larviana, Mariana, Melidore Gallatea & infinite others very well & judiciously handled by Mr: Rea, since the penning of this:

40. **[Margin note]** Some remove them to a second hott bed & with clod & all remove them when the violent heate is past & thence in May transplant in place shaded or in open sun, rich ground oft refreshed & so they will also produce good seede. They will also come in the open bed, but not so readily yet well enough **[continued in margin]** The greate purple which are hardy sow in Aprill: lesser purple at Those of divers colours & admirably oriental & shining with that of 3 colours in the H: bed to be set in potts like Gillyflo

41. **[Margin note]** Goldy locks ~~seeded~~ raised with ~~successe~~ greate care: put this last after Amaranthus it being arid.

sprinkled: this don ~~set a~~ set a glasse Bell over the pott: {giving some ayre in the warme gleames & cover at evenings} but do not water them:[42] when they are ready to transplant {usualy will be in about 6 weekes} take them out earth & all & ~~expose~~ {shew} them to the hott Sun, being shaded by the interposition of a Canvasse or mattre{a}sse a little moistned, so as the warmth thereoff may nourish not scorch them, then after five or six days you may expose them boldly:[43] {Ten yeares may be kept} The Seedes of this precious flower ~~may be kept good 10 yeares~~. {if a flower it be [44]lawfull to call it, which ~~calls it self~~ hardly calls it selfe one}[45]

{Here insert what fitts you out of Sr: T: Hanmer notes}[46]

---

42. **[Margin note]** old tufted rootes especially.

43. **[Margin note]** in a moneth more it flowers

44. **[Margin note]** here insert the story of the French Gentleman who gott precious seede on his cloake which ~~the Gar~~ the Neighbour florist would not sell or give:

45. **[Insertion on separate piece of paper]**

Dij non Sanguinem habent, sed quasi Sanguinem,

Dij non Corpora habent, sed quasi Corpora,

Sum Divis similis; non Ego Floribus

Consto, sed quasi Floribus

Cowley: 4: Pla:

46. **[Inserted text at page 298, in Thomas Hanmer's hand?]**

Of Beares Eares or Auriculers.

No flower of account agrees better with our climate then the Auriculer, Wee have the best of this kind certainly in the world, & hundreds of varietyes of very beautifull sweet flowers. ~~These be~~ The most valuable are such as 1 have many large flowers on a head standing close together, & not ragged 2dly that the stalkes or stemmes bee strong and grow high. 3dly that the Eye or bottome of each flower within bee large and pure white, or else of a strong yellow colour, but the white ~~are~~ is most beautifull. 4thly that the colour, of the flower bee new and not ordinary. Wee have only two or three sorts of them with dowble flowers, one whereof is haire colour, the other a dirty cinnamon, the double have no eyes. The single sorts are almost of all colours, and two or three of them strip't as Bugges Nonpareille of a reddish purple strip't with limmon colour, the blew murrey strip't with white, and a cinnamon markt with white.

The proper earth for Auriculars is a rich mold full of rotted dung, their station somewhat shady, their tyme of flowring March & Aprill chiefly, and a little in Autumne. They may bee planted at any tyme, but best in August & September, when the {great} rootes are fittly to bee devided. I choose beds rather then potts to sett them in & little or no housing of the potts, in the beginning of March put rich fresh earth upon that. They grow in about the rootes, up closse to the leaves.

The seed is ripe in June, & best sowed in October and in this manner which is now known to many but was a secret a long tyme.

In October put a foote deepe or more of good rich kitchin garden mold in the bottome of large wooden troughes or earthen pans with holes in them that the water may passe away, then on that earth sift three or fower inches thicke of finer mold mixt with a good deale of very rotten cow dung, and on that an inch or two of sifted willow earth taken from the bodeys of old decayed willowes, kept dry till it be usd,

Auricula ursi Beares-eares is of the nature of the {Paralysis &} *Primula*, infinitely various & therefore greately esteemed, & rarely becomming the flowring embrodery: They are raised, multiplied, & diversified by being sowed in large shallow panns or cases in *October* {September which is better then Spring} in mould made light with the willow earth, sifting it thinly over them, & kept moyst: It will be five or six moneths 'ere they peepe being placed where they may enjoy the morning Sun onely, when they have gotten 2 or 3 leaves as broad as a groate take them up earth & all with a knife, & plant them in lines ~3~ {4} or ~4~ {6} inches distant each from other keeping them daily watered, & then at Spring transplant them into the beds, where you will have them to continue: But if you desire them very faire, rather in Potts:[47] Also do they wonderfully propagate by dividing the rootes, which will easily be separated.[48]

---

presse downe a little with your hand or trowell this willow earth and then having mixt your seed well with some dry sand scatter your seed thin, then searce a little very fine rich earth on the seed only to cover it, all the danger is in covering it too much with earth for if you doe this small seed will never come up. Then set these pans or troughes in your garden to stand abroad in all weathers. **[Insertion continued on another piece of paper at page 298]** all the wynter in some place where they may bee a little shelterd from violent wynds & stormes of raine. In Aprill or the beginning of May they will come up very thicke & small closse to the ground without any stalkes but only with small leaves, in dry weather then water them a little with a very small waterpott & in July or the beginning of August they will be ready to remove into other troughes or beds of rich mold as aforesaid where they may have more roome to spread and grow, & if you please remove them againe before wynter into other such beds where they have yet larger roome to spread in. This is all that is to bee done with them, only let them grow in a shady part of your garden then where much hott sun may shine on them in the sommer following. They will beare their flowers the next spring following, some perhaps sooner if the beginning of wynter bee open & warme. Cast away the yellowes and common flowers, & reserve the best. The ~Seed~ best seed is that of orenge colour or cinnamons or such like with good eyes which is to bee gatherd in the end of July or thereabouts, & kept in the house till October when it is to bee sowed as aforesaid.

47. **[Margin note]** old tufted rootes especially

48. **[Insertion on separate piece of paper]** Mr: Rea, who has most exactly & freely described the culture of this pretty flo: ~advises~ teaches us to cutt of the stake of the Seede Vessell so soone as you perceive a small round hole in the top of it, & ~to~ keeping them upright for feare of sheding, to tie them up in bundles & expose them to the Sun in setting them in some glasse window which will perfect their maturity, then towards the end of Aug: or commencemnet of Sept: to sow them in boxes of 10 inches deepe & competent bredth with ~bares~ {holes} at bottom to draine superfluous moisture, filled 3 parts with fine sandy earth sifted, one halfe of which should be well rotted neats dung, exactly mingled & layd smooth with a trowell, then a finger thicknesse of fine willow earth sifted, on this to sow the seedes mingled with wood ashes, for direction to sow them more suitably by their colour, sow them pretty thick, for all come not up. Then cover them half a finger with the same willow earth etc: & presse them lightly downe, so expose them in the sun & aire till they begin to peepe,

{in March or better end of Aug: {~~they will spring small, the double & hose in hose~~ ~~are pretty, they love shade: The ordinary Cowslip beares no seede but is increased of~~ ~~slips from the roote~~ **[continued in margin]** ~~in spring or autumn, the topps cutt off,~~ ~~& so must you do when they have don blowing & so also order the green cowslip~~ ~~for bordures it is~~}[lxxviii] The oyle thereoff is excellent for wounds, beside inumerable virtues which it containes.

[**Page 293**] *Asphodelus* grow naturally in *Spaine & Italy* is of 7 or 8 kinds,[49] it delights in a rich Soyle & moist, planted 3 fingers deepe & 5 distant to be removed every two yeares. {& when taken up soon replanted} The vertues of this plant are very many in our *Botanists*: but what fewer of them mention, is, that the head shaven & rubbed with the rootes of it makes the haire to come curled for which the *Italian* Gent: much esteeme it, & the same roasted under the embers is a *cosmetique*, rubbing the face with it hott: whereby takes off the scurse & roughnesse & so 'tis used by the *Italian Ladys*: But of the farther perfections of it, reade *Dioscorid*: L: 2: c: 159.

[50]*Aquilegia*, Columbine comes from Seede {sowes itself} in greate & beautifull

---

which may be about Apll: Then remove them into the shade & gently water them now & then when of any considerable bignesse, take those up which prove too thicke, immediately plant them in a ~~bed~~ prepared bed 6 or 8 inch distant, where let them stand till they flower, transplanting the others out you left in the box at the end of Aug: let the bed be reset. His reason (which is good) of this early sowing (contrary to the opinion of some others) is the aptnesse of the seedes decaying if longer kept: To raise varietys procure the seedes of the best flo: ~~Let the place~~[?] Such as the Purple or fair downham, & Mr Goods, Austines, Buggs Whetmore, Fransway, black Imperiall, Rickets, purple stripd, purple & lemon striped; Scaret; Rose colourd, Blushes, most of the Lethercoates which are numerous, some of the white etc: let the beds you plant in rich & not to loamy, somewhat shaded: & in planting open a wide hole leaving a rising in the middle of it, spred the fibers of your rootes upon it & so cover & water it; those that are rarest plant in potts, almost half full of sifted neates dung, the rest good sand earth mixed with the same dung: Set them about the end of May, but not too deepe & place them in the sun all winter covering them with glasses in over wett seasons which is better then housing {& then uncover anew at dryer weath:} & at spring remove them into more shade till they have don blowing: For those in the bedds after mid August take them up every other yeare, refreshing the soile with sifted neats dung: then slip & trim & part the rootes for encrease, & so replace them. Thus for **[continued on verso]** the most ingenious Mr: Rea: To these he adds the ~~white~~ Burrage leavd Auricule somewhat rare {though not of the tribe but name} & to be treated as the flos Cardinalis & the Beares eard Sanicle or Cortusa Mathioli, raisd of seedes & conserved in a pot as the former:

49. **[Margin note]** of which best are the flesh coloured, the large white, the striped the minor & minimus of the same colour, the first of which is tender: But of the Lily kind there is the bloush & white very rare, the yellow more common: & of the day lilly most common of all:

50. **[Insertion on separate piece of paper]** The best are the double inverted, double rose, etc: of greate varietys, but the most rare is the Virginian which if not maintained by fresh seed are apt in time to degenerate:

varieties & dubled, there is no difficulty in raising them, being exposed to the Sun {& good Earth} they flourish wonderfully, {about} & their vertues are knowne by every House-wife. {& may be seperated {the old stock 5 or 6 years &} else continue leaving in the ground: Sow them in Aug: a bordur flo: if too thick they grow single & small. But the large double are propagated by slips rather & are more choyce & rare tender.}

Bellis is that pretty daisie which stares in our faces in a hundred varieties, some of them are of exquisite incarnadines; & ~~deepe and~~ araied in scarlet every leafe being a hollow pipe, & others grow in multitudes upon the same stalke, or daisie upon daisie, {also the large white, & great red & white **[continued in margin]** the double greene & childing} They are easily raised of Seedes, [51]~~and planted or~~ {but best} propagated of rootes, {Spring or Autumn} being divided & planted as the primerose, & doe wonderfully adorne the edges of borders whilst they are in flowers {in May & june} & for the lower embroderie: {it should be removed now & then to preserve the faire, the spring yearly} It is an excellent vulnerary, & by its *Signature* a usefull *Collyrium*.[52]

Canna Indica, {from the roote {or knobb thereoff:}} to be preserved in the Store in Winter: {a case-plant} {it beares flowers:} {& sometimes refreshed with water:}

Διὸς ἄνθος {Se Cowley note p: 238 plan: l: 4:} The Flower of the Gods {or as we call them}

Caryophyllus Carnations are amongst the flowers which[53] are highly esteemed

---

They do well succeed ~~July~~ in the Summer moneths when other flo: are rare: All bring seed, sow in Aprill in your flo: Nursery, & cull the best for your Garden after the 2d yeare that you have seene the flo: every 4 or 5 years tis good to renew them else they degenerate; take onely the best markd flo for seede, & to make that good pinch off the superfluous ~~budds~~ & seeds whose colours please not & that are but of one colour, as most of the best plants will have some

51. **[Margin note]** they must not stand much in the sun unlesse pleasantly watered:

52. **[Insertion on separate piece of paper]** Balsamina Fæmina or the Balsom Apple an Annual to be raised in the hot bed, & then removed & well & often watred in the hott season: ~~it~~

Blattaria or the Moth Mullen annuals & may be raised of Seedes ~~but~~ bearing ~~not the~~ second yeare; such are the greate Yellow & the white: But the purple & the Sweete yellow, ~~all whic~~ may be best propagated by their {seperating}{ed} rootes which are lasting:

53. **[Margin note]** Se Sr T Hanmer notes [at page 298]

Now briefly of Gilliflowers and Auriculars which are the only Fibrous flowers I shall speake of as being the principall.

of Gilliflowers

Mr: Rea hath named {& described} in his booke the best sorts then knowne about London when his ~~booke~~ {worke} was publisht, but there are since more new sorts of great ones, & many very fine ones are raised yearely in Holland & fflanders from whence they are brought to London. The reason that wee raise few large ones in England is because the great kinds seldome perfect their seed with us, the least wett in the end of Sommer spoiling it, but some dry yeares wee may have some good seed, as wee had the last being 1667, and I doubt not but wee may raise as good flowers

both for their aromaticall odor & variety of colours, in which it even emulates the
Tulip it selfe: They are raised either by Seeds or Layers: The Seede is to ~~ge~~ be gatherd
acording to the foregoing rules, {before the raines of Autumne} though some advise that the pods should stand till the end of *October*, & then the stemme being cutt
off, be hanged up in the conserve till spring: But it shall suffice that the ~~gap~~ yawn-
ing huske present it black & dry, & that you reserve that ~~onely~~ chiefly which resides
in the bottome of ~~these~~ {uppermost} Etuies {for the higher most produce single flo:
others say the ~~lower~~ lower most:} That the white Flower commonly produces the
most & best variety is the judgement of most as being *rasa tabula* as it were suscep-
tible of all colours; yet is also the Orange tawny greately commended, & some of the
Speckled; but all of them dubble. If the weather be not too sharpe, you may sow in
mid *Aprill*, but in *Italy* they sowe **[page 294]** in *September* {some in August} when
we frequently transplant them. Sow them ~~in~~ thinly in light {spongy yet rich {& that
rather naturally so}} earth & in cases or secure ⁵⁴Beds, sifting the mould proportionally upon them, kept continually moyst & exposed, as the ~~Amaranth~~ *Auriculas*
to the rising Sun: Within a fortnight being thus treated the will appeare. We have
begun almost a moneth sooner at the increase of *March* & succeeded well; but then
the Season was propitious: when they have put forth fowre or five leaves,⁵⁵ cherish
them by sifting a little fine mould amongst them, & by the end of June, {~~though some
let them alone 3 2 moneths longer~~} being about 4 fingers high you may transplant
them, the Moone also improving; {shade at first} but the very best Season, is, as we
sayd in September, for so they will produce excellent flo: in the yeare following: {Our
owne seede commonly degenerates after 2 years therefore change} They increase likewise so fast from the Slipps & Layers produced of the Mother plants about the end
of *October*, so as you will hardly be able to bestow all your store. But they ought to

---

as they doe abroad when wee have such. There is no difficulty in sowing them or
ordering them afterwards.

Any good rich blacke sifted garden mold will serve the turne, sow them thin, in the
beginning of Aprill, and remove them into the like earth as soone as you can which
will not bee before they have six leaves. Water & weed them well upon **[continued
on another piece of paper at page 298]** removing, & sett them not too thicke, remove them againe into the like earth before Michelmas, & there let them stand abroad
all wynter in beds or cases as you please till they flower. Cast away the small flowerd
ones & preserve the other. The other way of increasing Gilliflowers is by layers, which
is taught by soe many already that I shall omitt it. More dye by the wynds in March
then {all} the ffrosts in wynter, putting of fresh rich mold about the rootes in that
moneth preserves them much, & betters the flowers. The earth from woodstackes,
and where Melons or Cowcumbers have growne the yeare before is very proper for
them. I have had more dye yearely in potts housed then abroad in bedds. Suffer not
too many flowers on one roote, but nip of many of the small ones & cutt downe
many of the spindles to strengthen the roote against wynter, otherwise much bearing
often kills them.

54. **[Margin note crossed out]** or sowed at beginning of March
55. **[Margin note]** for such as put forth but 2 or 3 are commonly single &
little worth

be planted immediately after they are taken off, which if it be at the Full, some affirme they will come dubble; & this would be practised both *Spring* & *Autumne* the
mould well refreshed: But for the choyce & of which you have had experience of
their beauties, set them in large potts, ~~with earth & all~~ & when you take them thence,
let it be with earth & all ~~paring~~ {trimming} away the loose {& stragling {brad topp &
under blades, without leaves}} fibers, & then refresh the potts with excellent mould
mingled with {rotten} cow dung, loame & *oxes-blood* well subdued, & dulcified. {&
which will sift [56]} And then either place the bottome of the pot in a flatt larger vessell
filled with water, {for a while} or ~~let~~ feede it now & then with a *lingula filtrating* the
water *guttatim*.[57] {but not on the leaves, nor do this often, **[continued in margin]**
nor much after Aprill} In the winter you must be carefull to house your choycest
plants & layers to keepe them from the frosts & snow especialy[58] ~~or co~~ & comfort
them with exquisitely macerated dous-dongue, mingled with ~~so~~ mould & watring
them with its infusion: {or in water in which ~~flesh~~ flesh Rus has ben worked.} But
you shall not neede to be over indulgent to them, for so they are preserved from
the bitter winds {snow} & extreame severity of the weather, they shall hardly neede
the stove.[59] {which they abhorr as above all places most affecting free ayre if you do
store them now & then in gentle weather & possibly to prevent moisture} But in the
Spring produce them to the Celestiall Influences, & *æquinox* raines, & expose them
all Summer to the open & free aire where they will wonderfully flourish, onely be
not over hasty, especially in *March* for the wind & the Sun of that moneth is worse
then a Winter to them, Therefore use them to the aire very discreetely. {& take heed
also of over wetting them, especially their leaves, least you rott the strings:}[60] About
mid *May* you shall slip them, leaving not above 2 or 3 Spindles upon a roote, which

---

56. **[Insertion on separate piece of paper]** some commend the castings of
molehills in defect of better; note that they cannot endure sand {or clay} unlesse well
mingled with neates dung: There is an excellent mould also of an hazel colour found
on the topps of tyle {or brick} Earth, especially if taken {just} under the turfe in some
pasture, which if farr superior to what land has ben ploud mixing one part of neates
dung with 3 of this mould, yet strive not to make it over rich, for in such though the
plant flourish the flowers will be but leane: a mediocrity is best:

57. **[Margin note]** thus some but others I have knowne never water above once
a weeke when very dry; & when they cary them into the conserve hardly all winter,
so as they come out all in dust & yet prove rare.

58. **[Margin note]** or it shall suffice to cover them with bottomlesse potts which
will preserve them sufficiently & so they will also indure in the raisd bordure but not
blow so fayre but potts are also preferrable because of removing to any place by which
meanes experiments may be made to continue them longer in flo: & sooner: etc.

59. **[Insertion on separate piece of paper]** For even in the severest winters,
if set under a south wall, with a frame of moveable boards over them, which may be
taken off when the weather is temperate, is the best way of all: when if over dry, some
refresh them with water qualified with a little sheepe dung: especially after ~~long &~~
sharpe & binding frosts

60. **[Insertion on separate piece of paper]** in over wett season lay the potts
on the sides, till the weather change:

Figure 68. A method to propagate plants by slips, illustrated in text at page 295.

will ~~produce~~ furnish Layers enough to store you; sustaining the Spindles ~~in a gentle~~ within a cradle of wire, or whales bone **[page 295]** put through a square stitch at competent distance, & sufficient height, as the figure below will teach you: {nipping off superfluous budds &} Watring them ~~every~~ once every {3d} 4 or 5 daies 3 daies in Summer: {morning & evening if too dry} & securing them from excessive stormes & suddaine Gusts. {~~upon~~ In each pott sett a stick & a cane on it to destroy the black bob & coralls which devour them but will be cautch [caught?] in the evening & the morning} If the pod extreamely swell as to threatten bursting, prevente it by a {narrow} band cut out of hoggs bladder ~~&~~ {or rather gold beaten filme} which being wett clap on, needes no other ligature, & being transparent will not obscure the foote. The rootes of the slipps are to be transplanted soone after {S.} *Bartholomew tide*, especially if the season be moist: {The manner of slipping Se: c: 4: or thus from May to August: take the slips as you can, cutt of the topp, slit the stalke you slip'd & put them in the ground, replant in Spring} The *Layers* are bent into layer potts, bending the branch into the notch, being first a little slitt {at a knott **[continued in margin]** slit it upwards to the next joynt.} & then by pressing downe the sliding plate, hold it under the earth: {the slip upright then water it} After a moneth or six weekes, they may be separated & cutt of from the mother, & planted in other potts, {& shaded a while}[61] & this is don from February to mid *March*: ~~& indeede~~ {also {July &} in August when the season beginns: **[continues at side of illustration]** March be sure to take the lustiest slips to lay. Some affirme laying tis best from mide June to mid July in this let the groth direct rather sooner than later & to be taken off with their groth about them at the beginning of September: & potted but not over watred them for feare of rotting the strings:}

[illustration, see Fig. 68]

{Note that the morning Sun is best for Gilly flo: both when you first plant them & when in flo:}[62]

---

61. **[Insertion on separate piece of paper]** Thus you may plant 6 or 8 in a pott, to save roome in Winter

62. **[Insertion on separate piece of paper]** If you plant in beds, let them be

But there is a way amongst the Artists of Grafting the branches of Carnations, not onely the splicing invention, & in the smale twiggs of trees, but by helpe of a very curious instrument & so placing of severall coloured flo: on every branch, so they be sufficiently woodie; also by boaring of holes in ~~tal~~ the stemms of tall trees, an Inch deepe or more, & filling them with mould, & thus may a great tree be adornd with Carnations, pinkes, & severall other flowers, ~~which~~ {by} a very sweete & surprising varietie. {~~Towards Winter you must new earth them~~} {The Clove dos come of Seede but it is rarely proved; & those propagated of slips rather about August & remov'd in March ~~at full~~ a little before the full}[63] (vide infra*) There is also a camophyllus marinus or Thrift which I onely mention for its use in adorning the edges of borders & bedds to be planted in Spring once for all of slipps & is tonsile} The~~ir~~ cordiall & exhilerating virtue of this precious flower is universally knowne. *{The ordinary Pinke {or wild Giliflo: & double Pinke} is sowed in Aprill, flowers not 'till the 2d yeare, & when don bearing to be clip'd close, also are they propagated of slips {in September} the Birds eye or French pinke will matt prettily for bordures being so governed; flo: in May: Set them both of Seeds in Spr: or of slips in March or August} **[Page 296]**[64] *Cyclamen* Sow-bread is ~~ab~~ of about 20 kinds:[65] They [66]are raised of Seedes {sowne as soone as ripe} in 3 or 4 yeares, & ~~in~~ affects shady places, {especially the Autumnal} also are they propagated by the pieces of the roote: {~~in June~~} But both the *Vernal* & *Autumnal* thrive best in {large} potts ~~in good mould~~, two fingers deepe & in speciall mould preserved from the cold: One Roote being cutt, multiplies exceedingly, but this must be don after the leaves are withered, keeping the ~~cutt~~ divided parts dry that the wounds may heale & recover; for which some emplaster them with wax; but they

---

so situated as the Sunn may be off by 12 in the Somer monethes, for in May June & July, the {afternoon} Sun is apt to sterve them: & every 4th yeare renew the Earth: nay in potts you may lett them stand as long by onely renewing the mould above the roote, unlesse the roote be dead, then plant not a new one in that mould: in all watring of this plant new sett, give but little at a tyme: for too much wett, in so stiff ground is apt to rott the fibers: Therefore remove over raine drenched potts upon occasion to dryer exposures till the season be dryer

63. **[Insertion on separate piece of paper]** It is sayd that pease straw rotted to dust & scattered 2 fingers thicke above their rootes preserves them in the Severest Winters: but over much wett is also their enemy, & snow which is to be shaken off: but most of all the Eastern winds to be secured by Pease straw lightly cast over them, if the place protect them not otherwise:

64. **[Insertion on separate piece of paper]** Cistus mas {Ledon & others} are shrubby plants produce pretty flo: & a sweete Gumm, especially the latter that rare & usefull Lactanum: They are all raised of seedes & to be carefully ~~housed~~ {conserved} in winter in the Greene house: & therefore to be set in potts:

65. **[Addition at top of page]** The chiefest are the Antiochenum double flo:; the dry leavd Angustifol, the Lemans, the Spring & Summer Cyclamens, the autumnal both white & purple, etc:

66. **[Margin note]** all the allys of of [*sic*] Morins Garden planted or edged with Cyclamen the large lying flat make a rare grotesco: planted before the bordur at the edge of the ally: cf Dr: Needham:

would not be watered 'till they begin to [67]appeare. That which you raise of Seedes {as the dry leavd Autumnal & Roman} is to be sowne the one in *Spring*, the other in *Autumne* transplanting it after 3 yeares. It frequently varies the Colour.[68] The Water of the *tuberous* rootes be much in esteeme [69]for the taking away the spotts & cicatrices of the *Smale pox* & also to clarifie the skin: It is likewise put into *Catharticks* against pituitous humours, & the juice of it ~~composes~~ {makes} noble *Errhinon* for the Eyes & Affects of the head: what a *Philter* may be compose with it, we shall not neede to describe, because an expert Gardiner is worthy of {native beauty} & a virtuous love. ~~Crocus of all sorts & Colours & even the common Saffron which of all the flowers in nature containes the most innumerable virtues~~ [lxxix]

Consolida regalis

Delphinum or Larks spurr is also of greate variety, [70]dubble, ~~stra~~ straked & curiously spotted, They are easily and onely, produced by Seede in the Autumne, {will also sow themselves} and are a very greate ornament in our Coronary Gardens. {{sow them} in a sunny place in Octob: {or} when you plant out your Tulips: even among them in March:}[71,72]

~~*Dens carinus*~~ may be planted like other Bulbous rootes.

Flos Affricanus {annual for most part} ~~must~~ is best[73] raised in the hott bed, & afterwards transplanted: {about May} But the lesser sort of *French Marigolds* are sowne in the open bed, & continue long: {The other is an Annual Seed ripe in Sept: to which

---

67. **[Margin note]** the purple sort hath a sent so admirable & it possibly exceedes the very violet

68. **[Insertion on separate piece of paper]** Mr Rea gives us the most exact culture of this flo: & teaches us to transpl: in June or July, that of the Summer & Roman excepted, which should be planted before they put out their budds for flowers: Indeede {as} he tells us they rarely come of rootes to any purpose, but by seede rather, which should be sown in cases as soone as ripe in good light earth, covered at first a finger thicke, & when up, & that the small green leaves are dryed, seift more earth to them, & house & cover them the first winter, especially the Vernal, & after they will be sufficiently hardy, for 2 years after you may transplant them where they must abide at 9 inches distant.

69. **[Margin note]** they neede not be oft removd:

70. **[Margin note]** some sow them in Aprill {in lines} they flo in {July &} Aug: annuals: for bow potts:

71. **[Insertion on separate piece of paper]** they come sooner or later according to time of sowing; but for good seedes sow them in a warm {well} defended place as soone as ripe & these will produce admirable seed far surpassing the Spring sowne:

72. **[Insertion on separate piece of paper]** Dittany: especially of Creete produces a pretty flower, there is also a white: being touched smell agreably: they require a suny place, midling soile, & to be sometimes watred:

73. **[Insertion on separate piece of paper]** the rarest is the maximus multiplex, & the seedes produce greate varietys, 2 that cald the hollow leavd flower, & the lesser {double} French Marigold, all which bring variety by Seeds but are annuals & to be sowed in Aprill, some on hott bed, as the 2 first Sorts, & removed to a rich soyle & sunny, well watred: preserving only the seeds of the double:

tyme from Aug: they are in flo: if you crop the heads & hang {them} up, it will ripen better: every 3 or 4 years twill degenerat, therefore then change it}

{*Fraxinela*} [74]

Geranium or the Cranes bill is propagated of rootes {(in spring)} [75] & so is the Nocte olens & by Seede with care.{by bending downe the heads every morning that the deaw contracted in the night remaine not in the cupps which hinder it from maturity} [76]

[77] *Gladiolus*, & what resembles it the *Digitalis* of both Coloures which are to be planted in the face of the Sun; in a leane earth fower fingers deepe & as farr distant. [78] {this plants roote hath a rare virtue discutient of tumors mixed & mealted with hoggs greace;}

Gentiana major {Se p: 301}

Gentianella verna a most beautifull flo: & to be propagated by the roote {with greate facility & without care or trouble, & in a cooler place:}

[Globe Flower] [79]

---

74. **[Insertion on separate piece of paper]** Fraxinella: with red, white & other Colours; fit for bordures being of a tall woody kind: raised of Seede {in Aprill}, all bring many varietys but the seede, if not secured, will be lost: therefore easiest propagated by plants in March. It indures many yeares:

75. **[Insertion on separate piece of paper]** they increase so aboundantly: the rarest of them are the purple bleau & white, the red-rose, the sweete, but above all the knobbed, but there are divers more common kinds

76. **[Insertion on separate piece of paper]** maturity: Sow them in a pott, plunged in an hott-bed; with care you may preserve them in winter, abroad, setting the pott under a south wall, & covering it with mosse, & a bell glass, or better in the Conservatory, where it may be sure to be kept from wett which it abhorrs:

77. **[Margin note]** Seede in June sowd in August, flo: the 2d yeare: the roote remaines but should be removed in Spring else they grow too thick. a bordur flo: The Indea flag is choycer & is ~~bis annual~~ to be set in boxes & preservd in your greenhouse at winter: of the rest the bright red, white & Bizantine are choycest: to purge your ground, take then up when dry till Tulip season, & then you may cluster halfe a dozen together for the better shew:

78. **[Insertion on separate piece of paper]** Digitalis may be raised of Seed also in Spring {tenderly govern'd} but is 2 yeares {with oft transplanting} 'ere it produce flo: which come in July: they seede in Aug: after which cutt the drye stalkes: ~~tis a~~ the best way is by rootes, they are very prolifique, & hardy ~~at last~~ when growne, & should be removed once in 3 yeares: se another paper **[continued on separate piece of paper]** The choycest of these are the Ferruginea to be plan[t]d in a warme place & defend from frosts, & so they will continue the longer: The Orange tawny to be propagated yearly by the Seede: The Greate White & the lesser which is rarer: The greate yellow whose roote continues: The Small pale yellow, yet longer lasting: They may all be raised of Seedes {in rich Earth in Aprill} which produce flo: the 2d year, to be removed out of the flo: Nursery in Sept: into bordures:

79. **[Insertion on separate piece of paper]** Globe-flo: if you raise of Seeds

Hepatica should be planted in rich earth & moist, 2 fingers in depth, they shall neede no often removing but for increase: & must be shaded: {The single produce by seedes, but it is best trusting to plants which are very divisible: The most estimable are the doubles, especially the double white:} *Heleborus,* the *white,* is planted of rootes, & for bearing its flo: in winter is very commendable.[80]

Hermodactyles, set in leane ground, & a sunny, 3 fingers deepe & as neere as to touch. The *pilula* de Hermodactyles are prepar'd by every *Apothecary ad juncturarum affectus*
                         here comes in Frittellaria p. 297

[Page 297 continued from page 290] be somewhat fat of itselfe, & exposed to the Sun: They may be taken up in Autumne,[81] & within 15 days after replanted:[82] The *Stamina* of the ordinary *Saffron* or *shives* should be gathered morning & evening.[83]

[Continued in margin] {In re medica: applied outerwards ~~dra~~ extracts thorne, molifies tumors etc: & is used in some Cathartic Medicines: *viz* the rootes, but not being moyst, for it will choake like a halter: *Dosis* 3 [dram]*1 cum Zimzib: et pipere pulveriz etc.* but its vertues are so well known for its heate, drying, dissipating, opning, & corrobrating as nothing more onely we may not omitt this famous antidote against the Pestilence: *Elect: liberant ducis, pulv: Card: Nicot. Trochis: de barb pilux. Aleophanus* in which composit: *Crocus* is all the principall}

Frittillaria, or the variegated Lilly, *Dudoneus Flos Meleagris,* ~~are~~ the lesser is darke &[84] yellow, {red & Sabell} also early white, a kind of chequerd worke, {some are double} It is an early Flower & very pretty: Their Seedes sowne come not up till 3 yeares & bring later & more degenerate flowers: They have sometymes increased to 10 leaves, but then they seldom keepe so: They shall neede no taking up but for off-setts: yet delights it in a fatt Soile allways shady, & would be planted 4 fingers deepe 3 distant, kept continually moyst; Some thinke it best to plant them in potts, & advise, that in cropping the flower you {nipp} ~~take~~ the stalk very short, because it much injures the roote: They may be taken up in *October,* {July & planted in Aug:} or (as we sayd) continued in the ground, Their Seedes {of which the white is best} producing ~~no~~ {little} varieties within 10 or 12 daies replant them. {The signature of this plant ~~made~~ gave light to an knowing Chymistry to find an excellent successe & rare water to take away spotts & freckles out of the skin & face & to recover Sunburnt:

Spr: best of Slipps which roote in {mid} March: it flo: in May, is for ~~potts~~ bordures & potts:

80. **[Insertion on separate piece of paper]** But the true Black {Helibore: & albus atro rubens these} ~~is~~ {are} the rarest: ~~The first abides~~ neede no removing: give them reasonable good earth: of this tribe is Calceolus Mariæ {or the Heloborines} white, & purple: but these are in flo: in Spring; the true Helebor in Winter, yea at Christmas: The Heleborines plant of rotes in moderat soile:

81. **[Margin note]** but the Colchium or meadow Saffron about St James tide if you please:

82. **[Margin note]** every 3 or 4 yeares:

83. **[Margin note]** Se the Calinder for Saffron

84. **[Insertion on separate piece of paper]** Greenish, Black, Portugal, Spanish, etc:

[85]*Hyacinthus* The Iacinth of which also the Eastern Countries are very full, ~~are~~ be of severall Sortes: for the Seede take it out of the fairest, & when the flo: is neere faded, cropp the stalkes & reserve three or 4 onely for Seede: which in September sow in potts very thin, but transplant not till two yeares & preserve them both from excesses of weather, keeping it all ways moist, earthed up the 2d yeare: & in the 3d it will flowere, & come to perfection in the 4th, but yet {are best raised by the bulbes; ~~& may continue in the earth 4 or 5 yeares:~~ They delight most in a free aire, good, yet light soile: They may continue without remove 4 or 5 yeares, except the white Brumal which is exceedingly prolific & may be taken up the 2d yeare: Set them a good space asunder: But the *Botroydes inodorus*, the *Belgic* & the *Spanish* neede lesse depth & distance:[86] The white tuberous Iacynth would be sufficiently watered in dry Seasons[87] Set him deepe, & ~~observe~~ {remove} it ~~in~~{ab}out the ~~end~~ {middle} of ~~March~~ {Aprill}, keeping it from greate cold; or for more particular directions. Put the *Oriental* {of which the white double is rarest} in fine earth, & a sunny place 4 fing deepe, taking it up every 3 yeares in July, & replant in September after a greate raine.[88] The Serotine Iacynth delights in a very fatt earth & the sunny side. But the Serotine white rather in the Shade, Set a span distant: The Iacynth of Peru in reasonable mould, not much in the Sun, planted 5 fingers deepe, and as far distant.[89] The Seedes of the Oriental *Hyacinth* mixed with Treacle, as perfect remedy as *Alui Profluvijs*: etc:

[90]*Iris* of severall colours & vertues love a moyst {& shady ~~yet light~~} ground: They

---

85. **[Margin note]** Se Sr: Tho: Hanmer's notes **[insertion from page 290]**
Of Hyacinthes
They are to be ordered as the Irises. Those from Portugall & Spaine will seldom beare flowers with us; though the rootes will continue many yeares, & put forth leaves.

86. **[Insertion on separate piece of paper]** The Muscari plant warme:
The Indian potted in the hott bed in Aprill, in naturall earth, {next the bulb} & some richer about it, when it springs take the pot out, set it in Sun: water it well (but give it no water in the H-Bed till it springs) twill flo: in ~~Aprill~~ {August} take out the bulbs in Octob: before the raines, preserve in dry papers in a store moderate warme: **[continued on separate piece of paper]** The Oriental Zumbial {or Sweete Smelling} may be taken out of the earth yearly & the bulbes kept dry:

87. **[Margin note]** best in potts in hot bed

88. **[Margin note]** The white take out every 2d yeare for to clense of offsetts:

89. **[Insertion on separate piece of paper]** Note that all the Grape flowers loosing yearly their fibers may be yearely also removed about midsommer, but not long unburied: not so of the Hyacinth who do preserve their fibers:
The fairest & most esteemed are the Hyacinth Stellatus flo: albo: The double white, & double bleu. The Indian, Oriental Zumbul: The Comosus ramosus elegantior etc: Se the Catalogue:

90. **[Margin note]** Se Sr Tho Hanmers notes
[Insertion on separate piece of paper]
Of Bulbous Irises
They are of two sorts Greater & Lesser, soe calld from the biggnes or Smallnes of their rootes {as well as flowers}. The Greater sorts are most esteem'd because their flowers are larger, and will endure the raines and heates better then the lesser.

are both *bulbous* & *tuberous* {double, single,} propagated ~~loosely~~ {best} by offsetts.[91] They delight {not} in a fat {yet light} earth, especially the tuberous, & should be planted 2 fingers deepe & span distant, but neede never be watered: {nor so fatt a soile.} The Bulbous as deepe more, but at lesse distance, ~~fro~~ the{y} ~~others~~ {both} increase wonderfully, {& about Autumne use to swell above ground without damage} & this last may be taken forth about the end of July & planted againe at the end of September;[92] but the *Persian Iris* would be let stand, unlesse you desire multiplication: In setting them, spread the rootes well, & have care of breaking them: {especialy the

---

These greater are commonly but of one colour, some few are a little striped or markt, but the lesser bulbous Irises are of wonderfull varietyes. The names and colours are sett downe in Monsieur Moryns little printed catalogue of his flowers to which I refer you both for Irises and Tulipes, and Anemons & Ranuncules. If any dung come to your Iris rootes which is not absolutely rotten, they certainly perish, although they thrive exceedingly in a good ordinary garden mold. They should not stand in too hott a Sun nor bee over removed, never pott them, but let them stand alwayes in the full earth abroad. All the sorts yeild perfect seed with us, which being sowed almost at any tyme from the tyme it is ripe till Christmas will grow, & that of the smaller kinds will produce new varietyes, but seldome that of the great sorts. They come up as Tulipes doe the first yeare with rush leaves, the second yeares they are of the shape they will bee, and the third or fourth yeare they will beare flowers. You may let them stand where they are sowne in beds till they beare, or remove them the second or third yeare as you please.

91. **[Margin note]** though they will come also of seede: The very stalke of the Iris before the flo: blow will thrive & blow & hape being cutt off & set in water.

92. **[Insertion on separate piece of paper]**

Iris

The greate Bulbosa of Clusius is more tender & must be guarded in winter, in a warme quarter: ~~in removal be carefull of the bottome protuberances~~: The greate white purple strip'd bulbosa is very rare: The {greate} yellow bulbosa should be taken up before they are quite dry after flowering, before they put forth new fibers, & replanted in Aug: in moderate ~~groound~~ naturall Earth exposed to the rising, rather than the meridian Sun.

The Yellow Spanish is a good flo:, but the angustifolia bulbosa persico flower is the richest of all the Iris: {it is tender, cultivate it as the greate yellow:} the rootes of these for loosing their fibers, may be removed yearely: The Seedes of the bulbosa major flo: albo et purpureo variegata produce pretty varieties: governed as we are taught in Tulip Seeds: others not so rare afford aboundant offsetts. Of the Tuberous are the Chalcedanians & such of them whose fibers rott, ~~remove~~ take up {at Midsome} & plant in Autume in a warme exposure in fine Earth ~~not over~~ {pretty} rich: & cover them in sharp winters: The Alba versicolor is a **[continued on separate piece of paper]** a neate flo: & so are many of the Chamæiris's & the better for being hardy: yet they deserve good soile: remove & plant them in Sept moderately deepe & distant:

[Margin note] The rootes taken up in Spring must be dryed in the Sun for powder, tis also a better sternutative then Tobacco.

bottom fangs} from the seede expect no {greate} varietie: {whatever Laurenbergius affirmes **[continued in margin]** about the 4th yeare: yet in Apr: it may be sowne, & carefully governed for 3 yeares 'till they flower:} but infinite are the remedies which the rootes aford. The *Elect, Rotulo Diairios,* are well knowne, especially against the Asthma couggh etc: and it enters into *Theriacle & Mithridale* those famous *Electuaries*: we might fill a sheete to describe the perfections of the sweete roote, there is nothing becomes the breath more, making it smell like violets, & the perfumers cannot be without its powder. {The leaves will serve to bind branches & flowers with: Wine coopers or seacretly insert the roote into the Commisures or the Vessells *Leucoium* **[Page 298]**

⁹³Lathyrus
⁹⁴*Leucoium* or *stock Gilloflower* {is of no lesse then 42 sortes} being dubble is a very beautifull & sweete smelling flower. it grows best in moist places, but must be first sowne {in dry gravelly, but good Earth} of choice seedes in {March or} Aprill ~~new~~ {full [moon cresent] very thinly} and then being 1/2 foote high transplanted, {into richer earth {the next full}}⁹⁵ it is a tender plant & had neede be often irrigated; they will continue many yeares well governed.⁹⁶,⁹⁷,⁹⁸,⁹⁹

---

93. **[Insertion on separate piece of paper]** Lathyrus ever lasting pease, pl: in ~~Apr: in Gardens that~~ {March: next a wall} or pole that it may climb, they flo: in June or before, but many times not the 1 yeare; it neede never but once sowing: Orbus Venetus is another sort of this, raised alike & alike lasting

94. **[Margin note]** Reform this by all your papers & markes:

95. **[Insertion on separate piece of paper]** When they have grown ~~then to~~ a little more {in a wett Season} remove them a fresh {in the same amended bed} to cause them grow neerer the ground & fuller & not run up too high: then lastly remove them with clod & all carefully & set them where they are to continue shaded & refreshed sometime: let the single stand for seede, for they onely beare it, & sow in annualy, casting away the single such as you reserve not for seede: you may know what will be double by tumer of the budd: those that bear the best are such as are the single of the best of the double kinds: now the best of the double are such as are of most varietys of Colour, the double striped {the yellow etc} from the singles of these colours double are raised: also they are raised of slips {& cuttings} (especialy such as have no single) & indeed do so continue longest & fairest. Mr: Rays way is to be preferred: to choose an oblong branch, cutt it off some distance from the stock, so it be not over long, slit downe the barke at the end of the slip half an inch in 3 or 4 places, equidistant as the bignesse advises which peel as far as the slitts & turne up; cut of the naked woody part close to the rind thats turned up, set it 3 fingers deepe in a wide hole spreading the barke, cover shade & water it: so you may treate gilly flo: **[continued in margin]** or any woddy plant or you may lay them as they do gill: flo:

96. **[Margin note]** also thus are increased of Slipps.

97. **[Insertion on separate piece of paper]** In transplanting the Stock–Gillyflo: some observe that the curled heads are most apt to produce double, then againe in the full of Septr: to impeade their flowering the Spring, & shelter them well in Winter; therefore sow ~~them in~~ & plant ~~in~~ under some warme border & wall: Then in the full of March after transplant againe in yet richer earth, & where you will

Lilium The Lilly {of *Persian* extraction} is both white & red, {of which the red double, & yellow especialy **[continued in margin]** also the Byzantine & double white are most esteem'd ayre improves all lillys for doubling the flo: & furniture on the stalke} a lovely & noble Flower though common, they are propagated of their bulbes [100]& Seedes, which *in re medica* are of admirable use: some write it is propagated by its owne juice or teares, so as is no other flower, but we condemne it as fictitious. The polyanth red lilly has sometymes produced 84 leaves: They would be taken up about *St: James tyde* & replanted as soone as you please after. {Plant lillys in sunny dry ground in August, remove them after some yeares to come ample they continue forever}
[101]*Lilium Persicum*, ~~a rare & curious flower~~: The Wild Lilly may be taken up as soone as they have don flowering, separating the greene stalke:
Lilium Convallium {an honorable & excellent plant} requires a very ~~rich~~ {moderat} Soile, & would be planted[102] in *March* or *October* so neere as almost to touch, ~~alm~~ 3 fingers depth when the weather is drie, but the place shady: but first they are to be divided from their inexplicable intertextures with a knife, & so neede never be

---

have them stand for good: ~~they will~~ thus you shall have the double, & the fairer if you prune them ere they flo: The single are little esteemed, & may almost at any tyme be sown: ~~they~~ {even the double} are propagated of slips {at} the full in May, stripping off the under leaves, watring them frequently with rich compost water; thus they will last 4 or 5 yeares: They may be also ~~sow~~ set in rowes even so near as to ~~almost~~ touch & they will become an headg of flo: & may be kept in order exactly by clipping

98. **[Insertion on separate piece of paper]**
{The Viola lutea or} Wall-flo: resemble the Stock Gilly-flo: ~~love dry ground, & stony places shallow earth~~ continue long, ~~sowes itself after the first~~ is raised of slipps all the spring or autumn {in a warme place which will protecct such sorts as are tender} those set in Sept: flo: early in spring, they will grow woody, prune them therefore, & refresh the Earth they will be fair & double: **[Continued on separate piece of paper]** The best & rarest Sorte {of the Keris} are the double white, & the greate single double yellow which must be defenced in some winters: The double red, the simplex majus ~~&~~ the greate double ~~etc.~~ & pale yellow etc: **[end]** The very common Wallflo: is sown of Seedes & sowes itself shall neede no description, onely it flo: almost all winter & smells pleasantly

[Continued on another piece of paper] Lucoium Bulbosum or bulbous Violet is both early & latter, greate & lesse Some call them Snow flowers, estimable for their early appearing, though the majus bulbosum is a may flo: They aboundantly augment by the rootes & offsetts, & may be removed or let continue for offsetts; & to be governd much as the Narcissus, of which it is a species:

99. **[Insertion on separate piece of paper]** Leucoium Melancholeum is a kind of dull Gily flo: placed of slips in Spring, or Autumn in borders; ~~tis a the lea~~ they may be usd in flo: potts: & have greene leaves when young may be usd in Salads, tasting like rockett: the roote springs yearly:

100. **[Margin note]** The Lilly Water distilled is held a rare cosmetic for Face & hands.

101. **[Margin note]** not very rare, remove it seldom, & that in September:

102. **[Margin note]** but take them up in June:

removed, the earth nowe & then refreshed: Some cutt with a knife & set them in tufts:[103] The vertues of {all} their {oyles} are incomparable:[104]

Lychnis is of severall kinds: The rarest is the {dubble} *Chalcedonica* to us an admirable flo: both for colour & shape: {also **[continued in margin]** the double white & blush coloured single:} it is best propagated by dividing the rootes with a knife like *Lilium Conval*: ~~at spring,~~ {or end of August or September} & planted in rich earth pretty deepe to the top of the sprout, water & preserve it from the cold: {both the one and other being in Flo:} should be shaded, & in taking of the young pare with it **[continued in margin]** a little of the mother roote though without fibers: The wild must be also shaded ~~&~~ allways waterd & planted in fatt mould; {& loves yet the Sunn, especially in Spring}[105] There is also the ordinary *Campion* & the *Hortensis* or Batchelors Buttone, quite of another kind, & well knowne, easily governed & propagated by Seedes: {Slipps with a little of the roote; planted in Aug: it flo: in May etc: plant in spring it flo: not till after midsommer: when past flowering top it: it needes but once planting the light:}

Martagon [106] delights in a fat moyst & shady earth, it would be planted 4 inches deepe, & as farr distant: when they begin to peepe, {& indeede once in 2 yeares} take away some of the old earth, but touch not the ~~rootes,~~ {fibers **[continued in margin]** nor move the maine roote but clense it of offsetts} & supplie it with new: {& twill greatly multiply & increase flo:} Remove not the rootes unlesse for increase, {& to magnifie the flo:} & that not till the flower decay; {replant it immediately} but it is propagated

---

103. **[Margin note]** besides the comon white, there is one of a redish hue which is more rare

104. **[Insertion on separate piece of paper]** {All beauty attributed to rose & lilly

Vel mista rubent ubi lilia multa

Rosa alba: tales virgo dabat ore colores.

12 Æn:[68]}

And the Flower so famous that in poetic sense the Lilly above all that Nature had of sweete & beautifull, for ~~so it~~ to this sense {or having lost its virginity; hence God is sayd ex omnibus floribus sibi elegisse lillium; mysticaly thought to be Christ the Son of the B: Virgin, & though the French king meanes himself &}

Manibus date lilia plenis as Homer by his λείριος, the Junonian rose when here milke overflowed, the Galaxia was staind: lilly was taken for all fine & rare flowers & the Spouse in the Cant: will have that to face amongst the lillies: c. 2. 16, Solomons glory not comparable

[Margin note] tis calld the Vergin flo: because nothing sweeter till touchd or broken & then nothing more stinking

105. **[Insertion on separate piece of paper]** These hardier Non–Such's so taken from onely old rootes may be placed in March when ~~pr~~ of pretty stature; & may be raised also of seedes:

106. **[Insertion on separate piece of paper]** The Martagon or mountain lilly is of many sorts, as the spotted, white, Imperiall, Americane, ~~Byzantine~~ Pompenian, ~~Panonian etc:~~ Byzantinium, Panonicum, which is the noblest: ~~& of som~~ {all which} Martagons differ in colour & ~~Speckels~~ Speckles & season of flowering:

also by the very Squamous leaves which will grow boulbes being plunged into the earth: The Seedes produce no varietie: {& seldom ripening. The Indian or American Martagon must be planted in potts, & conserved in winter.}

Mirabile peruvianum is raised of Seedes, & sowes it selfe, & will keepe long in the ground, provided it be carefully defended in winter: {So likewise by taking up the rootes early, wraping them in paper {or wollen} & setting againe at spring: for Seedes take onely that of the most variable flo:}[107]

Muscipula without this ~~dilligence~~ indulgence:

{*Nasturtium indicum*, raised by seede in the hott bed {or without if well secured}: a beautifull flower: & to be ~~potted~~.}

Narcissus The Daffodill hath above 60 kinds, & thrives well in a leanesh sandy & light mould, they would be planted generaly 4 Inches deepe, {as far distant}, & now & then removed {about April when don flowering} to be clensed of their offsetts, but the purple Verginian seldomer, {&} the Indian {& Sea daffodill} not at all {removed}: whither they vary colour upon semination is not yet found that we know, nor do all ~~bea~~ produce seede.[lxxx] But to particulars The *crowned Narcissus* will have a fatter earth, be planted 4 fingers deepe & but 3 distant; {if you will take up, let it be in June kept dry till Septr} The Dubble yellow {~~cipriott~~ **[continued in margin]** Cypriot} in good Earth also, which has a warme aspect about the same depth & distance.[108] It is sometimes difficult **[page 299]** in flowring, & therefore may be delivered by making a smale incision; it wo[u]ld be watered unlesse the place be sufficiently moist.

The *Smale Narcissus* & the *Autumnale* should be set in fresh good earth, & may be planted at neerer distances. {Let us heare[109]} An admirable water is to be distilled from

---

107. **[Insertion on separate piece of paper]** Mirab: peru: is single & doub: the doub: will be preserved 2 years with shelter: Set the Seeds in Mar: in H bed: or rich mould in Apr: will flo: late, it fades immediately being gatherd, but is of strange & unconstant variety, fitt onely for large bordures etc:

108. **[Margin note]** Some pot them {especialy the Indian} to have early & winter them but needlesse:

109. **[Insertion on separate piece of paper]** Let us heare this beautifull flower of himselfe after the best of Poets:

Ut quondam pueris Puer
Sic Flos emineo Floribus omnibus
Nec causam poteris dare,
Cur mi forma minus nunc placent mea.
Demissum teneo caput,
Antiquam Speculum cernere gestiens,
Da Fontem mihi limpidum
Antiquis videas servere amoribus,
A Nymphis & adhuc color,
Et nostris decorant tempora floribus,
Me gestant tepidu sinu,
An mallent Puerum dicere, nescio.
Cowley: L: 3 Flora: [p 168]

The double white Virginian {Byzantine & Cyprian} ~~is~~ {are} tender & not for your sharper Winters {without care, under a warme wall unmoved} The doub: White ordinary if taken yearly up at midsomer & purged of its offsetts, & planted in Septr: againe will produce a noble large flo:

The Brimstone coloured is estimable both for colour & sent: Of the Pseudo Narcissus, Tradescants is the noblest & doublest: The Angustifolius aureus: is estimable: ~~The time of planting most daffodills is from~~ Most of these rarer sorts of Narcissus the Indian especially do best in potts.

the *Narcissus* against the *Epilepsia* washing the head therewith; but the chymicall Oyle is much superiour to it.[110,111]

Juncifolius or *Junquilia* is also another, & is of many sorts: {yielding a **[continued in margin]** rare essence for the Ladies: To these also is of affinity the *Leucoium bulbosum*, or bulbous Violet: set them 3 fingers deepe, in 3 yeares take up & separate offsetts; replant suddenly:} {plant 6 fing deepe & 2 distant, water when beginning to}

Orchis is of severall sorts, ~~but~~ {and} the *Satyrium* {or Bee Flower} is {a} ~~flo~~{or} the ~~Gar~~ Coronary garden [112] onely; it requires a humid Soile, {& shade} & would be set 5 fingers deepe: Crollius wonderfully exhalts the *Aphrodisiastic* essence thereof, to re-invigorate, & retarde old age. {This has the propriety to smell in the night not in the day tyme, seldom removed:}

Ornithogallum or starre of *Bethlehem*, *Hungarian*, *Spanish Neapolitan*, *Arabic*, etc: are to be cultivated much like the *Narcissus*; but the Indian {Arabic & Æthiopic} would be planted in potts and wintered in the conservatory, or else taken out of the bed from September till Feb: {the greate white is not altogether so tender} They affect a leane {sandy} earth & sunny, & may be interred 6 fingers deepe, & a span distant. {The Neapolitan to be annualy taken up, & freed of its too numerous progeny: but the yellow will abide longer:}

Pæony is a ~~wo~~ glorious {goodly} & rutilant flower, {Male & Femal} common & [113] well

---

110. **[Insertion on separate piece of paper]** But the Tuberous Narcissus {cf if this be not the Hyacinthus rather} requires more care, viz, that the roote be planted in naturall earth in a pott, & above that earth some excellent consumed & richer earth so as the fibers (not the roote itself for that would too fast increase the offsetts which would impaire the flower) may suck from it; then plunge your pot in the hot bed about beginning of Aprill, & when it comes up water it well & frequently, but not before {& then draw it out of the hotbed & set the pot where you please} After the same manner treate the incomparable flo: the Narcissus of Japan which we now have out of ~~Jersey~~ {Garnsey}, where they thrive with much lesse care, & came first thither: when they have don blowing at latter end of Aug: carry in your pott, & when the Earth is pretty dug, paper your rootes as formerly taught: Some of these Exeter plants beare yet with us but once, & the reason is they come impregnated from their own Country, but are never fruitefull more: When the The D: of Orleans first saw this plant in Morins Garden at Paris, asking the prise, he told him {as if then} his dukedom would not purchase it.

111. **[Insertion on separate piece of paper, originally inserted erroneously at page 199]** Nasturtium Indicum an Annual sowd in Aprill ~~{some raise them in hott beds}~~, but needlesse: you may lead them up by a pack thred for they are climers: I have had them sow themselves severall years: Their budds pickled is an excellent ~~Caper~~ succedance to the Capers, & ~~the~~ {both} leave & flo: ~~not~~ fitt for sallets: & it admirable aydes the scorbut.

112. **[Insertion on separate piece of paper]** There are of these that resemble both bees, Flys, Gnatts & Butterflies, whenc they have their severall adjuncts, & are pretty though ordinary flo: & should be transplanted with the turfe & all as you find them in the fields, in shady rich soyle: paring away the grasse when well fixed:

113. **[Insertion on separate piece of paper]** The Double purple, & double red, ~~double blush~~, carnation, & double striped ~~all femals~~ & double blush or whitish, which

knowne: {**[continued in margin]** a rare flo: as a ground may be furnished: though common:} it delights in the shade & needes not be taken up, unlesse for increase, & then in October: {or Spring} The earth where you plant him would be fatt, set ~~7 In~~ 6 inches deepe and 3 spanns distant: not watered: but the earth now & then renewed without touching the roote:[114] when you have occasion to transplant[115] take not the cake of earth which is about it, but plant it in the clod: The roote of the male is much celebrated by *Dioscorides* for {~~bear~~ pregnant} women, & that of the single peony against the Epilepsia & for children.

~~Pinkes, dubble~~, the *Partridge Eye or Spanish pinke above all, raised of seedes, & slipps: etc.*

Papaver The *poppy* being dubble is of great varietie, {the rarest of which is the golden-yellow **[continued in margin]** double particoloured red sriped, scarlet etc} a caduce but glorious flower propagated of Seede, they continue long & love the Eye of the Sun:[116] their *Anodyne* qualities is well knowne: {especialy to conciliat ~~sweete Rest~~ Sleepe which the poet has thus celebrated in praising this plant}[117]

---

is the rarest: are all females[.] The Males beare single flo: of which the best are that of Constantinople, the large blush: etc: transpl: in Autumne, & take such as have duggs at their extreames for they onely are fruitfull: but of the double every piece wil grow

114. **[Insertion on separate piece of paper]** Yet you may much increase your stock if you cutt {or breake} the roote into pieces, ~~whi~~{ea}ch ~~pi~~ morcell will grow & flo: the 2d yeare but not before: & they may also be propagated by the suckers of old rootes without molesting the mother, & improve her:

The Male is more choyce, & therefore by Somer set in a pott or ~~box~~ case: The ordinary peonys produce seede, which you may sow when blush & ripe, but they are are [*sic*] some years ere they bring a flo:

115. **[Margin note]** The double peony will grow of its own seede & bring varieties, but not in every yeare

116. **[Insertion on separate piece of paper]** popys, if too thick, pull up & sow them in a line in borders, July they flower. You may also sow ~~in~~ at end of Aug, & then they flo: In May following: They sow themselves afterwards, but tis best to extirpate & trust to new because they will come dissorderly:

117. **[Insertion on separate piece of paper]**
~~Upon the Popy.~~

> Somne, lenimen placidum Doloris,
> Gaudium Curæ, Requies Laborum,
> Sola Morborum Medicina grata,
>   Somne beate.
> Somne, non fallax Miserorum Amice,
> Hospes agrestis sine fraudetecti,
> Pauperum Fautor, Deus Innocentum,
>   Optime Somne.
> Somne, qui Mundum vicibus gubernas
> Cum Jove æquatis, mediumque Numen
> Inter & Plutona es, & inter illum
>   Maxime Somne
>   Cowley 4: Plantas [p. 232]

To which I add the old Ænigma

Phalangium or Spider wort.

Primula veris of all sorts are of admirable varieties, especially the dubble, [118]which be-come a parterr the best of any being planted thick, because they couch low, and may be wrought in rare imbroderies the colours well sorted: They delight in a good & ~~mo~~ naturally rich mould, moyst & well shaded, are propagated both of Seede[119] & by rootes, ~~but best of all by the rootes~~ which increase aboundantly: ~~Set th~~ plant them in Autumne:[120] Both the syrup & conserves are excellent against arthriticall indispo-sitions, but this especially the Cows=lip.[121,122]

[123]{Periploca Verginiana}

Ranunculus[124] or the *Crowfoot* is of wonderfull diversities & desire a speciall rich mould;

Grande mihi caput, & inter sunt membra minuta

Per unus solum, sed pes longissime idem

Et me somnus amat, proprio nec dormio somno.

118. **[Margin note]** & purple that flo: twise a yeare:

119. **[Insertion on separate piece of paper]** Seeds especially from these the red ~~hose in ho~~ hose in hose primrose & those of deepest colours etc: to be cultivated as the Auricula: but without all their curiosity, & so the mould be good, for they are hardy plants: they are also propagated by rootes whole or divided:

Note that the common cowslip is not apt to beare Seede, but is increased from slipps in Spring or Autumne, the topps cutt off; & so treate them also when they ~~have~~ are past flowering & they will spring fresh:

The Oxlip is of a more early kind, set also of Slipps; all of them fitt for edges & borders, & neede [be] transplanted only for increase & inlargement of the flowers:

The Jerusalem Cowslip or Pulmonaria flo in Spring, planted also from offsetts

The most choyce of ~~both~~ all the sorts are the ~~hose~~ Geminated flowers {or hose in hose} the double Cowslip, & double greene, the Jacknapes on horseback, the jagged hose, the red primroses of infinite diversities, the Scarlet, double red, Orange coloured Red birds Eyes etc:

120. **[Margin note]** cutt off the dry leaves when flowering is don.

121. **[Insertion on separate piece of paper]** There is a taller plant, which they call the Primerose tree, producing a flo: in June, & sowes itself, but is best propagated by setts & slipps, & though they sometimes seeme in the winter to perish, yet they Spring againe:

122. **[Insertion on separate piece of paper]** Princes feather is a sort of Ama-ranth raised of Seede all the Spring {to have early in hot bed} but {as well in a rich earth} Sprinkle the Seede with other {dry} earth because tis very small, else you will sow it too thick; in dry Season water it, remove them when of competent strength & water them: flo: in July:

123. **[Insertion on separate piece of paper]** or Virginian silke, though a mel-ancholy flo: yet is held a rarity, & rather to be planted amongst the simples: is raised of Seede, & remaines many years, increases & runns much without greate care, though some cover it with Soyle in Winter: It would never decay in my Ground so I exter-pated it quite:

124. **[Margin note]** Se Sr: T: Hanmers note

[Insertion on separate piece of paper]

they may be planted after *October* very well shaded, 3 fingers deepe & 2 distant; their rootes well covered & watered which are wont to get out, & irrigated when it wants refreshing. The *Byzantine* or *Asiatic Ranunculus* may be first soaked in water for 24 howers before planting, & that about *September*[125] buried two fingers deepe at 4 distant, or more, from any other flower, especially the *Anemonie* which 'tis sayd to burne: But Therefore, do they best in potts, because at first they require more Sun, & being in flower, the shade: when fir you perceive the leaves begin to dry take it immediately up. The *Yellow* and the *white* [page 300] must be planted againe in September; but the {Asiatic &} last neede not be removed except for increase: {at end of Winter & immediately replanted [continued in margin] but let the rootes dry before you separate the offsetts: {& keepe them in Sand, especially the more nice & tender such as the {severall} *Monsters pianisco* Puvoine of Rome Sang de Beuf the Parisian Plumach

---

Of Asian Ranuncles

I come now to the Glandulous flowers, amongst which the only considerable are the Asian Ranuncles, called in ffrance commonly Ranuncules de Tripoli. Wee have severall single sorts, as the White, the Gold yellow, the Lemmon or pale yellow, the Blood colour or deepe Crimson, the Murrey, the Gold colour strip't through with Scarlet, the Aurora, yellow on the inside of the flower and red on the backside or outside, the Rose frize, white within and Rose colour without, the palle Rose, White within, and Damaske rose colour without. The Chamois The Roman, chamois colour within, and Chamois and red on the backe. The African, yellow within and yellow and scarlet without, the Besancon yellow within and pale yellow and red without, The Cloath of Gold. The Melidor, Isabella colour within, and without crimson borderd with Isabella. The Parmesan, yellow within, and gold colour bordered with Crimson without, The Satinne, white within, and white and red without. The Sidonian, Chamois colour within, and chamois & red without.

Of the Dowble flowerd kinds, wee have only the scarlet. The greater Orange, strip't a little with yellow, the lesser Orange, called Boswell, Orange neatly markt with yellow, The Pevoine a greate dowble flower of a rich deepe scarlet colour, and the Monster, of the like fiery rich scarlet, bearing such large thicke flowers that it is wondefull that soe small a roote should produce soe great and thicke a flower. They have also in Paris a large dowble yellow which I have not seene about London.

All these Ranuncles both dowble and single flower in Aprill and May. They are all very beautifull & grow high upon strong stiffe stalkes, but they are all tender, and will neither endure the frosts abroad nor to bee long kept in a close roome within, or under close sheds of boards without as some use. The onely way I know to preserve them & have them beare well is not to put the rootes into the earth till the end of January, & then sett them in beds abroad, or in very large potts in rich blacke mold full of old sifted consumed rotten cow dung, where they may {have} much sun. Take the rootes up every June, and keepe them dry in the house till the time aforesaid of planting them.

The Dowble kinds yeild no seed anywhere, and the single but seldome in England, if you can procure any, sow it in rich mold in cases & house them in wynter.

125. [Margin note] but beware of either wett or winter after it, & therefore secure them with matresses shewing them Sun early

etc: these}[126] The *Globus* & round neede neither pott, nor disturbance but for propagation. {but} The *Tuberous* would be planted about Autumne as soone as taken up: The Rootes of the Ranunculus being stamped & applied heale the *Plague* sores: {remember againe that they are unsociale flo: & endure no other neere them & therefore require beds alone:}[127]

Salvia Sage, It will be wondered how this esculent plant came into our *Coronarie Garden*; but when you shall behold the immense & indicible varietie of the leaves their admirable & ~~various~~ stupendious variegations, colours & shapes, it will haply be as

---

126. **[Insertion on separate piece of paper]** These should be taken yearly up in mid June & preserved like Tulips in papers & boxes, & replanted about the beginning of Jan: in natural earth inrich'd {discreetly} & sanded, this is your securest season for this noble flower: When they begin to shew budds give them plentifull refreshments: Some will now & then lye dormant in their bedds & produce no flo: & the next year flo: againe

[Continued on separate piece of paper]

Ranunculus

But as we sayd pla: in Septr: they commonly perish with wett, though indeed the Sunn be proper, for it rotts with us the fibers, & then your plant will do no feates that yeare: but either stand at stay, or rott, or at most beares a pittifull flo: ~~& you wi~~ & accordingly you will find your roote lesse when you take it up that which have sett: fresh sand the under turfe earth is best for it, & in failur of that gett river–sand or Sea–sand which is best so it be exceeding fine, such as they scowre pewter with; get it in May or June & mix them to halfes, & with Kitchin–Garden mould, so let it ly till Septr or Jan, & then prepare your bedds, & plant 1 inch deepe laying any good earth at bottom, & sifting this mixture on it, then pl: your Ranunclus rootes, then cover them 2 inches with the same: If you plant in Septr: {or about} Michaelmas, cover them as soone at they peepe with matts, ~~unlesse the Weather be very dry, in the latter end of March & Aprill,~~ or Straw: But planting in Jan, you save the trouble unlesse the weather be very temperate & dry, in such dry weather water them once in 2 or 3 days in Mar & Aprill: If the frost prevent you this moneth, plant as soon after as you can, & if you cover, remember your rules for ayring as in Anemones; If you keepe either these rootes or Anemonys 2 yeares out of ground they will grow & blow never the worse so they be well dryed, & if over dry, so as sometimes to ly buried a whole summer without flowring, or even growing, yet another yeare they may take; Take them out when withered about June, & though they grew not, dry them yet well, for the next yeare they may prosper: verte

[Continued on verso] When you have ordered your earth as above, lay but a thin bed of ~~Earth~~ naturall Earth without mixture of dung about an inch thick, on your bed of prepared Earth, then place your roote, then ~~as~~ cover with as much naturall Earth, then your rich composition, Thus for all rare bulbs & Tubers; for though they love to grow in rich mould, yet the body of the roote is best in naturall Earth for reasons already presented.

127. **[Insertion on separate piece of paper]** This is an ordinary wild crow foote ~~a bi~~ of 3 or 4 colours, a bissanual raised of seeds; but better of slips in either Spring, ~~fitt for~~ a bordure flo:

much wonder'd ~~how~~ why it {was} kept so long out: but we referr the particulars, & the Seacret [128] of it to another place; in the meane tyme we know how it is propagated by slipps, in good earth, moderately moistn'd, and its virtues are innumerable for

Cur moriatur Homo cui Salvia

The *Solsequia* or *Heliotrops* are raised in warme rich grounds about {Aprill} the spring.[129] {frequently watered} 'tis an annuall plant of a stately {gigantine} & majesticall reguard: The Seedes of it are altogether as good (though not so greate) as the Pistacia, and as pleasant: & it ~~bl~~ yealds an excellent terpentine; but the *magneticall* qualities we shall describe hereafter.

Thrachelium Americanum {or the Cardinals flower} plant in potts the earth well macerated and preserved from th'extremitie of winter: They may {& ought} annually {to be} separated and transplanted about March, and the fibers buried 2 find{g}ers deepe, watered, & placed in the Sun, where most it thrives: The Seede yields no varietie (but its signature is for the throate.) {treate the pott in winter as you **[continued in margin]** are taught to do the Marum Syriacum planted in a warme exposure, mossed about, & covered with a bell till Spring: in mild weather expose it, for feare of moulding, set your pot 3 or 4 inch in earth above the brimms:}

Yucca, or *Indian bread* delights in a strong ground, shallow planted, in the spring it may be multiplied, otherwise not to be removed or disturb'd.[130]

Viola tricolor is of .3. or 4 Sorts, best propagated by plants but the Common *Violet* being dubble, multiplie exceedingly both [131] by seedes and strings being planted early, or in the Autumne in moyst & shady grounds: ~~The purple Colour, perfume with which they tinge the aire, & the delicious & usefull syrup advances this humble & modest plant flower above most of the Coronarie.~~ when they begin to bud for flo: clense them of their ~~flo~~ strings to maintaine the flo: the better, refresh them about *Octob*: & string them againe: The dubble do not beare Seede, but take such as of dubble degenerate & sow in *March*, {Aprill} or *Octob*: & *rescente luna*. {or for increase the **[continued in margin]** Seede of the Single} but of these [132] improvements hereafter, whilst the ~~purple~~ magistraticall colour perfume which they tinge the aire with ~~the~~ its delicious and usefull syrupe elevates this humble & ~~b~~ modest flower above most of the Coronary.

　　　And here we will make an end of this voluminous and endlesse talke Summarily

---

128. **[Margin note]** lib: 3. c: 1.

129. **[Margin note]** when 6 inch high transplanted

130. **[Insertion on separate piece of paper]** It is best {to pl: in Cases {in rich Earth} &} to house it in winter, yet it will support most winters abroad, & in the naked bed; I will teach you how to raise it; observe the duggs, ~~with~~ & tuberanes which the old rootes putt out on their sides a little[,] order the Earth, breake them off, putt them in good Earth, a little of the top peeping above ground, & plunge your pott in the hott bed: so you may increase them, it produces a beautifull stemm of flowers in July & Aug which will hang long:

131. **[Margin note]** Pansy

132. **[Margin note]** Cap: 1: lib: 3.

running over, or rather naming {onely} the lesse observable ~~which are~~ & easily governed, ~~which~~ by the rules already prescribed, which are such as follow.

[Page 301]

{Aster Atticus}[133]

Aconitum. Some of the kinds at least, as the *Napellus*, {of seede in Apr: for bordurs, an annual onely,} *Luteum Ponticum* etc. *Antirrhinum*[134] or *Snapdragon: Armeria* Sweete Williams.[135] {~~The Bel flower, an annual,~~} {Carduus[136]} {Crysanthemum[137]} {Cardamine}[138] {Camæmelum double set yearely of young slipps every Spring it being tender} {Cotula}[139] *Cyanus,*[140] Blew bottles, *Convoluulus,*[141] ~~Caccolus Mariæ~~, or our Ladys *Slipper, Chamæiris dwarfe flo: de luce*, {Companula or bells, of rootes, transplant now & then the rootes, ~~not too dee~~ shallow, else they will come late, & small: when don bearing & dry, cutt them}[142]

---

133. **[Insertion on separate piece of paper]** Aster starr–wort annual, but the Italian or blew Marigold ordinated, propagated by the roote

134. **[Insertion on separate piece of paper]** The Yellow {variegated white and} the best, the seeds ripe in Aug, sow, the 2d yeare they beare flo: & to preserve the old roote slip it {in the end of May} & treate it like the double stocke: take such slips as rise not to flo: some of mine have continued divers years without more trouble:

135. **[Insertion on separate piece of paper]** S: Williams raised best of slips {with a little of the roote} in Spr: or Autumne, after flo: cutt them: But the Pride of Lond: which is another sort propagated of seede in Spr: tis an annual: se another paper **[Continued on separate piece of paper]** The most choyce of these are the latifolia ~~an mo~~ & that singular pretty flo: cald the Velvet Armerias, & the double John etc:

136. **[Insertion on separate piece of paper]** Carduus globus Major & minor, may for its late flower & use in potts be addmitted the first raised of seedes {Spring} & beare the 2d yeare, but the latter: sometimes will abide many years without removing:

137. **[Insertion on separate piece of paper]** Crysanthemum corne Marigold an annual that of Peru & Candy or Sunflower of which I have raised gigantics, raised of seed easily & to be planted in some warme ~~Corner~~ place against the Sun & supported from wind: The double Marygold of Seedes the larger is most rare:

138. **[Insertion on separate piece of paper]** Cardamine Ladys smocks of Slipps {in Autumne} to edge bordures, & tonsile when the flo: is past: flo: Apr: & May.

139. **[Insertion on separate piece of paper]** Cotula {double:} propagated of slipps in {beginning of} Sep: & nipping off the first appearing flo: budds:

140. **[Insertion on separate piece of paper]** Cyanus blew bells: propagated of Seedes which brings greate varietys sown at Spring, it being an annual: The Sweete Sultan is of this but a far rarer kind frequently raised on the hott bed in Spring & then transplanted: The Snow–White of them is a beautifull flower: it must be frequently watered & yearly also renewed: The Spanish Corne–flower is another sort: Mr: Rea adds to these Parkinsons Jaceæ marina Bætica which is the vulgar greate blew bottle: & lastly the bastard Saffron or Carthamus Sativus whose Seede are brought us from Spaine:

141. **[Insertion on separate piece of paper]** Convoluulus are raised of Seedes commonly: the greate blew is sometimes raised in the hott bed, the rest require little care, but a stake or threid to climb by:

142. **[Insertion on separate piece of paper]** Campanula: the peach–leav'd, if

Dens Caninus {is one of the Satyrions, a pretty flo:}¹⁴³
Dragons–Claw of Seede sowd in Aprill & transpl: in Some by corner, they flo: from May 3 or 4 moneths, renew their raisings every 4th year for they seldom last longer: they are for bough potts etc:}
¹⁴⁴*Gentiana* major & *Pneumonanthe*
Gramina striata tremula etc:
¹⁴⁵{Hedyserum of various colours}
¹⁴⁶*Hollihocks* {in March {or Aprill} if you will have them early in H: bed, transpl: lat end of May: In no more earth they do as well; sow in spr: transpl: in Aug:: they flo: from July many moneths: Seede ripe in Sept: for bow & flo: potts: bordurs: garded from winds, not cutt but to take away the dry stalkes}
¹⁴⁷*Hesperis*:
¹⁴⁸*Lupines*
¹⁴⁹{The French Marigold raised in h: bed, at Sp: transpl: flowers in July as well though later flowering in natural earth, this an annual:}

---

the double may be had is rare, The Tracheliums are of this tribe ~~both~~ the Gyant etc: all of them hardy enough: plant the roote in Sept: in any ~~soile~~ coole ~~soile~~ place & Soile Se Flos Cardinalis: & set it next:

143. **[Insertion on separate piece of paper]** Dens Caninus: The white, red, purple & yellow etc: plant them in naturall earth in Aug early, covering them from all wett till they have taken hold, for 14 or 15 days. We do not easily multiplie them, but by the forraigne Flo: Merchants out of Flanders: ~~keepe~~ endeavor to preserve them early, & never keep them long unplanted:

144. **[Insertion on separate piece of paper]** Gentiana major may {in tyme} be raisd of seede, if you can have that which is mature; but by rootes in Sepr: in a warme rich ground securd from cold, & therefore the banke would be under some south wall:

145. **[Insertion on separate piece of paper]** Hedysarum Clypiatum or French Honysuckle an Annual flowers not till the 2d yeare & dye the next cold weather:

146. **[Insertion on separate piece of paper]** but the Holyhoc: sowd in Spring, seldome flo: the same yeare, ~~unlesse~~ but such as are sowed in Aug: do: last many yeares: The {double} black is counted rarest: which when you observe you may transplant the dunn beauty {in Octob:} Remember to preserve the first bearing of Seede: if you cutt Holyhoc neere Winter, the wett & cold will indanger it

147. **[Insertion on separate piece of paper]** Or Dames Violet & Queene Gilly-flo: are raised of slipps & branches, shaded & watred as (once for all) you should even do till such young things have taken rootes) nipping their budds at first appearance: The Singles are raised of Seedes: but the double are most prised, & of these the double striped: double purple, & double white etc: exceedingly sweete:

148. **[Insertion on separate piece of paper]** Lupines of various sorts, {the blew greate is best} ~~alw~~ set all the Spring long {especially Aprill} in bordurs, flo: in July, Seede in Aug: but they should be supported, ~~& do well~~ so the Scarlet kidney beane with a support set them in the Sunn:

149. **[Insertion on separate piece of paper]** Linaria of the white, yellow, & purple flo, the Sweete purple, Valentia, & the Broome Toad flaxes are the chiefe kinds

Moly {Indian & of Peru {The Homeric} in good strong earth, exposd to the Sun ~~seldom waterd~~ renew often the earth: The Montpeliense is tender & for the pott & conserve: Take all Molys up when the stalks dry, purge them of offsetts: See the incredible virtues in Hom Odyss: 10: & Plin: L: 25: c: 4: & Joseph: L: 7: c. 24: which some thinke to be the plant: Others say it mysticaly meanes membrum virile}

[150]*Nigella medica cochleata: Lurata, Spinosa* etc.

~~*Orbus venetus*~~ everlasting pease.[151] {*Pomum amoris*}

[152]*Pulmonoria* {Ptarmica the double white encreased of the stemm rootes:}

[153]*Phalangium* {Nor is the Popy to be omitted for its variety of Colours, & more stupendious Vertues, more shebendian offering Ergo}[154]

[155]{Radix cava}

& the last is best, the 2 first abide in the Winter: the rest die & must be yearely sowd in a warme place raised without difficulty:

150. **[Insertion on separate piece of paper]** Nigella The Spanish & double flo: annuall & the double sowe in Spring any where, & sometimes sowe themselves:

151. **[Insertion on separate piece of paper]** Pommum Amoris: Annual raised in hotbed: they are of 3 kinds, received for the beauty of the Apples not flo: if sowd in ~~ordinary~~ rich ground well watred (which they exceedingly require} they will succeede ~~well~~ sometimes within the hot bed:

152. **[Insertion on separate piece of paper]** The double Parthenium or Fellefew, propagated of slipps in the beginning of Septr:

153. **[Insertion on separate piece of paper]** Phalangium of Savoy: The non ramosum: The white Italian, & Virginian, plant in moyst ground, transplant in Septr: will endure 4 yeares without removing, & may be raised of Seedes in 3 or 4 yeares & produce varietys especialy the lilly Asphodills.

154. **[Insertion on separate piece of paper]**

Ergo sæcundum super omne germen

Ne Deus fecit, numeroque turbæ

vincit mea seminalis

Capsula Castrum.

fertiles crescunt homini Labores,

crescunt & ubique Morbi,

per totum vigil evagatur

Fertilis orbem.

hoc mundum miseratus ægrum,

Pater, viditque deditque nostram

Utque tantisque Antidotum Venenis

Fertiliorem.

Cowley: 4: Plant. [p. 235]

'Tis sowd in Spr: or Autumn, ~~afte~~ Flo: in May & then sowes itselfe: but the older the Seede the better & more double & various Colours it will produce:

155. **[Insertion on separate piece of paper]** Radix Cava. the white & blush shew themselves a moneth in Spring, & then suddainely disappeare: you may either leave it in, or take it out of the ground yearely: they increase & grow in any light shady ground:

Sisyrinchium The Spanish nut: {a kinde of Iris hardly flowering with us:} *Sanicula guttata major*

Soldanella, Scabiosa: {triannual}[156] *Scorpoides,* or Caterpillars of many Sorts:[157]

Saponaria flo: dupl: {Stramonium}[158] {Planta Sensitiva}[159]

{Speculum Veneris}

Thlaspi Creticum[160] {or} Candy Tufts: *Thalictrum Hispan:* {*album*} *Alpina,* white Spanish Tufts

Viola Lurasis {the white especialy:} Viola Mari{a}na[161] {also the Virginian yellow violet:}

[162]and infinite others. [163]{Then follow other *Annuals*} Most of which are propagated by seedes, Slipps, & Rootes without the least difficulty:

---

156. **[Insertion on separate piece of paper]** Scabius of Seede ~~Apr or Aug:~~ Spring or Autumne, but about St Bartho[lo]mus is the properest: ~~sow~~ mingle your Seede with dry Earth in sowing, else it will hardly strew: for bordures, & to be supported, cutt the ~~stalkes~~ stalkes of the seede when ripe, the plant will spring, & lasts 4 or 5 years without renewing: but then raise them againe: se the other paper (D)

[Continued on separate piece of paper] Our English white flowered Scabius: The Red Austrian Scabius, & Red Indian, whose Sede produce best varietys yearely sowd, unlesse it stand warme: To procure good Seede from the rest transplant young plants the beginning of June & that will keepe them back from running the first yeare to flower, & so you will have them in time the next: which sow in Aprill: reserve the Seede of the lightest & best mixed Colours: Se Mr: Rea:

157. **[Insertion on separate piece of paper]** a grovling plant & to be supported Sowd in Aprill, & only for curiosity not the flowers:

158. **[Insertion on separate piece of paper]** The Thorne Apple an annual, yet often they sow themselves & continue: to be planted in some wast[e?] corner for variety, not much ornament:

159. **[Insertion on separate piece of paper]** The Sensitive or Mimous plant is raised in the hott bed with great care as Melons are, & when risen to a handfull high, to be set with clod & all in a pott, & exposed to the hotest place of the Sun, plunging the pott in the Earth, & keeping it covered with a Glasse ~~all cold~~ when the Sun shines not out, unlesse the weather be very steady, there is also the humble plant, the one shrink from you, the other bend to the earth on the touch a Curiosity not for the flowers:

160. **[Insertion on separate piece of paper]** Thlaspi an annual to be sowed in Aprill; flowers in July: pretty for bordurs, changes colour with age, it often sowes itselfe some years, but dissorderly, for it would be sowd in rowes: for a Sommer flo:

161. **[Insertion on separate piece of paper]** The Viola Mariana {bearing bells} is an annual to be sowd in Spring: removed to a stake where it may climbe

162. **[Insertion on separate piece of paper]** The Aconites for their flowering & verdure in ~~Jan~~ Winter are received into our Garden: They are propagated of rootes any where from may to Septr: & neede not removal:

163. **[Insertion on separate piece of paper]** Ricinus: S: Palma Christi raised {in spring} of seede in the straw bed described in c: 4: in may ~~put in~~ remove it into a pot:

As for the *Aquatic plants* {which produce *Coronary* flowers} there may with the helpe of the Fountaine be fitted some corner for them, in some place that may not disorder the Garden: or else such as the *Nymphæa alba & lutea* may be cultivated in deepe potts, not perforated in the botome; let the earth be fatt, & as it were swimm with water: also the *Caltha Palustris*, refreshing the mould in *Autumne*; but the water needes not *Supernatare* as in the other, it will suffice that the Earth be always kept moyst, & that it be preserved from extreame frosts; & so it will flourish in Spring[164] and Autumne: {which is also their season for planting: & their rootes increase as other} Lastly, the *Trifolium palustre* etc. which shall suffice for the Aquatique, in case you think it not better to reserve them for the next chapter, where we bring in the Marshes: {But yet these for being so neere of kin to the Crow Foots, especialy the double we afford it place here:}

But now it has bin demanded by some, whither in our *Coronary Gardins* there be no admition for any of the *Esculent plants*: If we shall take them at large, & as *Pliny* has enumerated them under that title, there are truely very few of the ~~Kitchin~~ {Olitorie} Garden, which may not pretend to that honour: Especially the *Buglosse & Borrage*, whose flowers were frequently insertd **[page 303, i.e. 302]**[lxxxi] into Gyrlands & other flory workes: But there are some others, which rather for their agreable odor seeme in our opinion to challenge a better right to it: of which Sort are the ~~Marjoram Marum~~ {*Ocimum* Basil an annual: it is of 2 sorts sow it in Aprill} *Marum* or Mastic, {especialy the *Syriacum* is a rare plant, to be slipd, for even of the seeds we have raisd them with care, the potts in winter must be treated as the Cardinals flo: & with thornes in Summer defend from catts: the sent cures the hed ache **[continued in margin]** the other mastic is propagated of slipps in Spring, shaded & then exposd to the Sun {moderatly}, & defended in hard winter; it will indure: pruning it of the stickinesse} *Limon Tyme*

Lavendula {of 4 sorts} and some others; because without them a *Nosegay* cannot be compos'd without going out of our *Coronary Garden*; {is not to be wanting} ~~and besides as they may be disposed with the~~ {and besides as they may be disposed with the **[continued in margin]** common sweete Majoram is a well knowne annual, but that which is cald the Gentle is sweeter, an annual & to be sown in Aprill}

Majorana Aurea, {gilded, that of winter is most rare, raised of seeds & Slips that of the browne green leaves not gilded is sweetest:[165]

Salvia variegata {of which there are indeed stupendious varieties: some small, some greater, some musky & most rare; how to make it variegat we have spoke else where L: 3. c. 1. raised of slipps May:}

~~Crowfoote ordinary bissannual of several Colours raised of Seedes but best of the slip in~~ {either} ~~Spring, or a border flo:~~

~~(1) Crassula flowers in Aug:~~

The Caterpillar rather for curiosity than flo: is best raised by Seede in hott bed, replant, & water them: They seede about the beginning of Sept; an annual:

164. **[Margin note]** needs little moving but to multiply.

165. **[Insertion on separate piece of paper]** Pulegium though an Olitory plant the tufted sort may be addmitted: placed of roote in Spring are standard: in shady ground:

Rosemarium Aureum[166] yea and[167]

Caulis crispatus variatus (of which there are most rare & admirably coloured, and some that have a sent of muske) we say, as these may be disposed, they are not onely to be admitted, but so placed as to add a wonderfull Varietie.

And thus with what brevitie & certitude we were able, have {wee} gon ~~over~~ through the severall *Bedds*, {*Borders* &}, parterrs ~~& Compartiments~~ of our *Coronarie Garden*, and if what has bin sayd be not sufficient to give it the reputation which we designed, ~~it~~ it is because we have {not} yet visited such ~~bushes~~ *Trees*, *bushes* & *shrubbs* as have just title to their places, both for their flowers, sent, & verdure, & without which, the corners & centers of many ~~Contrivances, of~~ workes & compartiments as well as the Wales would remaine naked, ~~as~~ & be exceedingly deficient: A word therefore or two concerning them, before we present you with our Catalogue & shut up this Chapter:

Acacia Indica {flowers twise a yeare} 'tis raised by Seedes well soaked & sowen in Potts taken out of the Pods before they are too old: or planted in rich mould set in a very warme place: being decaied is renewed by cutting.

Alaternus[168] of which there are ~~3~~ {6} sorts {but 3 most knowne) very conspicuous, one of which is variegated with white, another with yellow: of all perenniall greenes, most to be preferred for *Contr'Espaliers* Divisions & Cabinetts in the *Coronary Garden*: Raisd by Seedes in good earth, also by Layers: to be transplanted at 2 years: It is a tonsile ~~plant~~ {shrubb}. Sow it in Spring or Autumne. {The ~~seedes~~ berries washed, dried, & broaken containe 3 Seedes in Each:}[169]

Althæa frutex has a pleasant flower, {the striped is rare: raisd of layers or graffed by approch:}

[170]*Arbor Indæ* {3 kinds} by every one knowne.

Amonium plinij[171] {The Arbutus, of Layers, seldom produces suckers; {English seede best} 'tis a most hardy plant, & may be set where it may have room enough.}

---

166. **[Insertion on separate piece of paper]** Rosemary: the Latifolia, Golden, Silverd, more rare, & double flowered: besides the Common Sort: all affect a Sunny Wall, propagated in March & latter part of August: the Season moyst:

167. **[Insertion on separate piece of paper]** Serpillum Time is the Limon, Muske, Tufted & Gilded, which last are rarer, propagated ~~both~~ of Seede, but best of slips in Spring; To these Mr: Rea adds the Abrotanum viridi flore amplo flowering in July, increased by Slips in March, preserved in potts in the shade in Summer, & from the cold in the house in Winter:

168. **[Insertion on separate piece of paper]** falsely cald Philirea (by our Gardners) as it was by Morin in Paris, not out of ignorance but to advance its price when he first brought it in regulation: etc:

169. **[Insertion on separate piece of paper]** Arbutus whose being is most oriental in the Autumne moneths: tis raised of Seedes & layers with care: & then an hardy plant, & is apt for palisad or standard:

170. **[Margin note]** which in regard of the lastingnesse of the flower, do beautifully at the corners of grand squares & knotts: to be encreasd of branches or layers:

171. **[Insertion on separate piece of paper]** Amonum Plin: raisd of the berys, conservatory in Winter:

Chamelæa. The *Mezereon*, planted in the shade, & a moist place. for the glorie of the berys & blossomes: {is raisd of seed in July: in a box they are lazy in comming up; remove in the 2 yeare.}

Clematis or perwinkle of ~~12~~ kinds, thriving best in the shade, & must be supported, the flo: are very beautifull: a knowne plant Cupressus, Cypresse The Male best for our purpose, and of all the Trees, admittable into the Coronary Garden The Principle, for his aptitude to be made pyramidal & slender, so as not to over shadow the beds, whose corners are most gracefull **[page 304]** adorned with them: They are onely raised by Seedes taken out of their *Galbuli* or nutts (in England {seldom or} never mature) & sowen in Cases about March: keepe them well watered & transplant them after a year in ordinary Earth, expos'd to the Sun after they have taken roote; but of these see cap: 4: The cuttings would [172] be saved to burne in the Garden amongst other Aromatiques of which hereafter:

Cerasus alb: multiflora, a white dubble flo: Chery; because our Coronary Garden is not alltogether to be without some fruit gratefull to the palate, as well as pleasant to the eye: It is graffed in the stock {or inoculated} as other cherys are: {Of the Megaziner hereafter:}[lxxxii]

[173]*Ficus Indica* {is rooted by plunging a leafe onely into the Earth: when it first begins to move in spring.}

Genista The white raised of Seedes first well macerated: also planted in rich earth, not too hott, & kept well watered. {The Spartum Hispanum makes a pretty heading, & also dos well for shew in standard as it may be raised of seede or succkerss: it dos also well in potts, rather raisd in hot bed:}

Granadile or Passion Flower, a sweete & glorious flower, ~~of Seedes~~ in May the Moone increasing, sow the seedes in fatt & spongy earth, much expos'd to the Sun, & secured from the winds: when it is very dry water it {aboundantly}, & being grown to some stature support it with a stake for it will else grovell, like the ~~Clem~~{Ivy}~~atis~~ or *Convolvolus*. In *Brasile*, they make curious Arbours and close walkes of them. Se: cap: 18.[174] {They continue divers years without sowing: but yet the stalkes die in winter: & must be defended if in Potts; set them in your Conserve; let them set if in the hott bed in Spring to hasten the flo:}

[175]*Jasminum* of this there is the vulgar in the white flo: best raised by layers {~~in good moyst & shaded ground~~} as other greenes are, leaving not above a bud or two uncovered & covering the rest: choosing a round smooth twigg about as big as a swanns quill: Also by suckerrs: When they are come to some height, keepe them low by cutting & pruning, but plant them in rich mould, shaded & frequently refreshed: The grow in all aspects, & in the open ground, being hardy enough to endure all ordinary weather, so that our Gardiner may have flowers enough for the making of oyles & essences in aboundance. {Also it may be formed into palisads etc.} There is

---

172. **[Margin note]** L: 2: c: 20: L. 2.

173. **[Insertion on separate piece of paper]** ~~Cytisus Maranthe for its early glorious flower~~

174. **[Margin note]** L: 2:

175. **[Insertion on separate piece of paper]** Hypericum frutex for his early flo: & perennial nature, raised by layers:

likewise the *Indian Jasmine* & Persian; These are more tender & should be planted in the Cases; & ~~carri~~ secured amongst the delicate: ~~plants~~ set in fine fat earth, expos'd to the Sun, watered, pruned in the decrease of March, when also it may be layed or graffed by Approch: {about Aprill or May} So also: {also the Indian Flavum or yellow: rare shining leafe, small most sweet flo: raisd of Layer: kept in Gr: house} The red *Indian Jassmine of Canada*, which must have a propp: or smale *Palisade* to sustaine it. {it will also be raisd of Seedes: or the stock of the common jasmine} The *Spanish* {or Catalonian **[continued in margin]** all the common white Jassmins} may be inoculated in *June* or *July* rubbing off all the ~~Smaler~~ budds, & smaler suckers, & keeping the grasse low. But at every 2d yeare take them Earth & all out of their Cases, & pare off the rootes & earth 2 fingers breadth with a knife & so replant it againe in new mould; and if you will[176] have it thrive gallantly cutt the branches within ~~an inch~~ {a little} of the stemm every spring of the yeare, it having first put forth the 5 or sixt bud:[177] Do this to the *Persian* ~~every~~ the 2d yeare from its graffing, & that neere the stock, & keepe the~~m~~ branches short, the 3d yeare they will be shott a foote, thus trimmed from yeare to yeare till the Tree be about a yard high, in which ~~posture~~ stature it may continually be kept, allways; as well in this, as in the other remembring to prune away the dry, & dissorderly spray, that it may not be choaked with too much wood. It is a tender plant as we sayd; yet at other tymes; the weather not being extreamely rigorous, it requires not so much care, & may endure a long while in the Porticos **[page 305]** Secured from the North & Eastern blasts: when you water it be careful not to bathe the leaves, for it kills them in Winter, but in the Summer you may irrorate them rather with a brush then the pott, this will wonderfully inliven them. ~~And~~ {Now} though (as we sayd & find by experience) the ordinary white ~~Gess~~ *Jassmine* ~~wel~~ support the winter well enough being expos'd; yet some, who are very curious, & would prevent all Accidents, will loosen the branches from the walls & *Palisads* to which they are affixed, & a little before the cruel winter frosts invade them gently incline & bend them prostrate to the Earth where they cover the Tree with matts till the spring, that they redresse it as before; but this may as well be done, & without so much trouble; by nailing matts before them. {There is also the double Spanish} Another *Indian* ~~Jassmine~~ or *American Jassmine* is also raised of seedes, exceedingly soaked & macerated in water ~~warm~~ {warmed in} the Sun: you may sow 2.or 3 in a pott of fatt earth {2 fingers deepe}: The season for this is from May till June; keepe them well moystned ~~at none~~ even at noone, & in a short tyme they will appeare if the Seedes be good: when they are two inches high, transplant them in Pots apart with the Earth & all, very plentifully refreshing them; or else set the potts in a larger Vessell of water, as we shewed of *Carnations*: when they begin to erect, set a stick or prop that it may cling about it, for it is a very weake plant of itselfe: Lastly prune off the exuberant branches, suffering it not to shoote too high. {There is also the Arabian, which flo: from Spring to Autumn but exceeding tender & therefore to be set in our Green–house} There is yet another *Indian* Jassmine of a crimson & noble Colour, which grows very tall being supported ~~which~~ & very well indures the

---

176. **[Margin note]** water it often

177. **[Margin note]** for a rule cut none of these above plants till they shoote a little

winter; but it must be watered from spring to Summer: It is ~~ra~~ propagated ~~by layers~~
& multiplied by layers:

{*Juniper* comes of Seedes, like the Cypresse, & may be shorne into boules[?] {hedges}
etc: I have seen an Ar - ca - ly[?] to contain 2 or 3 person cut in one road/round[?]
in England:}

[178]*Malus Punica*, especially the *Bulaustia hort: Eystitensis*
with the dubble flo: is one of the most glorious rutilant
& illustrious flowers of the *Coronary Garden* {aboundantly} suppling that
in colour which it wants in odor, *adeo nihil est ab*
omni parte perfectum, which we should cherish with all diligence:[179] All *Pomegranades*
may be raised of Seedes, but it is best produced of *layers & Suckers* {& is budded} it
loves a good mould, ~~&~~ to be exposed to the Sun, & frequently watered. They do very
well ~~planted~~ {preserved} in large Potts & Cases, or to be planted against a well defended south wall, & should be suffered to grow tall, else it becomes too bushy going
all into knotts & wood, nor beare they flo: as they otherwise would: being plashed &
kept as we have instructed [180]you in Cap: 15, concerning Citrons, by which meanes
your trees will also become charged with fruite, which otherwise, out of the conserve
you are in vaine to expect. They may also be aplied to ~~Palisade~~ & hedge worke; ~~in~~
~~whi~~ but then (for being on both parts perspirable) unlesse against a ~~wa~~ Southern wall,
you must cover them with frames of matts [181]in winter: of which consult: Cap: 7.

[Page 306] *Laurus*, of which there is besides the *Vulgar* {*Chamædaphne* raised of Seedes
& Cuttings} severall others whom we admitt in our Coronary Gardens for their[182]
perennial & pleasant greenes, ~~for the~~ berries & flowers: Especially the Oleander, raised
of layers, suckers etc: kept moyst. {So also the *Laurus Tinus*, {Cerastus}, *Laureola* {etc.
layer} a little before *August*.}

The *American* Laurals, governd like the *Myrtil*, but would not be much pruned: it may
also be raised of berries {or layers} like the common Bayes, & Laurell, {of which one
kind is better & more glossy & thick then the other} & afterwards transplanted &
governd either in standards, or *Palisads*. Se: L: 2. cap: .7 & 15. {Most of these Laurells
love ~~moist~~ shady ground & are hardy when old, the Oleanders excepted:}

Ligustrum privet: as the *Perwinkle*:

~~Len~~

~~Moly~~

Lentiscus Peru{*vi*}*ana* ~~or Moly~~ to be planted in excellent earth & a warme place, the
dry & arid twigs cutt away, the rest pruned, 'tis propagated by Layers, but which you
may not separate 'till 2. or 3 yeares after because they strike roote so slowly: also by
suckers they are multiplied.

{*Lignum vitæ* by layers:}

Myrtus the Myrtil {The {sweetest} Nymph of our Gardens} of all sorts must at no hand
be wanting in our Coronary Garden: we have the dubble Flowerd (so fortunately

---

178. **[Margin note]** place this after Laurus
179. **[Margin note]** but the rarest is that of the striped kind:
180. **[Margin note]** L: 2.
181. **[Margin note]** L: 2.
182. **[Margin note]** Laurocerasus; The L[aurus]: tinus of which 3 sorts

~~found~~ discovered by the ever noble *Perieskyus*.) The broad leaved, narrow leaved, single=flo:[183] in all 9 or 10 sorts (could we procure them) all which may be raised of Seedes, Suckers, Layers, & cuttings so they be kept exceedingly moyst for

> *Littora Myrtetis lætissima*
> Geor: [2.112]

There is nothing more affects it. If you ~~sow~~ raise them of Seede let it be in *March*, but choose such Seedes as come new over: & keepe them delicately till they ~~swell spring~~ are strong (for they are over tender which are thus produced & therefore we commend it not much) at 3 yeares transplant them deepe, & ~~cut~~ cut of their topps, within a handfull of the Earth. They rejoice in a rich mould & comfortable aspect, yet shaded in the excessive heates: They are best secured in Cases, & being a tonsile shrubb, may be shorne into any shape: to be placed in your Walkes & at the head of Beds & Compartiments: In Italy they are used like box (o delicious Country!) about their bordurs of flowers, & to forme the busie Parterre; & have bin knowne to grow in our *Elysium* expos'd: {likewise but then you must cover them with dry straw & matts in winter, & if any perish cutt at the foote the respiring: & yet even in Italy they had more then ordinary care of some of these sorts as we learn from Virgil: Dum teneras defendo a frigore Myrtos Ecl: 7: [6] & Ovid: Metuentum frigora myrtum & yet in another place Maro says Amanta frigora Myrtos & the hardiest with us is the Boetic latifolia.} Se: cap: 14.[184,185]

Oleaster, or Wild Olive, Is propagated by Suckers, in fat & moyst Earth, & in an airie place, yet well secured: {& the olive of luca is best}

[186]{Opuntia}

Peach bearing the dubble flo: is a *Coronary* Tree, & to be admitted for its beautifull flower, planted in rich Soile, & airy place, inoculated ~~in~~ {on an Abricott} the Moone increasing: pruned in Feb:

[Page 307] *Periclymenum*, {ordinary double} especialy the serotinum *flo: rubro*, which

---

183. **[Margin note]** the round leaved, the Boetic (a hardyer kind) the birds nest:

184. **[Margin note]** L: 2.

185. **[Insertion on separate piece of paper]**

Merisziere

The Merisiere or double blossom'd Chery may well for its shew & rarity be admitted into this Garden: There is another doub: flo: cherry which blossomes early, & would be joynd with the doub: flo: peach. Mr: Rea commends the graffing of this chery neere the ground in an able stock with the Flanders cluster cherry, to be plash'd to a wall for the rare succession of fruite:

186. **[Insertion on separate piece of paper]**

Opuuntia or the Indian figg:

Though an extravagant plant, bears a pretty pale yellow flo: succeeded with immature fruite: tis propagated by onely pricking a leaf into good ground which will take roote, but first let it a little sproute ~~some~~ {leaves} planted then abroad & they endured the most severe winters: The large sort is more tender, & must be set in potts for the Conservatory in Winter:

some call the bloody honysuckle: or *Caprifol*: raised in rich moyst earth, by layers &
Suckers, & for the rest treated like the white common ~~Gess~~ *Jasmine*: onely it shall not
require to be ~~trimmed~~ {cutt} so neere, but let grow to what stature you pleased supported with *Palisade* or Walls: but in no posture so gracious & glorious as when it is
governed ~~li~~ in forme of ~~the~~ a Cypresse {or globed} by being planted at the head &
{or} corners of *Coronary* beds, & sustaind by a stake at moderate [187]hight, to which
the plant being bound & suffered to rise no taller, free from suckers etc;[188] it should
be diligently clipt: for so will it thicken and blow in season from the very bottome
in most beautifull manner: {like a flowering obeliske: I would have some in Potts &
cases to carry in & perfume a roome.} {Clematis}[189]
{The Pyrocanth, raisd of berrys, a tonsile shrubb, & glorious in berries}
Phillyrea angusti folia comes well of Berries, & Layers: governed like the Myrtil, onely
it is so hardy as to indure all weather: This shrubb is of all others, one of the most
proper to forme into knobbs & boules for the decoration of the Coronary Garden in
fitting and convenient places: ~~such as~~ It is to be pruned now & then from the dead
wood:[190] But above all we may not forgett {~~The milke of Juno staind the~~ [continued
in margin] infra: ~~Chameastrys absurgens is raisd of seede & is fit for low hedges of
1 foote best to be kept clipt & to divide squares etc~~}
Rosa, Flos odorque divum etc etc:[191] The Rose would be planted (though also it ~~can~~ spring

---

187. [Margin note] yard before they spread:

188. [Insertion on separate piece of paper] In France they tie up the succkers
{about the main stemm} & clip them from a foote high, or even from the very earth,
till they come to what stature & shape they desire: but that upon a single foote seemes
to me the more beautifull.

189. [Insertion on separate piece of paper] next after Periclymenon:
Clematis or Virgins bower {(of which are both red & purple, & some double)}
is a bower plant for the Summer moneths in flo: propagated by Layers: Prune them
{short} in Spring both to ~~secure~~ take off what perishes in winter, & to inlarge the
flower:
There be no lesse then a dozen kinds of Periwinkles, which thrive well in shady
places; but should be supported; also they finely adorne bankes of earth in which they
will take roote, keepe them up, and beautifie with the flower: some of the leaves of
them are almost as large as a Lawrells

190. [Insertion on separate piece of paper] To this add the variegated whites
& yellow; tonsil (as the other) but of a taler kind, broad leafe, & more tender; yet with
some care when tis rooted, may endure the winter: The are propagated of Layers, &
planted in Spring, when they begin to shoote:

191. [Insertion on separate piece of paper]
A flower so universaly accomplish'd as that
Quicquid hoc Mundo superoque pulchrum est,
Optat et gaudet Roseum vocari,
Hæc Puellarum prope summa laus est,

Cowley: L: 3: Ro:

truly tis Porphirogenitra & comes crownd into the World Summa Dearum:
This is the flo: that Turks say sprang from the ~~blood~~ {sweate} of the Prophet: {& pro-

stormes & thick mists especialy in flowring tyme, & neede onely have the topps cutt off, the rest not much pruned; it is also a stoute plant. The *dubble white* may be bent & plied into any forme for intertexture with the rest; but loves no pruning, unlesse very old: {The Blush Rose} The {single &} *dubble Yellow* is reasonable hardy {plant it in standard somewhat shaded} & likewise abhorrs {much} cutting; yet to make them goodly ~~irradicate~~ {pluck} the supernumerarie: The suckers are transplanted at Spring. {Set this rose in the shade}[195] The muske rose[196] inoculated on the S: Brier should be pruned of its ~~dea~~ mortified branches, they are produced of Layers & cuttings: {The Spanish Muske}[lxxxiii] {The Guelder may be inoculated on the Damask: or propagated by suckers in Feb: as the rest are:} ~~Cneorum Ma~~ And what could be more pleasant then to behold a Palisade interwoven with all these {sorts of} roses some blushing, ~~others weeping, some~~ {others} pale, ~~others~~ red {& in a thousand varieties of Colour} with a bordure of Lilys under them! ~~misereons utile dulci~~ {Note that you may graff many sorts of roses on the Provence which flowering together & {t}will greatly delight you: But generaly for the Culture of Roses}[197] *Rhus* or *Indian Sumach* in Excellent Earth, and seasonably watered; but never pruned: It may be planted abroad & propagated by Suckers. {which it produces but too fast & will soone run over a ground} Lastly, for we
{The Rhus Myrtifolia is more rare, both of seede & rootes:} must conclude[198]
[199]Syringa, both blew {yellow} and white dubble flo: {of which the faire purple & white are rarest & that somewhat tender:} *Pipe-tree* They are all planted of Suckers {& layers} etc: One of them bearing nutts or *Balanus* is of admirable use; for the oyle

---

195. **[Insertion on separate piece of paper]** The culture of this Rose is by a particular processe accurately described by Mr Rea: To bud {a single yellow} in the Frankford stock neere the Earth & halfe a yard above the {place of this} bud when well shott put in a bud of the double yellow; {in this single yellow shoote:} preserve it from suckers, & rub off all the ~~roses~~ {budds} of the ~~stock~~ natural stocke: In 2 yeares it will beare, prune it neere in winter & cutt off all the small shootes, & abating the topps of the best & biggest as farr as they are small. In Spring rubb off the smallest bud leaves, leaving only some of the fairest, & when they appeare to flower nip also all supernumeraries if too neere one another:

196. **[Margin note]** of rare sent & commonly flower almost all the Autumne: plant it near a wall, it requires stature to beare:

197. **[Insertion on separate piece of paper]** Culture of Roses: they are best {singly} inoculated on the Damask, Wite, wild Eglantine, as soone as ~~first~~ early Budds can be procur'd, as about mid June: The stock kept cleane from succkers: Mr Rea shewes good reason for budding neere the ground that the sprout may be dextrously layd in the ground & take roote, which is much better than the budded trees for propagation: & such as do not afford succkers to increase, must be layd in rich earth:

Cut them pretty neere after bearing, & againe towards the spring with a knife towards a leafe bud, purging the old seare wood

198. **[Insertion on separate piece of paper]** The Rubus Indicus {or} Americanus with its ample purple & sweete flower & broade leafe a rarity worthy of this place, though with us it beares no fruite:

199. **[Insertion on separate piece of paper]** The shrub Solanum with variegated leaves may be admitted {for the flo:} & is raisd of layers; & so the Spiræa frutex:

of Seedes) of suckers {setts & layers} in a [192]rich mould, a Suny place, {they love not wetting round} a span deepe, & at a fathomes distance, & that in *Autumne*: This for the Generall: For there are many rare varieties of them, ~~especially~~ besides The Common Damaske, {red dwarfe double} Red, ~~Pro~~ White, Province As the Marble, Christall, Dubble Yellow, Ponfraict, {Vergin rose without thornes} Austrian, Muske, Rosa mundi, {which is but the striped red} Monethly or Italian {flo: pieno}, Yorke & *Lancaster*, Centifolia, Bataua, Inodura, Variegata, Velvet, China,[193] Cistus or holly rose, the Cynorrhodon or Eglantine, {double dugg rose} The *Sambucus*, or Elder rose {*Cneorum Matthioli* or the *Rock rose*:} with with [sic] many more, and which we have heard of that {a} Curious Gardiner had most of them growing upon the *Same* stocke For as the Muske yellow & dubble may be grafted {& inoculated} on the Sweet brier; so the rest upon other stocke to say nothing of the *Holly* because we are not ye satisfied: It is good to ~~prune~~ {clip} them after they have don blowing,[194] & in ~~afte~~ Octob: ~~&~~ {or} Novemb: {sometimes Christmas} to prune them of superfluous wood keeping them handsomly staked & upright, for so might this tree, which we usuall behold ~~to~~ growing very extravagantly, be shaped into a comely forme, & fitt for th *Coronary Garden*: especially the Monethly, & the Province, which dos most grace fully amongst the *Lillys*, and the {earlier} *Jasmine*: But the *Italian* or *Monethly* wou be oftner pruned, especially at the midst of *October* even neere the ground, & in th end of *March*, or earlier, leaving not above one or two smaler branches; & then a litt before the full; but then water it not in the ~~14~~ 12 or 14 dayes before: Now & the also rejoice it with with [sic] well digested Soyle the Earth stirred about the stem & roote, & then frequently irrigating it[.] **[Page 307a]** Also shall you secure it fro the excessive nipping frosts, & pull off all the præcoce & early roses at spring befc they blow freely, if you desire to have them late. The *Batavian Rose* is hardy, {sweet & a great bearer} prune of its old wood: The *Variegated Rose* should be preserved fro

---

phanly from the B V. concerned with the smell of it.} Se how prettily Philostra resembled it to Cupid which makes me wonder at the {odd} antipathy of some this glorious flo: & 'tis sayd of verte **[continued on verso]** of the Chevalier de Gu {like another of our Lady Henage {on whose cheek a rose would raise a blister, the Portugal Frier whom the smell of it killd, as Libanius reports:}} that could indure to here one name it, but he would sound, cui non dicta rosa est? all the Pc have abounded in its prayses:

192. **[Margin note]** white province. red province {& there is of it spott double white roses. The damask, sine spines, white damask, {variegated damask} F semper virens: Frankford rose Incarnat rose. The muske rose is multiple: simpl Italica: ~~Lutea~~ {yellow}: is of sing & double Cinamon is sing & doub: The Canir double. Rosa Dunensis African is the same with the Vitria The Rosa Coccinia I nonian The Semper virens The Apple rose

193. **[Insertion on separate piece of paper]** or Ferrarius his rose of a beauty, raisd of seede, in March, in a moneth springing comfort it, house it till spr in 3 years it bears an incomparable flower, it produces suckers also, cutt the top E cover them with wax, leaving one or two: They are yet strangers with us, but ben propogated in Italy:

194. **[Margin note]** for so I have had them blow all August:

pressed out is the body of all perfumes; & the flo: of the white, little inferiour to the Orange, were it rightly understood: {Note that the double white must be set in at winter planted in rich earth: All syringas must be yearly near[?] purged of their wood: For these and the Spiræa Theophrasti or mock willow & the Rubus for its pretty flower:}

~~The Yucca beares a noble series of flo: on a long stalk, plant the gourd under earth which twill pepe the pott plunged in the~~ [indecipherable] ~~hotbed:~~

[200]And this shall suffice to shew both what kinds, and what approach of trees

---

200. **[Insertion on separate piece of paper]** Laburnum {or Beane trefoile}: 2 sorts, one a greate sort, both raisd of cuttings etc:

Cytisus secundus Clusij: a noble Trefoile, encreased of seeds or succkers:

Colutea Vesicaria {& Scorpoides} Bastard Senas both: all raisd, from seeds, suckers, layers or cuttings:

Nux Vesicaria bladder nut, increasd by succkers of which if well purg'd rises to a pretty shrub:

Paliurus Christs thorne, by layers, is somewhat tender:

Hedera Virginian, is a wonderfull tall climbing plant & if it did not loose the verdure in winter would be admirable beautifull: raisd by cutting some rootes from the old stock & turning them up endways:

Tamarisks, that of the white leafe rarest & perennial both increasd by sukers & Layers:

Larix or Larch {not evergreen} from the nutts in the Cones like Cypresses: bears a beautiful Flower:

Castanea Equina raisd of succkers beares when old a beautifull flow:

Some do also for curiosity {& shew} plant these following evergreens in some corners of the Flower Gardens, though we rather reserve them for Groves {& Walks} & thicketts. especially Abies the severall Firr trees & Pines all raisd of the Kernells these for walks: but for hedges & Arbors:

~~Arb~~ Cypresse of seedes, excellent for ~~Pat~~ Contrespaliers, heads of knotts & Arbours, of which elsewhe: ~~Agrifo~~ tonsile:

Agrifolium Holly, of seeds freed from the mucilege when ripe, & of rootes, especialy rare is the variegated with gold yellow, to be propagated by layers: tonsile:

Pyracanth: Evergreen thorne beautifull for the berrys, increasd by succkers Layers & seede most of all, do well in hedge is tonsile

Celastrus the staff–tree a tall tree with age, increasd by Layers, tonsile & good for hedging:

Buxus in standard or hedge, ~~especially~~ {but} the dutch dwarfe is cutt finly close & well wrought excellent for knotts & parterr Embrodery, & keep up bordures; some reject it for the smell: There is divers sorts, ~~som~~ one edgd with gold the Auratus, & there is also a dwarfe gilded: to be propagated by slipps in the Spring:

Arbor vitæ, of seeds, ~~&~~ {but best & easiest of} layers: will plash to poles, but is graish in winter: of a medicinal & balsamakall property:

Ilex Arbor or Evergreen Oake: ~~prop~~ I have raisd them frequently of the leaves, but you may increase them of Layers:

Vermicularis frutex major or Stone–crop of Layers & Cuttings in Spring, well shaded & refreshed pretty for the variety ~~& flowers~~

may be alowed for the Ornament of our *Coronary Garden* and flowry Regions; for as the greater *Viridaria*, *Vireta*, Mounds, {taller} Groves, prospects & other magnificent *Relievos* be indeede the principles of ~~the~~ our *Elysium*, taking it in the grosse, and the ~~Coronary Garden~~ {thinner} sprinklings or bordures of flowers but accessories & trimmings: so are these to our *Coronary Gardens*, where onely the Flowers are the chiefe; & the ~~Spires~~ Trees, Shribbs Spires, boales & pyramids, of the taller plants, but the lesser Ornaments; of which if there seeme to have bin too many introduced in this Chapter, the Choice & admission is in the breast of our Gardiner, he may make what collation he pleases; but some he ought of necessitie to make best but for the perfecting & [?] [page torn] fortifing of Nose–Gays, Garlands, & other flowry ornaments which without some verdure will be grea[tly?] [page torn] defective: We have omitted the Orange & some other bearing **[page 308]** which are likewise to have place at the heads of some quarters, & in the allees, for their flo: & leave sake; but of that copiously in Chap: 14. whither we reccommend you & proceede next to our *Catalogues*: in which yet we do onely pretend to give you the names of the most illustrious Flowers, ~~thei~~ omitting their descriptions (for the most part) which would ~~take up~~ trespass too much upon our *Gardiners* patience, and prevent him one of the greatest diversions, which is to describe them himselfe, when he would exercise ~~his R~~ the Flowers of his Rhetoric.

Tulipes

Achate 54 sorts, of which the *Royal* is one of the best, being though but of 3 colours yet perfectly distinguished & separated, cleere purple with red, pennached within a greate field of white; the *Achate Robin* somewhat resembles him: ~~Agot~~ *Achate minime* has 4 {distinct} colours: *Achat indented*, etc *Albertine gredilin: Amaranth* {white botome purple strakes} *Amidor*, {cinnamon colour red, strake[?], etc: a rare flower when rectified} *Amarilis*, {dark purple & white} {*Aminte*} *Admiral* 21 sorts. Admiral of France is obscure purple, cleere Colombine, & white, Admiral of England, browne red, lively colombine & white: Admiral of Holland red & white. *Admiral of Delfe* rose red & white. etc: {Arch Duke Imperiall one of the best English: & the brown purple} *Augustine*; *Albertine* smale panaches of purple, with Grie di lin & pure white. Aurora: *English beauty*, a faire Colombine, red & white. Aurora: *English beauty*, a faire Columbine, red & white. *Amidor* is one of the ~~fo~~ noble{st} now in vogue: of a beane colour, cleere with a little read yeloish Isabell, & Amaranth colour: {præcoce} *Argus*, *Augustus* the greate, colour of glowing rose, & white: *Astrea Bell–rose* the *Blackish*, {Purple blondine, colombine upon chammy:} *Brabantine*, *Bruxelle*, *Bellbrune* a large flo: of Amaranth colour, browne & white: {Belle Fantasque} *Bells minione*, *Belle Trojans*, etc. *Ced~~a~~{e} nulli* or give place to none, a most incomparable *Tulipe*, purple violet with a little red & much white: The Charitie, *Celestine*, {*Cloth of Silver*: 4 sorts.} *China* a graish Columbine, read & chammy: Cadetts, purple & much white, *Calista*, *Cæsar*, ~~colour of honey~~ *Concubine*, columbine & white, Cupid, deepe purple, & white: *Celestial*, *Corinthian*, The Chancelour, violet & white: *Curate* præcox, *Cardinale*, *Crowne Royall* ~~etc~~: *Candyot*, faire colombine, its flower resembles the *Druide*, red & white chammy. {Colchique Trojan:} *Doris* milke white with lively red: Ducal faire w. & red: {Dutchesse: w: purple red} Dons .4. *Erimanthian*, *Eminent* Eugenia {iræ} & Elizabeth Eus[ebe/ebius],[lxxxiv] [Fla?]*ming Tulip of Tunis*: 6 more: *Flandrian* panached with a faire purple upon white: *Faustine* [page torn] white, pale red, & never demenishes to its dying day **[page 309]** *Felicity*, *Frier Andrew* obscure red mixed with white, a præcox: 2 more Friers: *Galatea*, yellow Isabell & golden red: Genouese {*Golden*}: Gyant, The *Glorious* a faire *Tulip*,

Isabelle a little upon the yellow & golden read. General *Picot* milke white ~~pur~~ straked
with a little purple: Gentile, {Hanmer Agot pale gredlin, scarlet, {white} ~~white~~ a
rare flo: & has its determinat from that noble knt: who first produced it here} *Her-*
cules, blood red, milke white: *Helena, Heliodorus,* {*Hazard* mediorall} *Hope* {red & yel-
low} etc. *Jaspored* 7 kinds: {that of Harlam, of Tudore} The English tristamine, red
& ~~yellow~~ whitish yellow. *Imperial*, browne purple, a little red, & milke white: *Iris,*
Incarnadine, Infanta, Isabella whipp't with white. *Incomparable, Ignaties, Josephus* Justice:
etc. *Loretta,* red somewhat rose colour & white: *Livia,* curiously straked violet upon
white, *Lucca, Leander, Lysa,* etc. {*Marquetries*} *Morillior* 27 sorts, the *Superlative* or little
Augustus Morillion is incarnadine, & ~~some~~ {much} white: *Montserat,* panachd upon
gri–de lin, mixed with red upon a faire white, *Marbled* faint gray incarnat & ~~whi~~ red:
Melidora: {*Maidenhead* scarlet, colombine & white} *Monster* dubble, The flo: seldome
comes perfect, yet has about 100, or 120 leaves, red, orange, & yellow. The single *Mon-*
ster so named from the ~~gre~~ largenesse of the flo: red & yellow, a kind of Cloth of
Gold: *Melicea, Melinda,* ~~morine~~, *Marvell of Amsterdam,* faire gri de lin, white. *Melissa,*
Morine incarnadine, penached on a faire white: *Newes from Holland,* white spotted with
a cleere purple: *Nicean Opale,* red, colombine, ~~yellow~~ golden, yellow & white: *Olinda*
smale panaches red & incarnadine on the edges which are white: *Olympia* mixed
with chammy, with pidgeons neck colour upon white *Medioral. Pallots* 14 Sorts, most
of them of burnt reads, & smoaky colours: yet very faire: *Parroquett* fueille–morte
colombine & greene: 7 sorts of Paroquetts more: *Panached,* five: *Palas,* purple & white:
Palamedes, Periander, Phrygian, Painter, Persian, Princesse, incarnat, fueille morte, citron,
& white: *President: Paragons* 5. *Proteus, Poliantha,* {*Phenix*} etc: *Quirinus, Quatricolor,*
fine, colombine, chammy, yellowish white. *Raphael,* Regular {faire} colombine, red,
& much white. *Raymond,* {præcoce} *Richmont:* curiously penached with gri de lin, &
red upon white. *Scipio,* lively red, & ~~yellow~~ whitish yellow: *Sultane* burnt red, obscure
grey, {& lavender colour} & white. *Swisse, Sabine* **[page 310]** panach'd ~~upon~~ {with}
lovely ~~white~~ greene upon white. *Satin'd* a faire white like satin, panach't with read.
Specious a noble purple violet, with panachs white & with blew so deepe that they appear black:. *Solimanæ* {starry} etc. *Tarantine, Triumphant,* Trojane: *Unique* 3 sorts, *Unique*
Evelyn panached with faire purple violet, murry, & white. *Venus* or *Cyprian* Brimstone,
faire colombine & red: *Venetian, Virginian* panached with incarnadine upon white,
with spotts like dropps of blood: Viceroy, *Widows* many kinds, The Common of ~~a~~
~~dryd rose~~ {murry} Colour & white, The rest are {chiefly} broune purple & white with
blew botomes: {*White præcox,* & *Seratine: Waned* an admirable flo: all white, but the
leaves; waning like a scallop worke edgd in white:} Zamet, colombine drawing to
a rose Colour, chammy & cleere red. *Zaiblon. Zeilane* with greate panaches, Bishops
violet, edged with fire colour upon a faire white. *Zurandale* 3 sorts, the Common has
her panaches red, very distinct & separated from the white, upon which they extend,
{*Zany* or Fooles coate:} etc. for we forbeare to speake of the White *præcox*, purple
præcoxes & early red, yellow etc: *Albus purpurea rubra, Media Lutea,* with many more of
the *Serotina* referring you to the *Herbals*; This note onely we shall add, That for the
better distinction of their Bulbes, the *Præcox Tulip* rootes are sharp at top, the Serotine
broader, which observation ~~is~~ {will be} of use when you plant, or purchase: otherwise
to pretend to name all the varieties were impertinent & impossible. *Monsieur Morine*
the ~~gr~~ famous Florist of Paris assuring me that himselfe had observed above 3000 sorts,
& that at length it exceeded his Arithmetick. {For those which desire more exact
marks, with the names & descriptions of such as are in the hands of our best & most

curious English Gardners may have them out of Mr: Reas excellent ~~worke~~ chapter on the flo: in his Flora: C; 9:} *Anemonies Albanian*, all white save a little incarnadine at bottome of the greate leaves & plush. *Albert*: flesh colour, clouded with incarnat, some call it the *Paragon*. *Albicant*, a dul white, the plush white at extremitie, rose colour: *Amaranth*, Angelique white, plush ~~de~~ gri de lin: Asiatique white mixt with incarnat, the plush granade flo: colour mixt with white, *Astrea*, Augustine, white mixt with incarnat, plush ~~wi~~ fire colour: ~~Vulgars~~ Blew, Blody, Boulonian, white, incarnat bottome, plush mixed with white & citron colour, it keepes flower long: Bakista greate red leaves, and plush mixt with a flesh[?] [page torn] colour. **[Page 311]** *Cardiot*, a whitish grey, the botome incarnat, the plush incarnat edged with {greenish} Fueille morte. *Cassander* all peach colour: *Carnea grossa* all flesh colour with large plush, an *Italian* flower. Celestine white, the plush white with lemon colour. *Clitia* flesh colour & incarnat, the plush rarely set like the dubble Marygold & is one of the noblest of ~~the~~ *Anemonies*. {The French Cordon violet has 5 colours, greate leaves & plush red. The russe Cordon violet, *Damaske*, incarnat & white distinctly straked, a very rare flo. *Eristea Extravagante*, white, red, greene: & of an extravagant plush: *Galipoly* fire colour mixed with white: *Incarnadine* of Spaine of a lively colour & well knowne: Julian, white mixed with incarnat:[201] {Hermaphrodites, many kinds:} *Mantuan* citron colour incarnat botome *Meliodore*, *Milanoise*, peach colour, a greate flower: Morescque. *Morine*, a ~~high~~ {high} deepe violet neere {to} purple, all over. *Natolian* white mixt with incarnat all over: *Olinda* violet leaves, sometymes edgd with white the plush all violet, *Oriental*, of a {a gray lavender color & upon} slate colour, large flower *Parisian*, greate white leaves, plush at first limon colour afterwards paler. *Parmesane, Pavonasse* {is our vulgar Violetts growes paler in fine: *Persian*:} Quatricolor of 4 sorts ~~greate leaves red, mixed with white, the plush browne Amaranth colour with a red~~ the rarest whereoff is that which has the greate leaves red, mixed with white; The plush Amaranth browne, except the middle which is incarnat. The *vulgar Red* & was one of the first plushed Anemonies brought into these parts Anno: *1598*. St Charles, Syrian, ~~Tuscane~~ {Pinapple: Swarthy:} {Syrian} *Toscane* ~~red~~ fading red sometymes fueille mort, dures long; *Tripolane* citron colour & growes very high. *Turky*, white botome incarnat, a tardy flower & very tall stalke. Victorious, the greate leaves flesh colour mixed with Incarnat, the plush fueille–mort & incarnate.{*Violet Isabell*; some *Anemonies* have 5 distinct colours:} But who is able to ennumerate the infinite varieties of such of these Flowers which are produced from Seede, & which are as changeable as the wind whose name they impart: This onely note that those *Anemonies* which beare those greate botomes resembling plush, are the most esteemed: The rest will hardly name. ~~that is The Carnation~~ those which come with the greater ivy forme leaves, the others are parsly leavd[.]

[Page 312] *Carnations* **[First paragraph crossed out]** [202]The fayre Elizabeth, The Queene G: flo: The white clove: The Dukes Amarillus, The Josephe Coate: ~~Savoy, Morelle, Burdeaux; gray Orleanes, Rum~~, Admiral of Zeland, Adam, Altezza, Black Imperial, Cardinal, Chrystal, White Carnation, Gyante head, Gen: Palma, Wiggon, Heart Oake, Incarnadine de Bleau, Morello non pareille, Nymph Royal, Prince of

---

201. **[Margin note]** Juno, white peach ~~colour~~ flo: a large flo:
202. **[Margin note]** Range & examine this better, consult Ray

Wales, Passe me not, Purple, Haloe {Common} Painted Lady, Royall white, Ravissant, Faire maids of Kent, Widdow, ~~Imperiall robe~~, Granade, The Charles, The Catrive,[?] The Russian Emperour, Persian Queene, English, & Coloign Virgins, Coridon, K of Bohemia, Greate Tamberlain,

According to Mr: Reas Catalogue

Red & white:

Char 2d: Q: Cather: Emperatoria, Emp: of Russia, Emperas Court, Persian queene, English & Coloigne Virgins, Coridon, K of Bohemia, Bohemian Crown, Emp: Rodulphus, Tamberlain the Greate: Q: Hesta, Floradine, Royal Oake, Grand Duke, Lacherbecken, Supereminent, de Camp, New bonaventure, Victoria, Marvel du mound, Countesse of Flanders, Bell & bonne, Prince de parma, Count de Castile, Samantua, Bel Infanta, Generall of Holland, Count Flores, Bel Rose, Browne favorite, Grand Boor, Kins sconce, Daris, Princes Court, New painted Lady.

Purple & white

K David, K Solomon, K of Assyria, {K of Portugal}, Q: of France, ~~Soph Solyman~~ {Q of Sweden} St Lewis, Royal March, Pr: Rupert, Solyman, Don John, Prince Henry, Pantaleon, Generall of the Indies, Triumph of Spaine, Purple royal, Dorilisant, Bel du mound, Bell Triumphant, Admirall of Spaine, House of Commons, Covenant of England, Marble Stone, Generall Wigon, Blew Crystal: Tapisere, Grave Florus, etc

Scarlet & white

German Emp: Alexander, Young Prince, Ethiopian King, Pr of Orange, Augustus, Count Mansfeild [*sic*], Bride of Holland, Carthusa, Lord Belle Yonton Oriental, the Jewell Greate Boor, Morning Star, Bel belvoise, Donanentur, Paragon, Brewer, Virgin of Orleans, Van Velson, Incarnad de Bezond, Dorothea of Holland, the Cock, Havaniere, Faire Frances, Salamander, etc. & some of these ~~have been~~ & of all the other Classes are knowne by severall other names which yearely beare according to the fancy of the raiser or possessor as the Faire Elizabeth, the Queen Gily-flo: **[page 313]** The White Clove, the Dukes Amarillis, Joseph Coate, Admiral of Zeland, Adam, Altezza, Bell Imperiall, Cardinal, White Carnation, Gyante Read, Gen: Palma, the Oake, Incarnadine de Bleau, Morella non Pareille, the Nymph Royal, P: of Wales, Passe me not, purple {& blew} Haloes, Royal white, the Ravissant & hundreds more to be reduced into what order you please:

Hyacinthus: see p: 316 & reforme:

The Botroides major, or greate yellow full of flo: & sweete smelling. The Cineritius also sweete, The Indian Tuberose incomparable sweete & a noble flo: purple, red, white The stellated of peru, bleu, black, white: The Comosus: Of {Botroides or} the Grape flower, the white, blew, ramasus, reddish, The larger Blew Hyacinth, the Orentalis major or Zumbal Indi. The Oriental Præcox, white ~~early~~ white doubble, Oriental, & blew, of the Starry the Vulgar {The Early} the white, Ash colour'd etc:

[Page 314]

Ranonculus's

Of the simple Ranunculus there are 5 kinds, as the white, yellow-gilded, pale yellow, citron Colour, browne red, which is also odoriserant. Of the Simple, the principle are the *African*: yellow gold *Aurora*, yellow panached [blank space] without, upon a botome pale yellow. *Asiatique. Calabrian, Cloath of Gold,* golden yellow mixt with red without the flo: *Melidoreus* ~~red~~ crimson edged with Isabell without: *Parmesan, Roman,* chammy spoted with red without, the botome chammy: *Sydonian,* chammy colour spotted red:

of the dubble, these have but one single Colour:

Gyant, all red a greate flower: That of *Constantinople*

Yellow with leaves like Rue: Italian yellow:

Dubble *Ranunc*: of double Colours:

The *Boswell* orange straked with yellow: *Gyant* straked with yellow, subject to varry, with some red, very rare. Most of these came from *Tripoly*, where they are called Asiatique: They have most of them black botomes.

Iris

Note that the bulbous ~~vio~~ Iris have ordinarily 9 leaves in every flo: ~~the~~ whereoff the extreames of the 3 ~~be~~ which incline {or fall} are calld chinns, the 3 that joyne with them & stand upright are named tongues {or Arches}; the 3 other which rise above these & forme the flower are called the standards or sailes, & the {large} yellow marke in the middle of the ~~leaves~~ straite leaves ~~in the middle of the~~ each chinn is calld the yellow Escutchion The *Ag{c}hate*: the chins ~~& body~~ {tongues} golden yellow, the standards gray panashed with violet: *Af[r]ican* ~~chins~~ {the falls} yellow mixt with blew the tongues cleer blew, the standards violet: *Alepo* the falls yellow, arches & standards white mixt with yellow: *Arabian*, falls ~~blew yellow gilt~~ golden yellow, tongues fueille mort, standards violet: *Armenian*, falls, yellow and fueille–mort, Arches pale yellow mixt with fueille–mort, standards violet: Antique, ~~Arabian~~, ~~Britton~~ Breton falls & arches yellow, standard a tarnished white: *Calabrian* has its flo: all yellow: *Chamblotted*, the ~~Arch~~ falls yellow & fueille morte, ~~arches~~ the standards like the neck of a Ring dove & fueille mort: Cardian falls, olive, Arches the same, intermixt with a ~~blue~~ pale blew, standards gri de lin. *Chinese* penached with blew, a dwarfe flo: *Damascus*, blew panashed with violet, ~~but if it panash~~ *Egyptian*, falls & arches blew the standards violet, *Florentine* is all white. *Florida*, falls, mixt blew, standards violet & gri de lin. *Gran Signior* falles, yellow edged with fueille mort, arches gri de lin, standards almost the same but deeper: *Grecian* falls & arches blew mixt with a little yellow: standards violet with white. *Quince*, Indian, falls & arches yellow, standards gri de lin mixt with violet[.] **[Page 315]** The Abbot has the falls, arches & standards a high purple tis a tardy flower & low. The ~~sheath~~ {scapbard} of the leaves is greene, spotted with purple or ~~red~~ purple red. *Levantine* falles Isabelle mixt with haire colour, the arches white & faire blew mixt with violet. *Lybian* falles yellow, tongues or arches & stands mixd yellow: *Macedonian* falls & arches Aurora & yellow standard col. of pidgeon nick: Maldivian falls straw yellow, the arches the same but somewhat bleuish, standards cleer blew mixt with yellow: *Melinda* is of the colour of the pansy: except the Escutchion which is golden yell, & is lesse then in any Iris: *Mexican*, *Milanese*, *Moluccan*, falls yellow & aurora, arches citron color & blew, the standards blew, bottomd with violet: ~~P~~ *Oriental* falls blew violet & yellow, arches violet, & standards violet panached with purple. This is one of the most rare & least common: *Perfect*, falls reddish violet falls, panached with purple: the arches violet mixt, standards a lively violet, a most rare flo: Parmisan, all violet, but very faire & much esteemd, *Poeticall*, falls olive greene mixt with blew, archs & standards blew: *Portugal* all violett, {a} very early & common Iris: *Pyrenian* fall yellow, arches yellow mixt with blew standards cleere blew: *Iris Royall* falls {pale} fueille mort panached with haire colour, arches {durty} fueille mort mixt with blew, standards gri de lin panached with violet. *Sauoyard*, *Swisse*, falls yellow, arches & standards yellow & blew: *Syrian*, *Tartarian*, *Turkey* falls light grey, arches blew & fueille mort, standard violet: *Venetian* falls blew mixt with white, arches blew, standards violet: *Vaudoit* is all blew except the {yellow} Escutchion {~~which is the~~} ~~yellow~~

~~fall which is in the~~ which is in the middle of every fall, & has usually 12 or 15 leaves in its flower: But the Climate & aire (as all other flowers) subject them to infinite changes; so as it were impossible to name them all: {for besides these, there are also the Tuberus etc: such as the Lusitanic twise flowering greate & lesse Calcedonian, Dalmatic & Asiatic Cerulia Versicolor, The Tripoly golden, Camerarius, the purple Iris; then the Augustifolia; also the severall Chamæiris & dwarfs etc:}

Narcissus

Polyanthes or full of flo: & dubble: which are of many sorts: The Chiefe as follows: *Atumnal white, Bastard Spanish,* {Gallic: African} *Bizantine,* {Brimstone colourd} *Corniculat* lesse & greater: *English, Epidaurian,* {Cipriot} *Faliosian Greene, Hispanica, Incomparable, Iuncifolius,* major & minor *luteus* etc, The white *Juncifol:* with pale & reflexed leaves: *Autumnal Juncifal:* white: *Indian,* another *Indian* of a red saffron colour & lilly leaved, *Indian* dubble with reddish ~~leaves~~ flower: The *Sweete Juncifol:* single & dubble: {*Long necked Indians,*} The *Mountaine Narcissus,* the flo: white & single ~~the cup~~ {with a} yellow cup: *Narbonian,* {Sea Daffodill} *Pseudo narcissus Iuncifol:* The wild *Rosy Narcissus* bigger & lesser: ~~The sweete~~ {The *Sphericall* Narcissus}, the *Virginian* Narcissus with a purplish flower, *White* of many sortes: The *Wild Starry Narcissus*; with innumerable others: **[page 316]** *Martagons* these are both red & purple: Severall sorts of *Orchis* resembling both sexes: so of the starr flowers *Ornithogalla,* especially the *Perigrinum Spicatum.*

{*Cyclamens* of *Verona,* rare, *Levanties, M: Libanon, Scy*[?] *Corke*[?] *Persian, Antiochian* **[continued in margin]** single, dubble, & so as to have flo: all the yeare}

Hyacinths, are of wonderfull variety, dubble & single, as the *Oriental,* the *white Brumal,* the *Præcox blew Sweete* The *Cyaneus, fuscus & crispus,* {Cyress's next}, The Swete *Byzantine, white violet, Ash coloured, Ruddy:* The white *Serotine:* of the dubble greate ~~changes~~ diversitie, as the *Pale blew, Greenish, Racæmosus, Rosy, English, Belgic, Spanish, Persian,* The white & red *Botryoide Indian* with tuberous roote etc above 30 sorts: {*Crowne Imperiall* with that greate flo: & severall stages dubble flo: yellow striped, etc.} Also of *Auricula red, purple, white yellow, leather coated,* murry, *scarlet,* tawny, *blood red, rose* colour, *blush, Aurora, haire colour,* variable, *Greene,* almost innumerable: In summ, he that can number the starrs in the heaven. may hope to perfect the Catalogue of the flo: or starrs of the Earth. As for the more vulgar sort of flo: though likewise different & various, to repeate their names & describe their colours would not much inlighten our gardiner or {greately} contribute to the dignity of this chapter: wherefore here we conclude: refferring our reader for the Latine {& Greek} names to the *Botanists,* whilst wee have ~~mentioned~~ {specified} these ~~are~~ for the most part which are best knowne to our Virtuosi & such as delight in the Coronary Garden, ~~&~~ {but} lesse taken notice {of} by the other.

And by this it dos sufficiently appeare how impossible it were to governe this numerous or rather innumerable people, the glorious inhabitants of our *Coronary Garden* without a greate deale of dexterity, polity, Art, & particular oeconomie, so that without an accurate ~~Rescension~~ Recension & enroulement, our Gardiner {who is the Monarch & Generall of all this multitude} shall never be able to take a ~~severall~~ just accoumpt of his severall subjects & Souldiers: Let therefore our Gardiners *Albus Memoriæ* be a narrow folio of Paper {~~fairely~~} ~~well bound & a competent thicknesse~~ {to be inserted or taken ~~out~~ at pleasure out of a {faire} cover ~~fairely~~ so you may renew & change at pleasure & as you yearely alter etc.} ~~accounting~~ {and} corresponding to his art & furniture of greater or lesse portatile volume: at the Front whereoff let his Coronary

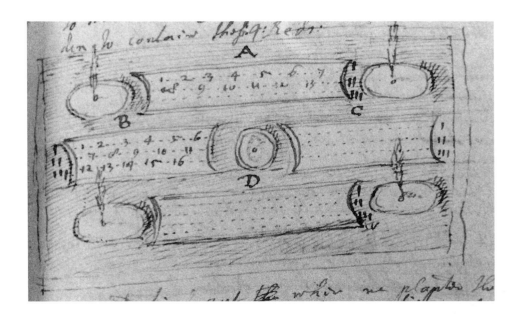

Figure 69. Plan of a coronary garden, divided into four beds, illustrated in text at page 317.

Garden be exactly delineated & plotted with each bed, bordure, & Allee according to exact scale: Let every of these beds be letterd Alphabetically: A.B.C.etc and lined out answering to the ranges of his Flowers & rootes, as they stand in the Garden, and those againe numberd with the {numeral} Cyphers I.II.III.IV. etc: and the *Tallys* or *Tesseræ* (which are smale plates of lead 5 Inches long & a quarter broade the thicknesse of halfe crowne ~~figured~~ {stamped} with the barbarous figures 1.2.3.4.etc) pricked downe & ~~set~~ placed ~~next~~ within an Inch or lesse of the stalke ~~of your flower~~ or roote of your {choycest} flowers, referring to the like number in the lines of your Albus expressed by {those smale} poynts, which run the length of the beds: This drawne & ~~well~~ proportioned as we designe, let the rest of the booke be divided into Catalogues or Tables. The First referring to the Alphabets ~~of~~ or Letters of the Bedds, for Example: The Bed: A. line: I. ~~In that~~ being **[page 317]** The Title of the first page, there sett {downe} underneath what ~~Flower~~ rootes, ~~& flowers~~ (the flo: exactly described) you planted in that range: Then in another *Page*: {Bed} A. l II etc. so of all the rest Bed: B. l. I.II. or III.IV. or Vt: by this meanes you shall have an immediate survey over your whole Garden, & know what is planted in every ~~P~~ Bed; The Second Catalogue. T~~abl~~he Index shall contain the whole furniture of your Garden Alphabeticall recorded, with the like references: As for Instance, to make it most perspicuous: Suppose the Coronary Garden containe these 4: Beds:

[illustration, see Fig. 69] [203]

    We would find out ~~the~~ where we planted the *Tulip Amarillis*, which is the 6t of our {first} Catalogue above Turne first to the letter T. and find *Amarillis* amongst the *Tulips* in the *Bed* A, *Line* or *Range* II ~~Tally~~ {figure} 9. ~~There seeke for the Tally~~ Goe then to the ~~Correspondent~~ bed in your Coronary Garden which correspondes to A in your *Plott*, and there at the Tally (9) you shall certainly find what you seeke: By these & the like locallities, in B. C. D: etc: there shall nothing escape your notice; ~~th~~ & it were

---

203. **[Margin note]** Make the beds so as to contain five lines: {& the plot like the K Garden ~~in~~ viz one of the pold squares at St James with carpet: etc:

therefore to be desired, that they were so digested before we began to plant our Garden at first: because it would so greately contribute to the accurate order & disposition of it; Moreover in this *Recension*, ought our Gardiner exactly to describe the peculiar colours, markes & age of every flo: ~~tha~~ the better to observe how it improves or degenerates, then which there can be nothing more delightfull & instructive. Finally our Gardiner should be very curious & circumspect even in the very Gathering his Flowers; for it will be fitting that he visite all the bedds ~~daily~~ every morning whilst the ~~pe~~ deaw lyes in smale pearles ~~upon them~~, the Son a little risen upon them, that they appeare smiling, halfe open & expiring their sweete sentes through their perfumed lipps. Of these he may gather some, & spare others, bringing them in for Nosegays, for shew, for the House etc. but in this ~~active~~ employment let him gather none by violent snatches which oftentimes violates the rootes & mortifies the stalke to the prejudice of the rest: ~~but be circumspect~~ therefore **[page 318]** rather crop them with ~~your~~ {his} naile, or cutt them with a smale falcated knife (without which he is never to be at any tyme working in the Garden) & that with circumspection, for some are not to be gathered so neere the ground as others.

Neither let our *Gardiner*, gather all the flowers from one plant, but choicest, ~~&~~ sparingly {~~& with judgment~~} through the whole Garden, that no place remaine remarkable naked & disfurnished, which were a very greate deformity. Neither shall he cutt or pull off all the leaves after the flower is gon, as some (for want of judgment) doe, seing it frequently kills the roote, by too greate & universal transpiration, through the multitude of wounds & overtures: In this case rather turne the more exuberant leaves inward, as those of the Narcissus, or being flaggs & ~~sprawling~~ stragling knitt them in an easie knott & contracted, or bind them up to a stake; but such as are ~~dead~~ withered & quite mortified may safely be pulled away without any detriment. And what can now be more ravishing and {innocently} tempting then the glorious & incomparable varieties of ~~our~~ such a *Coronary Garden!* ~~ub ubi~~ when the season inviting ~~CAP. XVII~~

> *Flores nitescunt discolor Gramine*   *Maro cf*
> ~~Of the Philosophihco-Medicall Garden~~
> and that our Gardin~~er~~{s} are in their prime,
> *Jam ver perpetuum, jam versicoloribus anni*
> *Fetibus {Alma Parens} cingi sua tempori gaudet*

For then the statues of our most renound & illustrious Gardiners are celebrated with Elogies, Garlands and Festoones, which the {cheerfull & busy} Nymphs crowne ~~their~~ {them} with all ~~every~~ {every return} {of} Spring, when these renascent flowers ~~indi cover~~ {embroider} the bedds & the Parterrs {with their beauties} & that our *Coronary Gardens* {glorious} triumph having gotten the victory over the last cruell Winter; For this is a universall Jubilee to them: Or if we will *Philosophise* and contemplate the wonderfull and stupendious processe of {polydedula} Nature. That those minute, despicable & tender ~~seedes~~ {Atomes} cast into the womb of so austeer a mother & rotting (in all appearance} under ~~the~~ her cold & miserable embraces should yet at last, after so long a ~~tyme~~ {captive abandond to} such {wett} showers fresh; {killing ~~and~~ nipping} {~~dea killing~~} snow & {hedious} stormes emerge {& come up} ralling their smale particles, ~~&~~ & putting forth ~~now little~~ {their slender} rootes, ~~penetra~~ serpenting in the mould: ~~& penetrating from whence it~~ whose milke & blood they {now} suck in revenge, & as the tyme approaches, penetrating the hard surface of the geniall bed, peeping out at first, but with a smale ~~white~~ {pale} thried, tipt with a faint greene mantle in which now it swells, & explains it self, discovering at last {through all this darke cloud} the raies of a long conceald, but admirable beauty, in stalling leaves, ~~flo~~ buds, & flowers which it delicately unfolds ~~and displaies modestly displaies~~ unplaiting the tresses ~~which nature~~ & modestly displaing the virgin beauties which are some-tymes guarded with vulnerating pricles **[page 319]** and fenced with sharp thornes, till being kissed open by the soft whispers of the rosy {~~fingered~~} Zephyr, they are tempted to peepe upon the ~~beauty~~ glorious Eye of the World the Sunn, that greate Luminary so propo[r]tions to them, and then as awakend out of their pretty cradles wherein the winds had ~~now~~ {gently} rocked them {asleepe}, they rise from their ~~beds sleepy~~ {drowsy} beds, and now apparel~~d~~{l} themselves like sommery Eastern Queenes, ~~&~~ {or} Goddesses; ~~What~~ Whith what delight & satisfaction dos our Gardiner {then} be-hold some {of these} moddest {&} flowery {Nymphs} mantled in their greene scarfes, others halfe dressed {in the ~~lawn~~ smocks of lawne} or indeede hardly borne! You would take some to be clad in white sattin {or so much figured snow} pinked plaited, chambletted ~~&~~ embroiderd & chammare'd with gold; some have the resemblance of a soft mother of pearle, or a tender Emra{u}ld; some like golden bells, silver, & of {flexible} Saphire, others ~~like little panniers~~ present you with inammeled capps, pretty paniers, & boxes lined with crimson damaske, ~~&~~ {with} vasetts of chrystall {achates} & rubies {of a gemmy luster} Their colours are ~~white~~ purpurine, celestiall: incarna-dine, blushing Aurora, & virgine–white so innocent, so faire {& smiling upon you} sparkleling lively, orient, flaming & radiant: They peepe ~~with~~ {out of} their buds as out of so many Eyes {mealting & trickling into tears of joy} & turne themselves into a hundred thousand formes & protean changes: Some stand errect, others are reflexed, some be pendant, {others} arched, {spiralling} slantt, {smooth} soft, stiff, {serpentine} wreathed, {jagged} eschalopt, {panached,} single, dubble, curled, {dim-pelld} tufted, trussed up {&} decked in plumes, {& plush} striped, & crowned with admirable variety. not omitting their sweete & odoriferous ~~perspications~~ undulations, tinging & perfuming the aire {with their briske, **[continued in margin]** poignant lively, delicate ~~faint~~ arromatique & agreable sents} beyond all ~~the abl~~ artificiall com-positions whatsoever & refreshing the senses {&} drawing {out our very} ~~the~~ soules ~~of~~ into admiration of other perfections; Then to examine the rest of the ~~anatomie~~ {principles & parts}; The Seedes lurking & nestling in the fiber cotton & d{o}wny ~~under~~ furrs, the ~~leaves~~ {foliage} like so many Umbrellas shading the ~~stalkes~~ {flowers} ~~budds circumvested with the tender which~~ supported with the knap, & studds, so correspondent & regular; not to riske the more interiour parts of the heart, rootes, fibers, curious reines, & reticulate contextures of the ~~parts~~ {particles} which supplie and maintaine them with juice life & spirits, to preserve their caduce & deciduous leaves ~~for~~ so long upon the {slender} stemms, displaing their glories flaggs & streamers as on so many stately masts & silken banners: ~~Here~~ Cast your Eye upon these beauti-full Tulips the pearles & Regents of {the} flowering {~~region~~} {Parterrs} ~~it resembles a flame~~ They resemble so many {flames trembling upon their socketts} torches ~~flaming up their~~ & illustrating the whole ~~Parterrs~~ {Region} with their Splendor ~~& flattring the us with a thousand tempting dimples varieties; They Some What~~ {a} ~~blushing roses are here~~ {considerate Lilies} what innocent & virgin ~~lillys~~ {candles} ~~be~~ here hiding their ~~heads~~ {bashfull} faces amongst yonde blushing roses, dimpl'd & smiling: O faire

Carnation, ~~rich~~ {royall} Amaranth, Golden Heliotrop, pretty enameld Pansy, ~~Royall~~ rich Anemone, stately Crown Imperiall, painted Iris, noble Hyacinth, lovely Myrtil, Sweete Jassmine, ~~what a Paradise is here, what an Elysium; what a Constellation of Earthly Starrs, yea what a heaven upon Earth, for so our Gardiner treads every day upon new borne Miracles as often as he walkes~~ For so were the *Athenean Tempes* imbroderd, where the faire *Proserpine* **[page 320]** used to {froliq &} divert herselfe: ~~walks upon his beds of Violetts, flowering bankes, conversing with the most abstracted & purest of human delights & such as the Gods themselves do emulate~~

> *tot fuerant illic, quot habet natura Colores*
> ~~O Vitæ tuta facultas~~
> *Pictaque dissimili flore nitebat humus*
> ~~Munera non dum intellecta Deum!~~

~~Such as the Gods themselves do emulate, or enjoy:~~
And so it was in that tempting Bower of Blisse:

> ~~And~~ {Where} all about grew every sort of flower
> To which sad lovers were transform'd of yore,
> Fresh Hyacinthus, Phoebus Paramore
> [And dearest love]
> Foolish Narcisse, that likes the watry shewe,
> Sad Amaranthus, made a flower but late,
> Sad Amaranthus, in whose purple gore
> Mee seemes I See Amintas wretched fate
> To whome Sweete Poets verse hath given endlesse date
> > *Spencer: L: 2: Cant: 12.*[lxxxv]

And now what a Paradise, what an Elysium is here! What a Constellation of Earthly Starrs, yea what a heaven upon Earth, For so our Gardiner treads every day upon new {borne} Miracles as often as he walkes upon his bedds of Violetts & Flowering bankes, conversing with the ~~most~~ purest & most abstracted of human delights. O Vitæ tuta facultas Munera nonndum ~~intellecta Deum!~~ {Intellecta Deum}
Such as the Gods themselves do emulat, & the wisest men onely {cultivate &} enjoy: ~~I will~~ {But} we ~~will shut~~ close this ravishing contemplation & exstasie with that of [204]*Pliny et de mira florum varietate: In Hortis seri et coronomenta jussit Cato, ine{na}rrabile Florum maxime subtilitate quando nulli potest facilius esse loqui, quam rerum Naturæ pingere lascivienti præsertim et {in} magno gaudio fertilitatis tam varie ludenti.*
or rather with that of the ~~best of~~ [205]incomparable Cowley

> tanta tot istius spectacula dædala lucis
> > Pingere tu, credo, solus Apollo, potes.

---

204. **[Margin note]** L: 21. C. 1.
205. **[Margin note]** L: 3d: Flora: [p. 141]

Tu qui peniculo radiorum pingis, Apollo,
      Hoc varium mundi multicoloris opus.
An possis plane dubito describere versu,
      Plantarum & Vatum sis licet ipse Deus
[206]Cowley

[Page 321]

---

206. [Continued on separate piece of paper]
Confiteor rem tantam operum non esse meorum;
      Pauca legam, ritu praetereuntis Apis.
Fasciculus nobis e tanto parvulus horto,
      Sufficiens unus, sit modo dulcis, erit.

CAP: XVII

Of the Philosophico-Medicall Garden:

In pursuite of the Divisions mentioned in cap, the first, & first Booke of this Worke, we are now arived to the *Medical Garden*, as that which is indeede the most naturall, usefull and *Philosophicall*, and therefore doubtless to have a principal part assign'd it in this our *Elysium*; ~~as being~~ For what can be more convenient & full of diversion, then the contemplation of ~~their~~ infinite varieties, & wonderfull effects of those Plants which are best known by the names of Simples {&} of which our Botanists have filled such {prodigeous} volumes, & the shops of the Apothecarius are {almost entirely} furnished; and therefore to discourse of them in particulars, as they have don, or {ever} hope to introduce their innumerable kinds into this ~~compendium~~ {narrow compasse} is not any ~~part~~ {portion} of our designe: It shall suffice that as an ornamentall ~~part~~ addition {to} ~~of~~ these our Royal Gardens, we alow it a chapter in this work, and such an ample plott or division within the precincts of our Wales, as may suffice to comprehend the ~~chi~~ principall & most usefull plants, {&} ~~and~~ to be as a rich & noble compendium of what the whole Globe of the Earth has ~~growing~~ {flourishing} upon her boosome: Besides we have by this means enlarged our roome & opportunities for new & rare experiments for enfranchising strange plants & civilizing the wild & rude; for the easier knowledge of Physical Simples, for the culture {& entertainment} of forreigne plants, for the composition of medicines & the use of the Family & lastly (by all these) for the contemplation of Nature & the accomplishment of our Elysium.

Let therefore the *Medicall Garden* be situate in some part of our large Enclosure, ~~which has the~~ the most obliged to the Sun, & which has the greatest variety of Grounds; for if that do not naturaly ~~happen~~ {occur}, it must be so made by art: the wild & the irregular ground being the most desirable: For here it is that we finely admitt & make use of the Mountaine & the March, the Woody, & the Champion, the Cold & the hott, dry & moyst ~~in Summ~~ the Sandy, Clayie, stonie, rockie, chalky, fat, leane, watry, hott, hungry, whatsoever ~~may best~~ is most variable and so for the differing aspects, that they varie, & imitate all the Climates & Seasons; And therefore in case these ~~va~~ accomplishments happen not (as rarely they doe) to encounter, our industrious Gardiner must study, & contrive **[page 322]** how he may assemble them by Arte: by raising of hills depressing of Vales, digging profundities, & changing the face of the ground into all ~~advantages~~ shapes: for here to affect uniformity would be ridiculous & uselesse; nor would it so well resemble the face of Nature upon which the {various} furniture of this Garden ~~dos grow~~ is produced.

Concerning the Extent it would be best to consult the inclination of the Person; It is almost incredible what ~~an aker or two~~ {smale compasse} will entertaine; but if the designe be publique & more August, the roome must be accordingly amplified; although even some of those, & which yet are much celebrated, containe not above an aker or two, for such is that of *Padoa* ~~in Italy~~ stored with *Italian & Greeke* plants: *Pisa* about the same extent, ~~full~~ & much alike furnished: *Leyden* somewhat bigger, full of *Indian* Plants: That at *Montpelier* .5. or .6. Akers abounding with the Alpestrall & pyrennial productions: Ours of Oxford of [blank space] {not to mention *Genoa, Florence, Bloys*, etc}[1] But that of *Paris* containing no lesse then eighteene Akers ~~the rest~~ one of the best furnished and Contrived of any in Europe; because not onely ~~abou~~ affording simples & plants for demonstration & pleasure onely, but for use & experience {also}, & which may truely be ~~sayd~~ esteemed an excellent pattern for our Imitation. For here are Groves, & hills, Meadow ground, & ~~levell~~ {flatt} Marshie, and upper grounds accommodate ~~severall~~ to all Situations, & proper for all sorts of Simples: & what is most to be desired & rarely found the situations of these naturall & unconstrained: besides that most of these have added to them whatsoever art can contribute ~~to richly~~ nobly adorned & nobly endowed: ~~That of Paris~~ This of Paris being founded Anno 1626 by the King of France, ~~at~~ {&} the care of the Greate Cardinal, who engaged even the Parliament itselfe about it {in the designe} ~~and~~ The Chancellour & most of the Grandees of that nation to contribute to the finishing of it: for to this is built a most decent {& noble} structure fit for the President. An Elaboratory,[2] Conservatory & ~~other~~ {whatsoever other} conveniences; ~~to~~ may seeme to be requisite.

Now though {it} is possible that even a flatt has sometimes furnished a very greate variety of Simples, as we have exemplified in those of *Leyden, Pisa, Oxford,* & *Padoa* itselfe, yet since as *Hippocrates* has most ~~commended~~ celebrated the *Mountaines* commanding his scholar *Cratenes* to gather his herbes from thence, ~~and~~ as {the} ~~most~~ best & most favored, & not in the lower grounds; yet that we may entertaine nothing which is imperfect in {this} our *Elysium*, for the accomplishment of ~~our Phy~~ {this part} **[page 323]** Let our Gardiner (in case he find none) raise a mount of 150 foote Square exactly situate according to the Cardinal poynts, which being elevated upon one ~~quarter~~ (hundred foote} ~~part~~ {square} of the Inclosure destind for this employment, may hollow & abate a proportionable part, so as gradualy to forme a declivity {& at last a botome} fitting for the more cold *Lacustrall, Juncipalustral,* ~~&~~ *Arundinat* & plainly *Aquatique* plants and, that of ~~Seve~~ various Situations & Aspects. ~~Divide therefore the plot into four {three} unequall parts, out of one whereoff we cast the mount {forming the} on a second is the declining ground out of which the mount is raised; the 3d is a levell square for the more upland plants, & the fourth and last is for the grove or woody part, & for trees, shrubbs, & such Simples as delight in their shadows.~~

Divide therefore the plott into 3 unequal parts, whereoff the first shall be on the North 80 foote broade 350 long: out of which at the foote of the mount let there be a Theater of 40 foote broade ranging with the mount: 150 long {as above described} for plants that love the coold & ~~fresh~~ {shady} places: The Second of the full breadth viz: 350 of the whole garden, shall be for the elevating of the mount, ~~taking~~ allowing 100 foote {square} one each side East & west: This (as we sayd) for aquatick plants, &

---

1. **[Margin note]** & Morgans at Westminster, not inferiour for furniture to some of these:

2. **[Margin note]** endowed with a Professor & lecture twise a yeare opning in a course of Chymistry & curiosities of the Simples:

such as affect fresh & coald places bottomed so deepe as to ~~end~~ end in the watry & slushie[.]³ The 3d & last is a square of 350 foote lying full South for such Simples as grow best in levell places exposed to all the aspects: So that the whole area ~~in amounts to~~ contains 350 foote in breadth, & 550 in length, comprehending the Grove, Mount: and the Southern plott, whose dimensions wee have described more exactly in the following Ichonisme.

Thus have you the ground fitted for all sorts of Simples, The Septentrion parts secured by the Grove & mount, & the rest inlightned & exposed by severall degrees of heate: But because it is necessary that our Mounte be made of a considerable {altitude} ~~height~~ (for the higher the better) besides the mould which the ~~lo~~ sinking of the marshes & pitts on the East & west sides, will afford; we would from other places procure & bring in other divers varieties of Earth & quarry, so as to represent the gravelly, rocky, chalky, sandy, lomie, marly & all other sorts of terraine: for ~~so~~ we shall find divers plants (especially the mountaine & Alpestrall) to require such ~~a~~ moulds & diversities of earth: And to facilitate this, & the better stability of what you erect, ~~lay~~ {raise} the earth in Cascades of sufficient declivity. This may easily be effected, by making the ascent one {the middle of} the south side onely, {Thus} every Cascade being 6 foote high, the whole will amount to **[page 324]** 72, and 13 broade: so that 12 such ~~ascents~~ cascades will reach to the top after that computation: out of this breadth of 13, reserve 4 for the bed, & 2 for the passage or ~~ally~~ Allee: which may ascend either climbing or upon an exact levell, which we rather approve, to be ~~ascended~~ mounted by stepps of stone, ~~as the fi~~ from ~~Allee to Allee~~ Cascade to Cascade as the figure represents; it rendring a noble & very agreable effect to the area below: The flatt at top is reserved for the most mountainous plants & such as best support the rigours of the weather: Such a situation, ~~if~~ so ~~found~~ formed by nature, as ~~or capable~~ {of it selfe} to yeald a fountaine: or capable of it by ~~the~~ deriving water from some other eminence had all the perfections which could be added to it. Upon the South & North Basis of the Mount let there be Caves arched over, so as to serve for the best of Conservatories; they may well be ~~20~~ {10} foote broade, and if ~~they passe also~~ & ~~12 foote~~ of what hight you please after they are past the first 13. for which purpose we designe that the face of the first cascade be of ~~brick or~~ {rude & extravagent} stone, which we would have layed without Mortar, & as naturaly as might be: That cave on the North side neede not be the whole face of the pedistall of the mount, but be made circling & in meanders, for congelations and other ~~Physo~~ Philosophicall experiments, & therefore if neede be would like wise be made to descend in some part ~~below~~ as farr below the area of the plaine as were possible. ~~But for~~ {Or ~~else to~~ else} the Southern Conserve may have its uttmost face either walled regularly with windoes at convenient distances, or may be arched upon pillars, ~~to be closed wth temporary~~ the intercollumniations shut or opned at pleasure by temporarie closures made of ⁴boards, as we described in Chap: 15. We have already shewed the necessity of the severall earths & moulds whereoff we desire the mount should be composed: But our Gardiner must likewise dispose in other places of the Gardene ~~bed~~ other beds to further the experiments, some whereoff may remaine longer unaltered some againe to be oftner renewed: And for this Effect,

---

3. **[Margin note]** transcribe the making this box out of Sharrok p: 136
4. **[Margin note]** L: 2.

besides his variety of flatt beds, for the accellerating of severall plants, some would
be helped with forraine soyles, & especialy by the Balast of shipps, Sea sand, & by
the stalkes & fruites of Indian & ~~forrei~~ exoticque plants ~~made~~ reduced into pouder:
For so we reade of Earth thus transported **[page 325]** out of Egypt, & brought into
Italy, which ~~brought~~ produced forreigne plants, & their rootes ~~bar~~ branches & seedes
contused and blended together with the {other} Earth, & watered with warme water
brought forth divers of these Countries Simples as it were spontaneously: And it is
my Ld: *Bacons* ~~rule~~ expedient how to acquire varieties of simples in their naturall
perfection by severall kinds of Earth: And therefore for some plants it will be better
to transplant them together with their naturall Soile, bring in a good quantitie of
it at a tyme, & furnishing some whole beds with it a good depth: And here it will
be reasonable to examine what we have written concerning *Composts & stercoration*,
& to consider that[5] some plants are spoyled by our unreasonable application of too
rich a mould; & then againe how some Plants prepare & fitt the Soile for the entertainement of others, better then ~~all~~ {any composition} we can devise; as *Corne* we see
dos for the *blew–bottle, Poppy, Fumitorie* and as my Ld *Verulames,* more at large exem-
plifies concerning *Sympathie*[6] & *Antipathie.* It would likewise be essaied whither the
same Earth layd & combed in severall postures, & altered againe in severall seasons
will not produce different plants: For if ever, here is the place to try severall conclu-
sions; ~~as to~~ and experiment how one may temper ~~the~~ even the heavens as well as the
Earth by Art: Seing we find ~~the~~ {our} greatest impediments to proceede from the
cold & the over much raine which in these Septentrion climats marrs most of our
labours in this kind: Here therefore let us exercise what we know concerning the re-
dubbling of the sun beames, ~~length lengthn~~ {repercussions & reflections} prolonging
of Autumne, præoccupating the Spring, preventing & moderating the {severity of}
winter, reversing the violence ~~of wi~~ & ~~& ill~~ {noxious} effects of the winds {& blasts}
to make such choice even of Plants, as may warme & prepare ~~the~~ both the soile & the
aire for others, & lastly to study what imbibitions, & waters are to be compounded
for them: & finaly whatsoever may facilitate their perfection & groth. Some plants
are best raised ~~of~~ without seede, or rootes, some onely by them: Wild plants, now &
then more valuable then the Garden, & some from bare Hills, ~~&~~ heathes, & Valies,
preferrable to those which grow in the richer {& more luxurious} Valies: These & all
other trialls, precautions, & instruction are of absolute necessitie for the ~~more even~~
{well} peopling our *Philosophico–medicall Garden.*

   All things in this order, the next ~~thing~~ to be considered is its furniture: And
for this expedient supposing our Correspondence ample, the Simples may either be
planted confusedly, & according to their severall aspects & soile which the best affect,
or more methodically and **[page 326]** in Alphabet: But this last, though it exceedingly
assist the memorie; yet in reguard of the differing application of site & soyle as we
sayd it will be very difficult, almost impossible to succeede so well in this method: We
therefore resolve upon the first, as the most consonant to the nature of the Simples,
& according to which their *localities,* may with a little industrie, be so methodised
as to be easily inserted into our *Album memoriæ* which should be a Booke purposely

---

5. **[Margin note]** C: 9: L:1.
6. **[Margin note]** Hist: Nat: cent: 5.

designed for this Garden. where~~in~~ they may be entered in Alphabeticall Catalogues, referring to their severall situations, bedds, & places, as we demonstrated in the precedent Chapter. The rest of the divisions of our Gardin, may be disposed into bordures & beds, so as may be most comprehensive; for here it shall be less necessarie to introduce knotts, Cabinets, Labyrinths, Aviaries and the like ornaments; because it is ~~onely culti~~ solely dedicated to the culture of Naturall varieties: onely the larger Area lying South of the *Mount* & Aquatique Quarters, would be cast into the best forme of Beds that it were capable of, & should by all meanes have an ample fountaine in the meddle, with sutable Walkes both to & about it: and if there be a moderate mixture of such Stattues as represent to the life the Effigies & memorie of the most skillfull & illustrious Botanists, Physitians & Philosophers[7] ~~it~~ which {~~they~~} may be rarely placed upon the Ascents of the Mount, & in some other signall places about the Garden, what can it want of the ultimate perfection & accomplishment of this part of our *Elysium*[.]

~~We will now give our Gardiner a Specimen~~ {For the furniture whereoff with ~~Speede~~ {the best} expedition &} choyce, we shall do well to imitate those who errect & ~~collect~~ collect great *Libraries*, to consult the best Catalogues that are extant especialy {of} the Publique Physick Gardens which are most flourishing & best stored: [8]We will exemplifie {in} that of Paris; Or the *Hortus Regius Blesensis* belonging to the late *D: of Orleans* or any other which we most ~~fa~~ esteeme, & out of them to make our collections; & provide our furniture: Likewise to visite our owne *Herbals* especialy those who treat of *Indigene* plants, least we put our selves many times to paine & expense for what growes {in} ~~at~~ our owne ~~doores~~ fields, & about o[ur] houses: But ~~before~~ for the better encouragement [o]f **[page 327]** our Gardiner, & facillitating this {noble & usefull} enterprise, we will ~~conclude this chapter~~ here add a ~~Speciment~~ few directions concerning the planting & situating of simples, serving onely as a {generall & familiar) Specimen.

On the Mount East:
[9]*Sedum* on the Mount walle, *Telephium* major and minor, set in the *crevasses* of the rocks: or more moyst:

On the Mount West:
Apocynum below, *Cnaphalium* [Gnaphalium] on the M: barren Earth, *Melissa, Laurus, Cuminus* below, *Libanotis, Alypum Montpeliens: Hippoglossum, Lachrymæ Jobi, Laserpitium* in a pot, *Rubia* on the rocky part. *Alyssum, Mezerion* below, etc.

On the Mount North:
{*Abies*} *Cedrus, Cypressus, Dentaria. Juniperus* {at top}, ~~*Cacalia*~~, *Larix. Gentiana, Poligonatum, Eryngium, Parietaria* on the rocky part & barren sides, *Sesili Æthiopicum, Aconitum bacciferum, Pinus* ~~top:~~ *picea* both only top, *Fragraria* ~~Aconite~~ *Circæa, Alkakengi, Hyoscyamus, Ladanum.*

On the Mount South:
Germander, Scordium in a gravelly part, *Heliotrophia, Nicotianum* under the wall of the mount: *Amygdalus* on the 4th Cascade; *Aloes*; Euphorbium, *Galanga, Lamium, Caryophyllata* shaded, *Balsamina, Balsamum, Moringa, Ornithopodium* on the barrenest part:

---

7. **[Margin note]** Apollo Soloman Chiron: Pliny, Theophrastus: etc:
8. **[Margin note]** printed at Par: 1655
9. **[Margin note]** Place these Alphabeticaly

Lycia, Buxus, Jucca, ~~*Camo*~~*[?] Schœnunthum, Myxos, Capparis,* on the wales & rocks, *Cedrus* at the top, *Agnus Castus, China radix, Officin: Citrullus, Vaccinia nubium* on the summite: *Polium* ~~*Curo*~~, *Xylum, Palma* in a Case, on the upmost Cascade: *Draco arbor* {in a case} above *Accacia, Scammonium, Ficus* ~~onely~~ {neere} Wall below, *Arbor Thurifera* in case, *Arisarum* below neere the foote. *Gallœ arbor, Zinziber, Mandragora, Tragacantha* in a pot, *Cardamomum, Erica, Helliboras, Cistus, Paliurus, Zizypha* in a pot, *Marum, Lentiscus, Myrobalanus* in a case, *Lunaria, Sesamum* in a pot, *Olea* plasted to the walls:[10] *Piper* in potts, *Quajacum* in a Case, *Polium [p]rotanum, Malus punica, Oryza, Dictamnum, Rhubarbarus, Crithmum* in the wall, *Sabina, Santalum* in a Case: [indecipherable] in a pot: *Prunella* in the gravelly soile: *Sena Herba mi[mo]sa* ~~raised~~ in a pot: *Barba Jovis* {frutex} in a case. *Arbor tristis* **[page 328]** ~~in a Case~~. *Abrotonum, Nardus* in a pot, *Celastrus* in a case, *Staphis* in a pot, ~~*Brunellus* amongst gravelly Earth~~, *Styrax arbor* in a case, *Rhus* g[r]avelly part: *Flos solis, Tamarindus, Arbor Vitœ, Curcuma* in a pot: *Terebintha* only top: *Cubabœ* in a Case, *Arbor Lanifera* in a case, *Arbutus, Amomum, Arbor brasilia* in a Case, *Camphora* in a pot, *Coccos* in a Case, *Galanga* in a pot, *Herba viva* pott, *Leucoma Ind* pot, *Payca herba* pot, *Spinosa herba, Lactuca Syl: Pumila* potts: *Melo: Carduus Americanus,* Myrrha potts: *Herba Sensibilis* pot {raised in hot bed in Aprill with care as Melons} *Herba impatiens* pot: *Lignum Nephritisum* case *Melochia, Herba Cassiana, Sarcocella,* Herba *Pomum arenosum, Flos Corvinus, Stipes Punctatus, Penna terrœ Paradisea, Aloe,*[11] *Gossypium, Ambrosia, Aphyllantes, Apocynum Asclepius, Lignum Rhodium, Pistacia, Botrys, Calamus Aromaticus, Caprificus, Capsicum, Colocynthis, Corallus arbor, Ephemerum, Crassula, Cytisus,* and many other rare exotick plants & Simples to be raised in the hott bed annualy for the most part are to be tenderly preserved in Cases or potts, & to be exposed to the Sun on the South ~~part of~~ aspect of the mount with greate care:

Palustrall and Aquatique. To be planted in the Marshes & Pitts sunke at the East & west sides of the Mount:

East aspect:

Angelica, Argentina, Thalictrum, Numilaria, very moist *Millefolium, Bedagaris, Polygonum, Consolida,* ~~*Capilli Veneris*~~ neere the water but *Amara daliis,* Cruciata, Cyperus, Myrtus, *Brabantica, Jacobea, Arundo* in the very marsh, *Satyrion,*

On the *Western* aspect

Serpentaria, Scrophularia, Moly, Bistortus, Tussilago, Lysimachia Sagittaria, Persicaria, ~~*Bechium Dracunculus*~~ *Scorpoides, Tamariscus, Dipsacus, Draba repens,* etc.

On the *Northern* Aspect

Morfus Diaboli, Scolopendra, Scordium, Enula Campana, Perficaria, ~~*Aldertia*~~ {Alnus}, *Willow,* ~~*Sallow*~~ {Salix}, *Paralysis, Nidus avis, Aragallis aquatica, Typha, Ophris* etc:

On the *Southern* aspect

Atriplex Sylvestris, {Caltha Trifolium palustre} *Capilli veneris, Dracancula, Ros Solis Herba doria* etc.

---

10. **[Margin note]** olea some question whither olives will come of stones, if so, they must be graffed & that often we tryed without successe, tis best to purchase a tree, The Wilder suppose old best, but the sweete worst. **[Continued in opposite margin]** Virgil says: Non ulla est olivis cultura, it needs no dressing:

11. **[Margin note]** Cotton will come of seedes in a dryish & stony ground sowne in Autumne 'till Spring 3 or 4 foote high:

[Page 329] In the Shady Theater twixt the Wood & the North side of the *Mount Umbilicus terræ, Castanea, Adiantum aureum, Bupleurum, Scabious* Sandy, *Quinquefolium, Chelidonium, Ulmaria, Epimedium,* ~~Basil~~ {*Ocymum*}, *Virga aurea* {in rich Earth} *Tormentilla, Asarabacca,* ~~Arum~~ {*Arum*}, etc.

In the flatt & open part of the Garden to the South of the Mount *Eastward Ulmaria, Centauria, Sanicle, Elaterium, Ebalus Mercuriale, Calcitrapa* in a rough ground, *Plantago, Dictamnus, Bursa pastoris* in barren earth, ~~So Fælix, Darinicum~~

Westward

Polygonon, Eupatorium, Fumaria, Filix barren Sand *Perforata* in dry leane ground, *Aster Atticus, Onos, Absynthium, Romanum,* or *Ponticum Staphisagria, Psillum, Petasites, Caprifolium, Ruta Lotus Arbor, Campanula* in a sandy place, *Carum, Muscipula, Myrris, Coriandrum, Clycyrrhiza* in a deepe fat mould, *Ricinus, Platanus, Baccharis Monspel, Cochlearia, Eringium, Fistularia, Laburnum, Larix, Stramonium,* etc

Northward

Op[h]ioglossum in fat soyle, *Enula Campana, Milium Solis,* etc

Southward

Carduus benedictus, ~~Verraine~~{bena}, *Veronica, Saxifragium* in light ground, so also *Pæonia,* ~~Acanthus~~ *Acantus* in Sandy, *Aristolochcia* both kinds, *perforata* in gravelly earth, *Piperitis,* ~~Picinus~~, *Marrubium, Libanotis, Coronopus* in a Sandy *Consolida* in a stony part, *Fraxinella* in fat & hot soil, *Scorzonera, Clematis* good mould, *C{h}amelæa, Glastum, Ruta* {The Suggar Cane is planted in bulbs, & rootes, in excellent Earth, pruned at a yeare old, & if you cut them within a yard of ground before winter, & raising a little cover over them, with a ~~little~~ some warme Soyle spread over the roote etc, it will neede no more care, & will thrive:}

In the Wood

Alchimilla, Imperatoria, Androsæmum, Serratula, Saxifragia, Fragraria, Aster Atticus, Chamædris, Viscum, Primula veris, Viola, Betonica, Bistorta, etc. {Or you may range them after an Alphabetical order for the more commodious remembring them; or in ~~Cla~~ their several Classes {& quarters} as *Jonstonus*[lxxxvi] has ~~d~~ assigned them in his Notitia Regni Vegetabilis ~~cited by us lib: 3: cap: 3~~ which together with ~~that~~ what we have sayd in ~~that~~ {Cap: 7} Chap: {7: lib: 3} concerning this study may here be fittly consulted.}[lxxxvii]

And this may suffice for a briefe direction as it concernes the furniture & culture of our *Physical Simples,* & from hence has the ~~Master of~~ Lord of our *Elysium, distilled Waters, Syrups, Conserves, Condited rootes, Oyles,* ~~powders~~ {Species} *Decoctions, Unguents, Emplasters, Antidotes, Bathes, Clysters* **[page 330]** and whatsoever else is needefull upon any emergency or suddaine accident, ~~as in~~ {for the care of} Tertians, Obstructions, Losse of Appetite weakenesse of Stomack, or Liver, Swelling, Wormes in Children, Wounds, {Contusions} Ackes, Scorbuticall affections, Exulcerations, Purges, Vomits, Pills, {Bathes} etc: for all which, who knows not the use & Souraine excellencies of Cochlearia, pyrrethrum, Tabaccum, Alchimilla, Angelica, Rue, Scordium, Artemesia, Asperula, [blank space] and thousand of other plants the virtues whereoff every Herbal will tell us, Besides what externall instructions {& helps to discou[r]se} we learne from the Names, Signatures, Authors, Places, Seasons, & incredible ~~&~~ varieties which they present to our eye; besides I say their interiour perfections, qualities & virtues, of which a more then ordinary tincture will be requisite in our {phytriatic} Gardiner

There are yet who have discoursed of {an} other *Philosophicall* Garden, which concernes the Vegetable worke in *Physick* whose principle fire is the stomac of the *Estrich,* the mould the best vegetable *Saturne,* made contrite by the ~~imbi~~ fruitefull

Figure 70. Illustration of a "garden of simples," or medicinal plants, in perspective in text at page 330.

imbibitions of the *Aqua Cælestis*. which produces most strange {miraculous} & glorious plants, flo: & trees, such as yet we have never encountred amongst the spontaneous growers of nature; but we referr the curious Reader to the true Sonns of Art, whilst we shall in the next chapter {present him} with some natural rarities, for the most part strangers to our Elysium as yet, not in lofty words, but plaine & veritable narrations, & in such Instances as will become both our ~~Wonder~~ {wonder &} astonishment ~~and~~ But first ~~we~~ behold our ~~Physi~~ Garden of Simples {thus reppresented} in Perspective:[12] **[illustration, see Fig. 70]** [13]

[Page 331]

---

12. **[Margin note]** or rather Round like that at Paris.
13. **[Margin note]** insert Dr: Morisons method:

CAP: XVIII.

Of Wonderfull and Stupendious Plants

He that shall skillfully {& dilligently} examine the admirable natures & properties of the severall plants which we have already enumerated in the two foregoing chapters, will find himselfe sufficiently engaged with wonder and amazement, ~~Since our Elysium~~ & to be so taken up with the {use &} contemplation of what we have there presented him, as not to imagine our Elysium in the least defective; though we should have omitted this Chapter of Prodigies and Stupendious plants: But since there were some rarities of that kind, which we could not so ~~well~~ happily introduce into our Philosophicall Garden with such relations & circumstances {as} are due to their severall natures {& strange effects}, we have thought fitt to assigne them this Chapter; and to divert our Gardiner {a while} with a briefe description of such ~~plants~~ wonderfull plants, as, though not all of them denisons in our *Britanique Elysium*, may {yet} by his industrie & curiositie be in tyme procured & ~~cultivated~~ {elevated: serving} in the interim ~~serve~~ to dignifie ~~and advance~~ (& indeare &} ~~this present worke~~ his proffession, & {to} advance the reputation of our present worke: Since there is in Nature nothing ~~more {so}~~ {more} admirable, ~~and~~ stupendious {& ~~so much~~ approching to miracles} then the vegetable productions of the earth, & furniture of what he {so diligently} cultivates. But we should indeede fill a Volume, not a chapter to ~~run~~ {passe} through halfe the varieties of this kind which nature {& our Gardens} presente us: we do not pretend it: It shall suffice us to have made such a Collection, as will not easily be encountred else where, without the interposition of some more vulgar, or lesse worthy our admiration: we ~~will~~ {do} therefore begin with the *Aloes*; & shall take ~~them~~ {the rest} as they ~~follow~~ {succeede} in that order.

The *Aloe*, a plant well knowne to the curious, and no stranger ~~to~~ {in} our ~~Phi~~ Medicall Garden, though more frequent in the hotter countries, remaines a low plant displaing it selfe in thick & poynted leaves onely, and not shooting up **[page 332]** into a stemm till after an hundred–yeares, when at length this plant breakes forth with such a horrid fragor & report as if some ~~greate Canon~~ {piece of Artillerie} were discharged; and then immediately rises up in a Trunke, with such {impetuousnesse &} celeritie, as in 4. or 5 daies to equal the ~~altitude~~ {stature} of an ordinarie Oake; bearing on its summite certaine floweres {&} triumphing as it were at its {prodigious} release, after so long {& hard an} imprisonement: And in this action, the motion is so speedie, as even to be discerned by the vigilant eye of the Patient Gardiner: Such a plant did not many yeares since exalt it selfe in the Garden of *Monsr: Perier* an *Apothecarie* at *Montpeliers* ~~in France~~ which in 4 daies attained to the height of 30 handfulls,[lxxxviii] & in bulke exceeding a mans thigh: The same likewise happned before the {late} *King* of *France* and *Cardinal Richlieu* in the Citty of *Piscerna* of the same Province, which in six and thirty howeres {space} rose 28 handfuls in height, & was judged so portentous & rare; as that ~~his Matie~~ *Lewes* the 13th caused the portraiture of the Tree to be exquisitely ~~drawne~~ {reppresented} to the Life, & preserved it as a very great ~~raritie~~ {curiositie};

And truely it is so rare; that it is to be wondered how the mention of such an effect should totally escape all our late *Botanists*, & that (besides *Clusius* who indeede seemes to mention such a *Phoenomenon* ~~at~~ that hapned at *Avignion* .Anno: 1599, which all the whole Country ran far & neere to behold) neither *Matthiolus, Dodonaus Fuchsius, Delcampius, Lobel, Ger{h}ard* or *Parkinson* should so much as ~~mention~~ take notice of it, 'till of late the industrious *Borell* recorded it in his ~~Ph~~ *Medio–Physical centuries*; upon whose ~~relation~~ {credit} yet, ~~of~~ {concerning} a thing so altogether wonderfull & stupendious we did not acquiesse till we had obtained an autoptical Authentique from an honorable person, who ~~resided lately resided at Mont~~ {residing at *Montpelier* con}firm'd the whole ~~relation~~ {passage} to us, in the same manner as we have described; and from who~~m~~{se} {testimony} there is not the least reason to appeale: {But we will subjoyne} his wordes. ~~are these: Concerning~~

{Touching} the *Aloe* Tree you mentione, I have informed my selfe, & can assure there is such a one, and saw it in the *Kings–Garden* heere: It is 100 yeares in growing, and at the 100 years expiration: from being an humble plant becomes in few daies a very ~~high~~ {lofty} tree; but breaking forth with so greate ~~impetuositie~~ violence & celeritie that it even rends the Earth, & make a wonderfull ravage {about it}; yea, so greate a noyse, that I heard affirmd from a credible *Merchant* in this Towne, who has himself heard it, ~~&~~ that it may very well equall the report of a Cannon; & not onely so; but has likewise (as he ~~affirmd to~~ depos'd to me) apparantly **[page 333]** seene it rise in the celeritie of those few daies groth:

There are many of these plants in Languedoc, ~~&~~ {which} are a spurious {kind of} *Aloes*. I informed my selfe likewise of an intelligent Apothecarie (a greate friend of Sr. K: Digby, & kinsman to the defunct Monsr. Perier, whom you nam'd to have the Tree in his Garden) about it, who confirm'd what the other had ~~sayd~~ {related} before.

Thus for, our {noble} correspondent in ~~his~~ {a} letter {dated} from *Montpellier: 25: Sept: 1656.*

Now what is in this instance most stupendious consists not altogether in its *Elephantique partus* and long stay: for so the Palme, Lachryma Cerui & some other trees are sayd ~~to~~ not to make their productions till after 100 years have passed over them: But what is {most} ~~prodigious~~ {wonderfull} is the fragor & celeritie with which it emerges {out of the earth}, carring up a stemm of that altitude in so short a space: but so ~~it~~ {this thick & Viscous} {plant} seemes to have laien ~~hid~~ conceald that it might amasse & collect {what was necessary for} such an ~~strength~~ Architectonique Spirit, ~~&~~ ~~Strength~~ {heate, force} ~~to make the prodigious effort &~~ {&} to digest the intrinsicall matter, give it heate & force sufficient to worke so prodigious effects. It is reported of the warie Mulberie–Tree, that she produces both her leaves & fruite in one night with a prævious gentle murmure; & so it is sayd also of the Walnutt, about St *Johns tyde*; but these are immaginations, what we have related of the Aloes is certaine; & for its admirable nature, worthy to be recorded in this Chap, and consecrated to posteritie: If such trees ~~were~~ {had bin} yearely ~~planted~~ & frequently planted; their effects would not be {now} ~~so~~ strange to us, & like the *Ludi–Seculares* amongst the *Romans*. ~~But let this suffice~~ But we dwell too long upon it.[1]

---

1. **[Margin note]** ~~Here set the Ichonisme:~~

{I here[?] now present you the Figure of the Plant} **[illustration inserted on separate piece of paper; see Fig. 71]**

The *Ampouli* is a plant growing in the Ile of St *Laurence*, the leafe whereoff burnt in perfume, dos hinder inchantments; so as 'tis credibly reported, whilst it sends up its fume, the Sorcerer ~~of~~ amongst these miserable Gentiles, can have no power to do mischief. {This may relate something to that of 6: Tabit: 16. & who can tell but such a plant might have hindred ~~the~~ even the Delphic Enthusiastics, **[continued in margin]** for tis reported they were struck as it were with a vapour issuing out of the Earth: Thus the Tripos upon which these {frantick} [sacred?] lesse sate bare: See Dr: [indecipherable] Delphique[?]}

The *Anramitaco* a plant growing in the same Ile: about 2 cubits high, bearing on the poynt of its leaves, which are very long, a Flower or fruite ~~very~~ {so} hollow as to resemble a pretty cup, with its cover, containing in them neere a pint of fair water: The Inhabitants make some scruple of gathering them often, ~~becau~~ as having a tradition that it will certainly be a tempestious day. There are some of the red, others yellow which are greates{r}. The Ananas is the King–pine esteemed (as doubtlesse it merites) ~~is~~ the most ravishing & delicious fruite that the whole universe affords: It is frequently {found} growing in the Barbados, & all the *Antilles* It is so beautifull {to the eye}, so sweete of sent, & rich of tast, that Nature seemes ~~to h~~ in favour of this fruite {onely} to have displaied whatsoever she {had} reserved of most **[page 334]** rare & preciouse in all her Elysium. It grows upon a stem of about a foote high, which is invested with 15 or 16 leaves about the length of those of an Artichock, large as your hand & in figure resembling those of the Aloes whereoff we have discorsed. For they are sharp at top, & a litle below towards the middle, armed on either side with smale spines, which are extreamely ~~sharp picant~~ {picant} The Fruite emerges {from} betweene these leaves, elevated on its stalke & being in bulke about the size of a melon, & in forme not much unlike to the pine–apple: The rind, which is ~~armed~~ {embossed} with smale compartiments in manner of scales some what of a pale greene colour, edgd with incarnate upon a ground of yellow, is tufted without with many smale floweres, which according to the different aspects of the Sun, change into as many severall colours as there be in the Raine–bow: These flowers fall off as the fruite matures: But that which gives him the greatest lustre, & has acquired him the title of the King of ~~Flowers~~ Fruites; is the Diadem which crownes the Summit like a ~~nosegay posy festoon'd with plumes~~ tuffett of rare & solid flowers indented & of a lively & ~~shining~~ shining red, which adds a marvelous grace to it.

The pulpe or ~~meate~~ edule part which is under the ~~pulpe skin~~ {integument} is something fibrous; but dissolves all into juice when it is in the mouth; & has a gusto so supreame, & so particular, that those who have essayed its perfect description, not being capab[l]e to reach it {by} ~~under an~~ single comparison, have borrowed ~~all that~~ whatever they have bin able to find of most delicious in nature: For here is the flavour of the Nectarine ~~& strawbery~~ the freshness of the strawbery, the richnesse of the Muscat Grape, the tast of the Pipin. & of {at least} 10 severall fruites {besides} & after all, this a new ~~relish~~ {sette} of severall rich & high tasts, flowing in so fast, that ~~men are~~ the most [well fed?] Epicure {must} consider himself at a losse, & that his very imagination is not able to keepe pace with the {delicious} ravishing variety which it ~~yields~~ presents him.

The germe which perpetuates the fruite, neither consists in the roote, or little ~~grai~~ peppin which is usually found in the pulpe; but in the ghirland which crownes

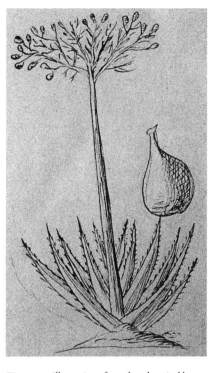

Figure 71. Illustration of an aloe plant in bloom, inserted at page 333.

it, which being stucke in the ground failes not to take roote, & yearly to fructifie: we sometymes find of these fruites, which beare no lesse then 4 of these glorious heads: & there are also of severall sorts of the fruites, which the Inhabitants distinguish by their Colours, figure, & Savor: ~~The~~ but that which we have described is much superiour to them all; & of which (besides what we have already attributed) affords a most incomparable beverage ~~to the Ta~~ nothing inferiour to the best Malvoisie being a little kept: being ~~preservd~~ {condited} it yeilds one of the ~~best~~ noblest preserves which ~~the whole~~ {comes from} the Indies: for they cutt the rind in two parts, & preserve it drye with a few of its thinest & most delicate leaves; after that joyning the parts exquisitely together, they incrust it **[page 335]** with an icy coate of suggar, which perfectly conserves the ~~figure~~ {shape} of the fruite & leaves & which maugre the ~~heates~~ excesses of the torrid zone presents these happy countries with a sweete image of the sad productions of our {rugged} Winters[.]

    Nor is this universall Fruite destitue of admirable effects as to Medicine, (though but of late detected) for experience has taught that it is ~~most~~ of rare virtue to recreate the spirits elevate~~d~~ & raise the depressions of the heart, it wonderfully corroborates the stomach, vanquishes the weaknesse of it, & totaly reestablishes the lost appetite: most efficacious are its properties for the asuaging the torments causd by the gravell, or suppression of Urine, in sume, it is an approved Antidote against ~~most~~ {all} poyson & is as it were a kind of *Panacea*. But the waters extracted by the Alembiq is of a speedier operation; but for being somewhat of a corrosive nature, it is to be taken with caution, & {the} advice of a skillfull Physitian.

[illustration, see Fig. 72]

{But his Majesty having had divers of these sent him over, & even ripening after they were here in his Garden at St James, we are not altogether to disparagd propagating them} Ramusius has given us a relation of the greate Melon or Gourd growing in the Capaseo mountaines in Tartarie which being cutt open & ripe, produces a little creature like a sucking lamb: The History is affirmed with wonderfull asseveration, and it is no other then the Scythian *Borametz*, described by *Scaliger* in his exercitations against *Cardan*: to be propagated by a seede like a Melon, & growing about a yard high: that if wounded it will bleede & beare a fruite ressembling a Lamb, which being fastned by the navill with a stringy stalke, lives onely so long as by that ligament it ~~can~~ is suffered to reach & feede on the subnascent hearbes: that wolves are extreamely greedy of them, & severall other stories of it: But these descriptions are ~~much more~~ {very} uncertaine, ~~then~~ & did give us no smale ~~reason~~ {cause} of suspect upon the whole matter, till we mett with those exact & pleasant relations of *Olearius*, who was late Secretary **[page 336]** to that extravagant, though most magnificent Embassy, of the D: of *Holsteine*, into *Persia*: whose enquiries have hitherto afforded us the best satisfaction & he~~is~~ ~~describes this~~ {mentions} {relation is} thus:

    They told us also that neere to *Samaxa* betweene the *Vuolga* & the *Don*, there grew a kind of melon, or rather pompion in forme of a lamb, that fruite extreamely resembling it, & having a stalke which fastned it to the earth by the navill: that in growing it changed its place, & dried up the grasse where ever it lay, which the *Moscovites* call feeding, & add, that when it dies the stalke ~~dries~~ withers, & the fruite re~~in~~vests itselfe with a {kind of} velvet skin, which may be taken off dressed & employed instead of furr: This Fruite they call *Boranez*, ~~that~~ which imports a *Lamb*: They shewed us some skins of it, which they had torne of from a bed Coverlett, & swore to us that it was made of that fruite, ~~though we~~ which we had some difficulty to

Figure 72. Illustration of an ananas *or "king" pineapple in text at page 335.*

Figure 73. Illustration of a banana tree and fruit in text at page 337.

believe. They were covered with a tender, curled wooll, much resembling that of ~~an~~ new fallen, or abortive lamb: & in summe, theire relation dos extreamely quadrate with that of Jul: Scaliger Exercit: 181, already mentioned:

Thus far *Olearius*, concerning this prodigious *Zoophyte*; {nor is the *Urtica marina* to be here forgotten, which grows on the rocks, & is not fed by the rootes but we passe it:}

The *Bananier* {or Banana} is a tree or shrub of about 15 foote high, {beautifull} leafe of an ell & a quarter ~~large~~ long, 18 Inches large, & such as may very well serve instead of Towells or Napkins; & being dried for ~~Matts~~ Bed matts: The pulpe of the fruite is white as snow, & being cutt in the middle as you would an Orange, ~~gi~~ presents you with the lively forme of a Crucifix {which Mr Ligon ~~affirmes the~~ espressed}[2] which therefore the Spanyards will by no meanes touch with a knife, for reverence sake: This Fruite is 13 Inches long, a little turning at the extreame, & about the bignesse of a mans Arme. The whole Bunch or Groupp is ordinarily the charge of a man, & sometymes so heavy, as they are faine to beare it betweene two wth a Coal-staff, as the Spies did the fruites of Canan; And there are some that will not be persuaded but that it was the Forbidden fruite wch our Grandmother was so licorish after, & the rather for the largenesse of the leafe, so convenient to cover their nuditie: How ever it were, the figure within the fruite may well afford matter of much divine & usefull speculation to those who on these occasions use to spiritualise upon the secrets of Nature. The figure follows, which yet much differs from Mr Ligons who makes it more to resemble the Plantane described hereafter in this Chapter:

[Page 337] [illustration, see Fig. 73]

The *Barnacle* describ'd by Hector Boetius is another wonderfull tree produc'd in the northern parts of our Elysium of Greate Britannes & which may well contend with the whole universe againe for its prodigious Fruite, if with *Parkinson*, it prove not at last to be a Scotch Imposture. {Se Sr R: Moray R Society}

---

2. **[Margin note]** Get the descrip: & cite it at length: in his: hist: Barbado: p. 82.

[Page 338] There is a certaine Beane in the American Iles which produces scane [skein] cropps without renewing: & are never seene without ripe fruite upon them, greene fruite, & faire flowers; so as it seemes to present you all the seasons at a tyme: but these are not to be thought more admirable then the spontaneous Pease which spring out of the stony beach, cast up in mounts of an incredible height, ~~in~~ at *Oxford* in Suffolke, whose roote is so profound as not to be investigated, nor dos there the least atome of Earth appeare about them: With these they feede their sheepe & hoggs, & sometymes (in a famine) the poore people of those coasts who call them Selfe Sowne Pease; There is likewise a kind of Cole-wort, which grow thereabout after as strange a manner: {but now we Speake of beanes, most stupendious is the variety of ~~them~~ such as have bin gatherd on the Sea Costs of *Cornewale*, a collection whereof the *Lady Killigrew* showed to *Lobell* that were droven thither; & so are yearely when the winds set westward; & which by their shapes are wafted from the very Indies themselves:} There is in the Ilands of Cimbabon, by the report of Scal: Duretus, Scaliger, Acosta, & especialy of M: Anton Pigofeta, a Tree, whose leaves do much resemble {that of} the Mulberie, which has on both sides little short {& strong} feete, not much like to those of a Batt, which falling on the Ground, if any offer to touch it, crawls away: Pigasetta ~~says~~ affirmes that he kept one of these leaves eight dayes together in a box, which at any tyme he would handle did ~~crawle away~~ {walke} about the box, & dos believe that they lived by the aire, for it could not be perceived that it tooke any other nourishment.

The Crowne-Imperiall is an ordinary ~~Plant flower~~ plant, but never the lesse ~~renownd~~[?] to be admired for the beauty of its flowre, ~~and~~ in the middle whereoff there depends a faire pearle in appearance, ~~&~~ proportion & orience, which will not {drop} ~~fall~~ off without violence, but taken with the top of your finger, it is to the last {more} ~~as~~ delicious ~~th~~ then any hony; & that succeedes with another about an hower after.

The Coco tree growes like the Palme, after a wonderfull order & uniformity; but it is the fruite of it, of which such things have been reported, especially those of the East Indies, which do much exceede those of America, from whence yet we have had of them that have weighed {about 10} pounds: They grow upon the Trunk of the tree it selfe, which from the tyme it **[page 339]** once begins to beare is never naked of fruite, for it produces them monethly: The shell of the fruite is so hard, as to endure the politure & engraving of any figures for the enriching & ornament of drinking cupps & severall Vessells of Elegant forme, for the service of the house: Whilst the rude & stringy integument of the outsides will be drawne out into threids to occam the shipps, & serves for Cordage The Nut being opened, the first that presents itselfe is a ~~pulpe~~ firme pulpe white as the driven snow, & of tast not inferiour to the best Almonds, & that in so plentifull quantity, as one is sufficient to fill an ample dish; in the middle or cavity of this there is contained a good glasse full of a cleere & {most} agrable liquor like the Frontiniaque grape in tast; in Summ, this blessed fruite presents us with a wholesome & rich collation, Sufficient for a repast: It is this water alone which containes the seminal part, & sends forth the sprouts, besides it has the property to etch out & explaine all wrinkles of the face, being washed with this water so soone as the fruite falls & is mature: Besides this, the Tree perforated in due season yields a most pleasant & wholesome liquor or Wine: And of its timber they make houses, beames, coverings, wales, boards, shipps, nailes, masts, sailes, {cloath}, Cordage, Tables, potts, cupps, spoones, all sorts of Utensils. And for its universall effects in

Medicine *Avicen, Serapion, Mesue* & others, do extreamely commend it. But what more ads to the history of this Tree, is the Travell & strang voyages which it ~~mak~~ sometymes makes For the Inhabitants of *Magdagascar* ~~affirme it~~ where yet it plentifully growes, affirme it no indigene of their Iland; but the fruite ~~made a voyage~~ {wafting} through those vast seas, came on shore upon the strands, and tooke roote in the Sand; when after twenty yeares it was hardly observed, 'till a certain King of the Iland being by chance ~~fallen~~ tempted to repose himselfe under its goodly shadow, one of the Nutts falling, knockt him o' the head & killed him: And ~~they~~ since that, they have observed divers of the nutts cast upon the shores when the wind sits East—north—East, from whence they conjecture that they {came} ~~set out~~ from some of the Ile situate under the Æquinoctial: And by this meanes it is likely many such encounters may happen in other places, were it dilligently observed, & that transmigrations of other plants may have hence had their so admird originals.

[**Page 340**] The *Cotton-tree* {of which there are severall kinds} growes about the height of a Peach having a broune rind, & narrow leafe divided into three & beares a flower as big as a rose of 5 leaves of a golden yellow colour: These floweres are succeeded by an oval fruite, about the bignesse of an ~~Filbert~~ haisell nutt, with its huske: when ripe it is very black without, but by some overtures discovers the white wooll, ~~which~~ {which} in so prodigious a quantity is stired & enclosed within that narrow compasse. There is another ramps like the Vine without a propp, & is that which produces the most excellent Cotton, of which is made so much cloath, & divers sorts of stuffes, so universally usefull.

The *Corall* is found to be a plant or Lythophylon which ~~are~~ {is} of a dirty colour till the Barke is taken off; But being tender & Squeezed a little ~~they~~ {it} ~~send~~{nds} forth a juice like unto milke as the fig tree dos, onely it is exceedingly caustick & burning, & ~~which~~ is thought to be the principle or Seede of this stony plant, ~~of~~ which in a little tyme being exposed to the ayre & artificially polished, becomes none of the most contemptible jewells. There is shewed ~~at~~ in a collection at Pisa Coral growing upon the skull of a man. Of this plant there is both a black & a white sort, whose pores seeme much more perspicuous, we have of the white sort which dos ~~arbore~~ perfectly arborescere a ~~pl~~ branch as big as a mans thigh. {~~Of such a nature might be the~~ And to this we might shew the tree or *Antipaten* of *Dioscorides*, The *Charitoblepharon* or *Isidos placamon Plinij.*}

The *Copeia* is a plant which beares leaves that serve like paper, & will ~~le~~ preserve the characters which are engraven upon both the sides, becomming very hard, & retaining the~~m~~ letters forever: But the *Xagna* hath a leafe of that amplitude, {as} out of which may be cutt whole skinns as it were of parchment, being a kind of pergamenifera.

The *Dutroa* [Datura] is a plant, the flower whereoff being given in drinke renders a man a laughing {& forgettfull} sott; for after a while it casts him into such a trance that for 24 howers he seemes as dead: This is the Ingredient which the *Indian* & *Portuguesse* {salacious & lewd} Women use to mix with their *philters*, &, ~~mix~~ scatter with amongst their Sweete meates, when they have a mind to be planting upon [**page 341**] their husbands foreheads, & which ~~after this~~ whilst the ~~operation~~ stupifactine operation of this lasts, they do with all the boldnesse & impudence imaginable, playing the wantons before their open eyes, pulling them by their beards, & abusing them with all ~~the~~ {sort} of reproches, whilst the poore {abused} sott dos nothing but grins & laughs; but what is most strange, when he comes to himselfe againe, he remembers no more what has passed, then if realy he had bin dead all that while. We should with some scruple ~~admitted~~ have admitted the effects of this wonderfull plant, had not the ~~fare~~ great Traveller *Mandeslo* confirmed the truth of it by his owne experience {at *Goa*} as he describes it in one of his letters, ~~sent~~ written from *Magdagascar*: in the yeare 1639, & printed at the end of the fore mentioned *Olearius*'s voyage into *Persia*, where he tells, how they ~~take~~ {can vanquish} of this charme at pleasure, by washing a certaine part of the body {namly the feete}. And in some others we have read, how slaves & servants give it frequently to their masters, when they would rob or pick their pocketts: But it seemes 'tis to be warily mixed, for being taken in to[o] great a quantity it kills out right: ~~Besides~~ But besides the former washing, a Vomite & frictions {or the Patients face put in Cowdung.} dos usually recover such as are surprised. {Of this ranke & quality is also the *Bangue* or Indian dreamer.}

There is ~~an~~ {a plant called *Teomath* or} Exhillerating ~~tree~~ {plant}, growing in Perù, ~~and~~ which being taken & held in the hand of a sick person dos immediately prognosticate ~~whith~~ the successe of his indisposition; for if he shall dye he becomes very sad & will be surprised with a wonderfu[l] consternation; if his sicknesse be not to death, he will ~~be~~ shew ~~such~~ a cheerfull countenance, and seeme as if he were perfectly recovered: Monardus protests that he has ~~frequently seene~~ {bin assured of} the experience of this strange effect from a person of greate honour who resided in the Indies, and that the Indians {physitians} of Peru use it as ours doe, when they would judge of a disease by the Water: but others, more probably, that the juice of it being dranke, if vomited up, is an ill prognostick, but otherwise, a Signe the Patient shall recover.

[illustration, see Fig. 74]

The Entsasacale is a tree in the Ile of St Laurence, the fruite whereoff is borne upon the very barke, and that without either leaves or branches; but, as we sayd upon the rind, ~~&~~ from the Sumit to the ~~roote of it~~ very ends of its roote, although under **[page 342]** although a greate depth under the Earth: Some also grow out at the ~~end~~ {extremities} of the leaves, and some emerge out of the very middle of the leafe: so as not to be assigned to any certaine place, nature being strangely extravagant & various in its production. The tree it selfe about the ~~sta~~ bignesse of an Almond, having leaves like the walnut, out of which hangs a fruite not unlike the Cassia

The Ebenie is the heart of a ~~Tree~~ greate Tree bearing small leaves like to the greater myrtil, of an obscure greene colour, the rind blackish: Of this there are two sorts. {but trees in the W. Indies so much harder as to sound & cutt like yron.}

The Endrachendrach is a tree whose wood being yellow is of that wonderfull hardnesse, as to indure in the Earth or whereever it is used, equaly with marble itselfe; & therefore hath a name imparting everlasting; it hath also the weight and hardnesse of yron. There are divers plants ~~and flo: which~~ and fruites which seeme to have letters and caracters upon them, for which famous is the *Hyacinth*,

> *Littera communis medijs pueroque viroque*
> *Inscripta è folijs: hæc nominis illa querelæ.*
> Met: 13.

~~The Ficus Indicus growes in the~~
{The Maccu–bay is the name of a plant in Ireland [Iceland?] bearing a pretty yellow

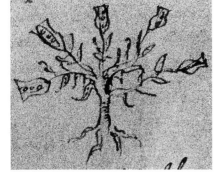

Figure 74. Illustration of an "Entsasacale" tree in text at page 341.

flo: which being but held in the hand or smelt too (or ~~as some say~~ more effectualy sat over) dos wonderfully & successfully purge by seige}

The *Ficus Indicus* growes to be of wonderfull stature in some places, and to sustaine itselfe thrusts out of its sides divers spurrs or buttresses from the roote to the very branches 4 or five foote about it, which forme many deepe arches and beautifull *Nices*: Another sort of them which they call the Goa Mangle lets downe certaine shining threads from the boughs resembling smale coards or cables of Silke, which no sooner touch the Earth, but immediately they take root, springing and putting forth large ~~boughs~~ branches, which againe take hold of the Earth as before *in infinitum*; so as that one tree dos often make a whole wood, in which the Indians cutting away some of the stemms ~~ma~~ forme them selves most sweete & natural bowers, for the archment above being impervious to the Sonn are like so many Caves or Nices, & so cloose and wonderfully disposd, as oftentime to yield an Echoe that will reverberate the voice 4 or 5 times, no otherwise then if it rebounded from so many hills, or solid buildings. It is reported that a thousand persons have inhabited under one of these trees, nay some affirne 3000: The tree it seemes was not a stranger to the Antients, *Theophrastus*, *Strabo*, *Pliny*, & others making mention of some thing very like it.

[illustration, see Fig. 75] [3]

[4]

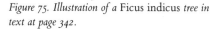

Nor may we passe over the more Common Tuna, whose leafe {being both roote & stemm} is supernascent the leafe for severall serieses; of these are severall sorts bearing flowers & wholesome fruite. The thornes yeilding needles to the Indians

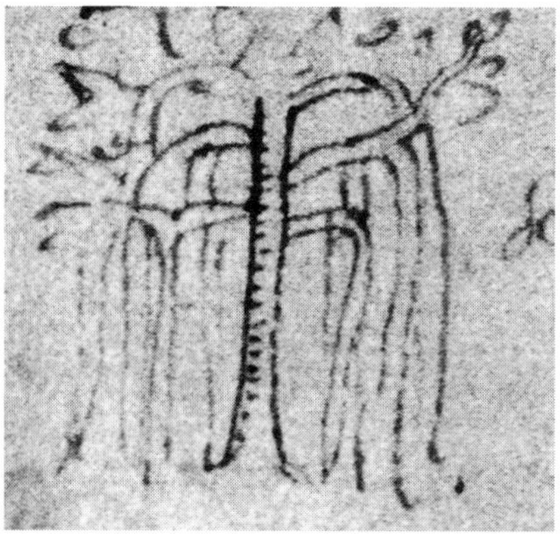

Figure 75. Illustration of a Ficus indicus *tree in text at page 342.*

---

3. **[Margin note]** Se: Parkinson: p: 1499:
4. **[Margin note]** Se the next Volume:

Complete Annotated Version
of Table of Contents and Related Material[i]

ELYSIUM BRITANNICUM.[1]
[2]OR THE[3]
ROYAL GARDENS
IN
THREE BOOKS

Præmissis præmittendis, etc.
BOOK I.

Præface Pr: pages:

Chap 1   A Garden derived, and defined, with its distinctions and sorts.   1
     2   Of a Gardiner, and how he is to be qualified.   3

---

1. **[Insertion above title]** A Diagratis or Plan towards the ~~The Plan of a Royal Garden~~ accomplish[men]t of a Royal Garden

2. **[Margin note (crossed out)]**
The Plan of a
Royal Garden
~~described~~
in 3 Books
towards the Accomplishment of
shewing the severall
Subiects, ~~the Horticulture~~
~~Horticulture in of~~
describing & shewing the Amplitude of that part of {Georgics}
Agriculture
which ~~the Horticulture~~ is belongs to Horticulture
in its noblest Extant.

3. **[Margin note (crossed out)]**
The Royal Garden
Paradisum Revisitum
A Plan o
A Plan, or Table of
~~Chapters~~. digested into ~~Heads~~

BOOK II.

Chapters, ~~towards the~~
towards the ~~Accomplishmnt~~
of a Royal Garden

4. **[Margin note]** with an account of the causes of Vegetation & Fertility. Se:
Malphigi & Dr: Grew:

5. **[Margin note]** Addendum: Transact: P. 797 ad 801.

6. **[Margin note]** part of this is printed. Syl[va]

BOOK III.

---

7. **[Margin note, printed]** This is already publish'd, being but a Chapter of this work.

8. **[Margin note]** Se: *Malphygius* 2d part

shew the riches, beauty, wonder, plenty, delight, and universal
use of a Garden. {Garden Buriale etc}

FINIS

J EVELYN [9]

A Table leading to the notes in the loose [10]
Sheetes to be inserted into the Elysium Britannicum:

Lib: j.
Cap: *Page*

---

9. **[Manuscript note crossed out on verso of title page]** note that when leaves dry the fibers rott: with bulbes loose the fibers should be yerly taken up which do not may remaine, but for offsetts. ~~bulbes~~, tamis {or} chives

10. **[Margin note]** Notes for the use of this Table:

note that {in} the loose papers to which these figures referr: the first stands for the book, the second for the chapter: as {in the margent} 2 – 8: that is the 2d book: chap: 8. viz Transplants, & so of the rest remembering to look on both sides of any sheet or page mentioned. & see how often the same signes occurr least you misse of many quotations.

Note also that though you find divers citats consulted as having served for a Chapter: yet if it have severall reference of number and Chapter it may possibly serve for severall Chapts; but then you are to consult what has already been used of it, & so be the more carefull in repeating of it

There is a packet of other loose papers marked (*) which are also referred to these chapters.

11. **[Margin note]** ~~This I feare must be againe explained~~

Lib: ij

Cap:

---

12. **[Margin note]** This also.

13. **[Margin note]** These must be examined again I doubt

31. 36. 55. 56. 61. 63. 67. 74. 75. 76. 79. 84. 88. 91. 125. ~~129,~~
~~130~~ 130. 133. 134. 143. 158. 160. 164. 165. 166. 168. 169. 170.
171. 172. 173. 174. 175. 180. 182. 185. 187. 189. 191. 196. 205.
210. 212. 213. 214. 215. 217. 220.

IX.   Famous Gardens etc ——————— 2. 20. 22. 23 {24.} 25.
30. 32. 48. 52. 59. 60. 61. 63. 64. 65[?]. 67. 74. 75. 80. 83.
88. 90. 104. 105. 106. 107. 108. 112. 114. 115. 116. 117. 125.
126[?]. 127[?]. 140. 145. 146. 147. 148. 149. 150. 158. 159.
184. [*sic*] 174. 187. 190. 198. 199. 203. 205. ~~209.~~ 209.
213. 214.

X.   Villa etc ——————— 17. 25. 34. 40. 103. 123.
127. 142. 172.

XI.   Corollary etc —

Præface. 133. 143. 162. 212. 220.

Stages[?]: 38. 63. 125. 169. 172. 175. 187. 191

[Separate sheet of paper inserted into text block] Loose papers to
be at leisure Inserted in their places:

{See the papers where these Uncial numbers are put; namely in the
packet marked ✪}

Captars   *Lib:1.*   *Preface* Signing (2) or Pr:

1 Book   *Title*   ✪ (1)

    I.   1   Garden defin'd & distinctions etc
    II.   2   Gardner qualitys[14]
    III.   3   Principles & Elements
    IV.   4   Fire
    V.   5   Air & Winds
    VI.   6   Water
    VII.   7   Earth
    [VIII.   8   ]
    IX.   9   Four Seasons.
    X.   10   Mould & Soile
    XI.   11   Composts
    XII.   12   Generation of Plants

2 Book
    XIII.   1   Instruments & use
    XIV.   2   Situation extent
    XV.   3   Inclosing, plotting, disposing
    XVI.   4   Seminary & propagating Graffing

---

14. **[Note to right]** For more loose papers upon this Subict Se Rolls ✣ loose
Notes and papers ⊖⊖ ✿ ✪

Note that the Chapters are in all XLVII: which serve for directions to which
these common places & collections referr in the bundles marked ✿ ⊠ ⊖⊖

XVII.	5	knots, parterrs, Embossements
XVIII.	6	Walkes, Alys, Carpets, Malls, etc
XIX.	7	Groves, dædales relievos
XX.	8	Transplanting
XXI.	9	Fountaines Water Work Canales
XXII.	10	Rocks, Grotts, perspectives, dials ~~statues~~
XXIII.	11	Status, obelisks, Vasas, perspectives paintings
XXIV.	12	Echos, Automats, Hydraulics
XXV.	13	Apiaries, Vivaries, Insects
XXVI.	14	Verdures, perennial greens, perpetual Springs
XXVII.	15	Orangeries, Oporotheca, Conservatorys
XXVIII.	16	Coronary Gardens, Flours, Vertues Gardners register
XXIX.	17	Philosophical Medical
XXX.	18	Wondrous Plants. {Sensitive etc.}
XXXI.	19	Ortyard, Olitory, & Esculent, Sallets
XXXII.	20	Vineyard making Wine
XXXIII	21	Watring, pruning, clipping, Rolling, Mowing
XXXIV.	22	Enemys
XXXV.	23	Almanack

3 Book

XXXVI.	1	Conserving properating Transmuting etc
XXXVII.	2	Elaborating vertues
XXXVIII.	3	Hortus hyemalis
XXXIX.	4	Painting fls & artificiall flours
XL.	5	Crownes Chapletts Garlands
XLI.	6	Laws
XLII.	7	Study hortulan Library
XLIII.	8	Entertainmnts Use {& abuse} of Gardens
XLIV.	9	Famous Gardens
XLV.	10	Villa
XLVI		Corollarys
XLVII		Books {that have been & are} to be consulted on all these Heads
[Verso]		Table of Chapters

To which the loose sheet

of

✪ and ⊖⊖

Bundle ~~for~~ ✾ for

Elysium belong:

APPENDIX 2

On the Conduct of Water

[Nine-page insertion at page 118]
[Page 118a]

Elysium Brit. Interserenda:

L: 2 . C. 9:

That we may therefore proceede on this so noble & ~~usefull~~ indispensible ornament of
our Elysium with all necessary precautions and Instructions; and the rather, for that
fruitelesse and improsperous attempts on this precious *Element*, and for the most part
very chargeable & expensive: Let us take notice ('ere we too hastily advance) of some
few Animadversions, and necessary *postulates*, which may exceedingly conduce to the
pretences of this *Chapter*, as it alltogether relates to the Hydraulicks, & to the conduct
of Waters for our Garden, {in which} the principal affaire, & onely difficulty seemes
to consist in the Finding, & raising of the Water. The first, we have already touched,
concerning the other; if Nature prove not so propitious, as to serve our Garden spontaneously with that, without which it will soone become a Wildernesse: Arte must
supplie our needes, and the Sonns of ~~Ctsibes~~ *Ctesibes* come in & hasten to our ~~ayde~~
{assistance}.

Now there are severall Inventions which do usualy, if not onely, contribute to the artificiall elevation and conduct of Waters: viz, the force of *Men*, *Beasts*, of *Conterpoises*,
Compression, *Siphons* & *Suctions*. But of these fower, there are, which do more immediatly ~~concerne~~{curr to} the motion of Waters for Fountaines and the ~~delight~~ ravishing
& delightfull effects of them. The first of these is the *Attractive* force, either for the
filling or evacuating, by which even this ponderous Element as it were forgettfull of
its owne nature takes to it self Wings, daunces and leapes for joy The 2d is the Expulsive, by which {is avoyded} all corporall penetrations ~~is avoided~~ when compressed
with some {other} harder or closer body: The 3d is the Rarefactive and Condensative,
which either attracts or expells the Water; Lastly The naturall and selfe gravity of the
Element which {unless powerfully opposd,} has ever a tendency to ~~run~~ {glide} into
the {more humble &} lower places. etc. He that rightly ~~knows~~ skills {how} to applie
and governe these fower principles, is to despaire of nothing which he may not hope
to accomplish for the use & ornament of a Garden; seing that all ~~the~~ Waterworkes &
Hydraulick inventions {whatsoever} are the products of one of these[.] **[Page 118b]**
But to treat of these minutely would fill a volume & our intent is not to ~~Epitomise~~
~~Vitr~~ exceede our Institution, beyond what shall be found necessary for our ingenious
Gardinr to comprehend for the better conduct of his water: refering the rest to the
writing of Vitruvius L: 10 . c: 9: ad 14: Mercennus, Porta Kerkir, Cause, ~~&~~ Schotti,[ii]
& those who have written ex professo It shall suffice us then to ~~consider~~ {observe to
you} these ~~following~~ {few) *Præcognita* following:

Theorem

The *Radius* of Water is the spout or *jetto* (i) the {confind} streame it selfe whither perpendicular & verticall, *inflexed* or *horizontall* all these proprieties have their severall

forces & distances, which are reduced to certaine Rules, by the height of the Tube or pipe, & the bore thereoff

Theorem: 2.

[1]All Waters ~~by~~ descending by naturall motions, & flowing out of ~~Tubes~~ Pipes, do imitate the Lawes & proportions of other ~~heavy~~ {weighty} things descending likewise by naturall motion: see proposit: 1. prob: 1.

Theorem: 3.

When more runs into the Cisterne then issues out at the pipes it suffices for continuall running of a artificiall Fountaine derived from that Cisterne.

Theorem: 4.

The more the pressure & depth of the Cisterne is, the higher is the Radius mount; because the Columne of {the incumbent} Water pressing is higher & therefore according to the altitude of the pipe, the swifter is the velocity of the jetto also.

Proposit: 1: probleme: 1

[illustration, see Fig. 76]

Let the pipe be ABCD, the bore B, divide the tyme allowed for the descente of the water into 5 equall parts; by the figures oppos'd to each other 'twill appeare, that the velocity of the descent of the water, will increase or diminish, according to the progresse of unequall numbers, & the spaces run, have a duplicat *ratio* to the tyme allotted, as you may ~~see~~ {deduce] by ~~the~~ comparing the numbers of the side AB, to the side CD.

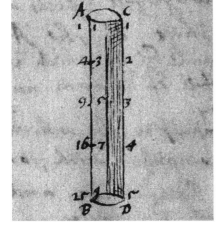

Figure 76. Theorem 4, proposition 1, problem 1 of water conducting, illustrated in inserted text at page 118b.

[Page 118c]

Theorem: 5.

The velocity of the motion of the descending water {&} flowing out by *tubes* of equall bore, but unequall altitude, have a subduplicate ratio of the height or pipes; that is according to the progresse of of [*sic*] unequall numbers, as before we did demonstrate: And all these Propositions will hold, whither the pipes be full or not.

Theorem: 6.

If pipes (full or not allways full) be of the same height but unequal bores, the same *ratio* or proportion of water to water holds, as it ~~did~~ dos of bore to bore; at least Physically, and to the sense, though not exactly mathematical~~ly~~: But the difference is not considerable in almost any practicable case whatsoever.

Theorem: 7.

Tubes not allways full, equaly high, & of like bore, but unequall base, are evacuated in unequall Tyme: For the *ratio* of the tyme, is the same with the proportion of the *base*: And this also succeedes in all *Prismaticall*, or any other figur'd overture & bore.

Theorem: 8.

The proportion of the tyme of the efflux out of pipes of equall *height* & *base*, but unequall *bore*, is reciprocall, as their bores are:

Proposit: 2: Prob: 2.

[illustration, see Fig. 77]

The height & bore of the pipe allways full, being given, to find out the quantity of water which it will afford in the tyme given; and by this meanes, to find out the magnitude of the Cisterne which shall be filled within that tyme.

---

1. **[Margin note]** Set this after Theorem 4:

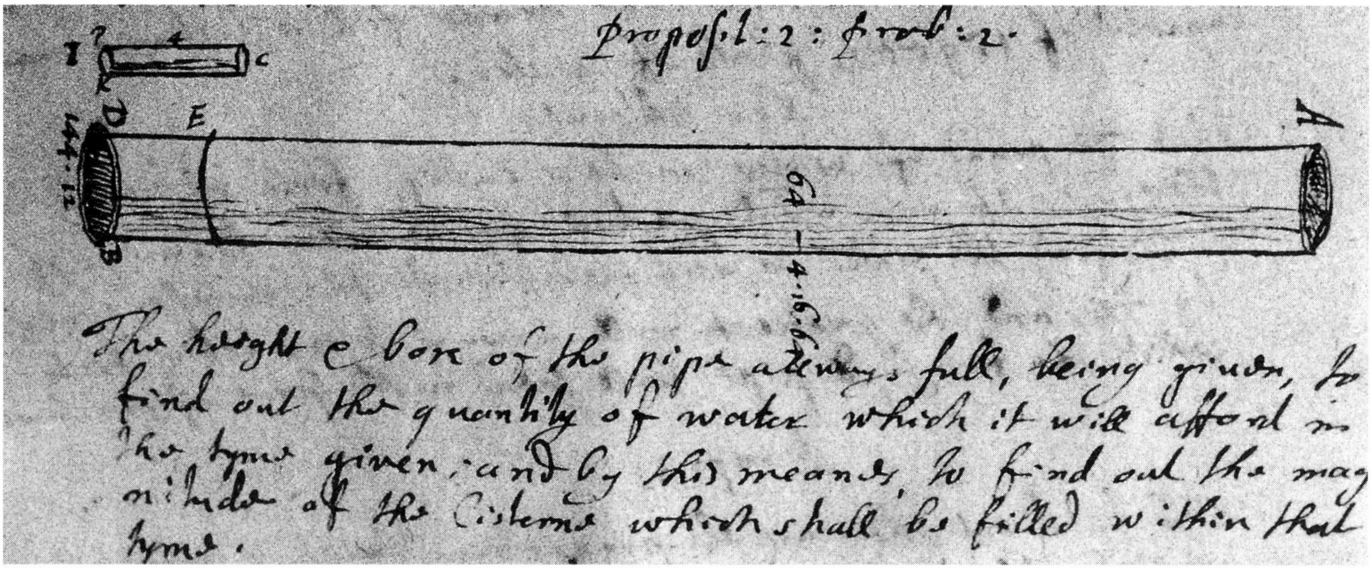

Be the altitude of the *Tube*, for instance ADB. 64 foote; the diameter of the *bore* DB.
an *Inche*; the tyme given an hower: You must first find how much water it will afford,
& what a Cisterne it fill in that space. Let therefore CPK reppresent a pipe 4 foote
high; take from the greater *tube* ADB a portion of 4 foote also: viz: EDB.: Now seing
the diameter of one *Inch* DB, is to the *linearie bore* PK, as 12. to .1. by the second *proposition* of *Euclid*: L. 2. The *bore* DB shall be to KP as a quarter is of the diameter DB, to a
quadrat of the diameter PK that is, **[page 118d]** as, 144. to .1. Therefore (by ~~the~~ {our}
6: Theorem) EDB. shall give 144 ~~more~~ greater quantity of water, than the tube CPK
shall, at the same tyme. But the pipe CPK issues a pound or pinte of water, in the
space of 13 *Seconds*; therefore the pipe EDB shall ~~at~~ {in} the same tyme give 144 pints.
{Therefore} ~~Since that~~ {also since} in one hower or 60 *minuts* 13 seconds are contain
about 277, if 144 pints of water (which the pipe EDB affords in 13 *seconds*) be multiplied by 277, the product will amount to neere 39888 pints which the tube or pipe
EDB will spend in one hower: Now there is found 'twixt 64 viz the height of the
pipe ADB, & 'twixt 4 the height of the portion EDB, {the} ~~the~~ middle proportion
16: Seing then, the water which the pipes ADB & EDB (allways full) do power out
in the same space, are in subduplicate proportion to the height (as *we shewd Theor: 5*)
The water spent by the pipe EDB in one hower, shall be to the water which the tube
ADB gives in the same space, as 4 is to 16, or as 1 to 4. ~~Therefore if so~~ And therefore
if as ~~4 to 16~~ 1. to 4. so 39888 (for so many pintes of water as ~~we~~ we demonstrated
the tube EDB) ~~So~~ to another number, viz. 159552, so many *Unites* as are herein contained, so many pints of water will the tube or pipe ABD (~~all~~ being allways repleate,
of Inch bore, & 64 foote high) give in the ~~same~~ space of an hower, {&} ~~& so~~ {conse-
quently,} Such a pipe, will in that one hower fill a Cisterne ~~equall~~ capable of 159552
pints of water.

Now observe

That 72 pound of water make a cubique foote of water, Therefore, if you would reduce (for the better forming of your Cisterne) the pintes to solid feete, divide the
number 159552 by 72, and the quotient will amount to 1216 cubique feete which the
fore sayd pipe will spend in the space of one hower.

*Figure 77. Theorem 8, proposition 2, problem 2
of water conducting, illustrated at page 118c.*

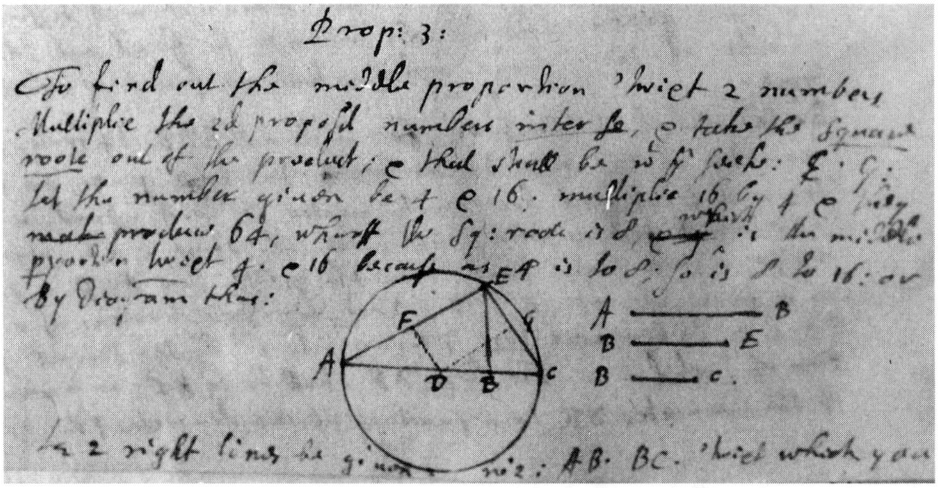

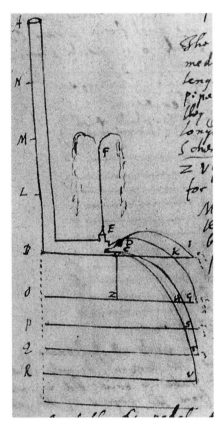

Figure 78. Theorem 8, proposition 3, geometry of proportions for a cistern, illustrated at page 118d.

Figure 79. Theorem 9, proposition 4, diagram illustrating the radius of water horizontally and medially spouted at page 118e.

Prop: 3:

To find out the middle proportion 'twixt 2 numbers Multiplie the 2d propos'd number *inter se*, & take the *Square roote* out of the product; & that shall be what you seeke: E.G: Let the number given be 4 & 16, multiplie 16 by 4 & they ~~make~~ produce 64, whereoff the Sq: roote is 8, ~~e.g.~~ {which} is the middle proportion twixt 4. & 16 because as 4 is to 8; so is 8 to 16: or by diagramm, Thus:

[illustration, see Fig. 78]

Le[t] 2 right lines be given, viz: AB. BC. 'twixt which you **[page 118e]** you would find out the medium proportionalem; conjoyne the lines AB . CD into one right continual line at the poynt B. viz, ABC, & that divided at D, describe a Semicircle or Circle AEC, at the intervall DA or DC; then at the poynt B. erect the perpindicular BE to the periferie, & BE shall be the quæsitum ~~as A~~ {& by the same operation a} 3d or 4th middle proportionale may be found. ~~by the~~ But consult Euclid: L: 6: prop: 11 & 12: And by these experiences may our Gardiner {learn to} calculate the tyme for the filling of any Basine, Lavor or Cisterne, with ~~a re~~ pipe of requisite bore, & so for the evacuating them againe by all verticall tubes: we might add many other examples, but these ~~shall~~ may aboundantly suffice.

Theorem: 9:

If your tubes be laterall, & the orifices not placed exactly in the base of the pipe, but at severall elevations, the former cases & propositions are subject to vast alterations, because the naturall gravity of the water is changed, & the *Virgula* or *Radius* also of the *Saliency* is different as to its mounting, stretch and spouting: whither the water issue vertically, inflexed medialy or horisontaly, which are all so modified by the descent, bending of the ~~issu~~ {flex} & disposing of the Cockes: Example

Prop: 4:

[illustration, see Fig. 79] The Radius of the water horizontally & medially spouted on the same horizon are in length a subduplicate proportion to the pipe ~~of the salient water~~ out of which they gush; & that we call the horizontall longitude of the saliency, which in this *Scheme* is the distance from the poynt ~~ZVG~~ ZVG to the poynt H: G. or G. for Instance: Make two pipes BL. of one foote, & the pipe AB of 4 foote: Let the Horizon be OHG, & horizontall issue of the pedal *tube* be CH. but of the quadrapedal tube BA. The salient CG. we say, the longitude of the salient issue of this pipe BL, viz, CH, will be subduple to the salient pipe BA. viz, CG. If therefore the longitude of the ~~issue~~ Salient pedal pipe be one foote, the longitude of the issue of the quadrapedall shall be 2 foote; and of the sendecupedall 4: of the 64 pedal, 8: & so of the rest, and the **[page 118f]** reason is from the velocity of the descending water: & this is wonderfull usefull; because you may heare know how brode & ~~wide~~ capacious your Basins are to be made, ~~that~~ that they may suite in due proportion with the jettos & the height of the mother Cisterns, pipes, Fountaines, etc: We would therefore ~~reccommend to~~ {that} our Fontaner furnished himselfe with a portabile Instrument or Tube made after this forme, of a determinate height & breadth as 1 foote longe & one inch diameter; for fixing a Cock, or stopping but with his finger at C, & then {the} pipe filld, turning the cock or {remove} ~~take away~~ his finger, so as but a little may ~~gush~~ issue forth & then againe stop it; he shall easily find out the proportion of ~~the~~ altitude & {the} distances of the salient water, the tearnes whereoff we have noted by the letters: K I H G S T etc

~~Theorem~~ Prop: 5

The Salient Horizontal & mediall radius's of the same pipe are by so much the longe & higher as the bore of the pipe is higher situated above the horizon: but if the height be excessive where the orifice is, the *radius* will not continue intire to that tarne ~~but~~ because it breakes into pearles, by the *reitering* of the aire into which it resolves, as is conspicuous in water which we cast from a very lofty place unlesse it be in exceeding plenty & a greate streame:

A Table of the Saliencies out of Mercennas
[illustration, see Fig. 80]
Theorem: 10:

The same is alwayes the altitude of verticall saliences in what ever elevation of the pipe above the Horizon; because it depends where upon the longitude of the tube & bore; but in meere Horizontals the depth depends also *from* the figure of the salient Water:

[Page 118g]

Theorem: 11:

Verticall & all other Saliences never equal the altitude of the original, because the gravity of the Water, & the resistency of the aire impeades the adæquation. And thus

A Table of the Saliencies out of Mercennas

[Altitude of the pipe above the Horizon: pedes]	Longitude of the Salient water: Digiti	
1	1	10
1½	2	0
2	2	6
3	3	0
4	3	5
5	4	0
6	4	4
12	5	6
18	6	6
26	8	0
50	10	0

Figure 80. "Table of Saliencies out of Mercennas," illustrated at page 118f.

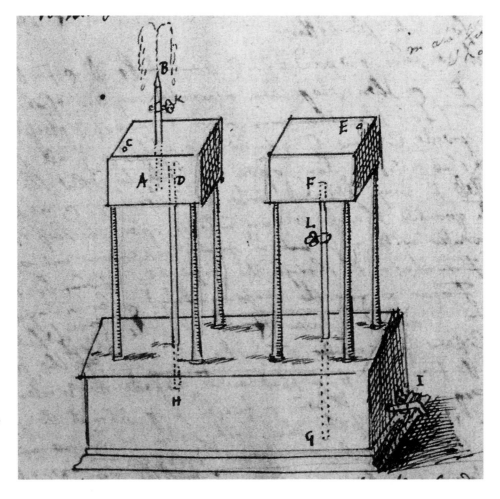

Figure 81. A device to demonstrate the expulsive force of water, illustrated at page 118g.

much ~~shall~~ {might} suffice, if before we proceeded to ~~the~~ what remaines concerning the common derivation of pipes to our Fountaine, we did not thinke it necessary to instruct our Ingenious *Hydroscope* with ~~su~~ a demonstration of the Expulsive force of Waters by {reason of} the impenetrability of bodys, conducing to the Elevation of the Element, & which {we suppose} dos somewhat exceed the Logick of our ordinary *Plumber*, but most requisite to be well understood of our Gardiner, as a Foundation of many ~~the~~ delightfull experiments in order to ~~the~~ Fountaines:

[illustration, see Fig. 81] [2]

Make 3 Vessels A F and G distinctly placed as in the Ichonisme or of any other shape: let the Vessells be exactly close, and ~~be sothred~~ if or ~~mettal~~ carefully solthred: let the under receptacle or Cisterne G have the cock I. by which the water may flow forth: let the Vessells A & F have two smale holes in the cover C.E by which to powre water with a tunnell into them, & afterwards be well stoppd againe. Out of the Vessell A, let there passe a smale pipe AB open at both extreames, but towards the bottome of the Vessell A place it at that distance as the water may flow ~~in~~ in & very straite at the orifice B, fit it also with its stop–cock K Then from the same Vessell A let there

---

2. **[Margin note]** make this in whatever shape you please

goe another pipe into the greater G, viz: DH, open also at both sides, but so as it do **[page 118h]** not touch the lid {D} of the vessell A, ~~towards but onely beare~~ comming short thereoff so much space, as may serve for ~~the~~ letting {out} the ~~aire in~~ aire: but ~~as~~ {at} H let it onely passe the cover of the Vessell or Cisterne G & no farther. Lastly from the Vessell F let another pipe descend into the Vessell G, viz: FG: open likewise at both extreames the poynt F onely peeping through the bottome of the Vessell & no farther {&} at G let the pipe be fixt at such distance from the bottome, that the Water may flow out, & let this pipe G. be fitted ~~with~~ with its stop–cock L. All these Vessells ~~must~~ & pipes must be exactly closed, so as not the least aire or water come forth save at the overtures mentiond: Also be carefull that the pipe AB be not so long as the pipe FG. Therefore the shorter the pipes be ~~above~~ & {the} lesse they appeare beyond the lid of the Vessell A, so much the better: The Machine thus prepared: Fill the Vessells A & F by the holes C.E. & then stop them accurately againe, especially the hole C. (for the other may remaine open if you please) but se that the great Cisterne G remaine empty & that all the Cocks be shutt: This don, open the Cocke L, that the water of the Vessell F may descend into the Cisterne G; & as soone as a smale quantity thereoff is run into it, open the stop cock K, & the water will rise ~~out~~ with greate vehemence out of the Vessell or Fountaine A through the pipe AB. ~~Thus~~ by the expulsive Force & ~~for the reasons alledgd~~ & to avoyde penetration: For the water of the Vessell F descending into the Cisterne G. ~~expells~~ {thence} protrudes the aire ~~up~~ {through} the pipe HD into the Fountaine A, & that aire {forces} expells the Water ~~& forces it up~~ contained therein & forces it up through the pipe AB; since it is impossible that both bodys should remaine together in the same place without {the} recession of one of them: This Instance we have exhibited as ~~a~~ {contaning the} principals {& Foundations} of all Hydropneumaticall Machines whereoff both in this of {~~Chap~~} {cap: 12} Fountaines & the Chap: of ~~Water~~ Hydraulique motions we shall have occasion to discourse more at large. Now when all the Water is thus spent, draw it out of the Cisterne G. by the Cock I & refund it againe into the Vessells A.F. Continuing it playing thus as long as you please: This we affirme to be the basis of many excellent Inventions ~~& usefull for water our Gardens the ornamentall part of Gardens by the~~ & therefore to be heedefully **[page 118i]** considered by our ingenious Gardiners: but then let him take along with him these farther Cautions: First, that the Fontaine A be as Capacious as the Vessell F {2ly} ~~2d~~ that the pipe FG be no bigger then AB, for by this meanes as long as the Water descends from F into G, so long will the water salie forth of the Fountaine A. by the pipe AB. though this be not absolutely necessary: secondly: 'Tis not necessary that the vessell F be at all; but the pipe G: which may have a Tunnell at the extreame F, provided it be larger then the pipe AB. 3dly It is alltogether requisite that the pipe FG be larger then AB, & the more it exceedes the higher will be the *radius* or *getto* AB. because it is the length of the perpendicular which causes the effect; & as that shortens by filling up the vessell G, so dos the spout at B deminish; 4ly You must not onely observe the proportion as to the longitude of the pipes AB & GF; but the Capacity also, least one be more lax then the other; ~~other~~ else will the aire be expressed with the over gravity & poise of the water. 5tly It is not materiall how high the pipe HD be ~~by~~ {through} which the aire mounts; since it concernes not the perpendicular; but it should not be ~~mo~~ {over} wide that it become not ~~we~~ to weake & ~~fee~~ altogether feeble. And thus have you the *Mysterie* of raising water by expulsion, & {which} may {upon ~~occasions~~ neede} serve for a temporary Fountaine ~~upon oce~~ in your Garden, or upon any ~~other~~ other occasion & Festivity;

{& more such directions I may meete with in that diligent collector the Jesuit Scotti}
And being hithertoo instructed how to manage our Water in all Seasons, where the
~~interposition~~ {presence & assistance} of Art is called to interpose, let us returne to
where we digressed, & shew what is to be don where Nature has bin so propitious
as of herselfe to furnish us with a plentifull source for the irrigation & refreshment
of our Elysium: So soone then as you have ~~liberated~~ considered these advantages, &
libe[r]ated the water; the next thing to be don is the sinking of our *Cisterne* into it
{(2) p:118 Elys: c. 9, ubi perge ut sequitur et C: apud which may be made of lead etc:}

APPENDIX 3

On Waterworks

[Four-page insertion at page 132]
[Page 132.1]

addenda ad: p: 132: Elysium Brit.

And these are {such} Waterworkes as consist of ~~a mixt principle~~ {machines that} are {either} mooved by the naturall fall of waters, or such as proceede from more mixt principles, ~~we w~~ for the better comprehending whereoff, & to facilitate the contrivance of these seeming wonders, let our ingenious Gardner learne by this Modell ~~all~~ the {whole} seacret of the arte[:]

The Ichonisme:[1]

[illustration, see Fig. 82]

Make of Copper or Laton, two vessells of what figure and dimention you think fitt, AB. CD. sustained at some competent distance with 3 or 4 pillars. {let} The covers of these vessells or Fountaines be some what hollow {or made} with a ledg about them so as to hold an Inch or 2 of water; ~~after the manner of Basins as~~ described by our ~~dubb~~ dubble line * * * *. Then through the columns BD. & CA deduce two *Siphons*, bending a little within the vessells, & peeping a little out ~~of the~~ in the middle of the Lavor at F. & N with a very smale orifice. Through the same ~~cov~~ let there likewise passe two other shorter pipes EI. PO. open at one extreame and not reaching to the bottome: This don, fill either of the Vessells with water as by the orifice .P. ~~of the cha siphon pipe~~ {(The machine inverted)} & when thus you have filled the vessell AB. turne the clepsydra in the posture it was before, & the water descending through the siphon HG. will rise like a Fountaine at the orifice F in to ~~ledg or B laver~~ The Basen or receptacle edgd about ~~upon~~ {the cover of} the Vessell .CD. & laying up in a smale gyrandala or raye of water till all be descended out of the {upper} Vessell AB. When all the water is thus spent turne the Clepsydra as before, & the water ~~de~~ swallowed up by the orifice (o) into the vessell CD shall descend by the other syphon KL & play at the orifice or Fountaine N. And so alternatively for ever, remembring only to turne the Machine, at what tyme the Gyrandola Ceases: By this invention ~~you may~~ you will easily comprehend the effects of the naturall & simple fall of waters; such **[page 132.2]** wee say, as Nature dos herselfe ~~produce~~ {use} in the production of ~~wate~~ fountaines both in valleys & Hills; & by this Artifice do the ~~contriv of~~ [s]killfull in Hydralick inventions raise up water into Towers & over Grotts, to precipitate through imperceptable pipes in showers & ~~dur~~ stormes, where otherwise they have not waters at Command & indeede by this Compression are most of those admirable workes of the Tiburtine & Tusculan miracles effected: Example of a Mixt Principle[2]

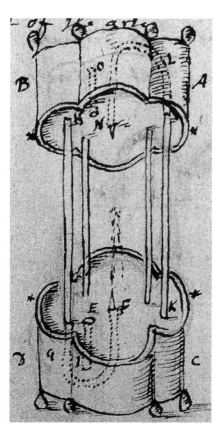

Figure 82. Illustration of Clepsydra or a waterwork displaying the force of naturally falling water in text of an insertion at page 132.

---

1. **[Margin note]** Examine the smale pipes by Schotti: p 255.
2. **[Margin notes]** Make the bird a Dove [;] Schotti p: 279

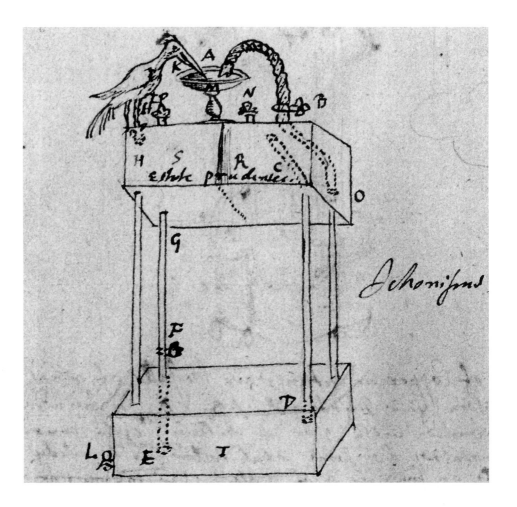

Figure 83. Illustration of a "mixt principle" waterwork with animal figures in text of an insertion at page 132.

[illustration, see Fig. 83]

Make two Vessells recipients of Water: RS.TE, distinguished ~~by~~ & supported by 4 Columns; part the uppermost Vessell by the *Diaphragma* R in the middle: & let each of the Vessells have a hole at the top, ~~viz~~ {denoted} at N.P. at which to fill them with water, & then to be stopped: Let A *Siphon* GE passe through one of the *Columns* having its stop–cock at F, the orifice of which *Siphon* G. must commence immediately above the bottome of the vessell RS, but the other extreame a little short of the ~~vessell~~ bottome of the Vessell ET. place also another smale *Siphon* HK to passe through the Leg & body of the Crane or {any} other fowle, or Image, even to the point of the bill. Lastly, make another pipe CD so as the extreame reach almost to the cover of the upper vessell RG. & another ~~smale~~ {shorter} siphon OBA. the orifice at ~~one~~ whose extreame may reach ~~at~~ neere the bottome of the upper vessell RC. viz: O. The other part ~~to passe~~ passing out of the cover in forme of a serpent having its head at A. To this *Siphon* make the ~~Turne~~ stopcock B. as also another in the neather Vessell ET. at L. by which to empty it. The Machine **[page 132.3]** Thus fitted, shut the cocks F.I.B, filling both the Vessells R S. by the holes N.P. then close them, & ~~se~~ place the Fountaine Bason M. in that sort betweene the Bird and the Serpent, that the beake of the one, and mouth of the other may enter within the ~~brim~~ margent of it. Let the lowermost Vessell ET remaine empty all this while: And when you desire to ~~make~~ {set} the Machine on worke, open the Cock F. and the water ~~of~~ {containd in} the Vessell S. shall descend by the siphon FG. into the ~~Vacuum~~ {empty Vessell} ET, and spout up into the Fountaine M through the siphon HK & to avoide vacuum in the vessell³ S, the water in the cup {Bason} M, will follow through the *Siphon* HK: And that it may not faile there, lax the cock B, so the water which descended by the pipe GF into TE, by being compressed by the aire shall be expelled through the pipe ED in the Vessell R. and protrude the water be contained in it through the serpent OA, & so into the Fountaine M. The Serpent still sup continualy suppling what the Dove {Crane} drinkes: Thus may be contrived a temporary Fountaine to serve in an Hortulan or other Entertainement, a Ganymede mixing water with the wind, filling the Basin or Cup with redwine, & the Receptacle .R with waters: But we will conclude these examples {Inventions} with this pleasant but unhappy device, after But we shall never etc: p. 132: Elysium which others may {also} be contrived for the Hortulan divertisement.

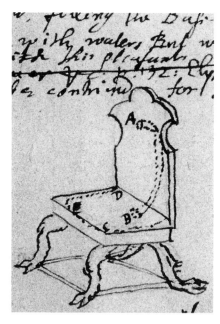

Figure 84. A "waggish invention," illustrated in an insertion at page 132.

[illustration, see Fig. 84]

How to make a chaire which shall wett those that sit upon it, though no water appeare
Frame a chaire of wood: ABC: and the back of it, being made somewhat thick, convey a siphon pipe within it AB. being a little crooked at either extreame, and so conceiled at the orifice A, that comming into the carvd head of a Lyon or some other beast it be not perceived: that the other extreame at B enter into a paire a false bottom, resembling a Lether Cushion, but within made of Leather like a {paire} bill paire of bellowes or sae large pouch, E.C.D. B. Fill these Billows with water by the siphon AB. & when any shall sit downe upon the seate the water by the orifice A, will spurt into his neck immediately; because of the pressure made **[page 132.4]** pressure, which forces it from beneath: This waggish invention we find in the Garden of the {pleasant} Villa belonging to *Sigr: Jovanni Laborne* a *French* priest at *Rome* & *Crosse-bearer* to the Pope: But we should never make an end etc: pag: 132 Elysium etc apud *

---

3. **[Margin note]** Examine all this

APPENDIX 4

On Bees

[Two-page insertion, written in a different hand, at page 223]
[Page 223.1]

The Method to Govern Bees is as follow's

1   In the buying them chuse the most weighty'st hives but if the party that lookt
to them bee dead, they will ~~thrive wi~~ not thrive with a succeeding ~~tender~~ {Master}
which is misterious;

2   The best way of preserving them is to gett good hives & cover them with a
Capp of small ~~hay~~ or chopt hay & cow dung tempered over them, or with small hay
& an earthern pan made fitt for the ¹topp of the hive, which will keepe them from
the scortching heat of Summer & from the severe frosts in winter & also keep mice
from eating into the crown of the hive, which they are subject too, when they stand
~~uppon~~ under a painthouse without such hard Capps,

3   Every hive must have a distinct forme to stand upon, otherwise the Bees of one
hive will rob the other

4   They must be placed against the south sun a little declining from the East, otherwise the Bees will fly out too early & be subject to the mischiefe of Cold Dews,

5   In Aprill they gather not honey but Bee bread for their young increas, & therefore must be fed about 5 or 6 a clock in the evening, if you feed them in the morning
they will be lazy & not worke,

6   At Michaelmas examin which Bees to keep, & which to Destroy {Taking &
keeping} Those hives that weigh about 30 pound that is hive Bees & honey is a good
hive to keep, those under that weight are not fitt to keep; **[page 223.2]** For a poore or
small swarme will require more feeding & tendance then a greate swarm the reason
is, that a hive full of Bees keeps a heat within which is nourishing, for the stomack
requires least meate in hott weather. If a hive weigh 50 or 60 pound then take it, it
being well stored with honey & perhaps too old to keep When you feed your bees
{(which let onely be with hony)} put in the trough That contains their meet on that
side the hive that ~~the~~ is most empty, & there admitt of no passage for the bees to pass
in or out but onely at there comon ~~en~~ passage When you are minded to look into a
hive first have in readiness dryed Cow dung which break over a Chafin dish of Coales
& lett the smoak fume on your face and hands then take off the hive gently & hold
it a little time over the smoake, after which you may turne up the hive; ~~for~~ & ~~vew it~~
view it as you please, for the Bees will all creep toward the topp of the hive, & not
minde to molest you Place your hive where they may have a cleare passage to flye,
if high trees stand in their ~~wey~~ way ~~they~~ it will interupt their flight, & also in the
season invite them to swarme on them which will give you trouble to hive them

---

1. **[Margin note]** *Cover*

APPENDIX 5

Catalog of Evergreens

[Insertion on separate piece of paper at page 260] which with some considerable improvement we shall not greeve to repeat in this place:

Trees for the Taller Shades & maine of the Grove:

3 Abies, 3 Acaceia Virg: Ægypt* 3 Agrifolium, 4 Alaternus, 1 Arbor vitæ, 2 *Arbutus*, 4 Buxus, Canella* 2 *Celastrus Theophrast*: Clus: 4 Cedrus, 3 Cupressus. *Dactylus Draco** 5 Ilex, {Cf} Larix, Laurus, 1 Limonia, 2 Lyma. Malus Medica vel Citria. Oliva, 2 Palma, Persea arbor* 2 Picea, 1 Pinaster, 9 Pinus. Santalum* Sassafras* 18 uber latifol: Tamarindus* 1 Taxus, 1 Terebinthinus, etc.

Shrubs for the Underwood & Thickett:

Asplenium or Ceterach, Anonis, Alp: frutes: purp: 1 Barba Jovis, Bruscus, 6 Capparis. Carub seu Siliq: dulcis: 2 Chamærodendron Alpin: fol oblong et subratend, Chamæcistus tetraphyll American: Chamælia, Chamærriphus, 28 Cistus, Cneorum Matthiol: Alb: Olea: flo: 2 Colutea. 2 Cytissus, 18 Erica, 2 Ficus Indica, 20 Genista :s: Spartum, Scorpius. 6 Hedera 2 Halimus, 3 Jasmine, Jucca, Iberis Cardamantica. 2 Laureola. 2 Laurus Alexand: 5 Laurus Tinus: 1 Lentiscus. Lidon, 2 Ligustrum. 9 Myrtus, 2 Oleander, Oxycedrus

7 Phillyrea. Phelodrys, Prunus Ægypt: 2 Pyracanthus, 3 Rosmarinus, Rosa Semp: virens, Rubus, Ruscus :s: Bruscus. 3 Sabina, Scorpius, Sedum arboresc: Seseli Æthiop 3 Smilax, Spina acuta: 6 Telephium 4 Teucrium arboresc: Vermicularis frutex 2 Vinca pervinca:

Herbs to be placed neere the earth under & betweene the former:

17 Abrotanum, {7 maj: 10 fam:} Aconitum hyemale. 14 Absynthium Acanthium Illyric: Cret: Lusitan:

Adiantum. Æthiopis. 4 Ageratum 21 Balsamita flo: alb. {B̶a̶l̶s̶a̶m̶u̶m̶} Alchimilla, Alipum Montis Ceti:

Allium montan fol Narciss: majus B. Pin. Aloes, Alsine, Althea Cret semp Vir: Amaracus

3 Angelica lucida Cornuti Canadensis. Anonis, Antirrhinum, Apha[r]ca. Apium, Aristolochia, 3 Asarum :s: Arum. Arisarum. Armenia. Asphodellus Luteus, Auricula ursi. 3 Barbarea. 4 Balsamum. 4 Bellis. 6 Beta. 5 Betonica Borago Semp: Vir: Bupthalmum Offi

Calamintha, 9 Camomilla, 24 Herbæ Capillares, Cardamine, Carthamus Perennis. Chelidonium maj: Clematis 2 Cochlearia, Cotyledon, 14 Coris. Crocus. 4 Crythmum. 1 Cymbalaria Italica, 1 Cynoglossum, Daucus lucida. Dorichnium Monspel: 2 Dictamus.

Doronicum Roman: Drabo repens. D̶r̶a̶c̶o̶ 14 Equisetum, 13 Eruca. 2 Euphorbium. Fœniculum, Gentianella vern: Gnaphalium marin. Hedisarum, Heliathemum. Helix. 15 Heleborus maj. 2 Hepatica nobilis. Hipericum Alexand: 10 Hyssopus.

2 Jacea Lusitan: semp: vir: Babylon: Jacobea. 3 Juncus Keyri. Lamium Luteum variega
1 Lapathus Sanguineum. 4 Lavendula. Lygusticum, Lillium, Linaria Sylvest:
Lingua Cervina. Majoram. 3 Malva hisp: Semp: vir arboresc: rosea. 2 Marum
Syrianum
8 Marrubium odorat: Matricaria. Millefolium, 5 Muscus. 6 Nasturtium. Nerium
Oenanthe apij fol: *Origanum Hisp: et Creticum.* Tragoriganum. Pentaphylla.
Portulaca marinu, 2 Pilosella ~~marin~~ min: 5 Pimpinella. 9 Polium montanum. Porrum
2 Primula Veris {et} Silvest: Prunella. Psyllium Plin. 2 Pulegium. 5 Pyrola. Rapum
5 Ruta. 10 Salvia. Sanicula. 6 Saturija. 33 Sedum semp: vir: Serpillum. Sison. Sion
Sophorea seu Ægypt vitiosa. Stachia Monspel: 20 Stæchas. 2 Tanacetum. Tarton raire
Thymolæa. 15 Thymum myrtifol: 8 Tithymalus et Esula. Trachelium Americanum:
4 Tragacantha. Trifolium bituminosum. Vaccinia nigr: Panon: Valeriana 3 Verbascum
virid: Luteum. purpur: 8 Veronica. 3 Viola Matronalis, 2 Viscum. Urtica Romana.
Yucca. Etc.

Now though all these are greene in Winter; yet may we not acurately speaking, name
them all to be perennial {& vivaces} because some of them shead their Seedes (especially the Herbes) and so renew themselves; Others produce succkers; and some are
{annual &} to be sowne yearely, Some bisannual, & others every three yeares; such
as are Angelica lucida bisan. **[Continued on verso]** Borage semper virens, Cæpia
paucij anual sowes itselfe. Jacea Lusitanica etc produc'd by Suckers, Malva arborescens, bis annual {&} by suckers: Trachelium Americanum annual: Verbascum viride
purp. annual etc which a little observation will perfect you in: The manner of farther
elevating & governing the rest

Excerpt from Cowley's *Poemata latina*

[Excerpt from Abraham Cowley's *Poemata latina, in quibus continentur, sex libri Plantarum* (London, 1668) bk. 3, pp. 141–143, inserted by Evelyn on a separate piece of paper at page 275]

ad p: 275: Coronary Gardens: begin:

Cum jam solennis pars magna peracta diei
    Esset odoratis magnificisque sacris
(Sacris quæ nec lingua potest humana referre
    Forsitan, et quæ sit forte referre nefas)
Iudicis tandem placuit certare jocoso
    (Sed res certe acta est acrius illa joco)
Reginam Hortorum regni si vellet amœni;
    Et quasi Pronumen diva creare suum
Quæ foret ingenti dignissima nomine planta
    Et tituli radijs nobilitanda novi,
Scena recurvatis stabat Topiaria ramis,
    Exigui formam Templi imitata cavam.
Multa arbor multusque frutex bene olentibus umbris,
    Et lepide pictis composuere Tholum.
Punica ibi, regale rubens et candida Jasmi
    Candidaque Idaliæ Myrtus amata Deæ
Et flore argento simile stetit Aurea Malus
    Tota odor; atque Maris Ros et utrumque Lilae
Lenta Perielymenos, vultuque Colutea flavo
    Intextusque Rosæ multus ubique decor.
Et pulcrum quicunque alius caput extulit alte
    (Emblema adjectum) Flos variabat opus.
Interius posita est summi testudine Templi
    Sub media, sedes Judicis alta Deæ
Conflata innumerabilibus (mirabile dictu)
    Ex folijs Horti versicoloris erat.
Quæ varijs oculos ludebant scita figuris,
    Non effabilibus consociata modis.
Vermiculatum opus egregie, gemmisque per artem
    Dispositis solidum, tesserulisve putes.
Nil opus est solido; sunt tenuia corpora Divis,
    Quæque super pappis firma sedere queant.
Illa sedet tota cum Majestate venusta
    Immensæ poterant quam dare Veris opes.

Illa Ariadnæa frontem stellata corona
    Indis & sesta veste superba sedet.
Ante Deæ solium & nullis non mite Tribunal,
    Stabat in Officijs turba parata suis
Mollibus et pictis, sed et, heu! pernicibus alis
    Subnixa Horarum bis duodena cohors.
Has prope ter deni stabant ex ordine pulchri
    Insignesque pedum mobilitate, Dies.

[Continued on verso]

Vos quoque bis seni sed vultu dispare Menses,
    Sedula Lunares gens agitare rotas.
Ver aderat roseus Juvenis, sua in ora ~~Deæ~~ notatus,
    Attrahere haud raro Judicis ora Deæ,
Pulchra quoque astabat, cultuque modestior Æstas,
    Spicea serta illi, flavaque vestis erat.
Pomonæque tumens, Bacchisque Autumnus honore
    Purpurea Vitis qui pede calcat opes.
Et parvo coutenta, famemque & frigora spernens,
    Tempestas plane stoica, pauper Hyems   etc:

Cowley: 4: Plant

For it is then etc:

APPENDIX 7

On Tulips

[Three-page insertion of Sir Thomas Hanmer's paper at page 282]
[Page 282.1]
Sr: T: Hanmers paper

Of Tulipes

The Tulipe is the Queene of Bulbous Flowers surpassing all others wee know in the richnes of colours, and variety of markings, and excellency of figure. It is only defective in odour, but hath no ill sent; It is the more estimable that it is hardy, enduring well abroad all wynter, and not quickly perishable by spring or sommer heate.

Wee value such most as consist of most colours, and which are not confused or brouillies (as the French say) but strong and distinct, but more particularly these things commend a Tulipe most. 1. that it bee of a good figure, not over great, nor very small, not very sharpe pointed, nor too long leaved, for then the flower will never open well, and the chiefe beauty is when the inside is fully seene, the colours being stronger and livelier within then on the outside; 2dly. every leafe of the flower must be equally markt or striped, which the French called pannach't, and the longer and bolder the pannaches are the more glorious the flower appeares, 3dly. the more colours there are in a flower the better, and the more unusuall and strange they are the more to bee esteemed, but it is necessary there bee either white or yellow stripes in every good Tulipe, for every mixture of other colours, without one of them two makes up but a dull flower, and there ought to bee good store of white or yellow, yet there may bee too much of them also. You shall seldome have more then three or fower colours in a flower, and commonly but two, and then they are of the lowest forme, except they bee of some very good violet and white, or deepe murrey or purple and white, which are well accompted of. 3dly. [*sic*] The stalke ought to bee strong and somewhat high, dwarfes are little worth. 4thly. The stamina, or tamyns as some call them in English and French too, (which are the little shaking speare {heads} which stand within the flower about the seed vessell) must bee of a rich purple colour, and not yellow nor pale greene as some are. 5thly, There must bee no part of the blew {or greene} bottomes, within the flower remaining, but as you will find hereafter it {they} must be breathed or streamed away into white or yellow pannaches. 6th. The colours most in request are purples, violetts, scarletts, gridelin shadowed and striped with white, or any odde durty rotten colours as some tearme them shadowed and markt with straw colour or stronge yellow; and these later sorts are called about London Modes, being a la mode de France, where such coloured Tulipes have of late yeares beene most prized and sought after.

It were but a vaine worke to give you the names of good Tulipes, they being soe numerous, and soe many Catalogues of them publisht, and soe many new sorts appearing yearly which are raisd by sowing the seed both abroad and in England, I will hasten therfore to their culture, and some observations on them not yet common. The ordinary Tulipes will prosper very well in a good ordinary garden soyle, but the **[page 282.2]** lime striped ones being more tender require a fine artificiall earth to bee planted in, compounded of two parts of fresh blacke naturall earth {out of the pasture} well sifted through a fine sive, and a third part of {sifted} cow dung which is quite turnd to earth, and hath lost all the ill smell, these being well mixed together, with a very little sand if you please, is absolutely the best earth for Tulipes, and indeed {for} many other bulbous and tuberous flowers, and this earth should be renewed every other yeare at the furthest, otherwise it will become spirittles, through the strong attraction of the vertues out of it by the naturall heate of the bulbes. Your beds ought to bee at least two foote deepe for to plant your Tulipes in, and raised halfe a foote higher then your alleyes, and convext or swelling a little in the middle thereof to cast of the water, for the rootes must not lye long wett, which ~~presently~~ rotts them as any new dung likewise doth. Your bigger bulbes may bee sett fower inches in this earth, the lesser two or three. We ~~pl~~ {never} plant any Tulipes in potts or cases, nor never house them, they love aire & moisture that passes quickly from them, and are not hurt by our ordinary frosts, but if very hard ones catch them {yong} as they peepe up, they are in some danger, and that is ever in January, when some cover them a little with straw or the like.

The best tyme to plant your choice Tulipes in England is in November, the neerer the end of it the better if your bulbes bee not too forward in shooting their greene out, as onyons doe in a house, but if they shoot much you must put them in the earth {the sooner} otherwise they will perish or become very weake and unable to flower well that yeare. Many plant them in September and October, but if the beginning of wynter prove warme and fayre those that are ~~planted~~ {sett} soe early, will come up before Christmas and are often caught by the frosts & soe nipt that they die or are ~~worse~~ much the worse for it, but if they begin not to appeare about the Earth till the middle or end of January, they are safe for that yeare, unles some extraordinary ill blasts in March strike them mortally, which seldome happens, & is not to bee provided against. Tulipes need no watering at all from the tyme of their planting to their deplantation. The early or Precoces Tulipes begin to flower in the end of March, and the rest about the middle of Aprill, and are all past by the end of May. In the end of June or in July wee take up our best Tulipes, and lay them in some roome that is not too close to dry the rootes, & earth cleaving to them, and then about a forthnight after cleanse them from the skins & earth & stalkes, & devide the offsetts from their mothers & soe keepe them dry in boxes {or basketts} secured from ratts, till November to bee then replanted as aforesaid Tulipes are encreased by offsetts or seed. Where they like the earth and ayre the old rootes encrease very much yearly in offsetts, which will seldome come diffirent in colours from their mothers, though some kinds will have in their infancy more white then their originalls & soe bee more beautifull for a few yeares, but then they become ~~of~~ like the old ones. **[Page 282.3]** By the sowing of the seed wee obteine all these late wonderfull varietyes of Tulipes, but there is a secrett in choosing of seed which will degenerate and produce flowers different from those kinds which yeilded the seed, for all seed hath not that vertue or weaknes if you will call it soe.

It is a great errour that the finest striped Tulipes yeild the best seed. The contrary thereof is certainly true, for many of the pannacht best sorts yeild no perfect seed, but afford only a chaffy unprolificall light matter in stead thereof, and the reason is obvious, the greate strength and vertue of the roote being soe much spent in the perfecting, and rectification of the flower, as they tearme it, that there is not sufficient left to produce vigourous seed. Some of the most pannach't or striped kinds afford seed perfect enough, but it seldome brings good striped flowers or any novelty at all. But the excellent seed must bee had from selfe colourd Tulipes, as wee call them, which are such as seeme to bee of one only colour, ~~but~~ and have neither white nor yellow visible in them, but they have an eye of some other colour or two in them which are confounded together & not distinct and shew in some like changeable silke stuffes. These single colourd Tulipes, whose stalkes are strong and high, and flowers large, yeild the seed from which you may raise rare new kinds, but all of them have not that vertue Those with strong blacke bottomes as the common red Tulipe hath, or {with yellow faint bottomes or} without any bottomes, as many are serve not ~~neither~~ for our use. The selfe colours which are good for seed are only such as have sweet celestiall blew bottomes and purple tamyns, or darke greene bottomes with the same tamyns as aforesaid.

From the tyme the seed is ripe untill November you may sow ~~the seed~~ {it} either in cases or bedds, but I like best of bedds. The Earth must be fine and light & somewhat sandy & without dung. cover the seed but lightly with fine sifted mold. Weed them well & water them if they be sowed in potts or cases, otherwise not, the first spring they will come up with rush leaves as onyons doe, the second yeare they will have a little leafe of the shape it will ever continue & soe the third & fourth yeare one leafe only from a roote. when the~~y~~ roote puts forth two leaves it will certainly beare a flower which is commonly the fowrth or fift yeare after sowing, very rarely the third, & never the second or first. Though all our fine new Tulipes are raised from such seed as is above mentioned, yet the first flowers ~~they~~ will bee only single colours, but those in tyme will stripe and variegate, not all in a yeare, but one leafe or two commonly begins and the rest follow, some sooner some later. As soone as the blew or greene bottome begins to breake & point with white or yellow, then the leaves begin to stripe, for all the white and yellow in striped Tulipes comes from those two coloured bottomes, and when a Tulipe is perfected or rectified as they say, that is when every leafe of the flower is well, {& alike} markt with stripes of white or yellow with other colours then there is none of the blew or greene bottome left, but all is streamed up into the leaves, & the colour changed, that is the blew into white, and the greene into yellow stronger or paler according to the strength **[page 282.4]** of the greene. This breaking & dividing of the bottome is the greate worke towards making a glorious Tulipe, but it is not the whole worke, In these selfe colours as I said before there are other colours latent or hid, which with age, will seperate and shew themselves, gathering themselves into severall shadowes of purples, orenges, gridelines or reds, and commonly the light self colours upon rectification become much sadder, and the sad lighter, which may seeme strange, but the cause is not hard to bee found out. After a florist is acquainted with the ~~art~~ secret of these self colours hee will bee as curious in making a collection of varietys of them, as of the best strip'd Tulipes, there being soe much hope and expectation of them, & none at all of the other. I know a Curioso in Paris who had at least a hundred sorts of these single colours, & valued them as highly as the dearest pannacht flowers, and had reason to doe soe, there being more money made out of such, which bring all the noveltyes, then out of the curious striped ones, which continue still but the same thing, or grow worse if not well ordered. I have beene too long on this subject, because of the beauty of this plant but I shall make amends in shortnes speaking of the other flowers, I shall only adde that the Tulipe prospers and flowrishes almost in every Climate hott or cold, and is as early in flower in these Northerne parts of England & Wales as at London, as I have ~~made~~ had the experience of severall yeares. The Encreases of Tulipes (as other Bulbous rootes) wee call offsetts, the French Cayeux, and the Italians Cipolletta'es.

APPENDIX 8

On Anemones

[Multi-page insertion between pages 290 and 291]
{Inserenda ad: p: 291:}

Of Anemones

Amongst the flowers with Tuberous Rootes, The Anemone is the principall and the only sort I shall say anything of. Wee have two chiefe kinds of them differing something in the rootes, more in the {greene} leaves, but most in the flowers. These are the Starr Anemones, which have a longer thicker more compacted knobby roote, larger harder & rougher greene leaves, and greater thicker flowers, whose leaves are like those of the Marigold flowers in shape & biggnes, and 2dly the Plush Anemones, whose rootes are flatter, with more appendixes, whose leaves are softer & smaller cutt and divided something like to Parseley, and whose flowers have generally six broad outward leaves encompassing a thrum or tuft of small threads fine and soft like silk: There is a third sort which we call Hermaphrodites, partaking of the rootes & greene leaves of the Plush Anemone, and yet much like to the Starrs in their flowers because theirs are onely composd of a good number of small leaves all of a bignes, without any great outer leaves as the Plush sortes have and these are apt to degenerate into single flowers or very little dubble, if not very carefully orderd by taking up yearly & planting in dung or spriggs and leaves of trees turnd to mould. Wee have of these Hermaphrodites some with scar[l]et flowers, some pinke coloured, some flesh colour, {some crimson}, other ashes colour & gridelines, but none of more then one colour that I have seene, neither are any of this kind soe common as of the other sorts.

The Starr Anemones, which are usually called in Latine Anemones latifoliæ & in French Anemones Lierrees, or Anemones durfurillage, have very large dowble beautifull flowers standing on strong high stalkes, like to the greatest dowble Marigolds as I sayd before; there are many of one selfe colour either scarlet, grideline, ash colour, murrey, crimson, or other redds, and some of two colours finely striped or markt, amongst which the scarlett and white is remarkeable called by the French Lierre de Paris, as also the Lemmon coloured and white called by some the Superitz I know not why, next in beauty to them are Belle d Arras tawney and white the Iccarasse crimson and white, and there are more now out of my memory.

The Plush Anemones are also lovely flowers of soe great varietyes in their colours and markings, & different figure of their plush or inner leaves as they come very little short of Tulipes, if they were as hardy as they, but the most curious sorts are tender, & are preserved with great difficulty more then a wynter or two in England. Those of one colour are the white, the Scarlet, the Carnation, the Peach, the Dove coloured, the Flesh coloured, the old crimson, the Grideline, the pale-Lemmon called in France La Tripolaine the sad murrey, called there la Ranunculee, the Deepe Violet called there la Morine, the flame-coloured called there Marguerite de Martiletti, and others. We have also many sorts of Plush Anemones of more then one colour and many more wee may have from Paris & Italy, the names of the best sorts with their colours and markings I shall not thinke it too much paines to insert by **[continued on another piece of paper]** translating of that part of Morines catalogue concerning Anemones, which perhaps many have not seene, nor can come by.[iii]

Albanoise white with carnation bottomes.

Albertine or Passescala, flesh coloured and carnation clouded

Angelica with white outward leaves, and pale grideline plush

Asiatique white and carnation leaves, scarlet and white plush.

Astrea or Asterie white and carnation.

Augustine, white and carnation leaves with scarlet plush.

Boulonise white leaves with carnation bottomes, plush carnation and lemmon

Briote white and carnation leaves, the plush carnation.

Bugi durty white and carnation, the plush very fine and small.

Candeote, the leaves whitish grey with carnation bottomes, the plush carnation, tipt with a greenish colour and a haire colour.

Cazertane, the leaves crimson borderd with brimstone colour, the plush deepe scarlet.

Celestine, the leaves white, the plush white tipt with Lemmon.

Celidee the leaves white and carnation the plush rose coloured mixt with another colour.

Clitie, flesh colour and Carnation.

Damasini, all carnation and white distinctly markt.

Dorismene, carnation and white leaves, with a reddish plush.

Extravagante, white, red, and greene.

Gabriele, white leaves, the plush greene white and carnation.

Galipoli of Sholough scarlet and white

Gartane, the first flowers purple and white, the following dove and peach.

Herisee, crimson outer leaves with some white sometimes, the plush scarlet.

Joliuett, the leaves flesh coloured and crimson, the plush bricke colour:

Juliane, the leaves white and carnation, the plush carnation.

Limosine much like to the Extravagant.

Lyonise, the leaves and ruffe whitish gray, with dove-coloured bottomes, the plush dove colour tipt with greene.

Mantuane, Lemmon coloured with carnation bottomes.

Melidor, deepe scarlett with white bottomes.

Meteline, all dirty grey mixt with greene and carnation

Moresque, grey mixt with carnation.

Morette, flesh coloured leaves with white plush tipt with red.

Natolie white and carnation.

Noiron, the leaves crimson, the plush crimson mixt with almost blacke.

Orientall of a blewish grey coloured like that of a slate.

Parisienne white leaves, the plush at first lemmon, but grows white.

Parmesanne, the leaves white with red bottomes the plush rose coloured. carnation and light haire coloured.

[Continued on verso]

Picarde or Juno, all over white and peach coloured.

Provensalle greene and peach throughout:

Regale, both the leaves and plush crimson stript & mixed with white.

St Charles, all white with red towards the bottomes.

Scala, the leaves durty white, the plush scarlett.

Sermonetta, scarlet and Lemmon colour all over.

Syrienne, the leaves pale Isabella clouded with flesh colour, the plush lightly greene and flesh coloured.

Toscane, a faded red with some haire colour.

Turquoise, leaves and plush white with carnation bottomes.

Victorieuse, the leaves flesh coloured mixt with carnation, the plush haire coloured and carnation.

Besides the Plush and Starr Anemones and the Hermaphrodites {all} which ~~all~~ three sorts have dowble flowers, though differing in shape from each other) wee have single Anemones of great beauty, almost of all colours & some finely striped with severall colours. Many about London call these Poppy Anemones ~~or~~ {some} French Anemones, others only single Anemones, & these are of two kinds the single hard leaved from whence come the starrs, & the single soft leaved from the seed whence come the Plush Anemones, & the Hermaphrodites.

The singler sorts are in flower in {the end of} ffebruary {and all} March and Aprill, and againe many of them at Michelmas & most part of Wynter. They are hardy and will endure abroad very well most wynters if the garden bee not too much expos'd to wynds & cold weather. Wee usually take them up every second yeare to free them from ofsetts, and that is best done in June and July & wee replant them againe in October or November & some in February. A loose garden mold enclin'd to sandy, without dung, agrees best with them.

Though these single kinds are hardy enough, yet all the other sorts are nice and tender, the aire must please them well as the earth must, otherwise they quickly perish. I have found the Starrs harder to preserve and blow well then the other sorts, but I have seene them at Mr Downtons at Thistleworth flowrish exceedingly in ordinary earth & under the shade of great trees in his orchard as it were wholely neglected.

The Starrs need a stronger good earth then the other doe, and ought to bee planted in September or October, and to be kept but a short time out of the earth, I think beds agree better with them then potts, except the stript starrs. The Plush Anemones which are of the curiousest sorts & come from Italy or France must be sett in very large potts or other wooden vessells in very fine sifted earth with a little sandy, & where~~in~~{with} there in some very old consumed cow dung mixt, or some fine sifted mold from old woodstackes.

[Continued on another piece of paper inserted at page 298] The surest way to preserve them from the Frosts with us is not to plant them before February, others plant them in the end of November either {time} may serve, as the yeare proves, the first, or last will doe best: but certanely to plant them betimes in Autumne is the worst way of all, for then the yong greene leaves will bee comming up when the greatest frosts are, & bee soe nip't therewith that they become not only abortive that yeare, but {dye downwards and} the very rootes perish. In very hard weather, house your potts but by no meanes in too close a roome, more dye by stifling, then by being all wynter abroad, and such as live abroad all wynter in the open ayre, & receave the raines, & frosts, beare the fairest and most beautifull flowers of all; & put forth most offsetts.

Take up your good sorts every yeare {in June or July} and devide the ofsetts from them, if they will easily part, but cutt nor breake none of ~~thos~~[?] {the} rootes to multiply them. No plant, nor flower delights more in a sweet warme delicate aire then the Anemone, which you may see by the ill blowing of these flowers ~~abou~~ in and neere London where every thing is smutted & the aire spoild with the smoake of sea coale. The best kinds should stand in borders or potts where the East and South East Sun may shine on them in the Spring when they flower, and bee waterd often in faire dry weather.

The Seed both of the single hard leav'd, and single Tenuifoliæs brings great varietyes of new sorts of single and Double ones, It is best sowing of it in cases in fine sifted rich earth as soone as it is ripe which is in June, & beginning of July, soe you may have {it} bring flowers the first yeare, as I have often had. The seed being small and wrapt in a woolly substance must bee pulld in small parts & may bee spread thin on the mold where you sow it & coverd ~~with~~ very thinly with very fine sifted rich mold of any kind, and a little waterd somtimes with a very fine {small} waterpott, &̶ your cases or potts must stand constantly abroad where a little sun may come upon them but nott too much. The Seed will come up in three weekes or a moneth, house your potts & cases before the great frosts come, & let them stand there till February & then sett them abroad where they may bee shelterd from the March winds, and yet have the Sun in the Spring.

The Seed of the Crimson flowers produces no varietyes, therfore choose your seed only of those of severall colours with bottomes differing from the upper part of the leaves. I have seene very few good Plush Anemones raisd in England the reason is because wee sow but small quantityes of seed here for amongst many hundreds you shall scarce raise one dowble, but in France & elswhere abroad where they sow somtimes halfe a quarter of an acre or more in the feild earth they raise many. And thus much for Anemones is enough, & more perhaps then needes for others have said the like almost, but I tell you my experience also. {Yet I will add that} I have had yearly in my garden very many come up yearly in the same paths betwixt my beds that have sowed themselves, & those rootes have beene strong & the flowers better then those I have sowed with all the care I could.

APPENDIX 9

On Daffodils

[Hanmer's essay inserted on separate piece of paper at page 298]
{Se Sr: T: Hanmers note}
{Interserenda p: 298 & the other {small} paper of the same mark}

   Of Bulbous Daffodills or Narcissi

The Indian kinds, which have all great rootes, and are exactly described by Ferrarius, prosper not in England. I have had many of them from the Barbadoes and other places, and could not with any art preserve them alive here above a yeare or two, some have borne flowers with mee the first yeare and then died, others have lived two yeares without bearing, & then have rotted away. Though it is generally lost labour to plant them, yet because possibly some may {have} better lucke then I have had, I shall sett downe here the likelyest way to preserve them. Set the rootes betimes in the spring in large potts in a sandy light earth mixt with some very old cow dung turnd to earth, then thrust the potts up to the brimms into a hott bed to draw out the fibres, which nothing but great heate will doe, as soone as the leaves come up remove the potts out of the hot bed into some border under a South wall, where sinke the potts to the verges, and cover the young plants with glasses all night, and in every cold day or part of the day, but giving them the sun in mornings & when it shines out in afternoones. As soone as the leaves grow somewhat bigger, water them often, but never before. House them from the middle of October **[continued on insertion at page 291]** till the end of Aprill, never take up the rootes, but yearly put good fresh sifted mold to them in the potts as they grow, if they live they will cast forth many offsetts, which you must take from the mothers carefully by scraping the earth softly by degrees from them to bare them that you may see what you doe. Take heed of crushing or break- ing of the fibres, for those ~~of~~ {that are} perennall (as these are) generally will hardly put out new ones, and soe consequently die. when you have gotten the offsetts away cover the old rootes well againe with such earth as is before mentioned. Perhaps if wee had good new seedes of these beautifull ~~Nar~~ Indian Narcissi, whose flowers are comonly large and single and of a scarlet colour or some other red, wee might raise plants that would prosper and continue with us, but all the rootes that I have seene which came from those hott climates would only beare the flowers here which they carried in their bellyes from thence and then die, or else perish before they bore any, their great fibres being commonly over dried and withered {or bruised too much} before they gett to us, soe that they rott and die and they will hardly put out new ones againe, without which they cannot subsist. All other Narcissi but the Indians, whither dowble or single flowerd, or whether polyanthes or but one flower on a stalke will prosper well in our gardens in bedds, the polyanthes are most tender but will endure the frosts indifferently well in warme places abroad. Wee have little good seed from the best kinds, and that produces no new sorts, it is to be sowen as Tulipe seede & will not produce flowers under fower or five yeares time.

.

Narcissus: the likeliest are the Nonparell, & greate Spanish both white & yellow, The large Junquille: sowed in Autumne, & 3 yeares after seminate removed about
mid=Somer & immediately interred till they flowere: But those of the Sea Narciss:
not stirred in 10 yeares, & then ~~preserve~~ later up & planted without wronging the
fibers immediately: & these & all of the Indian kinds must be propagated in boxes to
be governd in the Conserve as the Season requires for in winter they are tender & in
Summer thirsty:

APPENDIX 10

On Garden Design

[Four-page insertion at page 329]
[Page 329.1]
{Ad: p: 329.}

Designe of a Physical Garden[1]

Vegetabilium partes Solidæ Simplices per caro ~~pulta~~
|pulpa |~~vena~~ |Nervus |Vena |Membrana
Radix ~~est~~ et Scapus Caudir Cortex, lignum, Caro, Cor, etc
Folia: Flores, Fructus, Semina, partes liquidæ, Lacryma, Gummata
Specie, plantarum sunt
Arbor, Frutex, Suffrutex, Herba,

Arbores Pom aciniferæ:
    1 Class: 1 Pomus seu Malus. 2 Malus Cydonia: 3 Malus Citria 4 Limonia 5 Arantia.
6 Malus Punica, 7 pyrus etc
    2 Class: Ficus. 2 Sycomores. 3 Morus 4 Arbutus 5 Mespilus 6 Sorbus etc
Arbores Pom – ossifere
    1 Class: Malus persica 2 Armeniaca, 3 Persea prunus, 4 Myrobalanus 5 Sebestena
6 Ziziphus, 7 Cornus, 8 Lotus, 9 Ceras[s]us, 10 Chamæcerasus, 11 Oenooptia[?],
12 Aria, 13 Hamamelis
Arbores Nuciferæ
    1 Class 1 Juglandes, 2 Avelluna, 3 Castanea
    2 Class: Amygdalus, 2 Styrax,
    3 Class: 1 Pistacia, 2 Glans Unguetaria
    4 Class: Acer, 2 Gossypium.
    5 Class: Palma
Arbores Aromatica.
    1 Class: Nux Myristica, 2 Cassia, 3 Cinnamonum, 4 Mulalathrum 5 Betre.
6 Caryophyllus aromaticus 7 Piper 8 Culebæ 9 Amomum, 10 Cardamomum
Arb: Glandifera.
    1 Class 1 Quercus, 2 Phellodrys, 3. Suber, 4 Ilex, 5 Tagus
Arb: Bacciferæ
    1 Class: 1 Tilia, 2 Ostrys, 3 Viburnum, 4 Catanus, 5 Ricinus, 6 Sassafras
    2 Class: 1 Berberis, 2 Grossularia, 3 Ribes, 4 Sambucus, 5 Laurus 6 Laureola,
7 Camelæa 8 Thymelæa, 9 Cneorum.
    3 class: 1 Myrtus, 2 Ruscus, 3 Vitis idæa, 4 Buxus, 5 Olea, 6 Vitex {:s: Agnus
Castus} 7 Ligustrum et 8 Phillyrea

---

    1. **[Margin note]** make the classes to be bedds: Compare it to Mr Morisons: etc:

[no 4 class listed]

5 class: 1 Philyca, 2 Celastrus, 3 Rhamnus, 4 Lycium, 5 Rubus, 6 Capparis

6 Class: 1 Sabina, 2 Cedrus, 3 Juniperus, 4 Thuja, 5 Bruta, 6 Aspargus ~~Carruda~~

7 Class: 1 Taxus, 2 Draco

8 Class: Fraxinus, Rhus, Cocconilea, Azederach

Arb: Lachrymiferæ

1 Class: 1 Lentiscus, 2 Arbor Thurifera, 3 Terebinthus 4 Balsamum 5 Myrrhifera, 6 Bdellifera

2 Class: Cedrus Conifera, 2 Pinus, 3 Larix ~~Pitys~~ 4 Picea, 5 Abies 6 Cupressus

Arbores Siliquatæ

1 Class: Cytisus, Anagyris, 3 Laburnum, 4 Acacia, 5 Genista Spartium 6 Scorpius, 7 Genista non Spinosa, 8 Chamægenista, 9 Spartium, 10 Colusthea, 11 Sena, 12 Jovis Barba.

2 Class: 1 Siliqua, 2 Cassia fictutuus, 3 Tamarindus

3 Class: Evonymon, 2 Nerion

Arbores Rhodafloræ:

1 Class: 1 Rosa, 2 Cistus, 3 Chamæcistus, 4 Cistus ledum, {:S: Ladanum} 5 Ledum Alpinum

Arbores Miscellæ

1 Class: 1 Ebenus, 2 Guajocum

2 Class: Jasminum, 2 Syringæ

3 Class: Ulumus, 2 Betula, 3 Alnus, 4 Populus

4 Class: Salix, 2 Spiræa

5 Class: 1 Tamariscus, 2 Erica, 3 Camphorata, 4 Scopariæ omnes

6 Class: 1 Aspalathus, 2 Scintalum 3 Agallochum.

[Page 328.2]

Herbæ

Bulbosæ

1 Class: Iris bulbosa, 2 Iris tuberosa, 3 Sisyrinchium, 4 Gladiolus, 5 Hyacinthus, 6 Bulbus criophorus.

2 Class: Narcissus, 2 Leucojum bulbosum, 3 ~~Lilia narcissus~~ Tulipa, 4 Fritellaria.

3 Class: 1 Crocus, 2 Colchicum, 3 Ornithogalon.

4 Class: 1 Cæpa, 2 porrum, 3 Allium, 4 Scilla, 5 Moly.

5 Class: 1 Lilium, 2 Martagon, 3 Corona Imperialis.

6 Class: Orchis, 2 Satyrium, 3 Dens Canis, 4 Ophris, 5 Oroba[n]che.

Longicauli foliæ frumentaceæ

1 Class: Triticum, 2 Zea, 3 Hordrum, 4 Secate, 5 Avena, 6 Vitilago, 7 Oryza, 8 Frumentum Indicum, 9 Milium, 10 Panicum, 11 Sesamum, 12 Erysimum Cereale, 13 Phalaris.

Longicaulifoliæ diversi a frumentaceis generis

1 Class: 1 Gramen Carinum, 2 nodosum, 3 tremulum, 4 puniculatum, 5 Spicatum, 6 Sparteum, 7 Junceum, 8 ~~Cyperoides~~ {perfusum}, 9 Arundinaceum, 10 dactylon

1 Gramen Frugum Lolium, 2 Phœnix, 3 Holcus, 4 Panicum Sylvestre, 5 Herba Bromos, 6 Ægilops

2 Class: 1 Jurcus, 2 Nardus, 3 Cyperus, 4 Sparganium, 5 Uva marina, 6 Equisetum.

3 Class: 1 Arurdo Inodora, 2 Aromatica, 3 Indica, 4 Papyrus, 5 Typha.

4 Class: 1 Asphodelus, Phalangium.

5 Class: Xyris, 2 Iris, 3 Accrus, 4 Galanga, 5 Zingeber, 6 Zadoaria, 7 Costus, 8 Curcuma, ~~crocus Indicus~~

Nervifoliæ etc cum affinibus

    1 Class: 1 Helleborus, 2 Helloborine

    2 Class: 1 Gentiana, 2 Plantago, 3 Helosteum, 4 Coronopus, 5 Psyllium

    3 Class: Polygonatum, 2 Lilium Convallium, 3 Monophyllum, 4 Hippoglossum.

Rotundifoliæ etc cum affin:

    1 Class: 1 Pyrola, 2 Bistorta, 3 Limonium, 4 Potagometon [Potamogeton], 5 Nymphæ, 6 Dracontium, 7 Arum, 8 Colorasia, 9 Arisarum, 10 Asarum, 11 Tussilagy 12 Petasites, 13 Cacalia, 14 Lappa, 15 Tribulus aquatiq, 16 Sagitta.

    2 Class: Cymbalaria, 2 Nasturtium Indicum, 3 Balsamina, 4 Aristolochia, 5 Cyclamen, 6 Gramen parnassi, 7 Saxifraga, 8 Chelidonia minor, 9 Num[m]ularia.

Grassifoliæ cum affin

    1 Class: 1 Sedum, 2 Umbilicus, 3 Aloe.

    2 Class: 1 Radix Rhodia, 2 Telephium, 3 Scorp{i}oides, 4 Portulaca, 5 Cepæa, 6 Crithmum, 7 Kali, 8 Tragum

Asperifoliæ cum affin

    1 Class: Heliotropium, 2 Auricula muris, 3 Echium, 4 Onosma, 5 Anchusa, 6 Lycopsis 7 Buglossa, 8 Borago, 9 Cynoglossum, 10 Cerinthe, 11 Lithospermon, 12 Symphytium, 13 Pulmonaria, 14 Consolida media, 15 Brunella, 16 Bellis

    2 Class: 1 Pilosella, 2 Gnaphalium, 3 Leontopodium

Mollifoliæ et his congeneres.

    1 Class: 1 Malva, 2 Althæa, 3 Alcea, 4 Corchorus, 5 Geranium, 6 Sanicula, 7 Pes Leonie, seu Alchimilla, 8 Cannabis, 9 Eupatorium, 10 Pontentilla [Potentilla], 11 Herba moluccana, 12 Coryophyllata, 13 Dentaria, 14 Epimedium, 15 Pæonea, 16 Leontopetalon, 17 Chrysogonum, 18 Staphis agria.

    2 Class: 1 Quinquefolium, 2 Heptaphyllum :s: Tormentilla, 3 Fragrariæ, 4 Trifolium, 5 Lotus, 6 Melilotus

Stellatæ cum affinib:

    1 Class: 1 Rubia, 2 Aparine, 3 ~~Asperula~~ Molluga, 4 Gallium, 5 Cruciatu

    2 Class: 1 Ruta, 2 Thalictrum:

Capillares.

    1 Class: Phylittis, 2 Hemionitis, 3 Ophioglosson, 4 Asplenium seu Ceterada, 5 Lunaria minor, 6 Adiantum, 7 Trechomanes, 8 Ruta muraria, 9 Polytriochum aureum 10 Ros Solis.

    2 Class: 1 Filix, 2 Lonchitis, 3 Polipodium.

    3 Class: 1 Muscus, 2 Lichen, 3 Lenticula palustris

    4 Class: Muscus marinus, 2 Alga, 3 Androsace, 4 Alcyonium.

Discicorym biferie cum affin.

    1 Class: 1 Tanacætum, 2 Parthenium, 3 Chrysanthemum, 4 Buphthalmum, 5 Chamæmelum, 6 Cotyles, 7 ~~Belles~~

[Page 328.3]

    2 Class: 1 Abrotanum, 2 Artemisia, 3 Ambrosia, 4 Botrys, 5 Absynthium

    3 Class: 1 Helichrysum, 2 Conyza, 3 Aster Atticus, 4 Tripolium, 5 Alisma, 6 Virga aurea

    4 Class: 1 Anemone, 2 Pulsatilla, 3 Adonis, 4 Ranunculus

Cororariæ et semilis

1 Class: 1 Viola Martia, 2 Leucoium non bulbosum, 3 Viola matronalis, 4 Viola lunaria, 5 Lychnis, 6 Saponaria.

2 Class: Caryophylleos flores, ~~Ane~~ Armerios, etc:

3 Class: 1 Antirrhinum, 2 Linaria, 3 Linum, 4 polygala, 5 Orobrychis, 6 Glauci, 7 Stæcas Arabica, 8 Lavendula, 9 Rosmarinus.

4 Class: 1 Hyssopus, 2 Satureia, 3 Thymus, 4 Epithymum, 5 Cuscuta, 6 Serpillum, 7 Palium, 8 Ageratum, 9 Pulegium, 10 Dictamnus, 11 Origanum, 12 Tragoriganum, 13 Sampsuchus seu Amaracus, 14 Marum, 15 Clinipodium, 16 Acinus, 17 Erinus, 18 Ocymum sive Basilcum.

5 Class: 1 Mentha, ~~Sysy~~ 2 Sisymbrium, 3 Calamintha, 4 Melissa, 5 Marrubium 6 Galeapsis, 7 Urtica, 8 Alyssum, 9 Sideritis, 10 Euphrasia, 11 Melampyrum, 12 Betonica, 13 Serratula, 14 Behen, 15 Scrophularia, 16 Stachys.

6 Class: 1 Salvia, 2 Hirminum, 3 Verbascum, 4 Bluttaria, 5 Æthiopis, 6 Verbasculum S: primula veris 7 Sanicula Alpina seu Auricula Ursi, 8 Digitalis, 9 Ephemeron.

Umbellifferæ cum congenib:

1 Class: 1 Cuminum, 2 Fœniculum, 3 Anethum, 4 Meum, 5 Pyrethrus, 6 Ferula, 7 Thapsia, ~~Turpe~~ 8 Turbith, 9 Peucedanum, 10 Daucus, 11 Pastinaca, 12 Gingidium, 13 Chærephyllum, 14 Scandix, 15 Caucalis, 16 Apium, 17 Sison, 18 Sion Dioscoridis.

2 Class: 1 Elaphoboscum, 2 Sisarum, 3 Angelica, 4 Imperatoria, 5 Laserpitium, 6 Panax, 7 Spordylium, 8 Libanotis, 9 Carvi, 10 Coriandrum, 11 Anisum, 12 Ammis, 13 Pimpinella 14 Myrrhis, 15 Cicuta, 16 Cicutaria, 17 Seseli, 18 Ligusticum, 19 Bulbocastanum, 20 Oenanthe seu Filipendula, Pedicularis, 21 Barba Capræ

3 Class: Valeriana, 2 Nardus

4 Class: 1 Millifolium

Capitatæ etc:

1 Class: 1 Succisæ :S: Morfus diaboli, 2 Scabiosa, 3 Jacea, 4 Stærbe, 5 Cyanus, 6 Tragopogon 7 Scorzonera, 8 Caltha, 9 Helenium, 10 Verbena, ~~Capitatæ Spinosæ~~

2 Class: Capitatæ Spinosæus: 1 Carduus, ~~Corcus~~[?] {2 Carduus, [3] Cirsium dictus} 4 Attrachylis, 5 Acarnu, 6 Chamæleon, 7 Acanus, 8 Silybum, 9 Card: Sphærocephlus, 10 Acanthion, 11 Acanthus, 12 Scolymas, 13 Card: Spinocissimus, 14 Dipsacus, 15 Eryngium, 16 Card: stellatus, 17 Euphobia, 18 Tragacantha, 19 Poterium, 20 Drupis, 21 Anonis.

Siliquatæ etc:

1 Class: Fuba, 2 Smilax hortensis S: Phaseolus, {3 Pisum,} 4 Ochrus, 5 Lathyrus, 6 Vicia, 7 Aphaca, 8 Arachus, 9 Arachidna, 10 Lentes

2 Class: 1 Orobus, 2 Cicer, 3 Lupinus, 4 Fœnum Græcum

Subdivided of class

1 Class: 1 Hedysarum, 2 Ferrum Equinum, 3 Polygala, 4 Ornithopodium, 5 Tribulus

2 Class: Onobrychis, 2 Astragalus, 3 Galega, 4 Glycerhiza

3 Class: 1 Consolida regalis, 2 Fumaria, 3 Chelidonium, 4 Aquilegia, 5 Nigella:

Lactariæ etc:

1 Class: Tithynullus, 2 Pityusa 3 Apios, 4 Peplus :S; Esula rotunda, 5 Peplis 6 Chamæsycæ, 7 Lathyris, 8 Hippophæs

Scandentes :S: convolulæ:

1 Class: Scammonia, 2 Convolvulus, 3 Soldanella, 4 Smilax aspera 5 China, 6 Bryonia, 7 Lupulus, 8 Vitis Vinifera.

2 Class: Clematitis altera dioscoridis, 2 Clematis{tis} Indica :S: Lignum Colobrinum 3 Clematitis prima Veterum, 4 Periclymenum, 5 Apo{c}ynum, 6 Asclepias,

3 Class: Hedera, 2 Hedera terrestris,

Subclasses 1 pomiferæ scandentes, 1 Cucumis, 2 Melo, 3 pepo, 4 Anguria 5 Cucurbita, 6 Colocynthidi, 7 Cucumis Asirinus

[Page 328.4]

Noxiæ etc

1 Class: Solanum, 2 ~~Vesicarium, 3 Mandacum~~ 2 Mandragora, 3 Hyoscyamus, 4 Nicotiana, 5 Papaver 6 Hypocoum, 7 ~~Agrantum~~ Argemone,

2 Class: Aconitum, 2 Doronicum.

Olera et Oleratæ

1 Class: 1 Rupus, 2 Rapunculus 3 Trachelio, 4 Rapistrum, 5 Napus, 6 Raphanus 7 Lepidium, 8 Iberis, 9 Dracunculus Esculentus, 10 Eruca, 11 Sinapi, 12 Reseda, 13 Luteola, 14 Erysimum, 15 Hy[d]ropiper 16 Capsicum,

2 Class: Nasturtium, 2 Thlaspi, 3 Bursa pastoris, 4 Myagrum, 5 Drabæ 6 Alliaria, 7 Cochlearia,

3 Class: 1 Brassica ~~2 Lapathum~~

4 Class: 1 Glastum, 2 Lapathum, 3 Acelosa, 4 Spinachia, 5 Rho 6 Centaurium majus.

5 Class: 1 Beta, 2 Blitum, 3 Atriplex, 4 Halimus, 5 Amaranthus, 6 Parietaria, 7 Mercurialis, 8 Phyllon.

6 Class: 1 Lactuca, 2 Sonchus, 3 Lampsana, 4 Endivia 5 Cichorium, 6 Dens Leonis, 7 Hieracium, 8 Chondrilla, 9 Senecio, 10 Jacoba[?]

Herba Miscellæ

1 Class: Lysimachia, 2 Veronica, 2 [3] Teucrium, 4 Scordium, 5 Chamedrys, ~~6 Alsine, 7 Anagallis~~ 6 Chamapitys, 7 Alsine, 8 Anagallis, 9 Elatine,

2 Class: 1 Perfoliata, 2 Bupheurum, 3 Centaurium minos, 4 Cyratiola, 5 Hypericum, 6 Coris, 7 Symphytum Petræum, 8 Polygonum, 9 Anthyllis,

3 Class: 1 Fungi, 2 *Agarius*, 3 *Tubera*.

~~Etce: ex Jonstoni notitia regni vegetabilis~~

And though this might laudably supply ~~a Catalog~~ {it} yet if a more General Catalogue be requird, let our studious Gardner consult that of the Oxford Physic Garden, or ~~any~~ those of Leyden, Paris, Montpelle, Padua, etc: & ~~for a~~ but for our indegen & home–bud, that of the learned Dr. Merrett, in his aforementiond Pinax Se Morison

"To Encourage the Finishing of Elysium Britannicum"

To Dr Nedham upon the designe of Mr Evelyns Elysium Britannicum
Sr

Wee had an honor done us lately by Dr Stephens and as wee understand from him by your selfe in that you please to make some reference to our judgem[en]ts in the case of Printing a piece entitled Elysium Britannicum. The heads wee saw and perused; but thincke our selves farre too small for the grandeur of this reference & had much rather beg pardon & returne thanckes for the honor. How ever Sr to give you satisfaction wee are you see ready not onely to write but to make as it were this our common remonstrance that the piece will likely bee a Magnificent Worke & set to serve the Magnificence of Nobel persons. Some off the Heads containe matters of great and Comon Use & Profitt particularly the 10th 11th & 12 of the first booke & the 3d 4th 8th 13 14 & soe to the End of the Second booke & you know that profitt has that power to make any matter conduceing to it, at any time and in any method exceeding acceptable: Other heads and indeed the greater part referr to the Ornaments, state & Pompe of a Garden a theme altogether new to our writers as having not beene elaborated by any English pen that wee know and therefore very likely to bee most acceptable to our english nobility and gentry: many of {whom} we know have esteemed it a sufficient recompense for the paines of cost of a Journey not only to St. Jermins in France but of their travaile over the greatest part of Italy that they have thereby understood the beauty gallantry & state of such workes as ~~the Gentleman~~ {Mr Evelyn} is by us supposed to describe in this his Elysium a subject fit onely for a very extensive and very gentile witt: And wee hope that hereby Ventiducts Waterworkes for Musical especially and other motions (to the Vulgar stupendous) devices by the various casting reflecting & breaking of lights and shadows of Sounds likewise & Eccho's and other the Italian gloryes and pompous beauties may {be} one day brought (as farre as the temper of our Climate will give leave) into our English gardens (tis true wee have neither Materialls nor Mechanicians like those in Italy but wee suppose the Gentleman that writes this piece may bee able to propose wayes to helpe our Nation in this particular: and that the severall pieces proposed & workes will in the booke bee illustrated with figures and Cutts proportionable to the Noblenesse & State of the piece which by the Idea you have given us in the heads has putt an edge and Keenenesse on our appetites to see the whole made publique in doeing which the Gentleman shall greately delight & gratify his Nation & particularly oblige
   Sr
Oxon Jan: 20. 1659
   Your Faithfull Servants

Phil: Stephens
Walt[?] Browne
John Paris
Josiah Lane
Robert Sharrock
Rich: Inglett
Simon Welman
Jacob Bobert Senr
Will. Austin
Jho: Bannister
Arth: Smith
Jacob Bobert Junr

[Cover]   To our worthy friend
                   Dr Nedham thiese[?]
             London

Doctors & Heads of Houses
        & others Oxon: 20 Jan
             1659

To Encourage the finishing
        of Elysium Britannicum

APPENDIX 12

Catalogo Evelyni Inscriptus:
1665 Meliora retinete.

[This excerpt, which may have belonged to the "Elysium Britannicum," is now among the collections at the William Andrews Clark Library, University of California, Los Angeles]

xxxvi   *A Catalogue for Tryals*   xxxvi

1   Inoculate a rose bud on an Almond for early Roses:
2   Set a Rose tree in a Case, & Water it with warme Water dunged, & set it in all ill weather.
3   Prick Seedes into a Sea Onion or Squill, & trye how soone they will spring.
4   Lay slipps of young holly twisted[.] don: 5 Sept: 1662
5   Take some of the Ba old Barne Earth & plant Tulips, Anemonies, etc, in it
6   Set Seedes at several depths & take a role
7   Plant a Gourd, secure the Creeping vines from taking roote, by letting it run up a pole etc: & measure its groth every day, & weeke:
8   Graffe all sorts of Roses early in Spring to produce roses that yeare
9   Figures of Seedes pr: Micro Scopium
10 Set Fibrous, & bulbous rootes in severall Earthes, observe their groth & bignesse, & colour
11 See what ship balast from the Indies will produce.
12 Enquire of Mr Beale concerning Graffing of Seedes in Seedes etc[.] When they sproute to alter or mix the species
13 Try graines with composte Salts, Urine, blood etc
14 Putrifie living creatures & see what plants will be producd:
15 Seale some Earth hermeticaly up: Some dry, some wetter Exposd abrod & some Set in Earth
16 Innoculate a Lawrell on a black Cherry for a Standard

Sow holly berries in December or bury them in Earth S.S.S.[?] till spring like haws etc.
putt some rootes etc close in a pot of earth with a hole at top: se if they will coalesce:

Graffe an Apple on an Elme
Also an Elme on an Elme
Oake on oake, beech on beech
birch on birch,
Calcine a black holy-hock flower to see if it be not more Earth & Salt, than spirit in it compard to another coloured holy-hock of like weight: if so, blacknesse comes from the earthynesse:

[The following text is crossed out]
Graffe of his Coopers greate cherry
Mr: Waiths black cherry
Bro: Rich[ard] peare for perry:
Co: Tuke Apple:
Get, cuttings of cherys etc from Smith of G:wich
Get a Lewes lavender[?]
Mr: Cottles[?] bed little apple

[Appended note] The above fragment, in the hand of John Evelyn, the distinguished Author of the following Diary, is a portion of an unpublished work entitled "Elysium Britannicum." William Upcott, Islington, May 22, 1848.

The Vintage: The English Vineyard Vindicated

Gather your *Grapes* very *plump*, and *transparent*, which is when the *Seeds* or *Stones* come forth *black* and *clear*, not *Viscous* or *clammy*; that the *stalks* begin to *shrivel* at the part next the *Branch*, which is a signe it has done feeding. *Grapes* therefore cannot be *over-ripe*, and where they make the best *Wines* the *Clusters* hang till they are almost *wasted*, and the *Stalks* near quite *dry*; as in *Candy*, and *Greece*, and even in *France*, they stay till the *leaf* be ready to drop; nor do they much impair, though *Frost* or *Rain* do frequently surprise them, provided it prove *dry* one *Fortnight* before *Gathering time*.

It is best to *cut*, and not *pull* them from the *Vine*, in the *Moons* decrease, and to put them in *Baskets*, each sort apart, taking only the best-ripe, clean and unbruis'd.

In most places they *tread* them with their naked *Feet* in a *Vat* pierced full of *holes* at the bottom, through which the *Liquor* runs into a *Keeler* plac'd under it; but 'tis better to *void* it as 'tis *press'd* out; because it is found to carry with it too much of the *trash* and grosser parts: Others heap in so many, that the very weight of the *Bunches* press themselves; and *thus* is that rare *Lachryma* made, which is not obnoxious to that surcharge of *tincture* and *harshness* which the pressed Wines commonly betray.

If you would make *Claret*, let it remain with the *Murc* or hulks, till the *tincture* be to your liking: but the *White* are *Tunn'd* immediately, as soon as bruis'd, where they perfect their *fermentation* and working. The best course is to sink a Basket into the pressed *Murc*, and so to separate the *Must* from the *Husks*, and take out the pure *Liquor* only; the rest will remain behind, *subside* and sinke to the bottome of the *Vessel*, and may serve for *Claret*, or a ruder Wine.

When the *White* is *Tunn'd*, close it immediately and very accurately, fear not your *Vessel* if well made; since the force of the *working* (which may possibly continue *nine* or *ten* dayes) will not violate it, as some imagine; and therefore imprudently leave the *bung hole* open, to the utter loss of its *spirits*; to prevent which therefore, at the filling, leave *half a foot* or more, voide; and for *Claret*: somewhat above, which replenish at *ten* dayes end (when the fury of *working* is over) with some proper *Wine* that will not provoke it to motion again. This *process* must be frequently repeated if need requires; for *new Wine* will spend & wast somewhat till it be perfect; yea even to the very *Spring*, as far as *April*, leaving the more *soeculent* and grosser parts in the first.

This is the manner of *Languedoc* and Southern parts of *France*; but about *Paris* (which is the nearest in *constitution* to our *Country*) they permit the *Murc* to abide in the *Must* two dayes, and as many nights for White Wine, and at the least a *week* for their *Clarets*.

Some press their *White Grapes* by *themselves*, and afterwards *mix* them; and yet even *Red Grapes* will make a *White-wine*, if timely freed of the *Husk*; but the *Colour* follows the nature of the *husk*, and must therefore be treated accordingly as to the period of receiving *Tincture*, by frequent *tasting* it, and *experiment*, till it be to your *Eye* and *Palats* liking. But in this interim (lest too much *spirits* should evaporate) let an exact Cover of Wood (made like the lid of a round box) be fitted to your *Vat*, and to render it the closer, assist it with a *linnen cloth* that it may be exactly just, drawing out your *Must* by a *Spigot* at the bottom of the *Vessel*. In short, (to avoid the many inconveniences which happen to *Wines* by permitting them to abide *too long* macerating the *Husks*) 'tis better to dash it with a little *Art*, by mingling some *Red*, or other *Wine* naturally charg'd, than adventure the spoiling of the *Whole*, for this onely Circumstance, there being very few natural Wines, but what have this assistance, not to call it *Adulteration*.

In *Italy* they put the *Husks* and *Stones* together into that which is press'd, and so let it Work a fortnight, and then add a third part of *Water* to render it less *heady* and *strong*; but our *Wines* will by no means support this *dilution*. In some parts of *France* they *Tun* it when it has wrought in the *Keelers*, filling up (as we describ'd) what works out the first *three* or *four* dayes with what they *squeeze* from the *Husks*, which some think very practicable with us.

Whilest this *Working* and *Filling* continues, close up carefully the *North Windows* (if any) of your *Cellar*, lest it *sowre* your *Liquor*; and about the expiration of *March*, stop your *Vessel* for good and all. Some replenish their *Working Wines* with *water* onely, especially, the last time; provided it exceed not a *Quart* in a large quantity: Others, roll their *Casks* about the *Cellar* to blend with the *Lees*, and after few days re-settlement, *rack* it off with great improvement, about the same *season*.

When now your Must is *Tunn'd*, press your *Murc*; this, though no *delicate* Drink, will yet keep long, and is proper to mingle with other, and give it the *body* you desire. Others prefer the casting a convenient quantity of *Fountain*-Water on the *Husks* as soon as the best *Wine* is *trodden*, or forced out and tunn'd; and there let it *Colour*, drawing, and supplying it by degrees, as long as *tincture*, *tast* and *Virtue*, remains good. Be very careful to empty the *Vat* of the *Husks* as soon as ever your *Water* or mixture is drawn, lest it give such a *tang* to your *Vat*, as you can never *free* it of again; and therefore by all meanes I advise you to have *two Vessels*, that *one* of them alone may be destin'd to this employment of *mixing* your *Wines*.

The best *expedient* to multiplie *Wine*, is (when all is said) to fill your *Vat* with whole *Grapes* or *Clusters*, and *three* or *foure* dayes after, to draw out the *Must*, which will run off it selfe into a *Vessel* plac'd by the *Vat*, and well stopp'd: Afterwards, tread the *Grapes*, pouring in a good quantity of *Water*, and then immediately adding the *Must* that you before reserved to *worke*, and *ferment* together: *This* is esteem'd of all other the most approved way, and may promise a reasonable good *Wine* and fair success.

To Purifie Wine.

Put into your *Vessel* the *planings* of *Chips* of green *Beech*, the *Rind* carefully peel'd off; but first, *boyl* them in clear *Water* about an *houres* space, to extract their *ranknesse*; then *dry* them perfectly well in the *Sun* or an *Oven*: Lesse than one *Bushel* of *Chips* is sufficient to *sine* an whole *Tun* of *Wine*; and it will set your *Wine* in a gentle working, and *purifie* it in twenty four hours, giving it a good and agreable *flavor*.

These *Chips* may be *washed* again, and will serve the better upon the like Occasion, and even till they are almost consum'd. Let your *Chips* be *plan'd* off as *long* and *large* as you can get them, and put them in at the *bung-hole*. Lastly,

Some *dulcorate* and Sweeten their *Wines* (to prevent *harshness*) with *Raisins* of the

Sun, trodden into the *Vat*, and perhaps to good purpose a little *plump'd* before; or boyling half the *Must* in a *Vessel* a good hour, and *scumming* it, *tun* it up *hot* with with [*sic*] the other.

About *April* you may pierce your *Wine* to *Drink*, &c.

I could *dilate* much more upon all these *particulars*, but these *Rules* are *plaine* and *easie*, and more would be but *superfluous*. Dispose therefore of them as you think fit.

By *Must*, they signifie the *newly press'd Liquor*, whilst it *ferments* or remains in the *Vat*, and before it is tun'd.

By *Murc*, is meant the *Husks* of the *Grapes* when the *Liquor* is express'd.

Note, that some instead of *Trenching*, squeeze the *Bunches* 'twixt their *hands*; Others Press them in an *Engine* like a *Cedar Press*, putting the *Cluster* into a *Raisin-frail* or Bag of *hair cloth*.

FINIS.

An Account of Some Books

I. A Philosophical Discourse of EARTH, relating to the Improvement of it for Vegetation and the Propagation of Plants: By J. Evelyn *Esq; Fellow of the R. Society.* London, *printed for* J. Martyn, *Printer to the said Society. A. 1676 in octavo.*

This instructive and useful Discourse was presented by the Ingenious Author thereof to the *R. Society* in two Lectures *viz. April 19,* and *May 13* of this very Year.

In it he first describeth what he means by *Earth*; then endeavors to shew the several sorts and kinds of Earth, as they reside in their several Beds, together with the indications, by which we may discover their qualities and perfections; and lastly, how we may best improve it to the Uses of the Husbandman, the Forrester, and the Gardner; which is indeed of large and profitable extent, though it be but poor and mean, compared to Mines of Gold and Silver.

In the *second* part he not only takes notice, among the rest, of the fitness of our *Senses* in giving their verdict of the several qualities of Earths; but also acquaints us with the Microscopical examination he hath made of divers sorts both of Earth and Soils or Dungs; thereby encouraging others to inquire and observe, whether the very finest Earth, and best of Moulds, however to appearance mixt with divers imperfect bodies, do not consist more of *Sandy* or *Salin* particles, than of any other; and by such inquiry to find out the *principles* of Vegetation: Suggesting further several Quære's belonging to this argument; as, how far *Principles* might be multiplied and differenced by alteration and condensation? Whether Earth, stript of all heterogenity, retain only weight and an insipid siccity? And whether it produce or afford any thing more than embracement to the first rudiments of Plants; protection to the roots and stability to the stem; unprolific, as they say, till married to something of a more masculine vertue, but otherwaies nourishing only from what it attracts, without any active ore material contribution? &c.

In the *third* part he teaches *first,* How we may *improve* the best Earths, and apply remedy to the worst, only by labour, stirring, ventilating, shading and reposing; which being the least Artificial, approach the nearest to Nature: Where he notes, among many other excellent particulars, that the bare raking and combing only of a bed of Earth, now one way, then an other, as to the regions of Heaven and polar Aspects, may diversify the annual production. To which he subjoyns several *Mechanical* aids, (without *stercoration*) whereby the Soil may be rendred of a very extensive capacity for the entertainment of forreign and un-common Plants: Commending *Irrigation* or Watering as one of the richest Improvements that ever was put in practice, especially where fat and impregnate waters may be had, without grittiness, or being over-harsh and cold: Teaching also the cure of wet and boggy Lands, and such as are cold and dry, hungry and hot, to light and over-rank; and such as become unfruitful by the neighbourhood of other Plants, devouring the juyce of the Earth; or by the dripping of shadowy Trees.

Secondly, he delivers, what farther advancement we may expect from *Stercoration* or manuring the ground with *Composts*, and discovers to us the qualities latent in their several ferments, and how to apply them by a skilful and philosophical hand, without which they do alwaies more hurt, than good. Here, he *first* enumerates their several kinds, *viz.* from Animals, Vegetables, and of things promiscuous, and whatever is apt to rot and consume in any competent time, and is either salt, unctuous or fatty: To which he adds impregnating *Rains* and *Dews*, Cold and Dry Winters with store of *Snow*, which he reckons equal to the richest manures, impregnated as they are with Celestial Nitre. *Secondly*, he notes, what it is we chiefly seek for, and expect from Composts: Here he observes, that amongst these materials we may detect the causes of fertility more eminently than in other substances, partly from their *fixed Salts*, or some virtue contain'd in them, or rather drawn from without, and imparted to the exhausted and defective Earth; and that by such a process, as, by converting them into a *Chyle*, as 'twere, it facilitates their being insumed, assimilated, and made apt to pass into nourishment promoting Vegetation. *Thirdly*, How to treat Composts, so as to render them fit for our service: Which he takes to be a difficulty worthy the heads as well as the hands of the profoundest Philosopher; since it requires a more than superficial knowledge and penetration into causes. How skilfully he hath also acquitted himself of this part, the Curious Reader will best understand by perusing and considering the Discourse it self; from which we are unwilling any longer to divert him by an imperfect account.

Notes

John Evelyn and His "Elysium Britannicum"

Note to epigraph: Letter "To Dr Nedham upon the designe of Mr Evelyns Elysium Britannicum" from "Doctors & Heads of Houses and others," 20 January 1659. See Appendix 11 for the entire letter.

1. See Michael Hunter, *Science and the Shape of Orthodoxy: Intellectual Change in Late Seventeenth-Century Britain* (Woodbridge, Suffolk: Boydell, 1995), chapter 3, "John Evelyn in the 1650s: A Virtuoso in Quest of a Role," 67–98; quotation on p. 71. Biographies and biographical statements on John Evelyn can be found in the introductory volume of E. S. de Beer, ed., *The Diary of John Evelyn* (Oxford: Oxford University Press, 1955); Arthur Ponsonby, *John Evelyn, Fellow of the Royal Society: Author of "Sylva"* (London: Heinemann, 1933); Walter G. Hiscock, *John Evelyn and His Family Circle* (London: Routledge & Kegan Paul, 1955); John Bowle, *John Evelyn and His World: A Biography* (London: Routledge & Kegan Paul, 1981).

2. See Joseph M. Levine, "John Evelyn: Between the Ancients and the Moderns," in Therese O'Malley and Joachim Wolschke-Bulmahn, eds., *John Evelyn's "Elysium Britannicum" and European Gardening*, Dumbarton Oaks Colloquium on the History of Landscape Architecture 17 (Washington, D.C.: Dumbarton Oaks Research Library and Collection, 1998), 57–78.

3. De Beer, ed., *The Diary of John Evelyn*, 2:279.

4. For instances of the incorporation of correspondence material directly into Evelyn's text, see essays in O'Malley and Wolschke-Bulmahn, eds., *John Evelyn's "Elysium Britannicum" and European Gardening*, especially Douglas D. C. Chambers, "'Elysium Britannicum not printed neere ready &c': The 'Elysium Britannicum' in the Correspondence of John Evelyn," 107–130. See also two essays in Michael Leslie and Timothy Raylor, eds., *Culture and Cultivation in Early Modern England: Writing and the Land* (Leicester: Leicester University Press, 1992): Michael Leslie, "The Spiritual Husbandry of John Beale," esp. 162–166, and Timothy Raylor, "Samuel Hartlib and the Commonwealth of Bees," esp. 92, 97.

5. British Library Evelyn Manuscripts, letterbook no. 36.

6. Evelyn's famous gardens at Sayes Court were in Deptford, originally an independent town but now absorbed into the city of London.

7. Evelyn's letter to Robert Boyle, 3 September 1659.

8. See Charles Webster, *The Great Instauration: Science, Medicine and Reform, 1626–1660* (Cambridge: Cambridge University Press, 1975), and Mark Greengrass, Michael Leslie, and Timothy Raylor, eds., *Samuel Hartlib and the Universal Reformation: Studies in Intellectual Communication* (Cambridge: Cambridge University Press, 1994).

9. Geoffrey Keynes, *John Evelyn: A Study in Bibliophily & A Bibliography of His Writings* (New York: The Grolier Club: 1937), p. 3.

10. Evelyn records the fire in his diary; see de Beer, ed., *The Diary of John Evelyn*, 3:450–462.

11. See Douglas D. C. Chambers, *The Planters of the English Landscape Garden: Botany, Trees, and the Georgics* (New Haven: Yale University Press, 1993), chapter 3.

12. Pierre Morin, *Remarques necessaires pour la culture des fleurs* (Paris, 1658).

13. A comparison of the handwriting on several insertions at manuscript pages 282, 290, and 298 of the "Elysium" with the facsimile pages published in *The Garden Book of Sir Thomas Hanmer Bart* (London: Gerald Howe, 1933), xxxv–xxxvi, leads to this conclusion.

14. Graham Parry, "John Evelyn as Hortulan Saint," in Leslie and Raylor, eds., *Culture and Cultivation in Early Modern England*, 138.

15. Geoffrey Keynes, ed., *The Works of Sir Thomas Browne*, (London: Faber & Gwyer; Faber & Faber Limited, 1928–1931), 6:302.

16. William Bray, ed., *Memoirs, Illustrative of the Life and Writings of John Evelyn, ESQ. F.R.S.* (London, 1819), 2:88.

17. Parry, "John Evelyn as Hortulan Saint," 134.

18. B. Lamy, *A Treatise of Perspective, or The Art of Representing All Manner of Objects as They Appear to the Eye in All Situations . . .* (London, 1702).

19. John Evelyn's nineteenth-century sobriquet is courtesy of his most popular publication, which went through many editions: *Sylva, or A Discourse of Forest-Trees* (London, 1664).

20. "Actually [Lady Evelyn] was using some of [the manuscripts] to be cut up for dress patterns, so that Upcott is to be regarded (as are most collectors) in the light of a benefactor rather than a malefactor." Keynes, *John Evelyn: A Study in Bibliophily*, 29.

21. Upcott may have been responsible for having the "Elysium" manuscript bound at the same time as another volume with similar binding, also extant at the British Library, which contains miscellaneous notes on several subjects, principally, for *Sylva*. It seems that Upcott's access to the Evelyn manuscripts and his constant re-working of the diary and correspondence make Upcott a logical choice for having the manuscripts bound in their similar bindings.

22. See Appendix 11 for a copy of a letter to Dr. Jasper Needham, from Oxford supporters, such as Robert Sharrock, John Banister, the Bobarts, et al., in which Evelyn is encouraged to bring the "Elysium" to publication. As noted in the printed prospectus that serves as the table of contents, *Sylva* and *Kalendarium Hortense* had already been printed, while *Acetaria* would be published in 1699. See Frances Harris's essay on the Evelyn archive in this volume for additional information.

23. A copy of a different and earlier broadside, located at the British Library, lists four fewer chapters and some minor word changes; there is also no annotation (British Library, Add. MS 15950, f. 143). Courtesy of the late Dr. Helen Wallis. In contrast, the "Table of Contents" published in *Acetaria* in 1699 listed forty-two chapters.

24. Paraphrased in Parry, "John Evelyn as Hortulan Saint," 146.

25. Frances Harris addresses these points in this volume.

26. Michael Hunter, letter to John E. Ingram.

27. Keynes, in *John Evelyn*, 236, notes: "Portions [of the "Elysium Britannicum"] were probably removed by Upcott. One specimen 2 1/2 pp. 4to, headed 'A catalogue for [sic] Tryals', was sold at Christie's, 3 May 1967, lot 76, inserted in a copy of the *Memoirs*, 1819, with a statement by Upcott that it had belonged to the *Elysium Britannicum*." The excerpt is now among the collections at the William Andrews Clark Library, Los Angeles. Transcription in Appendix 12.

28. I plan to return to the British Library and complete a transcription of these

additional materials, and to make that information available to researchers in either printed or electronic format in the future.

29. Stephen Switzer, *Ichonographia rustica, or The Nobleman, Gentleman, and Gardener's Recreation. . . .* (London, 1718), xxx.

30. Specifically, the methodology chosen was that adopted by the Samuel Hartlib Papers project at Sheffield University, under the direction of Michael Leslie. Michael Hunter's guidelines for editing seventeenth-century manuscripts as outlined by him in "How to Edit a Seventeenth-Century Manuscript: Principles and Practice," *The Seventeenth Century* 10 no. 2 (1995 Autumn), 277–312, also proved extremely useful. I have retained both printed and electronic text files that reflect the more literal version of the transcription.

31. E. S. de Beer used a similar method in his 1955 edition of Evelyn's *Diary*.

The Manuscripts of the "Elysium Britannicum"

An earlier version of this essay appeared in *Garden History* (1997), 131–137. I am indebted to the editors for permission to republish it here.

1. For a summary account, see T. Hofmann, J. Winterkorn, F. Harris, and H. Kelliher, "John Evelyn's Archive at the British Library," *The Book Collector* 44 (1995), 147–209.

2. *The Miscellaneous Writings of John Evelyn,* ed. William Upcott (1825), 97–98; Geoffrey Keynes, *John Evelyn: A Study in Bibliophily* (Oxford: Oxford University Press, 1968), 46–47; see also Michael Hunter, "John Evelyn in the 1650s: A Virtuoso in Quest of a Role," in *Science and the Shape of Orthodoxy* (Woodbridge: Boydell, 1995), 94.

3. British Library Add. MS 15948, ff. 71–74: Paris, 13 September–25 October 1659. See Douglas D. C. Chambers, "Elysium Britannicum not printed neere ready &c': The 'Elysium Britannicum' in the Correspondence of John Evelyn," in *John Evelyn's Elysium Britannicum and European Gardening*, ed. T. O'Malley and J. Wolschke-Bulmahn (Washington, D.C.: Dumbarton Oaks, 1998), 124–125.

4. Sheffield University Library, Hartlib Papers (UMI Electronic edition, 1995), 67/22/1A: Beale to Evelyn, 30 September 1659 (copy).

5. Geoffrey Keynes, ed., *The Works of Sir Thomas Browne* (London: Faber and Faber 1931), 6:302: Evelyn to Browne, 28 January [1659/60] (misdated 1657/58 by Keynes; the correct date is in the copy in Evelyn's letterbook, Evelyn MS 39a).

6. E.g., W. Bray, ed., *Memoirs Illustrative of the Life and Writings of John Evelyn* (London, 1819), 2:90–91; and W. Bray, ed., *Diary and Correspondence of John Evelyn* (London, 1859), 2:394–395.

7. Their reply of 20 January 1659[/60] is inserted in the front of Evelyn MS 45; it is quoted in Peter H. Goodchild, "No Phantasticall Utopia, but a Reall Place': John Evelyn, John Beale and Backbury Hill, Herefordshire," *Garden History* (Autumn 1991), 105–106, but misdated 20 January 165[8/]9. See Appendix 11.

8. Keynes, ed. *The Works of Sir Thomas Browne*, 6:300–302: Evelyn to Browne, 28 January [1659/60].

9. Evelyn asked Dr. Wilkins that he not be expected to accept too many Royal Society commissions until he had finished the "Elysium" and asked for the Society's help; Bray, ed., *Diary* 3:103–131: 17 February 1660/61 (misdated 1659/60).

10. Evelyn MS 39a: Evelyn to Thomas Lloyd, 16 October 1668.

11. Margaret Denny, "The Early Program of the Royal Society and John Evelyn," *Modern Language Quarterly* 1 (1940), 490–491.

12. Bray, ed., *Diary* 2:392: Evelyn to Beale, 11 July 1679.

13. Denny, "Early Program," 491.

14. The latest edition of this is *Acetaria: A Discourse of Sallets*, ed. Christopher Driver (Totnes: Prospect Books, 1996).

15. Keynes, *John Evelyn*, 208–209. A Summary of this work was printed in the *Philosophical Transactions of the Royal Society* (1676) and is here reproduced as Appendix 14.

16. Ibid., 180–181. Headed "The Vintage," this was added to the second edition of *The English Vineyard Vindicated*, which was itself appended to the second edition of *The French Gardiner* of 1669. Here reproduced as Appendix 13.

17. Evelyn MS 61; Le Fèvre's work was published as *Traicté de la Chymie* in Paris 1660; see also F. Sherwood Taylor, "The Chemical Studies of John Evelyn," *Annals of Science* 8 (1952), 285, 290–292.

18. Evelyn MS 44, "A Booke of Promiscuous Notes & Observations concerning Husbandry, Building &c," includes notes about and an illustration of an engine for raising water.

19. It was written in response to Evelyn's request of 13 December 1667 and was acknowledged by him on 21 August 1668 (see Bray, ed., *Diary*, 3:201, 205).

20. For Upcott and the Evelyn archive, see Hofmann, et al., "John Evelyn's Archive," 200–204.

Book I

i. A complete annotated version of the "table of contents" with Evelyn's notes and changes is in Appendix 1.

ii. Cicero: *De Senectute* 16.56.

iii. Space left in manuscript.

iv. Interlineation lined through and indecipherable.

v. Evelyn's translation of Nicolas de Bonnefons's *Le Iardinier François, Qui enseigne a cultiver les Arbres, & Herbes Potageres Auec la maniere de conserver les Fruicts, & faire toutes sortes de Confitures, Conserves, & Massepans* (Paris, 1656). Keynes cites this edition.

vi. Jean de La Quintinie, 1626–1688, *Instruction pour les Jardins Fruitiers et Potagers, avec un Traite des Orangers, Suivy de Quelques Reflexions sur l'Agriculture* (Paris, 1690).

vii. Marcello Malpighi, 1628–1694, *Marcelli Malpighii Anatome Plantarum cui Subjungitur Appendix Iteratas & Auctas Ejusdem Authoris de Ovo Incubato Observationes Continens; Regiae Societati Londoni ad Scientiam Naturalem Promouendam Institutae Dicata*, 2 vols. (London, 1675–1679).

viii. Nehemiah Grew, 1641–1712, perhaps a reference to his *A Discourse Made before the Royal Society, Decemb. 10, 1674 concerning the Nature, Causes, and Power of Mixture* (London, 1675).

ix. Robert Boyle, *Origin of Forms and Qualities* (London, 1666).

x. Ralph Cudworth, 1617–1688.

xi. Paraphrase of *totam infusa per artus mens agitat molem*.

xii. Jacobus Gaffarellus, *De Fini Mundi* (Paris, 1629).

xiii. John Beale, 1603–1683.

xiv. Sir Thomas Browne, 1605–1682, *Pseudodoxia epidemica, or Enquiries into Very Many Received Tenents and Commonly Presumed Truths* (London, 1650, or edition unidentified).

xv. Insertion indicated but not present.

xvi. Insertion contained in Evelyn MSS: Miscellaneous XI.

xvii. Insertion indicated but not present.

xviii. Insertion contained in Evelyn MSS: Miscellaneous XI.

xix. Insertion contained in Evelyn MSS: Miscellaneous XI.

xx. Insertion indicated but not present.

xxi. Insertion indicated but not present.

xxii. Gabriel Plattes, *A Discovery of Infinite Treasure, Hidden Since the Worlds Beginning, Whereunto All Men of What Degree Soever, Are Friendly Invited to Be Sharers with the Discoverer* (London, 1639).

xxiii. *De Rei rusticae* 2.15–17.

xxiv. Peter Lauremberg, 1585–1659. *Horticultura, libris II comprehensa huic nostro coelo & solo accommodata; regulis, observationibus experimentis, & figuris novis instructa in qua quicquid ad hortum proficue colendum, et eleganter instruendum facit, explicatur* (Frankurt [1632]).

xxv. Gabriel Plattes?

xxvi. Insertion indicated, but not present.

xxvii. Chapter number and title supplied from printed table of contents.

xxviii. Pierre Gassendi, 1592–1655.

xxix. Insertion indicated but not present.

xxx. Christopher Merret, 1614–1695, *Pinax rerum naturalium Britannicum* (London, 1666 [1667]).

Book II

i. Paulus Orosius, *Pauli Orosii presbyteri hispani, Adversus paganos historiarum libri septem: vetustorum librorum auxilio a mendis vindicati, & annotationibus ex urtiusq linguae historicis illustrati, opera & studio Franc. Fabricii Marcodurani*, edition unidentified.

ii. Walter Blith, *The English Improver Improved*, London, edition unidentified.

iii. Lady Prudence Hartopp/Leith-Ross, in a letter to John Ingram of 17 November 1991, suggests that Evelyn may have been spelling, in his own creative manner, the word "foist," which can mean a cask.

iv. Johann Rudolph Glauber, perhaps his *A Description of New Philosophical Furnaces, or A New Art of Distilling Divided into Five Parts* (London, 1651).

v. Sir Henry Wotton, *The Elements of Architecture, Collected by Henry Wotton, Knight, from the Best Authors and Examples* (London, 1624).

vi. Peter H. Goodchild places Evelyn's description of the area in historical context in "'No phantasticall Utopia, but a reall place': John Evelyn, John Beale and Backbury Hill Herefordshire," *Garden History* 19, no. 2 (1992), pp. 105–127.

vii. William Oughtread, *The Key of the Mathematicks New Forged and Filed Together with a Treatise of the Resolution of All Kinds of Affected Æquations in Numbers . . .* (London, 1647).

viii. Marcus Porcius Cato, *De agri cultura* 3.1.

ix. Insertion indicated but not present.

x. Insertion indicated but not present.

xi. Two insertions indicated but not present.

xii. Insertion indicated but not present.

xiii. Pliny, *Naturalis historiae* 18.24.56.

xiv. Insertion indicated but not present.

xv. Robert Sharrock, *The History of the Improvement and Propagation of Vegetables* (Oxford, 1660).

xvi. John Parkinson, *Paradisi in sole, paradisus terrestris* (London 1629, 2d ed. 1656).

xvii. Pomponne II de Bellieure, 1606–1657.

xviii. Caspar von Baerle, *Rerum per octennium in Brasilia et alibi gestarum, sub praefectura . . . I. Mauritii Nassaviae &c. comitis, historia* (Kelve, 1660).

xix. Insertion indicated but not present.

xx. Two insertions indicated but not present.

xxi. Cardinal Enrico Caetani.

xxii. Insertion indicated but not present.

xxiii. Two insertions indicated but not present.

xxiv. Insertion indicated but not present.

xxv. Insertion indicated but not present.

xxvi. Insertion indicated but not present.

xxvii. Petrarch, *De secreto conflictu curarum mearum*, book 2.

xxviii. Insertion indicated but not present.

xxix. Insertion indicated but not present.

xxx. Two insertions indicated but not present.

xxxi. Agostino Ramelli, 1531–1590; Salomon de Caus, 1576–1630.

xxxii. Nine-page insertion in Appendix 2. Second insertion indicated but not present.

xxxiii. Sir Henry Wotton, *The Elements of Architecture*

xxxiv. Sir Philip Sidney, *The Countesse of Pembrokes Arcadia* (London, 1633) 1:3.

xxxv. Four-page insertion. See Appendix 3.

xxxvi. *Corpus Tibullianum Elergies* 1.27: "sed Canis aestivos ortus . . . ."

xxxvii. Blank spaces left for later addition of dimensions.

xxxviii. Edward Pierce/Pearce, fl. 1640–1666.

xxxix. Pierre Gassendi, *The Mirrour of True Nobility & Gentility. Being the Life of the Renowned Nicolaus Claudius Fabricius Lord of Peiresk . . .* (London, 1657).

xl. Meric Casaubon, *A Treatise Concerning Enthusiasme*, . . . , chap. 3.

xli. Robert Plot, *The Natural History of Oxford-shire, Being an Essay Towards the Natural History of England* (Oxford, 1677), pp. 8–12.

xlii. Insertion indicated but not present.

xliii. Athanasius Kircher, *Obeliscus Pamphilius hoc est, interpretatio . . . obelisci hieroglyphici . . .* (Rome, 1650).

xliv. Mario Bettini, *Apiaria vniversae philosophiae mathematicae, in quibus paradoxa, et noua pleraque machinamenta ad vsus eximios traducta, et facillimis demonstrationibus confirmata . . .* , (Bologna, 1642).

xlv. Athanasius Kircher, *Ars agna lucis et umbrae in mundo* (Rome, 1646).

xlvi. Pierre Borel, *A New Treatise Proving a Multiplicity of Worlds that the Planets Are Regions Inhabited and the Earth a Star* (London, 1658).

xlvii. Blank space, perhaps intended for an illustration.

xlviii. Evelyn did not include an illustration.

xlix. Evelyn did not include an illustration.

l. Kircher, Athanasius, *Oedipus Aegyptiacus*, Rome, 1652–1654.

li. Space left blank for Evelyn's translation.

lii. Line omitted by Evelyn: "thus doth h'invoke Sweetnesse by all her Names."

liii. Part of this inserted text was separated from the main manuscript of the "Elysium Britannicum"; it has now been placed correctly into Evelyn MS 45 at the British Library.

liv. Insertion indicated but not present.

lv. *De Re Rustica* 3.13.3.

lvi. The present transcription of the section on apiaries (pages 220–236) benefited from consulting D. A. Smith's edition in *John Evelyn's Manuscript on Bees from Elysium Britannicum* (Gerrards Cross, Bucks., England: Bee Research Association, 1966).

lvii. Smith, *Bees*, p. 34, notes that the lines come not from Horace, but from Asmenius, an "obscure poet who flourished about A.D. 400."

lviii. Two-page insertion on "The Method to Govern Bees," written in a different hand. See Appendix 4.

lix. Smith, *Bees*, p. 37.

lx. Ibid.

lxi. Space left blank for figure which is missing.

lxii. Space left blank for Evelyn's translation.

lxiii. Space left blank for Evelyn's translation.

lxiv. Pierre Belon, 1517?-1564.

lxv. Etienne de Flacourt, *Histoire de la grand isle Madagascar* (Paris, 1658).

lxvi. This word may have been lined through by Evelyn.

lxvii. Thomas Mouffet, *Insectorum sive minimorum animalium theatrum olim ab Edoardo Wottono, Conrado Gesnero, Thomaque Pennio inchoatum* . . . (London, 1634).

lxviii. Insertion indicated but not present.

lxix. Plutarch, *Moralia*, 2.876c.

lxx. Insertion on separate piece of paper, See Appendix 5. The first fifteen lines of page 261's text are lined through, the information supplied by Evelyn in Appendix 5.

lxxi. Nicolas Monardes, 1512–1588.

lxxii. Space left blank for Evelyn's translation.

lxxiii. Space left blank for Evelyn's translation.

lxxiv. Insertion on separate piece of paper. See Appendix 6.

lxxv. See Appendix 7 for Sir Thomas Hanmer's paper inserted by Evelyn at this point in the main text.

lxxvi. Insertion on separate piece of paper. See Appendix 8.

lxxvii. Insertion indicated but not present.

lxxviii. Insertion indicated but not present.

lxxix. Insertion indicated but not present.

lxxx. Insertion on separate piece of paper. See Appendix 9.

lxxxi. Evelyn misnumbered page 302 as page 303. He then caught up the correct page numbering by inserting page 307a.

lxxxii. John Harvey suggests that this reference is to the Meris(z)iere cherry. Cf. manuscript page 306.

lxxxiii. Insertion indicated but not present.

lxxxiv. Morin, *Remarques necessaires pour la culture des fleurs*, p. 189, includes a catalog of flowering plants with a tulip named "Eusebe."

lxxxv. Evelyn replaced Spenser's "shore" with "shewe." Evelyn's citation is from *The Faerie Queene*, bk. 3, canto 6, st. 45.

lxxxvi. John Jonstone, 1603–1675.

lxxxvii. Four-page insertion on "The Designe of a Physical Garden." See Appendix 10.

lxxxviii. The *Oxford English Dictionary* defines "hand" as a measure of four inches, so the plant reached a height of 120 inches in four days.

Appendices

i. Printed broadside to serve as title page and table of contents, to which starting page numbers for each chapter were added in manuscript and chapters are renumbered in sequential Roman numerals.

ii. Gaspar Schott, 1608–1666.

iii. John Harvey notes that only forty-five of seventy-two varieties are listed from Morin's 1658 catalog.

Index

Acknowledgments

The publication of John Evelyn's "Elysium Britannicum" owes its existence to the support, assistance, and knowledge of many people, who share equitably with the editor in whatever accolades the work may receive. Several individuals and institutions made exceptionally meaningful contributions to the successful completion of the project; others whose assistance may not have been quantifiably as great, nevertheless added qualitative contributions that substantively affected the work for much the better.

Patricia Gibbs, historian at the Colonial Williamsburg Foundation, and Terry Yemm, a Foundation gardener who truly wears the title of gardener as Evelyn most likely understood it, asked me to "take a look" at the "Elysium Britannicum" during a seminar in British librarianship at Oxford University in 1987. Without that request, this publication might still be waiting to be initiated.

Pearce S. Grove, former library director at Colonial Williamsburg, gave his encouragement, through both philosophical support and travel funding, that allowed me to conduct my first extended tour of transcription. Cary Carson, vice-president for research, and Susan Berg, director of the John D. Rockefeller, Jr., Library at the Colonial Williamsburg Foundation, provided both financial support and scholarly encouragement. To my colleagues at the Colonial Williamsburg Foundation Library who took up the slack while I spent almost six months at Oxford on the transcription, and who provided much needed collegial support during the period 1987–1994, I offer additional thanks, especially, L. Eileen Parris, Greg Williams, and Gail Greve, my associate curators in special collections. I must also thank the Colonial Williamsburg Foundation Audiovisual Department, which provided me with support for additional study of parts of the manuscript that I had photographed at Oxford.

At Oxford, my greatest debt of gratitude must be to John Wing, recently retired assistant librarian at Christ Church, who provided me a level of comfort and space in which to work on the transcription that I can only hope to extend to others in my own library career. John and his colleagues at Christ Church were without exception accepting of my project and supportive of it. The magnificent upper library at Christ Church afforded me an atmosphere that truly matched the merit of Evelyn's manuscript. David Vaisey, then Bodley's Librarian, and his secretary, Pam King, were extremely gracious to me, as was Bill Clennell, assistant secretary for the library. The late Helen Wallis, former head of the map library at the British Library, helped me obtain reproductions of important resources at that institution. Helen's much too early passing was a loss for the scholarly community and for me personally.

John Dixon Hunt was equally supportive in bringing this work to publication, first by writing in support of it to the National Endowment for the Humanities and the American Philosophical Society, and second by advancing its cause at Dumbarton Oaks through a roundtable in 1991 and setting it as the subject for the 1993 symposium in landscape studies there. The papers delivered at the symposium have been published as *John Evelyn's "Elysium Britannicum" and European Gardening*, edited by Therese O'Malley and Joachim Wolschke-Bulmahn, to whom I also owe great gratitude, as I do to all participants in that wonderfully enthusiastic meeting.

Mark Laird, Prudence Leith-Ross, and the late John Harvey each contributed of their special knowledge during the course of preparing this transcription by sharing a depth of history, understanding of gardens, and, in John Harvey's case, an intimacy with seventeenth-century botanical nomenclature that is perhaps solely his own. The institutions that have supported this effort through direct financial grants or through professional leave include the National Endowment for the Humanities (travel and summer stipend grants), the American Philosophical Society (research fellowship), the Colonial Williamsburg Foundation, and the University of Florida.

The final preparation of the manuscript for publication requires its own list of individuals to be acknowledged, including Frances Harris and Hilton Kelliher of the British Library, Michael Turner of Birkbeck College, and Dolores Jenkins, University of Florida, who read through the penultimate draft of the entire work. I also wish to acknowledge the editorial contributions of Michael Leslie and John Dixon Hunt to my introductory comments, which are the richer for their careful attention. The editorial staff at the University of Pennsylvania Press deserve a special note of gratitude and respect: Jo Joslyn, Ellen Fiskett, Noreen O'Connor, and the clear-eyed typesetter who noted that there is a difference between medial and final s in Greek.

This book is dedicated to Sophie Lemanowicz Ingram, my mother; to Pearce S. Grove, who gave me the confidence to begin; and to Alfred Browning Parker, who gave me a new enthusiasm for the work.